T0306191

Military Cost–Benefit Analysis

This is the first comprehensive book dedicated to military cost–benefit analysis. The aim is to help countries identify affordable defense capabilities that effectively counter security risks in uncertain and fiscally constrained environments. This volume offers several new practical tools designed to guide defense investments (and divestments), combined with a selection of real-world applications.

The widespread employment of cost–benefit analysis offers a unique opportunity to transform legacy defense forces into efficient, effective, and accountable twenty-first-century organizations. A synthesis of economics, statistics, and decision theory, cost–benefit analysis is currently used in a wide range of defense applications in countries around the world: i) to shape national security strategy, ii) to set acquisition policy, and iii) to inform critical investments in people, equipment, infrastructure, services, and supplies. As sovereign debt challenges squeeze national budgets, and emerging threats disrupt traditional notions of security, this volume offers valuable tools to navigate the political landscape, meet calls for fiscal accountability, and boost the effectiveness of defense investments to help guarantee future peace and stability.

A valuable resource for scholars, practitioners, students, and experts, this book offers a comprehensive overview of military cost–benefit analysis that will appeal to anyone interested or involved in improving national security. It should also be of general interest to public officials responsible for major programs, projects or policies.

Francois Melese is Professor of Economics at the Defense Resources Management Institute (DRMI) in the Graduate School of Business and Public Policy at the Naval Postgraduate School, USA.

Anke Richter is Professor of Operations Research at the Defense Resources Management Institute (DRMI) in the Graduate School of Business and Public Policy at the Naval Postgraduate School, USA.

Binyam Solomon is a Senior Scientist with Defence Research and Development Canada.

Routledge Studies in Defence and Peace Economics
Edited by Keith Hartley, University of York, UK and
Jurgen Brauer, Augusta State University, USA

In recognition of the

Defense Resources Management Institute (DRMI)

Graduate School of Business and Public Policy
Naval Postgraduate School
Monterey, California
www.nps.edu/drmi

Celebrating 50 Years

Excellence in Education since 1965

Military Cost–benefit Analysis
Theory and practice

Edited by **Francois Melese,
Anke Richter, and
Binyam Solomon**

Routledge
Taylor & Francis Group

LONDON AND NEW YORK

First published 2015
by Routledge
2 Park Square, Milton Park, Abingdon, Oxon OX14 4RN

and by Routledge
711 Third Avenue, New York, NY 10017

First issued in paperback 2017

Routledge is an imprint of the Taylor & Francis Group, an informa business

© 2015

British Library Cataloguing in Publication Data
A catalogue record for this book is available from the British Library

Library of Congress Cataloging-in-Publication Data
Military Cost–benefit Analysis: Theory and Practice /
edited by F. Melese, A. Richter, and B. Solomon.
    pages cm
    Includes bibliographical references and index.
    1. United States–Armed Forces–Appropriations and expenditures–
    Evaluation. 2. United States. Department of Defense–Appropriations
    and expenditures–Evaluation. 3. Armed Forces–Appropriations and
    expenditures–Evaluation–Case studies.
    4. Cost effectiveness–Government policy–United States.
    5. Operations research–United States.
    6. United States–Defenses–Costs.
    I. Melese, F., editor. II. Richter, A. (Anke), editor.
    III. Solomon, B. (Binyam), editor.
UA25.5.M55 2015
355.6'223–dc23   2014041462

ISBN 13: 978-1-138-49538-8 (pbk)
ISBN 13: 978-1-138-85042-2 (hbk)

Typeset in Times
by Sunrise Setting Ltd, Paignton, UK

Contents

Figures

Tables

Contributors

Diana I. Angelis is an associate professor at the Naval Postgraduate School in the Defense Resource Management Institute with a joint appointment to the Department of Systems Engineering. She studied accounting at the University of Florida and received a BS in Business Administration in 1977 and a BS in Electrical Engineering in 1985. She received her PhD in Industrial and Systems engineering from the University of Florida in 1996. Her research interests include cost accounting, activity-based costing, valuation of R&D and acquisition innovation. She was commissioned an officer in the US Air Force in 1984 and served as a program engineer until 1989. Dr Angelis is a Certified Public Accountant and retired in 2009 as a Lieutenant Colonel in the US Air Force Reserve. She joined the Defense Resources Management Institute's faculty in 1996.

Col. John T. Dillard, USA (Ret.), managed major weapons development efforts for most of his 26-year career in the US Army. He is now the Acquisition Academic Area Chair, Graduate School of Business and Public Policy, at the US Naval Postgraduate School in Monterey, California. Col. Dillard is also a 1988 graduate of the Defense Systems Management College.

Randall E. Everly Commander, US Navy, is a graduate of the US Naval Academy with a Bachelor of Science in Electrical Engineering. Originally from Plant City, Florida, Commander Everly is a Naval Aviator. He flew C-2A Greyhounds and E-2C Hawkeyes operationally, and instructed in the T-6 Texan II aircraft. He graduated from the Naval Postgraduate School with Master of Science in Information Technology Management and a Master of Business Administration. Commander Everly currently serves as the Deputy N7 in charge of Training and Education for Commander, Navy Reserve Forces Command in Norfolk, Virginia.

Col. Ross Fetterly is currently the Canadian Air Force Comptroller. He previously served as the Military Personnel Command Comptroller. Col. Fetterly has also been employed as the Section Head in Director Strategic Finance and Costing (DSFC) within Assistant Deputy Minister (Finance) at National Defence Headquarters responsible for costing analysis of all capital projects and major departmental initiatives, as well as the Section Head responsible for Strategic

Finance. Col. Fetterly completed a tour in February 2009 as the Chief CJ8 at COMKAF HQ, the NATO Base HQ at Kandahar Airfield, Afghanistan. While deployed he wrote the paper entitled "Methodology for Estimating the Fiscal Impact of the Costs Incurred by the Government of Canada in Support of the Mission in Afghanistan" with staff from the Parliamentary Budget Office. Col. Fetterly was employed as the Deputy Commanding Officer of the Canadian Contingent in the United Nations Disengagement Observer Force in the Golan Heights during the second intifada in 2000–2001. He has served as an Air Force Squadron Logistics Officer and at military bases across Canada. An Adjunct Assistant Professor at the Royal Military College of Canada (RMC), he teaches financial decision-making. Col. Ross Fetterly earned his PhD (War Studies) at the RMC. His fields of study were Defence Economics, Canadian Defence Policy and Defence Cost Analysis. His current research focus is defense resource management.

Dr David N. Ford is an Associate Professor at Texas A&M University and the US Naval Postgraduate School. In addition to teaching, he researches development project strategy, processes, and resources management. Dr Ford earned his doctorate from the Massachusetts Institute of Technology, and his master's and bachelor's degrees from Tulane University. He has over 14 years of engineering and project management experience in industry and government.

The Honorable Jacques S. Gansler, former US Under Secretary of Defense for Acquisition, Technology, and Logistics, is a Professor and holds the Roger C. Lipitz Chair in Public Policy and Private Enterprise in the School of Public Policy at the University of Maryland, and is the Director of the Center for Public Policy and Private Enterprise. As the third-ranking civilian at the Pentagon from 1997 to 2001, Professor Gansler was responsible for all research and development, acquisition reform, logistics, advance technology, environmental security, defense industry, and numerous other security programs. Before joining the Clinton Administration, Dr Gansler held a variety of positions in government and the private sector, including Deputy Assistant Secretary of Defense (Material Acquisition), Assistant Director of Defense Research and Engineering (electronics), executive vice president at TASC, vice president of ITT, and engineering and management positions with Singer and Raytheon Corporations. Throughout his career, Dr Gansler has written, published, testified, and taught on subjects related to his work. He is the author of five books and over 100 articles. His most recent book is *Democracy's Arsenal: Creating a 21st Century Defense Industry* (MIT Press, 2011). He is a member of the National Academy of Engineering and a Fellow of the National Academy of Public Administration. Additionally, he is the Glenn L. Martin Institute Fellow of Engineering at the A. James Clarke School of Engineering, an Affiliate Faculty member at the Robert H. Smith School of Business and a Senior Fellow at the James MacGregor Burns Academy of Leadership (all at the University of Maryland).

Dr Venelin Georgiev is a senior researcher in Department of Defense Resource Management at the Bulgarian Academy of Sciences. He has a distinguished career in the defense establishment with responsibilities that included designing processes and systems for resource management and managing projects. Dr Georgiev has held the positions of Chief of Defence Resource Programming Section and State Expert in Defence Acquisition Policy Directorate in the Bulgarian MoD. His research interests include defense policy, program and project approaches for economic development, defense resource management, risk management, innovation, investment, micro and macro-economics, administration, and institutional economics.

William L. Greer is Assistant Director of the System Evaluation Division at the Institute for Defense Analyses (IDA), a non-profit federally funded research and development center in Alexandria, VA. He specializes in air mobility cost and effectiveness analyses and has been involved in several recent large studies that address strategic and tactical airlift demands and the next-generation airborne tanker. Other work includes analyses of the Joint Strike Fighter, USAF long-range bomber force size requirements, ballistic missile defenses and naval surface forces. Prior to working at IDA, Dr Greer worked at the Office of the Secretary of Defense in the Pentagon, the Center for Naval Analyses in Alexandria, VA, and the Chemistry Department of George Mason University in Fairfax, VA. He has a PhD in chemical physics from the University of Chicago and a BA in chemistry from Vanderbilt University.

Jason K. Hansen, PhD, is an economist in the modeling and simulation group at the Idaho National Laboratory (INL). Prior to joining INL, he served on the faculty at the Naval Postgraduate School in the Defense Resources Management Institute as an assistant professor. Dr Hansen's research interests are in the economics of water resources, energy and public policy. His work is published in journals such as the *Journal of Benefit Cost Analysis, Journal of American Water Works Association, Hydrogeology Journal*, and the *Journal of Environmental Management.*

Professor Keith Hartley is Emeritus Professor of Economics at the University of York where he was previously Director of the Centre for Defence Economics. He was founding Editor of the journal *Defence and Peace Economics* (with Todd Sandler) and remained Editor from 1990 to 2007 and is currently Special Advisor to the Editor. He has acted as adviser and consultant to the UN, EC, European Defence Agency, various UK Government Departments and to the Parliamentary Defence Committee. He was a NATO Fellow and QinetiQ Visiting Fellow. Current research interests are in defense economics and include procurement, pricing, the costs of conflict, measuring defense output and the political economy of the aerospace industry.

Thomas Housel specializes in valuing intellectual capital, telecommunications, information technology, value-based business process reengineering, and knowledge value measurement in profit and non-profit organizations. He received his PhD from the University of Utah in 1980 and is currently a tenured Full Professor for the Information Sciences (Systems) Department at the Naval Postgraduate School in Monterey, California. His current research focuses on the use of Real Options models in identifying, valuing, maintaining, and exercising options in military decision-making. Prior to joining NPS, he also was a Research Fellow for the Center for Telecommunications Management and Associate Professor at the Marshall School of Business at the University of Southern California. Housel has been the Chief Business Process Engineer for Pacific Bell. He is Managing Partner for Business Process Auditors, a firm that specializes in training Big Six consultants, large manufacturing and service companies in the Knowledge Value Added methodology for objectively measuring the return generated by corporate knowledge assets/intellectual capital. His latest books include *Measuring and Managing Knowledge* (McGraw-Hill, 2001) and *Global Telecommunications Revolution: The Business Perspective* (McGraw-Hill, 2001).

Bohdan L. Kaluzny is a defense scientist with Defence Research and Development Canada, Centre for Operational Research and Analysis. Dr Kaluzny obtained his doctorate degree in computer science from McGill University in Montreal and his research interests include polyhedral computation, computational geometry, combinatorial optimization, multi-criteria decision analysis, and operational research.

Thomas J. Kniesner was born in Cleveland, Ohio, and received his PhD degree in Economics from The Ohio State University. He has recently joined the faculty of Claremont Graduate University as University Professor and continues to be a Research Fellow at the Institute for the Study of Labor (IZA). Dr Kniesner's specialty is the econometric examination of labor and health economic issues. His interests are labor supply, workplace safety, and health care costs and use. He has published articles in over 20 different professional journals including *The American Economic Review, Econometrica, Journal of Political Economy, Review of Economics and Statistics, Journal of Economic Literature, Journal of the European Economic Association, Journal of Mental Health Policy and Economics, Journal of Monetary Economics, Industrial and Labor Relations Review, Journal of Labor Economics, Journal of Risk and Uncertainty, Labour Economics, International Economic Review, Journal of Policy Analysis and Management, Journal of Health Policy, Politics and Law, Health Affairs, The Economics of Neuroscience,* and *Regulation.* He is the co-author of seven books, including *Labor Economics: Theory, Evidence, and Policy, Simulating Workplace Safety Policy, The Law and Economics of Workers' Compensation Insurance,* and *The Effects of Recent Tax Reforms on Labor Supply.* He is has served as co-editor of the *Journal of Human Resources,* co-editor of *Foundations and Trends in Microeconomics,* and associate editor of the *Journal of Risk and Uncertainty.*

C. J. LaCivita, Professor Emeritus, graduated in 1969 from the University of Detroit with a Bachelor of Electrical Engineering. He received an MBA from Valdosta State College in 1975, and a PhD in Economics from the University of California at Santa Barbara in 1981. Professor LaCivita served as a pilot in the US Air Force for five years. His current research concerns the relationship between accounting costs and economic costs and their use in promoting more efficient management of defense resources. He is a member of the American Economic Association and the American Society of Military Comptrollers. He is also a member of the commission that developed and oversees the Certified Defense Financial Manager Program. He was Assistant Professor of Economics at the University of North Carolina at Greensboro before joining the Defense Resources Management faculty in May, 1985. He served as Executive Director from 1993 to 2011 and was the Acting Dean of the School of International Graduate Studies at the Naval Postgraduate School from 2001 to 2002. He also served as a member of the oversight commission for the Certified Defense Financial Manager program from its inception through 2008. He has published widely in a number of areas in economics and defense resources management.

John D. Leeth is a Professor of Economics at Bentley University. He received a BA degree in political science from the University of Southern California and a PhD in economics from the University of North Carolina, Chapel Hill. Before coming to Bentley University in 1987, he was on the faculty of the Edwin L. Cox School of Business, Southern Methodist University in Dallas, Texas. His research areas include workplace safety, executive compensation, economic inequality, and mergers and acquisitions. His articles have appeared in various journals including *British Journal of Management*, *Industrial and Labor Relations Review*, *International Economic Review*, *International Journal of Industrial Organization*, *Journal of Finance and Quantitative Analysis*, *Journal of Risk and Uncertainty*, and *Regulation*. He co-authored the book *Simulating Workplace Safety Policy* (Kluwer Academic Publishers, 1995).

David C. Limmer Lieutenant, US Navy, earned his BS in Computer Science from Gordon College (2000) and his MS in Information Technology Management and MBA in Information Systems Management from the Naval Postgraduate School (2014). Lieutenant Limmer was commissioned through Officer Candidate School in Pensacola, FL and has since served as a Naval Flight Officer and Information Professional. He has flown the EA-6B and has been stationed overseas in Japan, Guam, and Italy.

Jonathan Lipow, PhD, is currently an Associate Professor at the Defense Resources Management Institute (DRMI) located at the Naval Postgraduate School (NPS). Prior to joining DRMI, he served as a professor at the Hebrew University of Jerusalem and at Oberlin College, acted as Bank of America's country representative in Israel, and worked as an economic advisor to Israel's Ministry of Defense. His military service was in the Israel Defense Forces'

Combat Engineering Corps. His research has focused on a wide variety of topics related to national security and defense economics, and he has published papers in journals such as *Defense and Peace Economics. Southern Economic Journal, Economics Letters, World Development,* and *Journal of Economic Behavior and Organization.*

William Lucyshyn is the Director of Research and Senior Research Scholar, at the Center for Public Policy and Private Enterprise, in the School of Public Policy, at the University of Maryland. In this position, he directs research on critical policy issues related to the increasingly complex problems associated with improving public sector management and operations, and how government works with private enterprise. Current projects include: modernizing government supply chain management, identifying government sourcing and acquisition best practices, and department of defense business modernization and transformation. Previously, Mr. Lucyshyn served as a program manager and the principal technical advisor to the Director of the Defense Advanced Research Projects Agency (DARPA) on the identification, selection, research, development, and prototype production of advanced technology projects. Prior to joining DARPA, Mr. Lucyshyn completed a 25-year career in the US Air Force. Mr. Lucyshyn received his Bachelor Degree in Engineering Science from the City University of New York, and earned his Master's Degree in Nuclear Engineering from the Air Force Institute of Technology. He has authored numerous reports, book chapters, and journal articles.

Cameron A. MacKenzie is an Assistant Professor in the Defense Resources Management Institute at the Naval Postgraduate School. His research and teaching focus on decision and risk analysis, with a particular emphasis on modeling the economic and business impacts caused by disruptions. He has analyzed the economic impacts caused by the 2011 Japanese earthquake and tsunami, and he has developed a resource allocation model to help an economic region recover from a disaster like the Deepwater Horizon oil spill. Previously, he consulted in the areas of defense and homeland security for former Defense Secretary William Cohen. He received a BS and BA from Indiana-Purdue University at Fort Wayne (2001), an MA in International Affairs from The George Washington University (2003), an MS in Management Science and Engineering from Stanford University (2009), and a PhD in Industrial Engineering from the University of Oklahoma (2012).

David Maybury received his BSc in Applied Mathematics from the University of Western Ontario and his PhD in Physics from the University of Alberta. He was a postdoctoral fellow with the Rudolf Peierls Centre for Theoretical Physics, University of Oxford, and with the high energy physics group at Carleton University. Currently, David is an operational research scientist, focusing on military applications of financial engineering, with Defence Research and Development Canada.

Francois Melese, is Professor of Economics and former Executive Director of the Defense Resources Management Institute at the Naval Postgraduate School (fmelese@nps.edu). He earned his BA in Economics at the University of California, Berkeley, his MA at the University of British Columbia, Canada, and his Doctorate at the Catholic University of Louvain, Belgium. He has over 25 years of experience conducting courses and workshops for military and civilian officials around the world. In 2005 Dr Melese participated in the US Defense Department's Quadrennial Defense Review (QDR), and in 2008 contributed to the Department's first Strategic Management Plan. He has consulted extensively, including for the Joint Chiefs of Staff (Comptroller), the Defense Business Board, and the Office of the Secretary of Defense (Directorate for Organizational & Management Planning). Dr Melese has earned several awards for teaching and research, and has published over 50 papers and book chapters on a variety of topics in economics and management including: public budgeting, economic development, energy markets, international trade, applied game theory, labor markets, public procurement, and defense management. At the request of NATO Headquarters and the US State Department he has represented the US as an expert in public budgeting and defense management at NATO meetings throughout Europe.

Dr Johnathan C. Mun is a research professor at the US Naval Postgraduate School (Monterey, California) and teaches executive seminars in quantitative risk analysis, decision sciences, real options, simulation, portfolio optimization, and other related concepts. He has also researched and consulted on many Department of Defense and Department of Navy projects and is considered a leading world expert on risk analysis and real options analysis. Dr. Mun received his PhD in Finance and Economics from Lehigh University, has an MBA in business administration, an MS in management science, and a BS in Biology and Physics. He is Certified in Financial Risk Management (FRM), Certified in Financial Consulting (CFC), and Certified in Risk Management (CRM). He has authored 12 books including *Modeling Risk: Applying Monte Carlo Risk Simulation, Real Options, Optimization, and Forecasting,* First and Second Editions (Wiley 2006, 2010); *Real Options Analysis: Tools and Techniques for Valuing Strategic Investments and Decisions,* First and Second Editions (Wiley 2003, 2006); *Real Options Analysis Course: Business Cases* (Wiley 2003); *Applied Risk Analysis: Moving Beyond Uncertainty* (Wiley 2003); *Valuing Employee Stock Options* (Wiley 2004), and others. He is the founder and CEO of Real Options Valuation, Inc., a consulting, training, and software development firm.

Dan Nussbaum, Professor at the Naval Postgraduate School, chairs the NPS Energy Academic Group, and provides leadership to the US Secretary of Navy's Executive Energy Education program. He teaches courses in cost estimating and analysis, and provides cost estimating and business case analyses for DoD organizations. He designs, develops and delivers distance learning courses in cost estimating and analysis. Prior to this position, Dan was a Principal, Booz Allen Hamilton. He has also been the Director, Naval Center for Cost Analysis, Office of the Assistant Secretary of Navy (Financial Management and Comptroller), Washington, DC. He directed all Navy independent cost estimates as required by Congress and senior Defense leadership on ships, aircraft, missiles, electronics, and automated information systems. Dr. Nussbaum has a BA in Mathematics and Economics, Columbia University; a PhD in Mathematics, Michigan State University; a Fellowship from National Science Foundation in Econometrics and Operations Research at Washington State University; and a fellowship in National Security from Harvard University's Kennedy School of Government.

Anke Richter, is a Professor of Operations Research at the Defense Resources Management Institute at the Naval Postgraduate School. She received a BA in Mathematics and French from Dartmouth College (1991) and a PhD in Operations Research from Stanford University (1996). Her graduate work was supported by a grant from the Office of Naval Research. Dr. Richter was previously a Director of Health Outcomes at RTI-Health Solutions, RTI International. Her research interests include resource allocation for epidemic control, disease modeling and economic impact assessment, and bio terrorism. Dr. Richter is a member of the Institute for Operations Research and the Management Sciences (INFORMS) and the International Society for Pharmacoeconomics and Outcomes Research (ISPOR). She has published in several peer-reviewed journals, including the *Journal of the American Medical Association, Journal of Clinical Epidemiology, PharmacoEconomics, Medical Decision Making, Clinical Therapeutics* and *Managed Care Interfaces*. While English is Dr. Richter's first language, she is also fluent in German and French.

Dr Binyam (Ben) Solomon is a senior scientist with Defence Research and Development Canada (DRDC), a special operating agency of the Canadian Department of National Defence (DND). Dr. Solomon is also an Adjunct Research Professor at Carleton University Canada and Co-Director of the Institute of Defence Resources Management (IDRM) at the Royal Military College of Canada. He has previously worked for the Department of National Defence as Chief Economist. He earned his BA in Mathematics, Statistics and Economics at the University of Regina, Canada, his Masters in Economics at the University of Ottawa, Canada, and his Doctorate at the University of York, United Kingdom. Dr. Solomon has more than 20 years of experience in economics research consulting and teaching. He has published articles and reports on various quantitative and defense economics issues ranging from time series analysis and economic modeling to the defense industrial base, peacekeeping, and defense resources management. Dr Solomon has represented Canada at a number of NATO research panels including a NATO System Analysis and Studies (SAS) on benchmarking (2006–2008), SAS 090 on the economics of international collaboration (2011) a Russia-NATO workshop on civil-military institutions (2003) and a NATO-Canada study on allied military training in Canada (1996). His research interests include economic aspects of international security, time series econometrics and defense resources management. Recently, he was named the Americas Editor of the *Defence and Peace Economics Journal* (Routledge).

Ryan Sullivan, Assistant Professor, received a PhD in economics from Syracuse University in 2010. Dr Sullivan joined the faculty of the Defense Resources Management Institute (DRMI) in that same year and has taught a variety of topics related to cost–benefit and cost-effectiveness analysis, marginal reasoning, budgeting, labor economics, and game theory. His research interests include program cost–benefit analyses with a specialization in value of statistical life (VSL) studies. He has published in several peer-reviewed journals, including *American Economic Journal: Economic Policy, Defence and Peace Economics, Economic Inquiry, National Tax Journal, Public Budgeting and Finance, and Public Finance Review*, among others. His work has been discussed in such prominent outlets as *Time Magazine, USA Today*, and *US News and World Report*. Dr Sullivan is a member of the American Economic Association and the National Tax Association. He served as a soldier in the US Army National Guard from 1998 to 2006.

Kent D. Wall, is a Professor at the Defense Resources Management Institute at the Naval Postgraduate School. He earned a PhD in Control Sciences from the University of Minnesota. After completing his studies he was awarded two postdoctoral fellowships in England, the first with the University of Manchester, and the second with the University of London. While in the UK he lectured at HM Treasury, the Bank of England, Queen Mary College, Imperial College, London School of Economics, and London Business School. He returned to the US as a Research Associate with the National Bureau of Economic Research in Cambridge, Massachusetts. Before coming to the Naval Postgraduate School he was an Associate Professor of Systems Engineering at the University of Virginia. His research interests focus on the development of quantitative aids in decision-making. He has published his work in many scholarly journals, and has been invited to present special courses at the University of Paris IX (Dauphine). He joined the faculty in August 1985 and served as Assistant Director for Academic Programs from 1993 to 1998.

Preface

This edited volume should appeal to anyone interested or actively involved in improving national security. It should also be of general interest to those responsible for major government programs, projects or policies. A valuable resource for scholars and practitioners, novices and experts alike, this book offers a comprehensive overview of military cost–benefit analysis (CBA). The goal is to help countries identify affordable defense capabilities that effectively counter security risks, in fiscally constrained environments.

The book consists of five parts: I) Introduction and problem formulation; II) Measuring costs and future funding; III) Measuring effectiveness; IV) New approaches to military cost–benefit analysis; and V) Selected applications. The seventeen chapters that make up these five parts showcase a diversity of international experts with both theoretical and hands-on experience. Lifting the veil on military CBA, this volume offers several new practical tools designed to guide defense investments (and divestments), combined with a selection of real-world applications.

Widespread employment of CBA offers a unique opportunity to transform legacy defense forces into efficient, effective, and accountable twenty-first-century organizations. A synthesis of economics, management science, statistics and decision theory, CBA is currently used in a wide range of defense applications in countries around the world: i) to shape national security strategy, ii) to set acquisition policy, and iii) to inform critical investments in people, equipment, infrastructure, services and supplies. As sovereign debt challenges squeeze national budgets, and emerging threats disrupt traditional notions of security, this volume offers valuable tools to navigate the political landscape, meet calls for fiscal accountability, and boost the effectiveness of defense investments to help guarantee future peace and stability.

Abbreviations

ABC	activity based costing
ACAS	airlift cycle analysis spreadsheet
ACF	autocorrelation function
ADF	augmented Dickey–Fuller
ADF	Australian Defense Force
AFB	air force base
AFM	airlift flow model
AFSAA	air force studies and analysis agency
AIMP	aurora incremental modernization program
ALM	airlift loading model
AMC	Air Mobility Command
AMOS	air mobility operations model
AoA	analysis of alternatives
APC	armored personnel carriers
ARDL	autoregressive distributive lag
ARIMA	autoregressive integrated moving average
AVF	all-volunteer force
BCA	business case analysis
BLS	Bureau of Labor Statistics
BRAC	base realignment and closure
BSC	balanced scorecard
CAF	Canadian armed forces
CAG	Comptroller and Auditor General
CAIG	Cost Analysis Improvement Group
CAIV	cost as an independent variable
CAPE	cost assessment and program evaluation (formerly PA&E)
CARD	cost analysis requirements description
CBA	cost–benefit analysis
CBO	Congressional Budget Office
CBP	capability based planning
CBS	cost breakdown structure
CC	conventional campaign
CCDR	contractor cost data reports

CEA	cost-effectiveness analysis
CER	cost estimating relationships
CES	cost element structure
CFDS	Canada first defence strategy
CFOI	census of fatal occupational injuries
COCOMO	constructive cost model
COEA	cost and operational effectiveness analysis
CORA	Centre for Operations Research and Analysis
CORE	cost-oriented resource estimating
CPS	current population survey
CRAF	civil reserve air fleet
CSIS	Center for Strategic and International Studies
CSS	combat service support
C-X	cargo-experimental
DAB	defense acquisition board
DACIMS	defense acquisition automated cost information system
DAES	defense acquisition executive summaries
DAMIR	defense acquisition management information retrieval
DAS	defense acquisition system
DASA	Defense Atomic Support Agency
DAU	Defense Acquisition University
DCARC	Defense Cost and Resource Center
DFARS	defense federal acquisition regulation supplement
DMDC	Defense Manpower Data Center
DND	Department of National Defence
DoD	Department of Defense
DOT	Department of Transportation
DPS	defense policy statement
ECCM	electronic counter-countermeasures
ECM	electronic counter-measures
EDA	European Defence Agency
EEoA	economic evaluation of alternatives
EIBA	European International Business Academy
EMD	engineering and manufacturing development
EPA	Environmental Protection Agency
ESBM	enhanced scenario-based method
EVMS	earned value management system
FAA	Federal Aviation Administration
FAR	federal acquisition regulation
FDI	foreign direct investment
FFRDC	federally funded research and development center
FLIR	forward looking imaging infra-red
FMTV	family of medium tactical vehicles
FO	fiber-optic
FPA	focal plane array

FV	future value
FY	fiscal year
FYDP	future year defense plan
GAO	Government Accountability Office
GDF	guidance for the development of the force
GDP	gross domestic product
GMOD	German Ministry Of Defence
GSA	general services administration
HALE	high altitude long endurance
HMMWV	high-mobility, multipurpose wheeled vehicle
ICEAA	International Cost Estimating and Analysis Association
IDA	Institute for Defense Analyses
IEDS	improvised explosive devices
IEP	Institute for Economics and Peace
IFB	invitation for bid
IIE	Institute of Industrial Engineers
IOC	initial operational capability
IRB	industrial regional benefit
IS	Islamic state
ISR	intelligence, surveillance and reconnaissance
IW	irregular warfare
JCIDS	joint capabilities integration and development system
JCTD	joint capability technology demonstration
JPG	joint programming guidance
JROC	Joint Requirements Oversight Council
KVA	knowledge value added
LBR	laser beam-riding
LCAC	landing craft
LCC	life cycle cost
LCTA	lowest cost technically acceptable
LMI	logistics management institute
LPD	landing platform dock
LRC	lesser regional contingency
MADM	multi-attribute decision-making
MAIS	major acquisition information system
MANET	mobile ad hoc network
MASS	mobility analysis support system
MAUT	multi-attribute utility theory
MCDM	multi-criteria decision-making
MCO	major combat operation
MDAP	major defense acquisition projects
ME	military expenditures
MEO	most efficient organization
MHE	materiel-handling equipment
MM	man-months

MoD	Ministry of Defence
MODM	multi-objective decision-making
MoE	measure of effectiveness
MOG	maximum on ground
MRC	major regional contingency
MRS BURU	mobility requirements study bottom up review update
MRS	mobility requirements study
MRTS	marginal rate of technical substitution
MSHA	Mine Safety and Health Administration
MTBF	mean time between failure
MTM/D	million ton-miles per day
MTTR	mean time to repair
NAO	National Audit Office
NATO	North Atlantic Treaty Organization
NDAA	non-developmental airlift aircraft
NGO	non-government organization
NM	nautical mile
NPV	net present value
NZDF	New Zealand Defense Force
O&M	operations and maintenance
O&S	operations and support
OECD	Organisation for Economic Co-Operation and Development
OLS	ordinary least squares
OMB	Office of Management and Budget
ONS	Office for National Statistics
OSD	Office of the Secretary of Defense
OT&E	operational test and evaluation
OUSD (A&T)	Office of the Under Secretary of Defense (Acquisition and Technology)
PA&E	program analysis and evaluation (now renamed CAPE)
PAA	primary authorized aircraft
PAA	program alignment architecture
PACF	partial autocorrelation function
PALYS	protection-adjusted life years
PAX	passengers
PBD	program budget decision
PCA	principal component analysis
PDM	programmed depot maintenance
PEM	program element monitors
PFC	Privates First Class
PGI	procedures, guidance, and information
POM	program objectives memorandum
PPBE	planning, programming, budgeting and execution
PPBES	planning, programming, budgeting, and execution system
PPBS	planning, programming, and budgeting system

PV	present value
PVA	present value analysis
PWS	performance work statement
QALYS	quality measures of healthcare based on quality-adjusted life years
QDR	quadrennial defense review
R&D	research and development
RAB	resource accounting and budgeting
RAID	rapid aerostat initial deployment
RDT&E	research, development, testing, and evaluation
RFP	request for proposal
RFQ	request for quotation
RM&A	reliability, maintainability, and availability
ROI	return on investment
ROK	return-on-knowledge
RP	risk premium
RTO	(NATO) Research Technology Board
SAB	Scientific Advisory Board
SAFMA	strategic airlift force mix analysis
SAR	selected acquisition report
SAS	system analysis and studies
SC	Schwartz bayesian criterion
SCEA	Society of Cost Estimation and Analysis
SDC	(US Army Materiel Systems Analysis Activity's) sample data collection
SDR	strategic defense review
SecDef	Secretary of Defense
SIPRI	Stockholm International Peace Research Institute
SLEP	service life extension program
SMOD	Sweden Ministry of Defence
SoS	system-of-systems
SOW	statement of work
SSC	Strategic Systems Committee
SSEB	Source Selection Evaluation Board
SSSP	steady-state security posture
SUR	structural unexpended rate
TAI	total aircraft inventory
TCE	transaction cost economics
TOW	tube-launched, optically tracked, wire-guided
TPFDD	time-phased force deployment data
TQM	total quality management
TRL	technology readiness levels
TWV	tactical wheeled vehicles
UAV	unmanned aerial vehicle
USAF	United States Air Force

USDOD	Under Secretary of Defense
USN	United States Navy
USTRANSCOM	US Transportation Command
VAMOSC	visibility and management of operating and support costs
VSI	value of a statistical injury
VSL	value of statistical life
WBS	work breakdown structure
WEKA	the WEKA project (data mining in Java)
WMD	weapons of mass destruction
WSARA	Weapon Systems Acquisition Reform Act

Acknowledgments

The editors are grateful to the series editors for valuable suggestions, and for reviewers' comments provided by Taylor & Francis that offered constructive guidance and support for this project. We would also like to thank the publisher for excellent editorial direction. Dr Melese is grateful to his wife, Heather, for her patient role as a sounding board, and especially to RADM James Greene, US Navy (retired) and his staff at the Acquisition Research Program at the Naval Postgraduate School for their early support of this book. Our recently departed defense economist colleague, Michael Intriligator, was an inspiration to us all. Finally, we are indebted to the authors for their outstanding contributions, as well as to current and past faculty and participants at the Defense Resources Management Institute (DRMI) and the broader defense economics community from whom we have learned so much over the years. The views expressed are those of the editors and authors and do not necessarily represent those of the US Department of Defense or the Canadian Department of National Defense.

Part I

Introduction and problem formulation

1 Introduction

Military cost–benefit
analysis: theory and practice

Francois Melese, Anke Richter, and
Binyam Solomon

1.1 Background

Military cost–benefit analysis (CBA) offers a vital tool to help guide governments through both stable and turbulent times. As countries struggle with the dual challenges of an uncertain defense environment and cloudy fiscal prospects, CBA offers a unique opportunity to transform defense forces into more efficient and effective twenty-first-century organizations.

Defense reforms typically involve politically charged debates over *investments* (in projects, programs, or policies) as well as contentious *divestment* decisions—from base realignment and closure (BRAC) to outsourcing and asset sales. A powerful contribution of CBA is to inform such complex and contentious decisions—carefully structuring the problem and capturing relevant costs and benefits of alternative courses of action. Lifting the veil on military CBA, this edited volume reveals several systematic quantitative approaches to assess defense investments (or divestments), combined with a selection of real-world applications.

The frameworks and methods discussed in the following chapters should appeal to anyone interested or actively involved in understanding and applying CBA to improve national security. These valuable approaches also have broader government-wide applications, especially in cases where it is difficult to monetize the benefits of a public project, program, or policy.

Unprecedented government spending to counter the global financial crisis has placed enormous pressure on public budgets. Combined with alarming demographics, many countries struggle to fulfill past promises to underwrite health care expenditures, social security payments, government pensions, and unemployment programs. As debt burdens grow to finance current operations, the risk of escalating interest payments threatens to crowd out vital future public spending. As the single largest discretionary item in many national budgets,[1] military expenditures make a tempting target. Especially vulnerable are military and civilian compensation (pay and benefits) and the purchase and operation of equipment, facilities, services, and supplies.

Anticipating future spending cuts, this book explores both conventional and unconventional approaches to contemporary defense decisions—from critical investments in facilities, equipment, and materiel to careful vendor selection to build, operate, and maintain those investments. Recognizing the value of systematic quantitative analysis, senior US Army leadership has "directed that any decisions involving Army resources be supported by a CBA."[2]

Faced with severe budget cuts and an uncertain threat environment, defense officials around the world confront urgent decisions on whether to approve specific *projects* (e.g. infrastructure—military housing; training, and maintenance facilities) or *programs* (e.g. weapon systems—unmanned aerial vehicles (UAVs), armored personnel carriers (APCs), cyber defense). Military CBA offers a valuable set of analytical tools to increase the transparency, efficiency, and effectiveness of critical defense decisions.

A synthesis of economics, management science, statistics, and decision theory, military CBA is currently used in a wide range of defense applications in countries around the world: i) to shape national security strategy, ii) to set acquisition policy, and iii) to inform critical investments in people, equipment, infrastructure, services, and supplies. This edited volume offers a selection of carefully designed CBA approaches, and real-world applications, intended to help public officials identify affordable defense capabilities that effectively counter security risks in fiscally constrained environments.

1.2   A brief history of cost–benefit analysis

The French engineer Jules Dupuit (Dupuit 1844) is widely credited with an early concept of CBA called "economic accounting." The British economist Alfred Marshall (Marshall 1920) later developed formal concepts that contributed to the analytical foundations of CBA.[3] In a pioneering survey, Prest and Turvey indicate that as early as 1902 the US River and Harbor Act required the Army Corps of Engineers to report on the desirability of any project, taking into account both the cost and the amount of "commerce benefited" (Prest and Turvey 1965). Widespread application of CBA in the United States is generally attributed to the 1936 Federal Navigation (Flood Control) Act. This required the Army Corps of Engineers to carry out projects to improve waterways when "the benefits to whomsoever they may accrue are in excess of the estimated costs" (Prest and Turvey 1965).

At the heart of CBA is the economists' concept of "allocative efficiency," in which resources are deployed to their highest valued use to maximize social welfare. A related and intuitively appealing definition called "Pareto efficiency" underpins CBA. An allocation is Pareto-efficient if no alternative allocation can make at least one person better off without making someone else worse off (Pareto 1909).

The link between allocations that yield maximum net benefits in CBA and Pareto efficiency is straightforward: If a public policy, program, or project has positive net benefits, then it is possible to find a set of transfers (side payments) that make at least one person better off without making anyone else worse off. Unfortunately, transfers necessary to achieve Pareto efficiency are difficult to implement in practice. Therefore, out of practical necessity, CBA relies on a related decision rule called the Kaldor–Hicks criterion (Kaldor 1939; Hicks 1940). This decision rule states that a public policy, program, or project should be adopted, if and only if gainers could potentially fully compensate losers, and still be better off.[4]

Application of this decision rule is relatively straightforward:[5] Adopt all projects that have positive net benefits.[6] An important caveat is that the Kaldor–Hicks criterion only applies when costs and benefits can be monetized. Given the prevalence of non-monetary benefits in national defense, this poses a serious challenge for the security sector.

The growing interest in CBA after WWII is often attributed to rapid developments in operations research and systems analysis—techniques that helped win the war by combining economics, statistics, and decision theory. Following the allied victory, Project RAND (launched in 1946 by the Army Air Corps) received government funding to maintain scientific expertise developed in WWII and to conduct independent and objective research in national security.

A key contribution of RAND's research was "systems analysis" pioneered by Ed Paxson and advanced by Charles Hitch who in 1948 founded RAND's Economics Division. Whereas operations research had a more immediate, wartime focus (e.g. finding the best short-run solution to a military mission, given a restricted set of equipment, etc.), systems analysis was more future-oriented, focused on finding the optimal mix of doctrine, forces and equipment necessary to accomplish a military goal at the lowest possible cost (or alternatively, for a given budget, to find the optimal mix that maximizes defense capabilities).

Working at RAND in the immediate post-war era, Hitch teamed up with another economist, Roland McKean, to publish a pioneering text entitled *The Economics of Defense in the Nuclear Age* (Hitch and McKean 1960). The authors emphasized two main ways in which military CBA can be applied: i) to guide defense *policy* (i.e. the allocation of resources between major missions or military goals) and ii) to guide defense *investments* (i.e. choices between alternative projects or programs to achieve a given mission or goal). A significant challenge in applying CBA to defense decisions is the complex and often controversial task of measuring "benefits."

At the highest national strategic level, "benefits" of a specific defense policy[7] might be measured in terms of its impact on long-term economic growth, peace, and prosperity—all key contributors to social welfare. For example, suppose resource costs to achieve specific military goals are viewed as insurance payments against hazardous states of the world. Suppose further that defense policy decisions that achieve specific military goals reduce risk premiums associated with domestic and foreign direct investment (FDI). Empirical evidence suggests that FDI boosts economic growth and in turn contributes to peace and prosperity.[8] In this example, high-level defense decisions could ideally be made with the aim of increasing social welfare by encouraging investment, boosting GDP, and thereby generating a virtuous cycle of peace and prosperity.

In reality, this high-level effort to capture monetary benefits of defense policy as growth in GDP is rarely explored.[9] Instead, it typically gives way to a more familiar perspective that makes up the bulk of chapters in this edited volume—where non-monetary "measures of effectiveness" (MoEs) of a policy, project or program substitute for monetary benefits.

Denied the opportunity to conduct controlled experiments or full-scale independent field tests to evaluate alternative policies, projects or programs, military officials and analysts are forced to resort to "proxy" variables. These include criteria and characteristics that reflect multiple objectives and that describe essential features of the alternatives being analyzed.[10] When benefits cannot be monetized, the terms "systems analysis" or "cost-effectiveness analysis" (CEA) are often used to describe military CBA.[11]

A related literature, alternately called multi-criteria decision-making (MCDM) or multi-objective decision-making (MODM), rapidly evolved after WWII to address the challenge of measuring non-monetary benefits of defense investments. The reader is encouraged to explore this literature for details on competing benefit measurement strategies, some of which are discussed in this volume. These measures have been in continuous development since the adoption of systems analysis by the US Department of Defense in the early 1960s.[12]

Following his election as President in 1960, John F. Kennedy appointed Robert McNamara Secretary of Defense. McNamara subsequently hired Charles Hitch as Comptroller to implement the Planning, Programming, and Budgeting System (PPBS) that Hitch had earlier helped develop at RAND. An output-oriented budgeting framework, PPBS relies heavily on systems analysis, or military CBA, to build a defense budget.

Prior to Hitch's tenure in the Office of Secretary of Defense, US defense budgets were largely based on the services' (Army, Navy, Air Force) proposals for annual incremental increases in inputs or "appropriation" categories (military personnel, procurement, operations and maintenance, military construction, etc.), often with little or no clear connection to defense outputs, joint missions, or national security goals. Having successfully employed a variant of PPBS called "program budgeting" as CEO of Ford Motor Company, McNamara recognized the value of building a defense budget that focuses on outputs (benefits) as well as costs.

The major innovation of PPBS is "programming," which bridges the gap between long-term military planning goals and short-term civilian budget realities. Designed as a constrained optimization underpinned by systems analysis, the "programming" phase was intended to produce a cost-effective mix of forces to maximize national security subject to funding constraints.[13]

Under certain conditions, the optimal allocation of a budget across various inputs (e.g. defense resources) that contribute to a common goal (i.e. increasing national security) requires the marginal contribution of each input towards that goal, for a given incremental cost, to be the same for any input. Since this decision rule is independent of the units in which the goal is measured, in principle it provides a valid test for allocative efficiency, satisfies the condition for Pareto optimality, and guarantees the most effective use of a defense budget.[14]

To implement PPBS, Hitch hired a RAND colleague, Dr Alain Enthoven, as Deputy Comptroller for Systems Analysis. In 1965, the impact of military CBA was reinforced when Dr Robert Anthony of the Harvard Business School replaced Hitch as Comptroller and elevated Enthoven's position to Assistant Secretary of Defense for Systems Analysis.[15] Throughout his tenure, Secretary McNamara consistently applied systems analysis to evaluate policy, project and program proposals from the military services and to build defense budgets submitted to the Congress.[16] Military CBA continues to provide an analytical foundation that guides PPBS decisions in the United States and in countries around the world.

It is clear that politics influences defense decisions. It is also true that public officials can manipulate CBA for their own personal strategic interests. Politicians likely win more votes highlighting a program's benefits and downplaying its costs, and public administrators may be similarly rewarded. While it is clear pork-barrel politics often plays an important role in defense decisions, this book attempts to take the high road. It encourages the application of military CBA with a strict focus on national security interests.[17]

While employment, income distribution, and regional impacts of defense investment decisions often play a role in political decisions, a clean CBA can inform the process by revealing the true (opportunity) cost of decisions that drift too far from the goal of making the best use of scarce resources for the security of the country. Ideally, a carefully constructed military CBA focused strictly on national security concerns could be used to inform voters and counter special interest lobbying and rent-seeking that often leads defense firms to inefficiently spread production across key voting districts to promote their programs.[18]

A risk for any military CBA is that benefit and cost estimates might be strategically manipulated by self-interested agencies or individual decision-makers.[19] As Robert Haveman and others have pointed out, politicians facing difficult re-election tend to prefer projects that concentrate benefits on particular interest groups that offer them support, and to camouflage or defer costs, or to spread them widely across the population (Haveman 1976). Fortunately, as nations around the world embrace civilian control of the military, and citizens insist on greater accountability (including tighter linkages between budgets and security), an increased premium is placed on transparency in defense decisions.

While politics still dominates major defense decisions, the importance of military CBA rises alongside growing demands for transparency and accountability.[20] Costly defense procurement scandals reinforce the need for objective CBA approaches to improve transparency in vendor selection decisions.[21] Meanwhile, painful recovery from the global financial crisis,[22] combined with emergent threats, fuel public demand to carefully apply tools such as military CBA to build efficient, effective, and accountable security forces.

1.3 Outline

This edited volume reveals how military CBA can reduce budget pressures and improve defense decisions that contribute to national security. The dual purpose of CBA is to encourage more efficient and effective allocation of society's scarce resources to increase social welfare.[23] Governments often employ CBA to rank (mutually exclusive) portfolios of projects or programs. The typical CBA involves at least eight steps:

1   Identify key decision-makers (and other stakeholders) to clarify goals, objectives, preferences, and constraints (including realistic funding projections).
2   Carefully structure the problem and identify feasible alternatives that contribute to those goals/objectives and that satisfy the constraints.
3   Determine the relevant time horizon over which the CBA will be conducted and select an appropriate discount rate.
4   Estimate relevant time-phased costs of each alternative over the relevant period.
5   Forecast time-phased benefits that will accrue over the relevant period.[24] This edited volume offers alternative approaches to structure a military CBA when benefits cannot be monetized. If benefits can be monetized, then the project or program with the highest net present value (NPV) can be recommended.[25]
6   The sixth step is to recognize uncertainty and conduct sensitivity analyses to determine whether results change with changes in key parameters (costs, benefits, budgets, discount rates, etc.).[26]
7   The seventh step is to report the results of the analysis (rankings of projects, programs, etc., along with key assumptions).
8   The final step is to make well-informed recommendations.

These eight basic steps of a CBA are explored throughout the chapters of this edited volume. The book consists of seventeen chapters divided into five parts.

1.3.1   Part I: Introduction and problem formulation

This part includes the first four chapters. Chapter 1 which you are reading offers a broad overview and outline of the book. Chapter 2 entitled "Allocating national security resources" sets the strategic tone of the book through the lens of US global security concerns. The Honorable J. Gansler (former US Under Secretary of Defense for Acquisition, Technology and Logistics) and his co-author W. Lucyshyn discuss challenges of wide-ranging international threats, domestic budgetary restrictions, and ongoing acquisition problems—including questions about future capacity to support current acquisitions. Revealing a possible mismatch between the National Security Strategy and the PPBS process, the authors highlight the need for military CBA at national, departmental, and program levels to make sound resource allocation decisions.[27] They also stress the vital role played by CBA in the continual process of reassessment and innovation necessary to maintain critical linkages between resources and requirements and to guarantee effective forces in a dynamic security environment.

   In Chapter 3, a prominent UK pioneer in defense economics, K. Hartley, and his Canadian senior defense scientist co-author B. Solomon (co-editor of this volume), confront the challenge of measuring defense outputs. While the economics approach discussed in "Measuring defense output: an economics perspective" is difficult to operationalize into a set of clear and unambiguous policy precepts, it does provide an important framework to help evaluate the benefits of defense outputs and activities. Combining theory and practice, the chapter describes attempts to measure defense outputs in the United States, Australia, New Zealand, and the United Kingdom and other European nations. Later chapters in this book provide several practical methods to help address challenges posed by the authors.

While maintaining the strategic themes of Chapter 2 and recognizing measurement challenges discussed in Chapter 3, Chapter 4 by F. Melese offers a comprehensive set of military CBA approaches to structure public investment decisions. Entitled "The economic evaluation of alternatives," six approaches are introduced that address a significant weakness in many conventional military "analyses of alternatives" (AoAs).[28] Historically, while AoAs correctly focused on lifecycle costs and operational effectiveness to evaluate alternatives, "affordability" was an afterthought, at best only implicitly addressed in final stages of the analysis.[29] In sharp contrast, the economic evaluation of alternatives (EEoA) encourages analysts and decision-makers to include affordability explicitly and up front in structuring a military CBA. EEoA places taxpayers alongside warfighters in the defense decision-making process. This requires working with vendors to build proposals based on different funding (budget/affordability) scenarios.[30] The decision map in the concluding section of Chapter 4 offers a comprehensive guide for practitioners to help structure an EEoA.[31]

1.3.2 Part II: Measuring costs and future funding

This part consists of three chapters. Chapter 5 entitled "Cost analysis" focuses on the first of the three main components of an EEoA—costs, budgets, and benefits. D. Nussbaum, who served as the US Navy's chief cost analyst, and his co-author, Professor D. Angelis, discuss approaches to collect, analyze, and estimate costs of proposed projects, programs, or activities. A unique contribution of this chapter is the explicit recognition of "transaction costs."[32] These include measurement, monitoring, management, contracting, negotiation, and other costs associated with government procurement. Depending on the nature of the transaction, it is conceivable that transaction costs could overwhelm the production costs of the desired product or service. Ignoring transaction costs creates a serious risk of underestimating the total costs of a project, program, or activity. In fact, the absence of transaction cost considerations in military CBAs may help explain the prevalence of cost overruns that often negatively impact expected returns on defense investments. To help address current biases and improve cost estimates in military CBAs, the authors recommend incorporating transaction cost considerations into traditional production cost calculations.

Chapter 6 entitled "Advances in cost estimating: a demonstration of advanced machine leaning techniques for cost estimation" presents recent technical advancements in cost estimation. The standard methods to estimate costs of defense systems in early design phases discussed in Chapter 5 include costing by analogy and parametric approaches. Analogy methods base the costs of new systems on historical costs of similar or "analogous" systems. The traditional approach is to ask subject matter experts to make subjective evaluations of differences between the new system and the old. This leads to the application of complexity factors to adjust the analogous (old) system's cost to produce an estimate for the new system. Rather than apply subjectively obtained complexity factors, an innovative proposal by Defence Research and Development Canada scientist B. Kaluzny explores the use of machine learning algorithms to estimate the costs of systems in early design phases. The author proposes a cost estimation by analogy approach that involves an agglomerative hierarchical cluster analysis and nonlinear optimization that requires limited subjective input. With limited information, traditional parametric approaches to cost estimation rely on basic statistical models to develop cost estimating relationships (CERs) to help identify major cost drivers. CERs can be as simple as a ratio or involve linear regression analysis of historical systems or subsystems. The author proposes a new parametric technique, the M-system of Quinlan (a combination of decision trees and linear regression models), for learning models that predict numeric values.

Having established the importance of treating affordability (or future funding constraints) up front in an EEoA, the challenge of forecasting long-term defense budgets is explored in Chapter 7. Colonel R. Fetterly and B. Solomon begin their chapter "Facing future funding realities: forecasting budgets beyond the future year defense plan" by highlighting the importance of strategic management methods, such as capabilities-based planning, to link existing military capabilities and force development goals to the future security environment. These strategic management approaches are coupled with a variety of forecasting models that take into account a nation's security threats, income, spillover effects of allies' defense posture, and competing demands for a limited public purse. The authors draw on data from a selection of NATO countries to develop several valuable budget forecasting models.

1.3.3   Part III: Measuring effectiveness

Chapters 8 and 9 offer a standard and novel approach, respectively, to develop military MoEs. Chapter 8, entitled "Multiple-objective decision-making," focuses on practical, conventional methods used to structure a military CBA when faced with the challenge of quantifying non-monetary benefits of defense projects, programs, or policies. Professors K. Wall and C. MacKenzie confront the challenge of non-monetary benefits leveraging the literature on multiple-objective (and multi-criteria) decision-making. The authors present a standard approach to help solve multiple-objective decision problems. Many contemporary decision problems in defense management and government resource allocation produce multiple, competing benefits. This chapter offers the widely employed analysis of alternatives (AoA) approach.

Chapter 9 offers a new, cutting-edge approach to conduct a military CBA focused on force protection investments. If the goal is to evaluate investments to protect soldiers, then monetizing the benefits of lives saved can help save the greatest number of lives. In this chapter, entitled "A new approach to evaluate safety and force protection investments: the value of a statistical life," Professors T. Kniesner, J. Leeth, and R. Sullivan cogently discuss how economists evaluate the benefits of safety investments by observing tradeoffs people actually make between safety and other job or product characteristics. The authors present a widely relevant application of their technique to evaluate the cost-effectiveness of adding armor protection to tactical wheeled vehicles. The value-of-statistical-life (VSL) approach presented in this chapter is an innovative military CBA technique highly recommended for future safety and force protection investments.

1.3.4 Part IV: New approaches to military cost–benefit analysis

In Chapter 10, entitled "The role of cost-effectiveness analysis in allocating defense resources," Professor K. Wall joins forces with C.J. LaCivita and Professor A. Richter (a co-editor) to present a new CBA approach to solve multi-level (multi-tiered) resource allocation problems. Their solution method re-interprets the conventional AoA model with a twist. Applying standard operations research techniques, they incorporate bounded rationality to realistically portray how decision-makers can and do cope with the complexities of multi-level constrained optimization.[33] The bounded rationality formulation employs subjectively assessed weights derived from the judgment and expertise of a central allocator (e.g. the Minister of Defense), that offer guidance to lower-level decision-makers (e.g. the Services: Army, Navy, Air Force) to balance costs and MoEs in building defense proposals.

Another new, groundbreaking military CBA approach is introduced in Chapters 11 and 14. Chapter 11 is entitled "A risk-based approach to cost–benefit analysis: strategic real options, Monte Carlo simulation, knowledge value added, and portfolio optimization." In that chapter renowned expert J. Mun and Professor T. Housel present their pioneering "real options" approach that estimates military returns on investment (ROI), combining risk analysis concepts and portfolio optimization techniques. Two dramatic events unfolded in recent history that fundamentally transformed the contemporary security landscape—the collapse of the Soviet Union and the tragedy of 9/11. From a single well-defined "cold war" nuclear threat, countries now face a wide range of diffuse risks: anything from failed states, terrorism, and arms proliferation to human trafficking, piracy, and cyber-attacks. This historic shift in the national security environment prompted many countries to switch from "threat-based" planning to "capabilities-based" planning (see Fitzsimmons (2007)). With emerging threats harder to predict, strategic planners recommend diversification—building broad portfolios of flexible defense capabilities to counter a wide range of possible security concerns. Chapter 11 offers a new, unconventional approach to military CBA designed to help build "capability portfolios." The strategic intent of the United States and other militaries is to maintain a military edge over rivals. Bureaucratic inertia and political lobbying by established defense firms, however, often result in too heavy a focus on prior conflicts. Research and development (R&D) expenditures represent a real options approach to future contingencies where some, but not all, research is expected to lead to the development of new systems. R&D payments are similar to premiums paid for financial options in that they grant the government the right—but not the obligation—to exploit, defer or abandon R&D investments. Periodic adjustments are made based on research results, new budget realities, and the evolving defense environment.[34] This innovative chapter introduces hands-on applications of Monte Carlo simulation, real options analysis, stochastic forecasting, portfolio optimization, and knowledge value added.

The real options approach attempts to make the best possible decisions under uncertainty and to identify, analyze, quantify, mitigate, and manage risks for military options. In Chapter 12, entitled "Extensions of the Greenfield-Persselin optimal fleet replacement model: application to the Canadian Forces CP-140A Arcturus Fleet," D. Maybury adapts other recent developments in financial modeling to construct a stochastic fleet replacement/overhaul model to predict the optimal timing of replacement. The chapter provides an interesting military application that features a popular maritime surveillance aircraft (the CP-140A Arcturus, a Canadianized version of the Lockheed P-3 Orion).

1.3.5   *Part V: Selected applications*

The last five chapters provide a selection of valuable applications and lessons learned that correspond to the methods and concepts discussed in the preceding chapters. Chapter 13, entitled "Embedding affordability assessments in military cost–benefit analysis analysis: defense modernization in Bulgaria," by V. Georgiev presents an application of the Economic Evaluation of Alternatives (EEoA) in Bulgaria's defense organization. The next two chapters each present real-world applications of military CBA, and are authored by subject matter experts with direct experience in high profile defense programs. Former program manager J. Dillard joins forces with Professors D. Angelis and D. Ford to review development of the Javelin anti-tank weapon system in Chapter 14 entitled "Real options in military acquisition: a retrospective case study of the Javelin anti-tank missile system." Study director W. Greer reviews the C-17 strategic airlift program in Chapter 15 entitled "An application of military cost–benefit analysis in a major defense acquisition: the C-17 Transport Aircraft." Whereas the former study provides a retrospective application of the "real options" approach, the latter offers a valuable historical perspective of traditional military CBA.

In Chapter 16, entitled "Cost-effectiveness analysis of autonomous aerial platforms and communications payloads," Commander (USN) R. Everly, Lieutenant (USN) D. Limmer and Professor C. MacKenzie build a traditional military CBA to evaluate investments in UAVs. The final chapter, by economists J. Hanson and J. Lipow, tackles a thorny issue: the so-called "social rate of discount." The debate among economists on whether, and by how much, to discount future costs in public procurement remains unresolved. Chapter 17, entitled "Time-discounting in military cost–benefit analysis" cogently summarizes the literature and contrasts it with current guidelines published by the US Office of Management and Budget

US OMB (1992). This final contribution offers valuable insights and a practical way forward that could help integrate the existing literature with government guidelines to improve the quality of military CBAs.

1.4 Conclusion

Tight budgets make for hard choices. The greater the pressure on public budgets the greater the opportunity to apply military CBA. Today, the impact of government deficits and debt on military spending is inescapable.[35] As one of the largest discretionary items in government budgets, military spending is an obvious target for cuts. While wise use of military power can underpin economic growth, it is equally clear that economic strength underpins military power. Shrinking budgets place a renewed premium on affordability. As sovereign debt challenges squeeze national budgets, and emerging threats challenge existing security forces, this edited volume offers a valuable set of tools and techniques to help navigate the political landscape and meet calls to increase the transparency, efficiency, and effectiveness of the defense sector.

Notes

1 According to the World Bank average, military expenditures globally account for 9.2 percent of government spending. http://data.worldbank.org/indicator/MS.MIL.XPND. ZS/countries/AU-C5-C7?display=graph (accessed February 7, 2014).

2 Office of the Deputy Assistant Secretary of the Army, *U.S. Army Cost–Benefit Analysis Guide*, January 12, 2010, p.6. In general, the US Federal Government's Office of Management and Budget (OMB) Circular A-94 provides guidance for the application of CBA across the entire Executive Branch. DoD Instruction 7041.3 "Economic Analysis for Decision Making" provides explicit guidance for the Department of Defense.

3 Notable among these is the concept of "consumer surplus."

4 Note that this criterion does not require transfers to actually occur and is occasionally debated on equity grounds (see Footnote 10).

5 Assuming policies, projects or programs are independent and there are no binding constraints on inputs.

6 In theory, selecting projects with positive net benefits maximizes aggregate wealth (e.g. GDP growth) which indirectly helps those that might be made worse off. Moreover, an implicit assumption is that costs imposed on some and benefits accrued to others will tend to average out across individuals. Where interactions occur among projects, the general rule is to choose the combination of projects that maximizes net benefits.

7 For example, benefits of a decision to allocate scarce financial resources among major military missions.

8 For example, see Brooks (2005) or Gartzke (2007).

9 Chapter 3 in this edited volume offers a notable exception.

10 Examples of proximate criteria or partial measures of effectiveness include speed, operating range, weapons accuracy, and armor protection.

11 For example, see OMB Circular A-94 *Guidelines and Discount Rates for Benefit-Cost Analysis of Federal Programs* published by the US Office of Management and Budget. Note that this edited volume will continue to use the generic term "military CBA" to refer to cases where benefits cannot be monetized. Although CEA also produces a ranking, there is no explicit information about whether the highest ranked alternative would

provide positive net social benefits. If all alternatives are mutually exclusive, and the status quo is among the alternatives, sharing similar scale and phasing of costs and benefits, then it is possible to apply CEA to select the most efficient policy.

12 Given the vast existing literature on building MOEs, this book instead focuses on the careful construction of military CBAs. Although we occasionally explore the question of developing non-monetary benefit measures, we encourage the reader to review the extensive literature on multi-criteria decision-making for alternative approaches to deriving such measures of effectiveness. (For example, see Keeney and Raiffa 1976; Buede 1986; or Kirkwood 1997.)

13 "The ultimate objective of PPBS shall be to provide operational commanders-in-chief the best mix of forces, equipment, and support attainable within fiscal constraints" (DoD Directive 7045, 14 May 22, 1984). The basic questions of systems analysis are twofold: i) given a fixed budget, which weapon systems are most cost-effective and, conversely, ii) given a fixed military mission, which system(s) could generate the desired level of effectiveness at the lowest cost? The basic ideas of PPBS were: "the attempt to put defense program issues into a broader context and to search for explicit measures of national need and adequacy;" "consideration of military needs and costs together;" "explicit consideration of alternatives at the top decision level;" "the active use of an analytical staff at the top policymaking levels;" "a plan combining both forces and costs which projected into the future the foreseeable implications of current decisions;" and "open and explicit analysis ... made available to all interested parties, so that they can examine the calculations, data, and assumptions and retrace the steps leading to the conclusions" (Enthoven and Smith 2005). http://www.rand.org/content/dam/rand/pubs/commercial_books/2010/RAND_CB403.pdf.

14 In practice, measuring contributions of various inputs towards a defense goal can be difficult and contentious, and these desirable results only hold under the assumption ("homotheticity") that optimal input ratios are independent of the budget and depend only on relative costs of each input. It is also important to recognize transaction costs associated with the application of military CBA (or systems analysis). For example, centralization of decision-making authority under Secretary of Defense Robert McNamara resulted in a proliferation of management systems to collect data required to evaluate the costs and benefits of alternative projects and programs (weapon systems). Increasingly buried in paperwork, the term "paralysis of analysis" was coined by some members of the defense establishment (personal conversation with A. Enthoven).

15 In 1972, the Systems Analysis division evolved into the Office of Program Analysis and Evaluation (PA&E) and later, in 2009, into the Office of Cost Assessment and Program Evaluation (CAPE). Prior to his departure, Dr Hitch launched an OSD-sponsored education institution to teach civilian and military managers in DoD (and partners and allies) basic principles of PPBS and CBA. Today it is known as the Defense Resources Management Institute (DRMI) located at the Naval Postgraduate School in Monterey, California. Two co-editors of this volume (Dr Melese and Dr Richter) are faculty members at this institution which celebrated its 50th anniversary in 2015 (http://www.nps.edu/drmi/; http://www.dtic.mil/whs/directives/corres/pdf/501035p.pdf).

16 McNamara relied heavily on systems analysis to reach several controversial weapon decisions. He canceled the B-70 bomber, begun during the Eisenhower years as a replacement for the B-52, stating that it was neither cost-effective nor needed, and later he vetoed its proposed successor, the RS-70. McNamara expressed publicly his belief that the manned bomber as a strategic weapon had no long-run future; the intercontinental ballistic missile was faster, less vulnerable, and less costly. Similarly, McNamara terminated the Skybolt project late in 1962. Begun in 1959, Skybolt was conceived as a ballistic missile with a 1,000-nautical mile range, designed for launching from B-52 bombers as a defense suppression weapon to clear the way for bombers to penetrate to targets. McNamara decided that Skybolt was too expensive, was not accurate enough,

and would exceed its planned development time. He claimed other systems, including the Hound Dog missile, could do the job at less cost.

17 Our view is that a clean military CBA is a valuable starting point for political debate. Careful analysis can constrain political attempts to turn defense spending into a jobs program or an opportunity to redistribute income. Since there exist considerably more efficient and effective ways to promote job growth and income distribution, if these are the goals, then they should be stated explicitly and explored using a separate CBA. This may prove a valuable avenue for future research.

18 An example is the case of the F-35 aircraft program. Lockheed-Martin claimed to have "created 125,000 US-based direct and indirect jobs in 46 states" http://www.businessweek.com/news/2014-01-22/lockheed-martin-inflating-f-35-job-growth-claims-nonprofit-says (accessed March 21, 2014).

19 Since costs (e.g. investment expenditures) tend to occur earlier with benefits appearing later, discount rates can also be strategically selected to make projects appear more or less attractive. (See Chapter 17.)

20 For example, see NATO's Building Integrity initiative at www.nato.int/cps/en/natolive/topics_68368.htm [last accessed June 24, 2014].

21 For example, see Camm and Greenfield (2005).

22 As public officials face growing resistance to tax increases, pressure increases on governments to work more efficiently and effectively.

23 National defense satisfies two key characteristics of a "public good." It is: i) non-rival and ii) non-excludable. In the former case, unlike private goods, if one person in a geographic area is defended from foreign attack or invasion, his or her consumption is non-rival in that others in the area can consume the same level of national security for little or no additional cost. In the latter case, if one person is defended, others in that same area cannot be excluded from the security benefits. This leads to a classic free-rider problem, making it difficult to charge people for national defense. The key here is that whereas it is generally agreed that the *provision* of national defense is a public good that must be funded with taxes, the *production* of national defense depends on the relative costs (including transaction costs) and benefits of public and private sector production, which can be evaluated using military CBA.

24 Since benefits of proposed defense investments are often difficult to monetize, various approaches have been developed to construct MOEs that capture the value or utility of alternatives. In theory, the benefits of alternative defense investments could be monetized if their contribution to security and stability encourages foreign direct investment that contributes to economic growth and social welfare. In practice, precise linkages between defense investments and economic growth are difficult to establish. As a consequence, the benefits of most military investments are not monetized, and instead various MOEs are constructed to conduct a CEA that is referred to in this volume as a military CBA (e.g. see OMB Circular A-94).

25 If benefits can be monetized, then calculate the discounted sum of net benefits (benefits minus costs) from each alternative over the specified time period, i.e. the discounted NPV. For example, consider two alternative military projects designed to achieve the goal of reducing the Navy's fuel budget. Suppose there is a fixed investment budget available, and the two mutually exclusive alternatives each require the same identically phased investment. The first proposal is to invest in a program to convert ship propulsion from conventional diesel to a less expensive bio-diesel. The second proposal is to invest in an energy conservation program at Navy installations. Since the two alternatives require the same identically phased investments, the CBA can simply focus on the stream of benefits (savings from cheaper fuel in the first case and reduction in fuel demand in the second) that accrue from each project. Assuming a preference for present vs. future savings, the discounted present value of each stream of savings can be calculated to determine the winning project. (See Chapter 17.)

26 Alternatively, a "Real Options" approach could be adopted, conducting Monte Carlo simulations assigning probability distributions to key parameters. (For example, See Chapters 11 and 14.)

27 The authors also warn that until new mechanisms such as CBA are adopted to address the continual failure to fuse requirements with necessary resources, DoD will essentially continue to create a disjointed, ineffective framework for addressing national security concerns rather than the vital cohesive plan required to confront the changing dynamics of modern, global warfare.

28 See Ullman and Ast (2011) and OMB Circular A-11 (2008) for discussions of AoAs.

29 In the US, AoAs are conducted in early phases (milestones) of major defense acquisitions. Since they frequently occur in early development before a project is fully funded, they rarely incorporate future funding forecasts. Instead, the budget estimate for the program or project is generated as an output of the AoA. As major budget cuts create funding challenges for new defense programs, "affordability" in terms of realistic budget constraints is gaining increasing importance in AoAs.

30 A key difference between traditional AoAs and EEoA is that instead of modeling competing vendors as points in cost-effectiveness space, EEoA solicits vendor offers as functions of optimistic, pessimistic, and most likely funding (budget) scenarios. A formal mathematical model of EEoA can be found in Simon and Melese (2011).

31 Following the recommended EEoA approach also provides a unique opportunity to achieve a significant defense reform: to coordinate the Requirements Generation System, Defense Acquisition System, and Planning, Programming, and Budgeting System (PPBS)—to lower costs, and improve performance and schedules.

32 For example, see Williamson and Masten (1999) or Melese *et al.* (2007).

33 Finding the optimal mix of forces to accomplish a military goal at the lowest possible cost, or alternatively, for a given budget, to find the optimal mix that maximizes defense capabilities.

34 The real options approach builds on what was previously referred to as incremental or "spiral" development of military programs and projects.

35 The response of many governments to the global recession was to bail out banks and businesses and to stimulate their economies. Combined with falling tax receipts, this led to unprecedented increases in government spending. The result in many countries transformed the financial crisis into a chronic sovereign debt crisis. Annual deficits soared and cumulative debt loads reached unsustainable levels. Aging demographics in some countries compounded the problem, placing impossible demands on social welfare programs and introduced further pressure on government budgets. Combined with an uncertain threat environment, the fiscal crisis makes a compelling case for widespread application of military CBAs to ensure future defense decisions to produce efficient, effective, and accountable security forces.

References

Buede, D. M. 1986. "Structuring Value Attributes." *Interfaces* 16(2): 52–62.

Brooks, S. G. 2005. *Producing Security: Multinatinal Corporations, Globalization, and the Changing Calculus of Conflict.* Princeton, NJ: Princeton University Press.

Camm, Frank, and Victoria A. Greenfield. 2005. *How Should the Army Use Contractors on the Battlefield: Assessing Comparative Risk in Sourcing Decisions.* Santa Monica, CA: RAND Corporation.

Dupuit, J. 1844. De La mesure de l'utilité des travaux publics. *Annales des Ponts et Chaussées, Memories et Documents* 2, 8: 332–375. Translated by R. H. Barback into English, "On the Measurement of the Utility of Public Works." 1952. *International Economic Papers* 2: 83–110.

Enthoven, A. C., and K. W. Smith. 2005. *How Much is Enough? Shaping the Defense Program, 1961–1969*. Santa Monica, CA: RAND Corporation.

Fitzsimmons, M. 2007. "Whither Capabilities-Based Planning?" *Joint Forces Quarterly* 44(1): 101–105.

Gartzke, E. 2007. "The Capitalist Peace." *American Journal of Political Science* 51(1): 166–191.

Haveman, R. 1976. "Policy Analysis and the Congress: An Economist's View." *Policy Analysis* 2(2): 235–250.

Hicks, J. R. 1940. "The Valuation of the Social Income." *Economica* 7(26): 105–124.

Hitch, C., and R. McKean. 1960. *The Economics of Defense in the Nuclear Age*. London: Oxford University Press.

Kaldor, N. 1939. "Welfare Propositions of Economics and Interpersonal Comparisons of Utility." *Economic Journal* 49(195): 549–552.

Keeney, R. L., and H. Raiffa. 1976. *Decisions with Multiple Objectives: Preferences and Value Tradeoffs* (Probability and Mathematical Statistics Series). New York: John Wiley & Sons, Inc.

Kirkwood, C. W. 1997. *Strategic Decision Making: Multiobjective Decision Analysis with Spreadsheets*. Belmont, CA: Duxbury Press.

Marshall, A. 1920. *Principles of Economics* (8th edition). London: MacMillan & Co. Ltd.

Melese, F., R. Franck, D. Angelis, and J. Dillard. 2007. "Applying Insights from Transaction Cost Economics to Improve Cost Estimates for Public Sector Purchases: The Case of U.S. Military Acquisition." *International Public Management Journal* 10(4): 357–85.

Pareto, V. 1909. *Manuel d'Economie Politique*. Paris: V. Giard et E. Briere. Reprinted, Paris: M. Girard, 1927; Geneva: Librarie Droz, 1966.

Prest, A. R., and R. Turvey. 1965. "Cost–Benefit Analysis: A Survey." *The Economic Journal* 75(300): 683–735.

Simon, J., and F. Melese. 2011. "A Multiattribute Sealed-Bid Procurement Auction with Multiple Budgets for Government Vendor Selection." *Decision Analysis* 8(3): 170–79.

Ullman, D. G., and R. Ast. September 2011. "Analysis of Alternatives (AoA) Based Decisions." *Military Operations Research Society, Phalanx* 44(3): 24–36.

US Office of Management and Budget (OMB). 1992. *Circular No. A-94, Guidelines and Discount Rates for Benefit-Cost Analysis of Federal Programs*. Washington, DC: Executive Office of the President. Available at www.whitehouse.gov/omb/circulars_a094/ [last accessed September 18, 2014].

US Office of Management and Budget (OMB). 2008. *Circular No. A-11, Preparation, Submission, and Execution of the Budget*. Washington, DC: Executive Office of the President. Available at www.whitehouse.gov/omb/circulars_a11_current_year_a11_toc [last accessed November 11, 2014].

Williamson, O. E., and S. E. Masten (Eds). 1999. *The Economics of Transaction Costs* (Elgar Critical Writings Reader). Northampton, MA: Edward Elgar Publishing.

2 Allocating national security resources

Jacques S. Gansler and
William Lucyshyn

Most innovations fail. And companies that don't innovate die . . . In today's world, where the only constant is change, the task of managing innovation is vital for companies of every size in every industry. Innovation is vital to sustain and advance companies' current business; it is critical to growing new business. It is also a very difficult process to manage.

Henry W. Chesbrough 2006, Haas School of Business
Berkeley California

2.1 Introduction

Private sector firms have accepted that they must continuously innovate to stay competitive in today's global environment. This innovation is not a one-time event, but a continuous exercise. Similarly, in a world of emerging and evolving challenges and threats, ministries of defense must be willing to continuously innovate. The constancy of change cannot be met with technology, training, or operational concepts that are outdated and inadequate. Equally important, as private sector firms have discovered, are innovations improving business processes. Within the US Department of Defense (DoD), one business process needs immediate attention—the one used to allocate national security resources. Military cost–benefit analysis (CBA) has an important role to play. To fully appreciate this imperative, one must understand and appreciate the environment that DoD finds itself in today. The willingness of DoD to adopt innovative CBA concepts to overhaul its resource allocation processes will directly affect the department's capacity to meet future threats to US and global security.

2.2 Background

During the cold war, US defense planning was, to a large degree, threat-based. The monolithic threat posed by the Soviet Union could sensibly, if not always accurately, be described in terms of troops, fighter aircraft, tanks, and missiles. The threat was remarkably stable and evolved slowly, simplifying the Pentagon's planning challenge—as well as the cost–benefit analysis of investments to cope with that threat.

With the dissolution of the Soviet Union, the relentless influence of the cold war upon the nation and its national security strategy vanished. Some, believing that mankind had reached the pinnacle of ideological evolution, wrote of the end of history with the United States as the world's lone super-power (Fukuyama 1989).

By the beginning of the 1990s, the United States found itself in the midst of a very different war—Desert Storm. This war showcased a new manner of warfare, involving precision strike capabilities used in conjunction with real-time information exchange—an early version of net-centric warfare. There was still much to be learned, however, and many additional advancements to be made. The Gulf War offered the first glimpse of technological capabilities, and these will continue to reshape warfare throughout the twenty-first century.

Immediately following Operation Desert Storm, powerful forces began to influence policy-makers as they anticipated a new era of change. These included the acceleration of the information technology revolution, globalization, the potential threat of terrorism, and perhaps most importantly the desire to reap a "peace dividend." With no clear rival in sight, the United States began a period of disinvestment, and it expedited efforts to downsize its military forces (Walker 2014).

Then, on September 11, 2001, the attacks on the World Trade Center and the Pentagon highlighted a new, global threat from terrorist organizations. The events of that day created an unprecedented urgency for innovative changes in the US defense establishment, and they laid the foundation for adjustment to the new global security environment. As the threats now addressed by the DoD were vastly different from those it faced in the previous five decades, this adjustment proved especially vital (Freier 2007).

While numerous earlier reports had highlighted the potential for transformation of the security environment (Cha 2000), the events of 9/11 provided the catalyst for reform. The formerly relatively stable Soviet threat was replaced by profoundly uncertain, fragmented, and complex threats that proved far more difficult to satisfactorily address. In addition to the threat from global terrorism, there were threats from failed or failing states that resulted in civil wars, humanitarian catastrophes, and regional instability. This tremendously unstable international security environment makes it extremely challenging to predict with any confidence what threats the United States, its partners, and allies might face in the medium or even the near-term.

2.3 The new security environment

The new security environment continues to pose unique operational challenges, making it difficult for a cold war-designed military to respond in a timely and appropriate manner. Recently, it is hoped that the presence and strength of the United States' armed forces can contribute to peace in some of the most important and dangerous places in the world.[1] As the United States's threats and enemies continue to adapt and transform, however, so too must its force structure.

The most recent shifts in the dynamics of warfare and threats to the United States have not been more evident than in the conflicts in Afghanistan and Iraq. There, US forces faced a new type of protracted, low-intensity conflict that seems to have defined a new paradigm for warfare. Counterinsurgency, nation-building, and protracted conflict—all hallmarks of US efforts in Afghanistan and Iraq— seem to offer insight into modern conflict and DoD's future requirements. How, and how well, DoD will prepare to confront new battlefield trends (including "war among the people"(Smith 2005)) remains to be seen.

The present security requirements demand that the US military be able to respond to disruptive, catastrophic, irregular, and traditional threats. These can be delivered by undetermined weapons and delivery systems to undetermined targets from often undetermined entities at undetermined times (Perl 2006). The pressure to counter these potential threats demands the development of a new, holistic view of security. Consider briefly some of these potential threats:

- *Global terrorism.* Global terrorism can be initiated at the national level or come from non-state actors, such as Al Qaeda, Hezbollah, Islamic State (IS), and other extremists groups. Some of these transnational groups are very well funded and have access to advanced weapons on the international market. Their actions, even on a small scale, can have significant effects. One of the greatest fears is that they will acquire and use weapons of mass destruction (biological, chemical, radiological, or nuclear). Their goals can be fairly narrow, such as the overthrow of legitimate regimes; or very broad, such as the establishment of a regional "caliphate" (Al-Salhy 2014). Terrorist groups most often target innocent citizens at home and abroad. While statistics vary widely in their accounting of terrorist attacks, the general consensus is that since 9/11 the number of events has rapidly increased each year (The Institute for Economics and Peace 2012). Most important for this discussion is to recognize that terrorists cannot be defeated solely by traditional military means.
- *Proliferation of weapons of mass destruction (WMD).* The proliferation of WMD, as well as their delivery systems, increases the possibility of their use, with the potential for significant casualties. Many countries already possess WMD, or they have the capacity to produce them. In addition, an increasing number of countries are in the process of acquiring and developing these capabilities. There is a growing interest among certain terrorist groups in acquiring such weapons.
- *Cyber warfare.* Although military systems are increasingly being designed to be hardened to cyber attacks, most of the nation's critical infrastructure is owned and controlled by the private sector, and it continues to be vulnerable. Successful cyber attacks on, for example, central banking systems, power distribution systems, or hospital computer systems could have devastating effects. There have already been major cyber attacks against other countries. Estonia, for example, suffered a major cyber attack in 2007 (believed to have originated in Russia). Further, prior to Russia's military incursion into

Georgia in 2008, the Georgian government's communications and information systems were disrupted with an extensive cyber attack (Schwirtz 2008). We can anticipate that future military operations will increasingly utilize cyber attacks to facilitate and amplify any kinetic conflicts.

- *Regional conflicts.* There are several recent examples of regional conflicts: the United States's "Global War on Terror" that involved large-scale operations in Iraq and Afghanistan, Israel's conflicts with Hezbollah in Lebanon in 2006 and with Hamas in 2014, and recent events in Ukraine. These can be fought against national governments and/or against groups of insurgents. In addition, there exist several potential regional conflicts, such as between North and South Korea; between China and Taiwan; between India and Pakistan, some of which could easily draw in the United States.

- *Potential future peer competitors.* The most frequently identified potential future peer competitor is mainland China, but others, such as India or even a resurgent Russia, cannot be dismissed. It is important to note, however, that there is no current "peer" to the overwhelming strength of the US military establishment (Perlo-Freeman 2014). Nonetheless, the United States should not ignore the potential of a future peer competitor as that would signal weakness in future geopolitical negotiations with any nation with ambitions of building a strong, regional or global military presence.

- *Non-traditional national security challenges.* There are several potential non-traditional security challenges that the United States may face. First, there is a real possibility of devastating global pandemics (for example, outbreaks of infectious disease, such as the Avian flu) that can spread quickly and rapidly overwhelm national healthcare systems. A second non-traditional security challenge is the increasing global demand for scarce strategic resources such as lithium, or possibly (with the worst-case global warming scenario), even drinking water. Third, international criminal activities have taken on a scale where they generate budgets as large as the GDP of many countries, corrupt the political process, and are often linked with the terrorist community. Finally, as some nation-states fail to maintain their own internal security, there is a strong possibility that the United States may be asked to contribute to stability—for humanitarian reasons—or to assist threatened neighboring partner or allied countries.

Although military CBA can help DoD as it shifts its portfolio of capabilities to meet these new challenges, the current force structure is still far from being able to fully respond to this spectrum of new challenges. As a result, the Department is faced with difficult investment decisions to bridge this gap, while simultaneously responding to current operational challenges.

2.3.1 Domestic spending pressures on the defense budget

Similar to many countries, the United States faces several long-term budgetary challenges to meet the rapidly rising burden of domestic entitlement programs.

Interest payments on the federal debt, required to meet the nation's mandatory spending, will soon directly impact the DoD's ability to transform its forces. The United States will suffer an escalating financial burden as baby boomers age (by 2020, the number of people in US population between the ages of 65 and 84 is expected to rise by nearly 50 percent (US Census Bureau 2004)), and mandatory spending on programs such as social security and Medicare will necessarily increase.[2] Unlike annual appropriations, which specify how much can be spent on a specific program in that year, the laws that govern these entitlement programs specify formulas to calculate benefits and eligibility criteria that automatically determine the level of spending, and do not require Congressional action.

Social security remains only the largest of the "must pay" costs expected to significantly increase in coming decades. Medicare and Medicaid, as well as interest on the national debt, will also continue to increase significantly as a percentage of GDP.[3] Based upon US Government Accountability Office (GAO) projections, 93 cents of every federal dollar will be spent in one of these three categories by 2020 (GAO 2010). The Congressional Budget Office (CBO) also projects continued growth within these three major programs.[4] Compounding the problem, net interest payments on the national debt are projected to grow to 8 percent of GDP by 2030, placing a substantial additional strain on the federal budget (GAO 2010). While CBO and historical trends suggest further increases in US economic output and a continually growing GDP, DoD's budget is projected to continue to shrink as a percentage of GDP. Since 1971, defense budgets have fluctuated from 7.3 percent of GDP to a historical low of 3.0 percent in 1999, 2000, and 2001.

Although defense spending and budgets have since increased, largely in response to conflicts in Afghanistan and Iraq, this upward trend is reversing after the military drawdown. CBO has stated that DoD budgets—given the most likely drawdown rate—will decrease from its current level of 4.6 percent of GDP to 3.1 percent by 2020 (see Figure 2.1).[5]

The trend is clear: mandatory domestic spending, specifically social security, Medicare, and Medicaid, as well as interest on the national debt, will increase well beyond historical levels, and will inevitably put downward pressure on future DoD budgets. This will serve to constrain funds available for recapitalization, modernization, and transformation. Future investments guided by military CBA will increasingly be constrained by shrinking DoD budgets, requiring hard decisions and a reengineering of current processes to ensure the most efficient use of scarce resources.[6]

2.3.2   *Internal defense budget challenges*

As new military missions and requirements emerge in response to the evolving security environment, the danger is that funding for equipment, personnel, operations and maintenance (O&M), and homeland security will increasingly depend on the crisis of the moment—especially given the new fluid environment which makes long-term planning difficult. Further, this problem is only exacerbated by

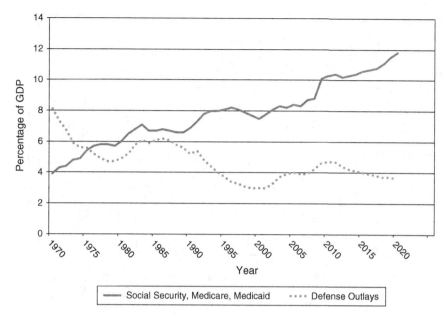

Figure 2.1 Defense and selected entitlement spending as a percentage of GDP.

Source: CBO 2010.

the year-by-year Congressional budget process which constrains the ability of DoD to identify and evaluate long-term funding options.

Further constraining defense budgets is the rising costs of military personnel compensation, annual healthcare, and facilities programs, which make up a sizable portion of "defense discretionary" spending already earmarked for future defense "must pay" requirements. Meanwhile, current operations and support funding represents nearly two-thirds of the DoD budget. Funds dedicated to future modernization represent only roughly one-third of the budget. CBO projections reveal major future increases in spending in areas such as personnel (including healthcare) and O&M, which are projected to rise from US$373 billion in financial year (FY) 2009 to US$425 billion in FY 2028 (in constant 2010 US dollars).

Even though defense budgets are currently well above the cold war average (as shown in Figure 2.2), they will likely decline significantly with troop drawdowns. At the same time, funds invested in research, development, testing, and evaluation (RDT&E) are projected to decline from US$81 billion in FY 2009 to US$54 billion in FY 2028 (in constant 2010 US dollars)—a reduction of approximately 33 percent; which threatens to significantly constrain future investment in modernization (see Figure 2.3) (CBO 2010).

Although budget projections for defense procurement do not currently indicate significant cuts, many defense analysts are skeptical. "Generally, the first thing to go is procurement," Michael Bayer, Chairman of the Defense Business Board was

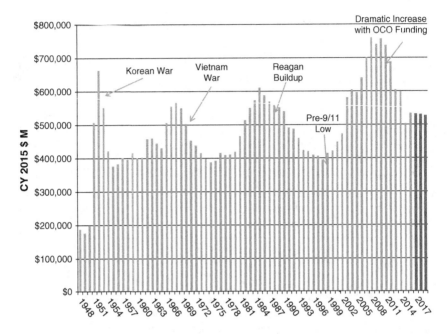

Figure 2.2 DoD total budget authority.

Source: National Defense Budget Estimates for FY 2015, Office of the Under Secretary of Defense (Comptroller), April 2014.

Note: FY 2016–2018 are projected estimates from the President's FY2015 budget.

quoted as saying. "With the spending declines following the Vietnam War and the post-Reagan years, the decline in procurement was steeper than the rate of decline in the overall defense budget" (Boessenkool 2009). In the present environment, it is likely that increasing O&M costs for legacy systems, along with projected rising personnel expenses, will be financed at the expense of future R&D and procurement within DoD.

2.4   Acquisition challenges

In addition to all of these environmental stresses, DoD continues to face several acquisition challenges. In terms of resource allocation, three of the most critical are continued program cost and schedule growth, the generation of requirements, and system-of-systems development.

2.5   Cost and schedule growth

> DoD's major weapon system programs continue to take longer, cost more, and deliver fewer quantities and capabilities than originally planned.
>
> Michael J. Sullivan, GAO 2008 (Sullivan 2008)

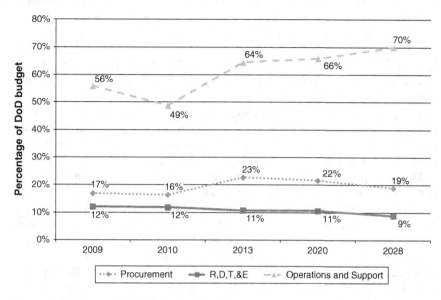

Figure 2.3 Resources for Defense in selected years as a percentage of total DoD budget.

Source: CBO 2010.

Note: 2009 and 2010 include supplemental funding of US$74 billion and US$130 billion.

Acquiring major weapon systems efficiently has proved to be difficult. During 2007 for example, programs that comprised DoD's Major Defense Acquisition Projects (MDAPs), which make up roughly 80 percent of the DoD's acquisition budget in a given year (Younossi *et al.* 2007), had an average program cost growth of 26 percent when compared to initial estimates. These increases represented approximately US$295 billion dollars in additional costs. These programs also experienced, on average, a 21-month delay in delivering initial capability to the warfighters (Sullivan 2008).

Unfortunately, these difficulties are not new. DoD has experienced similar development problems since at least the 1950s (Frank 1997). Despite data limitations, numerous reports issued over the past 50 years have noted high program cost growth. This growth is defined as the positive difference between actual costs and initial (budgeted) costs estimated in the original military CBA. Chapter 5 provides a detailed discussion of cost estimation techniques used in military CBA. Due to its relative ease of measurement, cost growth provides a simple measure to help gauge the efficiency of the acquisition process.

DoD has attempted several reforms to control program and unit cost growth, but most have had limited impact. The V-22 program is a good example. The V-22 Osprey is an innovative, tilt-rotor aircraft developed for Marine Corps, Air Force, and Navy use. The program's concept exploration phase began in 1981, and full-scale development was started in 1986. The V-22 achieved its initial operational capability (IOC) in mid-2007. By 2008, total program cost estimates increased from US$39.1 billion to US$56.1 billion, a 43 percent increase from the 1986 estimate (with reduced quantities!). This was due in large part to increases in R&D costs, which grew from an original estimate of US$4.1 billion budgeted to US$12.8 billion (a 209.6 percent increase). This increase was combined with increases in procurement costs, largely from fixed costs being spread over fewer units as the original program quantity was cut nearly in half (reduced from 913 to 458). While a 2010 GAO report suggested marked improvement in V-22 performance, pre-operational performance tests of the V-22 revealed multiple software and practical operational problems. These problems have continued to drive unit costs up. Unfortunately, this program is not unique. Other major programs, such as the F-22 and most recently F-35, have experienced similar problems, suffering from overly optimistic cost and performance estimates in the original military CBA.

If history is any indication, we can anticipate that many future programs will result in cost overruns during the R&D phase. This in turn results in increased total program costs, increased unit costs, stretched-out programs, and ultimately a reduction in the number of units procured. Unrealistic cost and performance estimates result in flawed military CBAs that require DoD to reassess its programs and change procurement outcomes. Given the nation's other pressing financial obligations, DoD must find ways to improve its military CBA decision-making (both in the initial selection of programs, as well as in its response to inevitable change orders) so that required capabilities can be developed and acquired as economically and efficiently as possible.

2.6   Weapon system requirements

As previously discussed, the current threat environment is pushing the DoD in several different directions. These include fighting the war on terror, deterring future conflicts, and investing in force transformation. Consequently, the focus of twenty-first-century acquisition must lie in several areas, including intelligence, unmanned systems, professional services, and advanced information systems. Emphasis on enhancing these "mission-oriented" areas marks a movement away from "platform-centric" thinking to more "network-centric" thinking in terms of integrated systems-of-systems (with large numbers of relatively inexpensive, distributed, sensors and shooters, all interlinked with complex and secure command, control, and communication systems). This increases the importance of robust military CBA approaches to help guide the acquisition of highly technical, game-changing systems. Examples include manned and unmanned (sensor-based) aircraft systems, net-centric communications systems, and advanced air and ground weapons systems.

All of these systems rely upon technological superiority to maintain their dominance, but if they are not constantly updated to remain ahead of potential threats, they could be rapidly rendered obsolete.

The drive to develop these high-tech systems often requires an extended period to mature and integrate technology. Yet military operators (users) often believe they must get *all* of their requirements included up front or risk losing the opportunity to obtain the complete benefits. Chapters 11 and 14 offer a novel so-called "real options" approach to CBA that attempts to address this concern.

Insisting on including all requirements up front lends itself to a process of identifying and developing requirements for these weapon systems that "is overly cumbersome, but also lacking in the expertise and capacity required to truly vet joint military requirement" (Reform 2010). Further, once requirements are approved, there is a great reluctance by the Services to trade them off for cost reductions or schedule accelerations. This results in programs being stretched out and running over budget. Compounding the problem is that historically DoD's requirements process is not resource-constrained; and, as a result, generates a demand for more new programs than fiscal resources can support. This concern for "affordability" is explicitly addressed in the "economic evaluation of alternatives" presented in Chapter 4.

Major investments in new systems are mostly the responsibility of the military services who recognize that they compete for funding with the other services. The result can be unhealthy. To secure funding for their programs, there is an alarming tendency in military CBAs carried out by the services to keep the program's cost estimates aggressively low—often resulting in program cost growth (Arena *et al.* 2006).[7]

Improving requirements generation and defense acquisition processes is critical. An unbiased military CBA framework is needed so that when a requirement is validated, the expectation should be that it is based on mature technology with more predictable costs and benefits, and that it is programmatically realistic so that it fits into forecasted available future funding (see Chapter 4). Today, that is generally not the case.

Finally, because "traditional" platform-based programs (ships, planes, tanks, etc.) are strongly supported by the services (and industry and Congress), and many of these programs are in current production and operational, the DoD budget has only 10 percent of the total acquisition dollars allocated for equipment optimized for emerging threats such as counterinsurgency, security assistance, humanitarian operations, etc. (Gates 2010). Thus, a significant shift in resource allocation is needed; and this begins with the "requirements process" that establishes security needs (benefits) for the future.

2.7 System-of-systems

With major advances in information technology, many of DoD's weapon systems are now interconnected to form interdependent systems-of-systems. A system-of-systems (SoS) is a set of individual systems that is integrated to operate optimally as a single system. SoS development provides the DoD with the unique ability to integrate and field a full range of assets (new and legacy) to provide required military capabilities. Although one can conceive of developing an entire SoS from scratch, most of DoD's SoS efforts consist of synthesizing existing capabilities of legacy systems, combined with selected newly developed systems to address additional capability needs.

Since it must pull together numerous projects and combine them into a cohesive whole, the size and scale of a SoS complicates any military CBA and the development of these integrated programs. The challenge for DoD is that, although the systems will be integrated in this fashion, they are still developed as individual systems.

In the traditional engineering framework, the goal of a typical development project is to optimize the performance of a particular system (e.g. platform). Since there are multiple systems within the overall SoS, each element is individually optimized (to derive maximum individual performance). In this framework, it is believed that the whole is equal to the sum of its parts.

A problem with this narrow engineering approach is that it fails to take into account how changes in one component of the interrelated whole may affect the performance or requirements (or costs) of other components of the entire system. If one system relies upon a second system having a minimum threshold capability that is not realized, the first may have to be modified to achieve the desired effectiveness. Conversely, optimizing the performance of an individual platform may not necessarily increase the performance of the SoS and it may, in some cases, degrade its overall performance. Due to the size and interconnected nature of SoS, one problem may have ripple effects throughout. Optimizing each individual system can produce a sub-optimal result at the SoS level. The goal must be to optimize the performance of the SoS as a whole and not individual component systems.

Currently, a SoS program generally spans multiple organizations. As a result, a number of authorities may be in a position to influence the decision-making process. Managing the component systems should be done using a portfolio approach with some flexibility to shift resources within the portfolio to meet the SoS requirement. In this way, there would be a level of flexibility not available with the "platform-centric" approach. Ideally, these SoSs will be able to leverage the unique advantages of each component system and result in a capability greater than the sum of its parts.

In the most likely future of limited resources, however, there is another problem with optimizing individual systems versus the overall SoS: namely "affordability" (see Chapter 4). SoS is a potentially valuable innovation that creates new challenges for military CBAs. In a resource-constrained environment, the focus of military CBA should be to optimize overall performance at an affordable price (often integrating lower-cost individual elements).

2.7.1   *Resource allocation within Department of Defense*

The biggest issue facing the Defense Department will be the mismatch between requirements and funds available.

General Charles Krulak, Former Marine Corps Commandant,
Elaine M. Grossman, *National Journal,* May 30, 2008

The nation's approach to allocating resources within the DoD, imperfect under the best conditions, will be severely challenged in the face of an increasingly unpredictable threat environment coupled with expected budgetary constraints. Yet, even today, a great deal of effort is placed on identifying shortfalls and the requirements to overcome them. Often this does not include the identification of the necessary resources or where they will come from. In a most likely future resource-constrained environment, a premium will be placed on resource-constrained planning (see Chapters 4 and 7). The relationship between the congressionally approved DoD budget and yearly outlays places great urgency on the ability to fuse requirements planning with necessary budget funding. Planning, that has always been difficult, based on the size and scope of the DoD enterprise, is growing increasingly more complex and uncertain.

Defense planning takes place through the planning, programming, budgeting, and execution (PPBE) process. The PPBE is the DoD's internal management and information system used to plan the allocation of resources to acquire the capabilities believed necessary to accomplish the DoD's missions. A key output of the PPBE process is the defense budget included in the President's budget submitted to the Congress. This system has evolved from the planning, programming, and budgeting system (PPBS), which was first introduced by Secretary of Defense Robert McNamara in the early 1960s. It was developed to coordinate three major facets of the DoD: planning, programming, and budgeting. As the name implies, the system attempted to draw together these three facets of DoD within an internal budgeting process.

The Congressional Budget and Impoundment Control Act was passed in 1974. This established the statutory basis for an integrated Congressional budget process, and provided for the annual adoption of a concurrent resolution on the budget as a mechanism to facilitate Congressional budgetary decision-making. It also established the current US federal fiscal year from October 1st to September 30th. Changes continued and in 1986 the Department of Defense Authorization Act was passed, requiring DoD to submit a two-year budget. While this was intended to help promote more accurate forecasting within the DoD planning process, as well as to shelter DoD from the unpredictability of annual Congressional review and approval, the Act placed an even greater emphasis upon DoD's ability to forecast external global actions, internal US politics, and internal changes in DoD. To date, the process has largely remained an "annual budget" process (in terms of commitments).

In 2003, the PPBS was changed to the PPBE process. This change—an attempt to place more emphasis upon "execution"—did not significantly change the framework from which DoD plans, programs, budgets, or even executes its budgets.

The first and arguably the most important step in the PPBE process is planning. A key element in the planning process is the quadrennial defense review (QDR). The QDR, conducted every four years, attempts to provide a "comprehensive examination" of DoD's national strategy, internal workings, and budget plan in an attempt to frame and structure national defense strategy and programs.

Mandated by Congress in 1997 through the National Defense Authorization Act, the QDR was intended to establish a cohesive longer-term framework for defense programming—with direct involvement of the Chairman of the Joint Chiefs of Staff Popescu (2010).

Critics argue that QDR planners from the various services, in an attempt to preserve their favorite weapon systems or increase their branch's budget within DoD, simply compete for prominent positions within this broad strategic framework. The result is a document where the only non-bureaucratized portion is a set of strategic, although sometimes unfocused and unconnected, bullet points somewhat detached from the reality of DoD's year-to-year PPBE process until the next QDR is launched.

During the planning process, the results of the QDR, along with other planning guidance (including the National Military Strategy), are reviewed, and the process ends with the development of the *Guidance for the Development of the Force* (GDF) and the *Joint Programming Guidance* (JPG). The GDF provides broad guidance in the form of strategic goals and desired capabilities, while the JPG addresses specific programs and provides dollar thresholds. These planning documents, along with broad fiscal guidance from the OMB, provide DoD Components with direction on defense policy, strategy, force and resource planning, and fiscal matters. The Components use them to develop their *Program Objective Memorandum* (POM), which extends six years into the future (Keehan 2008). These Component developed POMs are reviewed to ensure they conform to guidance provided by the Secretary of Defense in the planning phase, and changes are made as required. "Although the programming phase is a debate about means—which program choices best achieve the stated goals—it often reopens the debate about those goals, revisiting choices made in the planning phase" (Chu 2003).

While DoD's PPBE process attempts to address shifting requirements and defense spending, there remains a mismatch between long-term DoD strategy and resource allocation mechanisms. For example, the QDR—designed to provide a long-run framework for US defense planning—inadvertently contributes to this mismatch when it fails to pair the necessary future funding realities with identified requirements. Chapter 7 in this volume attempts to address the challenge of forecasting future budgets.

Direct Congressional action on or intervention in DoD's PPBE creates another possible mismatch. Administrations can be unpredictable enough, but Congress requires another level of forecasting: With 535 members, Congress can radically change the direction of its funding decisions in off-year elections. With an exceptional number of opinions and votes to consider, forecasting domestic actions at the Congressional level could baffle even the most skilled political analyst.

The high-level significance placed upon requirements generation, in processes such as the PPBE and the QDR, do not address two overarching problems. First, DoD finds itself in a world with a large number of complex and uncertain threats with an unprecedented potential for convergence (e.g. terrorists and WMD), and it has no precise mechanism to address these changes. DoD planning relies, to a large degree, upon attempts to forecast this unstable threat environment, often resulting in obsolete projections due to the rapidly changing landscape. This is complicated and made more difficult within the context of continually changing Congressional dynamics.

Second, although greater weight has been placed on strategic requirement planning (QDR) and the execution of those requirements (PPBE), two major facets of the process—programming and, more importantly, budgeting—are not only de-emphasized as a result, but remain unconnected to the strategic requirement or execution phases. Moreover, the POM process has a great deal of inertia and significantly reduces flexibility. When a new mission need is identified, there is often a two-year wait until funding for that purpose can be inserted in the next POM. At that point, funding is often severely restricted over the first few years.

The combination of complex and uncertain threats, downward budgetary pressure for the foreseeable future, and continuing acquisition challenges creates a need for a more rigorous, analytic process to compare alternatives at the system level, SoS level, and the enterprise level. This is one important goal of this book.

Based upon anticipated domestic budgetary challenges, the DoD must seek ways to acquire and maintain the required force structure at minimum cost. Basing budget sourcing decisions upon cost minimization alone, however, could result in just that—cost minimization at the expense of quality or effectiveness of DoD weapon programs and IOC sustainment needs. Furthermore, the implications of cost minimization on the execution of DoD operations could prove harmful, resulting in a failure to acquire the necessary capability, in both quantity and quality of advanced weapons systems, essential to address anticipated threats.

DoD must not simply resort to cost-minimizing strategies, but must instead identify the appropriate cost-performance trade-space and then make the necessary tradeoffs using military CBA, ensuring the most efficient and effective defense spending. This CBA approach is needed to ensure that DoD works within budget constraints: it forces a new, long-term planning approach which incorporates requisite resources into requirements identification and implementation processes.

Military CBA can also help decision-makers to identify and address the level of uncertainty in their estimates and, then, it can be used to test their sensitivity to various assumptions. Private sector firms have found that although there can be inaccuracies associated with some of the estimating involved, these analyses provide a meaningful framework for the selection of capital projects (Gordon 2000).

Some defense organizations already use military CBA, albeit at a much more tactical level. For example, according to Army Lt. Gen. William G. Webster Jr., as part of the planning for the drawdown of forces in Iraq, US Central Command's (United States CENTCOM) 3rd Army (Logistics) conducted "a cost–benefit analysis of every piece of equipment in Iraq, including the costs of transporting it out." Based on the outcome of the analysis, equipment was either transported back to the United States, shipped to Afghanistan, or left (or destroyed) in Iraq Carden (2010).

Current DoD policy requires Services (or joint sponsors) to conduct an analysis of alternatives (AoA) before they initiate major defense acquisition programs and begin system development at Milestone B.[8] The purpose of the AoA is to compare the operational effectiveness, costs, and risks of alternative solutions that address operational needs and requirements. However, a recent GAO report found that most of programs reviewed "either did not conduct an AoA or conducted an AoA that focused on a narrow scope of alternatives and did not adequately assess and compare technical and other risks of each alternative." GAO found programs that conducted a limited assessment generally did not do as well as those that conducted a more robust AoA (Sullivan 2009).

While these limited efforts should be lauded, we believe military CBA can provide a useful framework for acquisition decisions during all phases, at all levels, and throughout DoD. Unfortunately, at the enterprise level, the analysis becomes even more complex as one considers the interdependent nature of many of the systems. Therefore, new programs need to be considered within a portfolio or part of a SoS. On occasion, systems may look attractive on an individual basis, but when considered in the broader perspective, in combination with other new systems or legacy systems, they may, in fact, not provide the anticipated benefits. A military CBA conducted at the portfolio level would provide DoD with the ability to make more effective budgetary tradeoffs and program decisions and to help bridge the gap between requirements and available and future funding.[9]

2.8 Conclusion

Challenges facing US National Security begin with an increasingly complex and uncertain environment of global threats and also include domestic budgetary constraints that will significantly limit the resources available to address those threats. Coupled with top-line budgetary pressures, DoD must also deal with the challenge of the year-to-year line-item budgeting process and ongoing acquisition challenges, all of which threaten to severely limit DoD's capacity to support current acquisitions. All of this must be done while balancing the need for new systems to address evolving missions, such as "irregular" operations, missile defense, and cyber-defense. And, of course, sound acquisition decisions require accurate forecasts of vendor costs and future defense budgets. This "witches' brew" of conditions calls for the wider implementation of military CBA-guided resource allocation decisions throughout DoD. The goal is for the nation to receive the best value for every dollar it invests in defense programs.

Until new mechanisms are adopted that explicitly incorporate military CBA to address failures to fuse requirements with necessary resources, DoD will risk a disjointed, ineffective approach that may not properly address national security concerns. A comprehensive military CBA approach such as that proposed in this volume is vital in confronting the changing dynamics of modern, global warfare. Even if this approach is adopted, however, DoD must still engage in a continuing process of reassessment and innovation in order to retain the strong bond between resources and requirements these innovations may bring. This ability to constantly innovate will be central to remaining effective in the face of an increasingly complex and uncertain national security environment.

Notes

1 For example, in Somalia 1992, Iraq 2003 and Libya 2011.
2 In recent updates of Social Security financial projections, the US Congressional Budget Office (CBO) notes that the Social Security deficit will grow to be significantly larger by 2020 than previously expected (CBO 2010).
3 Social Security, Medicare, and Medicaid have reached 10.1 percent of GDP (2009) and are projected to continue increasing as a percentage of GDP to 11.8 percent in 2020, 15.5 percent in 2040, and 21.1 percent in 2075 (CBO 2010). According to GAO, these programs will near 30 percent of GDP by 2040.
4 Both CBO and GAO have conducted long-term studies surrounding the federal budget. Both have noted the dramatic increases in entitlement spending and interest on the national debt. GAO projections have been carried out until 2084 based upon CBO assumptions and projections ending in 2020.
5 This current projection was diverted from the baseline after an assumption that the US will draw down troops in Iraq, Afghanistan, and elsewhere to 60,000 by 2013. Other projections based upon different troop levels or different spending freezes, however, place DoD's budget even lower as a percentage of GDP.
6 Compounding future funding challenges is the fact DoD has come to rely on "supplemental" funding which is being significantly reduced. The Administration requested US$33.0 billion in 2010 supplemental funding on top of the US$129.6 billion already provided and a total of US$159.3 billion for its 2011 overseas contingency operations (OMB 2010).
7 The Cost Analysis Improvement Group (CAIG) launched by what is now known as CAPE (Cost Assessment and Program Evaluation) was meant to be responsible for providing independent cost estimates for the US Secretary of Defense: see www.cape.osd.mil [last accessed November 25, 2014].
8 Milestone B is normally the formal initiation of an acquisition program (see DoD Instruction 5000.02, November 25, 2013, http://www.acq.osd.mil/osbp/sbir/docs/500002_interim.pdf [last accessed February 9, 2015]).
9 Chapter 10 offers an interesting theoretical framework that captures aspects of a more general portfolio approach, while Chapter 4 explicitly addresses the issue of affordability.

References

Al-Salhy, S. and T. Arango. June 12, 2014. "Iraq Militants, Pushing South, Aim at Capital." *New York Times*: A1.

Arena, M. V., R. S. Leonard, S. E. Murray, and O. Younossi. 2006. *Historical Cost Growth of Completed Weapon System Programs* (Technical Report Series). Santa Monica, CA: RAND Corporation.

Boessenkool, A. November 11, 2009. "Analysts: U.S. Procurement Drop Coming as Costs Mount." *Defense News*.

Carden, M. J. April 8, 2010. "Army Command Sustains Logistics for Warfighters." *Fort Hood Sentinel*.

CBO. 2010. *The Budget and Economic Outlook: Fiscal Years 2010 to 2020*. Congressional Budget Office.

———. 2010. *Long Term Implications of the Fiscal Year 2010 Defense Budget*. Congressional Budget Office.

Cha, V. D. 2000. "Globalization and the Study of International Security." *Journal of Peace Research* 37(3): 391–403.

Chesbrough, H. W. 2006. "Open Innovation: A New Paradigm for Understanding Industrial Innovation." In *Innovation: Researching a New Paradigm* (Chapter 1). Oxford: Oxford University Press.

Chu, D. S. C., and N. Berstein. 2003. "Decisionmaking for Defense." In *New Challenges New Tools for Defense Decisionmaking*, edited by M. L. Stuart and G. F. Treverton. Santa Monica, CA: RAND Corporation.

Frank, D. F. Summer 1997. "A Theoretical Consideration of Acquisition Reform." *Acquisition Review Quarterly* 4(3): 279.

Freier, N. 2007. *Strategic Competition and Resistance in the 21st Century: Irregular, Catastrophic, Traditional, and Hybrid Challenges in Context.* Author via CreateSpace Independent Publishing Platform (a DBA of On-Demand Publishing LLC, part of the Amazon group of companies).

Fukuyama, F. Summer 1989. "The End of History." *The National Interest*: 3–18.

Gates, R. M. May 3, 2010. *Remarks as Delivered by Secretary of Defense Robert M. Gates* (cited May 5, 2010). Gaylord Convention Center, National Harbor, MD. Available at www.defense.gov/speeches/speech.aspx?speechid=1460 [last accessed November 25, 2014].

Gordon, L. A. 2000. *Mangerial Accounting: Concepts and Empirical Evidence* (5th edition). Columbus, OH: McGraw-Hill Higher Education.

Grossman, E. 2008. "Marine General Lays Groundwork for Unprecedented Change." *Government Executive.* May 30,2008. Available at www.govexec.com/defense/2008/05/marine-general-lays-groundwork-for-unprecedented-change/26953/ [last accessed November 25, 2014].

The Institute for Economics and Peace (IEP). 2012. *Global Terrorism Index 2012: Capturing the Impact of Terrorism for the Last Decade* (IEP Report Series). New York: The Institute for Economics and Peace.

Keehan, M. P. 2008. *Planning, Programming, Budgeting, and Execution (PPBE) Proccess* (Teaching Note). Fort Belvoir, VA: Defense Acquisiton University.

Perl, Raphael. 2006. *Terrorism Expert Calls for a Redefinition of National Security.* US Department of State, Office of International Information Programs, Washington, DC.

Perlo-Freeman, S. and C. Solmirano. April 2014. "Trends in World Military Expenditure, 2013." S*tockholm International Peace Institute Fact Sheet.*

Popescu, I. C. March 1, 2010. "The Last QDR? What the Petagon Should Learn from Corporations about Strategic Planning." *Armed Forces Journal*: 26.

Panel on Defense Acquisition Reform. 2010. *Interim Findings and Recommendations.* Washington, DC: House Armed Services Committee.

Schwirtz, M., A. Barnard, and C. J. Chivers. August 9, 2008. "Russia and Georgia Clash Over Separatist Region." *New York Times.*

Smith, R. 2005. *The Utility of Force: The Art of War in the Modern World.* London: Allen Lane.

Sullivan, M. J. 2008. *Defense Acquisitions: Fundamental Changes are Needed to Improve Weapon Program Outcomes* (GAO-08-1159T). Available at www.gao.gov/products/GAO-08-1159T [last accessed November 25, 2014].

———. 2009. *Many Analyses of Alternatives have not Provided a Robust Assesment of Weapon System Options* (GAO-09-665). Available at www.gao.gov/products/GAO-09-665 [last accessed November 25, 2014].

United States Census Bureau. 2004. Available at www.census.gov [accessed November 15, 2007].

United States Government Accountability Office. 2010. *The Federal Government's Long-Term Fiscal Outlook.* GAO-10-468SP.

US Office of Management and Budget (OMB). 2010. *President's Budget for FY 2011.* Washington, DC: Executive Office of the President.

Walker, D. July 15, 2014. "Trends in U.S. Military Spending." *Council on Foreign Relations.* Available at www.cfr.org/defense-budget/trends-us-military-spending/p28855 [last accessed November 25, 2014].

Younossi, O., M. V. Arena, R. S. Leonard, C. R. Roll, Jr., A. Jain, and J. M. Sollinger. 2007. *Is Weapon System Cost Growth Increasing? A Quantitative Assessment of Completed and Ongoing Programs.* Santa Monica, CA: RAND Corporation.

3 Measuring defense output

An economics perspective

Keith Hartley[1] and Binyam Solomon

3.1 Introduction

Measuring defense output is a necessary step to successfully apply military cost–benefit analysis (CBA) to evaluate alternative security investments. Other chapters in this book focus on what economists call "intermediate outputs" (e.g. military forces). This chapter offers a higher-level "macro" perspective of overall defense output that encompasses total defense spending.

In most countries, the defense sector absorbs substantial scarce resources that have many valuable alternative uses (schools, hospitals, etc.). Whereas defense expenditures are well known within each country, there is no single indicator of value (or benefit) of overall defense output. This contrasts with the valuation of private sector outputs in market economies. In defense, the economist's solution to measuring output assumes output equals inputs (a convention widely used across the public sector), or that the value of defense output is roughly equivalent to expenditures made to produce that output.

In sharp contrast, measuring the value of market outputs is not usually regarded as a policy problem. Market economies 'solve' the problem through market prices that reflect choices of large numbers of buyers and sellers. Defense, however, differs in several key ways from private markets, which helps to explain the challenge in measuring and valuing defense output.

An important step in applying military CBA to evaluate security investments is to discuss output measures. This chapter examines the measurement of defense output from an economics perspective. Specifically, the chapter identifies key questions which need to be addressed in measuring overall defense output. These include: What is defense output? How can it be valued? Under what conditions is it a worthwhile investment?

Economic theory offers some policy guidelines for determining the optimal defense output for any society. As an optimizing problem, the rule is to aim at the socially desirable or optimal level of defense output. This is achieved by equating additional or marginal costs of proposed defense expenditures with additional or marginal benefits. While the economics approach is difficult to 'operationalize' into a set of clear, unambiguous policy guidelines, it does provide a framework for designing valuations for defense outputs and activities.

This chapter is organized as follows. Section 3.2 reframes the defense output measurement issue as an economic problem utilizing insights from public goods, public choice, and principal-agent models. Section 3.3 presents the military production function as an early attempt to quantify defense outputs, and reveals some challenges in operationalizing the model. Section 3.4 discusses more recent attempts at measuring defense outputs through the transformation of defense budgets reporting. Section 3.5 analyzes both economic and non-economic benefits of defense, while Section 3.6 surveys international experience in measuring defense outputs. Nations surveyed include Australia, New Zealand, the United Kingdom, the United States, and a group of European nations.

3.2 Economic theory as a guide

3.2.1 Public goods

Defense is a classic example of a public good, and its desired outcome in the form of peace is also a public good. A public good is non-rival and non-excludable. For example, living as neighbors in the same city, my consumption of air defense protection does not affect your consumption and, once provided, I cannot exclude you from its consumption nor can you exclude me. In sharp contrast, private goods such as motor cars and TV sets are rival and excludable. Your payment and consumption of those items means that I cannot simultaneously use them (unless you choose to share), and private property rights guarantee your exclusive ownership, so that you can legally exclude me from using them.

The public goods features of defense provide incentives for free-riding. Since I cannot exclude you from the benefits and you cannot exclude me, each of us is inclined to let the other pay for protection. Free-riding is a contentious issue both within a nation and between nations in a military alliance (e.g. NATO, or US–Canadian security). This ultimately results in a nation's citizens failing to reveal their true preferences for, and valuations of, defense. A challenge for the state in providing and financing defense is that it does not know the true preferences of the potential beneficiaries of defense: it cannot easily quantify the volume of the defense public good demanded by consumers and estimate the true price the beneficiaries are willing to pay (Engerer 2011).

Theoretical solutions exist to estimate the optimal amount of a public good, but are difficult to operationalize in practice (Cornes and Sandler 1996). Public opinion polls can be used, but these are a limited mechanism for accurately assessing society's opinions on defense spending and defense policy and the willingness of citizens to pay for defense (Zaller and Feldman 1992).

Alternatively, one can frame the question of "how much defense is enough?," presenting it as an optimization where the economic decision rule is to achieve a socially desirable or "optimal" defense output. In principle, this is found by equating marginal costs with marginal benefits. This approach is difficult to 'operationalize' into a set of clear and unambiguous policy guidelines. As discussed in the introductory chapter, marginal costs and especially marginal benefits of many defense investments are not immediately obvious, and are difficult to quantify.

The economic model assumes a social welfare function showing society's preferences between defense (security) and civilian goods: again, this is an attractive concept but not one which is readily operationalized or easily identifiable for any society. Moreover, the benefits of defense are complicated by its public good and free-riding characteristics. Voting systems may also not be reliable and accurate methods of revealing preferences for specific public goods and services. Typically, elections involve choices between political parties that offer various tax and spending policies, where defense budgets and security policies are often buried in a wider policy platform. Problems can also arise in attempting to aggregate voter preferences into a ranking for society as a whole (the voting paradox: Tisdell and Hartley 2008). Further problems arise since the economic model assumes maximizing behaviour on the part of individuals, when most agents might instead be satisficers, willing to settle for acceptable solutions short of the optimum (Hartley 2010b).

3.2.2 Markets

There are several major differences between private markets and public (defense) markets. Private markets involve prices that reveal society's valuation of outputs, where these prices reflect market incentive and penalty mechanisms. Goods that are 'private' rather than public are characterized by both excludability and rivalry; large numbers of private consumers and buyers; rivalry between firms; motivation and rewards through profits; and a capital market that imposes penalties on poor economic performance through take-overs and the ultimate sanction, bankruptcy (with managers often losing their jobs).

Public bureaucracies such as the armed forces lack such incentive and penalty mechanisms, and they consequently tend to be slow to adjust to change. Often, change in the armed forces results from budget pressures, new technology, victories and defeats, and occasionally, views of senior military leaders (Solomon *et al.* 2008). In contrast to private markets, there is no market price for publicly provided defense forces: for example, there are no market prices for submarine or tank forces.

Although some rivalry exists between suppliers (Navy, Army, Air Force, etc.), there is no profit motive for public suppliers, nor capital market pressures corresponding to takeovers and bankruptcy in private markets. Defense has another distinctive feature reflected in the state-funding and state provision (ownership) of its armed forces. Governments are monopsony buyers and monopoly providers of armed forces.

This contrasts with private markets where there are large numbers of buyers and rivalry amongst suppliers. State-owned and funded defense markets are less likely to undertake worthwhile changes (Tisdell and Hartley 2008, Chapter 10). There is also a unique military employment contract which differs drastically from private sector employment contracts. The military employment contract requires military personnel to obey commands which relate to type, duration, location, and conditions of work (e.g. world-wide deployments) with significant probability of injury and even death. Such a contract contains elements resembling indentureship and command systems.

Each of the armed forces is a monopoly supplier of air, land or sea systems with monopoly property rights in the air, land or sea domains. There are barriers to new entry which prevent rival internal armed forces from offering competing products. For example, armies often operate attack helicopters and unmanned aerial vehicles (UAVs) which are rivals to close air support and surveillance provided by air forces. Similarly, land-based aircraft operated by air forces are alternatives to naval carrier-borne aircraft. Efficiency requires a mechanism for promoting such competition; instead, each service guards its traditional monopoly property rights in the air, land, or sea domain, thereby creating barriers to new entry.

This has an impact on efficiency. Specifically, is the correct amount of output being produced? Is the correct mix of inputs being used? As monopolies with significant barriers to entry, each of the armed forces lacks strongly competing organizations, and hence has less incentive for efficiency improvements and for innovation (where efficiency embraces both allocative and technical efficiency).

Allocative efficiency requires the choice of socially desirable output, and technical efficiency requires the use of least-cost methods to produce that output. Again, problems arise in determining allocative efficiency (see a discussion below on principal-agent models). Technical efficiency, however, can be assessed by allowing activities traditionally undertaken 'in-house' by the armed forces to be 'opened-up' to competition from private suppliers (market testing leading to military outsourcing). Indeed, military cost–benefit formulation of such competitions can offer improvements in allocative efficiency (e.g. by inviting competition for different levels of service in order to identify true marginal costs for different levels of output or service).[2]

Internal defense markets lack other incentives of private markets. There are no profit incentives to stimulate and reward military commanders to search for and introduce productivity improvements or to identify new and profitable opportunities (for example, the role of entrepreneurs in private markets). The absence of a capital market also means that military managers are unlikely to lose their jobs for poor performance and there are no capital market opportunities for promoting and rewarding mergers and take-overs. For example, a military commander of a regiment cannot merge with another regiment to achieve economies of scale and scope, nor can an Army regiment acquire Air Force or Navy transport units where such mergers might offer both cost savings and output improvements (such as horizontal, vertical, or conglomerate mergers).

Uncertainty dominates defense policy. Defense policy has to respond to a range of future threats, some of which are unknown and unknowable. Assumptions are needed about likely future allies and their responses to threats, the location of threats, new technologies, and the time dimension of threats (e.g. today, in 10–15 years, or 30–50 years ahead where uncertainties are greatest). These uncertainties mean that forces have to be capable of adapting to change, and that today's defense investments must be capable of meeting tomorrow's threats. Admittedly, the private sector also faces considerable uncertainty about future markets and new technologies, and these unknowns extend over lengthy time horizons. Defense is different, however, in that uncertainties are dependent upon, and determined by, governments, nation states, and some non-state actors, rather than by the actions of large numbers of private individuals as consumers, workers, and shareholders.

There is one further key difference between defense and private markets. Defense aims to avoid conflict, but where conflict arises it often destroys markets and valuable infrastructure and creates disequilibrium as resources are re-allocated to military forces to gain strategic advantage, with consequent opportunity costs in civilian goods and services. War involves the destruction of labor and capital. In contrast, private markets seek the optimal mix of labor and capital to provide goods and services through voluntary trading and exchange. Resource allocation is based on price and profit signals that lead to "creative destruction" reflected in continuous investment in new innovations, inventions and the output of new goods and services.

3.2.3 Public choice and principal-agent models

Defense decisions are made in political markets, which is another reason for their departure from the economist's optimizing solution. Political markets comprise voters, political parties, bureaucracies, and interest groups—each pursuing their own self-interest. Voters as taxpayers are "principals." They want something provided by government and appoint "agents" to perform the necessary tasks. The challenge for principals is to design incentive mechanisms to ensure that agents pursue the aims of the principals rather than their own objectives. For example, voters as principals seek peace, security, and protection, but the priority of their agents in defense ministries and the armed forces might be to subsidize costly local goods and services because doing so offers jobs, new technology, or export benefits which contribute to re-election of the governing party.

Limitations of the voting system as a means of expressing voter preferences for defense spending constrain principals (voters) in their attempts to guide their agents (elected politicians and bureaucrats). Free-riding further affects the willingness of voters to accurately reveal their preferences for defense. Principals also often lack the necessary information to make informed and rational defense choices in their voting decisions. The result is that agents often have a wide scope in shaping national defense policy and in pursuing their own self-interests (e.g. re-election).[3]

The principal-agent model has implications for CBA, resource-use, and efficiency in defense markets. It also has implications for measuring the benefits of defense outputs where these reflect a combination of principal and agent choices. The model can also be linked to the political market where defense choices are made. In political markets:

- voters and taxpayers as principals will seek to maximize the benefits (satisfaction) from their votes;
- political parties are vote-maximizers; governments seek re-election and are the agents of voters;

- bureaucracies can be modelled as budget maximizers acting as agents of the government;
- producer (e.g. defense industry) groups are profit- or rent-seekers in their roles as agents of the defense procurement agency or military bureaucracy.

The principal-agent and public choice models provide a useful analytical framework to help understand the military-industrial-political complex and its influence on defense choices and outputs. As principals, voters are generally poorly informed about defense policy so they defer to various agents to make their defense choices—namely, governments, civil servants in defense ministries and procurement agencies, and the armed forces. In turn, these agents are influenced by powerful producer groups in the form of large defense contractors (e.g. via lobbying) seeking lucrative defense contracts.

Examples of the influence of the military-industrial-political complex on defense choices abound. Government ministers will be aware of the vote-consequences of defense choices (e.g. impacts of base and plant closures and the benefits of awarding defense contracts to firms in marginal constituencies). Defense ministries and the armed forces as budget maximizers are tempted to overestimate the threat and underestimate the costs of their preferred policies and projects. Exaggerating the threat from terrorism enables the armed forces to obtain larger defense budgets. Understating costs of a new weapon system in a CBA allows the project to start, and once started projects build interest groups and become difficult to stop (a key factor in the 'optimism bias' that often leads to contract cost overruns).

Defense contractors also have an incentive to make optimistic claims to pump up perceived benefits and increase their chances of being awarded valuable defense contracts. For example, claiming that the contract will contribute valuable jobs, technology, spin-offs, exports, and that it is 'vital' to the future of the national defense industrial base. Rarely is attention given to opportunity costs: namely, whether the resources used in the defense project might provide even greater net economic benefits if used in alternative sectors of the economy. Overall, public choice and principal-agent models reveal how special interest groups influence military investment decisions and defense outputs.

3.3 The military production function

Another contribution from economic theory to output measurement comes in the form of the military production function. This is an input-output relationship that attempts to relate all defense inputs to a final defense output. Inputs comprise technology, capital (bases, equipment, spare parts, etc.), and labor (military personnel in the form of conscripts and/or volunteers, civilians, contractors, etc.). A formal expression of the function is

$$Q = f(A, K, L) \qquad (3.1)$$

where Q is defense output and A, K, and L are inputs of technology (A), capital (K), and labor (L).

While the model appears attractive, there are at least four major caveats. First, a production function assumes factor inputs are combined to minimize costs. This assumption is unrealistic in view of the lack of efficiency incentives in internal defense markets: there are few rewards or penalties to achieve least-cost production. Second, all defense inputs have to be identified and correctly valued. Third, defense output is simply asserted without recognizing the problems of identifying and measuring output, including the multi-product nature of overall defense output. Fourth, the model simply identifies defense outputs resulting from various inputs: there are no criteria for determining society's preferred defense output (the "optimal" defense output).

Two central problems with military production functions arise over inputs and outputs. Consider the problem of identifying and valuing all relevant inputs. These comprise technology, capital and, labor, and include the following items:

- technical progress as reflected in inputs embracing new equipment and new military facilities, including communications;[4]
- physical capital comprising a mix of equipment, military bases, land, and logistics (repair and maintenance);
- human capital comprising military personnel reflected both in their numbers the skills and productivity of the military labor force.[5]

While measuring inputs is a challenge, identifying, measuring, and valuing defense output is even more challenging. Economic theory simply asserts the concept of defense output without exploring its definition and multi-product nature. Few published studies have estimated military production functions. Typically, such studies have estimated readily identified measures of effectiveness, such as providing an air defense capability, the numbers of aircraft destroyed, or the number of aircraft sorties per day. This approach is used in cost-effectiveness studies that focus on intermediate defense outputs (Hildebrandt 1990, 1999).

For example, a military CBA of air defense would compare the costs and effectiveness of alternatives such as land-based air defense missiles versus manned fighter aircraft; or anti-submarine capability would compare land-based maritime patrol aircraft versus naval frigates; or anti-tank capability would compare missiles and attack helicopters. A different approach used in a more recent study estimated a military production function where various defense inputs were used to estimate the probability of winning in various conflict scenarios (Middleton *et al.* 2011).

A variant of the military production function is a defense R&D production function. This shows that current defense R&D determines future military equipment quality, with an impact on future defense output. The relationship between defense R&D and equipment quality is positive, but subject to diminishing returns and substantial lags. For example, today's military equipment quality was determined by defense R&D spending some 10–15 years ago.

It can be informative to convert equipment quality into a time advantage. Thus, over the period 1991–2001, US military equipment was six years ahead of that of the UK, seven years ahead of France, and twelve years ahead of Sweden (Middleton *et al.* 2006). The defense R&D production function can be expressed as

$$E_q = f(RD_d, Z) \tag{3.2}$$

where E_q is military equipment quality (e.g. British versus US tanks), RD_d represents defense R&D, and Z captures all other factors.

The defense R&D production function needs more theoretical and empirical work. For example, 'other factors' might contribute to equipment quality and these need to be identified specifically in the model. Furthermore, links between equipment quality and military capability need identifying, including the role of variables such as military skills which also contribute to final defense output. The model is also limited in focusing on aggregate defense R&D spending without any analysis of the most effective mix of R&D spending. More empirical work is needed to determine the most cost-effective ratio of research to development work within total defense R&D budgets, and the impact of that R&D on equipment quality and future output/capabilities.[6]

Traditionally, defense outputs were measured on an input basis, where input costs were assumed to equal the value of outputs. Table 3.1 presents some input data of the type typically used for measuring some of the inputs in a military production function.

Table 3.1 Defense inputs for a group of nations (2009)

Country	Defense spending (US$ million, 2009 prices)	Defense share of GDP (%)	Armed Forces personnel (000s)	Defense R&D (US$ million, 2000 prices)[c]
Australia[a]	20,109	1.8	58	242.7
Canada[b]	19,869	1.5	67	201.6
China[a]	98,800	2.0	2,285	Not available
France[b]	54,446	2.1	243	3,643.5
Germany[b]	47,466	1.4	254	1,103.2
India[a]	36,600	2.6	1,325	Not available
Italy[b]	30,489	1.4	197	64.9
New Zealand	1,358	1.2	9.8	Not available
Spain[b]	16,944	1.2	134	1,666.5
Sweden[a]	6,135	1.3	13	218.7
UK[b]	59,131	2.7	197	2,559.9
USA[b]	574,070	4.0	1,368	65,896.0

Sources: NATO (2010); OECD (2010); SIPRI (2011).

Notes
a Defense spending data in 2008 prices: source SIPRI (2011).
b Data for NATO nations is provided from one source and is on a consistent basis.
c Defense R&D data are in US$ millions 2000 prices and PPP rates.

3.3.1   Technical spin-offs

Defense R&D can also contribute to wider economic benefits in the form of technical spin-offs and spill-overs (external benefits: positive externalities or external economies). Among numerous examples are: jet engines, avionics, radar, composite materials, the internet, and the application of helicopter rotor blade technology to wind turbines. These positive externalities might be regarded as part of the benefits of defense investments contributing to defense output that need to be included in a military CBA. But such views need to be assessed critically. Technology spin-offs are not the main aim of defense spending, which primarily seeks to provide peace, protection, and security. Any technical spin-offs can be regarded as a windfall benefit of defense spending. Moreover, a list of spin-off examples fails to address the central question of the market value of such spin-offs, and whether there are better alternative uses of defense R&D resources. Consideration also needs to be given to the wider economic impacts of defense spending.

3.3.2   Defense-growth relationships

A considerable literature has developed on the relationship between defense spending and the benefits to a nation's economic growth. There are two alternative hypotheses. First is the view that defense spending favourably affects an economy's growth rate (a positive impact: Benoit 1973). Second is the contrasting hypothesis that military expenditure adversely affects a nation's growth rate (a negative impact: Deger and Smith 1983). Some of the literature has widened the possible relationship to include the impact of defense spending on other macroeconomic variables such as employment, unemployment, inflation, exports, and R&D (Hartley 2010a).

Both hypotheses are dominated by myths, emotion, and special pleading. Plausible explanations can be provided for either a positive or negative impact of defense spending on growth, and there is evidence supporting both! The divergent results reflect the need for a properly specified model of economic growth. Typically, defense spending is simply added to a conventional growth model without careful consideration of its causal impact on growth.[7]

A considerable literature has used Granger causality tests to examine the relationship between military spending and the economy. A critique of this literature concludes that parameters may not be stable over different time periods, different countries, and that:

> Granger causality test statistics are uninformative about the size and direction of the predicted effects and Granger causality measures incremental predictability and not economic causality.
>
> (Dunne and Smith 2010, 440)

This particular critique ends with the need to provide "measures of the political and strategic determinants of military expenditures, such as threats" (Dunne and Smith 2010, 440).

3.4   Assessing defense outputs: problems and challenges

Defense outputs involve a complex set of variables concerned with security, protection, and risk management, including risks avoided, safety, peace, and stability. Private markets routinely provide benefit measures such as sales, labor productivity, and profitability. Unlike private markets, there are no precise benefit measures for defense output.

Defense inputs are more easily identified, measured, and valued than outputs, as reflected in many nations' annual input-oriented defense budgets. For economists, questions then arise as to whether annual defense budget information provides sufficient data to assess the efficiency and effectiveness of military expenditure: how do expenditures on inputs correspond to desired defense outputs? Do defense budgets provide policy-makers and politicians with the sort of data needed to conduct military CBAs?

Typical questions include assessing the benefits and costs of alternative defense forces; expanding (or contracting) the Army, Navy, or Air Force; substituting equipment (capital) for military personnel (labor); or substituting national guard and reserves for regular (active) forces. Various defense budgets used by nations include: input budgets, output budgets, management budgets, and resource accounting budgets.

3.4.1   Input budgets

Input budgets provide some limited information on defense inputs such as the pay of military and civilian personnel, as well as the cost of land, machinery, and internal financial transactions, such as write-offs of various types of losses (see Table 3.2). The information in Table 3.2 and particularly the first ten items show the inputs used by the Canadian Department of National Defense (DND) in the production of national security outputs. More than half of the budget is spent on personnel, but there is no information on the proportion dedicated specifically to civilian, regular, and reserve personnel. The last two items referred to as "transfers" and "subsidies" detail payments in the form of grants and contributions to various national and international organizations, capital assistance (subsidies) to industry, research grants, and other assistance towards research carried on by non-governmental organizations. These might be considered as intermediate outputs.

Crucially, however, such budgets have major limitations for assessing efficiency. First, the budget fails to show any final defense outputs other than under the vague heading of "defense." Second, it does not relate inputs to specific intermediate outputs (e.g. air defense; anti-submarine defenses). Third, inputs focus on the current year only and do not reflect life-cycle cost implications of current procurement decisions. Fourth, inputs are not always valued in terms of market values. For example, some resources such as military bases and land for training might have been purchased years ago and are assumed to be free or available at a zero price, while other resources such as conscripts are not priced at their true labor market

Table 3.2 Annual defense expenditures FY 2012–13

	CDN$000
Personnel	10,438,096
Transportation and communications	768,058
Information	13,666
Professionnal and special services	2,982,038
Rentals	383,972
Purchased repair and maintenance	1,465,091
Utilities, materials and supplies	1,017,831
Construction and/or acquisition of land, buildings and works	500,631
Construction and/or acquisition of machinery and equipment	2,434,609
Transfer payments	181,705
Total subsidies and payments	221,561
Total gross expenditure	**20,407,258**
Total revenue	429,068
Total net expenditure	**19,978,190**

Source: Public Accounts Volume II. Receiver General of Canada (RGC 2013).

values. These and other limitations led to the development of output budgeting (Hartley 2011).

3.4.2   *Output budgets*

Output budgets, also known as program budgets, are much closer to the economist's production function model of defense budgets (Hitch and McKean 1960). Together with their costs, they provide information on some intermediate outputs of defense such as nuclear strategic forces, air defense, aircraft carriers, infantry regiments, and reserve forces. Output budgets also provide information on substitution possibilities (e.g. between nuclear and conventional forces, or between reserves and regulars).[8]

There are at least two major limitations with output budgets. First, the expenditure figures used in output budgets are unlikely to be least-cost solutions, because of the lack of competition and market incentives. Second, whilst they are known as output budgets, there remains a problem in identifying the overall output of defense. Often, outputs are defined in terms of the numbers of military personnel, aircraft squadrons, warships, and infantry regiments. These published data, however, are measures of intermediate rather than final outputs such as protection, security, safety, peace, and stability.

For example, the quantity of military personnel can be a misleading measure if training, productivity, and readiness for operations is ignored. Similarly, the numbers of aircraft, tanks, and warships are misleading without data on their average age and their operational availability. Also relevant are the combinations of military personnel and equipment required for effective forces with an ability to be deployed and sustained in different overseas locations for long periods.

3.4.3   *Management budgets*

Management budgets attempt to focus on efficiency. Top level and lower level budget holders are identified and awarded cash budgets where delegated financial powers allow military commanders and managers to combine resources to achieve agreed objectives. Inevitably, however, there are problems with management budgets. Budget holders (e.g. commanders of bases and units) often face constraints on their freedom to vary the mix of inputs of capital and labor (equipment and personnel). It is not unknown for large items of expenditure to be pre-committed, leaving base and unit commanders with choices about relatively minor items of expenditure (e.g. window cleaning, catering, and transport).

Efficiency incentives are also reduced if cost savings are automatically transferred to the defense ministry or the national treasury. Nor can efficiency be achieved without clearly specified defense output targets. Cost savings can always be realised by reducing the quantity and/or quality of output, especially if output targets are not clearly specified!

3.4.4   *Resource accounting and budgeting*

The UK adopted resource accounting & budgeting (RAB) in 2002 to bring public sector accounting practices into line with those in the private sector. The key feature of RAB is that costs are accounted for as they are incurred (as with "accrual accounting") rather than when payments are made (Table 3.3).[9] There is an annual balance sheet for the Ministry of Defence (MoD) showing fixed and current assets, provisions, and liabilities. Data on the value of the MoD's fixed assets includes valuations for fighting equipment and the defense estate (e.g. military bases and land for training). By revealing the costs of holding assets, RAB provides incentives for efficiencies such as the disposal of surplus spare parts, land, bases, and even estates. Canada's DND example of RAB and output budgets, known as Program Alignment Architecture (PAA), is provided in Appendix 3.1.[10]

The adoption of private sector management and accounting practices such as RAB or PAA by themselves will not lead to overall efficiency in the MoD. The private sector has a range of mechanisms and incentives for achieving efficiency, including competition, the profit motive and the capital market with the threat of take-overs and bankruptcy. Such mechanisms and incentives are absent from the MoD (and most other public agencies).

All parts of the public and private sectors consist of individuals and groups with incentives to pursue their own self-interests (recall the principal-agent model). The task for the MoD is to provide efficiency incentives equivalent to those in the private sector. Here, the challenge of measuring defense output remains a serious obstacle to assessing efficiency in the defense sector.

Both the UK RAB and the Canadian PAA are necessary steps towards connecting outcomes and resources but they require modifications and refinements. Both describe processes that tend to equate inputs to outputs. "Administration" in RAB and "internal services" in PAA are catch-all activities that include fixed costs and outputs (see Appendix 3.1). For example, government-wide

Table 3.3 MoD resources by budget area FY 2010–11

Top level budget holders	FY 2010–11 current £ million[a]
Departmental expenditure limits (DEL)	**48,463**
Request for resources 1: Provision of defence capability	**44,516**
Resource DEL	**36,221**
Commander-in-Chief Navy Command	2,294
General Officer Commanding (Northern Ireland)	*
Commander-in-Chief Land Forces	7,189
Air Officer Commanding-in-Chief RAF Strike Command	*
Commander-in-Chief Air Command	2,826
Chief of Joint Operations	480
Defence Equipment & Support	16,869
Central	2,401
Defence Estates	2,136
Administration	2,026
Capital DEL	**8,295**
Request for resources 2: Conflict prevention	**3,946**
Resource DEL	**2,862**
Capital DEL	**1,084**
Annually managed expenditure (AME)	**7,881**
Request for resources 1: Provision of defence capability	**6,918**
Request for resources 2: Conflict prevention	**28**
Request for resources 3: War pensions & allowances, etc	**935**

Source: Defence Analytical Services and Advice (DASA) 2011.

Notes
a Current £million, 2011.
* No value or not reported.

initiatives on accountability and environmental stewardship, while important, do not link directly to security outputs. To make both RAB and PAA more relevant for the assessment of MoD's and DND's efficiency and effective management of resources, the re-design must be linked to a strategic planning framework and costing tool that displays the total ownership cost resources (Solomon *et al.* 2008).

3.4.5 Challenges

Two growing pressures make it essential to focus on the size of a nation's defense budget and the efficiency with which defense resources are used. The first pressure is to reduce defense budgets and reallocate resources to other public spending programmes, especially education, health, and welfare (including care for the increasing elderly populations). Second, added pressure on defense budgets comes from the increasing costs of defense equipment. A simple example shows the importance of rising unit equipment costs which affects all nations (all figures are for unit production costs in 2010 prices):[11]

- Spitfire unit costs (1940): £154,850
- Typhoon unit costs (2010): £73.2 million
- Typhoon replacement in 2050: £1+ billion

Increasing unit costs and constant or falling defense budgets (in real terms) suggest difficult defense choices cannot be avoided. The challenge in divestment discussions as in investment decisions is to establish useful measures of defense outputs, or in the absence of such measures, to develop proxies to enable CBA.

This chapter, having identified multiple issues and obstacles involved in developing defense output measures; next reviews the experience of several nations. Many chapters in this book offer valuable techniques to develop proxy measures of intermediate outputs at lower levels of the organization in support of military CBA.

3.5 Defining defense outputs: the benefits of defense

In principle, defense provides an output in the form of goods and services which offers a stream of current and future benefits to a nation's citizens and to the citizens of other nations who might also receive such benefits. The benefits are both economic and non-economic. The economic benefits of defense usually take the form of services which contribute to national output. The non-economic benefits of defense include foreign policy benefits, peacekeeping, and its contribution to a nation's 'feel good' factor. This includes its involvement in being a responsible international citizen and valued member of the international community.

Economists rarely address the concept of overall defense output apart from vague references to security. Government statisticians and the national accounts have traditionally measured defense output on the convention that output equals input (Office for National Statistics (ONS) 2008). Improving this limited measure requires that the concept of defense output be further developed and explored.

3.5.1 Security

In principle, defense provides security, which itself is a multi-product output embracing protection, safety, insurance, peace, economic stability, and risk avoidance or reduction (Solomon *et al.* 2008). Further dimensions include prosperity, individual and national freedoms, liberty, and a 'way of life.' These are all difficult to measure and might be influenced by factors other than defense. Also, these aspects of security are public goods which are not marketed and include non-marketable services involving no tangible and physical products.

Security is sometimes defined as the absence of threats or risks (Baldwin 1997; Engerer 2011). A world of no threats or risks, however, does not and cannot exist: the real world is characterized by continually emerging threats and risks.

Questions then arise about which threats and risks can be reduced, by whom, and at what cost.

Recent developments have led to security referring to issues other than military security (creating fuzzy boundaries). Individuals are faced with threats to their lives, health, property, other assets, and their prosperity (e.g. from criminals and terrorists, disease/pandemics and ill health, natural or man-made disasters, and economic recessions). Threats to individuals augment the threats to nation states (e.g. military threats from other nations and environmental problems originating from other nations) which raises questions about which threats should be handled privately and which publicly.

Where threats are handled publicly, which is the most appropriate and least-cost solution? For example, military solutions are appropriate for external military threats whilst internal police forces are more appropriate for internal threats from criminals (e.g. physical violence to individuals involving injury, death, and robbery). Threats to an individual's state of health require dietary, medical, and care solutions (e.g. from doctors, nurses, and care homes). Threats to prosperity require government macroeconomic and microeconomic policies to promote full employment and economic growth (e.g. opportunities for education, training, and labor mobility—although some of these activities can be funded privately).

Technical progress and changing consumer preferences have resulted in shifts from the public provision of security to private protection measures provided and financed by individuals (e.g. private security guarding, camera surveillance of property, and creation of neighborhood watch schemes providing local club goods). Security also has important geographical dimensions.

For example, defense can be viewed as a means of protecting a nation's property rights over its land, sea, and air space. A nation's defense forces, however, might also be used to protect other nations' citizens so that the public good becomes international which further increases the problem of obtaining and financing the optimal amount of the international public good (including peace). Overall, security measures can be analyzed as national or international public goods, club goods, and private goods—each with different solutions and each embracing different industries (e.g. security and defense industries: Engerer 2011). These different industries have different customers, products, and technologies (Sempre 2011).

3.5.2   *The economic benefits of defense*

Defense contributes to individual and collective security and protection, both of which are valuable commodities. It protects households and their assets, firms and their assets, the national infrastructure, national institutions, and national freedoms (e.g. democracy, freedom of speech and movement, etc). It also protects national interests, including independence and 'appropriate sovereignty' (e.g. protecting a nation's interests in a globalized world, including leverage and status in world politics and diplomacy). How can these commodities be valued? There are at least three approaches.

First, estimate a nation's per capita defense spending and then ask whether its citizens are willing to pay at least such a sum for the annual protection offered by its armed forces. Comparisons can be made with other public spending programmes, such as health and police forces. Second, value-of-life studies can be used to estimate the value of lives saved and injuries avoided resulting from the provision of armed forces (see Chapter 9, and Jones-Lee 1990).[12]

Health economists have developed measures of health output benefit measures in the form of quality-adjusted life years or QALYS (but these are not valued). The defense equivalent of QALYS would be protection-adjusted life years (PALYS: Hartley 2010b). In addition to estimating the benefit of lives saved by defense, there are further gains from valuing property saved by avoiding damage and destruction (i.e. estimating both human and physical capital saved).

Third, consider defense as insurance in response to various current and future known and unknown threats and contingencies. These contingencies can involve time periods of some 25–50 years into the future: the result lags in the relationship between inputs and defense outputs, meaning that defense productivity cannot be based on the standard relationship between inputs and outputs within a calendar year. The insurance approach has private market comparators. Individuals and firms pay for a variety of insurance policies and other forms of protection. Examples include households buying insurance for homes, motor cars, driving, healthcare, international travel, and retirement.

In addition, households buy further protection in the form of household security (e.g. alarms and guard dogs), purchasing safer motor cars, locating in a safe neighborhood, and joining neighborhood watch schemes (through payments-in-kind). Similarly, firms make various insurance payments to protect their assets: they employ security guards and introduce measures to protect their staff and assets from terrorist attacks. Admittedly, these are private rather than public goods but, nonetheless, the payments in cash and kind provide some indication of the willingness of households and firms to pay for protection; such willingness to pay might then be applied to estimating the minimum level of a nation's defense spending. Further spending for protection is reflected in expenditure on a nation's police forces and internal security. The result is a substantial expenditure for private and public spending on internal security. Again, such sums provide an estimate of the lower bound of national defense spending.

By providing security and protection for a nation's citizens, defense spending on the armed forces creates the conditions allowing and promoting beneficial voluntary trade and exchange within and between nations. Protection of national property rights over land, sea, and air space (and more recently cyber-space) promotes national market exchanges whilst protection of international trade routes promotes beneficial international trade and exchange. For example, a nation's navy protects its international shipping and trade routes, including protection from piracy.

National and international market exchange contributes to improve society's welfare (especially compared to societies that lack well-developed national markets). In the context of national markets, the armed forces provide a capability to respond to national emergencies and provide aid to the civilian community. Without the armed forces, civil powers would have to provide more resources for emergencies (a relatively high cost for capabilities only required infrequently), or ignore such contingencies.

Ideally, defense spending on a nation's armed forces helps to prevent and avoid conflict; and where conflict occurs, minimizes its duration and effects on citizens, as well as contributing to more rapid post-conflict recovery. In this context, defense provides a deterrent aiming to persuade potential adversaries that conflict is not worthwhile. Where deterrence fails, defense spending aims to provide a warfighting capability to achieve a 'successful' conclusion by minimizing the costs of conflict.

These features are economic benefits that can be reflected in cost savings from avoiding conflict or minimizing its duration, and contributing to post-conflict recovery and restoration of market activity. Again, it is difficult to measure cost savings for events which do not occur. Indeed, such problems raise the general methodological issue of the counter-factual: what would have happened in the absence of defense spending?

Defense spending as a form of fiscal policy provides some direct national economic benefits comprising jobs, new technology, spin-offs, exports, and import-savings. The armed forces are a source of employment, and their spending in local areas further increases employment and provides a source of trained and skilled labor for the rest of the economy. In addition, public spending on the nation's defense industrial base contributes to jobs, advancing technology, spin-offs, and the balance of payments.

As discussed earlier, however, these economic benefits need to be assessed critically: there are serious doubts about many of these claimed economic benefits. For economists, a major concern arises over the alternative-use value of the resources employed in the armed forces and national defense industries. It needs to be asked whether the resources used in the military-industrial complex would make a greater contribution to jobs, technology, spin-offs, and exports if these resources were used elsewhere in the economy (Hartley 2010b).

Bilateral military alliances might provide additional economic benefits. For example, the US–UK special relationship provides the UK with access to US technology for its nuclear-powered submarines and missiles for its nuclear deterrent; with a leading role in the F-35 programme; and enables major UK defense firms' (e.g. BAE and Rolls-Royce) access to the US defense market. Also, the US provides security and protection for the UK which might otherwise require a larger defense budget. Similarly, Canada benefits from US defense spending and protection, leading to lower Canadian defense spending.

3.5.3 *Non-economic benefits of defense*

Defense spending also contributes major non-economic benefits to a nation and it might be that non-economic benefits are more valuable than many economic benefits. Non-economic benefits are those which do not explicitly contribute to national output. They comprise political, military-strategic, and international benefits.

These non-economic benefits include the ability to pursue national interests and foreign policy objectives; to add to a country's international reputation, standing, and status in the world (the feel good factor); and to increase its position in the world power hierarchy. These non-economic benefits might be reflected in a nation's position in the United Nations (e.g. membership of the Security Council), its membership in world economic organizations (e.g. OECD, IMF; G-8, and G-20 groups of nations), its leadership positions in international military alliances (e.g. NATO), and its ability to influence the behaviour of other nations. For example, military-strategic benefits can arise from bilateral or multilateral military alliances (e.g. benefits from standardization of equipment and tactics, some of which are economic in the form of cost savings).

There are other ways in which a nation can obtain non-economic benefits.

- *Prestige and international reputation.* A nation may provide military forces for international peacekeeping and peace enforcement, leading to world peace. Such peacekeeping contributions, however, are not costless.
- *Feel good factor.* Further non-economic benefits arise when a nation's armed forces contribute to international efforts on humanitarian aid and disaster relief. These contributions provide a 'feel good' factor (national pride) for the contributing nation's citizens (e.g. national spending on child protection and social services: Hartley 2010b).
- *Compulsory club membership.* Some nations may contribute to peace missions because they value (or feel compelled by) a relationship with a dominant ally or neighbor. This type of alliance or relationship can be considered as a compulsory club membership with clear obligations and benefits (Berkok and Solomon 2011).

3.6 The evidence: the international experience with measuring defense output

3.6.1 UK experience

Before 1998, the UK published traditional input and intermediate measures of defense output. Typically, these comprised numbers of armed forces military personnel and their formations, including numbers of aircraft squadrons, infantry regiments, tank units, and warships. The published data on unit numbers were available in varying degrees of detail (e.g. aircraft squadrons by types of aircraft, types of warships, etc). The amount of published data and its detail have improved over time. Data were also published on the numbers of regular and reserve forces and the numbers of civilian personnel employed by the MoD.

During the cold war, the armed forces focused on preparing for and deterring a direct military attack on the UK or Western Europe. After the cold war, there was no longer a direct military threat to the UK. In 1998, the publication of the

Strategic Defence Review (SDR) marked a significant change in published defense output measures.

The 1998 SDR represented a pioneering contribution to UK published data on defense output measures. For the first time, the UK published data on its defense capabilities, which are a more meaningful indicator of defense output. These defense capabilities are viewed as planning commitments. The 1998 SDR committed the UK to be a 'force for good' in the world with an associated global military expeditionary capability. On this basis, the UK armed forces were capable of supporting continuing commitments (e.g. Northern Ireland at that time) able to:

- respond to a major international crisis of a similar scale and duration to the Gulf War (an armoured division, 26 warships, and over 80 combat aircraft); or,
- undertake a more extended overseas deployment on a lesser scale (e.g. Bosnia) while retaining the ability to mount a second substantial deployment if this were made necessary by a second crisis (e.g. combat brigade and supporting air and naval units).[13]

These defense capabilities were subject to various constraints of readiness, location, duration, and concurrency. Different levels of readiness involve different cost levels: maintaining continual high readiness is costly. Similarly, location and duration affect force requirements: regional conflicts outside the NATO area and for an indefinite duration require different sizes and structures of armed forces compared with short-term deployments to, say, Bosnia or Kosovo.

Concurrency is a further issue involving the number of operations which can be conducted at any time including their scale, location, and duration. SDR identified the core regions of Europe, the Gulf, and the Mediterranean. The UK was committed to conducting two medium-scale operations concurrently (SDR 1998). Surprisingly, the government's actual military commitments exceeded these planning assumptions!

Following the 9/11 terrorist attacks on the US, the 1998 SDR was modified. A modified policy was announced in 2003/04 (comprising Cmnd. 6041 2003 and Cmnd. 6269 2004). The revised policy adopted new planning assumptions including:

- the ability to support three simultaneous small to medium-scale operations where at least one is an enduring peacekeeping mission (e.g. Kosovo),[14] or
- the ability at longer notice to deploy forces for large-scale operations while running a concurrent small scale peace-support operation, or
- the ability to project military force to sub-Saharan Africa and South Asia as well as a capability to respond to international terrorism; and
- the most demanding operations will be conducted as part of a coalition, usually involving the United States This requires the UK's armed forces to be interoperable with US Forces.[15]

Further changes occurred with the *Strategic Defence and Security Review* of 2010 (Cmnd. 7498 2010). Following the 2010 planned budget cuts, the UK's Defence Planning Assumptions (DPAs) and its defense capabilities were reduced to:

- an enduring stabilization operation around brigade level (up to 6,500 personnel) with air and naval support; and
- one non-enduring complex intervention (up to 2,000 personnel); and
- one non-enduring simple intervention (up to 1,000 personnel); or
- alternatively, three non-enduring operations if not already engaged in an enduring operation; or
- for a limited time, and with sufficient warning, committing all the UK's effort to a one-off intervention with up to three brigades with air and naval support (about 30,000 personnel);[16] together with
- maintaining a 'residual defense capability' for unforeseen emergencies or to reinforce existing operations or to respond to scenarios where the UK acts alone (House of Commons (HCP) 992 2011, 20).

MoD budgets pay for the UK force elements to be ready for operations as outlined in the DPAs. The costs of these missions, however, are funded from the government's contingency reserves. Over time, the rising unit costs of defense equipment and of volunteer military personnel will result in smaller armed forces and reduced defense capabilities (as defined by the UK MoD).

More important would be an assessment of the costs of achieving these defense capabilities compared with other nations providing similar capabilities (i.e. is the UK providing its capabilities at least-cost?). Within MoD, measures of defense training activities are used to assess performance. These include flying hours, days spent at sea, and Army personnel data on gains to trained strength and data on military exercises (ONS 2008).

The MoD publishes an annual performance report which offers some further insight into its defense capabilities (HCP 992 2011).[17] Useful though such information might be, it is both qualitative and vague (i.e. "success" in Afghanistan) and focuses on input costs which are unhelpful data for measuring output by themselves. On force readiness, the MoD's *Performance Report* admits that "Measuring and aggregating readiness is complex, not least because it is based on judgements of what is required to enable the armed forces to respond to a wide range of potential challenges" (HCP 992 2011, 21).

The MoD also reports on where there are "critical and serious weaknesses" in UK Forces.[18] The MoD's *Performance Report* also included a section on implementing the 2010 *Strategic Defence and Security Review* which provided further information on the UK's defense capabilities.[19]

The UK's defense capabilities output measures are an improvement on the traditional input approach but there are deficiencies at least in terms of publicly available information. For example, the National Audit Office has reported that the UK MoD has a good system for defining, measuring, and reporting the readiness of its armed forces which compares well with other countries (e.g. Australia, Denmark, and US: NAO 2005). It is recognized that 100 percent readiness is too costly. The published data on readiness, however, refers to whether there are serious or major weaknesses, which is useful but not very illuminating (e.g. without knowing what and where such weaknesses arise and their impact on force effectiveness). For instance, a statement that 50 percent of UK Forces had no serious or critical weaknesses suggests that the remaining 50 percent suffered serious weaknesses, which should be a source of concern!

Moreover, these performance assessments are mostly undertaken by MoD personnel, which could raise questions of independence and objectivity. An NAO report on the performance of MoD in 2009–10 presented and reviewed performance indicators (NAO 2010). The report focused on financial management information (e.g. management of stocks and assets) and made no mention of defense output measures. Though there was mention of defense output indicators, these only included qualitative measures: 'success on operations;' the existence of serious and critical weaknesses in readiness; manning levels in relation to manning balance by Service (with no data); and flying hours achieved against targets (again, without any data). In relation to the MoD aim of global and regional reductions in conflict, no output measure was reported (NAO 2010).

The NAO also publishes value-for-money reports (a type of retrospective CBA)—for example, on the multi-role tanker aircraft capability—and annual reports on MoD's major projects. These project reports assess major defense projects against their contractual commitments on cost, delivery, and performance, usually identifying cost overruns, delays, and any failures to meet performance requirements. Such value-for-money reports are a useful addition to knowledge but do not include the wider industrial and economic benefits of major projects, nor do they provide any assessment of the "battle-winning" performance of defense equipment (e.g. as demonstrated in conflicts such as Afghanistan or Iraq).

Overall, the UK's defense capabilities are useful measures of defense output but deficiencies remain. Some indicators of force readiness are qualitative: readiness is a variable measure depending on circumstances (readiness for what, when and where?); capabilities are not all identified; benefit values are not attached to capabilities; and the capabilities cannot be aggregated into a single measure of overall defense output.

None of the output measures address the contribution of defense to conflict prevention and its contribution to minimizing the costs of conflict, including saving lives. In fact, MoD economists examined different approaches to capturing output used in various parts of the MoD. As Davies *et al.* (2011, 399) put it:

> These include a number of partial aggregations and a balanced scorecard approach covering the three main areas of activity: success in military tasks, readiness to respond, and preparing for the future... and... it was confirmed that no existing technique offered a solution. Although it is hoped that in

the longer term progress will be made on the direct measurement of defense outputs and productivity, this remains an elusive goal.

The UK's experience in measuring outputs in other parts of the public sector and in the private sector is given in Appendix 3.2, offering selected insights for defense.

3.6.2 Australian experience

The Defence White Paper of 2009 outlined Australia's defense policy and force structure to 2030 (Department of Defence (DoD) 2009). It specified Australia's strategic interests including (ranked in order of priority):

- the defense of Australia against armed attack with the capability to act independently so as not to be reliant on foreign military forces. This principal task requires the Australian Defence Force (ADF) to control the air and sea approaches to Australia;
- the security, stability, and cohesion of Australia's immediate neighborhood which is shared with Indonesia, Papua New Guinea, East Timor, New Zealand, and the South Pacific Island states;
- an enduring strategic interest in the stability of the wider Asia-Pacific region; and
- a strategic interest in preserving the world international order which restrains aggression, manages other risks and threats, and addresses the security impacts of climate change and resource scarcity.

These objectives are to be achieved by Australia acting independently, by leading military coalitions, and by making tailored contributions to military coalitions. As a result of these priorities, the ADF of 2030 will need to invest especially in its maritime capabilities as well as enhancing its air capabilities.

Part of the funding for these capability improvements is to be achieved through efficiencies and savings (of AUD$20 billion) which, it is claimed, will not compromise effectiveness (DoD 2009, 14). Also, to fund ADF of 2030, the government has committed to real growth in the defense budget of 3 percent to 2017–18 and then 2.2 percent real growth to 2030 (DoD 2009, 137). The 2009 White Paper recognizes that defense planning is about managing strategic risks, that uncertainties remain, and that it is not possible to eliminate all risks (an ideal warning time of 10 years is reported: DoD 2009, Chapter 3, 28).

The 2009 White Paper deals with preparedness embracing readiness, sustainability, and concurrency. It recognizes that preparedness comes at a cost (but provides no data on the marginal benefits or costs of different levels of preparedness). Sustainability refers to the ability to undertake tasks and operations over time, whilst concurrency deals with the ability to conduct a number of operations in separate locations simultaneously. The White Paper provided an extensive list of the required capabilities of the ADF including:

- the capabilities needed for sea and air control around Australia;
- the ability to deploy a brigade group for combat operations for a prolonged period of time in the primary operational environment (for shorter period beyond that area);
- the ability to deploy a battalion group to a different area of operations in the primary operational environment;
- the ability to maintain other forces in reserve for short-notice, limited warning missions;
- the ability to provide tailored contributions to operations in support of Australia's wider strategic interests (e.g. special task forces group); and
- the ability to provide assistance to civil authorities (e.g. fisheries protection, terrorist incidents, support for major events, emergency responses, humanitarian and disaster relief in Australia and its neighbors, provision of search and rescue support, etc).

The list of capabilities is extensive with no ranking and little indication of the military resources available for each capability. Some of the capabilities are clearly military; others, including aid to civil authorities, are a general 'catch-all' which might be used to justify public support for defense spending. Further data on capabilities is provided by the annual defense budget.

Australian defense budgets show published data on expenditure on various overseas operations—the sources of planned cost savings, and capital investment programmes. There is data on the extra costs of overseas operations and on the numbers of military personnel by service (permanent, reserves, and numbers of high readiness reserves). Further budget data are presented on planned performance and outcomes for each of three defense outcomes comprising the protection and advancement of Australia's national and strategic interests and support for the Australian community and civil authorities (including expenditure by military base area). Some limited performance (intermediate output) indicators are published, such as the number of unit ready days for the Navy and flying hours for each of the services (DoD 2011).

A review of defense accountability was published in 2011 with the aim of improving accountability across defense (Black 2011). The review recommended the introduction of specific, measurable, and achievable outcomes with individuals given ownership and made accountable for their outcomes. The review recognized that there was a lack of specific outcome-based language in defense and an insufficient use of measurable outcomes. Particular focus was placed on performance measures for shortfalls in equipment delivery to date, including costs and quality (e.g. average delays of 28 percent or 2+ years; cost overruns of 52 percent: Black 2011, 60–61). The review, however, focused on management-organizational issues (e.g. too many committees) and not on the development of defense output measures and their consequences.

In June 2011, the Australian Minister for Defence announced a Defence Force Posture Review designed to assess whether the ADF is correctly positioned geographically to meet Australia's modern and future strategic and security challenges. These include:

- the rise of the Asia-Pacific and the Indian Ocean rim as regions of global strategic significance;
- the growth of military power projection capabilities of the Asia-Pacific countries;
- the growing need for the provision of humanitarian assistance and disaster relief following extreme events in the Asia-Pacific; and
- energy security and security issues associated with expanding offshore resource exploitation in Australia's North West and Northern approaches.

The ADF *Force Posture Review* considers how the ADF will support Australia's ability to respond to a range of activities including deployments on overseas missions and operations; support of operations in Australia's wider region; and engagement with the countries of the Asia-Pacific and Indian Ocean rim in ways which will help to shape security and strategic circumstances in Australia's interest. The *Force Posture Review* also makes recommendations on basing options for Force 2030. There is also a *Submarine Sustainment Review* to assess sustainment of Australia's Collins Class submarines (ADF 2011).

The Australian Defence White Paper of 2013 identified the capabilities the ADF will need in the future, reflecting the withdrawal from Afghanistan and the Solomon Islands. It emphasized air, naval,[20] special-forces, intelligence, and cyber security. The commitment to spending 2 percent of GDP on defense became a long-run target.

The 2013 White Paper presented a broad description of future forces but provided little detail on their capabilities. Interestingly, the 2013 White Paper referred to productivity and the need for "defence to become more efficient and prudent in its use of resources to remove waste and achieve better economies of scale." This is a politically attractive phrase, but does not explicitly address the challenge of preserving an adequate level of overall defense output and corresponding measurement challenges (DoD 2013).

3.6.3 New Zealand experience

New Zealand has a considerably smaller defense effort compared with the UK (see Table 3.1; Hartley 2010b). Nonetheless, it has devoted substantial resources to measuring its defense output. This section describes and assesses the development of its output indicators as published in 1991, 1993, 2011, and 2013.

In 1991, the New Zealand Defence Force (NZDF) published defense output measures in its *Annual Plan* (NZDF 1991). At this time, the output of the NZDF was grouped into two main categories: namely, retained outputs and current outputs.

Retained outputs are military groupings of operational forces which are retained to provide the government with a basis of military power from which force may be applied. Current outputs reflect the range of current activities undertaken by the NZDF which reinforce foreign policy goals and contribute to the well-being of the nation. Current outputs were further divided into core (military activities which contribute to military outcomes) and non-core (services provided to the community).

Published intermediate output data were provided for the two final outputs. For example, retained outputs consisted of eleven intermediate outputs: namely, naval combat forces; mine countermeasure forces; naval control and protection of shipping organizations; strategic assets (force troops); ready reaction forces; infantry brigade group and force maintenance; long-range maritime patrol force; offensive air support force; long and medium-range air transport force; medium and short-range air transport force; and the utility helicopter force.

Each intermediate output included performance targets and performance achievements. For example, the performance target for the infantry brigade group required deployment for operations within 90 days, and the performance achieved was for such a force to be available for sustained low-level operations at 90-days' notice. Offensive air support required 3,760 flying hours by Skyhawks, but there was a shortfall of over 400 hours against this target.

Changes were made and announced in 1993 (NZDF 1993). Seven output classes were identified: protection of New Zealand's territorial integrity and sovereignty; provision of military advice; provision of intelligence; provision of ancillary services; contribution to regional security; mechanisms for participation in defense alliances; and contributions to collective security.

Each output class was divided into sub-groups, each with performance targets and achievements. For example, the sub-group of "countering terrorism" had a performance target of two counter-terrorist exercises but only one such exercise was conducted. Similarly, for the sub-group called "deterring intrusions," there was a performance target of sustaining a naval presence for up to 30 days in the New Zealand area, and it was reported that this capability was demonstrated and achieved.

Whilst an impressive amount of detail was published, there are serious deficiencies with the outputs reported and performance indicators used. First, the outputs and performance indicators reported are mainly inputs or intermediate measures of output. Second, several outputs are unusual for defense outputs: namely, the provision of advice, intelligence, and ancillary services which includes civil defense assistance, support services to the community, and ceremonial support for the state. Third, the published data provide no weighting to indicate the relative importance of the various intermediate defense outputs to overall security. Is the provision of advice and intelligence ranked as highly as protection of New Zealand's territorial integrity and sovereignty? Fourth, some defense outputs might more appropriately be the responsibility of other government departments.

The defense outputs were refined and developed over time and with experience. The New Zealand position in 2011 is reflected in the NZDF Statement of Intent (NZDF 2011) which outlined the country's defense policy over the next 25 years. It specified the primary mission of the NZDF as securing New Zealand against external threat, protection of its sovereign interests, and the ability to take action to meet likely contingencies in the country's strategic area of interest. This primary mission recognizes that the country's national interests affect both the security and prosperity of the nation.

New Zealand must trade to survive, which requires that New Zealand has unfettered access throughout the Asia-Pacific region to engage in business. "Instability, conflict and war, even far from New Zealand's shores, can therefore directly affect New Zealand's social and economic well-being" (NZDF 2011, 9). Recognizing that the primary mission of the NZDF is broad, a number of subsidiary or intermediate outcomes have been developed.

The NZDF main and intermediate outcomes are currently not linked to a formal set of measures, mainly due to the complexity of measuring outcomes which deliver security and protection: there is no single measure of success in delivering protection. "There is no definitive way of knowing what might have happened, but did not happen, because of the activities of the NZDF" (NZDF 2011, 34).

The NZDF has 37 outputs in 16 output/expenses classes. Its output/expenses classes include naval combat and support forces, mine countermeasures, land combat and support forces, naval helicopter forces, airborne surveillance, and fixed wing and rotary transport forces.

Other output categories include unusual components such as military hydrography, military advice, and multi-class output appropriations (e.g. support to youth development and support to military museums: NZDF 2011). The NZDF also stresses its links with the community, reflected in the provision of skills to society, promotion of a 'healthy' defense industry, and a "buy New Zealand" procurement policy (NZDF 2011, 11). It is now explained, however, that these links to the community arise as by-products of the NZDF (NZDF 2011, 11).

The NZDF uses a measure of military capability which shows the combined effect that inputs have on operational effectiveness. Military capability is assessed using two elements: namely, preparedness and force components, described by the acronym PRICIE.[21] The elements are comprised of personnel, R&D, infrastructure, concepts of operations and training, information/technology, and equipment and logistics (NZDF 2011, 48).

The NZDF recognizes that its output measures often appear as inputs rather than outputs. Inputs are used as proxies for military capabilities (e.g. 500 flying hours of a specific type of aircraft will provide a certain military capability), but the actual measurement systems and capabilities are classified. Following the New Zealand *Defence Review*, however, concerns were expressed that the current system is too input-focused, amid a desire to measure military impacts and outcomes and cross-sector security outcomes. Where complex relationships are involved, it might not be possible to easily identify and measure cause and effect (Comptroller and Auditor General (CAG) 2011). No valuations of output are provided.

These concerns continued in the NZDF *Annual Report* of 2013 which reported its aggregate level of preparedness as "substantially prepared" (asserted without supporting data). The 2013 report did publish some output measurements, including objectives, measures, and outcomes (NZDF 2013). Overall, the NZDF has made commendable efforts to recognize and address the challenge of measuring defense output.

3.6.4   European experience

The focus here is on major European defense spending nations that publish their data in English. These nations are France, Germany, Italy, Spain, and Sweden.

3.6.4.1   France

A new French defense policy was announced in 2008 with the aim of making the French armed forces more flexible for rapid deployment from the Atlantic to the Indian Ocean. France aims to provide the necessary resources to ensure the security of its citizens, to safeguard national independence, and to consolidate the nation's military and diplomatic power. Under the new policy, France will be able to project 30,000 personnel with 70 combat aircraft, one carrier group and two naval battle groups within a six-month period for up to a year (a force capable of dealing with one major war or crisis at a time). Nuclear deterrence remains a key military mission, but terrorism is the most immediate threat, and there are also public service missions. There will be reductions in the numbers of military personnel and investment in new equipment. Some equipment is of poor quality: for example, only 50 percent of Leclerc tanks are mission ready; refuelling aircraft are 45 years old; and some Puma helicopters are 30 years old (Penketh 2008). In 2010, the UK and France signed an Anglo-French Defence Treaty with the potential for greater bilateral co-operation between their armed forces and defense industries.

By 2014, French defense policy was adjusting to a "difficult financial situation" leading to further reductions in the numbers of military personnel, ships, tanks, helicopters, and transport aircraft. A Joint Reaction Force was created, with 2,300 personnel and the ability to deploy up to 15,000 troops in a single overseas deployment. Plans were in place to cut the defense budget to 1.5 percent of GDP.

3.6.4.2   Germany

NATO remains the centrepiece of Germany's defense policy. The new defense policy announced in 2011 involved major changes for Germany's armed forces: reductions in the defense budget; abolishment of conscription replaced by an all-volunteer force; improvement of Germany's expeditionary capabilities; and closer military co-operation in Europe, especially in procurement and training (German Ministry of Defense (GMOD) 2011). Under the new policy, Germany plans to increase the deployment of the Bundeswehr outside Germany from the current 7,000 to some 10,000 soldiers (but there is no statement of the extent of geographical coverage of these expeditionary forces). There are also plans to reduce quantities of equipment (aircraft, helicopters, and ships). In 2014, however, Germany announced a review of its commitment to overseas military deployments, including its military contribution to the international pooling and sharing of military resources.

3.6.4.3 Italy

Despite cuts in defense spending due to Italy's austerity programme, Italy retains an expeditionary capability. Reports suggest the Air Force has been particularly affected by defense cuts. There were also reports that in 2010, Italy planned to reduce its involvement in peacekeeping missions in the Balkans and possibly in Lebanon, concentrating instead on Afghanistan where force levels peaked at 4,000 soldiers (Nativi 2010).

Italy's *Military Policy Review* of 2013 aimed to reduce the numbers of military personnel to 150,000 and civilian personnel to 20,000 by 2024. This represents a lengthy adjustment period. Italy also identified reductions in the numbers of senior military personnel within the reduced total numbers (i.e. fewer admirals, generals, colonels, and naval captains). The plan is for a defense budget of 0.84 percent of GDP.

The 2013 *Military Policy Review* declared that "available resources will be used on developing systems that combine high operational efficiency, adequate cost-effectiveness, and a development/growth margin that allows them to be integrated into complex and net-centric systems."

3.6.4.4 Spain

Reductions in defense spending were part of Spain's austerity programme. The 2011 budget reflected four objectives: the safety of the troops (force protection via operating and logistics expenditure); operational readiness; the maintenance of weapons systems; and international operations and fulfilment of Spain's international commitments. New tools were announced for improved oversight and management of defense expenditures.

3.6.4.5 Sweden

A new defense policy was announced in 2009 with an emphasis on mobility and flexibility of Sweden's armed forces. The plan is for it to be possible for an entire operational organization of some 50,000 people to be used within one week after a decision on heightened alert. In contrast, today only one-third of the national operational organization is equipped and prepared for an operation within one year. Some defense capabilities were listed in terms of inputs: numbers of military personnel (e.g. deployment of 1,700 people for continuous international peace-support operations) and numbers of Gripen aircraft (100 of the C/D model). An all-volunteer force will replace compulsory military service and there will be substantial reserve forces (e.g. four mechanized battalions). For the Army, only a small proportion of its soldiers will be full-time. Sweden specified its area of national interest: namely, the Baltic Sea or the northern area (Sweden Ministry of Defence (SMOD) 2009).

3.6.5 The European Defence Agency

The European Defence Agency (EDA) publishes defense data for its member states. These include annual financial data such as levels of defense spending and shares of GDP for member states, equipment procurement and R&D expenditures, spending on infrastructure and construction, defense expenditure that is outsourced, and expenditures on collaborative equipment programs. Input data is also published that include numbers of military, civilian and internal security personnel, personnel expenditures, as well as data on numbers of different types of equipment (combat aircraft tanks and warships).

Most of the data published is for inputs rather than defense outputs, although some EDA officials regard indicators such as quantity of military personnel as intermediate output measures. There is, however, data which are clearly a measure of intermediate output and proxies for defense output: namely, operation and maintenance expenditure, operational costs, average numbers of troops deployed, and the average numbers of sustainable (land) forces (EDA 2011). Comparative analysis of such data could be useful in revealing variations in efficiency and effectiveness across member states.

3.6.6 The United States

The United States is unique in its global power commitments and large-scale defense spending. US national security strategy requires a "comprehensive global engagement aimed at supporting a just and sustainable international order" (Under Secretary of Defense (USDOD) 2011, 2–1). The United States remains the only nation able to project and sustain large-scale military operations over extended distances. Its main objectives are to prevail in today's wars, prevent and deter conflicts, prepare for a wide range of contingencies, and preserve and enhance the all-volunteer force (AVF). Three of these objectives refer to actual and potential threats or outputs/outcomes, but the commitment to the AVF is an input, not an output! Funding for these objectives is to come partly from efficiency savings, including cancelation of unwanted and poorly performing equipment programs.

The US DoD publishes a massive amount of data of varying degrees of usefulness in terms of measuring defense outputs. For example, its aims include sustaining military capabilities to fight two wars, confront global terrorism, and provide humanitarian assistance and disaster relief, but no measures or valuations are attached to any of these objectives.

It also presents extensive data on performance results relating to its primary warfighting goals and its supporting goals (e.g. preserving the AVF and implementing the defense agenda). It is claimed that 75 percent of DoD performance goals were met in 2010 with 25 percent not met—"winning our nation's wars" was apparently 100 percent met even though, at the time, the final outcomes in Afghanistan and Iraq were still unknown! Similarly, for defense of homeland security, it was reported that 67 percent of goals were not met, a surprisingly high failure rate for such a core defense function (i.e. protecting US citizens: USDOD 2011, 7–11).

US defense budget data only marginally enhances the understanding of defense outputs in terms of capabilities and valuations. Performance results are recorded by DoD staff who may have a not entirely unbiased interest in reported outcomes. Budget data tend to be input-oriented, showing annual expenditure on military personnel, operations and maintenance, R&D and procurement, and family housing and military construction—all published by totals and by service.

The 2014 *Quadrennial Defense Review* (DoD 2014) described "tough choices" being made in an era of fiscal austerity. These choices were reflected in a reduced force structure, modernizing the forces, investing in readiness and innovation to meet future challenges, and protecting the health of the AVF in undertaking these reforms. Within this framework, the United States retained its capability to simultaneously engage in two regional conflicts.

3.6.7 *Evaluating international experience*

Since the great recession, financial austerity played a major role in formulating defense policy, especially in the US, UK, and the rest of Europe. It is under these constraints that measuring defense output can be particularly helpful in improving CBAs to guide difficult defense choices. Unfortunately, the response to austerity often resulted in indiscriminate across-the-board force reductions to accommodate politically determined budget choices. While the armed forces cannot ignore budget constraints in policy formulation, sensible policy choices require recognition of defense output implications of smaller budgets and the need to formulate better measures of defense output to guide future CBAs.

3.7 Conclusion

This chapter has identified a set of important questions that arise in efforts to measure defense outputs. Indeed, it has raised more questions than answers, but this investigation contributes to further the understanding needed to address the central research questions: What is defense output? How can it be valued? Under what conditions is it a worthwhile investment?

In its published form, the international experience of measuring defense output reveals some useful intermediate output measures, usually in the form of specific defense capabilities.[22] These are improvements on the traditional reporting of inputs that have typically included numbers of military personnel and equipment (e.g. combat aircraft, tanks, and warships). By themselves, input measures offer little indication of the value of overall defense capabilities such as peace, protection, deterring conflicts, and insurance against future threats.[23]

A starting point in answering the central research questions is to apply CBA: to identify the costs of defense and then ask whether defense provides at least a comparable level of benefits in the outputs produced. It is also important to capture non-economic benefits in addition to measurable economic benefits in measuring the overall benefits of defense spending. For example, if defense spending costs \$X billion, does it provide overall benefits of a similar value? Similar questions can be asked about the costs and benefits of conflict and peacekeeping operations.[24]

Next, the CBA can focus on incremental (or marginal) changes. If defense spending is increased or decreased by 10 percent, what are the effects on defense outputs (benefits)? Such marginal analysis can be assessed as a whole (on overall defense output), or by each military service (e.g. what would be the impact of a 10 percent increase or decrease in the size of the Army?).

Specifying the important questions is the first stage in any evaluation; but who raises and answers the questions? In a democracy, elected politicians are ultimately responsible for determining the size of military expenditures and its allocation among each of the services. Typically, unelected agents within the military propose many of these choices.[25] This reinforces the importance of developing meaningful defense output measures to guide future military investment and divestment decisions.

Appendix 3.1: Program Alignment Architecture (PAA)

The PAA is part of a broader government policy on managing resources and reporting results that directs all departments to have clearly defined and measurable strategic outcomes. DND's articulation is depicted in Table A3.1 and it intends to show what defense does and the results it is striving to achieve.

As shown in Table A3.1, the third strategic outcome states that "Defense operations improve peace, stability and security wherever deployed." This statement is rather vague on the military capabilities required to achieve the outcome. Is this a peacekeeping or peace enforcement mission? Is it exclusively the provision of strategic lift to transport aid and soldiers or air patrol? How quickly could the Canadian armed forces (CAF) provide an effective fighting force for an operation in North America? The statement also asserts with certainty an outcome, without any probabilities attached (e.g. defense operations *might* improve peace, stability, and security).

Strategic outcome 4, which states "Care and support to the Canadian armed forces and contribution to Canadian society," is equally ambiguous. The care and support to CAF members can be considered an input (part of recruitment and retention) while contribution to society could be a grant/subsidy program. Even if we make the assumption that outcomes and outputs are the same, there are still challenges in measuring the outcome/output. How do you measure international peace?

Appendix 3.2: UK experience in other parts of the public sector and the private sector

Other parts of the UK public sector have addressed the issue of measuring their outputs. Examples include health, education, public order and safety, transport, and social protection. The problems of measuring UK public sector outputs were

Table A3.1 Canadian Program Alignment Architecture 2011–12

Strategic outcome	Program	Actual spending 2011–12 CDN$000[a]	Alignment to Government of Canada outcomes
1. Resources are delivered to meet Government defence expectation		**4,334,325**	
2. National Defence is ready to meet Government defence expectations		**10,169,909**	
3. Defence operations improve peace, stability and security wherever deployed	3.1 Situational awareness	599,459	A safe and secure world through international engagement
	3.2 Canadian peace, stability and security	336,917	A safe and secure Canada
	3.3 Continental peace, stability and security	202,580	A strong and mutually beneficial North American partnership
	3.4 International peace, stability and security	1,980,673	A safe and secure world through international engagement
Sub-total		**3,119,629**	
4. Care andsupport to the Canadian Armed Forces and contribution to Canadian society		**1,516,338**	
5. Internal services		**1,078,558**	
Total		**20,218,759**	

Source: Department of National Defence (DND) 2013.

Note

a Current CDN$000.

reviewed by Atkinson (2005). This review started by recognizing that government output is generally non-marketed output and it is the absence of market transactions which underlie many of the problems of measuring public sector outputs. The traditional approach used in national accounts' statistics is the "output equals input" convention (Atkinson 2005). The review recognized that in the case of defense it is hard to identify the exact nature of the output (Atkinson 2005, 12). Some principles were suggested. Can we borrow from private sector experience (where the focus is on value-added)? Also, government output should be adjusted for quality changes (which is a problem for defense).

The Atkinson Review reported on experience of output measurement in public sectors such as health, education, public order and safety, and social protection. In health, it reported on the use of an aggregate output index constructed from separate series such as total numbers of in-patient and day cases. It recognized quality issues where healthcare embraces saving lives and extending the lifespan and preventing illness. It reported on the possibilities of using quality measures of healthcare based on quality-adjusted life years (QALYS).

Education output was measured by such indicators as examination results and the numbers of full-time school pupils (but numbers fail to reflect attendance). Public order and safety embraced police, fire, law courts, and prisons. Outputs were measured by such indicators as number of nights spent in prison, fires fought, and the number of crime-related incidents. Social protection includes the residential care of children and adults and output is measured by the numbers in residential care (Atkinson 2005). Experiences of measuring outputs in these parts of the UK public sector provide some guidance for measuring defense outputs.

Measuring health outputs which involve saving lives and preventing illness have parallels in defense (as mentioned earlier, Chapter 9 of this book is another illustration). The development of QALYS for health might be extended to defense in the form of protection-adjusted life years (PALYS). Since the Atkinson review, the ONS has continued to develop and improve output measures for various parts of the UK public sector. For example, education output measures are now adjusted for attendance and for quality changes (e.g. annual changes in examination points' scores: ONS 2010). But often the output measures are aggregate indices with no valuation of actual outputs.

Experience of measuring output in the UK transport sector has addressed a key issue raised in defense: namely, the value of life and the value of lives saved by transport improvements. The value of life is based on a person's willingness to pay (e.g. for good healthcare and for road safety improvements). On this basis, the UK Department of Transport valued a life at £1.57 million and a non-fatal serious injury at £176,215 per person (2009/10 prices).

Experience in the UK private sector might provide guidance on the possible valuations to be placed on defense output. In the private sector, individuals and households allocate resources to protection and safety. Examples include insurance policies for protecting property; household security measures (e.g. cameras, fencing, alarms, and dogs); car insurance and purchase of safer cars; location of homes in 'safe' areas; and the purchase of private medical and life insurance. In addition, there are public expenditures on protection, including police, fire and rescue services, prisons, as well as healthcare. Expenditures on these 'comparator sectors' provide an indication of society's willingness to pay for various measures of protection.

Notes

1   This chapter is based on a report prepared by Keith Hartley for the Defence Research and Development Canada under contract number DND-10/23136. Parts have been updated to 2014.
2   See also Williamson (2000) for more nuanced discussion.

3 For example, a nation's international peacekeeping contributions might provide considerable satisfaction to the country's prime minister, senior ministers, and civil servants able to attend international meetings at the UN and to participate in regional meetings. The principal-agent and public choice analysis raises the general question of who gains and who pays for these defense policies (e.g. international peacekeeping, national procurement of defense equipment including offsets). Ultimately, taxpayers pay and receive some defense benefits whilst agents consume some benefits not explicitly supported by the majority of voters and taxpayers.

4 For example, compare today's space satellite communications systems with the military communications facilities in 1914 (e.g. observation balloons).

5 Skills and productivity differ between regular forces, conscript, and reserve forces. Other complementary or substitutable labor inputs include civilian labour, contractors, national guard and reserves, and even police forces (e.g. police forces substituted for British Army troops in policing Northern Ireland: Ridge and Smith 1991).

6 Chapter 14 offers an interesting application of a new "real options" cost–benefit analysis of R&D investments.

7 The varied results in this field reflect different economic and econometric models, combinations of variables, time-periods, cross-section and time-series studies; a heterogeneous set of countries; and the use of data with varying degrees of reliability and scope of coverage.

8 With output budgets, a distinction needs to be made between the budget available to the MoD and the budget released to Parliament and the public. The published version of the budget does not reveal all the information available to the MoD and the basis for the choices which are reflected in the publicly released version of the budget (Davies *et al.* 2011, Chapter 17).

9 As an example, note that in Table 3.3 capital departmental expenditures limit (DEL) is part of overall resource DEL and reflects investments spending (cash) which appears in MoD's balance sheet to be consumed over a number of years. The resource DEL includes depreciation and cost of capital changes.

10 Formerly known as Program Activity Architecture.

11 Norman Augustine famously forecasted that with continued rising unit costs, by 2054 the entire US defense budget will purchase just one aircraft which would have to be shared between the Air Force and Navy (the Marines would have it for one day in leap years). He also forecasted that the UK and France would reach this position two years earlier (Augustine 1987, 143).

12 See Chapter 9 in this book for a novel application of the statistical value of life.

13 It was not expected that both deployments would involve warfighting or that they would be maintained for longer than six months. One might be a short warfighting deployment; the other an enduring non-warfighting operation (SDR 1998, 23).

14 "Small scale" is defined as the UK's deployment to Macedonia in 2001; "medium-scale" as Afghanistan (2001); and "large scale" as operation TELIC (Iraq).

15 When part of a coalition, the optimum ratio for prolonged commitments was 3–4 ships and 5 Army and RAF crews/units for each one deployed (Cmnd. 6269 2004).

16 This is about two-thirds of the force deployed to Iraq in 2003.

17 For example, its 2011 report focused on success in Afghanistan reflected in the costs of operations; the costs of its force elements (e.g. a ship at an annual cost of £28 million; a fixed wing combat aircraft at £6.5 million per year); and the direct costs of Service personnel (£49,000 per Service personnel per year: HCP 992 2011).

18 Interestingly, MoD's Performance Report included a section on Defence exports where one aim is to support British industry and jobs (HCP 992 2011). Defence exports are not an obvious output indicator for the MoD.

19 There is a NATO (NATO 2010) commitment to spend at least 2 percent of GDP on defense; an aim of achieving savings from contract renegotiations with the defense

industry; a goal to retain a surface fleet of 19 warships; a commitment to reduce the force of main battle tanks by 40 percent; and, lastly, a commitment to scrap the Nimrod MRA4 fleet (at a savings of some £200 million per aircraft: HCP 992 2011).

20 The decision to replace the Collins' class submarines was confirmed but the life of the Collins' class was extended by seven years.

21 Compares to "Lines of Development" in the UK and DOTMILPF (doctrine, organization, training, material, leadership and education, personnel, and facilities) in the US.

22 None of the nations reviewed in this chapter addressed the challenges of measuring and valuing overall defense output. The nearest to an intermediate output measure consisted of the identification of various defense capabilities, but these were not always comprehensive. For example, the UK did not identify all its capabilities, including defense of the UK homeland and its nuclear deterrent, and no valuations were provided for the assorted capabilities. Nonetheless, the focus on defense capabilities is an improvement over the traditional focus on input measures such as numbers of personnel and equipment. The next challenge may be to assign weights to the mix of capabilities and aggregate them into an index that represents an overall measure of defense output.

23 Nor should it be assumed that there exists a single "best" indicator: performance indicators can often give unexpected and perverse results (e.g. the operation was a success but the patient died).

24 For example, was the Iraq conflict a worthwhile investment for the US?

25 Governments could use representative samples of voters to form focus groups which would offer their views on the size of alternative defense budgets and force structures. These focus groups could receive advice from officials and military personnel. Focus groups are not an ideal solution (e.g. free-rider problems remain; groups have to be selected; and they will have their internal momentum and dynamics), but would provide politicians with an additional mechanism for identifying voter preferences on defense spending and policy.

References

Atkinson, Sir A. B. 2005. "Measurement of Government Output and Productivity for the National Accounts." In *Atkinson Review: Final Report*. Basingstoke, England: Palgrave Macmillan.

Augustine, N. R. 1987. *Augustine's Laws*. London: Penguin Books.

Australian Defence Force (ADF). August 25, 2011. *Australian Defence Force Posture Review Public Consultation and Submission Process*. Canberra, AU: Department of Defence.

Baldwin, D. A. 1997. "The Concept of Security." *Review of International Studies* 23: 5–26.

Benoit, E. 1973. *Defense and Economic Growth in Developing Countries*. Boston, MA: Lexington Books.

Berkok, U. G., and B. Solomon. 2011. "Peacekeeping, Private Benefits and Common Agency." In *Handbook on the Economics of Conflict*, edited by D. L. Braddon and K. Hartley. Northampton, MA: Edward Elgar Publishing.

Black, R. 2011. *Review of Defence Accountability Framework*. Canberra, AU: Australian Government Department of Defence.

Comptroller and Auditor General (CAG). June 2011. *Central Government: Cost-effectiveness and Improving Annual Reports*. Wellington, NA: Comptroller and Auditor General.

Cornes, R., and T. Sandler. 1996. *The Theory of Externalities, Public Goods and Club Goods* (2nd edition). Cambridge: Cambridge University Press.

Davies, N, T. Turner, A. Gibbons, D. Jones, S. Davis, and N Bennett. 2011. "Helping Secure the 'Biggest Bang for the Taxpayers' Buck:' Defence Resource Management in the United Kingdom." In *Handbook on the Economics of Conflict*, edited by D. L. Braddon and K. Hartley. Northampton, MA: Edward Elgar Publishing.

Defence Analytical Services and Advice (DASA). 2011. *U.K. Defence Statistics Compendium 2011*. London: The Stationery Office Limited.

Deger, S., and R. P. Smith. 1983. "Military Expenditure and Growth in Less Developed Countries." *Journal of Conflict Resolution* 27(2): 335–353.

Department of Defence (DoD). 2009. *Defending Australia in the Asia Pacific Century: Force 2010*. Canberra, AU: Department of Defence.

——. 2011. *Defence Portfolio Budget Statements 2011–2012*. Canberra, AU: Department of Defence.

——. 2013. *Defence White Paper 2013*. Canberra, AU: Department of Defence.

—— 2014. *Quadrennial Defense Review*. Available at www.defense.gov/pubs/2014_Quadrennial_Defense_Review.pdf [accessed 10 September, 2014].

Department of National Defence (DND). 2013. *Department of National Defence: Report on Plans and Priorities 2013–14*. Ottawa, CA: Department of National Defence.

Dunne, P., and R. P. Smith. 2010. "Military Expenditure and Granger Causality: A Critical Review." *Defence and Peace Economics* 21(5–6): 427–441.

Engerer, H. 2011. "Security as a Public, Private or Club Good: Some Fundamental Considerations." *Defence and Peace Economics* 22(2): 135–145.

European Defence Agency (EDA). March 31, 2011. *Defence Data 2009*. Brussels, BE: EDA.

German Ministry of Defense (GMOD). May 2011. *Defence Policy Guidelines*. Berlin, DE: GMOD.

Hartley, K. 2010a. "Defense Economics." In *The Economics of Human Systems Integration: Valuation of Investments in People's Training and Education, Safety and Health, and Work Productivity*, edited by W. B. Rouse. Hobeken, NJ: Wiley.

——. 2010b. The Case for Defence. *Defence and Peace Economics* 21(5–6): 409–426.

——. 2011. *Defence Output Measures: An Economic Perspective*. Defence R&D Canada–CORA. Contract Report: DRDC CORA CR 2011-178.

Hildebrandt, G. G. 1990. "Services and Wealth Measures of Military Capital." *Defence Economics* 1(2): 159–176.

——. 1999. "The Military Production Function." *Defence and Peace Economics* 10(3): 247–272.

Hitch, C. J., and R. N. McKean. 1960. *The Economics of Defense in the Nuclear Age*. London: Oxford University Press.

House of Commons (HCP) 992. 2011. *Ministry of Defence Annual Report and Accounts 2010–2011* (including Performance Report). London: The Stationery Office Limited.

House of Commons Defence Committee. 2003. *Delivering Security in a Changing World*. 2003 Defence White Paper: Cmnd. 6041, Volumes I–II. London: The Stationery Office Limited.

House of Commons Ministry of Defence. 2004. *Delivering Security in a Changing World: Future Capabilities*. 2004 Defence White Paper: Cmnd. 6269. London: The Stationery Office Limited.

Jones-Lee, M. E. 1990. "Defence Expenditure and the Economics of Safety." *Defence Economics* 1(1): 13–16.

Middleton, A., S. Bowns, K. Hartley, and J. Reid. 2006. "The Effect of Defence R&D on Military Equipment Quality." *Defence and Peace Economics* 17(2): 117–139.

Middleton, A., K. Copsey, and K. Hartley. 2011. *Estimating a Production Function for Military Power (Mimeo)*. Malvern, UK: Economex Limited.

Military Policy Review 2013. Available at www.difesa.it/Primo_Piano/Documents/2013/gennaio%202013/Direttiva%20Ministeriale_ENG.pdf [accessed 10 September, 2014].

National Audit Office (NAO). 2005. *Assessing and Reporting Military Readiness* (HCP 72). London: The Stationery Office Limited.

———. 2010. *Performance of the MoD 2009–10.* Briefing to House of Commons Defence Committee. London: The Stationery Office Limited.

National Security and Intelligence. 2010. *Securing Britain in an Age of Uncertainty: The Strategic Defence and Security Review.* (Cmnd. 7498). London: The Stationery Office Limited.

Nativi, A. November 19, 2010. "Italy Protects Defense Modernization Spending." *Aviation Week.*

New Zealand Defence Force (NZDF). June 1991. *Annual Plan: G55.* Wellington, NZ: NZDF.

———. 1993. *New Zealand Defence Force Annual Report 1993.* Wellington, NZ: NZDF.

———. 2011. *New Zealand Defence Force Statement of Intent 2011–2014.* Wellington. NZ: NZDF.

———. 2013. *New Zealand Defence Force Annual Report 1993.* Wellington, NZ: NZDF.

North Atlantic Treaty Organization (NATO). 2010. *Financial and Economic Data Relating to NATO Defence.* Brussels, BE: NATO, Press and Media.

Office of Under Secretary of Defense (USDOD). 2011. *US DoD Fiscal Year 2012 Budget Request.* Washington, DC: Department of Defense.

Office for National Statistics (ONS). 2008. *Scoping Paper on the Possible Improvements to Measurement of Defence in the U.K. National Accounts: U.K. Measurement of Government Activity.* Newport, SW: ONS.

———. 2010. *Annual Report 2009–10.* Newport, SW: UK Centre for Measuring Government Activity.

Organisation for Economic Co-operation and Development (OECD). 2010. *Main Science and Technology Indicators.* Paris: OECD.

Penketh, A. June 18, 2008. "The Big Question: What is the New French Defence Strategy, and Should we Follow Suit?" *The Independent Newspaper.*

Receiver General of Canada (RCG). 2013. *The Public Accounts of Canada Volume II.* Ottawa, CA: Government of Canada.

Ridge, M., and R. P. Smith. 1991. "U.K. Military Manpower and Substitutability." *Defence Economics* 2(4): 283–293.

Sempre, C. M. 2011. "The European Security Industry: A Research Agenda." *Defence and Peace Economics* 22(2): 245–264.

Solomon B., P. Chouinard, and L. Kerzner. October 2008. *The Department of National Defense Strategic Cost Model* (Volume II: Theory and Empirics, Defence R&D). Ottawa, CA: Canada-CORA.

Stockholm International Peace Research Institute (SIPRI). 2011. *Military Expenditure Database* (Database). Solna, SE: SIPRI.

The Strategic Defence Review (Cmnd. 3999). 1998. (See also Supporting Essays). London: The Stationery Office Limited.

Sweden Ministry of Defence (SMOD). March 19, 2009. *A Functional Defence.* (Press Release by the Sweden Ministry of Defence).

Tisdell, C., and K. Hartley. 2008. *Microeconomic Policy: A New Perspective* (2nd edition). Cheltenham, UK: Edward Elgar Publishing.

Williamson, O. E. 2000. "The New Institutional Economics: Taking Stock, Looking Ahead." *Journal of Economic Literature* 38: 595–613.

Zaller J. R., and S. Feldman. 1992. "A Simple Theory of the Survey Response: Answering Questions versus Revealing Preferences." *American Journal of Political Science* 36(3): 579–616.

4 The economic evaluation of alternatives

Francois Melese

An AoA [analysis of alternatives] *is an* analytical comparison *of the* operational effectiveness, suitability, *and* life-cycle cost *of* alternatives *that satisfy established* capability needs.

US Department of Defense (DoD 2006, Section 3.3)

4.1 Introduction: making the case for "affordability"

Military cost–benefit analysis (CBA) is routinely used to shape future forces and influence military spending. It underpins the "analysis of alternatives" (AoA)[1] in the United States and the concept of "value for money" in the United Kingdom. A standard definition states: "An AoA is an analytical comparison of the operational effectiveness, suitability, and life-cycle cost of alternatives that satisfy established capability needs" (DoD July 7, 2006 Section 3.3). Missing from this definition is "affordability."

A weakness in the traditional application of military CBA in the United States is that while AoAs correctly focus on life-cycle costs and operational effectiveness of alternatives, forecasts of future funding rarely appear.[2] As former chairman of Lockheed Martin Corporation, Norm Augustine, once noted: "affordability is rarely considered."[3]

As ministries of defense struggle to obtain the best value for every dollar they invest in defense programs, affordability is a growing concern.[4] In an age of fiscal austerity, where deficits and debt require rethinking defense budgets, affordability increasingly takes center stage.

The latest US defense guidance emphasizes the importance of affordability, but offers only nominal suggestions about how to include it in an AoA.[5] This chapter reveals several concrete approaches to structuring public investment decisions that emphasize affordability. We refer to this set of military CBA approaches as the "economic evaluation of alternatives" (EEoA). The goal is to encourage analysts and decision-makers (DMs) to integrate affordability (funding and other resource constraints) early and explicitly in the acquisition process alongside estimates of operational benefits and life-cycle costs.

The EEoA approach to military CBA brings taxpayers up front alongside warfighters in the defense acquisition process. This requires working with vendors to build proposals based on future funding (budget) scenarios.[6] EEoA clearly separates the life-cycle costs (or "price") of an alternative, its expected operational effectiveness or benefit (performance and schedule), and the resources (funding or budget) likely to be available (i.e. affordability) for the overall program.[7]

4.2 Integrating requirements generation, defense acquisition, and PPBS

A focus on affordability offers a unique opportunity to achieve a significant defense acquisition reform—to closely couple requirements generation systems and defense acquisition systems with financial management systems such as the Planning, Programming, and Budgeting System (PPBS). The primary goal of PPBS is to build an "optimal" mix of forces that maximizes national security within fiscal (affordability) constraints (DoDD 2013). A brief review of defense budgeting and acquisition highlights the valuable role EEoA can play in improving investment outcomes.

The requirements generation process naturally fits into the planning phase of PPBS. The first step in any investment analysis is to identify the derived demand for a key capability, program or project.[8] The focus of EEoA is on materiel investments identified to fill critical capability gaps. This is accomplished through DoD's Requirements Generation System.

Operator demands ("requirements") are identified and refined in the planning phase of the PPBS process. Whenever major "materiel" solutions are recommended, prospective military investments are identified that serve as the basis for a military cost–benefit AoA. AoAs underpin the development of major acquisition programs in the Defense Acquisition System (DAS).[9]

Ideally, the planning phase of PPBS establishes fiscally constrained guidance and priorities for the military services. This guidance on readiness, sustainability, modernization, etc., provides direction for DoD Components (military departments and joint defense agencies) in the programming phase of PPBS. In the US component programs and new investment proposals are summarized in what the services (Army, Navy, Air Force, and Marine Corps) call their *Program Objectives Memorandum* (POM).

Service POMs provide detailed resource-allocation decisions (funding, personnel, etc.) for programs projected six years into the future. A comprehensive summary of service POMs is captured in the Future Year Defense Plan (FYDP) database. A challenge for EEoA is that evaluations of major investments require DAS life-cycle cost estimates that project well beyond the six years of the FYDP. This concern is addressed in Chapter 7.

Each POM is subsequently reviewed by the Joint Staff and senior leadership in the Office of the Secretary of Defense (e.g. Cost Assessment and Program Evaluation—CAPE) to ensure that it satisfies strategic planning guidance, and that the overall FYDP is effective and affordable. Today, in the US, budgeting in PPBS occurs concurrently with programming. The budgeting phase converts the programming phase's (output-oriented) benefit or military capability perspective into the (input-oriented) cost format required for Congressional appropriations.[10]

The Under Secretary of Defense Comptroller and the Office of Management and Budget (OMB) jointly review budget submissions to ensure that programs are affordable in the budget year—i.e. satisfy current fiscal year constraints.[11] Once accepted by the Secretary of Defense, this spending plan is included in the President's overall federal budget submission to the Congress for approval.

In principle, AoAs should contribute to requirements generation in the planning phase of PPBS, helping to identify investment alternatives and the benefits and costs of those alternatives. Through the DAS's decision milestones, AoAs should also influence the programming phase of PPBS.[12] According to GAO, however:

> [T]he vast majority of capability proposals that enter the [Requirements Generation] process are ... approved without accounting for resources [funding/budgets] that will be needed to acquire the desired capabilities.[13]
>
> (GAO 2009, 6)

This concern about future financial resource availability ("affordability") is the primary focus of EEoA. In considering alternative funding scenarios (that partly rely on accurate FYDP forecasts), EEoA injects an explicit constrained-optimization approach into defense investment decisions that parallels one already embedded in the programming phase of PPBS: choosing an optimal mix of forces, equipment, and support that maximizes national security subject to fiscal constraints.

4.3   Integrating affordability assessments into military CBA

In practice, military requirements are often approved without fully accounting for resources available, including future funding realities. While AoAs attempt to estimate costs and benefits of competing alternatives, affordability is addressed as a separate exercise, and then only ex-post.[14] This results in the following observation: "at the program level, the key cause of poor outcomes is the approval of programs with business cases [AoAs] that contain inadequate knowledge about ... resources [funding] needed to execute them" (GAO 2009, 7). Ironically, this directly contradicts the department's own policy outlined in DoD Directive 5000.01 which explicitly states:

> All participants in the acquisition system shall recognize the reality of fiscal constraints ... DoD components shall plan ... based on realistic projections of the dollars ... likely to be available [and] the user shall address *affordability* in establishing capability needs.
>
> [emphasis added] (DoD 5000.01 2007, Enclosure 1, 5)[15]

According to the *US Defense Acquisition Guidebook*, the purpose of an affordability assessment is to demonstrate that a program's projected funding requirements are realistic and achievable:[16]

> In general, the assessment should address program funding over the six-year programming [FYDP] period, and several years beyond. *The assessment should also show how the projected funding fits within the overall DoD Component plan.*[17]
>
> [emphasis added] (DoD July 7, 2006, Section 3.2.2)

EEoAs provide a mechanism for analysts and DMs to embed affordability assessments directly into AoAs. In preparing affordability assessments, the FYDP offers a valuable source of data.

4.4 An intuitive guide to the economic evaluation of alternatives

Nesting the requirements generation and DASs within PPBS suggests formulating the military's acquisition problem in terms of identifying and funding investments that maximize benefits (performance or effectiveness) for a given budget. Structuring the military investment problem as a constrained optimization, i.e. maximizing military effectiveness subject to a budget constraint or, alternatively, minimizing costs of obtaining a given level of effectiveness, are the first two of the six approaches recommended in the EEoA.[18] Either approach would boost the value of an AoA, since they both require and promote explicit assessment of higher level (joint) resource allocation decisions in the planning and programming phases of PPBS.

Multiple criteria decision-making (MCDM) techniques typically applied to structure AoAs do not currently lend themselves to this interpretation (see Chapter 8 for example). As a consequence, rather than being constrained by budgets, a budget for a new program or project is generated as the output of an AoA, producing so-called "funding requirements."[19] The third of the six possible approaches proposed to structure an EEoA turns this on its head.[20] Instead of generating a budget through the AoA process, forecasts of optimistic, pessimistic, and most likely funding scenarios are produced as part of the PPBS process, and then vendors are asked to build alternatives which fit within that budget envelope.[21]

According to the *US Defense Acquisition Guidebook*, affordability assessments should also provide details on how excess funding demands will be accommodated by reductions in other mission areas or in other accounts.[22] This marginal analysis across programs is the last of the six approaches proposed to structure an EEoA, labeled the "opportunity cost approach." The fourth and fifth (modified budget and modified effectiveness) approaches to EEoA involve attempts to level the playing field across alternative vendors; in effect converting the problem back to the first two constrained optimization approaches.

Whereas funding decisions for major programs take place through the PPBS process, the GAO finds that:

> ...the process does not produce an accurate picture of the department's resource needs [funding/budget requirements] for weapon system programs... Ultimately, the process produces more demand for new weapon system programs than available resources can support.[23]
>
> (GAO, March 18, 2009, 6)

EEoA directly responds to these challenges. It also responds to other concerns highlighted by GAO that continue to confront DoD's DAS. This includes: "(1) [to make] better decisions about which programs should be pursued or not pursued given existing and expected funding; [and] (2) [to develop] an analytical approach to better prioritize capability needs" (March 18, 2009, Highlights).

In sharp contrast with the MCDM approach used in most contemporary AoAs, EEoA approaches explicitly identify and emphasize funding (budget or affordability) constraints. In generating alternatives under optimistic, pessimistic, and most likely funding scenarios, EEoA requires explicit input from the PPBS process. As a consequence, widespread application of EEoA would directly contribute to the goal of achieving:

> ...greater consultation between requirements, budget, and acquisition processes [that] could help improve the department's... portfolio of weapon programs... [and guaranteeing] decision makers responsible for weapon system requirements, funding, and acquisition execution... establish an investment strategy in concert... assuring requirements for specific weapon systems are clearly defined and achievable given available resources [funding/budgets].
>
> (GAO, July 2, 2008, 10 and 14)

The next section offers a brief description and critical evaluation of the status quo. This includes two common decision criteria widely used in cost-effectiveness analyses. The first is the popular "bang-for-the-buck" or benefit/cost ratio.[24] The second criterion is essentially a weighted average of cost and effectiveness, a decision rule generated by the standard MCDM approach to cost-effectiveness analysis that underpins most contemporary AoAs (see Chapters 8 and 16, for example). Section 4.6 illustrates the six approaches to structure an EEoA. The final section concludes with a decision map to guide analysts and DMs in selecting which of the six approaches is best suited to their circumstances.

4.5   A critical evaluation of the status quo: two popular decision criteria

Today, most modern military investment (and divestment) decisions are supported by some form of CBA. The US DoD applies CBA to anything from milestone decisions for major defense acquisition programs and major acquisition of information systems (MDAPs and MAISs) to outsourcing (OMB Circular A-76; Eger and Wilsker 2007), public-private partnerships, privatization, asset sales, or base realignment and closure (BRAC) actions (see OMB Circulars A-94; Federal Acquisition Regulations (FAR); Defense FARs; DoD 5000 series, etc.).

When benefits can be quantified, but not monetized, analysts rely on so-called "measures of effectiveness" (MoEs) in which case CBA is generally referred to as "cost-effectiveness" analysis.[25] (US OMB 1992) The most common methodology and approach for building MoEs and for structuring cost-effectiveness analyses is alternately referred to as multiple-criteria decision-making (MCDM), multi-attribute utility theory (MAUT), or multiple-objective decision-making (MODM) (see for example French 1986; Keeney and Raiffa 1976; Clemen 1996; Kirkwood 1997; Parnell 2006; Ramesh and Zionts 1997).

This chapter describes some limitations of the two decision criteria used in most AoAs and proposes an alternative methodology derived explicitly from the constrained-optimization approach recommended for an EEoA. The latter approaches are closer in spirit to the economic origins of cost-effectiveness analysis found in Gorman (1980); Hitch and McKean (1967); Michael and Becker (1973); Stigler (1945); Theil (1952); etc.—and most often attributed to Lancaster (1966a, 1966b, 1971, 1979).

A key difference between the MCDM approach to an AoA and EEoA approaches is that instead of modeling decision alternatives from competing vendors as points in cost-effectiveness space, EEoA models alternative vendor proposals as functions of optimistic, pessimistic, and most likely funding (budget) scenarios. The EEoA approach directly responds to GAO's observation that affordability needs to be an integral part of any business case (AoA):

> [o]ur work in [uncovering] best practices has found that an executable business case [requires] demonstrated evidence that . . . the chosen concept can be developed and produced *within existing resources* [funding/budgets].
> [emphasis added] (GAO September 25, 2008, 6)

Benchmarking against the private sector, GAO further emphasizes that:

> . . .successful commercial enterprises. . .follow a disciplined integrated process during which the pros and cons of competing proposals are assessed based on strategic objectives. . .*and available resources* [budgets/funding].
> [emphasis added] (GAO 2009, 5)

A distinctive feature of defense investment decisions is that multiple criteria such as cost and effectiveness cannot easily be combined into a single, overall objective such as "government profitability." The challenge of ranking public investments when benefits cannot be monetized has generated a broad literature across management science, operations research, and decision sciences. Techniques that mostly fall under the umbrella of MCDM are routinely used by analysts and DMs (such as AoAs) to guide public investment decisions. (See Chapter 8.)

This literature models investment alternatives as bundles of measurable character-istics (criteria or attributes). The development of MoEs,[26] combined with life-cycle cost estimates (Chapter 5), are used to help rank alternatives. (See Chapters 8 and 16) An ongoing concern is how to integrate costs and effectiveness in the selection process (see Henry and Hogan 1995; Melese and Bonsper 1996; Melese *et al.* 1997; etc.).

In their pioneering work applying economic analysis to defense, Hitch and McKean (1967, 158) define a "criterion" as the "test by which we choose one alternative...rather than another" (p. 120). They stress that "[t]he choice of an appropriate economic criterion is...the central problem in designing a [cost-effectiveness] analysis."

The two most popular decision criteria used to integrate cost and effectiveness in AoAs are 1) to construct benefit/cost (or MoE/cost) ratios, and 2) to assign a weight on cost relative to effectiveness and construct a weighted average of cost and effectiveness (using a linear, separable, additive "value" function) as demonstrated in Chapter 8. The latter decision criterion is a common prescription for AoAs that emerges from MCDM. Both approaches can be problematic. We first focus on what is arguably the most widely applied criterion—benefit/cost ratios. Next, we move to the most common MCDM decision criterion—to assign a relative weight to the cost (price) of alternatives in an overall value function.

At first glance, the benefit/cost (MoE/cost) ratio or "bang-for-the-buck" cri-terion is appealing. It turns out, however, to be largely meaningless unless alternatives are constructed with a specific budget (funding/affordability) scenario in mind or to achieve a specific level of effectiveness. Meanwhile, the second deci-sion criterion can also turn out to be misleading in the absence of a specific budget (funding/affordability) constraint or clear understanding of "opportunity costs."[27]

4.5.1 *"Bang-for-the-buck" (benefit/cost) ratios*

It is well known that the application of a benefit/cost ratio (or "bang-for-the-buck") decision criterion to rank alternatives is largely meaningless unless alternatives are constructed for a specific budget (funding) scenario or to achieve a specific level of effectiveness. The problem of ranking public investments when benefits cannot be expressed in dollars has spawned an extensive literature in management science, operations research, and decision sciences:

1   In a military text entitled *Executive Decision Making*, the author offers that "[w]hen we cannot fix cost or effectiveness, we might combine them to help us choose between alternatives... If neither can be fixed... we can establish a cost/effectiveness ratio" (i.e. a cost/benefit ratio) (Murray 2002, 6–3, 6–10).
2   In presenting what they claim is a "novel cost–benefit analysis" for the "com-prehensive evaluation of competing military systems," authors in the *Acquisi-tion Review Quarterly* define a "merit function" as "a single number...[that] reflects the ratio of benefits derived to dollars spent" (i.e. a benefit/cost ratio).

The article asserts: "with this . . . approach, the cost-effectiveness of competing systems can be compared and "provides for objective and reliable decision making," where "a large system merit [benefit/cost ratio] is preferable to a small one" (Byrns *et al.* 1995).

3 Similarly, in a section entitled "Comparing Costs and Benefits," the US Department of the Army's *Economic Analysis Manual* states: "When the results yield unequal cost and unequal benefits [. . .] in this situation all alternatives [. . .] may be ranked in decreasing order of their benefit/cost ratios" (DoA February 2001, 32).[28]

Each of these examples recommends using a benefit/cost ratio as the decision criterion. Each also neglects to include either an affordability (cost or budget) constraint or a performance (effectiveness or capability) constraint (see Appendix 4.1). As legendary RAND analyst Gene Fisher (1971) clearly points out in his classic text *Cost Considerations in Systems Analysis*:

> The use of [benefit/cost] ratios usually poses no problem as long as the analysis is conducted in [a] framework . . . with the level of effectiveness or cost fixed. However, it is common to encounter studies where this has not been done, *with the result that comparisons [are] essentially meaningless.*
> [emphasis added] (p. 11)

In applying economic analysis to defense, Hitch and McKean (1967) warn:

> One common 'compromise criteria' is to pick that [alternative] which has the highest ratio of effectiveness to cost . . . [M]aximizing this ratio is the [decision] criterion. [While] it may be a plausible criterion at first glance . . . it allows the absolute magnitude of [effectiveness] or cost to roam at will. In fact, the only way to know what such a ratio really means is to tighten the constraint until either a single budget (or particular degree of effectiveness) is specified. And at that juncture, the ratio reduces itself to the test of maximum effectiveness for a given budget (or a specified effectiveness at minimum cost), and might better have been put that way at the outset . . . .[29]
> (pp. 165–7)

The first two ways to structure an EEoA, as well as the fourth and fifth approaches, follows their advice:

> The test of maximum effectiveness for a given budget (or alternatively, minimum cost of achieving a specified level of effectiveness) . . . seems much less likely to mislead the unwary.[30]
> (p. 167)

The conclusion is that the use of benefit/cost ratios as a decision criterion in AoAs does not pose a problem as long the analysis is structured paying close attention to affordability (i.e. a budget/funding constraint) or operational performance (i.e. a fixed level of effectiveness or MoE).[31] Since AoAs typically evaluate vendor proposals that differ in both costs (price) and benefits (MoEs), using benefit/cost (or effectiveness/cost) ratios to rank alternatives is at best "misleading."[32] Partly as a consequence, decision scientists developed another approach to rank investment options, the MCDM criterion routinely applied in AoAs. This second widely prescribed decision criterion is examined below.

4.5.2 Weighted averages of cost and effectiveness: assigning a weight to cost as a proxy for affordability

MCDM is often used as an umbrella term, and we will do so here. "In the literature, the terms multi-attribute decision making (MADM), multi-criteria decision making (MCDM), and multi-objective decision making (MODM) are used almost interchangeably" (French 1986, 105). In a typical MCDM evaluation, a DM is asked to identify desired criteria (characteristics or attributes) of a project, program or system to fill some critical capability gap, given a specific threat scenario. Next, the DM is asked to reveal agreeable tradeoffs among those attributes. An exercise of this sort helps analysts to uncover the DM's underlying utility function—similar to the economist's indifference curves that reflect a consumer's "utility" function—to help generate an MoE for each alternative.[33]

To uncover a DM's utility function, beginning with Saaty (1977), decision scientists bridged an important implementation gap. Multiple-objective (analytic) hierarchy approaches were developed to help reveal underlying utility functions.

The objectives hierarchy approach can help a DM to work down from a high-level objective (provide national security) to a relevant set of sub-objectives (an effective airlift capability) to specific attributes that underpin those sub-objectives (mobility, transportability, etc.) and, finally, to measurable characteristics (mobility = speed (S), range (R); transportability = payload (P), weight (W), etc.). The outcome in this example is a utility function for airlift capability: $U = U(M(S, R); T(P, W))$, where the desired characteristics (speed, range, payload, weight) might be measured respectively in mph, miles, cubic feet, and pounds.

The standard procedure in the literature is to define a linear, additive separable utility function.[34] This generates an MoE for each alternative, roughly analogous to a weighted average of its attributes (see Chapter 8 for example). There exists a vast literature concerned with eliciting preference weights and the normalization of characteristics data that involves several important issues for future research.[35]

Momentarily overlooking these issues, it is interesting to note in passing that maximizing a linear multi-attribute utility function subject to a budget (affordability) constraint yields a decision rule analogous to the benefit/cost ratio criterion discussed above. Under the assumption of a fixed budget and a linear, additive separable utility function, the benefit/cost decision rule can indeed be used to rank alternatives. In this case, the winning alternative is the one that generates the highest MoE per dollar or the biggest "bang-for-the-buck" (or in the dual, cost minimization, the lowest "cost-per-kill"). With a more general (non-linear) utility function, the equivalent optimization generates a more complex marginal benefit/marginal cost decision rule.[36]

In reality, MCDM techniques that underpin most AoAs do not involve an explicit discussion of budgets, affordability or funding (resource constraints) to structure the decision problem. As a consequence, the problem is typically not structured as described above.

Instead of structuring an AoA as a constrained optimization, the most common decision-analysis approach is to simply attach a weight to cost and introduce it directly into the utility function.[37] (see Chapter 8 for example). The relative weight assigned to the cost of alternatives under consideration is the proxy for affordability. As opposed to a benefit/cost (or effectiveness/cost) ratio, this popular MCDM approach generates an overall "value" function that is essentially a weighted average of cost and effectiveness.

Alternatives are ranked and selections made through an unconstrained optimization where the best alternative is the one that maximizes the "overall effectiveness" or "value" function, $V = V(\text{MoE, COST})$.

According to two prominent authors:

> Deterministic decision analysis is concerned with finding the most preferred alternative in decision space by constructing a value function representing a decision maker's preference structure, and then using the value function to identify the most preferred solution.
>
> (Ramesh and Zionts 1997, 421)

The linear, additive separable version of this value function is frequently used to calculate a positively weighted MoE and negatively weighted cost for each alternative (for example, see Beil and Wein 2003; Che 1993; Clemen 1996; French 1986; Hwang and Yoon 1981; Keeney 1994; Keeney and Raiffa 1976; Kirkwood 1997; Liberatore 1987; Pinker *et al.* 1995; Vazsonyi 1995).

The typical decision sciences' (MCDM) approach to an AoA[38] thus involves:

> Given several alternatives, select the preferred alternative that provides the best value, i.e. Maximize: V(MoE,COST) = w1***MoE** − w2***COST**.

This requires two important modeling efforts: 1) *Building an effectiveness (MoE) model* (non-cost–benefit factors; MoE = quality, schedule, etc.); and 2) *Building a cost model* (costs/prices; estimate total system life-cycle costs, total ownership costs—see Chapter 5). Once these independent modeling efforts are completed, the challenge is to integrate the two either using benefit/cost ratios (discussed earlier) or by assigning a relative weight to cost (a value for w2 in the example above) as a proxy for affordability.

The typical recommendation in the applied literature to integrate cost and effectiveness is to ask the Decision Maker (DM): "How important is cost relative to effectiveness?" The US FAR and both the General Services Administration (GSA) and the OMB explicitly promote this approach:[39]

> The solicitation shall state whether all evaluation factors other than cost/price, when combined [i.e. an MoE], are significantly more important than, approximately equal to, or significantly less important than cost/price.
> (GSA, DoD, NASA, March 2005, Section 15.101-1(2))

> The specific weight given to cost or price shall be at least equal to all other evaluation factors combined unless quantifiable performance measures can be used to assess value and can be independently evaluated.
> (OMB Circular A-76, B-8)

An early proponent of this (MCDM) decision methodology offers an example of administrators evaluating alternative pollution control devices being asked to answer questions such as: "Which is more important, costs or [reducing] pollutant concentrations [i.e. effectiveness]?" (Keeney 1994, 797). As the author is quick to point out, the problem with this approach is that without some estimate of the *total budget available* or any knowledge of *opportunity costs*, one cannot expect the DM to provide a sensible answer. The author (ironically an early adopter and prolific advocate of this MCDM approach) warns: "I personally do not want some administrator to give two minutes of thought to the matter and state that pollutant concentrations are three times as important as cost"[40] (Keeney 1994, 797).

Figures 4.1 and 4.2 offer illustrations of alternative vendor offers. Figure 4.1 reflects a situation where the DM believes costs to be important enough (and thus assigns a sufficiently large relative weight to cost, reflected in the ratio w2/w1) that the preferred alternative is A1 (the low-cost option). The opposite case is illustrated in Figure 4.2.[41] Similar graphs are presented in Chapter 8.

How does a DM decide on an appropriate weight to assign to costs? Consider an extreme case. Suppose affordability is not an issue, so funding is not an issue. In that case the budget is not binding, making costs irrelevant. Clearly this means a zero weight should be assigned to costs and the alternatives can be ranked exclusively on the basis of their MoEs (e.g. A2 wins). As a consequence, any weight applied to the costs of the alternative proposals (w2) must reflect an implicit concern about affordability (future funding or budget realities).

A key hypothesis in the EEoA is that if a DM pays any attention to costs (i.e. places a weight on cost), it is because they acknowledge an implicit funding/budget or affordability constraint, or recognize the opportunity cost of funds committed to the program. Future funding and opportunity cost concerns are directly related to the earlier discussion of affordability, and close coordination of requirements generation, defense acquisition, and PPBS.[42]

The irony, as Keeney (1994) rightly observed, is that to assign any weight to costs requires the DM to have some understanding of affordability (funding/budget realities) and an appreciation of opportunity costs. If this information is known, then analysts and DMs have no reason to take the MCDM approach and assign a weight to costs since the more robust, constrained-optimization (mathematical programming) EEoA approach is available (Simon and Melese 2011).

In fact, it is relatively straightforward to demonstrate that even if the DM had perfect information about future funding (budget/affordability) and attempted to interpret that information through a weight assigned to the relative cost (price) of alternatives (as illustrated in Figures 4.1 and 4.2), vendor rankings that resulted

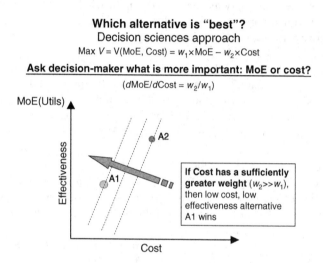

Figure 4.1 When cost is relatively more important than effectiveness.

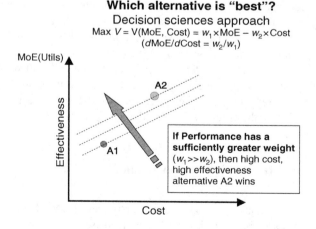

Figure 4.2 When effectiveness is relatively more important than cost.

would only coincidentally correspond to rankings obtained under the full information constrained-optimization EEoA approach (where MoE is maximized subject
to the budget constraint).[43]

This is a damning result that clearly undermines the way MCDM is typically
applied to support AoAs. If there is no guarantee that the MCDM approach will yield
consistent results under full information (including affordability), then using this
criterion with less than perfect information (i.e. in the absence of explicit assumptions about future funding/budgets) is clearly problematic. In fact, GAO emphasizes
"[w]ith high levels of uncertainty ... funding needs are often understated. .." (GAO
2009, 9). A very real risk in applying the MCDM approach is that if AoAs
"fail to balance needs with resources [funding/budgets] ... un-executable programs
[are allowed] to move forward, [and] program managers ... are handed ... a low
probability of success" (GAO 2009, 10).

In conclusion, the popular MCDM decision sciences approaches that underpin
most AoAs either ignore affordability and apply a benefit/cost (effectiveness/cost)
ratio criterion, or implicitly attempt to capture affordability through a relative weight
assigned to cost in a value function such as: Maximize $V = V(\text{MoE}, \text{Cost}) = w_1 \times$
$\text{MoE} - w_2 \times \text{Cost}$.[44] Again, to quote economists Hitch and McKean (1967):

> One ubiquitous source of confusion is the attempt to maximize gain
> [w1*MoE] while minimizing cost [w2*Cost] ... *If a person approaches a*
> *problem with the intention of using such a [decision] criterion, he is con-*
> *fused to begin with* ... [A] criterion in which the budget ... is specified has
> the virtue of being aboveboard.
>
> [emphasis added] (pp. 165–7)

Rather than attempt to get a DM to reveal affordability concerns through
a weight assigned to costs (or prices) of alternatives, EEoA recommends a
more transparent approach—to treat "cost as an independent variable" (CAIV).
The relevant CAIV concept follows a definition posted on the Office of the
US Under Secretary of Defense (Acquisition and Technology) website in early
1999. It states that CAIV is the "DoD's acquisition methodology of making ... performance a function of available budgeted resources" (see Lorell and
Graser 2001, 33).[45] According to the *Defense Acquisition Guidebook* "all participants ... are expected to recognize the reality of fiscal constraints" (July 7,
2006, Section 3.2.4). This reflects a direct concern for affordability. The next
section illustrates how affordability can be explicitly incorporated in military
CBAs through the EEoA.

4.6   Six ways to structure an "economic evaluation of alternatives"

There are six ways in which analysts and DMs can structure an EEoA. The first,
third, and fourth approaches are in the spirit of CAIV. It is also useful to distinguish
between: i) intra-program analysis approaches (1–5) and the ii) inter-program

analysis approach (6). In the case of intra-program analysis, the DM associated with the program is assumed to have sufficient information to be able to select an alternative without reference to competing programs. That is not the case in inter-program analysis, which requires a higher level "opportunity cost approach." The six EEoA approaches are shown in Table 4.1.

Two possibilities are highlighted within the intra-program analysis approach outlined in Table 4.1. The first possibility is that DMs (analysts) are able to construct/define/build alternatives ("endogenous alternatives"). The second possibility is that alternatives are already constructed/defined/built (pre-specified) and must simply be evaluated ("exogenous alternatives"). This section describes each of the six EEoA approaches in some detail.[46]

A quote from Hitch and McKean (1967, 167) cited earlier highlights the first two EEoA approaches: "[A] criterion in which the budget or level of effectiveness is specified has the virtue of being aboveboard." Starting with the first of the EEoA approaches, the fixed budget approach, it is useful to recall another quote from Hitch and McKean (1967, 167): "The test of *maximum effectiveness for a given budget* seems much less likely to mislead the unwary." [emphasis added]

4.6.1 Fixed budget approach

In his groundbreaking book, *Cost Considerations in Systems Analysis*, Fisher (1971) describes the first approach to EEoA:

> In the fixed budget case, the alternatives being considered are compared on the basis of effectiveness likely to be attainable for the specified budget level (p. 12). The analysis attempts to determine that alternative (or feasible combination . . .) which is likely to produce the highest effectiveness.
>
> (p. 10)[47]

Table 4.1 Six approaches to structuring an EEoA

I) INTRA-PROGRAM ANALYSIS

   A) Build alternatives:

      1. Fixed budget approach
      2. Fixed effectiveness approach
      3. Economic (expansion path) approach: (Construct alternatives as cost-output/effectiveness relations or "response functions.")

   B) Modify existing alternatives: "Level the playing field"

      4. Modified budget approach: GOTO 1.
      5. Modified effectiveness approach: GOTO 2.

II) INTER-PROGRAM ANALYSIS

      6. Opportunity cost/benefit approach

EEoA build alternatives

1. Fixed budget approach

Maximize effectiveness subject to budget constraint
(*construct alternatives for given budget*)

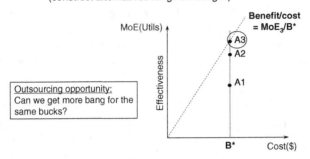

Figure 4.3 Fixed budget approach.

Drawing on these observations, the fixed budget approach to EEoA leverages Lancaster's (1966a, 1966b, 1971, 1979) "characteristics approach to demand theory." Building on studies by Gorman (1980), Stigler (1945), Theil (1952), and others who provided early foundations for the MCDM literature, Lancaster offered economists (and defense analysts) a familiar way to analyze the consumer or defense DM's choice problem (to choose among alternative defense investments).

In Lancaster's model, different vendors generate different bundles of characteristics evaluated by DMs ("consumers"). Applying Lancaster's model to choose among alternative bundles of characteristics (say, computers) offered by different vendors, defense DMs would maximize a utility function defined over a desired set of multiple attributes or characteristics, subject to a budget (funding/affordability) constraint.[48] In this approach, the cost-effective alternative is the one that, for a given budget (funding or affordability level), generates the best mix of characteristics determined by the DM's utility function.

The fixed budget approach illustrated in Figure 4.3 is the first of six ways proposed to structure an EEoA. In Figure 4.3, the budget (funding or affordability level) forecasted for the program is set at B*. The three vendor offers received for this budget are A1, A2, and A3. Given its superior performance (i.e. MoE), vendor A3 wins the competition which, in this case of a fixed budget, also corresponds to the vendor with the highest benefit/cost ratio.[49]

4.6.2   Fixed effectiveness approach

The second way to structure an EEoA is the dual of the first: select the vendor that minimizes costs of achieving a given MoE. Figure 4.4 offers an illustration. The least cost vendor for a fixed MoE is A1, which also offers the greatest benefit/cost ratio.[50]

A good example of the fixed effectiveness approach for structuring an EEoA appears in US Federal guidance for public-private ("competitive sourcing" or what

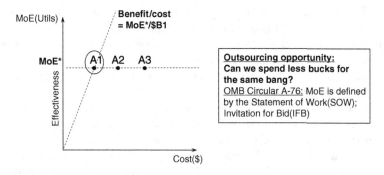

EEoA build alternatives

2. Fixed effectiveness approach

Dual: Minimize costs subject to effectiveness constraint
(construct alternatives for given MoE)

Figure 4.4 Fixed effectiveness approach.

the British call "market testing") competitions conducted under *OMB Circular A-76*, which "requires . . . a structured process for [evaluating] the most efficient and cost-effective method of performance for commercial activities" (OMB May 29, 2003). This process, sometimes referred to as Lowest Cost Technically Acceptable (LCTA), involves four steps: 1) develop a Statement of Work (SOW) or Performance Work Statement (PWS) to define desired performance/effectiveness; 2) construct the Most Efficient Organization for the in-house competitor; 3) issue an Invitation for Bid (IFB) for well-defined, routine commercial activities; and 4) compare bids or proposals, and select the "least cost." This offers an illustration of the fixed effectiveness approach: minimizing costs of achieving a given MoE (e.g. defined by the SOW or PWS).[51]

4.6.3 Economic (expansion path) approach

In an earlier quote, Hitch and McKean (1967) strongly hint at the third, and most general, approach to structure an EEoA:

> The test of *maximum effectiveness for a given budget* seems much less likely to mislead the unwary.
>
> (p. 167)

> As a starter, . . . *several budget sizes can be assumed.* If the same [alternative] is preferred for all, . . . budgets, that system is dominant. If the same [alternative] is not dominant, the use of several . . . budgets is nevertheless an essential step, because it provides vital information to the decision maker.
>
> (p. 176) [emphasis added]

This third way to structure an EEoA provides the underlying foundation for the first five EEoA approaches. It is described intuitively here and formally modeled in Simon and Melese (2011).

The model involves a three-step process that includes multiple players. For ease of exposition, assume three players: the military buyer and two competing private vendors.

The first step is for the military buyer to publish a solicitation for bids (or "request for proposals"). This solicitation states all significant non-price factors (e.g. criteria, attributes, characteristics) that the agency expects to consider in evaluating bid proposals, and is combined with an affordability assessment— e.g. optimistic (B1), pessimistic (B2), and most likely estimates of the budget (funding) for the program.

Once the solicitation is issued in the form of a Request for Proposal (RFP) or IFB, interested vendors submit their offers and the selection process begins.[52] Each vendor is assumed to have different production and cost functions which they use to build proposals with the desired attributes.[53] Assuming the award is made without discussions (pursuant to *FAR* 52.212-1 and 52.215-1), the military buyer employs a (secret) scoring rule to rank vendors that is only revealed after award of the contract.[54]

The model is illustrated in Figure 4.5 and briefly described here. This third EEoA approach describes the military buyer and competing vendors as follows:

Military buyer goal
Select an alternative that:
Maximizes MoE = Utility function = U (non-cost factors/attributes), subject to BUDGET constraint.

Vendor goal
Select a mix of non-cost factors that:
Maximizes Q = Production function = Q (non-cost factors/attributes), subject to sum of costs of attributes = $c_1 \times a_1 + c_2 \times a_2 + \cdots \leq$ budget.

Military buyer requirements
MoE: Build-effectiveness model (non-cost factors: performance = quality, schedule, etc.)
COST: Build-cost model (costs/prices: estimate total system life-cycle costs, total ownership costs—see Chapter 5);
AFFORDABILITY: Estimate budget (forecast future funding available for the program—see Chapter 7).

Private vendor requirements
Production function: possible attribute mixes given vendor-specific technology;
Total costs: vendor-specific costs of producing each attribute;
Vendor proposal constructed as a function of buyer's revealed funding/budget constraint.

This three-stage procurement auction briefly summarized in Table 4.2 is formally modeled in Simon and Melese (2011).

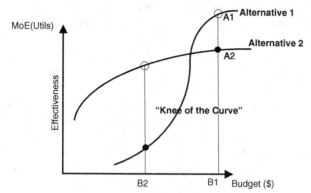

EEoA build alternatives
3. Expansion path approach (Engel/response curves)
(Alternatives are cost-effectiveness relations, not points)
Explore impact of budget cuts/increases *(Identify vendor responses)*

Source Selection Decision: A2 for pessimistic budget; A1 for optimistic budget

Figure 4.5 Economic (expansion path) optimization approach.

Table 4.2 Three-stage multi-attribute procurement auction—economic (expansion path) optimization approach (Simon and Melese 2011)

---

1) First stage: (cost as an independent variable – CAIV)
   - *The DoD provides notional budget guidance,* (B), *to possible vendors for the program.* DoD searches for the optimum product (procurement) and/or service (R&D; O&M) package that it can obtain at that price, B. *DoD also reveals optimistic and pessimistic budget guidance.*
   - *The DoD defines the set of characteristics/attributes that it values*: This is known to vendors. DoD's precise utility function over those characteristics, however, is unknown to vendors (secret scoring rule).
2) Second stage: (target costing)
   - *Vendors have different costs and production functions* for generating the products or services defined as bundles of characteristics.
   - *Each vendor maximizes its output offer* (an optimal mix of the desired characteristics) *subject to their particular budget constraint* (which includes DoD's budget guidance and the vendor's individual costs to produce a unit of each characteristic).
   - *This is the product and/or service package (output) a particular vendor is able to propose for each possible budget,* (B), given their production function (technical production possibilities) and their vendor-specific costs of generating those characteristics.
3) Third stage: (selection)
   - *With the latest budget* forecast, *DoD selects* from the optimized characteristic bundles proposed by each *vendor* the *bundle/alternative* (total product/service package) *that maximizes DoD's utility function* (or MoE).

This third and most general EEoA approach follows Hitch and McKean's (1967) earlier recommendation:

> As a starter ... several budget sizes can be assumed. If the same [alternative] is preferred for all ... budgets, that system is dominant ... If the same [alternative] is not dominant the use of several ... budgets is nevertheless an essential step, because it provides vital information to the decision maker.
>
> (p. 176)

This approach is illustrated in Figure 4.5 with two notional forecasted future funding/budget levels: B1 (pessimistic) and B2 (optimistic).

The expansion paths for each vendor reveal combinations of attributes each vendor can offer at different budget levels (e.g. pessimistic, optimistic, and most likely). In Figure 4.5, each vendor's expansion paths are transformed (through the government's utility function) into cost-utility or cost-effectiveness response functions (A1 and A2). These response functions reveal each vendor's proposal under different budget scenarios and represent the most general description of "alternative vendor proposals" in the EEoA. Given a range of likely budgets for the program, the most effective vendor over that range of budgets can be selected by the buyer.[55]

A key difference between traditional AoAs and this economic (expansion path) approach is that instead of modeling competing vendors as points in cost-effectiveness space, EEoA solicits vendor offers as functions of optimistic, pessimistic, and most likely funding (budget) scenarios. This approach explicitly addresses a key concern voiced by GAO:

> A cost estimate is ... usually presented to decision-makers as a ... point estimate that is expected to represent the most likely cost of the program but provides no information about the range of risk and uncertainty or level of confidence associated with the estimate.
>
> (GAO 2009, 9)

Whereas the first three ways to structure an EEoA assume alternatives can be constructed or built based on budget or effectiveness considerations (endogenous alternatives), the last three approaches assume alternatives are exogenously determined, so that DMs must evaluate pre-specified alternatives. The most interesting cases are where an alternative (vendor proposal) costs more but offers greater utility (MoE), while others cost less and offer less utility (MoE).

4.6.4   Modified budget approach

Suppose alternatives are provided that have been developed exogenously—for example, on the basis of a manpower or squadron constraint (one computer per person, or a certain number of aircraft per squadron, etc.). If the overall budget or desired level of effectiveness (MoE) for a program is not available, and analysts and DMs have not structured the problem explicitly recognizing affordability, then

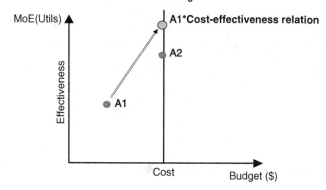

EEoA: Modify existing alternatives
("Level the playing field")

4. Modified budget approach (GOTO 1 & 3)
Modify alternatives to equalize budget
(Identify vendor MoE responses to budget increase)
Revealed budget

Figure 4.6 Modified budget approach.

it is likely these pre-specified alternatives solicited from different vendors have different costs and yield different MoEs.

The first step commonly prescribed in evaluating these alternatives is to create a scatter plot of effectiveness versus cost (see Figure 4.6 and illustrations in chapters throughout this book). In the absence of any other information, given two alternatives A1 and A2 that differ in both costs and effectiveness, leveling the playing field requires the DM to determine the highest cost alternative he/she is willing to consider (say the price of A2). This can then be used as an implicit budget for the program. The fourth way to structure an EEoA recognizes that the highest-cost (highest-utility) alternative DMs are willing to consider (A2 in Figure 4.6) reveals their (implicit) budget constraint.

Then, in order to "level the playing field," the DM asks the lower cost, lower utility vendor (A1) how it might use the difference in funds (between their costs and the high cost proposal) to increase the utility/MoE of their proposal (say from A1 to A1*).[56] Note that this effectively returns the problem to the first (and third) way of structuring an EEoA—"maximize effectiveness (MoE) for a given budget."

4.6.5 Modified effectiveness approach

Similarly, the fifth way to structure an EEoA levels the playing field for a specified choice of utility or effectiveness (MoE) revealed by one of the vendors. This returns the problem to the second (and third) way of structuring an EEoA—"minimize the cost of achieving a given level of MoE."

For example, in Figure 4.7, anchoring the desired MoE at a target level such as that revealed (offered) by vendor 2 (A2), the government asks vendor 1 how much

**EEoA: Modify existing alternatives
("Level the playing field")**

5. Modified effectiveness approach (GOTO 2 & 3)
Modify alternatives to equalize MoE
(Identify vendor COST responses to higher MoE requirement)

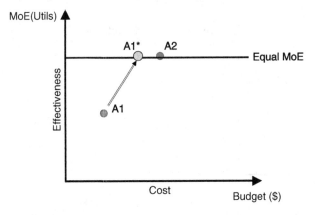

Figure 4.7 Modified effectiveness approach.

it would cost to achieve the same target level of MoE.[57] In Figure 4.7, vendor 1 is preferred since the response (A1*) minimizes the budget required for the program.

4.6.6   *Opportunity cost (or effectiveness) approach*

Finally, suppose DMs find themselves in a situation where (due to legal, information or other constraints): i) alternatives cannot be modified to obtain response functions, and ii) future funding is unknown and a specific desired target level MoE cannot be determined. In this case, it is likely some alternatives (bundles) offered by vendors will cost more but offer more effectiveness, while others cost less and offer less effectiveness. For example, consider Program A in Figure 4.8.

The sixth and final approach to structure an EEoA involves marginal analysis and an inter-program comparison called the "opportunity cost approach." Rather than modify the alternatives to level the playing field as in the fourth and fifth EEoA approaches, the opportunity cost approach requires a more challenging inter-program analysis to choose between lower-cost, lower-effectiveness alternatives (say A1 in Figure 4.8) and higher-cost, higher-effectiveness alternatives (A2).

The main challenge in selecting an alternative in this context is that the DM must reach beyond the immediate program (A) into higher-level inter-program considerations. If alternatives are exogenously determined and it is not possible to level the playing field, then to find the most cost-effective solution requires information about other competing programs (Program B in Figure 4.8).

This involves a higher-level inter-program analysis illustrated in Figure 4.8. The DM must consider the incremental (marginal) loss in utility (MoE) in other

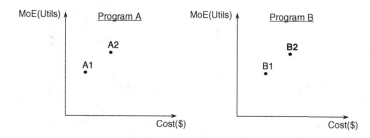

EEoA: Inter-program analysis
6. Opportunity cost approach

A) Question: Where is the extra money coming from if I buy the high cost alternative?
B) Question: Where is the extra money going if I buy the low cost alternative?

Figure 4.8 Opportunity cost approach.

programs that must be sacrificed (e.g. a budget cut in Program B shifting the decision from B2 =>B1) for funds to be released to purchase greater marginal utility (MoE) in the program under review (e.g. boosting the budget of program A to shift the decision from A1 =>A2). "[T]he assessment should provide details as to how excess funding... demands will be accommodated by reductions in other mission areas, or in other... accounts" (DoD July 7, 2006, Section 3.2.2).

Alternatively, the DM can explore how much additional utility the extra money might generate somewhere else if the low-cost alternative (A1 in program A) was chosen. These are tough but useful questions that break through the suboptimization of most traditional AoAs. As a consequence, EEoA encourages critical communication between different layers of the organization and a seamless interface between the requirements generation system, the acquisition system, and PPBS.[58]

The bottom line is that it is often more transparent, efficient, and effective to develop MoEs that are independent of costs. Equally important are the roles of budget (funding) forecasts and opportunity costs in helping structure defense investment decisions. Structuring an Economic Evaluation of Alternatives (EEoA) using one of the six approaches summarized in Figure 4.9 can help achieve the primary goals of defense acquisition, to lower costs and improve performance and schedules.

4.7 Conclusion: a decision map for decision-makers

This chapter has identified several major challenges that face a conventional military cost–benefit AoA. It also critically examined key assumptions and decision criteria typically used by the military to structure investment decisions. An alternative set of military cost–benefit approaches is proposed. Based on microeconomic

Decision Map to Structure an Economic Evaluation of Alternatives (EEoA)

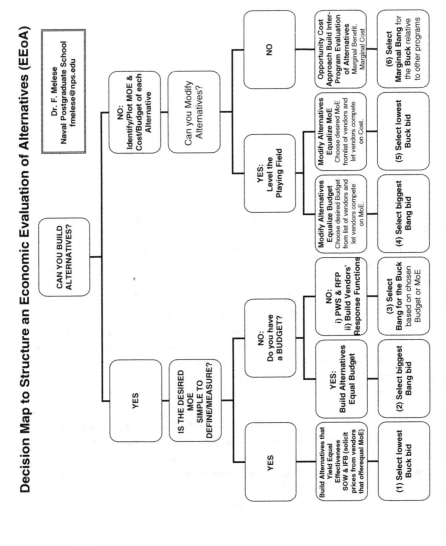

Figure 4.9 Decision map to structure an EEoA.

foundations, the six alternative approaches to structure a cost–benefit analysis are collectively referred to as the economic evaluation of alternatives (EEoA).

A significant weakness in the multi-criteria decision-making (MCDM) approach that underpins many contemporary AoAs is that while they correctly focus on life-cycle costs and the operational effectiveness of alternatives, "affordability" is an afterthought, only implicitly addressed through a weight assigned to costs. In contrast, EEoA encourages analysts and DMs to embed affordability directly into AoAs. This requires working with vendors to build investment alternatives based on different funding (budget/affordability) scenarios. Supported by a static, deterministic, multi-stage, constrained-optimization, microeconomic production (procurement auction) model, EEoA explicitly addresses affordability (see Simon and Melese 2011).

The key difference between the traditional MCDM approach to AoAs and the EEoA approach is that instead of modeling decision alternatives from competing vendors as points in cost-effectiveness space, EEoA models alternatives as functions of optimistic, pessimistic, and most likely funding/budget scenarios. In demonstrating how to embed affordability directly into an AoA, EEoA represents an important step in the long-running effort to achieve a significant defense reform: to integrate the requirements generation system and the defense acquisition system with PPBS to lower costs and improve performance.

The primary goal of this chapter was to demonstrate ways to improve defense investments. The decision map illustrated in Figure 4.9 offers a summary guide for analysts and DMs to select which of the six EEoA approaches is best suited to their circumstances. Carefully structuring military cost–benefit analyses using EEoA should improve defense decisions, leading to better use of scarce resources and greater national, regional, and international security.

Appendix 4.1

A simple example helps to illustrate the danger in using benefit/cost ratios without anchoring either the budget (here measured in dollars) or a specified measure of effectiveness (MoE) (here measured in "utils"). Suppose Alternative A1 in Figure A4.1 costs $10 million and yields an MoE of 10 utils, while Alternative A2 costs $1 billion and yields an MoE of 900 utils. Applying a benefit/cost ratio criterion indicates that A1 has a bigger "bang-for-the-buck" since it returns 1 util per million dollars, while A2 only offers 0.9 utils per million dollars. (In Figure A4.1, the slope of any ray from the origin represents the (constant) benefit/cost ratio anywhere along that ray: the steeper the slope, the greater the benefit/cost ratio.)

Using benefit/cost ratios to rank alternatives, however, is dangerous in this case since it ignores the absolute magnitude of the costs involved. Now suppose the situation was reversed and that A2 offered a higher benefit/cost ratio than A1. Anyone who chooses A2 in a simple ranking of alternatives strictly on the basis of "bang-for-the-buck," ignoring affordability, would be in for an unpleasant surprise: a $1 billion vs. $10 million commitment!

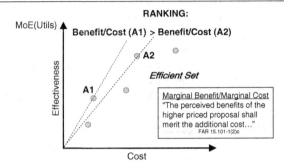

Figure A4.1 The inappropriate application of cost–benefit ratios.

Since affordability and opportunity costs are always a concern in public investment decisions (and especially so through the interdependence of the Requirements Generation System, DAS, and PPBS), it is imperative that analysts and DMs explore budget and opportunity cost implications of going with the high-cost alternative (for example, the extra $990 million to obtain an additional 890 utils of MoE) or, equivalently, of the savings in going with the low-cost alternative.

Notes

1 This study often uses the term "analysis of alternatives" (AoA) in its broad, generic sense. Although focused on defense acquisition, the results of the study apply to any public-sector procurement where benefits can be quantified but not monetized. It should be clear in context whenever the term AoA references major defense acquisition programs (MDAPs) or the acquisition of major automated information systems (MAISs).

2 For examples of the theoretical foundations of AoAs, see Clemen (1996), French (1986), Keeney (1982, 1992, 1994), Keeney and Raiffa (1976), or Kirkwood (1997).

3 As quoted in E. Newell "Business group urges reform of Pentagon contract requirements process," Government Executive, www.govexec.com [last accessed July 27, 2009].

4 The US Government Accountability Office (GAO) emphasizes that a major challenge facing the Department of Defense (DoD) is to "achieve a balanced mix of weapon systems that are affordable" (GAO, 2009, 5). Section E1.1.4, "Cost and Affordability" of US DoD Directive 5000.01, states: "All participants in the acquisition system shall recognize the reality of fiscal constraints. They shall view cost as an independent variable, and the DoD Components shall plan programs based on realistic projections of the dollars and manpower likely to be available in future years ... The user shall address affordability in establishing capability needs" [The Defense Acquisition System, DoDD 5000.01 (certified current as of November 20, 2007)].

5 "Affordability means conducting a program at a cost constrained by the maximum resources the Department can allocate for that capability" [quote from "Better Buying

Power" *Memorandum for Acquisition Professionals* from Ashton Carter, Undersecretary of Defense for Acquisition, Technology and Logistics (dated September 14, 2010)]. Available at www.acq.osd.mil/docs/USD_ATL_Guidance_Memo_September_14_2010 _FINAL.PDF [last accessed November 11, 2014].

6 Instead of modeling decision alternatives from competing vendors as *points* in cost-effectiveness space, EEoA generates vendor proposals as *functions* of optimistic, pessimistic, and most likely funding (resource/budget) scenarios.

7 The DoD uses the Planning, Programming, Budgeting And Execution (PPBE) process as its principal decision support system to provide the best possible mix of forces, equipment, and support within fiscal constraints. Two other major decision support systems complement the PPBE process: a Requirements Generation System to identify military investment opportunities and the Defense Acquisition System (DAS) to develop and procure new weapon systems. In explicitly addressing affordability up front, EEoA provides a unique opportunity to achieve a significant acquisition reform to lower costs and to improve performance and schedules by tightly integrating requirements generation and defense acquisition within the PPBE.

8 Based on US strategic guidance (the National Security Strategy, National Military Strategy, Quadrennial Defense Review, Strategic Planning Guidance, etc.), the Requirements Generation System reviews existing and proposed capabilities and identifies critical capability gaps. To fill those capability gaps, senior leadership examines the full range of "doctrine, organization, training, materiel, leadership and education, personnel and facilities" (DOTMLPF). (JCIDS 2007, A-1; DoD 5000.2 2008, 14) The DAS provides principles and policies that govern major defense acquisition decisions and milestones. To ensure transparency and accountability and to promote efficiency and effectiveness, various instructions (e.g. FAR; DFARS; DoD Directive 5000.01; DoD Instruction 5000.02; etc.) specify statutory and regulatory reports (e.g. AoAs) and other information requirements for each milestone and decision point of major defense investments.

9 Major Defense Acquisition Program (MDAP) and Major Acquisition Information Systems (MAIS) proposals that emerge from the planning process enter the DAS and are incorporated into the programming phase of PPBE.

10 Translating the budget implications of these decisions into the usual Congressional appropriation categories [military personnel, procurement, operations and maintenance (O&M), military construction, etc.] generates the nation's defense budget and FYDP. While DoD's biennial defense budget projects funding only two years into the future, it includes more financial detail than the six-year POMs.

11 Office of Management and Budget (OMB) *Circular A-11* titled *Preparation and Submission of Budget Estimates* is the official guidance on the preparation and submission of budget estimates to Congress. The Army's acquisition guidance emphasizes "the requirement for presenting the full funding for an acquisition program—that is the total cost [for] a given system as reflected in the most recent FYDP [...] pertains to all acquisition programs" (DoA July 15, 1999, 41).

12 Current DoD directives require that an AoA be performed at key milestone decision points (i.e. A, B, C) for all MDAPs and MAISs. "Affordability Analysis should be conducted as early as possible in a system's life cycle so that it can inform early capability requirements trades and the selection of alternatives to be considered during the Analysis of Alternatives (AoA)" (USD (AT&L), November 25, 2013, 120). The EEoA offers a mechanism to embed affordability assessments into AoAs.

13 "A 2008 DoD directive established nine joint capability-area portfolios, each managed by civilian and military co-leads [...]. However, without [...] control over resources [funding/budgets], the department is at risk [...] of not knowing if its systems are being developed within available resources [funding/budgets]" (GAO 2009, 11).

14 "Typically, the last analytical section of the AoA plan deals with the planned approach for the cost-effectiveness comparisons of the study alternatives" (DoD July 7, 2006,

Section 3.3). Note that there is no mention of "affordability," but instead only an ex-post cost-effectiveness tradeoff that implies a concern for affordability. Moreover, this tradeoff occurs at the end of a process in which alternatives under consideration have been developed independently of any cost/budget/funding/affordability constraint.

15 One of the multiple cost analysis tasks prescribed in the US Air Force AoA *Handbook* is to: "provide funding and affordability constraints..." and "describe the appropriate CAIV [cost as an independent variable] methodology for the AoA" (US Air Force 2008, 32 and 49). Yet in its explanation of the final vendor selection process, the *Handbook* states "There is no formula for doing this; it is an art whose practice benefits from experience" (p. 41). In sharp contrast, Figure 4.9 at the end of this chapter offers explicit guidance to help analysts and decision-makers structure an EEoA with a focus on affordability.

16 "Since this assessment requires a DoD Component corporate perspective, the affordability assessment should not be prepared by the program manager nor should it rely too heavily on the user. It requires a higher-level perspective capable of balancing budget tradeoffs (affordability) across a set of users" (DAU, 2006, Section 3.2.2).

17 A first step in the program's affordability assessment is to portray the projected annual modernization funding (Research, Development, Test and Evaluation (RDT&E) plus procurement, measured as Total Obligation Authority (TOA)) in constant dollars for the six-year programming period and for twelve years beyond. Similar funding streams for other acquisition programs in the same mission area also would be included. What remains to be determined is whether this projected funding growth is realistically affordable relative to the DoD component's most likely overall funding. This chapter proposes structuring the EEoAs not only for a "most likely" budget, but also for an "optimistic" (higher) and "pessimistic" (lower) budget.

18 These dual constrained optimization approaches represent the first two of six ways proposed in this study to structure an EEoA. See Figure 4.9: A decision map.

19 A Senate report (Acquisition Advisory Panel 2007) states that "Awards are made on the basis of the solicitation of factors and sub-factors by a Source Selection Official who, using his or her discretion and independent judgment [e.g. guided by an AoA], makes a comparative assessment of [...] competing proposals, trading off relative benefits and costs" (Chapter 1, Commercial Practices, 65). The Senate Committee's recommendation is that "Regulatory guidance [...] be provided in the FAR [Federal Acquisition Regulations] to [include] a minimum weight to be given to cost/price" (p. 102). Missing in this discussion is an explicit and realistic acknowledgement of "affordability"—the resources, funding, or budgets available for the procurement—something only indirectly and implicitly addressed in assigning a "weight" to cost.

20 The first and second EEoA approaches are the standard fixed budget or fixed effectiveness techniques. In the former case, the recommended alternative offers the greatest effectiveness for a fixed budget and in the latter case the lowest cost to achieve the desired level of military effectiveness. More interesting and realistic cases involve decisions among alternatives that offer somewhat greater (less) effectiveness for somewhat higher (lower) costs.

21 This is in the spirit of the Army's *Acquisition Procedures*, which explicitly states that "Cost as an Independent Variable (CAIV) applies to all defense acquisition programs [...and] treats cost as an input to, rather than an output of, the materiel requirements and acquisition processes." The Army guidance emphasizes "CAIV is focused on [...] meeting operational requirements with a solution that is affordable [... and that does] not exceed cost constraints [and to] establish CAIV-based cost objectives (development, procurement, and sustainment costs) early in the acquisition process. Moreover, the "RFP must [...] solicit from potential suppliers an approach [...] for meeting CAIV objectives" (DoA July 15, 1999, 63).

22 This offers an alternate approach to defense investment decisions based on explicit funding (resource/budget/affordability) scenarios that supports the "...long-standing DoD policy to seek full funding of acquisition programs..." [*Defense Acquisition Guidebook*, Chapter 3.23: "Full Funding, Defense Acquisition" University, https://akss.dau.mil/dag/DoD5000.asp?view=functional (accessed April 18, 2009)].

23 The cost of many programs reviewed by the GAO exceeded planned funding/budget levels (GAO July 2, 2008).

24 The inverse cost/benefit ratio is also used and sometimes calculated as a "cost-per-kill." For an example, see the case of the Javelin anti-tank missile in Chapter 14.

25 Fisher (1965) argues that "numerous terms [...] convey the same general meaning [...] 'cost–benefit analysis,' 'cost-effectiveness analysis,' 'systems analysis,' 'operations analysis,' etc. Because of such terminological confusion, [...] all of these terms are rejected and 'cost-utility analysis' is employed instead" (p. 185). Although the terms "cost–benefit" and "cost-effectiveness" are used interchangeably here, the assumption throughout is that neither "benefits" nor "effectiveness" can be measured in monetary terms.

26 "[E]ffectiveness analysis...is built upon the hierarchy of military worth, the assumed scenarios and threats, and the nature of the selected alternatives....In many AoAs involving combat operations [a] typical classification would consist of four levels: (1) system performance, based on analyses of individual components of each alternative or threat system, (2) engagement, based on analyses of the interaction of a single alternative and a single threat system, and possibly the interactions of a few alternative systems with a few threat systems, (3) mission, based on assessments of how well alternative systems perform military missions in the context of many-on-many engagements, and (4) campaign, based on how well alternative systems contribute to the overall military campaign." (DAU, Section 3.3.3.5).

27 Ironically, if a budget scenario is specified, there is no need to take the MCDM approach that underpins most AoAs since it is possible to adopt the EEoA approach. The EEoA approach constructs alternatives to fit within a budget envelope, converting the problem into a straightforward MOE maximization (see next section).

28 A fourth example involves a recent landmark RAND study on capabilities-based planning. The author falls into the same trap. In a section entitled "Choosing Among Options in a Portfolio," Paul Davis (2002) develops "A Notional Scorecard for Assessing Alternatives in a Portfolio Framework," where alternatives differ in both their costs and effectiveness. Nevertheless, the decision criterion recommended by the author to select an alternative in "[t]he last column is the ratio of effectiveness over cost" (pp. 45–6).

29 The authors continue: "Of course, if the ratios did not alter with changes in the scale of achievement (or cost, the higher ratio would indicate the preferred system, no matter what the scale [...]. But to assume that such ratios are constant is inadmissible some of the time and hazardous the rest" (Hitch and McKean 1967, 167).

30 The third (and most general) approach to EEoA follows another of Hitch and McKean's (1967) recommendations: "As a starter [...] several budget sizes can be assumed. If the same [alternative] is preferred for all [...] budgets, that system is dominant [...]. If the same [alternative] is not dominant the use of several [...] budgets is nevertheless an essential step, because it provides vital information to the decision maker" (p. 176).

31 An additional (necessary and sufficient) condition is a linear, separable, additive objective function.

32 "Usually, ratios are regarded as potentially misleading because they mask important information" (DoD July 7, 2006, Section 3.3.1).

33 "Measures of Effectiveness [...] provide the details that allow the proficiency of each alternative in performing the mission tasks to be quantified [...]. A measure of

performance typically is a quantitative measure of a system characteristic (e.g. range, etc.) chosen to enable calculation of one or more measures of effectiveness ... The cost analysis normally is performed in parallel with the operational effectiveness analysis. It is equal in importance in the overall AoA process [...]. [I]ts results are later combined with the operational effectiveness analysis to portray cost-effectiveness comparisons" (DoD July 7, 2006, Section 3.3.1).

34 It is often implicitly asserted certain key assumptions are satisfied for this utility function to be valid, such as "additive independence" (see French 1986; Keeney and Raiffa 1976; and Keeney 1994).

35 For example, one issue is that normalization is not necessary, and worse, can be misleading. The author is aware of several applications where relative weights were assigned to different attributes based on soliciting acceptable tradeoffs among *measurable characteristics* from decision-makers, but then later those same weights were applied to *normalized values* of the characteristics to obtain MOEs (personal correspondence with DoD officials).

36 This corresponds to the first of the six EEoA approaches presented in this chapter—the fixed budget approach.

37 "In the European Union, a legislative package intended to simplify and modernize existing public procurement laws was recently adopted. As before, the new law allows for two different award criteria: lowest cost and best economic value. The new provisions require that the procurement authority publishes ex-ante the relative weighting of each criteria used when best economic value is the basis for the award" (see EC 2004a and EC 2004b).

38 "An AoA is an analytical Comparison of the operational Effectiveness, suitability, and Life-cycle Cost of Alternatives that satisfy established Capability needs" [*Defense Acquisition Guidebook*, Chapter 3.3: "Analysis of Alternatives," Defense Acquisition University. https://akss.dau.mil/dag/DoD5000.asp?view=functional (accessed April 18, 2009)].

39 According to US Federal Acquisition Regulations (FAR), "source selection" is the decision process used in competitive, negotiated contracting to select the proposal that offers the "best value" to the government: "In different types of acquisition, the relative importance of cost or price may vary" (General Services Administration 2005, Section 15.101).

40 Surprisingly, the author has continued to write prolifically in this field and continued to promote this decision criterion, apparently never taking the time to reflect back on these key observations.

41 Note that the slope of the straight-line indifference curves that reflect the DM's relative preference (or tradeoffs) between effectiveness (MOE) and cost are given by the relative weights assigned, the ratio $-w2/w1$.

42 The Army's *Economic Analysis (EA) Manual* states that "good EA should go beyond the decision-making process and become an integral part of developing requirements in the PPBE process" (DoA February, 2001, 12).

43 The weight on cost in the unconstrained optimization (MCDM approach) roughly corresponds to the Lagrangian multiplier (shadow price) of the budget constraint in the constrained optimization (the EEoA approach). (See Chapter 10 for an alternative interpretation.)

44 In a section describing *Building a Model*, Fisher (1965) comments: "Since by definition a model is an abstraction from reality, the model must be built on a set of assumptions. These assumptions must be made explicit. If they are not, this is to be regarded as a defect of the model design" (p. 190). It is easy to inadvertently conceal the importance of affordability (budget/funding) issues in the MCDM decision sciences approach that underpins many AoAs. In sharp contrast, the EEoA approach encourages explicit affordability (budget/funding) assumptions.

45 The OMB Circular A-109 for Major Systems Acquisition mentions the goal of "design-to-cost." "Under the CAIV philosophy, performance and schedule are considered dependent on the funds available for a specific program."

46 The technical model can be found in Simon and Melese (2011). The static, deterministic, multi-stage, constrained-optimization, microeconomic production (procurement auction) model developed in that study underpins the third, and most general, approach to EEoA, called the "expansion path approach."

47 In a footnote, Fisher (1971, 10) adds: "[T]he fixed budget situation is somewhat analogous to the economic theory of consumer [optimization] ... For a given level of income [budget/funding] the consumer is assumed to behave in such a way that he maximizes his utility."

48 Note that we refer to the usual deterministic "utility function" that is a conventional term used in the economics literature. This is in contrast to the way a utility function is typically defined in the decision sciences and operations management literature as a stochastic function. The "value function" described in the latter literature is similar to our "utility function," except that costs can enter into a value function and are excluded from our utility function since they appear as part of the budget constraint.

49 Note that in the first and second EEoA approaches, since either the budget (funding level) or MOE (level of effectiveness) is anchored in the constrained optimization, the benefit/cost ratio decision criterion can be used as a decision rule in the selection process. The steeper the slope from the origin through an alternative (A1, A2, A3), the bigger the "bang-for-the-buck."

50 An example of this second approach to EEoA is RAND Corporation's AoA study for the KC-135 recapitalization program: "in this AoA, *the most 'cost-effective' alternative* [fleet] means precisely *the alternative whose effectiveness meets the aerial refueling requirement at the lowest cost*" (Kennedy *et al.* 2006, 7).

51 Title 10, Subtitle A, Part IV, Chapter 146, Sec. 2462 of the US Code reads: "A function of the Department of Defense ... may not be converted . . . to performance by a contractor unless the conversion is based on the results of a public-private competition that ... examines the cost of performance of the function by Department of Defense civilian employees and the cost of performance of the function by one or more contractors to demonstrate whether converting to performance by a contractor will result in savings to the Government over the life of the contract" (January 3, 2007). This law concerning public-private competitions offers another illustration of the fixed effectiveness approach, minimizing the cost of achieving a given MOE.

52 Budget announcements are analogous to an agency exploring in order to uncover its true reservation price for the product (given competing demands for scarce budgets). Adoption of this approach of evaluating vendor proposals under different "reservation prices" could eventually lead to greater use of fixed-price contracts. Note also that although requiring vendors to offer multiple bids based on different budget scenarios increases vendors' bidding costs, the government's ability to make a superior vendor selection with the extra information should more than compensate for any incremental price increase charged by vendors or for extra costs the government might incur to compensate bidders for their higher bidding costs.

53 The vendors' constrained optimizations define distinct expansion paths, one for each vendor (for example, two vendor expansion paths are illustrated in Figure 4.5). From the Envelope Theorem, the Lagrangian multiplier in each vendor's constrained optimization problem reveals the marginal product [the extra output or attribute mix they are capable of producing) if the military buyer (DoD) relaxes its funding constraint (i.e. corresponding to a more optimistic budget)].

54 The buyer reveals desired attributes/characteristics of the investment to the sellers, but not the relative importance weights, and requests a single offer from each seller based on a pre-specified budget (affordability) constraint, and then he selects the one he prefers

among the submitted offers. "We call this procedure a 'single-bid auction with secret scoring rule'" (Asker and Cantillon 2004, 1). A more general construct is presented in Simon and Melese (2011).

55 For example, if the PPBS process ultimately results in narrowing the budget/expenditure constraint for the program around B2, then alternative 2 (A2) is selected. Note that if the planning process allows the optimistic budget assumption, B1, to persist, then A1 would have been selected, but when reality struck and budget B2 was all that was available, choosing A1 would have turned out to be highly inferior decision (see Figure 4.5). This EEoA approach relies upon and reinforces the importance of closely coupled iterative interactions between the requirements generation system, defense acquisition system, and PPBS.

56 Alternatively, different valuable uses for the money saved by choosing the lower-cost alternative could be brought into the effectiveness calculation. Some will recognize this search for the "next best alternative use of funds" as the standard economic definition of opportunity costs. This sets the stage for the sixth way to structure an EEoA.

57 Note that the response function (expansion path) for vendor 1 includes points A1 and A1*.

58 Fisher (1965, 182) quotes Secretary of Defense Robert McNamara: "Suppose we have two tactical aircraft which are identical in every important measure of performance [MOE] except one—aircraft A can fly ten miles per hour faster than Aircraft B. Thus, if we need about 1,000 aircraft, the total additional cost would be $10 million. If we approach this problem from the viewpoint of a given amount of resources, the additional combat effectiveness ... of Aircraft A would have to be weighed against the additional combat effectiveness which the same $10 million could produce if applied to other defense purposes—more Aircraft B, more or better aircraft munitions, or more ships, or even more military family housing ... This kind of determination is the heart of the planning-programming-budgeting ... problem with the Defense Department."

Bibliography

Acquisition Advisory Panel. Report to the US Congress, Commercial Practices (Chapter 1), Jan. 2007, pp. 31–157. Available at www.acquisition.gov/comp/aap/24102_GSA.pdf [last accessed November 22, 2014].

Asker, J., and E. Cantillon. December 2004. *Equilibrium in Scoring Auctions*. FEEM (Fondazione Eni Enrico Mattei) Working Paper No. 148.04.

Beil, D. R. and L. M. Wein. 2003. "An Inverse-Optimization-Based Auction Mechanism to Support a Multiattribute RFQ Process." *Management Science* 49(11): 1529–1545.

Byrns, Jr., E. V., E. Corban, and S. A. Ingalls. 1995. "A Novel Cost–Benefit Analysis for Evaluation of Complex Military Systems." *Acquisition Review Quarterly*, Winter: 1–20.

Carter, A. Undersecretary of Defense for Acquisition, Technology and Logistics (AT&L). 2010. *Memorandum for Acquisition Professionals*. Office of Secretary of Defense (OSD), Washington DC.

Che, Y.-K. 1993. "Design Competition through Multidimensional Auctions." *RAND Journal of Economics* 24(4): 668–80.

CJCS. May 2007. *Joint Capabilities Integration and Development System* (JCIDS) (CJCSI 3170.01F). Washington, DC: Author.

Clemen, R. T. 1996. *Making Hard Decisions: An Introduction to Decision Analysis* (2nd edition). Belmont, CA: Duxbury Press.

Corner, J. L. and C. W. Kirkwood. 1991. "Decision Analysis Applications in the Operations Research Literature, 1970–1989." *Operations Research* 39(2): 206–219.

Davis, P. K. 2002. *Analytic Architecture for Capabilities-Based Planning, Mission-System Analysis, and Transformation.* Santa Monica, CA: National Defense Research Institute, RAND.

Defense Acquisition University. 2006. *Defense Acquisition Guidebook.* Section 3.2.2: AoA Study Plan—Affordability. Available at https://dag.dau.mil/Pages/Default.aspx [last accessed November 18, 2014].

Defense Federal Acquisition Regulation Supplement (DFARS) and Procedures, Guidance, and Information (PGI). Available at www.acq.osd.mil/dpap/dars/dfarspgi/current/ [last accessed September 12, 2014].

DoA. July 15, 1999. *Pamphlet 70–3.* Washington, DC: US Army Headquarters.

——. February 2001. *Economic Analysis Manual.* Arlington, VA: US Army Cost and Economic Analysis Center.

DoD. May 22, 1984. *The Planning, Programming, and Budgeting System* (PPBS) (DoD Directive 7045.14). Washington, DC: Author.

——. April 9, 1987. *Implementation of the Planning, Programming, and Budgeting System* (PPBS) (DoD Directive 7045.07). Washington, DC: Author.

——. November 7, 1995. *Economic Analysis for Decision making* (DoD Directive 7041.3). Washington, DC: Author.

——. 1998. *DoD Guide to Cost as an Independent Variable* (DA PAM 70–3). Washington, DC: Author.

——. July 7, 2006. *Department of Defense (DoD) Defense Acquisition Guidebook.* Chapter 1.1 (Integration of the DoD Decision Support System); Chapter 1.2 (Planning, Programming, Budgeting and Execution Process; Office of Management and Budget (OMB) and the PPBE Process). Available at https://acc.dau.mil/CommunityBrowser.aspx [last accessed March 16, 2009].

DoDD. November 20, 2007. *Department of Defense Directive Number 5000.01,* USD (AT&L) (SUBJECT: The Defense Acquisition System).

——. January 25, 2013. *Department of Defense Directive Number 7045.14,* USD (C) (SUBJECT: The Planning, Programming, Budgeting and Execution Process).

DoDI. December 8, 2008. *Department of Defense Instruction Number 5000.02,* USD (AT&L) (SUBJECT: Operation of the Defense Acquisition System).

Dyer, J. S., and R. K. Sarin. 1979. "Measurable Multiattribute Value Functions." *Operations Research* 27: 810–822.

Dyer, J. S., P. C. Fishburn, R. E. Steuer, J. Wallenius, and S. Zionts. 1992. "Multiple Criteria Decision Making, Multiattribute Utility Theory: The Next Ten Years." *Management Science* 38(5): 645–654.

Edwards, W., D. von Winterfeldt, and D. Moody. 1988. "Simplicity in Decision Analysis." In *Decision Making: Descriptive, Normative, and Prescriptive Interactions,* edited by D. Bell, H. Raiffa, and A. Tversky, pp. 431–464. Cambridge, England: Cambridge University Press.

Eger, R. J., and A. L. Wilsker. 2007. "Cost Effectiveness Analysis and Transportation: Practices, Problems and Proposals." *Public Budgeting and Finance* 27(1): 104–116.

European Commission. March 2004a. *Coordinating the Procurement Procedures of Entities Operating in the Water, Energy, Transport and Postal Services Sectors* (Article 55 of the European Commission Directive 2004/17/EC of the European Parliament and of the Council of March 31, 2004).

——. March 2004b. *On the Coordination of Procedures for the Award of Public Works Contracts, Public Supply Contracts and Public Service Contracts* (Article 53 and 54 of the European Commission Directive 2004/18/EC of the European Parliament and of the Council of March 31, 2004).

Ewing, P. L., W. Tarantino, and G. S. Parnell. 2006. "Use of Decision Analysis in the Army Base Realignment and Closure (BRAC) 2005 Military Value Analysis." *Decision Analysis* 3(1): 33–49.

Federal Acquisition Streamlining Act of 1994 (Public Law 103–355).

Federal Acquisition Reform Act of 1995 (Public Law 104–106).

Federal Activities Inventory Reform Act of 1998 (Public Law 105–270).

Fisher, G. H. 1965. "The Role of Cost-Utility Analysis in Program Budgeting." In *Program Budgeting*, edited by D. Novick, pp. 61–78. Cambridge, MA: Harvard University Press.

——. 1971. *Cost Considerations in Systems Analysis*. New York: American Elsevier Publishing.

Fowler, B. W. and P. P. Cason. 1998. "The Cost Exchange Ratio: A New Aggregate Measure of Cost and Operational Effectiveness." *Military Operations Research* 3(4): 57–64.

French, S. 1986. *Decision Theory: An Introduction to the Mathematics of Rationality* (Ellis Horwood Series in Mathematics and Its Applications). Cambridge: Ellis Horwood.

Gansler, J. S. June 2003. *Moving Toward Market-Based Government: The Changing Role of Government as the Provider* (New Ways to Manage Series). Arlington, VA: IBM Endowment for the Business of Government.

GAO. July 2, 2008. *Defense Acquisitions: A Knowledge-Based Funding Approach Could Improve Major Weapon System Program Outcomes* (GAO-08-619). Washington, DC: Author.

——. September 25, 2008. *Defense Acquisitions: Fundamental Changes are Needed to Improve Weapon Program Outcomes* (GAO-08-1159T). Testimony of M. Sullivan, Director of Acquisition and Sourcing Management before the Subcommittee on Federal Financial Management, US Senate. Washington, DC: Author.

——. December 2008. *Defense Logistics: Improved Analysis and Cost Data Needed to Evaluate the Cost-Effectiveness of Performance-Based Logistics* (GAO-09-41). Washington, DC: Author.

——. March 18, 2009. *Defense Acquisitions: DoD must Prioritize its Weapon System Acquisition and Balance them with Available Resources* (GAO-09-501T). Testimony of M. Sullivan, Director of Acquisition and Sourcing Management before the Committee on the Budget, House of Representatives. Washington, DC: Author.

General Services Administration, Department of Defense, National Aeronautics and Space Administration. March 2005. *Federal Acquisition Regulation* (FAR). Washington, DC: Author.

Golabi, K., C. W. Kirkwood, and A. Sicherman. 1981. "Selecting a Portfolio of Solar Energy Projects Using Multiattribute Preference Theory." *Management Science* 27: 174–189.

Gorman, W. 1980. "The Demand for Related Goods: A Possible Procedure for Analysing Quality Differentials in the Egg Market." *Review of Economic Studies* 47: 843–856.

Henry, M. H. and W. C. Hogan. 1995. "Cost and Effectiveness Integration." Military Operations Research Society's *PHALANX*, 28/1.

Hitch, C. J. and R. N. McKean. 1967. *The Economics of Defense in the Nuclear Age*. Cambridge, MA: Harvard University Press.

Howard, R. 1988. "Decision Analysis: Practice and Promise." *Management Science* 34(6): 679–695.

Hwang, C.-L, and K. Yoon. 1981. *Multiple-Attribute Decision Making: Methods and Applications*. New York: Springer-Verlag.

Keeney, R. L. 1982. "Decision Analysis: An Overview." *Operations Research* 30(5): 803–38.

———. 1992. *Value-Focused Thinking: A Path to Creative Decision Making*. Cambridge, MA: Harvard University Press.

———. 1994. "Using Values in Operations Research." *Operations Research* 42(5): 793–813.

Keeney, R. L. and H. Raiffa. 1976. *Decisions with Multiple Objectives: Preferences and Value Tradeoffs*. New York: John Wiley & Sons.

Kennedy, M., L. H. Baldwin, M. Boito, K. M. Calef, J. S. Chow, J. Cornuet, M. Eisman, C. Fitzmartin, J. R. Gebman, E. Ghashghai, J. Hagen, T. Hamilton, G. G. Hildebrandt, Y. Kim, R. S. Leonard, R. Lewis, E. N. Loredo, D. M. Norton, D. T. Orletsky, H. S. Perdue, R. A. Pyles, C. R. Roll, Jr., W. Stanley, J. Stillion, F. Timson and J. Tonkinson. 2006. *Analysis of Alternatives (AoA) for KC-135 Recapitalization*. Santa Monica, CA: Project Air Force, RAND.

Kirkwood, C. W. 1997. *Strategic Decision Making: Multiobjective Decision Analysis with Spreadsheets*. Belmont, CA: Duxbury Press.

Lancaster, K. J. 1966a. "A New Approach to Consumer Theory." *Journal of Political Economy* 74(2): 132–157.

———. 1966b. "Change and Innovation in the Technology of Consumption." *American Economic Review* 56(2): 14–23.

———. 1971. *Consumer Demand: A New Approach*. New York: Columbia University Press.

———. 1979. *Variety, Equity, and Efficiency*. New York: Columbia University Press.

Larsen, R. and D. Buede. 2002. "Theoretical Framework for the Continuous Early Validation Method." *Systems Engineering* 5(3): 223–241.

Liberatore, M. J. 1987. "An Extension of the Analytic Hierarchy Process for Industrial R&D Project Selection and Resource Allocation." *IEEE Transaction on Engineering Management* 34(1): 12–18.

Lorell, M. and J. Graser. 2001. *An Overview of Acquisition Reform Cost Saving Estimates*. Santa Monica, CA: RAND Project Ari Force.

Melese, F. May 17, 2007. "Outsourcing for Optimal Results: Six Ways to Structure an Analysis of Alternatives." In *Proceedings of the 4th Annual Acquisition Research Symposium* (Creating Synergy for Informed Change). Monterey, CA: Naval Postgraduate School.

Melese, F. and D. Bonsper. December 1996. "Cost Integration and Normalization Issues." Military Operations Research Society's *PHALANX* 29(4).

Melese, F., R. Franck, D. Angelis, and J. Dillard. January 2007. "Applying Insights from Transaction Cost Economics to Improve Cost Estimates for Public Sector Purchases: The Case of US Military Acquisition." *International Public Management Journal* 10(4): 357–385.

Melese, F., J. Lowe, and M. Stroup. 1997. "Integrating Cost and Effectiveness: An Economic Perspective." Military Operations Research Society's *PHALANX* 30(3): 13–17.

Michael, R. T. and G. S. Becker. 1973. "On the New Theory of Consumer Behavior." *Swedish Journal of Economics* 75(4): 378–396.

Murray, C. H. 2002. *Executive Decision Making* (6th edition). Newport, RI: National Security Decision Making Department, US Naval War College.

Office of Aerospace Studies. 2008. *Analysis of Alternatives (AoA) Handbook*. Air Force Materiel Command, Kirtland AFB, New Mexico. Available at http://www.ndia.org/Divisions/Divisions/SystemsEngineering/Documents/Forms/AllItems.aspx?RootFolder

=http%3a%2f%2fwww%2endia%2eorg%2fDivisions%2fDivisions%2fSystemsEngine-ering%2fDocuments%2fCommittees%2fMission%20Analysis%20Committee%2fSupp-ort%20Documentation&FolderCTID=0x0120003F6EF07406A5714EB4933D54BF88 1105 [last accessed November 19, 2014].

OMB. April 5, 1976. *Major Systems Acquisitions* (OMB Circular A-109). Washington, DC: Author.

——. October 29, 1992. *Guidelines and Discount Rates for Benefit-Cost Analysis of Federal Programs* (OMB Circular A-94). Washington, DC: Author.

——. May 29, 2003. *Performance of Commercial Activities* (Public-Private Competitions) (OMB Circular A-76, Revised). Washington, DC: Author.

Parkes, D. C. and J. Kalagnanam. 2005. "Models for Iterative Multiattribute Procurement Auctions." *Management Science* 51(3): 435–451.

Parnell, G. S. 2006. "Value-Focused Thinking Using Multiple Objective Decision Analysis." In *Methods for Conducting Military Operational Analysis: Best Practices in Use Throughout the Department of Defense*, edited by A Loerch and L. Rainey, Chapter 19. Alexandria, VA: Military Operations Research Society.

Pinker, A., A. H. Samuel, and R. Batcher. December 1995. "On Measures of Effectiveness." Military Operations Research Society's *PHALANX*, 28/4.

Quade, E. S. 1989. *Analysis for Public Decisions* (3rd edition). Englewood Cliffs, NJ: Prentice Hall.

Ramesh, R. and S. Zionts. 1997. "Multiple Criteria Decision Making." In *Encyclopedia of Operations Research and Management Science*, edited by S. Gass, and C. Harris, pp. 538–543. Boston, MA: Kluwer.

Retchless, T., B. Golden, and E. Wasil. 2007. "Ranking US Army Generals of the 20th Century: A Group Decision-Making Application of the Analytic Hierarchy Process." *Interfaces* 37(2): 163–175.

Ruefli, T. 1971. "PPBS—An Analytical Approach." In *Studies in Budgeting*, edited by R. Byrne. Amsterdam: North Holland.

——. 1974. "Analytic Models of Resource Allocation in Hierachical Multi-Level Systems." *Socio-Economics Planning Science* 8(6): 353–363.

Saaty. T. L. 1977. "A Scaling Method for Priorities in Hierarchical Structures." *Journal of Mathematical Psychology* 15(3): 234–281.

——. 1980. *The Analytic Hierarchy Process*. New York: McGraw-Hill.

Simon, J., and F. Melese. 2011. "A Multi-Attribute Sealed-Bid Procurement Auction with Multiple Budgets for Government Vendor Selection." *Decision Analysis* 8(3): 170–179.

Smith, J. E. and D. von Winterfeldt. 2004. "Decision Analysis in Management Science." *Management Science* 50(5): 561–574.

Stigler, G. J. 1945. "The Cost of Subsistence." *Journal of Farm Economics* 27: 303–314.

Theil, H. 1952. "Qualities, Prices and Budget Enquiries." *Review of Economic Studies* 19: 129–147.

Thomas, C. and R. Sheldon. 1999. "The Knee of the Curve." *Military Operations Research* 4(2): 17–24.

US Code. January 2007. *Title 10—Armed Forces, Subtitle A, Part IV, Chapter 146, Section 2462*. US Government Printing Office. Available at www.gpo.gov/fdsys/granule/USCODE-2006-title10/USCODE-2006-title10-subtitleA-partIV-chap146 [last accessed November 19, 2014].

US Congress. 1997. *Clinger-Cohen Act—Information Technology Management Reform Act of 1996* (Public Law 104–106). Washington, DC: Chief Information Officers Council.

USD (AT&L). November 20, 2007. *The Defense Acquisition System* (DoD Directive 5000.01). Washington, DC: Author.

——. November 25, 2013. *Operation of the Defense Acquisition System* (DoD Instruction 5000.02). Washington, DC: Author. Available at: http://www.acq.osd.mil/osbp/sbir/docs/500002_interim.pdf [last accessed February 9, 2015].

Vazsonyi, A. December/January 1995. "Multicriteria Decision Making." *Decision Line* 26(1): 13–14.

Willard, D. 1998. "Cost-Effectiveness, CAIV, and the Knee of the Curve." Military Operations Research Society's *PHALANX* 31(3).

Winterfeldt, D. and W. Edwards. 1986. *Decision Analysis and Behavioral Research.* Cambridge, England: Cambridge University Press.

Zahedi, F. 1986. "The Analytic Hierarchy Process—A Survey of the Method and its Applications." *Interfaces* 16: 96–108.

Zionts, S. 1980. "Methods for Solving Management Problems Involving Multiple Objectives." In *MCDM: Theory and Applications*, edited by G. Fandal, and T. Gaul, pp. 540–558. New York: Springer-Verlag.

Part II

Measuring costs and future funding

5 Cost analysis

Diana I. Angelis and Dan Nussbaum

5.1 Introduction

Military cost–benefit analysis (CBA) requires careful consideration of future costs. Cost estimating is the process of collecting and analyzing historical data and applying quantitative models, techniques, tools, and databases to predict the future cost of an item, product, program or task. The term "cost analysis" is broadly used to include not only the process of estimating (measuring) the cost of a project but also the process of discovering, understanding, modeling and evaluating the relevant information necessary to estimate the cost as well as the cost uncertainty and risk.

Some might make a distinction between the cost estimating techniques and analysis used for commercial off-the-shelf items (where a competitive market determines the price), and products developed specifically for defense (where there is no obvious market price). When comparing total life-cycle costs of alternatives, the techniques and practices presented in this chapter apply equally to both cases. The only distinction is whether the acquisition price is determined by the market or through contract negotiations.

It is important to note that cost analysis and estimating, as applied to financial management throughout government and industry, provides for the structured collection, analysis, and presentation of life-cycle cost (LCC) data to assist in decision-making for weapon systems capabilities throughout their useful life. Examples of the components of LCC analysis conducted during each phase are:

- research and development (R&D)—complexity and innovation studies;
- production—performance, scale, and process studies;
- operations and support (O&S)—crew levels, training, fuel consumption support, reliability and maintainability, and logistics studies;
- disposal—feasibility and tradeoff studies.

There are three main applications of cost estimating in the Planning, Programming, Budgeting, and Execution System (PPBES) process: (1) preparation and justification of budgets, (2) making choices among alternatives, and (3) source selection (contracting). Descriptions of these applications are given below.

- Preparation and justification of budgets. Cost estimates are performed within all phases of the acquisition process to determine the budget amounts required to fund the program (or "funding requirements") throughout its life-cycle.
- Making choices among alternatives. This is further subdivided into the following areas:

  o   acquisition cost forecasting;
  o   analysis of alternatives (AoA).

- Source selection (contracting), through its phases of:

  o   acquisition planning;
  o   contract formulation;
  o   contract management and administration;
  o   contract close-out.

Cost estimates for the AoA requires forecasts of time-phased cash flows that occur over the life of a system. This forms the basis for estimates of the total LCC of a system. The LCC estimates are usually developed using constant dollars,[1] and cost comparisons of alternatives are based on the present value[2] of the total LCC.

Cost estimating for budgeting assumes that the choice has been made and we are interested in the near-term implementation cost of the chosen alternative. Budget estimates must include the effects of expected inflation over the budget years and are therefore stated in current (or nominal) dollars.

While the planning phase of PPBES is conducted with some resource constraints, it is not an intensive consumer of cost estimating support. The execution phase is primarily focused on actual costs rather than estimated costs and the difference between the two can be a source of much consternation, and is one of the main reasons credible and accurate cost estimates are so important. Additionally, the execution phase often uses the earned value management system (EVMS), which has its roots in cost estimates, both to identify planned vs actual cost variances, retrospectively, as well as to forecast cost variances, prospectively.[3]

5.2   Cost estimating process

According to the International Cost Estimating and Analysis Association (ICEAA), formerly called the Society of Cost Estimating and Analysis (SCEA),[4] estimating is "the art of approximating the probable worth or cost of an activity based on information available at the time." An estimate is a judgment, opinion, forecast or prediction. A cost estimate therefore is a prediction of the likely future cost of a process, product, project, service, program or system. The *Cost Estimating and Assessment Guide* published by the Government Accountability Office (GAO) provides a framework for understanding the cost estimating process as displayed in Figure 5.1.

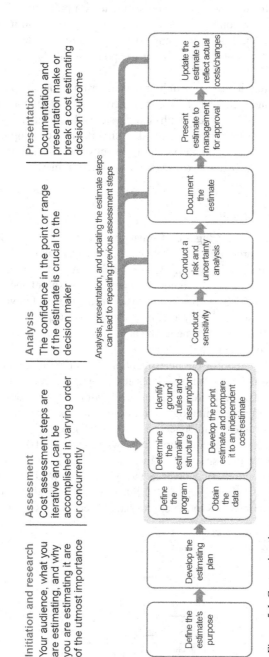

Figure 5.1 Cost estimating process.

Source: GAO 2009.

In the defense acquisition process, a cost estimate is a prediction or forecast of the complete costs of a complex program or weapon system, and it is often a time-phased estimate. The first step in any cost estimate of complex systems is to understand the attributes of the program or weapon system whose cost is to be estimated.

Traditionally, this requires understanding and describing the weapon system in terms of physical and technical parameters, operational and support concepts, mission requirements, and interfaces with other systems. Understanding the program's schedule and acquisition profile is also important in developing a cost estimate. The goal is to understand the relationship between key weapon systems' attributes and cost. The next step is to develop an explicit framework for the cost estimate.

5.3   Cost breakdown structure

A cost estimate is organized using a cost breakdown structure (CBS). The CBS is a hierarchy that captures the totality of the inputs and activities required to develop, produce, operate, and retire a system. A CBS is developed by subdividing a product, process or service into its major cost elements and sub-elements. At the highest level, the system CBS can be organized according to the life-cycle phases of a system: R&D, investment, operating and support, and disposal. Under each phase, a hierarchical structure documents the activities and resources required to complete the work associated with that phase.

For example, the hierarchy for the investment phase (commonly referred to as the work breakdown structure or WBS) defines at an aggregated level what is to be procured and consists of at least three program levels with associated descriptions. The WBS contains uniform terminology, definitions, and placement in the input-oriented family tree structure. Guidance on work breakdown structures for US Department of Defense (DoD) acquisitions is provided in MIL-HDBK 881.[5] An example of a program WBS is shown in Figure 5.2.

The level of detail in the WBS evolves as the system is defined and developed throughout its life-cycle. After a program WBS has been approved, the contractor will then extend a contract WBS to the appropriate lower levels to provide better

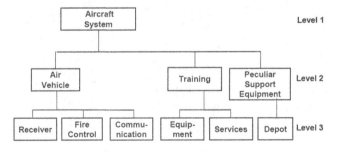

Figure 5.2 Program WBS.

Source: US DoD 2005.

definition of the complete scope of the contract. When integrated with the program WBS, the extended contract provides a complete WBS for the acquisition program. Similar to the economists' production function, WBS reveals all the key inputs required to generate the ultimate output/product. Further details on WBS, including examples for various weapons classes, can be found in MIL-HDBK 881.

Operations and support (O&S) costs are also organized in a hierarchy (commonly known in the US DoD as a cost element structure or CES). The Cost Analysis and Program Evaluation (CAPE) team in the Office of the Secretary of Defense (OSD) defines standard O&S cost structures and cost elements that cover the full range of O&S costs that could occur in any defense system in their *Operating and Support Cost-Estimating Guide.*[6] An example of a cost element structure is shown in Figure 5.3.

The final step is to develop a cost estimate. From the CBS perspective, the total cost estimate of the system is obtained by adding up the cost estimates of the individual elements (inputs) in the hierarchy across the levels of the CBS. To do this, a cost estimate must be generated for each element of the CBS. The level of detail of the cost estimate depends on the amount of information available about the system. In early stages of development, only rough estimates are available of the system parameters and attributes; therefore, only the highest levels of the CBS cost can be estimated using "rough order of magnitude" or "top-down" techniques such as analogy and parametric approaches.

It should be noted that parametric estimates are usually underpinned by the statistical technique of regression analysis, and they result in equations called cost estimating relationships (CERs) that relate cost to underlying technical and performance parameters.[7] For example, the estimated cost of a new aircraft may be modeled as a function of the weapon system's key inputs and attributes, such as

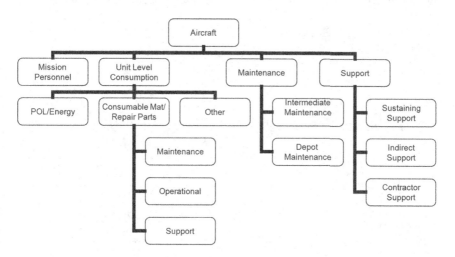

Figure 5.3 Cost element structure.

Source: OSD 1992.

empty weight, speed, useful load, wing area, power, and landing speed. This model estimates the total cost of the aircraft based on a set of parameters independent of the WBS structure.

As more information about the system becomes available, more detailed estimates can be developed for lower levels of the CBS using a variety of techniques. A cost estimate is now developed for each element at a given level of the CBS. For example, the cost of the aircraft wing may be estimated using historical data for weight, area, and materials. While this estimate is still based on the parametric technique, the level of detail (a wing) corresponds to a CBS element. As the system matures, the work and resource requirements are sufficiently well defined to use "bottom-up" techniques such as engineering estimates and actual costs obtained from prototypes and early production models. An engineering (production function) estimate would be based on the labor, material, and overhead required to complete a particular element of the CBS. Obviously, this sort of estimation requires a great deal of information about how the system is built—data that is usually not available until early phases of production. Figure 5.4 shows the relationship between estimating techniques and the evolution of a system. We will have more to say about cost estimating methodologies later in this chapter.

While the CBS framework provides an excellent accounting system for cost estimates, it does have a few drawbacks. First, although it captures the functional relationship between inputs and cost elements, it does not explicitly show potential correlations among those cost elements. If there is a correlation between two cost elements that are assumed to be independent, the variability of the cost estimate can be significantly increased. Second, the program CBS is input-oriented, not relationship-oriented; it therefore largely overlooks transaction costs such as search and information costs, decision and contracting costs, and monitoring and enforcement costs (for example, see Melese *et al.* 2007). While it might be

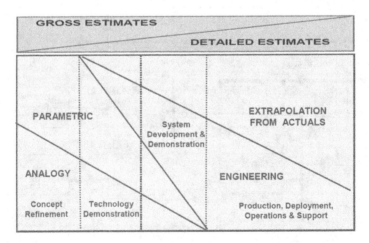

Figure 5.4 Cost estimating techniques as a function of acquisition phases.

Source: Angelis *et al.* (2007).

argued that these costs are implicitly considered in the cost estimates of the various CBS components, it is likely that most are underestimated or ignored, thereby possibly leading to overly optimistic cost estimates, that is to say, underestimating future costs.

5.4 Functions of cost estimating

Cost estimates are designed to inform users about the cost realism, the cost validity, and the cost reasonableness of proposed alternatives, contracts, and budgets. Initial descriptions of these functions are given next.

Cost realism helps to determine and communicate a realistic view of the likely cost outcome, and it can form the basis of the plan for executing the work. Cost realism also clarifies questions about technical competencies, technology maturity, and budgetary defensibility. More specifically, cost realism addresses the following questions.

- Is it clear from the cost estimate or proposal that the estimator/vendor understands the technical requirements of the project?
- Is the cost proposal consistent with the technologies and technology readiness levels (TRLs) described in the Cost Analysis Requirements Description (CARD) and the technical proposal?
- Are the budgets that support the program defensible?

In the acquisition arena, cost validity supports decisions on program viability, program structure, and resource requirements, while in the arena of "making choices among alternatives," cost validity measures the degree of confidence that the government has in its cost estimates. Often, the metric is a level of uncertainty such as standard error or one of the statistically grounded goodness of fit measures, such as a correlation coefficient (R^2).

In the "source selection" arena, cost validity measures the degree of government confidence in the vendor's ability to perform within the proposed cost. This assists in both the source selection process and in the engineering processes of design and analyzing tradeoffs in the design phase. In both of these arenas, i.e. in the acquisition arena, as well as in the "making choices among alternatives" arena, cost reasonableness addresses two questions, namely:

- Is there a complete identification of cost drivers? The underlying thought is that no cost estimate can be credible if it does not address all the elements of cost that the project will incur.
- Is the proposed profit margin commensurate with the understanding of the risk in the program? While the usual mechanism for adjudicating and balancing the inherent risk of the project between buyer (government) and seller (vendor) is the contract type (e.g. cost plus fixed fee, firm fixed price, etc.), an analysis of the vendor's proposed profit margin can also provide insights

into whether the buyer and seller have a shared appreciation of the intrinsic program risk.

5.5   Environment of cost estimating

In pursuing its objectives, the US DoD leverages large administrative and decision systems: the requirements generation system, known as the Joint Capabilities Integration & Development System (JCIDS); the financial and resources management system, known as PPBES; and the Defense Acquisition System (DAS). Cost estimating, as described next, plays an important role in each of these three systems, and, therefore, cost estimating plays a critical role in supporting administrative and decision processes within DoD.

Cost estimating in the DoD is organized within either the financial management/Comptroller or the engineering communities. The dual structure represents historic legacies and philosophies. At the OSD level, the CAPE office was established in 2009 as directed by the Weapons Systems Acquisition Reform Act of 2009.[8] It is useful to think of the CAPE as the functional manager for cost estimating processes within DoD. According to the Defense Acquisition University website:[9]

> The Director, CAPE is the principal staff assistant to the Secretary of Defense for Cost Assessment and Program Evaluation. The Director's principal responsibilities include:
>
> - analyzing and evaluating plans, programs, and budgets in relation to US defense objectives, projected threats, allied contributions, estimated costs, and resource constraints;
> - reviewing, analyzing, and evaluating programs, including classified programs, for executing approved policies;
> - providing leadership in developing and promoting improved analytical tools and methods for analyzing national security planning and the allocation of resources;
> - ensuring that the costs of DoD programs, including classified programs, are presented accurately and completely;
> - assessing effects of DoD spending on the US economy, and evaluating alternative policies to ensure that DoD programs can be implemented efficiently.

Each service has, as part of its Assistant Secretary for Financial Management and Comptrollership, its own service cost center, as follows:

- Department of Army—Office of the Deputy Assistant Secretary of Army for Cost and Economics (DASA-CE);[10]
- Department of Navy—Naval Center for Cost Analysis (NCCA);[11]
- Department of Air Force—Deputy Assistant Secretary for Cost and Economics).[12]

Within each service, there are cost estimating organizations located in the acquisition communities. To a large extent, these organizations support program managers and program executive officers in the PPBES and acquisition processes. For example:

- In the Army Material Command there are cost estimating organizations within:

    o   Communications and Electronics Command (CECOM);
    o   Aviation and Missile Command (AMCOM);
    o   Tank and Automotive Command (TACOM).

- In the Air Force Systems Command, there are cost estimating organizations within:

    o   Space and Missile Command (SMC);
    o   Aeronautical Systems Center (ASC);
    o   Electronics Systems Center (ESC).

- Within the Navy and Marine Corps, there are cost estimating organizations within:

    o   Naval Air Systems Command (NAVAIR);
    o   Naval Sea Systems Command (NAVSEA);
    o   Space and Naval Warfare Systems Command (SPAWAR);
    o   Marine Corps Systems Command (MCSC).

5.6   Data collection and sources

Perhaps the most difficult part of developing a credible cost estimate is finding reliable data to inform and support the estimate. Although the cost estimate is a prediction about the future, that prediction relies on historical information, including data about the physical, technical, and operational parameters of similar systems and the cost of similar systems, efforts or components. In addition, other information including prior experience with schedule, production, and operations is used to support cost estimates.

The first problem is finding relevant historical data (if it exists). Once data has been collected, the cost analyst must verify the validity of the information and assess how it relates to the current system being estimated. To do this, the analyst needs to have an understanding of what was included in the historical records.

The historical data needed for a cost estimate will likely come from a number of different sources. Seldom is all the technical and cost data available in one location. Typical sources of cost data include accounting records, cost reports (often required for earned value management), cost proposals, documentation associated with prior cost estimates, contracts and budget documents.

Sources for technical data vary by the type of information required, but often include acquisition documents, such as the CARD,[13] system specifications, contract documents, operational and maintenance records, vendor descriptions and numerous other records and documents. In addition to system documents, cost and technical data may be provided by subject matter experts, developed using special studies or market analysis or even collected from different websites. Finding data sources is a challenging process and can be disappointing when cost analysts discover that desired data was never collected or recorded.

Once potential data sources are identified, the data must be collected. Extracting and organizing data from different sources can prove to be a time-consuming effort. Often historical records are not automated and the data must be manually transferred to a computer for further analysis. Even when the records are digitized, they may only be copies of original documents that must be reviewed individually to find and extract the relevant data. Often the data is contained in different databases that must be combined to provide useful information. Unfortunately, much of the historical cost and technical data collected by contractors to prepare proposals for new weapon systems is considered proprietary and may be difficult, if not impossible, to obtain.

In general, the acquisition cost collected in DoD databases is not standardized. For a given category, the data collected may be inconsistent over time and across programs. If there are changes in data categories, there is no mapping from the old categories to the new categories. Differences between databases need to be reconciled prior to using the data for cost estimates.

The US Defense Acquisition Management Information Retrieval (DAMIR) system contains various data sources that the acquisition community uses to manage acquisition programs and thus can be a useful source of technical, cost, and schedule data. This database includes information on contract performance and program cost from a variety of reports, such as Selected Acquisition Reports (SAR) and Defense Acquisition Executive Summaries (DAES), as well as other reports.

The SAR is prepared by the program manager and documents estimates of the program cost, schedule, and performance for major acquisition programs. The DAES reports program assessments, unit cost, current estimates of the program baseline parameters, exit criteria, and vulnerability assessments. Historically, program managers only report on the six largest, currently active contracts (excluding subcontracts) that exceed US$40 million in then-year dollars for a given program; thus, the totals are moving targets. In addition, information reported in this database does not necessarily track to the information reported for the same program in the OSD budget.

Contractor cost data in the US is documented in Contractor Cost Data Reports (CCDR) and includes the Cost Data Summary Report (DD form 1921, CDSR) and the Functional Cost Hour Report (DD form 1921-1, FCHR). While there are inconsistencies in reporting program costs from contract to contract and from company to company, the reports are based on the program WBS, so the reporting is usually consistent over time for a given contract. The Defense Acquisition Automated Cost Information System (DACIMS) houses all CCDR data collected by the Defense Cost and Resource Center (DCARC).

Information on operations and maintenance for major weapon systems is maintained in historical databases managed by each service:

- Navy—Visibility and Management of Operating and Support Costs (VAMOSC);
- Air Force—Air Force Total Ownership Cost (AFTOC);
- Army—Operating and Support Management Information System (OSMIS).

What are known as Budget Item Justification sheets in the OSD budget can also provide useful information on cost and schedule for major weapon systems, albeit at an aggregated level.

A critical step when using historical data is to first "normalize" the data before using it to estimate future costs. Appendix 5.1 offers a comprehensive overview of data challenges and the importance of data normalization in cost estimates.

5.7 Cost estimating methodologies

Estimating future costs is always challenging, and is one of the most difficult tasks facing analysts. The three basic methods recognized for use within the professional cost estimating community are:

- analogy—using costs of similar systems to determine the cost of the subject system;
- parametric—generalized relationships between system characteristics and costs;
- engineering (also called bottom-up or industrial engineering analysis).

These approaches rely on statistical properties and logical relationships, and are largely based on historical data. One view of these three approaches is often heard at cost estimating conferences, such as the one put on annually by the International Society of Cost estimating and Analysis (ICEAA, formerly called the Society of Cost Estimating and Analysis (SCEA)):

- "It's like one of these" (Analogy)—subjectively compares the new system with one or more existing similar systems for which there is accurate cost and technical data.
- "This pattern holds" (Parametric)—sometimes known as the statistical method, this technique generates an estimate based on system performance or design characteristics. It uses a database of elements from similar systems. It differs from analogy in that it uses multiple systems and makes statistical inferences about the CERs.
- "It's made up of these" (engineering)—a "bottom-up" method of cost analysis that is the most detailed of all the techniques and the most costly to implement. Each WBS element must be costed to build an estimate for the entire program.

Analogy-based cost estimating, which can also be called "It's like one of these," subjectively compares the new system with one or more existing similar systems for which there is accurate cost and technical data. With this approach, an analyst selects a system that is similar to or related to the system for which costs are being estimated, and adjusts for differences between the two systems. This approach works well for derivative or evolutionary improvements. Therefore, a relevant starting baseline must exist to apply the method successfully. The analogy estimating approach is faster than the other two approaches, yielding more immediate cost estimates.

The parametric relationships used for estimating costs are called cost estimating relationships (CERs). According to the *Parametric Cost Estimating Handbook,*[14] "a parametric cost estimate is one that uses CERs and associated mathematical algorithms (or logic) to establish cost estimates." Parametric methods are usually based on a statistical technique that attempts to explain the correlation between the dependent variable (typically cost) as a function of several explanatory variables such as technical and performance characteristics, independent variables derived from project parameters, such as:

- intended performance and in-service date (hedonic);
- overall system design characteristics (parametric);
- sub-system design characteristics (synthetic);
- inputs to program work packages (resource-based).

The relationships between these variables and cost are frequently determined using a statistical technique, such as ordinary least squares (OLS) regression.

The flowchart in Figure 5.5 shows the steps taken in developing a CER.

An example, taken from the Constructive Cost Model (COCOMO)[15] used to estimate the cost of developing software, is:

$$MM = 2.4(KDSI)^{**}1.05$$

where MM = man-months of development effort and $KDSI$ = thousands of delivered source instruction.

This estimating equation indicates the expected number of man-months (MM) of development effort for a programming project (the dependent variable), depends exclusively on delivered source instructions in thousands (the independent or explanatory variable). More specifically MM is equal to 2.4 times the delivered source instructions (in thousands) to the power 1.05.

Parametric analysis has some advantages for estimating costs. These advantages include:

- after the basic parametric estimating relationship has been defined, it is straightforward to apply;

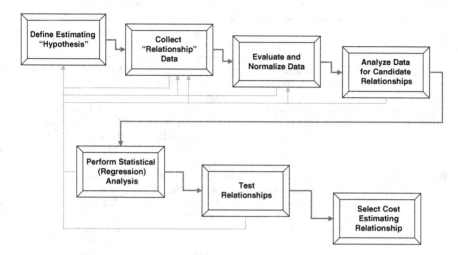

Figure 5.5 Steps used to develop a cost estimating relationship.

Source: Nussbaum class notes, OA 4702, NPS 2013.

- the analyst is not required to be a technical expert; however, to apply the method, the analyst must first obtain values for all the explanatory variables (e.g. cost drivers);
- parametric relationships generated using OLS also provide information on the uncertainty underlying the forecasted value. That is, the power of the underlying statistical methodology permits a result of $y \pm \text{\euro}$ where $\text{\euro}$ is related to the error terms of the regression. This uncertainty value can be just as informative as the predicted value.

The bottom-up approach relies on detailed engineering analysis to determine an estimate. To apply this approach to estimate future aircraft engine production costs, an analyst would need the detailed design and configuration information for various engine components and accounting information for all material, equipment, and labor. A conceptual engine design is built from scratch (hence the name "bottom-up"). This approach generates a fairly detailed forecast.

One of the advantages of this approach is that many issues can be addressed, and the effect of each issue can be well understood. For example, we could isolate the effect of choosing a new material in construction or a new manufacturing method.[16]

The bottom-up method, however, has some drawbacks. First, the analysis is time consuming. Often, a great deal of time must be spent generating the conceptual design and corresponding cost estimate. Some companies have automated the process by creating sophisticated database tools, but these systems can be expensive to develop.

A second drawback of the bottom-up approach is that the analyst must be an expert in the design of the technology being employed. Specific design details

Table 5.1 Advantages and disadvantages of cost estimating methodologies

Model category	Description	Advantages	Limitations
Analogy	Compare project with past similar projects	Estimates are based on actual experience	Truly similar projects must exist
Expert judgment	Consult with one or more experts	Little or no historical data is needed; good for new or unique projects	Experts tend to be biased; knowledge level is sometimes questionable
Bottom-up	Individuals assess each component and then component estimates are summed to calculate the total estimate	Accurate estimates are possible because of detailed basis of estimate (BOE); promotes individual responsibility	Methods are time-consuming; detailed data may not be available, especially early in a program; integration costs are sometimes disregarded
Parametric models	Perform overall estimate using design parameters and mathematical algorithms	Models are usually fast and easy to use, and useful early in a program; they are also objective and repeatable	Models can be inaccurate if not properly calibrated and validated; it is possible that historical data used for calibration may not be relevant to new programs

Source: Nussbaum class notes, OA 4702, NPS 2013, danussba@nps.edu.

must be considered to apply the method correctly. The user (i.e. cost estimator) must also understand design tradeoffs and the current state of technology.

A third disadvantage is that the system must be well defined, i.e. there is little allowance for unknown factors. For example, a component's cost must be estimated even though that component might represent a first-of-a-kind technology. Finally, the user of the bottom-up approach must have access to, or maintain an extensive and detailed database of, development, production, operating, and support costs for the particular technology.

Table 5.1 summarizes the advantages and disadvantages of each approach. A fourth approach, "expert judgment," is included, which can be used when historical data is not available. Note, however, that there are no statistics associated with an estimate based upon this method.

5.8 Cost uncertainty and risk

A cost estimate, by definition, is uncertain. That is, since we do not know the future, we will have to make assumptions in order to estimate a future cost. A good cost estimate must therefore include information about the uncertainty surrounding the estimate. This requires the statistical analysis (using either actual data or simulations) to estimate a distribution for the cost estimate, as well as a confidence interval around the point estimate.

We arrive at a point estimate by evaluating the available data and calculating a mean. This represents the most likely cost for a given project or program. The variability of the cost data provides the information necessary to build a confidence interval which consists of the estimated mean cost plus or minus some number of standard deviations. The number of standard deviations chosen depends on the desired level of confidence. For example, we can state that we are 95 percent confident that a construction project will cost between US$4 million and US$6 million dollars with the most likely cost being US$5 million dollars. In this case, our estimate of the mean is US$5 million and the standard deviation (or standard error) is US$0.5 million dollars. To build a 95 percent confidence interval, we use plus or minus two standard deviations to arrive at our statement of cost uncertainty.

Statistical analysis can also be used to assess the cost risk. First we must define what we mean by "cost risk." The standard quantitative risk assessment paradigm focuses on the following triplet of questions articulated by Kaplan and Garrick (1981):

1   What can go wrong?
2   What are the associated likelihoods?
3   What are the consequences?

Once these critical questions have been answered, the greater challenge of risk management is to address and control the following three issues articulated by Haimes (1991):

1   What can be done and what options are available?
2   What are the trade-offs in terms of costs, benefits, and risks?
3   What are the impacts of current decisions on future options?

We will focus on the first set of questions when assessing cost risk. For cost estimates, we pose the following three questions:

1   What can go wrong with the cost estimate?
2   What is the probability of a cost overrun?
3   What are the consequences of a cost overrun?

For a cost estimate, the answer to the first question is: the actual cost of the program exceeds the program budget (a cost overrun). Note that while it is certainly possible that the actual cost of the program is less than the budget, this is not a "risk" since it is a desirable outcome. In addition, there are a number of reasons why cost overruns are much more likely than cost underruns, as data and analysis from RAND has shown (see Figure 5.6). The next section reviews these reasons in examining biases in cost estimating.

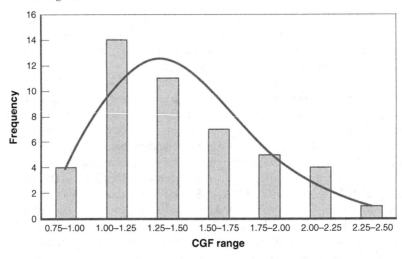

Figure 5.6 Distribution of cost growth (difference between estimate and actual costs).

Source: Arena *et al.* (2006).

The answer to the second question (what is the probability of a cost overrun?) depends on how much money is programmed in the budget. The real question is: how much money should we put in the budget? We could start with the mean estimate for the cost of the project. If we budget the mean and the cost distribution is approximately normal, the risk of exceeding the budget (for any particular program) is about 50 percent. In other words, the risk of a cost overrun is 50 percent, not a very attractive number if you are the program manager.

If we budget less than the mean for each program in a portfolio of programs, there is a higher risk of individual program cost overruns (not necessarily for the total portfolio), but it permits funding more programs in a portfolio. Of course, funding a program at such a high level of risk may imply to program managers that a cost overrun is expected. It also reduces the amount of funds available for contract negotiations, management reserves, and performance incentives.

We can reduce the risk of cost overruns if we budget an amount greater than the mean. This will lower the risk of an individual program exceeding its budget, but it may leave dollars on the table if actual costs are less than the amount budgeted. Of course, this less risky approach means fewer programs can be funded in the portfolio. It also provides less incentive to program managers to control costs, but it increases the funds available for management reserves, contract negotiations, and performance incentives.

The third question (what are the consequences of a cost overrun?) may provide some insight into why defense programs are more often than not underfunded (resulting in cost overruns). What are the consequences of a cost overrun in a defense program? Cost overruns tend to result in either a reduction in the number of units purchased (for example, cost overruns in the B-2 program forced the US

Air Force to cut the number of aircraft procured from 132 to 21) or an extension of the schedule, so that less units are procured each year. Understanding production costs is essential to evaluating the impact of such actions. Often, cutting the quantity of units produced increases the unit cost, resulting in less capability, as fewer units can be purchased for a given budget.

Funding shortfalls may also lead to a reduction in scope or capabilities and sometimes even program cancellations, but such outcomes are less frequent. Much more likely is that one program will be cut to fund another (higher priority) program to maintain a robust portfolio of capabilities. While some of these consequences, such as cancellation of the program, are highly undesirable, historically they have been rare and as such present less risk. As a result, the US DoD has been willing to accept the risk of cost overruns, perhaps judging that the consequences are manageable and thus not very risky.

It is common for CBA to focus on a comparison of the capabilities (effectiveness) and total cost of each alternative. It is also useful to compare the cost risk of different alternatives. To do this, we need the cost distribution for each alternative. In some cases, one alternative dominates the other, meaning that regardless of the funding (budget) level, the risk of a cost overrun is always lower for the dominant alternative. In other cases, the comparison is not as clear. Consider the alternatives A and B shown in Figure 5.7.

Alternative A has a lower cost risk up to a certain funding level (US$1,770), and alternative B has a lower risk beyond that level. Figure 5.8 illustrates how risk curves can be used to highlight this information and help decision-makers make better choices.

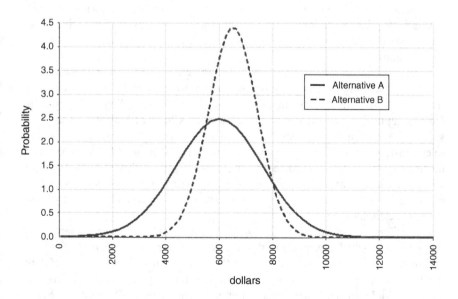

Figure 5.7 Cost distribution for two alternatives.

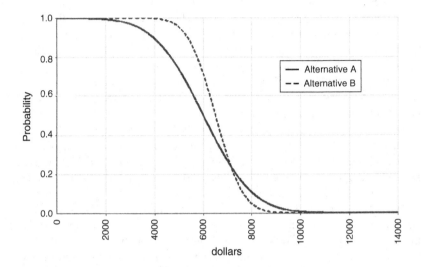

Figure 5.8 Cost risk curves for two alternatives.

5.9   Cost estimating biases

The two factors commonly used to explain "unrealistic cost estimates" are bad incentives (due to optimism bias (psychological explanation) or perverse bureaucratic incentives and strategic misrepresentation of budgets (political-economic explanation)) and bad estimates (imperfect forecasting techniques such as an omitted variable bias (methodological explanation)). It is helpful to examine these factors in the context of the PPBE process used by the DoD to build the nation's defense budget.

In theory, "programming" involves a constrained optimization in which investment and operating decisions are made to maximize national security subject to fiscal constraints. In the US, the Secretary of Defense (including CAPE and the DoD Comptroller) and the Chairman of the Joint Chiefs of Staff have good reasons to prefer accurate cost estimates given their global optimization perspective. In contrast, given their sub-optimizing perspectives, Combatant Commanders and the military services (for instance) may be more subject to a bias toward optimism and to perverse bureaucratic incentives. Since their primary focus is on performance and military capability, they have reason to be less critical (and realistic) in their cost estimates.

According to McNicol (2005, S-4), "statistical analysis is consistent with the well-established presumption that the military services tend to prefer [...] optimistic procurement cost estimates." Program Element Monitors (PEMs) in the US, for example, act as advocates for the funding of their programs and are responsible for defending those programs throughout the PPBE cycle. Since all programs compete for the DoD's limited resources in particular funding categories, PEMs are well aware that resource allocation is a competitive, zero-sum game. Given their job descriptions, PEMs are drawn to lower cost estimates that fit their advocacy agendas, rather than to higher cost estimates which make defending their programs more difficult. Moreover, since they do not always possess a higher-level perspective, they may not fully appreciate how underestimating costs can impact other programs.

Since this makes their programs more attractive to the DoD and the Congress, defense companies also have good, strategic reasons at the beginning of a program to underestimate costs. Once a program is accepted as a "program of record," and the DoD has accepted that the future capabilities associated with the program will become available, the incentive to underestimate costs declines.

Given the complexity and uncertainty of many major, technologically advanced weapon systems, contracts are necessarily incomplete; i.e. they cannot cover all possible contingencies. As a consequence, the incumbent company can be confident it will recoup overruns from multiple change-orders (generally for added scope) anticipated over the life of the contract. In fact, firms have an incentive to anticipate, but strategically omit, some of these elements in the original contract negotiation. Moreover, by strategically hiring workers in key Congressional districts, the company can pressure Congress to retain the contract and approve compensation for cost overruns to preserve jobs. This combination of strategic behaviors could explain some of the systematic bias in initial cost estimates.

In an early attempt to address the factors that lead to biased cost estimates, US Secretary of Defense Melvin Laird directed that independent parametric cost estimating be made a part of the DoD acquisition process. Legislation to this effect followed. The OSD launched an independent Cost Analysis Improvement Group (CAIG) that began operations in the spring of 1972. Eventually, the CAIG was assigned the statutory responsibility of providing independent life-cycle cost estimates for all major weapon acquisition programs.

Whereas independent cost estimation is an important step that clearly attenuates the impact of psychological and political-economic factors, the challenge of developing a more comprehensive cost estimating/forecasting methodology remains. Cost estimating techniques must properly anticipate transaction costs such as measurement, monitoring, management, and re-negotiation costs that may overwhelm initial production cost estimates and which vary according to the nature of the transaction. If transaction cost considerations are not properly anticipated, the result will be that cost estimates will continue their downward bias, and programs will continue to suffer cost overruns. One possible means to improve cost estimation is to add transaction cost considerations to the current production cost focus in cost estimating methods.

5.10 Summary

In this summary section, we provide recommendations on future research directions. In many disciplines, research is driven by both demand-side and supply-side considerations. The demand-side represents the research which is done in response to what users of the discipline are demanding, while the supply-side represents those new techniques driven by researchers internal to the profession.

In cost estimating, the impetus for research is driven almost exclusively from the demand-side, which encompasses changes in various ministries of defense and military acquisition strategies. From this perspective, the most important developments in the US are:

- the passage of the Weapon Systems Acquisition Reform Act (WSARA) in 2009;
- continued problems in estimating the costs of science and technology and software;
- renewed emphases on affordability; and
- the ability to provide quick turnarounds of cost estimates in the early stages of a program.

There are also some internal challenges within the professional community to make sure that the next generation of cost estimators, with the right academic background, are properly identified and developed in order to provide a better level of service to the next generation of defense leadership.

Finally, there is the ever-present challenge of data availability. In this regard, there have been some major improvements in data collection in the US over the past 15 years, such as the development and maintenance of extensive data collections like VAMOSC[17] and DCARC[18] (see Appendix 5.1). More recently, OSD/CAPE has been working to consolidate all DoD cost data sources into the Cost Assessment Data Enterprise, a unified initiative to collect, organize and use cost data across the cost community. These and similar databases must be continuously updated and maintained to support future cost estimates that are a critical input in military CBA.

Appendix 5.1: Data normalization

Using historical data to predict future costs requires that the data not only be relevant to the system under consideration, but that it match the assumptions of the cost estimating model. For example, cost data is recorded in accounting records based on transactions that occur over time. The cost of each transaction reflects the buying power of the currency at the time the transaction was completed. Over time, if a country is experiencing inflation or deflation, the buying power of the same amount of currency changes. As a result, cost information contained in accounting records incorporates inflation or deflation. These effects must be removed before they are used in a cost estimating model; otherwise the cost estimate will be biased.

There are many other factors that can corrupt historical data and lead to unreliable cost estimates. Data errors can arise from entry mistakes or software problems. Numbers are transposed, incompletely recorded, entirely missing or duplicated. In some instances, data is missing due to lack of documentation (so that it never enters the accounting system); in other cases, human or software mistakes lead to incorrect data. Data that undergoes any kind of aggregation or transformation is particularly subject to data errors. A simple check for possible outliers in a data set is a good first step in cleaning up the data. This process may reveal anomalies that require further investigation.

Anomalies in cost data can result from valid but unusual circumstances. For example, the production process may be interrupted due to a shortage of materials or a strike, leading to lower production rates and costs during a given period. An accelerated delivery schedule may lead to higher prices for materials (due to rush orders) and increased overtime expenses. A system modification may lead to significantly higher maintenance costs in one period. Understanding how such anomalies affect cost is critical to proper data normalization.

Data normalization is the process of making data recorded under different circumstances comparable. The circumstances may include time, location, quantity, technology, and operating tempo as well as many other variables that differ between data points. As mentioned earlier, cost data collected over time must be "normalized" to constant dollars to remove the effects of inflation or deflation.[19] In addition, cost data collected in different time periods may differ due to changes in accounting rules (related to what amount should be recorded or included in the cost of an item) or changes in the accounting system or software (which, for example, may lead to the same cost being recorded in a different category from one period to the next).

Over time we can expect that production or operating processes will change, perhaps becoming more efficient, and that materials and supplies used may change and either increase or decrease the cost of production and operation. In addition, quantities produced or operated will likely change and the cost of inputs such as labor, raw materials, and equipment will differ from period to period. These differences must be accounted for prior to using the data for a cost estimate.

One of the most important differences in costs over time in DoD arises from the difference between peacetime and wartime operations. The higher wartime operational tempo consumes significantly more resources, which, in turn, leads to higher costs. In addition, the attrition level is higher during wartime, and this may impact both acquisition costs and operating and sustainment costs. These differences should be recognized when estimating system life-cycle costs. Of course, predicting the timing of conflicts is an almost impossible task. For this reason, DoD uses peacetime assumptions when preparing cost estimates for weapon systems and budgets.

Often the cost of a new system is estimated using historical data from similar or related systems. The systems will differ to some degree in terms of configuration, materials, technology, missions, manning, and numerous other characteristics that lead to differences in development, acquisition, and operational cost. While such differences are unavoidable, it is the job of the cost analyst to adjust (or "normalize") data to account for the most significant differences to ensure costs are comparable.

Notes

1 Constant (or real) dollars are amounts that reflect the buying power in a base year and do not include inflation or deflation over time.
2 Present value analysis converts amounts paid or received in future years to an equivalent amount paid or received today. See Appendix 5.1 for a more detailed discussion.
3 Earned value management (EVM) is a project management technique for measuring project performance and progress by combining into a single system measures of scope, schedule, and cost (adapted from Wikipedia).
4 See www.iceaaonline.com/
5 *Department Of Defense Work Breakdown Structures For Defense Materiel Items.* www. acq.osd.mil/pm/currentpolicy/wbs/MIL_HDBK-881A/MILHDBK881A/WebHelp3/ MILHDBK881A.htm
6 *Operating and Support Cost-Estimating Guide* (OSD CAIG), Oct 2007. *http://dcarc.pae. osd.mil/reference/osd_ces/O_S_Cost_Estimating_Guide_Oct_2007.pdf*
7 An application of ordinary least squares regression appears later in the chapter.
8 Text available at http://www.govtrack.us/congress/billtext.xpd?bill=s111-454, or description available at
http://en.wikisource.org/wiki/Weapon_Systems_Acquisition_Reform_Act_of_2009
http://www.govtrack.us/congress/billtext.xpd?bill=s111-454)
9 See https://acc.dau.mil/CommunityBrowser.aspx?id=24463
10 See http://asafm.army.mil/offices/office.aspx?officecode=1400
11 See www.ncca.navy.mil/
12 See www.saffm.hq.af.mil/organizations/index.asp
13 See https://acc.dau.mil/CommunityBrowser.aspx?id=28858&view=w&lang=en-US
14 *Parametric Cost Estimating Handbook.* http://cost.jsc.nasa.gov/PCEHHTML/pceh.htm)
15 See http://sunset.usc.edu/csse/research/COCOMOII/cocomo_main.html
16 All representatives from engine producing companies interviewed during the course of writing this chapter indicated that they employ some form of bottom-up approach to estimating aircraft engine costs.
17 Visibility and Management of Operating Support Costs (VAMOSC). https://www.vamosc.navy.mil/
18 Defense Cost and Resource Center (DCARC). http://dcarc.cape.osd.mil/csdr/default. aspx
19 For example, we can't directly compare the nominal cost of fuel purchased by the US Navy in 1990 (US$1.35 billion) and 1997 (US$1.52 billion). We must first delete the effect of inflation since a barrel of fuel in 1990 cost US$30 while the same barrel of fuel in 1997 cost US$38. We can adjust the 1997 cost of US$1.52 billion to reflect 1990 prices using a price index ($38/30 = 1.27$); thus, the cost in real dollars is US$1.20 billion. Now we can compare US$1.35 billion in 1990 to US$1.20 billion in 1997.

Bibliography

Angelis, Diana I., J. Dillard, R. Franck, and F. Melese. 2007. Applying Insights from Transaction Cost Economics (TCE) to Improve DoD Cost Estimation. *Acquisition Research Sponsored Report Series*, NPS-GSBPP-07-008, Naval Postgraduate School.
Arena, Mark V., R. S. Leonard, S. E. Murray, and O. Younossi. 2006. *Historical Cost Growth of Completed Weapon System Programs.* Santa Monica, CA: Rand Corporation.
Defense Acquisition University (DAU). *Weapon Systems Acquisition Reform Act of 2009* (WSARA 09), DTM 09-027.
Fisher, Gene H. 2007. *Cost Considerations in Systems Analysis.* Santa Monica, CA: Rand Corporation.

Garvey, Paul R. 2000. *Probability Methods for Cost Uncertainty Analysis*. New York: Marcel Dekker.

Government Accountability Office. 2009. *Cost Estimating and Assessment Guide*. Available at www.gao.gov/new.items/d071134sp.pdf

Haimes, Y. Y. 1991. Total Risk Management. *Risk Analysis* 11(2): 169–171.

Kaplan, S. and B.J. Garrick. 1981. On The Quantitative Definition of Risk. *Risk Analysis* 1: 11–27.

McNicol, D. L. 2005. *Cost Growth in Major Weapon Procurement Programs* (2nd edition, IDA Paper No. P-3832). Alexandria, VA: Institute for Defense Analyses.

Melese, F., R. Franck, D. Angelis, and J. Dillard. 2007. Applying Transaction Cost to Improve Cost Estimates for Public Sector Purchases: The Case of US Military Acquisition. *International Public Management Journal* 10(4): 357–385.

Office of the Secretary of Defense. 1992. *Cost Analysis Improvement Group Operating and Support Cost-Estimating Guide*. Available from www.dtic.mil/pae.

Shrull, D., ed. 1998. *The Cost Analysis Improvement Group: A History*. McLean, VA: Logistics Management Institute (LMI).

Stewart, R. D. 1991. *Cost Estimating* (2nd edition). New York: John Wiley and Sons, Inc., Chapter 4.

US Air Force. 2007. *Cost Risk and Uncertainty Analysis Handbook*. Available at https://acc.dau.mil/CommunityBrowser.aspx?id=316093

US Department of Defense. 2005. *Work Breakdown Structures for Defense Materiel Items* (MIL-HDBK-881A). Available at www.everyspec.com.

6 Advances in cost estimating

A demonstration of advanced machine learning techniques for cost estimation

Bohdan L. Kaluzny

6.1 Introduction

> Defense cost analysis is an amalgam of scientific rigor and sound judgment. It requires knowledge, insight, and the application of statistical principles, as well as the critical interpretation of a wide variety of information known with imprecision.
>
> (Flynn and Garvey 2011)

6.1.1 Background

The International Cost Estimating and Analysis Association (ICEAA) *Cost Estimating Handbook of Knowledge* (CEBoK)[1] categorizes different costing techniques commonly applied for defense cost estimation. These include costing by analogy, costing by parametric approaches, engineering build-up approaches, and extrapolation from actuals. Figure 6.1 shows when each of these costing techniques are commonly applied relative to a program's life cycle. The figure shows the approximate proportional usage of cost techniques by phase. At the beginning of a program there is more emphasis on using analogies and parametrics. As the program matures, it becomes more defined, additional data is collected, and the estimates get more detailed. A challenge to cost analysts is developing good cost estimates during early design phases using costing by analogy and parametrics.

Cost estimation by analogy is typically accomplished by forecasting the cost of a new system based on the historical cost of similar or analogous systems. This requires a reasonable correlation between the new and historical system. The cost of the historical system is adjusted by undertaking a technical evaluation of the differences between the systems, deducting the cost of components that are not comparable to the new design and adding estimated costs of the new components. Usually subject matter experts are required to make a subjective evaluation of the differences between the new system of interest and the historical system, and subjectively chosen complexity factors are often used to adjust the analogous system's cost to produce an estimate. This subjectivity is a disadvantage of traditional analogy methods.

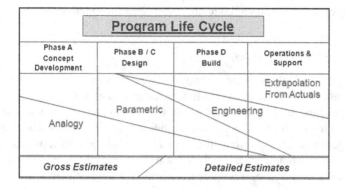

Figure 6.1 Defense Acquisition University (DAU) integrated defense acquisition, technology, and logistics life cycle management framework chart.

Parametric approaches to cost estimation use regression or other statistical methods to develop Cost Estimating Relationships (CERs). Strengths in parametric approaches are their potential to capture major portions of an estimate quickly and with limited information, their basis on consistent and quantitative inputs, and standard tests of validity, including a coefficient of correlation indicating the strength of association between the independent variables and the dependent variables in the CER. A major disadvantage of typical parametric approaches is that they may not provide low-level visibility (cost breakdown) and changes in sub-systems are not reflected in the estimate if they are not quantified via an independent variable. CERs may be mathematically simple (e.g. a simple ratio) or involve linear regression analysis (of historical systems or subsystems) on a single or multiple parameters (weight, length, density, etc.). Miroyannis (2006) noted that CERs are often insufficient and that other cost-driving factors must be incorporated to develop estimates of sufficient quality at the preliminary design phase. Furthermore, the relationship between the parameter(s) and cost may not be best expressed in linear form. While the field of regression analysis offers a multitude of alternative approaches (see Ryan 1997), linear regression is the most popular and easiest to understand.

This chapter explores recent advancements in costing by analogy and parametrics that were presented in the context of estimating the development and production costs of naval ships by the North Atlantic Treaty Organization (NATO) Research Technology Board (RTO) System Analysis and Studies (SAS) task group 076 on "NATO Independent Cost Estimating and the Role of Life Cycle Cost Analysis in Managing the Defence Enterprise." The NATO RTO SAS-076 Task Group (2012) report and associated publications (Kaluzny *et al.* 2011; Kaluzny and Shaw 2011) detail the data collection and normalization efforts and provide cost estimation results. The primary focus of this chapter is to highlight and further explore the methods published in the latter references. For this reason actual costs (data, normalization, results, etc.) are not discussed and only appear on occasion in figures and tables to facilitate understanding of the methods.

6.1.2 Leveraging machine learning

Witten and Frank (2005) define data mining as the process of discovering patterns, automatically or semi-automatically, in large quantities of data. Data mining often employs machine learning methods whose focus is on prediction, based on known properties learned from data. In this chapter we define machine learning techniques as mathematical algorithms for "best-fit" prediction. The application of data mining and machine learning techniques to cost estimation, or cost prediction, is natural and not new—regression analysis is a predominant machine learning technique utilized by cost analysts. However, advancements in the fields of data mining and machine learning have brought forward additional tools that can be leveraged to improve cost estimation. In this chapter two machine learning algorithms are discussed in detail and exemplified:

- A combination of hierarchical cluster analysis, principal component analysis, and nonlinear optimization can be used for a cost estimation by analogy approach that is void of subjective adjustment factors. The approach also considers multiple analogous systems rather than just one. Hierarchical cluster analysis identifies the historical systems that are the "nearest neighbors" to the new system. A hierarchy of clusters grouping similar items together is produced: from small clusters of very similar items to large clusters that include more dissimilar items. A matrix of distances (measure quantifying the similarity of two systems) among systems is calculated expressing all possible pairwise distances among them. These distances are then used to predict the cost of a new instance.
- Using an algorithm combining decision trees and regression analysis, a parametric approach for cost estimation incorporating a multitude of cost-driving factors, while remaining a "top down" approach applicable in early design phases of the procurement cycle, is described. The Quinlan (1992) M5 model tree algorithm combines features of decision trees with linear regression models to both classify similar systems (based on attributes) and build piecewise multivariate linear regression models.

6.1.3 Outline

The remainder of this chapter is structured as follows. Section 6.2 provides a very brief description of the dataset used to exemplify the machine learning algorithms discussed herein. Section 6.3 presents a machine learning algorithm for costing by analogy and Section 6.4 exhibits the application of M5 model trees to parametric cost estimation. Section 6.5 provides a combined discussion. Finally, the chapter concludes in Section 6.6.

6.2   Data

Data mining approaches are data intensive. Both the quality and quantity of the data drive the quality of the outputs of machine learning algorithms. While the appropriate level of data quality and quantity will be case-specific, to illustrate the application of machine learning algorithms a database of 59 naval ships compiled by the NATO RTO SAS-076 working group is considered. This dataset is subsequently referred to as the SAS-076 ship dataset. The database captures over 100 descriptive, technical, and cost attributes for 59 naval ships from 18 classes (of ships), from seven nations, commissioned between 1950 and 2010. The normalized costs also span multiple orders of magnitude.

The SAS-076 ship dataset contains military and civilian auxiliary (coast guard or similar) vessels that were judged to be more or less similar to Landing Platform Dock (LPD) ships. A benefit of employing machine learning algorithms is that they allow for, or can excel on, a greater variability in the input dataset—variability that could be questioned when using traditional costing by analogy or parametric approaches. The fidelity of costing by analogy and parametric approaches also depends on the size of the input dataset. In this case, the availability of ship cost data limited the size of the SAS-076 ship dataset. While the decision as to which ships were or were not included in the dataset was subjective, it was primarily driven by the availability of cost data.

Using machine learning terminology, each ship is an *instance* and together the ships listed in the SAS-076 dataset form a set of instances for input to a machine learning scheme. Instances are things that are to be classified, associated or clustered. Each instance is characterized by the values of a set of predetermined features or *attributes*. The matrix of instances versus attributes forms the input dataset (e.g. the SAS-076 ship dataset). The value of an attribute can be *numeric, nominal, ordinal, interval* or *ratio*. Numeric attributes measure numbers (real or integers) and are not necessarily continuous. Nominal, or categorical, attributes take on values from a prespecified, finite set of possibilities. These can take the form of distinct symbols or even words like "yes" or "red." Ordinal quantities are nominal quantities with a rank order (e.g. fast > slow > very slow). Interval quantities are ordinal but also measured in fixed and equal widths (e.g. temperature in degrees Celsius). Ratio quantities are relative; specified by an inherent zero-point (e.g. the distance between two objects).

Descriptive, technical, and cost data were gathered for each of the ships and broken down into categories, as shown in Table 6.1. Attribute units are expressed by either nominal values (e.g. "fixed pitch," "controlled pitch," "yes," "no"), or by numerical units such as meters, megawatts, knots, hours, nautical miles, etc. Unknown or missing data is permissible and is denoted by empty or "?" entries.

6.3   Data mining for cost estimation by analogy

This section describes how hierarchical cluster analysis is used for a cost estimation by analogy approach that is void of the subjectivityinherent (of traditional

Table 6.1 Categories of ship data

	Category	Number of attributes
I	Description	6
II	Construction	8
III	Dimensions	5
IV	Performance	8
V	Propulsion	9
VI	Electrical power generation	3
VII	Lift capacity	35
VIII	Flight deck	19
IX	Armament	13
X	Countermeasures	5
XI	Radars/sonars/sensors	13
XII	Combat data systems	1
XIII	Weapons control systems	1
XIV	Other capabilities	7
XV	Cost data	3
	Total	136

analogy approaches) in quantifying the cost of the technical and other differences between the historical system and the new system. The approach also considers multiple analogous systems rather than just one.

6.3.1 Hierarchical cluster analysis

Hierarchical cluster analysis is a data mining approach that facilitates cost estimation by analogy by identifying the systems that are the "nearest neighbors" to the new system. Hierarchical cluster methods produce a hierarchy of clusters grouping similar items together: from small clusters of very similar items to large clusters that include more dissimilar items. In particular, agglomerative hierarchical methods work by first finding the clusters of the most similar items and progressively adding less similar items until all items have been included into a single large cluster. Hierarchical agglomerative cluster analysis begins by calculating a matrix of distances among systems expressing all possible pairwise distances among them. Initially each system is considered a group, albeit of a single item. Clustering begins by finding the two systems that are most similar, based on the distance matrix, and merging them into a single group. The characteristics of this new group are based on a combination of the systems in that group. This procedure of combining two groups and merging their characteristics is repeated until all the systems have been joined into a single large cluster.

Hierarchical cluster analysis is a useful means of observing the structure of the dataset. The results of the cluster analysis are shown by a dendrogram (tree), which lists all of the samples and indicates at what level of similarity any two clusters were joined. The *x*-axis is a measure of the similarity or distance at which clusters join. The resulting clustering can be used to estimate the cost of a new system by taking a weighted average of the cost of historical systems based on the relative distances between the new system and the historical systems.

6.3.2 Application to SAS-076 ship dataset

Using the SAS-076 ship dataset, hierarchical clustering is used to define a ship distance function which takes as input ship attributes for a pair of ships and outputs a single value indicating the distance, or similarity, between the two ships. Formally, define

$$d_{ijk} = \text{distance between ship } i \text{ and } j \text{ with respect to attribute } k. \tag{6.1}$$

For numeric attributes, d_{ijk} is normalized to lie in the $[0, 1]$ range with $d_{ijk} = 1$ indicating that ships i and j lie at opposite ends of the observed spectrum for attribute k (e.g. shortest and longest length ships), and $d_{ijk} = 0$ indicating that the ships are the same with respect to attribute k. For nominal attributes, d_{ijk} is binary—set to 0 if ship i and j are the same with respect to attribute k, and 1 if they are not.

A variety of distance metrics can be used to calculate similarity of two ships based on the attribute distances d_{ijk}. Using a simple Euclidean distance metric, the aggregate distance between two ships i and j, is expressed as

$$d_{ij} = \sqrt{\sum_{k \in A} d_{ijk}^2}, \tag{6.2}$$

where A is the subset of attributes considered.

Computing the distances between all pairs of ships using Equation (6.2), the cost of a ship i can be estimated by computing the weighted-average cost of the other ships. Let C_j be the known cost of ship j, then

$$\tilde{C}_i = \sum_{j \neq i} \frac{C_j}{d_{ij}^2} \cdot \frac{1}{\sum_{j \neq i} \frac{1}{d_{ij}^2}} \tag{6.3}$$

is the estimated cost of ship i. Figure 6.2 plots the actual ship costs, C_i, versus the costs predicted, $\tilde{C}_i$, by the analogy method using hierarchical clustering based on a simple distance metric. The solid line running at 45 degrees represents perfect prediction. The measures of worth of the analogy method using hierarchical clustering analysis (simple distance metric) for predicting ship costs are $R = 0.48$ and $R^2 = 0.23$. The mean absolute percentage error is 49 percent indicating that this raw approach does poorly in learning the known ship costs and would likely yield poor cost predictions.

An assumption in the above approach is that all attributes are of equal importance; the (normalized) differences or similarities for each attribute contribute equally to the measure of similarity between ships. To potentially improve the

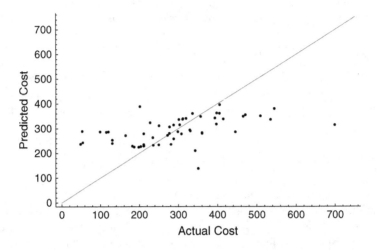

Figure 6.2 Hierarchical clustering with simple distance function: correlation plot of actual versus predicted ship costs.

predictive capability of the method, attribute weights can be defined. Let

$$w_k = \text{weight of attribute } k. \tag{6.4}$$

Using a weighted Euclidean distance metric, the aggregate distance between two ships i and j, is expressed as

$$\hat{d}_{ij} = \sqrt{\sum_{k \in A} (w_k \cdot d_{ijk})^2}, \tag{6.5}$$

where $\sum_{k \in A} w_k = 1$ and $w_k \geq 0$ for all k. As before, let C_j be the known cost of ship j, then

$$\hat{C}_i = \sum_{j \neq i} \frac{C_j}{\hat{d}_{ij}^2} \cdot \frac{1}{\sum_{j \neq i} \frac{1}{\hat{d}_{ij}^2}} \tag{6.6}$$

is the estimated cost of ship i using weighted attributes. The optimal allocation of weights is determined by minimizing the prediction error for the known ships,

$$\text{minimize} \sum_i (C_i - \hat{C}_i)^2. \tag{6.7}$$

The resulting mathematical optimization is a nonlinear convex program. With a large set of attributes the mathematical program may be too computationally intensive to solve in a reasonable amount of time. To reduce the dimensionality of the problem, a smaller subset of attributes can be selected. While there are numerous attribute selection algorithms (see Witten and Frank 2005), principal component analysis (PCA), a tool in exploratory data analysis and for making predictive models, is recommended. PCA involves a mathematical procedure that transforms a number of possibly correlated variables into a smaller number of uncorrelated variables called principal components. The first principal component accounts for as much of the variability in the data as possible, and each succeeding component accounts for as much of the remaining variability as possible. The reader is referred to Jolliffe (2002) for mathematical details of PCA.

Using PCA, the ship dataset was reduced to a set of 16 macro-attributes accounting for 95 percent of the original set's variability. Each macro-attribute is a linear combination of the original attributes. For example, macro-attribute A2 is

$$
\begin{aligned}
A2 = {}& 0.204 \times \text{length} \\
& + 0.196 \times \text{beam width} \\
& + 0.183 \times \text{vehicle space} \\
& + 0.18 \times \text{no. of expeditionary fighting vehicles} \\
& + 0.165 \times 1 \text{ if has a well deck, otherwise } 0 \\
& + 0.165 \times \text{width of the well deck} \\
& + 0.164 \times \text{length of the well deck} \\
& + 0.159 \times \text{no. of large personnel landing craft} \\
& + 0.156 \times \text{no. of Chinook helicopters supported} \\
& + 0.155 \times \text{full load displacement} \\
& + 0.153 \times \text{no. of combat data systems} \\
& + 0.150 \times \text{light load displacement} \\
& + 0.144 \times \text{well deck capacity} \\
& + 0.143 \times \text{no. of elevators} \\
& + 0.142 \times \text{vehicle fuel capacity} \\
& \text{etc.}
\end{aligned}
\tag{6.8}
$$

(Only the top 15 attributes—in terms of PCA coefficient size—are enumerated in Equation (6.8).)

Table 6.2 lists the macro-attributes and the respective percentage of data variability (cumulative) each accounts for.

Using the top ten macro-attributes, accounting for over 80 percent of the original dataset's variance, an optimal solution to Equation (6.7) for the macro-attribute weights was determined. The weights are listed in the last column of Table 6.2.

Table 6.2 Principal component analysis and optimal macro-attribute weights

| Macro-attribute | Percentage of data variability accounted | | Optimal weight |
	Proportion	Cumulative	
A1	17	17	0
A2	12	29	0.452
A3	11	41	0
A4	9	49	0
A5	8	57	0.334
A6	7	64	0
A7	6	69	0
A8	5	74	0
A9	4	78	0
A10	3	81	0.214
A11	3	85	
A12	3	88	
A13	3	90	
A14	2	92	
A15	2	94	
A16	1	95	

Only macro-attributes A2, A5, and A10 have non-zero weights. This is a typical extreme output of mathematical optimization software. There may exist other optimal solutions with other non-zero macro-attributes weights.

The hierarchical cluster analysis using the weighted distance function on the top ten macro-attributes determined by PCA (effectively the three macro-attributes assigned non-zero weight) is visualized in Figure 6.3. The figure illustrates the resulting dendrogram indicating the relative grouping of ships. As expected, ships within the same class (but different rank) are closely grouped together. The weighted distance function is used to determine the distances of each ship to a particular ship. For example, plugging in the macro-attributes weights of Table 6.2 into Equation (6.5) results in the list of computed distances to the Rotterdam LPD presented in Table 6.3.

Figure 6.4 plots the actual ship costs, C_i, versus the costs predicted, $\hat{C}_i$, by the analogy method using hierarchical clustering based on a weighted distance metric (the figure is based on Table 6.3 and Equation (6.6)). The solid line running at 45 degrees represents perfect prediction. The measures of worth of the analogy method via hierarchical clustering analysis (weighted distance matrix) for predicting ship costs are $R = 0.93$ and $R^2 = 0.86$. The latter coefficient of determination indicates that 86 percent of the total variation in the ship costs can be explained by an average cost of the known ships weighted by an optimized distance metric. The mean absolute percent error is 16 percent, a significant improvement over the hierarchical clustering based on the simple distance metric that yielded a 49 percent error.

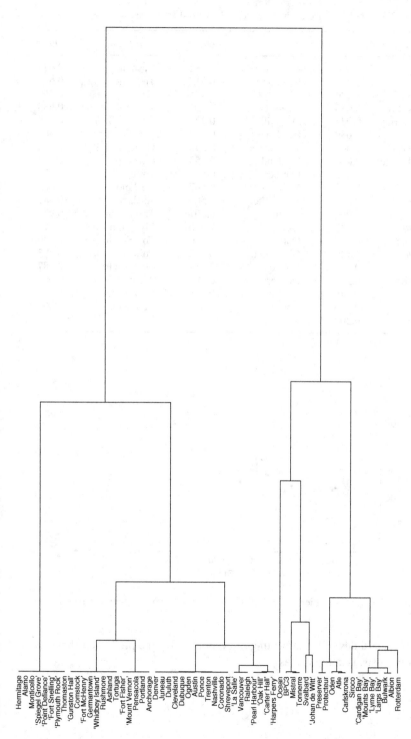

Figure 6.3 Dendrogram illustrating the arrangement of the clusters produced by the hierarchical clustering of ships (weighted distance function).

Table 6.3 Weighted distance of the Rotterdam LPD to ships in the SAS-076 dataset

Name	Distance	Name	Distance	Name	Distance
Rotterdam	0.000	Vancouver	0.312	Nashville	0.639
Largs Bay	0.034	La Salle	0.316	Trenton	0.646
Lyme Bay	0.034	Harpers Ferry	0.405	Ponce	0.650
Mounts Bay	0.035	Carter Hall	0.431	Whidbey Island	0.655
Cardigan Bay	0.035	Oak Hill	0.435	Germantown	0.659
Oden	0.039	Pearl Harbour	0.439	Fort McHenry	0.664
Carlskrona	0.044	Anchorage	0.546	Gunston Hall	0.668
Johan de Witt	0.046	Portland	0.550	Comstock	0.673
Atle	0.052	Pensacola	0.553	Tortuga	0.678
Albion	0.057	Mount Vernon	0.557	Rushmore	0.682
Bulwark	0.058	Fort Fisher	0.561	Ashland	0.687
Siroco	0.067	Austin	0.601	Thomaston	0.971
Svalbard	0.068	Ogden	0.606	Plymouth Rock	0.975
Protecteur	0.128	Duluth	0.610	Fort Snelling	0.979
Preserver	0.129	Cleveland	0.612	Point Defiance	0.983
Ocean	0.227	Dubuque	0.617	Spiegel Grove	0.987
Tonnerre	0.244	Denver	0.621	Alamo	0.992
Mistral	0.246	Juneau	0.626	Hermitage	0.996
BPC3	0.266	Coronado	0.630	Monticello	1.000
Raleigh	0.309	Shreveport	0.634		

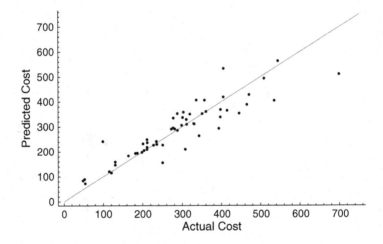

Figure 6.4 Weighted hierarchical clustering: correlation plot of actual versus predicted ship costs.

The standard deviation, indicating the variation that the predictions have from the actual costs, is computed as

$$\sqrt{\frac{\sum_{i=1}^{n}(y_i - \hat{y}_i)^2}{n}}. \tag{6.9}$$

To summarize, as an analogy costing approach, hierarchical agglomerative cluster analysis, principal component analysis, and nonlinear optimization were used to calculate a matrix of distances among the systems of a dataset. These distances can then be used to predict the cost of new systems. The fidelity of the estimation model is very dependent the dataset. It is a "top down" approach applicable in early design phases of the procurement cycle.

6.4 Data mining for parametric cost estimation

Parametric approaches to cost estimation use regression or other statistical methods to develop CERs, which are equations used to estimate a given cost element using an established relationship with one or more independent variables. The typical ship costing CER expresses the cost (dependent variable) as a function of the ships length (independent variable).

There are several advantages of a parametric approach to cost estimation, including:

- it can capture major portions of an estimate quickly and with limited information (which is often all that is available in early phases of the procurement cycle);
- the CER is objective—it is based on consistent and quantitative inputs;
- once the CER is established it is easy to perform sensitivity analyses (determine the change in cost subject to changes in the independent input variables); and
- CERs established using regression analyses include standard tests of validity, including a coefficient of correlation indicating the strength of association between the independent variables and the dependent variable in the CER.

A critical consideration in parametric cost estimating is the similarity of the systems in the underlying database, both to each other and to the system which is being estimated. A major disadvantage of the approach is that it may not provide low-level visibility (cost breakdown) and changes in sub-systems are not reflected in the estimate if they are not quantified via an independent variable.

This section describes a parametric approach for ship cost estimation that incorporates a multitude of cost-driving factors, while remaining a "top down" approach applicable in the early design phases of the procurement cycle. It combines features of decision trees with linear regression models to both classify similar ships (based on attributes) and build piecewise multivariate linear regression models.

6.4.1 The M5 model tree system

In 1992, Quinlan (1992) pioneered the M5 system for learning models that predict numeric values. The M5 system combines features of decision trees with linear regression models. M5 model trees are similar to regression trees; a decision tree induction algorithm is used to build an initial tree, recursively splitting the dataset based on the value of a chosen splitting attribute. The splitting attribute is selected to minimize the prediction error down each branch. Whereas the nodes of a regression tree each contain a constant value (prediction), each model tree node is a multivariate linear regression model. The attributes defining these regression models are the attributes that are involved in the tree's branching decisions.

Figure 6.5 depicts a simple example of a M5 model tree. The subfigure on the left shows a two-dimensional space of independent variables x_1 and x_2. This is a graphical representation of a dataset with two attributes (e.g. ship length and crew size), where each two-dimensional point in the x_1–x_2 plane represents an instance (a ship). The dependent variable, Y, represents the numerical value associated with each instance (i.e. ship cost)—the values for the known instances are not shown in the subfigure. To build a model to predict the Y value of a new instance, the algorithm proceeds in four parts. First, a decision tree is constructed using the same procedure as for regression trees: the tree is constructed recursively by splitting the training set (known ships) by selecting the attribute value that minimizes the error in the estimation of the known instances. For example, in Figure 6.5 the algorithm determines that splitting the dataset on attribute value $x_2 > 2$ yields a lower estimation error (predicted versus known cost of the ships) in comparison to a model without the split. The process is repeated on the half-spaces generated. The recursion stops when the estimation error is small (e.g. less than 5 percent) or when the sub-space contains only a small number of instances. The decisions to divide the space are represented by a model tree as shown in the right subfigure. The second part of the algorithm constructs multivariate linear regression models for each region, in other words at each node of the model tree, using only the attributes that are referenced by tests somewhere in the subtree of this node.[2] In the example illustrated, there would be eleven linear regression models, one for each of the six leaves and five internal nodes. Part three of the algorithm applies a tree pruning routine which eliminates subtrees of a node if the estimation error is higher in the lower branches than the estimation error when using the node's internal regression model. For example, if the combined estimation error of the linear regression models of leaves 5 and 6 was worse than the estimation error of the decision node labelled "$x_2 < 1$," then the algorithm would eliminate Models 5 and 6 and the subtree rooted at node "$x_2 < 1$" would collapse to a leaf. The last step

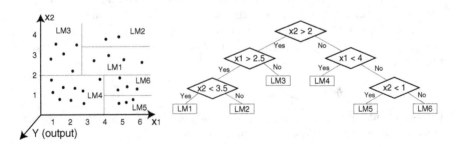

Figure 6.5 Example M5 model tree.

of the algorithm is a smoothing process. With the goal of improving prediction accuracy, the linear regression models of adjacent leaves are adjusted so that they are continuous and smooth (piecewise connected). In the example, the algorithm would adjust Model 1 to be piecewise connected to Model 2, Model 2 to be piecewise connected to Model 3, etc. This process is particularly effective when some of the linear regression models are constructed from few training cases.

To predict a value for a new instance (e.g. a new ship design), the M5 model tree is followed from the root down to a leaf using the instance's attribute values to make routing decisions at each node. The leaf contains a linear regression model based on a subset of the attributes, and this is evaluated for the new instance to output a predicted value.

6.4.1.1 Discussion

Regression trees are more accurate than straightforward linear regression, but the trees are often cumbersome and difficult to interpret (Witten and Frank 2005). Model trees are more sophisticated than regression trees as they approximate continuous functions by linear "patches"—M5 model trees are analogous to piecewise linear functions. M5 model trees have an advantage over regression trees with respect to compactness and prediction accuracy due to the ability of model trees to exploit local linearity in the data. Regression trees will not predict values lying outside the range of learned training cases, while M5 model trees can extrapolate. The M5 model tree algorithm is optimized both to learn known cases and predict unknown cases. The trees are also smaller, easier to understand, and their average error values on the training data are lower.

M5 model trees tackle the difficulties in considering a multitude of cost-driving factors; they determine the right set of independent variables (ship attributes) by construction. The effect of the M5 system is somewhat similar to the use of indicator variables in standard linear regression analysis, with the key difference being that appropriate indicators are identified and included based on an optimization algorithm.

M5 model trees have been shown to excel even when limited data is available (Wang and Witten 1997) or learn efficiently from large datasets. They can handle datasets which include systems with notable differences, missing data, and noise (as is the case for the SAS-076 ship dataset). The decision tree can branch on any variable type: nominal (e.g. military versus non-military) or numeric (e.g. tonnage less than 15,000 or greater than 15,000).

The use of M5 model trees for numeric prediction has increased since comprehensive descriptions, implementations, and refinements of Quinlan's method became available (Wang and Witten 1997; Malerba *et al.* 2004; Torgo 2000, 2002; Dobra 2002). Recently Chen (2006) and Sharma and Litoriya (2012) discussed the benefits of the system for estimating the cost of software development.

There are many other types of prediction methods that employ data mining techniques. For example, neural networks are commonly used for predicting numeric quantities, but suffer from the disadvantage of producing opaque structures that mask the nature of the solution. Their arbitrary internal representation means that there can be variations between networks trained on the same data. By comparison, the M5 system is transparent and the model tree construction is repeatable. The final tree and linear regression models are straightforward and clear.

6.4.2   Application to SAS-076 ship dataset

An easy-to-use implementation of Quinlan's M5 model tree is available as part of the WEKA project.[3] Witten and Frank's (2005) textbook provides documentation on both the theory and implementation (data formatting, execution, etc.) of the algorithm. The descriptive attributes, the complete set of technical attributes, and a normalized cost attribute for each of the ships in the SAS-076 dataset were used as input to the M5 model tree algorithm. Using WEKA,[4] the construction of the M5 model tree for the SAS-076 ship database takes on order of seconds of computation.

Figure 6.6 shows the resulting M5 model tree. The root of the decision tree divides the ships into two categories based on the number of air-cushioned landing craft (LCAC) that the ship is designed to carry. Internal nodes of the tree further split the dataset on attributes such as the number (#) of torpedo decoy systems on board, the ship's rank in class, the number of propeller shafts, the maximum number of helicopters supported, and the ship's range in terms of total distance in nautical miles. The tree branches out to seven leaves, where seven corresponding linear regression models are fitted. The regression models are presented in Table 6.4. In addition to the ship attributes used in the decision tree for branching, the linear regression models use the ship attributes of length (in meters), crew size, and number of elevators on board. Table 6.5 provides the minimum, median, mean, and maximum values found in the SAS-076 ship dataset for the attributes used by the M5 model.

The linear regression models output the log-transformed (decadic) cost of a ship. The individual linear regression models are mostly intuitive: the cost of a

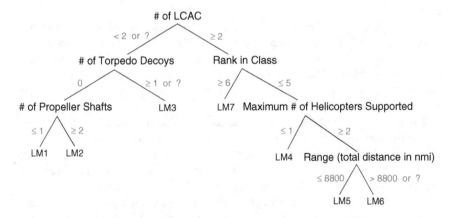

Figure 6.6 M5 model tree applied to the SAS-076 dataset.

Table 6.4 M5 model tree linear regression models

LM1	LM2

Log(Cost) = 7.8009
    − 0.0083 × rank in class
    + 0.0017 × length (m)
    + 0.0006 × crew size
    − 0.0450 × no. of propeller
        shafts
    + 0.0304 × no. of LCAC
    + 0.0218 × no. of elevators
    + 0.1897 × no. of torpedo
        decoys
	Log(Cost) = 7.7916
	    − 0.0083 × rank in class
	    + 0.0017 × length (m)
	    + 0.0006 × crew size
	    − 0.0450 × no. of propeller
	        shafts
	    + 0.0304 × no. of LCAC
	    + 0.0218 × no. of elevators
	    + 0.1897 × no. of torpedo
	        decoys

LM3	LM4

Log(Cost) = 7.8869
    − 0.0189 × rank in class
    + 0.0017 × length (m)
    + 0.0006 × crew size
    − 0.0203 × no. of propeller
        shafts
    + 0.0304 × no. of LCAC
    + 0.0218 × no. of elevators
    + 0.1285 × no. of torpedo
        decoys
	Log(Cost) = 8.1555
	    − 0.0226 × rank in class
	    + 0.0031 × length (m)
	    + 0.0001 × crew size
	    + 0.0216 × no. of LCAC
	    + 0.0155 × no. of elevators

LM5	LM6

Log(Cost) = 8.2675
    − 0.0349 × rank in class
    + 0.0029 × length (m)
    + 0.0001 × crew size
    + 0.0216 × no. of LCAC
    + 0.0064 × no. of elevators
	Log(Cost) = 8.4549
	    − 0.0303 × rank in class
	    + 0.0018 × length (m)
	    + 0.0001 × crew size
	    + 0.0216 × no. of LCAC
	    + 0.0038 × no. of elevators

LM7	

Log(Cost) = 8.4544
    − 0.0202 × rank in class
    + 0.0012 × length (m)
    + 0.0001 × crew size
    + 0.0216 × no. of LCAC
    + 0.0155 × no. of elevators	

ship increases as the length, number of elevators, crew size, number of LCAC supported, or number of torpedo decoy systems increase(s). The regression models also predict a shipbuilding learning curve as the cost of constructing a ship decreases as a function of the ship's rank in class. However, the negative coefficient preceding the number of ship propeller shafts in the regression models LM1, LM2, and LM3 is counter-intuitive. It seems unlikely that a ship will cost less if

Table 6.5 Statistics of attributes used in the M5 model tree linear regression models

Attribute	Minimum	Median	Mean	Maximum
Rank	1	3	3.6	12
Length	103.7	173.8	170.2	203.4
Range (total distance)	6,000	8,000	9,933	30,000
Crew size	15	352	321	491
No. of propeller shafts	0	2	1.7	4
No. of LCAC	0	2	1.9	4
No. of elevators	0	0	0.6	3
No. of helicopters supported	0	6	5	18
No. of torpedo decoy systems	0	0	0.5	1

the number of propeller shafts is increased. The SAS-076 ship data explains this anomaly: all but one of the ships captured in the SAS-076 ship dataset have at most two propeller shafts; only Sweden's Atle icebreaker has four. The Atle is also the lowest costing ship. Since there is no constraint on keeping the coefficients positive, the linear regression model LM2 uses the propeller shaft attribute to model Atle's low cost. The combination of Atle's low cost and unique propeller shaft attribute drives the negative coefficient sign. The smoothing process of the M5 model tree construction spreads this feature to the adjacent linear regression models LM1 and LM3. The M5 model can be potentially adjusted in an attempt to remove such anomalies by disabling the particular attribute (number of propeller shafts); however, there is no guarantee that the regenerated model will not substitute this attribute with another, also allocated a negative coefficient. Similarly, removing the instance (e.g. Atle) from the dataset provides no guarantees. Rather than subjectively diminishing the dataset, anomalies are noted and discussed as part of the results.

Figure 6.7 plots the actual ship costs versus the costs predicted by the M5 model tree. The worth of a regression-based model is most commonly measured by the coefficient of correlation, the quantity that gives the quality of a least squares fitting to the original data. Let y_i be the actual cost of ship i and $\hat{y}_i$ the predicted cost (using the M5 model tree), then the coefficient of correlation, R, of the M5 system is calculated as

$$R = \frac{n \sum y_i \hat{y}_i - \sum y_i \sum \hat{y}_i}{\sqrt{n \sum y_i^2 - \left(\sum y_i\right)^2} \sqrt{n \sum \hat{y}_i^2 - \left(\sum \hat{y}_i\right)^2}}, \tag{6.10}$$

where $n = 59$, the number of ships in the dataset, and each of the sums are over these 59 ships. By design R can range from -1 to $+1$ with $R = 1$ indicating a perfect positive linear correlation. A correlation greater than 0.8 is generally described as strong (Ryan 1997). The value R^2, known as the coefficient of determination, is a measure of how well the regression line represents the data—it is a measure determining how certain one can be in making predictions from

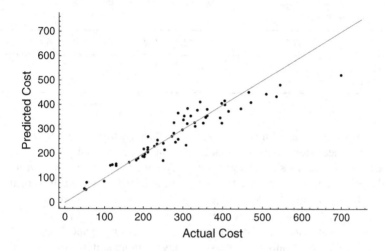

Figure 6.7 M5 model tree: correlation plot of actual versus predicted ship costs.

the model. R^2 is also the ratio of the explained variation (by the model) to the total variation of the dataset. The measures of worth of the M5 model tree for predicting ship costs are a strong $R = 0.9646$ and $R^2 = 0.9304$. The coefficient of determination indicates that 93 percent of the total variation in the ship costs can be explained by the linear relationships described by the M5 model tree linear regression equations. The remaining 7 percent of the total variation remains unexplained.

The mean absolute percentage error quantifies the amount by which the estimated cost differs from the actual cost. The mean absolute percentage error is computed as follows:

$$\frac{1}{59} \sum_{i=1}^{i=59} \frac{|y_i - \hat{y}_i|}{y_i}. \tag{6.11}$$

The mean absolute percentage error for the M5 model tree applied to the SAS-076 ship dataset is 11 percent. Mean absolute percentage errors specific to the individual M5 model tree linear regression models are shown in Table 6.6. In addition to absolute percentage errors, the standard deviation is also indicative of a model's accuracy. For the purpose of determining the standard deviation of a M5 model tree output prediction, the standard deviation over all the training data is more reflective of the M5 system than just the standard deviation of the training cases reaching the particular leaf node used for the prediction. By M5 model tree construction, each of the training cases influence the structure of the final model tree.

Figure 6.8 plots the residuals for attributes used in the M5 model tree linear regression models, providing a visual confirmation that the residuals are randomly

Table 6.6 Mean absolute percentage errors of known instances per individual M5 model
tree linear model

	LM1	LM2	LM3	LM4	LM5	LM6	LM7
Mean percentage error	24	22	10	13	12	7	6
No. of instances	3	3	16	9	12	6	10

scattered (indicating that a linear fit is suitable) for all attributes except for the
rank in class. The residuals for the rank in class attribute indicate more accurate
predictions the higher the ship's rank in class. This indicates that a linear fit may
not be the most suitable. Typically the construction of lower-ranked ships of the
same class benefit from labor learning curves and economies of scale. Learning
curves are nonlinear, taking the general form of $C_r = a \cdot r^b$, where C_r is the cost of
unit (of rank) r, and a and b are fitted parameters (see Goldberg and Touw (2003)
for more information). Nonlinear regression may be more suitable to model the
relationship of ship cost to the rank in class attribute, however this is outside the
capabilities of the M5 model tree algorithm.

The results presented in Table 6.4 show that linear regression model LM5 contributes the greatest to the standard deviation. LM5 models the nine highest costing
ships. Figure 6.7 reveals that in eight of these cases, LM5 underestimates the actual
cost. By the piecewise linear M5 model tree construction, LM5 is influenced by
the adjacent linear regression models LM4 and LM6. To evaluate the degree of
this influence, a separate multiple linear regression model was fitted to the ships
reaching the LM5 leaf using the same five ship attributes as LM5. The resulting
CER is as follows:

$$\text{Log}_{10}(\text{Cost}) = 8.6376 - 0.0651 \times \text{rank in class}$$
$$+0.0637 \times \text{number of LCAC}, \tag{6.12}$$

with an R value of 0.95 ($R^2 = 0.90$), and mean absolute percentage error of 7
percent. This result indicates that it is indeed possible to derive better models
for subsets of the data. This does not depreciate the M5 model tree algorithm,
whose strength is its optimization in predicting unknown cases (rather than simply
memorizing the known). Using the linear regression model of Equation (6.12) in
place of LM5 would leave adjacent linear models LM4, LM5, and LM6 sharply
discontinuous. The M5 system applies a smoothing process to construct piecewise
linear regression models. Experiments by Wang and Witten (1997) show that this
smoothing substantially increases the accuracy of predictions of unseen cases. The
M5 system smoothing process may be a reason for the underestimation of the most
expensive ships. When the smoothing procedure is disabled, the same model
tree depicted in Figure 6.6 is generated, but the linear regression models
differ.

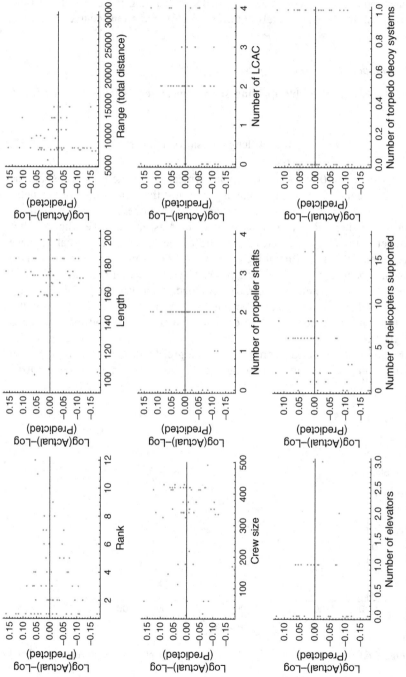

Figure 6.8 Plots of residuals for attributes used in the M5 model tree linear regression models.

Figure 6.9 plots the actual ship costs versus the costs predicted by the M5 model tree when the smoothing procedure is disabled. The R value is 0.985 ($R^2 = 0.97$). The unsmoothed M5 model tree does better in learning the costs of the most expensive known ships, but likely at the expense of prediction accuracy of unseen cases.

6.4.3   Comparison to linear regression models

The best CER returned by applying simple linear regression on the SAS-076 dataset is

$$Log_{10}(Cost) = 6.94 + 0.01 \times \text{length of ship (in meters)}, \tag{6.13}$$

with an R value of 0.75 ($R^2 = 0.56$). One typically tests the hypothesis that the linear regression fit is a better fit than fitting to just the mean length of the ships. Define the total variation to be the variance when a model is fit to just the mean length of the ships. Residual variation is defined as the variance when the linear model is fit. The F-statistic is the ratio of the model and residual variance and represents the proportional increase in error of fitting a mean model versus the linear model. The p-value is the probability of rejecting the null hypothesis that the linear fit is equal to the mean fit alone, when it is in fact true. A significant p-value (e.g. less than 5 percent) implies that the linear fit is a better fit than the mean alone. In this case the F-statistic is 74.2 and the p-value is 6.7×10^{-12}.

Applying multiple linear regressions with a greedy attribute selection method (step through the attributes removing the one with the smallest standardized

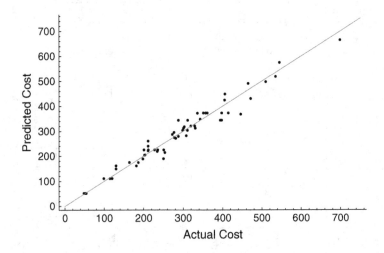

Figure 6.9 Unsmoothed M5 model tree: correlation plot of actual versus predicted ship costs.

coefficient until no improvement is observed in the estimate of the error given by the Akaike (1980) information criterion), yields the CER

$$
\begin{aligned}
\text{Log}_{10}(\text{cost}) = 5.7184 &- 0.0229 \times \text{ rank in class} \\
&+ 0.0125 \times \text{ length (in meters)} \\
&+ 0.0329 \times \text{ beam (in meters)} \\
&+ 0.1073 \times \text{ draught (in meters)} \\
&- 0.0001 \times \text{ full load displacement (in tonnes)} \\
&+ 0.0011 \times \text{ crew size} \\
&- 0.0830 \times \text{ number of propeller shafts} \\
&- 0.0223 \times \text{ number of guns of calibre } \geq 75,
\end{aligned} \tag{6.14}
$$

with an R value of 0.91 ($R^2 = 0.83$). Table 6.7 lists the F-statistics and p-values associated with each of the model attributes. The rank in class and number of propeller shaft attributes have a p-value near 10 percent, indicating that the fitted linear model should not be claimed to be a better fit than just using the mean values for these two attributes.

While the CER produced by applying simple linear regression is straightforward to understand, the negative coefficient signs of the multiple linear regression CER makes its interpretation non-trivial.

6.5 Discussion

Figure 6.4 shows that the analogy method using hierarchical clustering based on a weighted distance metric underestimates the cost of seven of the eight most expensive ships. This was also a characteristic of the parametric estimation presented in the preceding section. In the latter it was conjectured that the underestimation was likely a result of the smoothing and pruning functions of the M5 model tree algorithm, designed to optimize the predictive capability of the method. However, the underestimation of expensive ships in both methods is potentially an indication that the attributes (and their values) of the SAS-076 ship dataset do

Table 6.7 Multiple linear regression F-statistics and p-values

Attribute	F-statistic	p-value
Rank in class	2.7	1.0×10^{-01}
Length	169.6	1.1×10^{-17}
Beam	9.9	2.8×10^{-03}
Draught	6.3	1.5×10^{-02}
Full load displacement	43.7	2.5×10^{-08}
Crew size	15.0	3.1×10^{-04}
Number of propeller shafts	2.6	1.1×10^{-01}
Number of guns of calibre ≥ 75	4.5	4.0×10^{-02}

Table 6.8 Comparison of the M5 model tree and hierarchical clustering methods

	M5 model tree	Hierarchical clustering
Coefficient of correlation	0.96	0.93
Coefficient of determination	0.93	0.86
Mean absolute percentage error	11	16
Ability to learn known cases	✓	✓
Optimized to predict unknown cases	✓	×
Uses entire dataset	✓	×

not provide enough information to help distinguish the highest costing ships from their peers.

Multiple cost estimations are a good thing, especially during early design and developmental phases of a system. Multiple *independent* cost estimates are ideal, and strongly endorsed as best practice (see NATO RTO SAS-054 Task Group (2007) report). The two machine learning approaches described in this chapter are independent of each other; however, given their reliance on a common source of data (in this instance) the independence of the cost estimates they produce can be argued. Given multiple estimates, decision-makers must exercise sound judgment to assess and select a final figure. Properties of the machine learning methods discussed can provide guidance:

- The M5 model tree algorithms are optimized both to learn known cases and predict unknown cases. The attribute weights used in the hierarchical clustering method are optimized to learn the known cases.
- The hierarchical clustering approach uses PCA to reduce the dimensionality of the attribute space. Due to computational limitations, the weight optimization method could only be applied on the top ten macro-attributes, accounting for 80 percent of the original dataset's variability. In comparison, the M5 model tree algorithm is computationally superior as it efficiently learns from large datasets.
- The M5 model tree results in a better correlation measure, lower mean absolute percentage error, and smaller standard deviation in estimating the known cases.

Table 6.8 synthesizes the predictions and compares properties of the M5 model tree and hierarchical clustering methods.

Given this information, decision-makers could be advised that estimates generated by the M5 model tree should be considered to be the primary estimates and the hierarchical clustering estimates as secondary estimates.

6.6 Conclusion

Two novel approaches to cost estimation using machine learning algorithms are demonstrated. Both approaches incorporate a multitude of cost-driving factors and allow for a greater variability in the input dataset—variability that could be curtailed when using traditional approaches. As with other parametric and analogy approaches, the fidelity of the estimation models are very dependent the dataset, especially if the size of the dataset is small. Both are "top down" approaches applicable in early design phases of the procurement cycle.

As an analogy costing approach, hierarchical agglomerative cluster analysis, principal component analysis, and nonlinear optimization were used to calculate a matrix of distances among the systems of a dataset. These distances can then be used to predict the cost of new systems.

The parametric approach combined features of decision trees with linear regression models to both classify similar systems (based on attributes) and build piecewise multivariate linear regression models. The attributes of a new system can then be used to trace down the tree and as input to the resulting regression models which output a cost prediction.

Acknowledgements

Portions of this chapter reproduce work originally presented in the NATO RTO SAS-076 Task Group (2012) report, Journal of Cost Analysis and Parametrics article by Kaluzny *et al.* (2011), and Defence Research and Development Canada report by Kaluzny and Shaw (2011). The author is indebted to Sorin Barbici, Göran Berg, Renzo Chiomento, Dimitrios Derpanis, Ulf Jonsson, R.H.A. David Shaw, Marcel Smit, and Franck Ramaroson for their contributions.

Notes

1 See www.iceaaaonline.org [last accessed November 20, 2014].
2 The linear models are also tested to see if eliminating a set of attributes reduces the estimated error (a measure of accuracy of the model on unseen cases).
3 Data mining software in Java, available at www.cs.waikato.ac.nz/ml/weka/ [last accessed November 20, 2014].
4 The program's default parameters for the M5 model tree algorithm were used.

References

Akaike, H. 1980. "Likelihood and the Bayes Procedure." *Trabajos de Estadística y de Investigaciín Operativa* 31: 143–166.
Chen, Z. 2006. *Reduced-Parameter Modeling for Cost Estimation Models*. PhD thesis, Faculty of the Graduate School, University of Southern California.
Dobra, A. 2002. "Secret: A Scalable Linear Regression Tree Algorithm." In *Proceedings of the Eighth ACM SIGKDD International Conference on Knowledge Discovery and Data Mining*. New York: ACM Press, pp. 481–487.
Flynn, B. and Garvey, P. 2011. "Weapon Systems Acquisition Reform Act (WSARA) and the Enhanced Scenario-Based Method (ESBM) for Cost Risk Analysis." In *Proceedings of 44th Annual Department of Defense Cost Analysis Symposium Williamsburg, Virginia*.
Goldberg, M. and Touw, A. 2003. *Statistical Methods for Learning Curves and Cost Analysis*. Topics in Operations Research Series. Linthicum MD, USA: Institute for Operational Research and Management Sciences.

Jolliffe, I. 2002. *Principal Component Analysis*. New York: Springer.

Kaluzny, B., Barbici, S., Berg, G., Chiomento, R., Derpanis, D., Jonsson, U., Shaw, R., Smit, M., and Ramaroson, F. 2011. "An Application of Data Mining Algorithms for Shipbuilding Cost Estimation." *Journal of Cost Analysis and Parametrics* 4: 2–30.

Kaluzny, B. and Shaw, R. 2011. *A Parametric Approach to Cost Estimation During Options Analysis*. Technical Memorandum DRDC CORA TM 2011-069, Defence Research and Development Canada.

Malerba, D., Esposito, F., Ceci, M., and Appice, A. 2004. "Top-Down Induction of Model Trees with Regression and Splitting Nodes." *IEEE Transactions on Pattern Analysis and Machine Intelligence* 26(5): 612–625.

Miroyannis, A. 2006. *Estimation of Ship Construction Costs*. PhD thesis, Department of Mechanical Engineering, Massachusetts Institute of Technology.

NATO RTO SAS-054 Task Group 2007. *Methods and Models for Life Cycle Costing*. Technical Report RTO-TR-SAS-054, NATO Research & Technology Organization.

NATO RTO SAS-076 Task Group 2012. NATO *Independent Cost Estimating and the Role of Life Cycle Cost Analysis in Managing the Defence Enterprise*. Technical Report NATO RTO-TR-SAS-076 AC/323)SAS-076)TP/420, NATO Research & Technology Organization.

Quinlan, J. 1992. "Learning with Continuous Classes." In *Proceedings AI'92*, edited by A. Adams and L. Sterling. Singapore: World Scientific, pp. 343–348.

Ryan, T. 1997. *Modern Regression Methods* (2nd edition). New York: John Wiley & Sons, Inc.

Sharma, N. and Litoriya, R. 2012. "Incorporating Data Mining Techniques on Software Cost Estimation: Validation and Improvement." *International Journal of Emerging Technology and Advanced Engineering* 2(3): 301–309.

Torgo, L. 2000. *Inductive Learning of Tree-based Regression Models*. PhD thesis, Universidade do Porto.

Torgo, L. 2002. "Computationally Efficient Linear Regression Trees." In *Proceedings of International Federation of Classification Societies (IFCS) 2002: Classification, Clustering and Data Analysis: Recent Advances and Applications*.

Wang, Y. and Witten, I. 1997. "Inducing Model Trees for Continuous Classes." In *Proceeding of the 9th European Conference on Machine Learning Poster Papers*, pp. 128–137.

Witten, I. and Frank, E. 2005. *Data Mining: Practical Machine Learning Tools and Techniques* (2nd edition). Massachusetts: Morgan Kaufmann.

7 Facing future funding realities
Forecasting budgets beyond the future year defense plan

Ross Fetterly and Binyam Solomon[1]

7.1 Introduction

Introducing future funding realities is a critical component of any military cost–benefit analysis (CBA). Building a national defense force for future generations, planning missions that will be assigned to military forces in the coming decades, developing a capital equipment program to meet anticipated future operational requirements, and building the infrastructure and logistics system to support them are by their very nature long-term tasks. It is significant, therefore, that in defense departments around the world one of the biggest challenges is to plan defense budgets over the medium to long-term.[2] Indeed, "despite ferociously complex planning processes, coherence between strategic guidance, capability development and the budget remains elusive" (Thompson 2007, 3).

Forecasting future funding envelopes for defense programs is a daunting task. The challenge of allocating defense budgets among labor (military and civilian personnel) and capital (weapon systems, platforms and infrastructure) inputs is further complicated by three additional factors. First, the long-term planning horizon necessary in defense is in stark contrast to the relatively short-term planning outlook of most national governments, a consequence of the four to five year election cycles that exist in most modern democracies. Second, defense directly competes for discretionary funding with publicly popular programs such as healthcare and infrastructure spending. Third, defense faces external shocks in the form of dramatic changes in the international strategic environment, such as the end of the cold war in 1989, and the rise of multiple inter-state and intra-state conflicts throughout the world after September 11, 2001. Although some of these problems were anticipated by analysts, it is still difficult to predict the scale, scope and impact of those changes (Dorff 2005).

Given these challenges, no one strategic management approach or forecasting model can provide a completely robust framework for all nations that face different external threats, economic growth trajectories, and mutual defense alliances. One key element required to enhance defense resources management is the development of a more comprehensive approach to forecast and manage budgets within defense departments.

In this chapter three forecasting approaches and two management strategies are presented to help develop future funding lines (i.e. budget envelopes) for defense investments. The development of funding lines would allow defense planners to conduct more rigorous cost–benefit and tradeoff analyses using reasonable proxies of future budget constraints. While most multi-year planning exercises tend to be fiscally informed, future cost constraints are often not anchored by a reasonable approximation of a funding line.

The risk is that a capability acquired in the absence of careful budget estimates may impact other programs if funds are "borrowed" from those programs to fund the new program that exceeded the actual funding constraint. Alternatively, unanticipated budget cuts can seriously impact program performance sacrificed to accommodate the smaller budget.

Recognizing these challenges, a United States Government Accountability Office (GAO) report on cost growth in US defense acquisition stated, "the goal is to get a better match between budgeted funds and costs in order that the true impact of investment decisions is known" (GAO 2005). The major finding of a Center for Strategic and International Studies (CSIS) study adds that "resource constraints require a more integrated approach in defense" (CSIS 2005).

The rest of the chapter is structured as follows. The first section presents stylized facts about defense and fiscal frameworks. The second section examines management of the defense budget while the third section discusses defense cost drivers. The fourth section introduces various forecasting models and contrasts their uses to the challenges of optimal defense resources management. The last section concludes the chapter and highlights some future directions for research in forecasting defense budgets beyond the future year defense plan (FYDP).[3]

7.2   Defense and the economy: stylized facts

The development of a defense budget is a complex and time-consuming process. The results of this process are influenced by the dynamics of the political process, various organizations within the defense establishment, government officials, and the external environment. Each of these diverse groups has differing objectives (incentives) and responsibilities (see Chapter 3 for example). For the central government the challenge is to allocate tax revenues among competing demands.

For most NATO member nations, the standard of living of their citizens has grown significantly in the last three decades. As shown in Table 7.1, most of these nations displayed real (inflation-adjusted) GDP per capita growth of about 23 percent during the 1980s and 1990s and a more moderate rate of growth of about 13 percent during the 2000s. The next half decade to 2015 is forecasted to moderate even further to 9 percent. This moderation in the standard of living further complicates the central government's budget allocation process.

A nation's standard of living can be improved by increasing the labor participation rate of its citizens (demographics), the level of effort (hours worked), and/or productivity. The former two have natural limits in the form of demographics, immigration absorption and available hours of work. Productivity can be improved by increasing

Table 7.1 Real GDP per capita growth for selected NATO members

Country	1980s %	1990 %	2000s %	2010–15 %
Belgium	19.3	21.4	7.8	7.0
Canada	16.0	18.9	8.2	6.0
Czech Republic	n.a.	n.a.	30.0	16.0
Denmark	20.7	22.2	4.1	9.0
France	18.8	15.7	5.5	7.3
Germany	20.3	17.0	9.2	9.8
Greece	1.9	16.0	23.3	4.9
Italy	23.5	15.3	−2.8	3.2
Luxembourg	46.5	36.3	15.2	6.5
Netherlands	16.9	24.2	9.6	8.6
Norway	21.5	31.2	7.6	6.3
Portugal	35.8	28.6	2.1	3.3
Slovak Republic	n.a.	n.a.	48.8	20.9
Slovenia	n.a.	n.a.	26.1	13.5
Spain	25.9	25.4	7.1	7.6
United Kingdom	26.0	22.6	9.1	8.4
United States	23.0	21.7	7.1	8.7

Source: IMF (various years) World Economic Outlook.
n.a. = not applicable.

capital intensity and through innovation. These require investment in infrastructure, research and education. Meanwhile, increased demand for social programs by an aging population constrains budget resources available for defense.

Table 7.2 presents annual government fiscal positions as a proportion of income (GDP). The 2008 financial crisis has significantly eroded government finances. The selected NATO member nations with the exception of Norway are expected to face budgetary shortfalls at least until 2015. While stimulus spending and bailout packages to combat the financial crisis contributed to the worsening fiscal balance, automatic stabilizers such as transfer payments that automatically kick in during economic downturns (e.g. unemployment insurance, food stamps, income supplements and other services for the poor) further deplete tax revenues.

Competition for shrinking government funding can have large impacts on discretionary items such as national defense budgets. A powerful example of this comes from the Canadian experience of the 1990s. A newly elected Liberal government began its mandate in 1993 saddled with an inherited CAN$40 billion (and rising) public debt, which accounted for 70 percent of GDP by 1995 (combined public sector debt was close to 100 percent). In addition to the usual strategies of raising taxes and cutting and re-engineering transfer payments, the new government also formulated a new defense policy to reflect post-cold war realities (Stone and Solomon 2005).

As shown in Figure 7.1, both defense and non-defense spending were cut, albeit, at a different rate. Non-defense was cut by about 9 percent while defense absorbed a reduction between 24 percent (economy-wide inflation-adjusted) and 28 percent

Table 7.2 Government annual surplus/deficit per GDP

Country	2000	2010	2015
Belgium	−0.037	−4.784	−5.181
Canada	2.945	−4.933	−0.249
Czech Republic	−3.722	−5.411	−5.207
Denmark	1.804	−4.556	−1.09
France	−1.474	−8.002	−2.199
Germany	1.314	−4.496	−1.414
Greece	−3.692	−7.883	−1.956
Italy	−0.864	−5.111	−3.003
Luxembourg	5.968	−3.793	−0.711
Netherlands	1.972	−6.002	−4.055
Norway	15.374	11.14	11.756
Portugal	−1.093	−7.253	−5.818
Slovak Republic	−12.3	−8.018	−1.763
Slovenia	−1.235	−5.685	−0.829
Spain	−0.997	−9.272	−4.414
United Kingdom	1.345	−10.171	−2.417
United States	1.1	−11.085	−6.499

Source: IMF (various years) World Economic Outlook.

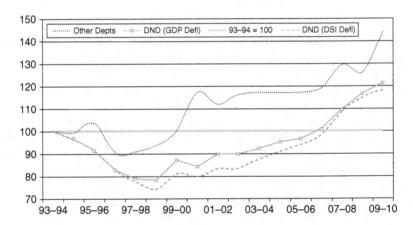

Figure 7.1 Trend in defense and non-defense spending: 93–94 = 100.

Source: Authors' calculations.

(defense-specific inflation). There is evidence that inflation inflicts considerable damage to the purchasing power of defense dollars (Solomon 2003; Kirkpatrick 2004). Defense inflation is discussed in some detail in subsequent sections.

By the end of 1997–98, the Government of Canada managed to balance the books and non-defense spending resumed its original growth path beginning in 1999. Defense spending, on the other hand, only reached its pre-reduction levels in 2007, about eight years later. The main point to take away from this Canadian example is that a country's budgetary constraints affects the level of funding available for defense, and defense tends to absorb a disproportionately large share of the cuts. Since defense often accounts for a large share of the discretionary budget, this is to be expected. Figure 7.2 shows how the recent financial crisis has forced the Government of Canada to revise its 20-year defense projections by CAN$1 billion beginning in 2013. Similarly in the United States, the US GAO long-term simulations show that "absent policy changes the federal government faces an unsustainable growth in debt" (GAO 2010).

In the US and elsewhere, the growing cost in non-discretionary (mandatory) budget items as a percentage of total government spending (medical care, social security, and other payments in economies with aging populations) is irrevocably changing the dynamics of federal budgets. Certainly, federal programs based on entitlements are relatively inflexible in the short-term and difficult to change politically. The implication for defense is that governments will be increasingly constrained in the way they fund defense budgets in response to conflicts or shifts in the international strategic environment, largely due to the increasing proportion of social welfare programs in the budget. Consequently, restoring a more equitable overall balance between revenues and expenses, as well as controlling cost growth in social welfare and defense programs, will be critical to a long-term fiscal policy capable of funding essential national security programs. The challenge for most Western governments is to achieve long-term sustainable defense funding in an environment where fiscal policy is likely to be "tightened sharply over the next several years" (World Bank 2010).

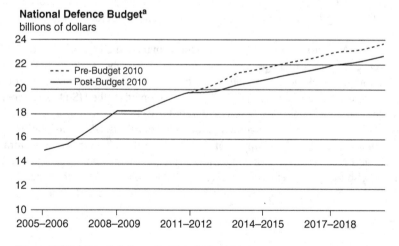

Figure 7.2 Projected defense funding, budget 2010.

Source: Department of Finance-DoF (2010).

Note

a Excludes incremental funding for deployed operations in Afghanistan and in support of the 2010 Olympics.

Senior finance department officials over the coming decade will find that national budgetary deficits have become to some degree structural in nature, and as a result will have a substantial continuing negative impact on the fiscal framework. The challenge, therefore, is to adjust and shape spending practices in defense to accommodate a medium-term environment of anticipated budgetary constraints. As a consequence, affordability needs to be brought up alongside operational performance as the principal criteria under which all defense programs will be assessed. In response to this multi-faceted and complex challenge, a broad-based and integrated response by defense departments is required.

7.3 Defense resources management

The defense sector has a number of very distinctive characteristics. Indeed, the relationship between factor inputs and outputs in the military production function is very specific. The inputs into the production function that produces "defense capability" include capital, labor and technology—which provide the personnel, infrastructure and equipment for national defense forces. From an economics perspective, the goal is to find the optimal mix of these inputs that maximizes national security subject to future funding constraints (see Chapter 3).

A distinguishing characteristic of defense budgets is that although flexibility in the current year may be minimal, current decisions on specific programs can have a significant impact on future year budgets. Therefore, today's budget decisions have a crucial long-term impact on the production of defense output. The long-term challenge is to manage over-programming (GAO 1994) in-year, while simultaneously dealing with systematic fiscal optimism in defense planning (Jordan 2000), and addressing a multitude of unanticipated in-year events: all while managing a capital program that extends several decades into the future.

Various NATO governments have introduced management strategies to tackle the defense resources management challenge described above. Some have introduced strategic-level and comprehensive approach such as the Planning, Programming, Budgeting and Execution (PPBE) process adopted by the US Department of Defense (DoD) and capability based planning (CBP) in Australia, Canada and the United Kingdom. These management strategies are discussed extensively in the literature and also in other chapters of this book. In this chapter, we concentrate on CBP and other short-term management strategies as they are being applied in Canada, with the goal of extracting more general lessons for other countries faced with similar challenges of forecasting future defense budget constraints.

7.3.1 Business planning

The need for a comprehensive long-term resources management strategy stems from the fact that governments do not explicitly incorporate the temporal asymmetry between defense, the holder of the largest discretionary budget and capital outlays, and other departments that deal with transfer payments and recurring operations. Thus in times of fiscal constraints, the temptation is to delay capital acquisition, and cut equipment maintenance funding and life-cycle maintenance of infrastructure to provide short-term financial relief to national governments. However, in the long-term, dramatic swings in defense funding can increase the cost of defense investments and result in sub-optimal allocation of scarce defense resources. Moreover, long-term budgetary planning is even more essential in defense "because of the lengthy lead times required to field new weaponry and force structure" (Jones and McCaffery 2005). In addition, effective management of defense budgets is complicated by the fast paced and changing international security environment, dominated by asymmetric threats.

The reality of simultaneously maintaining aging equipment, supporting new equipment, adapting to a transforming military force, and coping with shifting activities and activity levels compounds budgetary forecasting difficulties. The most effective approach to mitigate these issues is to develop an institutional level and in-depth knowledge and understanding of defense costs, as well as the establishment of a prioritized capability plan. Armed with this knowledge, politicians and defense decision-makers can develop a long-term affordable plan to manage and efficiently allocate resources to maximize national security.

7.3.2 Capability based planning

Using Canada as a case study, the central government decision-making process can be illustrated as follows. The federal government's policies and priorities are often communicated, in broad terms, through the Speech from the Throne. Allocating specific funds through the Federal Budget (often announced a few months after the Speech) operationalizes specific priorities outlined in the Speech. While the Speech gives the general short-term direction of the federal government, policy statements and White Papers provide more precise expectations and directions of the central government to specific departments or policy areas. The 2005 Defence Policy Statement (DPS) and 2008 Canada First Defence Strategy (CFDS) are examples of such direction, and a specific guide for defense spending.

CBP greatly enhances the information available to decision-makers and was developed with minimal changes in the financial reporting mechanism. CBP provides the tools through which the Defence Services Program can be linked to government policy and expectations (Chouinard and Wood 2007). CBP is employed through a process that creates scenario specific force-wide capability goals.

From an economics perspective, this process is a high-level constrained optimization whose objective is to select a mix of capabilities that achieves the optimal allocation of resources (maximize national security subject to fiscal constraints). CBP also explicitly encourages output-based planning by linking capability decisions to high-level strategic goals. By focusing on forecasted requirements for future capabilities to achieve the nation's strategic goals, decisions to upgrade existing systems or invest in new systems critically depend on how these investments are likely to impact future capabilities and strategic goals.

CBP consists of three interrelated steps. The first step assesses the future security environment. Step 2 deals with the linkage of the "concept of operations" to the capability framework and to validate the planning process. In Step 3, an operations research technique is applied to create a priority list of relevant activities for the given force development scenario (Department of National Defence (DND) 2008). In general, CBP assists senior managers to establish pan-Canadian Forces priorities within the budget, and to shift resources among defense programs—and across the military services—from less to more productive uses in response to changes in the future security environment. Another economic interpretation of the CBP is linking the future security environment and the policy intentions of political leaders to decisions on force structure, readiness, and modernization. This problem is equivalent to choosing a point on a "production possibility frontier" that represents intertemporal tradeoffs between "consumption" (current readiness) and "investment" (modernization or future readiness). In fact, the resources allocation challenge of the DND is a subset of the Government of Canada's own challenge of funding its policies and programs within available fiscal resources (Solomon et al. 2008).

CBP provides a clear linkage between military outputs and defense policy outcomes that policy and decision-makers can use. However, CBP does not answer the question of cost efficiency since there is no mechanism for ensuring genuine competition among the various service providers or appropriate incentives for minimizing costs. Certainly the right incentives in the form of gain-sharing (a portion of savings given as a reward for minimizing costs) may induce culture change in a public sector faster than resource budgeting (Melese 1997).

7.3.3 Lessons from capability based planning

CBP is now gradually starting to become a significant focus for planning staff at national defense headquarters in Western nations. This also includes increasing the effectiveness in the management of capital equipment life-cycle operations and support costs (GAO 2010). This shift in emphasis towards a more integrated approach to defense management requires increased involvement by leaders in defense headquarters in the financial management of defense resources. Furthermore, senior management need more comprehensive cost information when making resource allocation decisions. This, in turn, alters and challenges the manner in which the various staffs prepare senior defense officials for internal decision-making forums.

This shift in emphasis can be categorized as conceptual, structural and financial in nature. In essence, these developments are related to changes in how defense departments decide to purchase new capital equipment, what they purchase, and how departmental procurement organizations manage the acquisition process. In order to support the development of a management framework that itself supports a departmental investment plan that clearly responds to the direction provided in government policy, the following mechanisms are suggested:

- A long-term cost model that integrates procurement, as well as operating and personnel costs. Such a model can support the estimation and analysis of the affordability of future plans. In addition, structural changes are needed within defense procurement organizations to consolidate the management and oversight of many of the large complex capital projects under one organization.

- Enhanced Comptrollership and financial management within defense departments. The unique role and activities of defense departments within national government financial structures can be a challenge if defense is restricted to only utilize the government's standard financial reporting and management processes.
- A greater degree of integration of financial information within strategic levels of defense decision-making. This allows common linkages for conceptual, structural and financial changes needed within defense headquarters. This strengthening of defense administration processes also needs to extend beyond defense departments.
- A foundation that incorporates departmental priorities with fiscal realities through the alignment of financial resources with anticipated future requirements (DND 2007). This can be achieved through a range of assumptions in which funding gaps are identified. This planning process articulates previous decisions, as well as the funding available in the fiscal framework to support future requirements. The foundation is elaborated by a framework that provides a series of financial envelopes for the primary defense cost drivers. This includes personnel costs for military and departmental civilians, capital equipment acquisition, as well as operations and maintenance (O&M) costs. Estimate resource requirements with the explicit understanding that conventional analysis would likely understate Defense Department projections of future funding needs. The approach by the Congressional Budget Office of including unbudgeted costs (CBO 2010) in projecting defense resource requirements is an effective planning benchmark.
- Inclusion of medium-term transformation and modernization costs that incorporates the many new capabilities that will be introduced over the medium term (say next ten years), and retirements of obsolete older systems. As a planning document, it can be expected that funding is likely to be reallocated between financial envelopes as plans are further defined.

7.3.4 Absorption rate

Forecasting a likely funding line into the future, and building a capability portfolio constrained by this budget envelope, is only one element of a comprehensive strategy of managing cost growth. The other key element is absorption rate, or the demand for defense services.

An era of high operational tempo and demand for Western military forces began in the early 1990s and has continued through the present. The paradox is that the initial period in the post-cold war era brought a protracted series of substantial budget cuts to defense at the same time that there was increasing demand for peacekeeping and peace making operations. Despite a subsequent decade of budget increases to reflect this increased demand for defense services, the result is continuing pressures on resources and capabilities.

To manage the budget reductions during the 1990s, while maintaining the maximum level possible of military capability, the capital equipment budget and personnel (military and departmental civilians) were reduced dramatically, numerous bases were closed, and other major expenditures such as infrastructure repairs and maintenance were deferred. Substantial re-investment in defense by Western nations since September 11, 2001 strained the capacity of defense departments to absorb and spend resources effectively. Whereas cuts to defense capability can be made rapidly, rebuilding capability can take a number of years to regain the experience and expertise needed to operate effectively.

The nature of defense activities is such that defense departments are prime candidates to employ multi-year strategies that over the long-term could be a more optimal use of government funding than is currently the case. The unprecedented deployment rate of military personnel in coalition operations overseas will likely continue in response to the current international strategic environment, although perhaps at a more sustainable rate in the future.

Any supplemental funding made available to defense at the end of a fiscal year must go to capital, the operating budget or personnel. The ability to absorb incremental funding on personnel is small due to lengthy hiring and recruiting processes. For capital investments, unless the projects are well advanced and ready for contract, the absorption rate is low to medium. The critical mechanism for absorbing any supplemental funding is in maintenance O&M activities. The "absorption rate", or ability to spend any uncommitted or new incremental funding, can be increased to the extent that a strategic planning process is in place to identify and evaluate valuable capabilities and projects and to have them ready for contracts as soon as funding comes available. The ability of defense systems to reveal funding pressures in maintenance O&M activities, as well as to ensure capital projects are in a position to be funded, are essential strategies to anticipate opportunities for supplemental funding and to ensure value for money.

The wide range of cost drivers in defense ranging from personnel costs, activity rates and major equipment acquisition programs all contribute to demands on the defense budget. Managing within a fixed funding allocation from government, a significant possibility exists that considerable funds could lapse unexpended at the end of the fiscal year. Uncontrollable events, slippage and delays in approvals lead to unexpended funds that lapse at year-end.

Applying a Structural Unexpended Rate (SUR) as an over-programming mechanism to manage expected in-year under-expenditure is a strategy defense planners use through a balanced blend of risk management, spending controls and resources management. The objective of applying over-programming at the SUR is to plan early in the year to spend the entire defense budget incorporating over-programming (called the planning level), rather than strictly managing to the spending authority level. Implementing this over-programming mechanism reduces the potential for lapsed funds at year-end and more importantly avoids a year-end spending rush while expending the funds wisely with due regard for economy and efficiency.

In effect, enabling defense departments to "plan to spend" upcoming in-year surpluses at the beginning of the fiscal year and paying down the SUR over-programming throughout the year increases the effectiveness of resource allocations. This is particularly true in cases where these funds are targeted to areas that can generate future savings—such as increasing preventative maintenance of infrastructure on defense installations, or increasing funding to the capital program to replace equipment fleets before maintenance costs becomes excessive.

Legislative requirements to fully spend funding allocations prior to the end of the fiscal year can be a powerful disincentive to effective resources management. Government authority to carry-forward a certain level of the defense budget to the next year could support more efficient and effective use of resources. In the current defense resource environment, even a modest carry-forward authority for senior resource managers will not provide the necessary flexibility to manage multi-year projects or realign multi-year spending.

7.4 Cost drivers

In the event that the above-mentioned strategic management approaches, particularly CBP, are not truly institutionalized, the benefits of optimal resource allocation will not be realized and the effectiveness of the armed forces risks being eroded along with its purchasing power. One fundamental resources management problem has come from high-level commitments by Western governments to overseas operations, with a concurrent reticence to make critical disinvestment decisions to relinquish capabilities and realign force structure based on these new commitments within fiscal constraints.

Indeed, with the economic downturn in late 2008, changed fiscal realities have moved the necessity to address a resources/capability gap to the near-term. Specifically, the baseline funding in many Western countries to achieve a stable capital equipment program and to sustain existing capabilities is likely insufficient at current funding levels. To be sure, the ability of national security establishments to "craft, implement, and adapt effective long-term strategies against intelligent adversaries at acceptable costs has been declining for some decades" (Krepinevich and Watts 2009). The present constraining factors on the defense budget are defense-specific inflation, increasing personnel numbers and associated costs, as well as aging equipment fleets and infrastructure. These factors increase pressure on the defense budget and have the potential to draw limited defense resources away from new defense programs. This challenge is amplified by the steady growth in the cost of maintaining advanced military forces.

7.4.1 Personnel

Defense establishments are first and foremost people-driven organizations. As a consequence, personnel costs in a defense budget are often both the most significant and the least flexible expenditure category. The cost of military personnel and departmental civilians has an overwhelming impact on other expenditure categories and drives much of the remaining defense spending.

Consequently, the preliminary and possibly most significant step in defense decision-making is the determination of the required number of military personnel. Forecasted Army, Navy, Air Force, and Marine Corps personnel, to a large extent, guide the force planning process. The requirement for military bases, quantities of military equipment, training facilities, as well as O&M expenses all flow from decisions regarding personnel strengths. Government costs for military personnel includes direct pay, environmental and operational allowances, and the employer share of programs such as pensions and unemployment insurance.

7.4.2   Capital

The acquisition of capital equipment in defense is generally the most visible aspect of defense spending, because of the substantial annual allotment of taxpayer dollars and the expectations of industry to obtain contracts related to those planned expenditures. To maintain a viable and effective military capability, it is essential to have a well-conceived capital equipment replacement plan that is supported by a stable long-term financial commitment. And in order to develop a coherent and effective plan for the acquisition of new and modernized equipment there are always tradeoffs that must be made. Future tradeoffs include:

- number of personnel versus investment in high-technology equipment (capital/labor substitution);
- multi-purpose versus single purpose forces (i.e. specialized capabilities);
- regular force versus reserve force mix;
- the optimum balance between force elements (air, land, maritime and special forces).

In terms of goods and services procured and personnel employed, defense departments spend a large percentage of the overall federal operating budget and capital funds. This is significant because these categories of expenditure are highly visible, generate employment, and to a certain extent are discretionary; accordingly these expenditures are particularly vulnerable to spending cuts during budget crises.

7.4.3   Defense-specific inflation

Protection from the loss of purchasing power resulting from inflation in defense goods and services, and from required compensation increases for military and civilian personnel, are essential elements in forecasting future defense funding. However, given the specific nature of defense, the GDP deflator does not capture the anomalies of the "defense market" and is thus an inadequate measure of the inflation adjustment required to maintain stable defense purchasing power. The traditional defense perspective is that defense-specific goods and services experience greater price fluctuations during inflationary periods, which should be accommodated in both internal and external fiscal planning and budgetary considerations.

Defense-specific inflation is different for three reasons. First, the defense market is different from markets that produce civilian goods and services included in baskets underlying most aggregate measures of inflationary price changes. Second, imperfections in some segments of the defense market provide the potential for greater price fluctuations than prevail elsewhere in the economy. Finally, exchange rate fluctuations will have greater effect on defense, as defense is the direct final consumer, and as such is also susceptible to importing inflation, whereas in the economy as a whole, other factors tend to dampen the price level effects of exchange rate fluctuations[4] (Solomon 2003).

7.4.4 *International deployments*

Another potential cost driver is activities related to international deployments. Defense departments in NATO alliance nations all face a common set of financial pressures. The cost of ongoing overseas operations, investing in readiness, and intense investment in preparation for the future environment are creating significant internal budget pressures. To "succeed in this era of fiscal constraint, new ways of thinking, constructive change, and basic reforms are essential. Everything must be on the table and subject to scrutiny" (Dodaro 2010).

Increasing interoperability and specialization among NATO allies could assist in increasing alliance effectiveness and efficiency while lowering costs (Berkok 2005). Also, the growing involvement of non-governmental organizations (NGOs) and international organizations, as well as regional organizations in assisting failed and failing states since the end of the cold war has been significant and not always fully recognized. This has resulted in defense planning "becoming denationalized and far more plural" (Nelson 2001).

7.5 Modelling future defense budgets

Proper application of military CBA and CBP and other management strategies require an information management system that can attribute direct and indirect costs of military capabilities. Activity-based costing is one such approach. In the absence of such a system, hybrid systems can be used.

For example, Solomon *et al.* (2008) develop a strategic cost model by attributing expenditures in a given fiscal year to capabilities based on basic attribution rules. Thus, a typical intermediate output such as land training consists of assets such as a Land (Army) Warfare Centre, direct fire equipment such as tanks, artillery schools and common training. The civilian and military personnel that work in each of these organizations as well as their O&M costs make up the total cost of army training. These are linked to a number of final army outputs (capabilities) such as light infantry direct fire and brigade headquarters that use such training. The attribution of this training activity is based on the proportion of personnel each of the army capabilities will potentially use for the training. This proportion is based on the total cost of personnel in each of these final capabilities in the reference year (Solomon *et al.* 2008). Unfortunately, such information management systems and databases are not available in most nations and often decisions must be made in a data- and time-constrained environment. The modelling section presented below acknowledges these constraints.

Future defense budgets can be modelled using a variety of econometric techniques. The relevance and appropriateness of each model depends on the research question, data constraints and forecast horizon. The three econometric models used in this chapter are selected with the above mentioned goals and constraints in mind. We begin with the simplest model when data and governing theoretical frameworks are severely lacking.

7.5.1   Defense budget forecast model #1: an application of a univariate autoregressive integrated moving average (ARIMA) model

Univariate (single variable) ARIMA models which are based on the Box–Jenkins time series modelling process discussed in Appendix 7.1, describe a single series, such as defense expenditures over time, as a function of its own past values (Box and Jenkins 1970). As an illustration of the univariate ARIMA forecasting model we use time series data of Belgian military expenditures (ME) in real dollars. The data is extracted from the Stockholm International Peace Research Institute (SIPRI) and NATO databases.

The ARIMA modelling process starts with the identification of the time series and a differencing order of 1 was used to make the series mean stationary. The autocorrelation and partial auto-correlation (ACF and PACF) functions of the Belgian time series are calculated and shown in Appendix 7.1 (Figures A7.1 and A7.2). The initial identification seems to point to an autoregressive model of order 1. Currently, there are a number of statistical software packages that can automatically select models based on a series of diagnostic tests. One such software is Autobox (AFS 2000). As indicated in Appendix 7.1, Autobox is also one of the time series forecasting software packages that include automatic outlier detections. In fact the software package identified 1988 as a level shift and 1991 as transitory (pulse) shocks each of which is explicitly incorporated in the final forecasting model.

It is preferable if the modeller has a priori information on particular events that may affect the time series in question. For example, if there were any events or policy announcements in Belgium that might have affected defense expenditures, then these should be explicitly incorporated in the model. Of the two dates selected by the software, 1991 is consistent with Belgium's decision to reduce defense spending after the fall of the Soviet Union (Amara 2008).

The forecast horizons based on the univariate ARIMA models are presented in Figure 7.3. The first model uses the real Belgian defense expenditures without prior adjustments and the forecasts indicate almost flat growth (a small increase in the range of 0.7 percent to 0.5 percent) in real defense expenditures. The

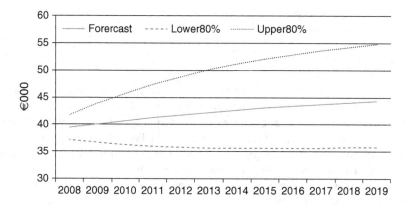

Figure 7.3 Belgian defense expenditures forecast based on an ARIMA model (000 euros).

model based on defense expenditures in logarithmic scale forecasts a more modest increase of about 1 percent in real terms for the next decade.

Stationarity (stationary time series with or without differencing) is an important aspect of the ARIMA class of models. This characteristic constrains the prediction of future values to be linear functions of the observations. Such a restriction, often a sufficient approximation of reality, does not cover every aspect of real life situations and thus a broader class of models should be entertained. The linearity assumption is somewhat relaxed when using a transformation of the original series as was done here for Belgian defense expenditures.

Unfortunately, forecasts based on univariate models cannot tell us whether growth is due to increases in the armed forces (people), or major weapon systems (capital). In addition, univariate models are not suitable for conducting simulation exercises on what effects changes in threat, income or government policies might have on overall defense budgets. For such broader simulation models with policy prescriptions we turn to a second set of models that rely on strong theoretical frameworks based on the neoclassical social welfare maximization models.

7.5.2 Defense budget forecast model #2: military demand models

Military demand models assume defense budgets are a result of the derived demand for national security, S. The most common theoretical specification for the demand for ME is based on the neoclassical model of welfare maximization (Smith 1989, 1995):

$$W = f(C, S, Z_n). \tag{7.1}$$

This standard welfare function includes economic variables such as consumption C and the population of a country,[5] as well as security S and other variables Z_n, which parameterize shifts in the welfare function, such as doctrinal changes or the politics of the party in power.

The limits on welfare maximization include the standard income constraint:

$$I = p_c C + p_m M \tag{7.2}$$

where I is aggregate income often proxied by GDP; M and C are real military expenditures and consumption, and the price for each are denoted by p_m and p_c respectively. Note that alternate welfare function specifications will use military and non-military expenditures and prices in the budget constraint model. For detailed discussions on the empirical estimation of demand for military spending models see Hartley and Sandler (1990) and Smith (1995).[6]

The other key constraint in the welfare maximization problem is the security function. Security can be represented as

$$S = f(M_1, \ldots, M_n, Z_s). \tag{7.3}$$

In a Nash–Cournot specification the ith country will take the military expenditures, M, of its $(n - 1)$ allies as given when establishing its own security needs. Note, however, that if other countries are hostile and pose a threat, this affects country i's national security posture.

In a Nash equilibrium, the first-order condition from maximizing Equation (7.1) subject to Equation (7.2) and (7.3) implies

$$S = f(I, p, Q, Z_n, Z_s) \tag{7.4}$$

Thus the security of a nation depends on its military forces and other countries' forces and other strategic variables that may affect the security environment.

Looking at the ME of other countries, allies' military expenditure may be seen as "spillin", thus

$$Q = M_{it} + \sum_{j=1}^{n} M_{jt} - M_{it}$$

where $i \neq j$. The resulting partial equilibrium determination of one country's forces, given those of the other nations, leads to the derived demand for ME, which defines military budget forecast model #2:

$$ME_t = \beta_0 + \beta_1(p_m/p_c) + \beta_2 I + \beta_3 Th + \beta_4 Q + \beta_5 Z + \varepsilon_t. \tag{7.5}$$

Recall that the ME of other nations elicit varied security postures depending on whether one is an ally or a threat. The reaction is captured as either Th (threat) or Q ("spillin"). Aspects that are unique to a nation, such as external conflict, new security policy or other exogenous effects are summarized as strategic variables (Z).

The empirical work on demand for military spending falls largely into two groups. The first group, popularized by the important work of Murdoch and Sandler (1982), supports a well-specified theoretical model that generates the military budget forecasting equation. The second group proposes an approach where the estimating equation is determined by the best fit to the data, based on rigorous statistical testing. Chowdhury (1991) is one example of the latter.

Recent studies have departed from these two groups in favor of a compromise strategy. This strategy, adopted in this chapter, starts with a model based on a general theory of the demand for military spending, followed by rigorous statistical testing to investigate the relative importance of strategic and other economic factors for the country(ies) under investigation. Smith (1989) and most recently Dunne *et al.* (2003) and Solomon (2005) employ such a strategy.[7]

For this application of model #2, we use Belgian and Canadian ME for the period 1955 to 2007 from SIPRI annual publications. To convert US and other NATO members' military spending data into constant dollars the IMF database was consulted. Note that the GDP deflator of each country was used. All figures are in US dollars. Belgium, Denmark, France, Germany, Italy, Luxembourg, Netherlands, Norway, and the United Kingdom were included in the NATO Europe sample. This variable (NATO_Europe) proxies the potential spill-ins from allied contribution. If the sign on this allied spill-in (Q) variable is negative, this suggests that the nation (Belgium or Canada) is a free rider. However, Canada and Belgium articulate their defense posture within the context of a multilateral security arrangement and thus a positive response to allies' ME is expected. To reflect the choices faced by decision-makers between socio-economic and security needs, government expenditures were obtained from the World Bank (removing ME from the aggregate). A negative association is theoretically predicted.

Various databases were consulted to identify potential enemies, militarized inter-state disputes and peacekeeping related expenditures and missions. Threat variables include USSR (sample period 1952–1990 and Russia for the period 1991–2006) on which data were obtained from the SIPRI (various years) year book, and Soviet/Russia Nuclear Equivalent Megatons and Intercontinental Ballistic Missiles (data from Jim Finan, Royal Military College, Canada). The latter was found to be a better proxy for the Soviet threat since the smaller NATO nations' primary concern was strategic capability and the potential nuclear fallout.

Data on foreign aid were obtained from the Organization for Economic Cooperation and Development (OECD). In addition various dummy variables were used to proxy various country-specific security policies. These were proxied according to the dates of the introduction or suspension of government documents that articulated the nations' security strategy. NATO doctrine changed from Mutual Assured Destruction (1952–1969 = 1, 0 elsewhere) to Flexible Response (1970–2001 = 1, 0 elsewhere; 1970 was used as the period of shift based on statistical properties) and was also used as a possible determinant of military spending.

Other standard variables from social welfare maximization, such as income (GDP) and the relative price between military and civilian good are anticipated to be significant and show positive and negative effects respectively. This is because defense is considered a normal good, and also reflects the tendency for governments to economize on military spending when it becomes relatively expensive. Note, however, that this variable is only estimated for Canada, for which military price data is readily available. In addition, public finance theory suggests that military spending may crowd out other government programs; as such, a significant and negative coefficient for non-military expenditures is anticipated.

Preliminary tests were conducted on the specification of the variables. Levels as opposed to shares of the variables were used, as these better explain the nature of the demand for ME (see also Hartley and Sandler 1995).[8] The estimated long-run coefficients for Belgium and Canada are presented in Table 7.3.

Examining results for Canada, country income, and US and European allies, both contribute positively to military spending. Surprisingly the threat from intercontinental nuclear attack is negative; this is discussed later in this section and turns out to be somewhat consistent with the theoretical prediction of the model. The price variable is not significant for Canada, indicating that rising military prices have little or no impact on government ME (resource allocation) decisions. On the other hand, the significance of the income variable for Canada suggests that income constraints have important long-run impacts.

The long-run coefficients for Belgium are mostly not significant, and only the threat variable proxied by nuclear arsenals was significant. This suggests that for Belgium, short-run effects tend to govern defense spending.

Table 7.4 presents the short-run effects through the error correction representation of the demand model;[9] see also Appendix 7.2.

It is important to point out that the short-term dynamics of the demand for military spending models in Canada are governed mostly by a complementary reaction to allied military spending, and budgetary inertia. The latter is evident for all the nations considered, and especially when observed from the perspective of peace support operations and defense procurement.

Peacekeeping and other military expeditionary operations, to be effective as a military response to the threat of international instability, are by necessity medium

Table 7.3 Long-run coefficients

	Constant	Income	Price	Spill-in	Policy	Threat
Belgium	8.6	−1.6	n.a.	−0.9	0.3**	0.11** NT
Canada	−5.7***	0.22***	0.49	1.23*** US 0.27**	n.a.	−0.13*** NICM

Notes
***1% significance level **5% and *10%; n.a. = not applicable; n.s. = not significant.
Sample period 1955–2007.
Policy = Defense policy changes (dummy variables); NICM = Nuclear Intercontinental Missile (USSR/Russia); NT = NICM plus surface; US = US Military Expenditures.

Table 7.4 Error correction representation

Variables	Belgium	Canada
ΔCONSTANT	1.28**	−2.14***
ΔME	0.85**	0.32***
$ΔME_{-1}$	n.a.	−0.30***
ΔQ	−0.14	0.45***
ΔQ(US)	n.a.	0.10**
$ΔTh_{(NTOT)}$	0.02**	n.a.
$ΔTh_{(NICM))}$	n.a.	0.02
$ΔTh_{(NICM))-1}$	n.a.	−0.071***
$ΔTh_{(NEX)}$	0.02**	n.a.
$ΔZ_{(policy)}$	0.02	n.a.
ΔPRICE	n.a.	0.18
ΔGDP	0.24	0.08***
$ΔZ_{(NONDEFENCE)}$	−0.21	n.a.
ECM_{-1}	−0.14**	−0.37***

Notes
Key: See Equation (7.5) for variable descriptions, and also Table 7.3.
* 10%, ** 5%, *** 1% significance.
Δ denotes the first difference of the variable; X_{-1} implies $X_{-1} - X_{-2}$.

to long-term propositions. Once commitments have been made by a nation to a coalition expeditionary mission, it is difficult to disengage. Similarly defense procurement is a lengthy process requiring several years to administer and deliver. Another unique aspect of this dynamic is Canada's short-term reaction to the USSR/Russia's strategic threat. While the change in the strategic threat is not significant for Canada, it is the lagged change effect that is negative and significant. This suggests that Canada reacted to the nuclear threat after engaging in other security changes not directly related to military spending (hardening targets, infrastructure spending, etc.).

Belgian short-run dynamics are governed by inertia and the proxies for threat (total nuclear arsenal and nuclear explosions). For the smaller allies, the USSR/Russia strategic assets (nuclear power) were the main concern. This is consistent with Hilton and Vu's (1991) assertion that non-nuclear allies in NATO may have perceived the Soviet threat beyond their capacity and thus tended to ignore it in their decision-making. The error correction factor of 0.14 indicates a moderate to long period adjustment to a shock. The general indication for Belgium is that other country-specific factors govern the demand for ME. (This also suggests that bureaucratic and political interpretation may provide important clues).

In general, models such as these based on the demand for ME can be used to simulate future budget scenarios by individually calibrating GDP (income) growth or changes in alliance posture or threat. As an example, Figure 7.4 shows a possible Canadian defense expenditures path given real GDP growth rate of 2 percent for the next 10 years, holding other variables at constant growth. This implies that defense will grow by about 0.44 percent in real terms given the elasticity estimate

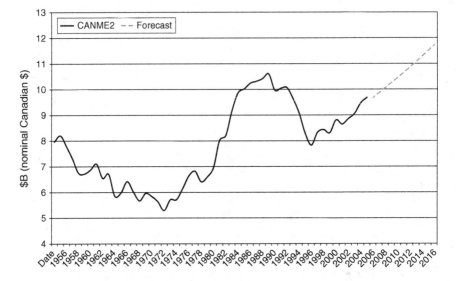

Figure 7.4 Canadian defense expenditures forecast based on constant GDP growth (2 percent).

of 0.22. Given the long-run estimate of GDP inflation at 1.5 percent, the forecast for nominal defense growth is around 1.9 percent.

7.5.3   Defense budget forecast model #3: Budget components based models

The preceding two models are based on strategic or macro-level assessments of ME. In this section, we offer a micro-level perspective that decomposes the ME data into the subcomponents that make up the defense budget. Broadly defined, these budget components (or defense appropriations categories) include people, capital and O&M costs. As shown in Table 7.5 each of these budgetary components are further divided to include type of personnel (military officers, conscripts, civilian and part-time soldiers), capital (equipment and infrastructure) and O&M attributed to people, equipment and infrastructure. Note that the variations in the primary inputs of labor and capital are due to technology and other cost drivers discussed earlier.

This is also the model we recommend when a strategic management system (such as CBP) is fully institutionalized, with an information management database linked to activity- and capability based costing as discussed in earlier sections. The model application again uses Canadian data. Following the budget identity equation in Treddenick (2000) for Canada, the defense budget can be disaggregated into several primary input variables including personnel (P), weapons (capital or equipment (E)), infrastructure (I), and O&M.

Table 7.5 Key variables to forecast or simulate

Personnel
    Military (officers and enlisted civilian)
    Reserve or other non-regular
    Inflation_Pay

Operations & maintenance
    People related
    Equipment
    Infrastructure
    Inflation_O&M

Capital
    Equipment
    Infrastructure
    Technology
    Procurement policy
    Defense inflation

Statutory and transfers
    Personnel related
    Other transfers

Exogenous
    Federal budgets
    Defense White Papers
    Other government initiatives

Grand total

Personnel costs can be further disaggregated into military and civilian personnel costs,

$$P_t = p_m P_{mil} + p_{ci} P_{civ} \tag{7.6}$$

where $(p_m P_{mil})$ is number of military personnel times the wage rate, and similarly civilian personnel costs are $(p_{ci} P_{civ})$. Equipment costs are represented as

$$E_t = (1 - \alpha e) E_{t-1} + E_{Ct} \tag{7.7}$$

and infrastructure costs as

$$I_{ft} = (1 - \beta w) I_{ft-1} + I_{Ft}, \tag{7.8}$$

where α and β are parameters.

While the above depicts possible weapons accumulation, with E_{Ct} depicting weapons expenditures, and I_{Ft} infrastructure expenditures, both at time t, it is possible to extend the mathematical formulation to include lagged adjustments to a desired/planned future stock.

In some nations, there are legal limits on the armed forces, in others where conscription has been replaced by voluntary forces, recruitment and retention requires careful calibration. In the Canadian case, the 2008 CFDS explicitly constrains the size of the personnel component to about 68,000 to 70,000 regular forces (enlisted and officers), 23,000 civilians, and about 30,000 reserves. Given an activity-based costing or an information management system that can be manipulated to calculate the cost of a military or civilian personnel, one can forecast future personnel-related costs.

The key cost drivers for personnel are inflation (both economy-wide and defense-specific), demography, and economic opportunities. The last two affect the available pool of recruits and/or retention of the most desired cohort. From the perspective of forecasting future defense budgets, the relevant question is the current strength of the armed forces and if this number is:

1   below the required goal, how long will it take to achieve the desired level given the attrition rates in basic training and regular attrition in the existing force?
2   above the required level, how would the reduction be achieved (e.g. to reduce recruitment until regular attrition reduces the number, or design an accelerated reduction program)?

In essence, the challenge is to estimate the growth/reduction in personnel until a steady state is achieved, and then use inflation rates to estimate future budgetary requirements for that steady state force. As mentioned in earlier sections, if one assumes defense-specific inflation, personnel component costs must be increasing faster than the civilian sector even after adjusting for productivity (quality) gains. Since measuring productivity is difficult in the government sector, the best inflation rate to use is the economy-wide inflation rate, and information from negotiated wage increases between public sector unions and the government.

For capital projects the assumption is that the defense department uses a strategic management technique that involves military CBA discussed elsewhere in this book, CBP or other management techniques. The key message from these management techniques is that the rationale for acquiring a platform or a weapon system is based on a clear need linked to defense policy or other relevant directive and the legal control of expenditures (Melese *et al.* 2004). Again, for forecasting purposes we assume that the list of capital programs for the forecast period are selected using such management techniques and the relevant forecast drivers are as follows.

• *National policies on procurement.* As discussed earlier, nations tend to leverage defense acquisitions to satisfy multiple objectives that are often mutually exclusive and unrelated to defense objectives. As indicated in Solomon *et al.* (2008), industries likely impose premiums to address government mandates like the Canadian Industrial Regional Benefit Program (IRB) that are estimated to be in the range of 13–22 percent.

- *Technology.* Kirkpatrick (1995) and Pugh (2007) offer excellent sources for the impact of technology on the cost of weapon systems. Specifically, Kirkpatrick (1995) has found that equipment costs have been rising by about 10 percent per year in real terms. Nations may want to customize the impact of technology by examining their own nation's trends in costs. Solomon (2009, Table 6.8) has found a rate of increase of about 6–7 percent for selected air force platforms in Canada.
- *Defense inflation.* For those nations that have estimates of defense inflation the forecasted increase in this inflation rate can be used, and for those nations that do not explicitly measure defense inflation, the GDP deflator is a good proxy. Note also that for forecasting purposes one can also use the mid-point of the inflation target used by the Central Bank. For example, if the Bank of Canada inflation target is currently in the range 1–3 percent, 1.5 percent can be used to project future inflation rates.

Finally, O&M costs can be forecast using projected inflation rates. Note that O&M expenditures depend on the number of personnel (P), infrastructure (I), and weapon stocks (E):[10]

$$OM_t = \delta_0 + p_{OM}I_f + p_{OM}E + p_{OM}(P_{mil} + P_{civ}). \qquad (7.9)$$

The model is applied to Canada. Baseline personnel numbers and expected capital acquisitions are taken from Canada's departmental plans and priorities (DND 2009). As shown earlier in Figure 7.2, the Federal Budget has reduced its own 20-year projection for defense, and this information is coupled with the fact that personnel numbers will hold steady.

Personnel-related costs are projected 20 years out (Figure 7.5). Projections for capital will depend on the ability of DND to re-scope and re-phase projects given the absorption challenges discussed previously. Specifically a report to Parliament indicated DND did not have the capacity to absorb the announced increases to its budget, and the result was a funding lapse of approximately $300 million (1.6 percent of the total budget; DND 2009). Projections on personnel, readiness, infrastructure and equipment are constrained by the CFDS 20-year funding ceiling but year to year growth is based on the 1.5 percent and then 2 percent increase expected by DND (DoF 2010). Figure 7.6 shows overall future funding projections for the defense budget by calibrating policy, technology and inflation projections.[11]

It should be reiterated that the funding line (budget envelope) projected here may or may not equal derived demand since the funding line will always be constrained by legislated personnel numbers, approved inflation funding, and force acquisition and elimination decisions based on CBP management decisions.

On the demand side the attribution rules generate, in input-output model parlance, technology coefficients that are updated annually. Long-term projections remain fixed on these updated technology coefficients. To the extent the modeller receives a priori information about a new in-service support arrangement

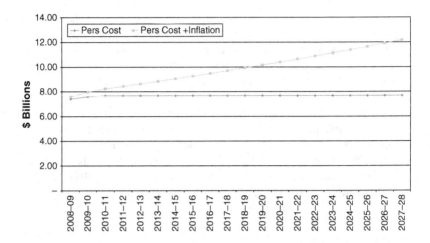

Figure 7.5 Personnel growth projections with and without inflation adjustment.

Source: Initial Personnel Numbers from DND (2009). Inflation projection based on DND (2008).

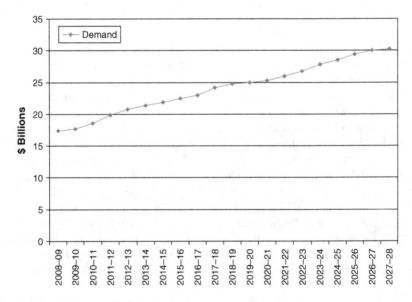

Figure 7.6 Demand based on cost driver.

or training that may affect factors such as the attribution of training, material and infrastructure support, these can be incorporated in long-term projections. For example, if the future security environment and capability planning favors an emphasis on the Arctic, then one example of "early warning" data is in-service support arrangements for Arctic patrol capability.

While this final model is closely linked to the strategic management strategy we outlined in preceding sections, each of the forecasting models discussed here have their merits depending on the maturity and availability of strategic and management information systems.

7.6 Conclusions and future directions

Long-term defense budget planning—under any circumstances—is challenging. The unique requirement to deal simultaneously with a continually shifting international security environment and the peaks and valleys of global business cycles adds to the complexity of trying to manage a multi-billion dollar defense portfolio. Under these conditions, the optimal strategy is to focus staff energies on the development and execution of a flexible and balanced approach that is aligned with government policy, has the necessary funding, and is supported by exercising careful and proficient management of the established plan.

CBP and other strategic management strategies discussed elsewhere in this book are important, but institutionalizing such systems has proven problematic. The literature on transaction cost economics and public choice may offer some important clues. Of the three defense budget forecasting models introduced, modelling the derived demand for military expenditures to forecast future defense budgets may prove the most useful. When future threats are not easily defined, a nation's defense posture is often governed by its bilateral and multilateral security arrangements, income constraints, and policy directives. Introducing future funding realities is a critical component of any military CBA.

Appendix 7.1: Box–Jenkins method

The process (Box–Jenkins) is a three-stage iterative process that reduces a given time series with underlying structure to pure randomness (white noise). The three stages are identification, estimation, and forecasting.

The identification stage entails choosing a preliminary model based on simple visual aids such as plots of the time series and selected key statistics such as the autocorrelation and partial autocorrelation of the time series. These key statistics are used to make the series stationary, where the mean and variance are constant over time. Mean stationarity is often achieved by differencing, and variance stationarity by applying the correct power transformation such as the logarithmic or square root of the original time series (Kennedy 1998). To determine the order of the differencing, the number of time periods between the relatively high autocorrelation is usually a good indicator (see Figures A7.1 and A7.2 for example). For variance stationarity the power transformation can be obtained from a flexible family of transformations introduced by Box and Cox (1964; Kennedy 1998).

Once a tentative model is identified, a nonlinear least squares or a maximum likelihood estimation based on the Marquardt Algorithm, is employed (Box–Jenkins 1970, 504–505). A pure auto regressive (AR 1) process sometimes known

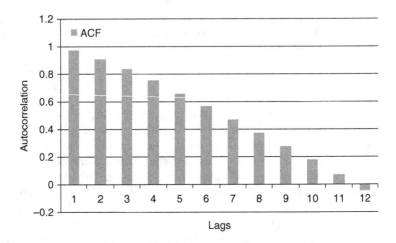

Figure A7.1 The autocorrelation function plot—Belgian defense spending.
Source: Box and Jenkins (1970).

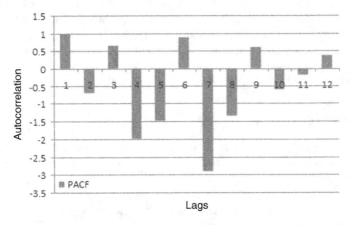

Figure A7.2 The partial autocorrelation function plot—Belgian defense spending.
Source: Box and Jenkins (1970).

as a "random walk" model can be estimated by linear methods. Whether the tentative model is appropriate for forecasting is assessed through a series of diagnostic checks or tests known in Box–Jenkins parlance as necessity, invertibility, and sufficiency tests. Each parameter included in the model should be statistically significant (necessary) and each factor must be invertible. In addition, the residuals from the estimated models should be random (model sufficiency).

The test for necessity is performed by examining the T-ratios for the individual parameter estimates. Parameters with non-significant coefficients may be deleted from the model in order to have a parsimonious model. Invertibility is determined by extracting the roots from each factor in the model. All the roots must lie outside of the unit circle. If one of the factors is non-invertible, then the model must be adjusted. The appropriate adjustment is dictated by the type of the factor that is non-invertible. For example, a non-invertible autoregressive factor usually indicates under-differencing, while a non-invertible moving average factor may indicate over-differencing. A non-invertible moving average factor could also represent the presence of a deterministic factor. Since the model structure is not really clearcut, the overall model must be considered when adjusting for non-invertibility (Box and Jenkins 1970). The residuals are then tested for white noise by studying the autocorrelation and partial autocorrelation of the residuals. Furthermore, a test statistics Q or "portmanteau test" is performed on the residuals autocorrelations of all lags. If the model is mis-specified or inappropriately fitted, the Q test tends to be inflated (Box and Jenkins 1970; Kennedy 1998).

The general multiplicative Box–Jenkins model as articulated in its standard form is (see Box and Jenkins 1970)

$$\varphi_p(B)\Phi_P(B^s)\nabla_s^D Z_t = \theta_q(B)\Theta_Q(B^s)a_t \tag{A7.1.1}$$

where s denotes periodicity of the seasonal component (4 for quarterly and in our case annual which is 1); B denotes the backward operator, i.e.

$$BZ_t = Z_{t-1}$$
$$(B^s)Z_t = (B^s)Z_{t-s};$$

$\nabla^d = (1-B)^d$ is the ordinary difference operator of order d; $^D\nabla_s = (1-B^s)^D$ is the seasonal difference operator of order D; $\varphi_p(B)$ and $\Phi_p(B^s)$ are stationary autoregressive operators (they are polynomials in B of degree p and in B^s of degree P, respectively); $\theta_q(B)$ and $\Theta_Q(B^s)$ are invertible moving average operators (they are polynomials in B of degree q and in B^s of degree Q, respectively); a_t is a purely random process (Box and Jenkins 1970). The general multiplicative model (1.0) is said to be of order $(p,d,q)\,(P,D,Q)_s$.

After the selection of the appropriate model that passes the relevant diagnostic checks, the time series model is forecasted. Specifically, the forecasting function of a typical random walk multiplicative model (1,0) can be expressed as

$$Z_{t+l} = Y_1 Z_{t+l-1} + \cdots + Y_m Z_{t+l-m} - a_{t+l} - P_1 a_{t+l-1} \ldots P_n a_{t+l-n} \tag{A7.1.2}$$

where $m = (p + s.P + d + s.D)$ and $n = (q + s.Q)$; $\psi(B) = \varphi_p(B^s)\nabla^d\nabla_s^D$ is the general autoregressive operator; $\pi(B) = \theta_q(B)\Theta_Q(B)$ is the general moving average operator.

Looking at the explicit form of the forecasting function, for $l > n = (q+s.Q)$, the conditional expectation of (2) at time t is

$$\widehat{Z}_t(l) - \Psi_1 \widehat{Z}_t(l-1) - \Psi_m Z_t(l-m) = 0.$$

For $l > m$ and the solution of this difference equation is

$$\widehat{Z}_t(l) = b_0(t) f_0(l) + b_1^{(t)} f_1(l) + \cdots + b_{m-1}^{(t)} f_{m-1}$$

for $l > n - m$. Note also that f represents functions of the lead time l and includes polynomials, exponentials, etc. The general autoregressive operator $\psi(B)$ defined above, which determines the mathematical form of the forecasts function, i.e. the nature of f. In other words, it determines whether the forecasting function is to be a polynomial, a mixture of sines and cosines, a mixture of exponentials or some combinations of these functions. As indicated in Box and Jenkins (1970), the above is called the "eventual forecast function", and since $n > m$ it provides the forecasts only for lead times $l > n - m$.

Outlier detection

Most time series based forecasting software packages include a routine that automatically detects the presence of outliers (isolated events such as strikes, earthquakes, etc.) or "shocks," and whether these shocks are transitory or induce a level shift. Often such events are modelled as "dummy" variables with a series of zeroes and one(s) for the time period(s) of the isolated event. The automatic outlier detection algorithm is obviously better than the theory-based method for cases when the modeller does not have a priori knowledge of when the event may have occurred. In addition, if the outlier causes a structural shift (such as new institutional legislation, defense White Papers, etc.) and if the impact of the event takes a longer time lag to affect behaviour, then the modeller risks biasing the effect of the outlier by choosing the day the event occurred as the break in the series.

On the other hand, theory-free methods have the "potential for finding spurious significance" during the testing of the hypothesis (AFS 2000). However, since many of these events may or may not be identifiable to the modeller, a theory-free detection algorithm is often desirable. The algorithm begins by first fitting a univariate ARIMA model to the series divided by a series of regressions at each time period to test the hypothesis that there is an intervention. After identifying an outlier the residuals are modified and the test will resume until all outliers are uncovered.

Some forecasters (see the 1990 AFS manual) argue that fitting a univariate ARIMA model does not necessarily imply that the series is homogeneous (the error term of the series is random about a constant mean). In such situations, the identification of the outliers become dubious due to the recursive process. The suggested solution is the testing of a more rigorous specification, i.e., the mean of the errors must be near zero for all time sections (AFS 2000). As an alternative, an endogenous determination of the timing of structural breaks can be more informative. Lanne et al. (2002) developed an Augmented Dickey–Fuller (ADF) type test on such a method by considering shift functions of a general nonlinear form that is used to add to the deterministic term. Lütkepohl and Saikkonen (2002) also argue that a shift may occur in various forms ranging from a shift that is spread out over a number of periods to a smooth transition to a new level. This method is employed in the next section to supplement dummy variable selection.

Appendix 7.2: The autoregressive distributed lag (ARDL) approach to cointegration

As discussed in Appendix 7.1, socio-economic time series are not trend stationary. In econometric parlance, such variables are said to be integrated of order 1 ($I(1)$ for short) and regression analysis based on these variables may lead to spurious results with high R^2.

One typical cointegration technique for estimating time series based models is the autoregressive distributed lag (ARDL) approach to cointegration introduced by Pesaran *et al.* (1996) and Pesaran and Shin (1999). Estimating a model using the ARDL approach to cointegration means estimating a model of the form

$$\theta(L, p)y_t = \alpha_1 + \alpha_2 T_t + \sum_{i=1}^{k} \beta_i(L, q_i)x_{it} + \varepsilon_t \tag{A7.2.1}$$

where: x_{it} are exogenous variables; T_t is a deterministic time trend; and $\Theta(L, p)$ and $\beta_i(L, q_i)$ are polynomial lag operators, with maximum lag of p and q_i respectively (Pesaran and Pesaran 1997). The order of the distributed lag function on y_t and the forcing variable x_t are selected using the Schwartz Bayesian Criterion (SC).

The Pesaran and Shin (1999) test consists of adding, in the first differenced version of Equation (7.5), lags of first differences of the variables so as to orthogonalize the relationship between the explanatory variables and the residual term g. Testing for cointegration then amounts to a F-test on the joint statistical significance of adding level regressors of the variables suspected to be cointegrated. Under the null hypothesis of no cointegration, the distribution of such an F-statistic is non-standard; so the usual critical values do not apply. Pesaran *et al.* (2001), tabulate the relevant critical bounds for $I(0)$ and $I(1)$. Instead of the conventional critical values, this test involves two asymptotic critical value bounds, depending on whether the variables are $I(0)$ or $I(1)$ or a mixture of both. If the test statistic exceeds their respective upper critical values, then we can reject the null of no cointegration regardless of the order of integration of the variables and there is evidence of a long-run relationship; if below we cannot reject the null hypothesis of no cointegration; and if it lies between the bounds, inference is inconclusive.

The error-correction form of (7.9) can be represented as

$$\Delta ME_t = \beta_0 + \sum_{i=1}^{n} \alpha \Delta ME_{t-i} + \sum_{i=1}^{n} \chi \Delta(p_m/p_c)_{t-i} + \sum_{i=1}^{n} \phi \Delta Q_{t-i}$$
$$+ \sum_{i=1}^{n} \gamma \Delta Th_{t-i} + \sum_{i=1}^{n} \varphi \Delta I_{t-i} + \sum_{i=1}^{n} \eta \Delta ME_{t-i} + \varepsilon_t.$$

A variable addition test where the lagged values of the level variables represented as

$$\theta_1 M E_{t-1} + \theta_2 (p_m/p_c)_{t-1} + \theta_3 Q_{t-1} + \theta_4 Z_{t-1} + \theta_4 I_{t-1}.$$

One can use the variable addition test to fit a more parsimonious model of demand for military expenditures. For example, if by dropping a variable x from the model it ceases to be cointegrated, then we can infer that x has a significant effect on the demand for military spending in the long run. However, if the reverse holds, then one can remove the variable. The use of the F-test to eliminate variables is similar to one employed by Beenstock (1998) to test significance of variables for cointegration in Israel's demand model. Specifically, if the null hypothesis testing for long-run relations is sensitive to the removal of the variable in question, then one can safely assume that the variable in question is likely a long-run forcing variable explaining military expenditure.

Notes

1 The views expressed in this chapter are the views of the authors and do not necessarily reflect the views or policies of the Canadian Armed Forces or the Department of National Defence.

2 National defense is a complex, high consequence of error, capital-intensive, knowledge-dependent, national security instrument. Categorization of defense in this manner results from the diversity of tasks assigned to the defense department and the military forces, the elevated level of technology employed within these organizations, the aggregate size of the budget, and the considerable annual capital investment in weapon systems. Indeed, management of the defense budget "is a highly constrained exercise in pricing the executability of programs within the parameters of affordability and political feasibility" (Jones 1991, 20).

3 While most of the examples used in this chapter have a Canadian flavor, selected NATO member nations are also discussed where data and information are available.

4 There is considerable debate on this issue. While Solomon (2003) makes the case for defense inflation for Canada as does Kirkpatrick (2008) for the United Kingdom, a special issue of the Royal United Services Institute (RUSI) dedicated a special issue on the subject (RUSI 2009) that needs to be considered to assess whether a separate index of inflation is required in defense costing.

5 The addition of population may seem peculiar given the fact that defense is a public good; however, consumption probably is not and as such, per capita consumption is assumed to matter for welfare. In other words, demand for defense spending may increase if it has a high-income elasticity and increase in population reduces the tax cost faced by the median voter (Dunne *et al.* 2003).

6 Most empirical studies in the literature, citing practical and conceptual difficulties associated with military price indices, make the assumption that the relative price differential between the military and civilian price is constant. Solomon (2003, 2005) discusses the arguments for and against this view as well as the implications for empirical work.

7 The conventional econometric method for estimating time series models is based on cointegration. (See Appendix 7.2.)

8 The log-transformation of the variables was preferred, based on non-nested tests. As such, these results are presented.

9 The ARDL (autoregressive distributed lag) estimates and the lag order were selected using the Schwarz Bayesian Criterion. The error correction term enters the equation with

the expected negative sign and is significant at the 1 percent and 5 percent significance for both countries considered. The results from the model in general do not point to any econometric problems, as the model successfully passes all the diagnostic tests.

10 If the information system or costing model allows further disaggregation then personnel can be limited only to operational and support personnel.

11 Initial calibrations are based on the official data from DND *Report on Plans and Priorities* (FY 2008–09) Section 3 Supplementary Tables A&B as well as Table 13 on all approved major capital projects.

References

Amara, J. 2008. "NATO Defense Expenditures: Common Goals Or Diverging Interests? A Structural Analysis." *Defence and Peace Economics* 19(6): 449–469.

Automatic Forecasting. Systems-AFS. 2000, 1990 and 1986. *User's Manual for Autobox Software*. Hatboro: Pennsylvania.

Beenstock, M. 1998. "Country Survey XI: Defence and the Economy in Israel." *Defence and Peace Economics* 9(3): 171–222.

Berkok, U. 2005. "Specialization in Defence Forces." *Defence and Peace Economics* 16(3): 191–204.

Box, G. E. P. and D. R. Cox. 1964. "An Analysis of Transformations." *Journal of the Royal Statistical Society Series B* 26: 211–243.

Box, G. E. P. and G. Jenkins. 1970. *Time Series Analysis: Forecasting and Control* (rev. 1st edn). San Francisco: Holdenday.

Center for Strategic and International Studies. 2005. *European Defense Integration: Bridging the Gap between Strategy and Capabilities* (Washington: Center for Strategic and International Studies). Available at www.csis.org/media/csis/pubs/0510_eurodefensereport.pdf [accessed April 12, 2007].

Chouinard, P. and I. Wood. 2007. *The Department of National Defence Strategic Cost Model: Development*. DND Centre for Operational Research & Analysis, Ottawa, p. 2.

Chowdhury, A. R. 1991. "A Causal Analysis of Defence Spending and Economic Growth." *Journal of Conflict Resolution* 35: 80–97.

Congressional Budget Office. 2010. *Long-Term Implications of the Fiscal Year 2010 Defense Budget* (CBO, Washington). Available at www.cbo.gov/ftpdocs/108xx/doc10852/01-25-FYDP.pdf [accessed July 23, 2010].

Department of Finance. 2010. *The Federal Budget 2010*. Ottawa: Public Works and Government Services Canada.

Department of National Defence. 2007. *Investing in the Future: A Ten Year Strategic Investment Plan* Framework *for the Department of National Defence*. Ottawa: Department of National Defence.

———. 2008. *Canada First Defence Strategy*. Ottawa: Department of National Defence.

———. 2009. *Report on Plans and Priorities*. Ottawa: Department of National Defence.

Dodaro, Gene L. 2010. *Maximizing DOD's Potential to Face New Fiscal Challenges and Strengthen Interagency Partnerships*. Government Accountability Office, Washington, p. 2. Available at www.gao.gov/cghome/d10359cg.pdf [accessed July 5, 2010].

Dorff, Robert H. 2005. "Failed States After 9/11: What Did We Know and What Have We Learned?" *International Studies Perspectives* 6(1): 20–34.

Dunne J. P., E. Nikolaidou and N. Mylonidis. 2003. "The Demand for Military Spending in the Peripheral Economies of Europe." *Defence and Peace Economics* 14(6): 447–460.

GAO. 1994. *Future Years Defense Program: Optimistic Estimates Lead to Billions in Over-programming*. GAO, Washington. Available at www.legistorm.com/showFile/

L2xzX3Njb3JlL2dhby9wZGYvMTk5NC83/ful24551.pdf [accessed July 28, 2010].

———. 2005. *Defense Acquisitions: Improved Management Practices Could Help Minimize Cost Growth in Navy Shipbuilding Programs* GAO, Washington). Available at www.gao.gov/new.items/d05183.pdf [accessed July 4, 2010].

———. 2010. *The Federal Government's Long-Term Fiscal Outlook: January 2010.* GAO, Washington. Available at www.gao.gov/new.items/d10468sp.pdf [accessed July 19, 2010].

Hartley, K. and Sandler, T. (Eds). 1990. *The Economics of Defence Spending: An International Survey.* London: Routledge.

———. 1995. *Handbook of Defence Economics, Volume 1* Amsterdam: North Holland.

Hilton, B. and A. Vu. 1991. "The McGuire Model and the Economics of the NATO Alliance." *Defence Economics* 2(1): 105–121.

International Monetary Fund (IMF). Various years. World Economic Outlook Database.

Jones, L. R. 1991. "Policy Development, Planning, and Resource Allocation in the Department of Defense." *Public Budgeting and Finance* 11(3): 15–27.

Jones, L. R. and Jerry L. McCaffery. 2005. "Reform of the Planning, Programming, Budgeting System, and Management Control in the US Department of Defense: Insights from Budget Theory." *Public Budgeting & Finance* 25(3): 1–19.

Jordan, Leland G. 2000. "Systematic Fiscal Optimism in Defense Planning." *Acquisition Review Quarterly* (Winter): 47–62.

Kennedy, P 1998. *A Guide to Econometrics* (4th edition). Cambridge: MIT Press.

Kirkpatrick, D. 1995. "The Rising Unit Costs of Defence Equipment – the Reasons and the Results." *Defence and Peace Economics* 6(4): 263–288.

———. 2004. "Trends in the Costs of Weapon Systems and the Consequences." *Defence and Peace Economics* 15(3): 259–273.

———. 2008. "Is Defence Inflation Really as High as Claimed?" *RUSI Defence Systems* 11(2): 66–71.

Krepinevich, Andrew F., and Barry D. Watts. 2009. *Regaining Strategic Competence.* Center for Strategic and Budgetary Assessments, Washington, p. vii. Available at www. csbaonline.org/4Publications/PubLibrary/R.20090901.Regaining_Strategi/ R.20090901.Regaining_Strategi.pdf [accessed August 21, 2010].

Lanne, M., H. Lütkepohl, and P. Saikkonen. 2002. "Comparison of Unit Root Tests for Time Series with Level Shifts." *Journal of Time Series Analysis* 23: 667–685.

Lütkepohl, H. and P. Saikkonen. 2002. "Testing for a Unit Root in a Time Series with a Level Shift at Unknown Time." *Econometric Theory* 18: 313–348.

Melese, F. 1997. "Gain-Sharing, Success-Sharing and Cost-Based Transfer Pricing: A New Budgeting Approach for the Department of Defense." *Military Operations Research* 3(1): 23–50.

Melese, F., J. Blandin, and S. O'Keefe. 2004. "A New Management Model for Government: Integrating Activity Based Costing (ABC), the Balanced Scorecard (BSC), and Total Quality Management (TQM) with the Planning, Programming and Budgeting System (PPBS)." *International Public Management Review* 5(2): 103–131.

Murdoch, James C. and Todd Sandler. 1982. "A Theoretical and Empirical Analysis of NATO." *Journal of Conflict Resolution* 26(2): 237–263.

Nelson, Daniel S. 2001. "Beyond Defence Planning." *Defence Studies* 1(3): 25–36.

Pesaran, M. H. and B. Pesaran. 1997. *Working with Microfit 4.0: Interactive Econometric Analysis.* Oxford: Oxford University Press.

Pesaran, M. H. and Yongcheol Shin. 1999. "An Autoregressive Distributed Lag Modelling Approach to Cointegration Analysis." In *Econometrics and Economic Theory in the 20th*

Century, edited by S Strom. The Ragnar Frisch Centennial Symposium, Chapter 11. Cambridge: Cambridge University Press.

Pesaran, M. H., Y. Shin, and R. J. Smith. 1996. "Testing for the Existence of a Long-Run Relationship." *DAE Working Papers Amalgamated Series*, No.9622, University of Cambridge.

———. 2001. "Bounds Testing Approaches to the Analysis of Level Relationships." *Journal of Applied Econometrics* 16: 289–326.

Pugh P. G. 2007. *Source Book of Defence Equipment Costs*. London: Pugh.

Royal United Services Institute (RUSI). 2009. "Defence Inflation: Myth or Reality." *Defence Systems* 12(1): 12–21.

SIPRI Yearbooks. Various years. *Armaments, Disarmament and International Security*. Stockholm International Peace Research Institute. Available from http://www.sipri. org/yearbook [last accessed February 9, 2015].

Smith, R. 1989. "Models of Military Expenditure." *Journal of Applied Econometrics* 4(4): 345–359.

———. 1995. "The Demand For Military Expenditure." In *Handbook of Defence Economics, Volume 1*, edited by K. Hartley and T. Sandler. Amsterdam: North Holland.

Solomon, B. 2003. "Defence Specific Inflation: A Canadian Perspective." *Defence and Peace Economics* 14(1): 19–36.

———. 2005. "The Demand For Military Expenditures in Canada." *Defence and Peace Economics* 16(3): 171–189.

———. 2009. "The Defence Industrial Base in Canada", In *The Public Management of Defence in Canada*, edited by Craig Stone. Toronto: Breakout Educational Network.

Solomon, B., P. Chouinard, and L. Kerzner. 2008. T*he Department of National Defence Strategic Cost Model: Volume 2 – Theory and Empirics*. DRDC-CORA TR2008-03, Ottawa.

Stone, J. C. and B. Solomon. 2005. "Canadian Defence Policy and Spending." *Defence and Peace Economics* 16(3): 145–169.

Thompson, M. 2007. *Improving Defence Management*. Canberra: Australian Strategic Policy Institute.

Treddenick, J. M. 2000. "Modelling Defense Budget Allocations: An Application to Canada." In *The Economics of Regional Security: NATO, The Mediterranean, and Southern Africa*, edited by Jurgen Brauer and Keith Hartley, pp. 43–70. Amsterdam: Harwood Academic Publishers.

World Bank 2010. *Global Economic Prospects Summer 2010: Fiscal Headwinds and Recovery*. World Bank, Washington, p. 2. Available at http://siteresources.worldbank. org/INTGEP2010/Resources/FullReport-GEPSummer2010.pdf [accessed July 5, 2010].

Part III

Measuring effectiveness

8 Multiple objective decision-making

Kent D. Wall and Cameron A. MacKenzie

8.1 Introduction

Imagine the the following decision problem for the fictitious country of Drmecia, a small nation with many security problems and limited funds for addressing these problems:

> The Army of Drmecia operates a ground based air-search early warning radar base located near the capital city, Sloat. The radar exhibits low availability because of reliability and maintainability problems. This exposes the country to a surprise air attack from its enemy, Madland. The Army obtained procurement funds two years ago and installed another radar of the same type as a back-up, or standby, radar. Unfortunately, the second radar unit also has exhibited low availability and too often *both* radars are off-line. The commander of Sloat Radar Base is now requesting funds for a third radar, but the Army Chief of Staff is very concerned. He knows that the defense budget is under increasing pressure and funds spent on another radar may have to come from some other Army project. In addition, two new radar models are now available for procurement at higher cost than the existing radars. It may be better to purchase one of these than another radar of the existing model.
>
> The Chief of Staff knows he must have a strong case if he is to go to the Minister of Defense and ask for additional funds. He wants to know which radar is best. He wants to know what he is getting for the extra money spent. He wants to know what is the most cost-effective course of action.
>
> The director of analysis for the Army of Drmecia knows that making a cost-effective decision requires two things: (1) a cost analysis and (2) an effectiveness analysis. The analysis of cost is a familiar problem and he has a staff working on it. The effectiveness part of the problem, however, is a concern. What is effectiveness in this situation? How can effectiveness be defined and quantified? How can the cost analysis be integrated with effectiveness analysis so that a cost-effective solution can be found?

The goal of this chapter is to develop a method to think about and quantify effectiveness in the public sector, specifically defense. Effectiveness can best be measured in the public sector by developing a framework for solving decision problems with multiple objectives. The framework will provide you with a *practical tool for quantitative investigation* of all factors that may influence a decision, and you will be able to determine *why* one alternative is more effective than others. This analytical ability is very important because many real-life decision problems involve more than a single issue of concern. This holds true for personal-life decisions, private sector business decisions, and public sector government resource allocation decisions.

Examples of personal-life decision problems with multiple objectives are plentiful: selecting a new automobile; choosing from among several employment offers; or deciding between surgery or medication to correct a serious medical problem. In the private sector, maximizing profit is often the sole objective for a business, but other objectives may be considered, such as maximizing market share, maximizing share price performance, and minimizing environmental damage.

Public sector decision-making almost always involves multiple objectives. State and local government budget decisions are evaluated, at least, in terms of their impacts on education programs, transportation infrastructure, public safety, and social welfare. The situation is more complex at the Federal level because national defense issues enter the picture. For example, consider the ways in which the US Department of Defense (DoD) evaluates budget proposals. Top-level decision-makers consider the effects of a budget proposal on (1) the existing force structure, (2) the speed of modernization, (3) the state of readiness, and (4) the level of risk, among other factors. Other national defense objectives include the ability to deter aggression, project force around the world, and defeat an enemy in combat regardless of its location or military capability. This multidimensional character permeates all levels of decision-making within a planning, programming, budgeting and execution system (PPBES). Acquisition decisions, training and doctrine policy changes, and base reorganization and consolidation choices all have multiple objectives (Buede and Bresnick 1992; Parnell *et al.* 1998; Ewing *et al.* 2006).

Government decisions in general, and defense resource allocation decisions in particular, have an added evaluation challenge. Outcomes are difficult, if not impossible, to represent in monetary terms. First, benefit cannot be expressed in terms of profit. Unlike the private sector, the public sector is not profit motivated and this single monetary measure of benefit is not relevant. Second, market mechanisms often do not exist for "pricing out" the many benefits derived from public sector decisions. Thus, it is not possible to convert all the benefits into monetary terms and conduct a cost–benefit analysis (CBA). In national defense, benefits are often characterized in terms such as deterrence, enhanced security, and increased combat capability (Dyer *et al.* 1998; Parnell *et al.* 2001). No markets exist that generate a price per unit of deterrence or a unit increase in national military security.

Solving these decision problems requires a structured systematic approach that aids the discovery of all the relevant objectives and makes it easy to work with objectives expressed in many different units of measure. It also must allow the decision-maker to account for the relative importance of the objectives and the importance of marginal changes within individual objective functions. Following such an approach can allow decision-makers to perform cost-effectiveness analysis (CEA) to compare programs and alternatives.

8.2 Problem formulation

A systematic approach to decision-making requires developing a model that reflects a decision-maker's preferences and objectives. We assume the decision-maker is rational and seeks the most attractive or desirable alternative. Goals describe what the decision-maker is trying to achieve, and objectives determine what should be done in order to achieve the decision-maker's goal(s). A model based on the decision-maker's objectives will allow the decision-maker to evaluate and compare alternatives.

For a decision problem with a single objective, the model for decision-making is straightforward. For example, consider the simple problem of choosing the "best" alternative where "best" is interpreted as the greatest range. Not surprisingly, the decision-maker should choose the alternative with the greatest range.

Things are never this straightforward when there are multiple objectives because the most desirable or most effective alternative is not obvious. For example, consider the selection of the Sloat Radar as discussed in the introduction. The decision-maker knows that range and interoperability are important. Maintenance and reliability are also concerns. How do we define effectiveness in this situation? Do we focus only on range? Do we focus only on interoperability? How can we consider all four objectives at the same time?

8.2.1 Issues of concern and objectives

The issues of concern to the decision-maker can always be expressed as objectives. For example, in selecting a radar system suppose two alternatives are equal in all respects except for range. In this case, the decision-maker chooses the radar with more range. This concern with range translates to an objective: the decision-maker wants to maximize range. Likewise, suppose that two alternatives are equal in all respects except for required maintenance, and the decision-maker selects the alternative with less required maintenance. The concern with required maintenance translates to an objective: the decision-maker will want to minimize required maintenance.

The rational decision-maker can always be shown to act in a way consistent with a suitably defined set of objectives. Hence, decision problems characterized by many issues of concern are decision problems in which the decision-maker attempts to pursue many objectives. In other words, the decision-maker confronts a *Multiple Objective Decision Problem* (Keeney and Raiffa 1976; Keeney 1996).

The set of objectives is fundamental to the formulation of this type of decision problem. If we have a complete set of objectives that derive from *all* the issues of concern to the decision-maker, we have a well-formulated problem. Furthermore, if these objectives are defined in sufficient detail, they tell us how to evaluate the alternatives in terms that have meaning to the decision-maker. In the radar example, each alternative can be evaluated in terms of its range, its interoperability, its required maintenance, etc. This knowledge is fundamental to the solution of this type of decision problem. It tells us how to quantify things or how to measure the attainment of the objectives. We seek to represent the alternatives by a set of numbers that reveal to the decision-maker how well each alternative "measures up" in terms of the objectives.

Let us introduce some mathematical notation to help with the formulation, and Table 8.1 defines all the variables used in this chapter. Let there be M objectives for the decision-maker. Let these be defined in enough detail so that we know how to measure the attainment of each objective. Let these measures be denoted x_i where $1 \leq i \leq M$. For example, $x_1 = $ range, $x_2 = $ interoperability, $x_3 = $ required maintenance, etc. Let there be N alternatives indexed by the letter j where $1 \leq j \leq N$. Thus, each alternative can be represented by a set of M numbers:

$$\{x_1(j), x_2(j), x_3(j), \ldots, x_M(j)\}.$$

These numbers become the *attributes* for the jth alternative, and each of the M numbers represents how well the jth alternative meets each one of the decision-maker's M objectives. Evaluating an alternative means determining the numerical value of each of the measures. These serve as the raw data upon which the decision is made.

The key to solving the decision problem is to explain how this set of M numbers is viewed in the mind of the decision-maker. This is done by constructing a *collective measure of value* that reflects how much the decision-maker *prefers* one collection of attributes vis-à-vis another collection of attributes. For example, how does the decision-maker value the set of attributes for the first alternative, $\{x_i(1)\}$, compared to the set of attributes for the second alternative, $\{x_i(2)\}$, where $1 \leq i \leq M$? Is the the set $\{x_i(1)\}$ more "attractive" than the set $\{x_i(2)\}$?

It is challenging for a decision-maker to compare alternatives if each alternative has several attributes (i.e., if M is greater than 3 or 4). Developing a function that combines the M attributes into a single number provides a method for the decision-maker to compare alternatives based on the attributes that describe each alternative. This single number is called the *Measure of Effectiveness (MoE)*.

8.2.2   Effectiveness

The function that measures the effectiveness of the jth alternative is called a value function, $v(j)$. This function incorporates the *preferences* of the decision-maker and converts each *collection of attributes* as represented by the set $\{x_i(j)\}$ into a number that represents the attractiveness or desirability of the collection in the mind of the decision-maker. It measures the extent to which the jth alternative helps the decision-maker pursue all the objectives while taking into account the relative importance of each. Effectiveness is a number. It quantifies "how far we go" towards achieving our goals as measured by the value of the objectives. The objectives are not all of equal importance, however, and $v(j)$ also takes into account the relative importance of each objective.

Table 8.1 Variable definitions

Variable	Definition
a	Assessed parameter in the exponential value function
b_1	Assessed parameter for squared term in the exponential value function
b_2	Assessed parameter for cubic term in the exponential value function
$c(j)$	Life-cycle cost of the jth alternative
c_{ideal}	Dollar amount at which the value of cost equals 1
$c_{too\ much}$	Dollar amount at which cost is too high or value of cost equals 0
i	A single objective or attribute
j	A single alternative
$k = \dfrac{1}{c_{too\ much}}$	Reciprocal of too high of cost
w_i	Importance weight for the ith attribute
w_A	Importance weight for availability
w_C	Importance weight for complexity
w_E	Importance weight for electronic counter-countermeasures (ECCM)
w_I	Importance weight for interoperability
w_L	Importance weight for cognitive load
w_P	Importance weight for performance
w_R	Importance weight for range
w_U	Importance weight for ease-of-use
$v(j)$	Measure of effectiveness for the jth alternative
$v_c(c(j))$	Value function for cost of the jth alternative
$v_i(x_i)$	Value function for the ith attribute
x_i	Measurement for the ith attribute
$x_i(j)$	Measurement for the ith attribute for the jth alternative
x_{ideal}	Ideal measurement for an attribute
x_{max}	Maximum measurement for an attribute
x_{min}	Minimum measurement for an attribute
$x_{too\ little}$	Too little for an attribute for more-is-better case
$x_{too\ much}$	Too much for an attribute for less-is-better case
z	Swing in attribute that contributes least to an objective
z_i	Difference between x_i and either x_{max} or x_{min}
K	Normalization constant for exponential value function
K_1	Normalization constant for quadratic exponential value function
K_2	Normalization constant for cubic exponential value function
M	Number of objectives or attributes
N	Number of alternatives
$V(j)$	Payoff function for cost-effectiveness of the jth alternative
V^* and V^{**}	Payoff values of cost-effectiveness
W_C	Importance weight for cost
W_E	Importance weight for effectiveness

The decision-maker desires to maximize effectiveness by choosing the alternative with the highest $v(j)$ subject of course to cost considerations. The fundamental problem in formulating the decision problem is defining $v(j)$ based on the set of attributes $\{x_1(j), x_2(j), x_3(j), \ldots, x_M(j)\}$ and then integrating cost with the MoE.

Formulating a decision problem with multiple objectives requires four pieces of information (Kirkwood 1997):

1   we need a list of the relevant objectives;
2   we need to know how to value the measures associated with each individual objective;
3   we need to know the relative importance of these objectives;
4   we need to know the relative importance between the cost and effectiveness of each alternative.

We proceed to address each of these needs in the rest of the chapter.

8.3   Discovering the relevant objectives

We must know what matters in a decision problem or the consequences that a decision-maker considers when thinking about each solution alternative. These are the issues of concern and are represented by objectives. We cannot judge alternatives without knowing the objectives of the decision-maker.

Discovering all the relevant objectives is the first step in solving the decision problem (Keeney 1996; Hammond *et al.* 1999; Clemen and Reilly 2001). It is helpful to employ a graphical construction called an hierarchy or "tree structure." (Think of a tree: a trunk with a few main branches that have many more smaller branches that have even more smaller branches—now turn that picture upside down and you have a picture of an hierarchy.) Figure 8.1 depicts a hierarchy with several levels. The hierarchy begins at the top most level with a single over-arching objective that captures in its definition all that the decision-maker is trying to do. For multiple objective problems in public policy, the overall objective is to *maximize effectiveness*. The objectives in the first level below the overall objective tell us how we define the top level hierarchy. We say the overall objective is refined or defined in more detail by the objectives listed on the next level down. The lower level provides more detail as to what is meant by the objective at the next higher level.

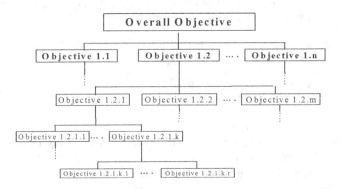

Figure 8.1 Generic hierarchy.

The definition is not operational unless it is useful in measuring things. We must have a way to develop the hierarchy in enough detail so that we get specific enough in our definition of the objectives that it becomes obvious to us (and everyone else) how "to measure things." What we need is a method of construction that takes us from the top level down to the lowest level where measurement is obvious. There are several ways of doing this but we will only discuss the "top-down" method and the "bottom-up" method.

8.3.1   The top-down approach

In the top-down approach you start with the obvious, to maximize effectiveness. This becomes the top-level objective. Because this objective can mean many things to many people and is too vague to be operational, the next step is to seek more detail. You proceed by asking the question: "What do you mean by that?" The answer to this question will allow you to write down a set of sub-objectives, each of which derives from a more detailed interpretation by the decision-maker of just what overall effectiveness means to him or her. For example, in the case of Sloat Radar the decision-maker may say: "Maximizing availability is part of maximizing overall effectiveness, I've got to have a radar that works almost all the time." He may also say that "I need a high performance radar that works almost all the time, so maximizing radar performance is also part of maximizing overall effectiveness." Finally, he may say that he needs a radar that is easy to use. Thus minimizing radar complexity for the user is also important.

The top-down approach continues in this way until there is no doubt what the objectives mean because we will be able to measure their value for each alternative. For example, in the first level down from the top we know exactly what we mean by acting so as "to maximize availability." Availability has a well-known precise definition: availability is the probability that a system will work at any given time. It can be measured either directly or by computation using the system's Mean Time Between Failure (MTBF) and its Mean Time To Repair (MTTR). Each alternative can be evaluated in terms of its availability, and maximizing availability is pursued by seeking the system that exhibits the highest availability.

Performance, however, does not have a precise agreed-upon definition that tells us how we can measure it. Here we must ask once again: "What do you mean by that?" The answer to this question will allow us to understand what is meant by maximizing performance. Suppose, for example, that the response to this question is: "High performance means great effective radar range, resistance to electronic countermeasures, and high interoperability." We do not need to ask any other questions here because we know how to measure (evaluate) range for each alternative. We know how to evaluate resistance to electronic countermeasures: a simple "yes" or "no" answer will do. Either an alternative has electronic counter-countermeasures (ECCM) capability or it does not. Finally, we know how to measure interoperability: we can count the number of communication links that can be operated by each alternative (so it can feed target information to the various anti-air forces).

Minimizing user complexity also requires refinement so we need to ask: "What do you mean by that?" The answer in our example may be that to minimize user complexity we need to minimize the cognitive load placed on the radar operator (measured by how many things the operator has to watch, sense, react to, adjust, and refine) and maximize the ease-of-use of the radar by the operator. Each alternative could be evaluated by cognitive psychologists and human-machine interface industrial engineering specialists. In this case each evaluation could result in a simple rating scheme that uses "high," "medium," or "low" coding. Therefore both objectives are specific enough to be measurable.

The end result of this top-down approach for the Sloat radar example is the objectives hierarchy depicted in Figure 8.2. The key to the top-down approach is repeated application of the question "What do you mean by that?" to provide more and more detail. You stop refining the structure when the answer to the question defines a quantity that can be measured, quantified or evaluated. When you have reached this point for each part of the hierarchy then you have completed the process and obtained what you desire—a complete description of what you mean by effectiveness and a way to measure it.

8.3.2   *The bottom-up approach*

The bottom-up approach starts where the top-down approach ends: with a collection of very detailed and specific measures. These are structured, or grouped, into a hierarchy in a way that assures we are not forgetting anything important and we are not double-counting objectives. The key to this approach is the repeated application of the question: "Why is that there?"

The construction of the list is accomplished in many ways. First, it can be considered a Christmas "wish list." The decision-maker can be asked to list everything he or she would like to have in an alternative. For example, with Sloat Radar the decision-maker may respond with the following. "I'd like to have maximum effective range and complete immunity to electronic 'jamming.' I'd also like to have it very easy to use so my least technically adept soldier could operate it." Second, specific measures can be found in the "symptoms" listed in the original problem statement. If the Army is upset with the existing radar availability then

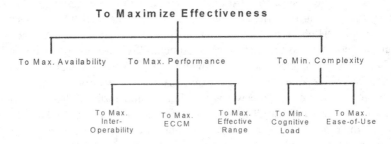

Figure 8.2 Sloat Radar objectives hierarchy.

it is obvious that the decision-maker would also be interested in improving or maximizing availability.

For each item listed the decision-maker is asked: "Why is that there?" The response to this question will provide information that aids in grouping the measures. This makes it easy to define higher level objectives for each group. For example, electronic countermeasure resistance and range are included so that "when the radar works, it has enough capability to do its job better than any other alternative." This response may bring to mind performance issues, and we group these two measures under an objective that seeks to maximize performance. Once performance is included as a higher objective it may provoke consideration of other ways one interprets performance, and this may make the decision-maker think of high interoperability. The same process applied to the ease-of-use measure would lead to considering cognitive loading on the operator and a general concern with user complexity.

Finally, this process aids the decision-maker in clarifying the higher level objectives. A structure emerges that helps insure nothing is forgotten and nothing is double-counted. For example, once the higher objectives of maximizing performance and minimizing complexity are evoked, the decision-maker will be able to see what is important: (1) the radar has got to work almost all the time, i.e., maximize availability; (2) when it works it must be the best, i.e., maximize performance; and (3) it should be easy to operate or else all the other stuff is not worth anything, i.e., minimize complexity. The result is a hierarchy of objectives as in Figure 8.2.

8.3.3 Which approach to use

Each approach has its advantages and disadvantages. The top-down approach enforces a structure from the very beginning of the exercise. It is, however, often difficult to think in general terms initially. Humans find it easier to focus on specifics, like range and availability. The bottom-up approach is more attractive in this respect, but this will not produce a logical structure without additional work. Producing an extensive wish list will, most likely, produce redundant measures. Oddly enough, the longer the list, the more likely something important will be forgotten. Long lists are harder to critically examine and locate omissions. This is where structure helps.

The best approach is perhaps a combination of the two. First, construct a hierarchy with the top-down approach, and then "reverse" direction—construct a hierarchy using the bottom-up approach. Critical examination of the results provides information for a more complete final hierarchy. The result should be a hierarchy that is (Keeney 1996):

1 mutually exclusive (where each objective appears once);
2 collectively exhaustive (where all important objectives are included);
3 able to lead to measures that are operational (can actually be used).

The bottom level of the hierarchy composes the M objectives or attributes necessary to build the function for effectiveness. The Sloat Radar hierarchy has $M = 6$ attributes (availability, interoperability, ECCM, range, cognitive load, and ease-of-use), which will be used to compare alternatives.

8.3.4 The types of effectiveness measures

The effectiveness measures that result from development of the objectives hierarchy can be of three general types: (1) *natural* measures; (2) *constructed* measures; and (3) *proxy* measures (Kirkwood 1997).

8.3.4.1 Natural measures

Natural measures are those that can be easily counted or physically measured. They use scales that are most often in common use. Radar range, interoperability (as measured by the number of communication links provided), and availability (as measured by the probability that the system will be functioning at any given time) are examples. Weight, payload, maximum speed, size, volume, and area are other examples. Whenever possible, we should try to refine our objectives definitions in the hierarchy to obtain this type of measure.

8.3.4.2 Constructed measures

This type of measure attempts to measure the degree to which an objective is attained. It often results when no commonly used physical or natural measure exists. For example, cognitive load is a constructed measure. It is assessed as high, medium, or low depending on the number of visual and audible signals to which the operator must attend. Suppose indicators of operator cognitive abilities as measured by aptitude scores, training rigor, and education level indicate significant error in operator function if the combination of audio and visual cues is greater than 5. A radar with 5 or more cues is then assessed as having a high cognitive load. Similarly, a combination of cues between 3 and 4 constitutes a medium cognitive load, and a combination of cues less than 3 constitutes a low cognitive load. Constructed measures are the next best thing to natural measures.

8.3.4.3 Proxy measures

These measures are like natural measures in that they usually are countable or physically measurable. The difference is that they *do not directly* measure the objective of concern. In one sense we could consider radar range to be a proxy for measuring how much an alternative helps to maximize warning time to react better to an airborne threat. The actual reaction time cannot be directly measured because we would need to know the exact attack speed of the threatening bombers. We do know, however, that the farther out we can detect an attack, the more reaction time we would have. So maximizing range is a proxy measure for maximizing time to react.

8.4 Decision-maker preferences

After building the objectives hierarchy, we know what is important and have created a list of the relevant objectives. Each alternative can be evaluated using the list of individual effectiveness measures for the different attributes, but these measures involve a variety of incommensurable units. We must develop a way to convert all these disparate measures to a common unit of measure. This common unit of measure represents value in the mind of the decision-maker.

Calculating the MoE for the jth alternative as represented by the function $v(j)$ requires two types of preference information: (1) information that expresses preference for more or less of a single attribute and (2) information that expresses relative importance between attributes. The first represents preference information *within* a single attribute, while the second represents preference information *across* different attributes (Kirkwood 1997).

The first is important because of the way a decision-maker values marginal changes in a single effectiveness measure. For example, in the Sloat Radar case, a decision-maker may value the increment in range from 200 km to 400 km more than twice as much as the same increment from 400 km to 600 km. The same increment in range (of 200 km) from 600 km to 800 km may be valued very little. This valuation is quite reasonable. More range is preferred to less range, but there is a point beyond which additional range has little additional value to the decision-maker. We already will have "enough" range for the purposes of early warning against air attack. Such information is very important for another reason. It allows us to construct an *individual attribute value function* that provides a scaling function to convert the natural units of measurement into units of value on a scale of 0–1. This has the advantage of removing any problem caused by the units of measurement for the individual attribute. For example, measuring radar range in terms of meters, kilometers, or thousands of kilometers can influence the numerical analysis and ultimately the answer. We need a process that is *independent of the units of measurement*. This is one of the important things we achieve with an individual attribute value function. Such a function also makes the process independent of the range of values of the individual effectiveness measures. This preference information will provide the answer to the question: "How much is enough?"

The second type of information is important because a decision-maker values some individual effectiveness measures of attributes more than others. For example, in the Sloat Radar problem, the decision-maker may feel it much more important to increase availability than to increase range. Such information implies that a decision-maker would be willing to obtain more availability at the expense of less range. This preference information will provide the answer to the question: "How important is it?"

8.4.1 How much is enough (of an individual attribute)?

Once we know all the relevant effectiveness measures, we need to describe how a decision-maker values marginal changes in each measure. This is done by constructing a function that converts the nominal measurement scale into a 0–1 value scale where 0 is least preferred and 1 is most preferred. There are several ways of doing this but only one method is presented here. It is a three-step procedure.

First, divide the nominal scale into "chunks," or intervals, over which the decision-maker can express preference information. For example, consider radar range. The decision-maker may find it difficult to express preferences for each additional kilometer of range but may find it easier to do so if we consider range in 100 km chunks.

Second, ask the decision-maker to tell you, using a scale of 0-10, how valuable is the first 100 km of radar range. Then ask how valuable is the next 100 km of range (the second increment from 100 km to 200 km). Repeat this process for each additional 100 km of range until you reach the upper limit of interest. Suppose this exercise gives the following sequence when applied to range measurements between 0 km and 1000 km: 10, 10, 8, 7, 5, 3, 1, 0.5, 0.1, 0.05. These are the *increases in marginal effectiveness* to the decision-maker.

Third, use this marginal information to create a cumulative value function scaled to give value scores between 0 and 1. The radar range example gives a total cumulative value (the sum of the marginal increments) equal to $10 + 10 + 8 + 7 + 5 + 3 + 1 + 0.5 + 0.1 + 0.05 = 44.65$. Divide all marginal increments by this sum: $10/44.65, 10/44.65, 8/44.65, 7/44.65$, etc. We obtain a sequence of smaller numbers that add to one. The cumulative value, calculated by adding the marginal values, is what we use to determine the value of a measure. For example, the value of 300 km range is equal to the value derived from increasing the range from 0 to 100 km plus the additional value derived from increasing the range from 100 km to 200 km plus the additional value derived from increasing the range from 200 km to 300 km. The cumulative value of these normalized marginal increments is presented graphically in Figure 8.3.

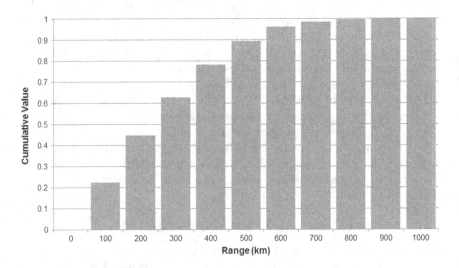

Figure 8.3 Radar range value function.

This process achieves two important things. First, if we repeat it for each attribute, we have a common unit of measure standardized to a 0–1 interval. Second, and most importantly, we now have a way of valuing radar range. A range of 700 km has a value of 0.985 and a range of 800 km has a value of approximately 0.997, which informs us that the decision-maker prefers 800 km to 700 km but that this increase is not highly valued (only an increase in value of 0.012). On the other hand, increasing the range from 200 km (with a value of 0.448) to 300 km (with a value of 0.628) is much more valuable to the decision maker. The increase in value here is 0.18. Thus we know the decision-maker prefers the 100 km increment from 200 to 300 km more than the going from 700 to 800 km.

The analysis of effectiveness is facilitated by converting this graphical information to algebraic form so that we can obtain a model of preferences that allows us to quantify these preferences for every possible numerical measure for an attribute. We construct a value function for an individual attribute where x_i represents the numerical value for the ith attribute and $v_i(x_i)$ is the value function for the ith attribute (Kirkwood 1997). A useful algebraic form for capturing the important characteristics of Figure 8.3 is the *exponential function*:

$$v_i(x_i) = \frac{1 - e^{-a[x_i - x_{min}]}}{K} \tag{8.1}$$

where $K = 1 - e^{-a[x_{max} - x_{min}]}$ is a normalization constant. This function requires three parameters: x_{min}, x_{max}, and a. The first two are known already because the decision-maker has specified the range of interest over which x_i will vary: $[x_{min} \leq x_i \leq x_{max}]$. The parameter a can be obtained using least-squares regression using the Solver "add-in" tool in Excel. The parameter can also be estimated graphically by adjusting a until the curve generated by the function $v_i(x_i)$ corresponds to the points representing the decision-maker's preferences in the cumulative value function as ascertained by the three-step method. More flexible but more complicated forms of this exponential function can be used (see Appendix 8.1). The purpose of these algebraic forms is to match the original cumulative value function given to us by the decision-maker as closely as possible.

Calculating a numerical value for a in $v_i(x_i)$ that corresponds to the information for the range of the radar, as depicted in Figure 8.3, is done in Excel using the Solver add-in tool. Figure 8.4 presents $v_i(x_i)$ corresponding to the data in Figure 8.3 when we use an exponential form with $a = 0.0033$, $x_{min} = 0$, and $x_{max} = 1,000$.

The preceding example illustrates a case where "more is better." Exactly the same approach is used when "less is better." For example, consider a man-portable field radio. Here less weight is preferred to more weight. Now the decision-maker is asked a series of questions relating to marginal value but we "start from the other end" of the measurement scale—we start with the heaviest weight and work backwards to the lightest weight. For example, suppose it is decided that field radios weighing more than 20 kg are useless because they weigh too much for a typical soldier to carry. Imagine we use marginal changes in weight of 2 kg.

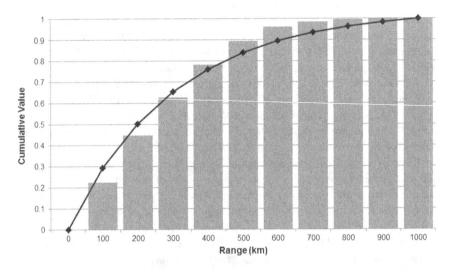

Figure 8.4 Fitted exponential value function for radar range.

We begin by asking the decision-maker to give us a number (on a scale of 0–10) expressing the value of a 2 kg reduction (from a weight of 20 kg to a weight of 18 kg). Then we ask what value is associated with a further 2 kg reduction in weight (to 16 kg). We repeat the process until we get an answer for the value attached to the last 2 kg of weight. Suppose we obtain the sequence: 10, 9, 8, 5, 3, 1, 0.4, 0.1, 0.0. These sum to 36.5 so we normalize the decrements by this total. The result is presented in Figure 8.5.

As in the case where more is better, the graph of cumulative value can be used to fit an exponential function for conducting analysis of effectiveness. Once again, exponential functions are very useful and can be used to represent this information:

$$v_i(x_i) = \frac{1 - e^{-a[x_{max} - x_i]}}{K} \tag{8.2}$$

where K is the same as before. Figure 8.6 depicts the results of fitting the cumulative value function for radio weight in Excel using the Solver add-in tool where $a = 0.21$, $x_{min} = 0$, and $x_{max} = 20$. Once again, closer fit can be obtained by using more terms in the exponent as described in Appendix 8.1.

A linear function can also be used to approximate the exponential function for either the more-is-better case or the less-is-better case. The linear function can use the same cumulative value function as described previously, or just two values can be assessed from the decision-maker. The two values necessary are a number corresponding to "not enough performance" and a number corresponding to "good enough performance." If more is better, the number corresponding to not enough performance is "too little" or $x_{too\ little}$. If less is better, the number corresponding

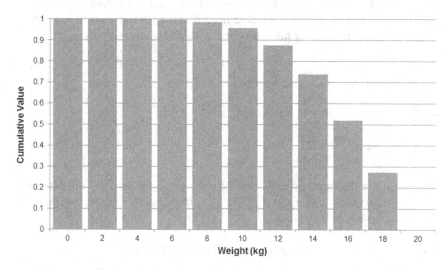

Figure 8.5 Radio weight value function.

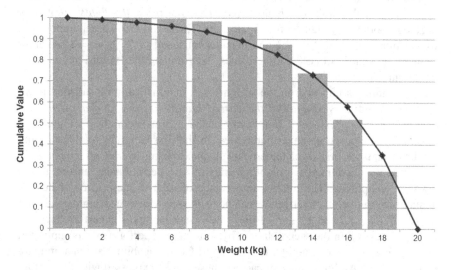

Figure 8.6 Fitted exponential value function for radio weight.

to not enough performance is "too much" or $x_{\text{too much}}$. In both cases, the number corresponding to good enough performance is "ideal" or x_{ideal}. For example, in the more-is-better example of radar range, 0 km can represent not enough performance or too little and 600 km can represent good enough performance or the ideal. We choose 600 km rather than 1,000 km as the ideal because the assessed value at 600 km is 0.963 and the increase in value from 600 to 1,000 km is only 0.037. In the less-is-better example of the radio's weight, we choose 20 kg as too much and 8 kg as ideal. Eight kilograms is chosen as ideal because the value at 8 kg is 0.986 and the increase in value from 8 to 0 kg is only 0.014. The linear value function is defined for more is better in which $[x_{\text{too little}} \leq x_i \leq x_{\text{ideal}}]$:

$$v_i(x_i) = \frac{x_i - x_{\text{too little}}}{x_{\text{ideal}} - x_{\text{too little}}}, \tag{8.3a}$$

and for less is better in which $[x_{\text{ideal}} \leq x_i \leq x_{\text{too much}}]$:

$$v_i(x_i) = \frac{x_i - x_{\text{too much}}}{x_{\text{ideal}} - x_{\text{too much}}}. \tag{8.3b}$$

If $x_i \geq x_{\text{ideal}}$ in the more-is-better case or if $x_i \leq x_{\text{ideal}}$ in the less-is-better case, $v_i(x_i) = 1$. Similarly, $v_i(x_i) = 0$ if $x_i \leq x_{\text{too little}}$ in the more-is-better case or $x_i \geq x_{\text{too much}}$ in the less-is-better case.

8.4.2   *How important is it (relative to the other attributes)?*

After assessing the preferences of the decision-maker for changes in each attribute, we need to know the preferences of the decision-maker among different attributes. The model for the MoE uses *importance weights* or *tradeoff weights* denoted by w_i, the importance weight for the ith attribute (Kirkwood 1997). Each importance weight must satisfy $0 \leq w_i \leq 1$ and together must satisfy $\sum_{i=1}^{M} w_i = 1$. A larger value of w_i signifies that the effectiveness measure for the ith attribute is more important.

The conditions imposed on the weights will automatically be satisfied if we apply the conditions to *each of the partial hierarchies that appear within the overall objectives hierarchy*. For example, the overall hierarchy in Figure 8.2 is actually composed of three hierarchies. In the first hierarchy, defined by the top level and the first level underneath it, maximizing overall effectiveness is supported by maximizing availability, maximizing performance, and minimizing user complexity. The relative importance of each of these three objectives to maximizing overall effectiveness can be expressed with three weights such that $0 \leq w_A, w_P, w_C \leq 1$ and $w_A + w_P + w_C = 1$ (A = availability, P = performance and C = complexity). In the second hierarchy, maximizing performance is supported by maximizing interoperability, maximizing ECCM capability, and maximizing range. The relative importance of each of these can be expressed with three more weights such that $0 \leq w_I, w_E, w_R \leq 1$ and $w_I + w_E + w_R = 1$ (I = interoperability, E = ECCM, and R = range). Finally, minimizing complexity is supported by minimizing cognitive load and maximizing ease-of-use. The relative importance of these two objectives can be expressed with two weights such that $0 \leq w_L, w_U \leq 1$ and $w_L + w_U = 1$ (L = cognitive load and U = ease-of-use).

Assigning weights in this fashion guarantees that the weights for all M objectives or attributes sum to one and are all within the range of 0–1. The Sloat Radar example has $M = 6$ attributes, and we need six importance weights, $w_1, w_2, w_3, w_4, w_5,$ and w_6 to correspond to each one of the attributes (availability, interoperability, ECCM, range, cognitive load, and ease-of-use). These six "global" weights can be derived from the "local" weights described in the previous paragraph. Availability stands alone in the hierarchy, and $w_A = w_1$ where w_1 is the global weight for availability. Performance is composed of three attributes, and $w_P = w_2 + w_3 + w_4$ where w_2 is the global weight for interoperability, w_3 is the global weight for ECCM, and w_4 is the global weight for range. Complexity is composed of two attributes, and $w_C = w_5 + w_6$ where w_5 and w_6 are the global weights for cognitive load and ease-of-use, respectively. Using the fact that $w_I + w_E + w_R = 1$ for the performance sub-hierarchy and $w_L + w_U = 1$ for the complexity sub-hierarchy, we can express the global weights for the six attributes:

$$w_1 = w_A \tag{8.4a}$$

$$w_2 = w_P \cdot w_I \tag{8.4b}$$

$$w_3 = w_P \cdot w_E \tag{8.4c}$$

$$w_4 = w_P \cdot w_R \tag{8.4d}$$

$$w_5 = w_C \cdot w_L \tag{8.4e}$$

$$w_6 = w_C \cdot w_U. \tag{8.4f}$$

Since each group of local weights sum to one, we know the global weights as calculated above will also sum to one:

$$w_1 + w_2 + w_3 + w_4 + w_5 + w_6 = w_A + w_P + w_C = 1.$$

Obtaining the weights requires solicitation of decision-maker preferences using a different set of questions from that used above. There are many ways to do this, and we consider five methods.

8.4.2.1 Direct assessment

The most obvious way to gain the information required is to directly ask the decision-maker for M numbers, w_i, such that $0 \le w_i \le 1$ for $\{1 \le i \le M\}$ and $\sum_{i=1}^{M} w_i = 1$. If there are no more than three or four effectiveness measures this is a feasible approach. Unfortunately many real-life problems have many more effectiveness measures and direct assessment becomes too difficult. The Sloat Radar example has six effectiveness measures, and this presents a formidable problem to the decision-maker. All is not lost, however, if we utilize the structure given us in the objectives hierarchy.

Consider the Sloat Radar hierarchy. We can ask the decision-maker to consider first just the relative importance of the three components that make up overall effectiveness: availability, performance, and user complexity. Directly assessing three importance weights at this level presents no insurmountable problem for the decision-maker. Next we can ask the decision-maker to consider the components of performance and tell us the relative importance of interoperability, ECCM capability, and range. Finally, we can ask the same question for the components of user complexity that requires only two importance weights be assigned. The results of this series of questions allows us to compute the complete set of six weights using Equations (8.4a)–(8.4f).

Using the hierarchy and this "divide and conquer" approach makes direct assessment feasible in many situations where otherwise it would appear overwhelming.

8.4.2.2 Equal importance

Direct assessment may result in the decision-maker stating that "all individual measures are equally important." In this case we must ask the decision-maker if this statement applies to all M attributes or to each part of the hierarchy. Different importance weights result depending on the interpretation of the statement.

If the decision-maker is referring to all M attributes, then clearly $w_i = 1/M$. In the Sloat Radar example this means that each measure would be given a weight of 1/6. It is important to realize that this weighting has implications for the corresponding weights in the hierarchy. As discussed earlier, the importance weight for performance equals the sum of global weights for interoperability, ECCM, and range, and $w_P = 1/6 + 1/6 + 1/6 = 1/2$. The weight for complexity equals the sum of the weights for cognitive load and ease-of-use, and $w_C = 1/6 + 1/6 = 1/3$.

Clearly, equal importance across the bottom level measures does NOT imply equal weights throughout the hierarchy. Thus, it is very important to go back to the decision-maker and ask: "Do you really believe performance is three times more important than availability?" "Do you really believe that minimizing complexity is twice as important as maximizing availability?" When phrased this way the decision-maker may be led to reassess the importance weights.

If the decision-maker is referring to the weights at each level in the objectives hierarchy, then we get a different set of weights for w_i. Figure 8.2 tells us that on the first level down availability, performance and complexity are all equally important:

$$w_A = w_P = w_C = 1/3.$$

This also means that all the component objectives for performance are equally important:

$$w_I = w_E = w_R = 1/3.$$

Finally, suppose the decision-maker says that maximizing ease-of-use and minimizing cognitive load are equally important, so then we know

$$w_U = w_L = 1/2.$$

These local weights translate into the following global weights:

$$w_1 = 1/3, \quad w_2 = 1/3 \cdot 1/3 = 1/9, \quad w_3 = 1/3 \cdot 1/3 = 1/9,$$
$$w_4 = 1/3 \cdot 1/3 = 1/9, \quad w_5 = 1/3 \cdot 1/2 = 1/6, \quad w_6 = 1/3 \cdot 1/2 = 1/6.$$

A very different picture emerges. Availability is three times more important than interoperability, ECCM capability, and range. Availability is twice as important as cognitive load and ease-of-use.

The structure of the hierarchy is a powerful source of information that we will continually find helpful and informative.

8.4.2.3 Rank sum and rank reciprocal

Sometimes the decision-maker will provide only *rank order* information. For example, in assessing the weights making up the performance measure, the decision-maker may tell us: "Range is most important, interoperability is second most important, and ECCM is least important." In such cases we can use either the *rank sum* or *rank reciprocal* method. Range has rank one, interoperability has rank two, and ECCM has rank three (Stillwell *et al.* 1981).

In the rank sum method, range has an un-normalized weight of 3, interoperability 2 and ECCM 1, based on the decision-maker's ranking. Dividing each of these weights by the sum $3 + 2 + 1 = 6$ returns the normalized weights: $w_R = 3/6$, $w_I = 2/6$, and $w_E = 1/6$.

In the rank reciprocal method, the reciprocals of the original ranks give

$$\text{Range} = 1/1,$$
$$\text{Interoperability} = 1/2,$$
$$\text{ECCM} = 1/3,$$

which sum to 11/6. Dividing the reciprocal ranks by their sum gives three numbers that satisfy the summation condition and represent a valid set of weights: $w_R = 6/11$, $w_I = 3/11$, and $w_E = 2/11$.

Both the rank sum and rank reciprocal methods only require rank order information from the decision-maker. The rank sum method returns weights that are less dispersed than the rank reciprocal method, and less importance is placed on the first objective in the rank sum method.

8.4.2.4 Pairwise comparison

Decision-makers find it easier to express preferences between objectives where there are only two objectives. This has led to a procedure for soliciting preference information based on pairwise comparisons. This allows the importance weights over M measures to be established by comparing measures only two at a time. This is a special case of the swing weighting method, which is described below.

8.4.2.5 Swing weighting

One method helpful with direct assessment that incorporates more than rank order information is *swing weighting* (von Winterfeldt and Edwards 1986; Clemen and Reilly 2001). Although more complex than the other methods, the swing weighting method can provide a more accurate depiction of the true importance the decision-maker places on each objective. Swing weighting is also sensitive to the range of values that an attribute takes, and different values for attributes can result in different weights. The method has four steps. First, the decision-maker is asked to consider the increments in *overall* effectiveness that would be represented by shifting, or "swinging," each individual effectiveness measure from its least preferred value to its most preferred value. Second, the decision-maker is asked to order these overall increments from least important to most important. Third, the decision-maker quantitatively scales these increments on a scale from 0 to 100. Finally the sum-to-one condition is used to find the value of the least preferred increment.

Let us illustrate this process using the performance part of the Sloat Radar hierarchy. We need to find three importance weights: w_I, w_E, and w_R. First, suppose that the least preferred under performance are 0 km for range, 0 communication links for interoperability, and no ECCM. This "least-preferred alternative" with 0 km in range, no communication links, and no ECCM has a value of 0 for performance. The most preferred under performance are 1,000 km for range, 5 communication links, and with ECCM. The decision-maker believes that a swing in range from 0 to 1,000 km will contribute most to performance, a swing from no communication links to five links will contribute second most to performance, and a swing from no ECCM capability to having ECCM capability will contribute the least to performance. Because range is the most preferred swing, we arbitrarily assign a value of 100 to a hypothetical alternative with 1,000 km range, 0 communication links, and no ECCM. We ask the decision-maker for the value of swinging from 0 to 5 communication links relative to the alternative with a value of 100 and the least-preferred alternative with a value of 0. The decision-maker may say that a hypothetical alternative with 0 km range, 5 communication links, and no ECCM has a value of 67. Finally, the decision-maker may conclude that a hypothetical alternative with 0 km range, 0 communication links, and having ECCM capability has a value of 33 relative to the other alternatives. Thus, we know the un-normalized weights are 100 for range, 67 for interoperability, and 33 for ECCM. Dividing each weight by the sum of the un-normalized weights gives the importance weight for each attribute: $w_R = 100/(100 + 67 + 33) = 1/2$, $w_I = 67/(100 + 67 + 33) = 1/3$, and $w_E = 33/(100 + 67 + 33) = 1/6$.

These weights express something very important in effectiveness analysis. When x_i is at its least preferred value, $v_i(x_i) = 0$. When it is at its most preferred value $v_i(x_i) = 1$. The weights, $\{w_i, 1 \leq i \leq M\}$, capture the relative importance of these changes. The ratio $w_i/w_{i'}$ expresses the relative importance between the changes from worst to best in the measures x_i and $x_{i'}$ for the ith and i'th attributes.

Swing weighting incorporates three types of preference information: ordinal (rank), relative importance, and range of variation of the individual effectiveness measures. Pairwise comparison uses rank and relative importance. The rank sum and rank reciprocal methods only use rank information.

8.5 Effectiveness analysis

The quantification of decision-maker preferences completes our model of effectiveness. We can begin assessing or analyzing the overall effectiveness of each alternative. All the ingredients are present: The objectives hierarchy tells us what is important and defines the individual measures of effectiveness. The individual value functions tell us how the decision-maker values marginal increments in these measures and scales them to a 0–1 interval. Finally, the importance weights tell us the relative importance of the individual attributes. The weights are combined with the values for a single alternative to calculate the overall effectiveness of the jth alternative:

$$v(j) = w_1 \cdot v_1(x_1(j)) + w_2 \cdot v_2(x_2(j))$$
$$+ w_3 \cdot v_3(x_3(j)) + \cdots = \sum_{i=1}^{M} w_i \cdot v_i(x_i(j)). \tag{8.5}$$

The MoE is calculated as the weighted sum of all the individual value functions. Nothing of relevance is left out, and everything that enters the computation does so according to the preferences of the decision-maker (Keeney and Raiffa 1976; Kirkwood 1997).

Evaluating the overall effectiveness of an alternative requires computing its $v(j)$. The result allows us to order all the alternatives from best to worst according to their MoE. The "best" alternative is now the alternative with the largest MoE. While this provides us a way to find "the" answer, we have a far more powerful tool at hand.

We can use Equation (8.5) to investigate why we get the answers we do. For example, what makes the best alternative so desirable? What individual effectiveness measures contribute most to its desirability? An alternative may be the best because of very high effectiveness in only one single measure. This may tell us that we could be "putting all our eggs in one basket." If this alternative is still under development, uncertainties about its development may make this alternative risky, and identifying the second best alternative may be important.

We can also assess the sensitivity of the answer to the importance weights. We can find out how much the weights must change to give us a different answer. For example, would a change of only 1 percent in one of the higher level weights change the ordering of the alternatives? How about a change of 10 percent? This is of practical significance because the decision-maker assigns weights subjectively, and this always involves a lack of precision.

Most important of all is the ability to assess the effect of uncertainty in the future condition. The decision-maker's preferences are a function of the future condition. If the decision-maker believes the future condition will change, then the preferences, value function and weights may change. The effects of uncertainties in the problem formulation can be readily evaluated once we have our model.

We illustrate each of these situations using the Sloat Radar example. Suppose there are four alternatives: (1) "do nothing" (keep the two existing radars at Sloat which is labeled as Sloat 2); (2) purchase a third radar for Sloat of the same type (which is labeled as Sloat 3); (3) purchase the new SkyRay radar; and (4) purchase the new Sweeper radar. The latter two alternatives are new, with better range, availability, interoperability and ECCM. These come at the cost of higher cognitive load and less ease-of-use. The costs of procurement for the two new radars are also higher than purchasing an existing radar. The data on which each of these four alternatives can be assessed are depicted in Table 8.2.

8.5.1   The components of success

The decision-maker preferences for the importance weights are $w_A = 0.60$, $w_P = 0.35$, $w_C = 0.05$, $w_I = 0.50$, $w_E = 0.0$, $w_R = 0.50$, $w_L = 0.50$, and $w_U = 0.50$. Individual value functions for availability and range are specified by value functions similar in shape and form to that portrayed in Figure 8.4. The individual value function for interoperability is similar but specified for integer values, 0–5. The individual value function for ECCM capability is binary, taking the value 0 for no ECCM capability and the value 1 for having ECCM capability. Cognitive load and ease-of-use are evaluated using a constructed scale of three categories: low, medium, and high. For cognitive load, $v_L(\text{low}) = 1$, $v_L(\text{medium}) = 0.5$, and $v_L(\text{high}) = 0$. For ease-of-use $v_U(\text{low}) = 0$, $v_U(\text{medium}) = 0.5$, and $v_H(\text{high}) = 1$. Combining these evaluations and preferences gives the values depicted in Table 8.3.

Table 8.2 Evaluation data for Sloat Radar

Alternative	Availability	Interoperability	ECCM	Range (km)	Cognitive load	Ease-of-use
Sloat 2	0.79	2 data links	No	250	Low	Medium
Sloat 3	0.87	2 data links	No	250	Low	Medium
SkyRay	0.98	4 data links	No	700	Medium	Low
Sweeper	0.97	2 data links	Yes	500	High	Low

Table 8.3 Values and weights for Sloat Radar

Alternative	Availability	Interoperability	ECCM	Range (km)	Cognitive load	Ease-of-use
Sloat 2	0.962	0.375	0	0.413	1.0	0.5
Sloat 3	0.982	0.375	0	0.413	1.0	0.5
SkyRay	0.998	0.938	0	0.909	0.5	0
Sweeper	0.997	0.375	1	0.774	0	0
Global weights	0.60	0.175	0	0.175	0.025	0.025

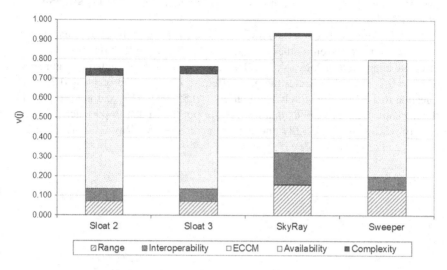

Figure 8.7 Components of overall effectiveness for Sloat Radar.

Multiplying each of the global weights by the each of the values and adding them together calculates an MoE for each radar, as pictured in Figure 8.7. SkyRay is the most effective alternative and we know why. It has the highest value for interoperability and range. Sweeper is second best because it has the second highest value for range. All alternatives possess approximately the same availability rating. Interoperability and range are the attributes that are most important in discriminating among these alternatives.

8.5.2 *Sensitivity to preferences*

The original importance weights produce an ordering of alternatives in which SkyRay is most effective, Sweeper next most effective, followed by Sloat 3 and then Sloat 2. Is this ordering robust to reasonable changes in the weights? If not, which weights are most influential? Questions like these are answered using the model to recompute the MoE of each alternative with different importance weights.

First let us fix $w_P = 0.35$ and vary both w_A and w_C over a reasonable range of values subject to the condition that $w_A + w_P + w_C = 1$. The result is shown in Figure 8.8. SkyRay remains the most effective alternative for the range of weights examined, which means that the most effective alternative is fairly robust to changes in the importance weights for availability relative to complexity. The ordering of the other alternatives changes if $w_A \leq 0.55$ or, correspondingly, when $w_C \geq 0.10$. As availability becomes less important relative to complexity, Sweeper becomes the least effective radar, and Sloat 3 becomes the second most effective alternative. When determining the second most effective alternative, the decision-maker needs to ask himself: "How confident am I that $w_A > 0.55$ when $w_P = 0.35$?"

Attention now focuses on the influence of w_P. We repeat the above analysis for w_A and w_C for different values of w_P. If $w_P = 0.25$, SkyRay remains the most effective alternative as long as $w_A \geq 0.5$ and $w_C \leq 0.25$. As depicted in Figure 8.9, if $w_P = 0.2$, Sloat 3 becomes the most effective if $w_A \leq 0.55$ or $w_C \geq 0.25$. The question to ask is: "How likely is it that $w_A \leq 0.55$, $w_P \leq 0.2$, and $w_C \geq 0.25$?" If the decision-maker responds that he will not put that much importance on complexity relative to availability and performance, then SkyRay remains the most effective alternative.

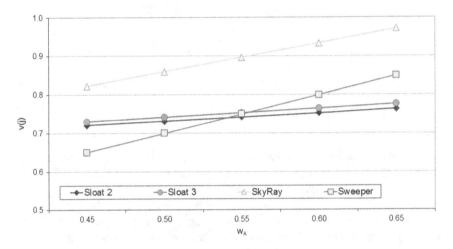

Figure 8.8 Sensitivity to w_A and w_C with $w_P = 0.35$.

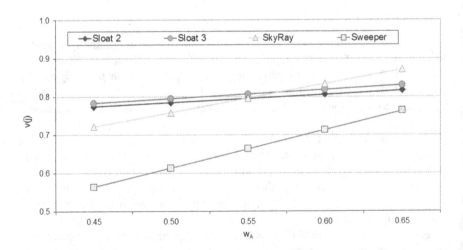

Figure 8.9 Sensitivity to w_A and w_C with $w_P = 0.2$.

8.5.3 Uncertainty in the future conditions

A new future condition or planning scenario may change the decision-maker's preferences and, consequently, the ordering of the alternatives. Investigating this type of sensitivity is very important when there is uncertainty in the future condition. Let us assume that the situation described in Section 8.5.1 and depicted in Figure 8.7 corresponds to a particular planning scenario we will call the baseline.

Now suppose that new intelligence estimates suggest the potential enemy will re-equip its bomber fleet with supersonic attack aircraft. This new scenario may change decision-maker preferences to place more importance on performance because of the enemy's increase in capability. For example, the importance weights defining the measure of overall effectiveness may change to $w_A = 0.30$, $w_P = 0.65$, and $w_C = 0.05$. Furthermore, the importance weights defining the components of performance could change to $w_I = 0.25$, $w_E = 0.0$, and $w_R = 0.75$. This preference structure gives the result depicted in Figure 8.10. The ordering of the alternatives is unchanged and the picture resembles that in Figure 8.7. There are differences, however, in the composition of the MoE for each alternative. Range plays a more important role, and availability plays a less important role. Nevertheless, the original ordering of alternatives is robust to this change in the future condition.

Now assume that intelligence reports indicate that the potential enemy cannot afford to reequip its bomber fleet with new aircraft. Instead, they have decided on an avionics upgrade to give the existing bomber fleet radar jamming capability or electronic countermeasures (ECM). Under this future condition the decision-maker may still favor performance over availability, and $w_A = 0.30$, $w_P = 0.65$, and $w_C = 0.05$. ECCM becomes important, and the weights within performance may change to $w_I = 0.10$, $w_E = 0.75$, and $w_R = 0.15$. The resulting MoE are

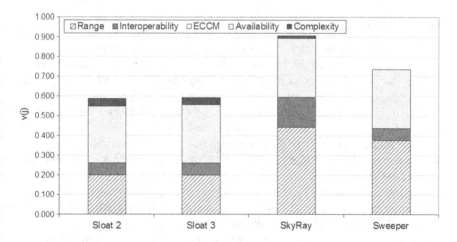

Figure 8.10 Supersonic attack scenario.

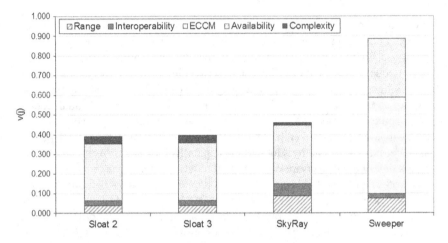

Figure 8.11 ECM scenario.

depicted in Figure 8.11. Sweeper is now the most effective alternative for this future condition because it is the only radar with ECCM capability.

8.6   Cost-effectiveness

Computing the MoE for each alternative allows the decision-maker to order the alternatives from most effective to least effective. This is only half the story, though, because cost also matters. Ultimately the decision-maker will have to integrate cost information with effectiveness and engage in *cost-effectiveness analysis* (CEA). This section presents the conceptual elements used in the analysis and outlines the process followed in the analysis.

8.6.1   *Conceptual framework*

The decision-maker ultimately pursues two overall objectives when searching for a solution: (1) maximize effectiveness and (2) minimize cost. An alternative j will be evaluated in terms of its MoE, $v(j)$, and its discounted life-cycle cost, $c(j)$. Drawing a picture of effectiveness and cost on a scatter plot can help us think in these two dimensions at the same time. Cost is plotted on the horizontal axis, and effectiveness is plotted on the vertical axis. If the four alternatives in the Sloat Radar example have the discounted life-cycle costs and MoEs (with the importance weights from the baseline) as in Table 8.4, Figure 8.12 depicts this information graphically.

This framework makes it easy for the decision-maker to see which alternative is cheapest or most expensive and which alternative is most effective or least effective. It shows the distance between alternatives—how much more effective and/or costly is one alternative compared with another. Such a picture provides all the information the decision-maker needs to choose the most cost-effective

Table 8.4 Discounted life-cycle costs and MoEs for Sloat Radar

Alternative	Cost (millions of dollars)	Effectiveness (MoE)
Sloat 2	23.9	0.752
Sloat 3	41.6	0.765
SkyRay	63.5	0.934
Sweeper	70.4	0.799

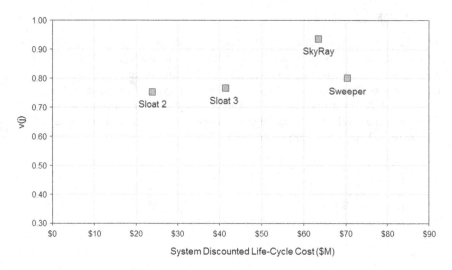

Figure 8.12 Alternatives in cost-effectiveness space.

alternative, the exact meaning of which requires understanding the many ways the solution can be interpreted.

8.6.2 Solution concepts

Multiple ways exist to define a solution that minimizes cost and maximizes effectiveness. The solutions are distinguished from each other based on the amount of additional information required of the decision-maker. First, we present two concepts that do not require any more information from the decision-maker. Second, we develop solution concepts that require a little additional information from the decision-maker. Finally, we conclude with a definition for the most cost-effective solution. This last concept requires eliciting additional decision-maker preference information and is the most demanding.

8.6.2.1 Superior solution

A superior solution is a feasible alternative that has the lowest cost and the greatest effectiveness. It does not matter if you are a decision maker who places all emphasis on minimizing cost or a decision-maker who places all emphasis on maximizing effectiveness. Both types of decision makers would select the superior solution if one exists. Figure 8.13 illustrates this concept. Alternative 1 is superior to all the others, and it is called the *dominant* solution because this alternative is the cheapest and the most effective. We do not need any preference information beyond that which we have already obtained in order to define effectiveness. No alternatives exist in the "northwest" quadrant relative to alternative 1 because no alternative is either cheaper or more effective than alternative 1.

8.6.2.2   *Efficient solution*

The efficient solution concept builds upon the superior solution concept. An *efficient* solution is one that is not dominated by, or inferior to, any other feasible alternative, and an alternative is not efficient because there exists another alternative that is superior to it. An example of this type of solution is found in Figure 8.14. Alternatives 4 and 6 are dominated by, or are inferior to, alternatives 3 and 5, respectively. Consequently, alternatives 4 and 6 should not be selected. Alternatives 2, 3, 5, and 7 are all efficient.

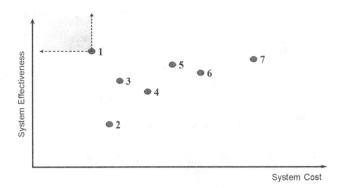

Figure 8.13 Superior or dominant solution.

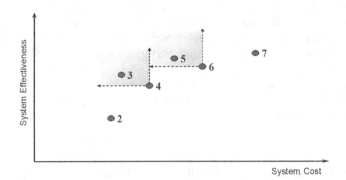

Figure 8.14 Efficient solution.

This solution concept does not necessarily yield unique answers. If only one efficient solution exists, it is the superior solution. If more than one efficient solution exist, a set of non-unique solutions or alternatives exists. This may not be a bad circumstance, however, because the decision-maker has flexibility, and several alternatives can be defended as efficient.

8.6.2.3 Satisficing solution

A satisficing solution is a feasible solution that is "good enough" in the sense that it exceeds a minimum level of effectiveness and does not exceed a maximum cost. This solution concept requires the decision-maker to state a desired MoE and a maximum life-cycle cost. An alternative that satisfies both of these requirements simultaneously is satisfactory. Like the efficient solution concept, the satisficing solution concept often yields non-unique answers. Figure 8.15 shows a situation where both alternatives 3 and 5 are satisfactory solutions because both alternatives are cheaper than the maximum cost ($cost_{max}$) and more effective than the minimum effectiveness level ($v(j)_{min}$). Because both alternatives are satisfactory, a decision-maker will need another solution concept to decide between the two alternatives.

8.6.2.4 Marginal reasoning solution

If a superior solution does not exist, marginal reasoning may be used to select an alternative. This solution concept begins with an efficient set of alternatives, such as those from Figure 8.14, which are reproduced in Figure 8.16. Suppose the decision-maker is considering alternative 3. Alternatives 2 and 5 are its closest neighbors: alternative 2 is similar in cost and alternative 5 is similar in effectiveness. Two questions can be asked: (1) Is the marginal increase in cost worth the marginal gain in effectiveness when moving to alternative 5? and (2) Is the marginal savings in cost worth the marginal decrease in effectiveness when moving to alternative 2? If the decision-maker prefers alternative 5 over alternative 3, the additional cost is worth paying to obtain the additional increase in effectiveness. If the decision-maker prefers alternative 3 to alternative 5, the marginal increase in effectiveness is not worth the marginal increase in cost. If the

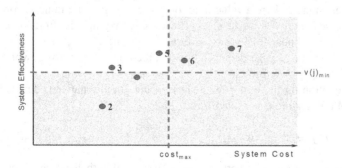

Figure 8.15 Satisficing solution.

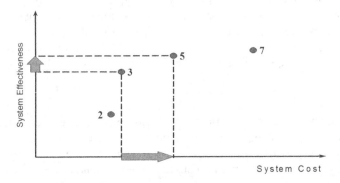

Figure 8.16 Marginal reasoning solution.

decision-maker cannot decide between alternative 3 and alternative 5, the marginal increase in cost is balanced by the marginal increase in effectiveness, or equivalently, the cost savings just compensate for the decrease in effectiveness. It is a "toss up" between the two.

This reasoning can be applied to each alternative in the efficient set. After all the alternatives have been considered, the decision-maker will arrive at one of two situations: (1) one alternative is identified as the most preferred alternative; or (2) two or more alternatives are identified as equivalent and, as a group, are more preferred than than all the rest.

8.6.2.5   *Importance weights for effectiveness and cost*

The most formal solution concept asks the decision-maker to determine the relative importance of cost to effectiveness. This means there exists *in the mind of the decision-maker* a payoff function that combines the two issues of concern: (1) maximizing effectiveness and (2) minimizing cost. The first objective is represented by the MoE $v(j)$. The second objective is a function of the cost measure $c(j)$ and represents a less-is-better preference relation. The decision-maker needs to determine a value function for cost similar to the example given in Section 8.4: "How much is enough?" where a value function for the weight of a radio is constructed. The value function for cost $v_c(c(j))$ can be an exponential function as in Equation (8.2) or a linear function as in Equation (8.3b) in which less is better. Figure A8.1 in Appendix 8.1 depicts a linear value function for cost in which $c_{ideal} = \$0$ and $c_{too\ much} = \$90$ million.

The payoff function for the cost-effectiveness of the jth alternative is denoted by $V(j)$ and follows a simple additive form:

$$V(j) = W_E \cdot v(j) + W_C \cdot v_c(c(j)), \tag{8.6}$$

where W_E and W_C are the importance weights for effectiveness and cost, respectively. Upper case letters distinguish these weights from those used in defining $v(j)$. W_E represents the importance to the decision-maker of maximizing effectiveness and W_C represents importance to the decision-maker of minimizing cost. The weights must satisfy $0 \leq W_E \leq 1$, $0 \leq W_C \leq 1$, and $W_E + W_C = 1$. The relative importance of these two conflicting objectives is captured by the ratio W_C/W_E.

Equation (8.6) represents the preferences of a rational decision-maker. When confronted by a choice between two alternatives equal in effectiveness, the decision-maker will choose the less expensive alternative because $v_c(c(j))$ decreases as the cost $c(j)$ increases. Similarly, when confronted by a choice between two alternatives equal in cost, the decision-maker will choose the alternative with the greater MoE because $v(j)$ is greater for the alternative that is more effective.

The overall cost-effectiveness function $V(j)$ defines a preference structure that allows us to develop valuable insights. We can see this graphically by rearranging the cost-effectiveness function and drawing a straight line to represent $V(j)$ on the cost-effectiveness graph. Express $v(j)$ as a function of $V(j)$ and $c(j)$:

$$v(j) = \frac{1}{W_E} V(j) - \frac{W_C}{W_E} \cdot v_c(c(j)).$$

For simplicity, we assume a linear individual value function—see Equation (8.3b)—for $v_c(c(j))$ in which less is better. If we assume $c_{ideal} = 0$, then $v_c(c(j)) = [c(j) - c_{too\ much}]/[-c_{too\ much}] = 1 - k \cdot c(j)$ where $k = 1/c_{too\ much}$. For a fixed value of $V(j)$, we see that $v(j)$ is a linear function of $c(j)$:

$$v(j) = \frac{1}{W_E} V(j) - \frac{W_C}{W_E} \cdot [1 - k \cdot c(j)]$$

$$= \frac{1}{W_E} V(j) - \frac{W_C}{W_E} + \frac{W_C}{W_E} \cdot k \cdot c(j).$$

This is the equation for a straight line when we interpret $c(j)$ as the independent variable and $v(j)$ as the dependent variable. The intercept for the line is given by $V(j)/W_E - W_C/W_E$ and the slope is given by $k \cdot W_C/W_E$. This line represents all combinations of cost and effectiveness corresponding to a given level of overall cost-effectiveness, $V(j)$. As $V(j)$ increases (for example, $V^{**} > V^*$ in Figure 8.17), this "isoquant" line shifts up and to the left. As we move closer to the northwest corner of the cost-effectiveness plot, we move to greater levels of overall cost-effectiveness.

Suppose the decision-maker is much more interested in minimizing cost than maximizing effectiveness. This decision-maker would select weights where $W_C \gg W_E$. The slope of the lines representing constant overall cost-effectiveness would be very steep. This situation is depicted in Figure 8.18. Alternative 3 is the best in this situation because it lies on the highest achievable isoquant of cost-effectiveness. A decision-maker who places more emphasis on maximizing effectiveness would choose weights that result in less steep lines of constant

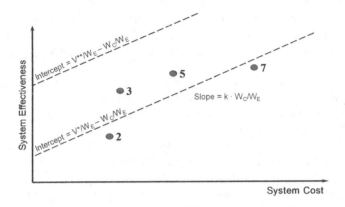

Figure 8.17 Cost-effectiveness linear preference.

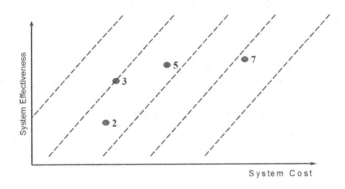

Figure 8.18 $W_C \gg W_E$.

overall cost effectiveness, which could yield a picture like Figure 8.19. Now alternative 5 is the most cost-effective. Finally, consider a decision-maker who places considerable importance on the maximization of effectiveness, which implies that $W_E \gg W_C$. The slope of the lines is very small resulting in nearly flat isoquants of cost-effectiveness as in Figure 8.20. Alternative 7 is now the most cost-effective alternative.

The above three cases illustrate the importance of the efficient set, and the most cost-effective alternative is selected from the set of efficient alternatives. The most cost-effective depends on the decision-maker's preferences for cost reduction versus effectiveness maximization. The answer to the decision problem requires elicitation of decision-maker preferences—we do not know what we mean by "cost-effectiveness" until we incorporate decision-maker preferences over cost and effectiveness.

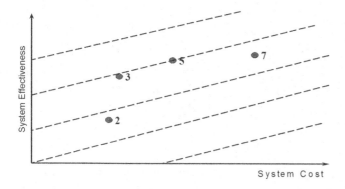

Figure 8.19 $W_E > W_C$.

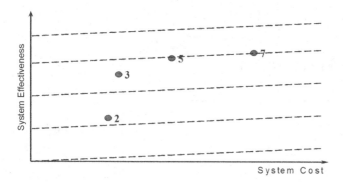

Figure 8.20 $W_E \gg W_C$.

8.6.3   Cost-effectiveness for Sloat Radar

Figure 8.12 shows that no superior solution exists among the four alternatives of the Sloat Radar problem and Sweeper is dominated by SkyRay. The efficient set is composed of Sloat 2 (the "do nothing" alternative), Sloat 3 (purchase a third radar of the type already installed), and SkyRay. The question is which of the three non-dominated alternatives in the efficient set is most cost-effective? The answer cannot be given until we solicit additional preferences from the decision-maker.

A marginal reasoning solution may begin with Sloat 2 by asking the decision-maker whether he is willing to spend an additional $17.7 million to achieve an increase in 0.013 in effectiveness (the difference in MoEs between Sloat 3 and Sloat 2). The increase in effectiveness occurs because Sloat 3 is available more frequently than Sloat 2. If the decision-maker responds that he is unwilling to spend the extra money for a small increase in effectiveness, we can ask him if he is willing to spend an additional $39.6 million to achieve an increase in 0.182 in effectiveness (the difference in MoEs between SkyRay and Sloat 2). SkyRay is more effective than Sloat 2 because it has more range, is available more often,

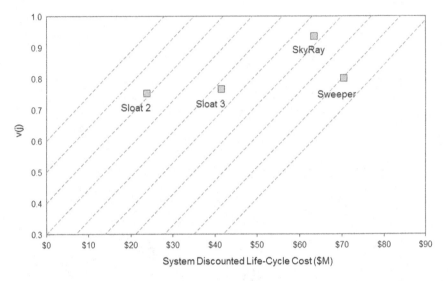

Figure 8.21 Cost-effectiveness: $W_C / W_E = 1.0$.

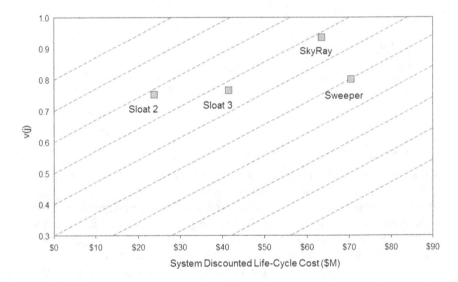

Figure 8.22 Cost-effectiveness: $W_C / W_E = 0.5$.

and has greater interoperability. Framing the questions in this manner can help the decision-maker understand precisely what additional capability he is getting for an increased cost.

The more formal manner of answering which alternative is the most cost-effective requires elicitation of the final set of importance weights, W_C and W_E.

Suppose the decision-maker believes cost and effectiveness are equally important. These preferences translates to $W_C/W_E = 1.0$ resulting in the picture given in Figure 8.21. The decision-maker would select the "do nothing" alternative because at least one isoquant line lies to the right of Sloat 2 and to the left of Sloat 3 and SkyRay.

If the decision-maker believes maximizing effectiveness is twice as important as minimizing cost, $W_C/W_E = 0.5$, which results in the picture given in Figure 8.22. Sloat 2 is still most cost-effective because at least one isoquant line separates Sloat 2 from Sloat 3 and SkyRay. If the decision-maker believes maximizing effectiveness is four times more important than cost reduction, $W_C/W_E = 0.25$. These preferences give the picture shown in Figure 8.23. SkyRay is the most cost-effective because at least one isoquant line lies below SkyRay and above Sloat 2 and Sloat 3.

This method also can serve to find the ratio between W_C and W_E which would make the decision-maker indifferent between two alternatives. For example, when $W_C/W_E = 1/3$ we obtain the situation in Figure 8.24. Here Sloat 2 and SkyRay are almost of equal cost-effectiveness. The analysis of cost-effectiveness afforded by the model reduces the management question to one of asking the decision-maker: "Do you feel that effectiveness is more than three times as important as cost?" If the answer is yes, SkyRay should be selected. If the answer is no then do nothing (Sloat 2) is the best alternative. The model helps to focus attention on critical information.

Now that we have found the critical value of $W_C/W_E \simeq 1/3$, it is of interest to consider the effects of uncertainty in the future condition. Two other planning scenarios besides the baseline were considered during the MoE discussion.

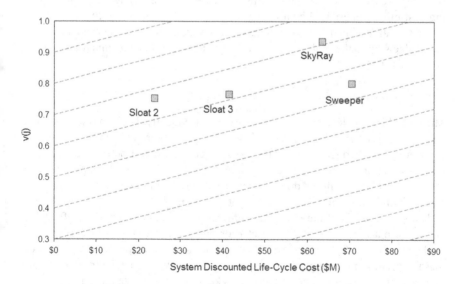

Figure 8.23 Cost-effectiveness: $W_C/W_E = 0.25$.

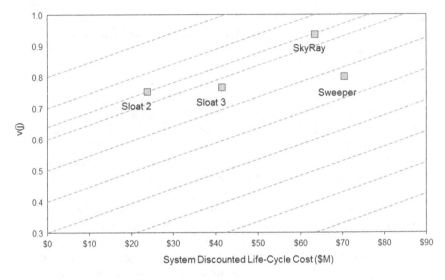

Figure 8.24 Cost-effectiveness: $W_C/W_E = 0.33$.

If the supersonic attack scenario is highly likely, then we use different weights in the definition of effectiveness. The $v(j)$ values change for all alternatives and Figure 8.25 shows that SkyRay is the most cost-effective if $W_C/W_E \leq 0.57$. The decision-maker should be asked: "Is effectiveness more than 1.75 times as important than cost?" If he answers yes, SkyRay is the best alternative. The ECM planning scenario changes the importance weights in effectiveness, and the resulting cost-effectiveness is shown in Figure 8.26. If $W_C/W_E = 1/3$, Sweeper is the best alternative. Under this scenario, Sweeper remains the best alternative as long as the decision-maker values effectiveness at least 1.4 times as much as cost, or $W_C/W_E \leq 0.74$.

8.7 Summary

Multiple objective decision problems arise very frequently. Their solution requires the decision-maker to first determine what really matters and list the issues or consequences of concern. This process of discovery should be pursued through the construction of an objectives hierarchy. It is the single most important step towards a solution. Without doing this we run the risk of not knowing "what is the real problem" and of not asking "the right question."

The lowest levels of the hierarchy define the individual measures of effectiveness. These are the natural, constructed or proxy measurement scales by which we begin to quantify the effectiveness of an alternative. The proper integration of these measures into a single MoE requires quantification of decision-maker preferences. First we need to know decision-maker preferences over marginal changes in the individual effectiveness measures—the answer to "How much is enough?"

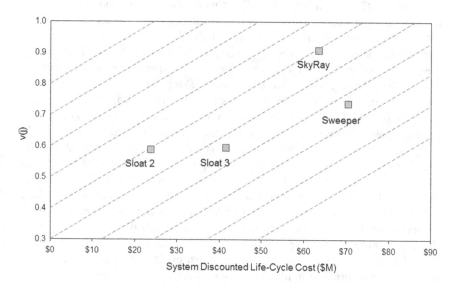

Figure 8.25 Cost-effectiveness for supersonic attack scenario: $W_C / W_E = 0.57$.

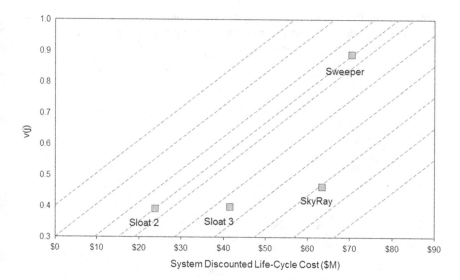

Figure 8.26 Cost-effectiveness for ECM scenario: $W_C / W_E = 0.74$.

These changes can represent increases (when more is better) or decreases (when less is better). This information allows us to convert the individual effectiveness measures into individual value measures on a 0–1 scale. Second we need to know decision-maker preferences across the individual measures—the answer to "How important is it?" This information allows us to combine the individual scaling functions using a weighted sum defined by the importance weights.

Next, we combine the resulting MoE with the discounted life-cycle cost. This provides all the information needed to conduct the analysis of cost-effectiveness. Viewing things in a two-dimensional framework expedites thinking about the solution by allowing visual inspection and making use of humans' ability at pattern recognition. In this framework, five solution concepts apply: (1) the superior solution, (2) the efficient solution, (3) the satisficing solution, (4) marginal reasoning, and (5) weighting cost versus effectiveness. The first concept should always be sought, and a superior solution (if one exists) is the best alternative regardless of the preferences for cost reduction versus effectiveness maximization. The efficient solution and the satisficing solution often yield non-unique answers and gives the decision-maker flexibility over which alternative to select. The set of efficient solutions is intrinsically important because because the most cost-effective alternative will come from this set. Selecting the most cost-effective alternative requires eliciting additional decision-maker preferences. We must know the decision-maker's preferences over cost minimization and effectiveness maximization before determining the most cost-effective alternative.

Appendix 8.1: Individual value functions

There are many functions for describing decision-maker preferences over marginal changes in a single effectiveness measure. The exponential function provides a good approximation to many preferences:

$$v_i(z_i) = \frac{1 - e^{-az_i}}{K}$$

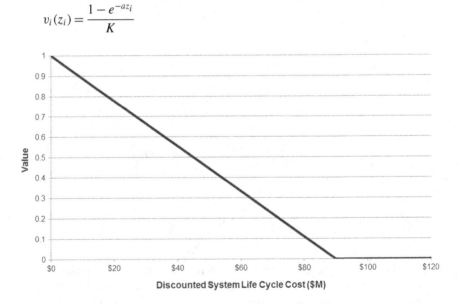

Figure A8.1 Linear value function for cost.

where either

$$z_i = x_i - x_{min}$$

(the more-is-better case) or

$$z_i = x_{max} - x_i$$

(the less-is-better case) and $K = 1 - e^{-a[x_{max} - x_{min}]}$ is a constant that standardizes the range of variation so that $0 \le v_i(z_i) \le 1$.

This function is flexible enough to include the linear value function. It can be shown using calculus that, in the limit as $a \to 0$, this function becomes

$$v_i(z_i) = \frac{z_i}{x_{max} - x_{min}}.$$

This describes a decision-maker who places equal value on marginal changes of equal amounts. For example, let $a = 0.001$, $x_{min} = 0$ and $x_{max} = \$90$ million. We obtain the function pictured in Figure A8.1. This represents a decision-maker who values a \$10 million cost savings the same, no matter if it is a reduction in cost from \$90 to \$80 million or from \$70 to \$60 million.

This exponential form can be expanded to include a quadratic term,

$$v_i(z_i) = \frac{1 - e^{-az_i - b_1 z_i^2}}{K_1},$$

or a cubic term,

$$v_i(z_i) = \frac{1 - e^{-az_i - b_1 z_i^2 - b_2 z_i^3}}{K_2},$$

where $K_1 = 1 - e^{-a[x_{max} - x_{min}] - b_1[x_{max} - x_{min}]^2}$ and $K_2 = 1 - e^{-a[x_{max} - x_{min}] - b_1[x_{max} - x_{min}]^2 - b_2[x_{max} - x_{min}]^3}$. The quadratic form with $a = 0$ allows value functions with an "S-shape" to be represented. The cubic form with $a = b = 0$ permits us to incorporate value functions that appear almost like "step" functions.

Higher-order terms can be specified but in practice are almost never needed. The additional terms permit a wider range of preference behavior to be modeled but are hardly ever worth the increased complexity.

References

Buede, Dennis M., and Terry A. Bresnick. 1992. "Applications of Decision Analysis to the Military Systems Acquisition Process." *Interfaces* 22:110–25.

Clemen, Robert T., and Terence Reilly. 2001. *Making Hard Decisions with DecisionTools*. Mason, OH: South-Western.

Dyer, James S., Thomas Edmunds, John C. Butler, and Jianmin Jia. 1998. "A Multiattribute Utility Analysis of Alternatives for the Disposition of Surplus Weapons-Grade Plutonium." *Operations Research* 46:749–62.

Ewing Jr., Paul L., William Tarantino, and Gregory S. Parnell. 2006. "Use of Decision Analysis in the Army Base Realignment and Closure (BRAC) 2005 Military Value Analysis." *Decision Analysis* 3:33–49.

Hammond, John S., Ralph L. Keeney, and Howard Raiffa. 1999. *Smart Choices: A Practical Guide to Making Better Life Decisions*. New York: Broadway Books.

Keeney, Ralph L. 1996. *Value-Focused Thinking: A Path to Creative Decisionmaking*. Cambridge, MA: Harvard University Press.

Keeney, Ralph L., and Howard Raiffa. 1976. *Decisions with Multiple Objectives: Preferences and Value Tradeoffs*. New York: John Wiley & Sons.

Kirkwood, Craig W. 1997. *Strategic Decision Making: Multiobjective Decision Analysis with Spreadsheets*. Belmont, CA: Brooks/Cole.

Parnell, Gregory S., Harry W. Conley, Jack A. Jackson, Lee J. Lehmkuhl, and John M. Andrew. 1998. "Foundations 2025: A Value Model for Evaluating Future Air and Space Forces. *Management Science* 44:1336–50.

Parnell, Gregory S., Ronald E. Metzger, Jason Merrick, and Richard Eilers. 2001. "Multiobjective Decision Analysis of Theater Missile Defense Architectures." *Systems Engineering* 4:24–34.

Stillwell, William G., David A. Seaver, and Ward Edwards. 1981. "A Comparison of Weight Approximation Techniques in Multiattribute Utility Decision Making." *Organizational Behavior and Human Performance* 28:62–77.

von Winterfeldt, Detlof, and Ward Edwards. 1986. *Decision Analysis and Behavioral Research*. Cambridge, UK: Cambridge University Press.

9 A new approach to evaluate safety and force protection investments

The value of a statistical life

Thomas J. Kniesner, John D. Leeth,
and Ryan S. Sullivan

9.1 Introduction

A fundamental tenet of economics is that public decisions should be evaluated in terms of benefits and costs. Such decisions include laws, rules, regulations, policies, and investments, and all are aimed at improving civilian safety and reducing military casualties. Economic welfare is only increased if the benefits of safety improvements exceed their costs. Whereas calculating monetary costs of safety investments is relatively well established—determined through engineering or accounting studies (see Chapter 5, for example)—monetizing benefits can be highly controversial. As we explain in this chapter, assessing the benefit of fewer fatalities and injuries requires both an accurate forecast of fatalities (and injuries) prevented or eliminated and an estimate of the monetary value of lives saved or injuries avoided.

Some contend that no monetary value can be placed on human life. The associated implication is that life is infinitely precious, so any action to improve safety regardless of the cost is worthwhile. The dilemma facing government officials can be stated as follows: although everyone believes saving lives is moral, societal resources are limited, so actions to save lives in one area come at the expense of other worthwhile goals, including the possibility of saving lives elsewhere. This chapter reveals how pricing lives can allow government officials to determine if the resources devoted to improving safety in one area might be better allocated to other areas or other programs. We urge governments with limited budgets to consider using the value of a statistical life (VSL) approach described in this chapter in any cost–benefit analysis (CBA) of alternative force protection investments. This will not only ensure resources are allocated to their highest valued use, but more importantly, may result in more lives saved.

Any military that operates as if human life had infinite value would soon be out of business. The focal message of our chapter is that hard choices must be made because complete safety is impossible. Approving every force protection investment (in armaments, technology or training) to reduce casualties or injuries would rapidly exhaust military budgets.

In reality, most of us do not behave as if our life has infinite value. Many make conscious decisions to drive small cars, knowing large cars are significantly safer, because small cars are cheaper to own and operate. We routinely engage in risky activities (skiing, biking, roller-blading, etc.), because the perceived benefits compensate for the risks. People smoke, drink alcoholic beverages, and eat unhealthy food, even though health hazards are well known, presumably because the immediate pleasure outweighs any possible long-run consequences. In short, people routinely make cost–benefit decisions that influence their own safety, and those decisions do not reflect an infinite value of life.

This chapter examines how economists evaluate the costs and benefits of safety improvements, and then provides a contemporary case study of a major recent force protection investment. The study examines the cost-effectiveness of adding armor protection to tactical wheeled vehicles (TWVs) to protect soldiers. We demonstrate how the conclusions depend on the measure called the "value of a statistical life," or VSL.

A common approach to value the benefits of greater safety is to observe actual tradeoffs people make between safety and other valuable job or product characteristics (Viscusi and Aldy 2003). Consider two identical jobs that only differ in terms of safety: one job is completely safe, but in the other job there is a 1 in 100,000 (or 0.00001) chance of a workplace injury resulting in death. The completely safe job pays US$80 less per year than the job with the slight chance of a workplace fatality.

This scenario offers two complementary perspectives. Workers in the safe job essentially sacrifice US$80 annually in the form of a lower wage to eliminate a 0.00001 chance of injury on the job that could result in death over the next year. Alternately, workers in the dangerous job demand a wage premium of US$80 extra annually to accept a 0.00001 increase in the chance of a deadly injury.

One possible interpretation is that if 100,000 workers were each willing to pay US$80 per year (a total of US$8 million) to avoid a 0.00001 probability of injury, then one life per year would be saved on average. Collectively, the US$8 million is the value workers implicitly place on that one life and implicitly on their own individual lives. Because the actual life that is saved is unknown, but in a sense is drawn randomly from the 100,000 workers, economists refer to the resulting figure (US$8 million) as the VSL.

The VSL in this case can be obtained by dividing the wage gain in the riskier occupation (US$80) by the higher probability of death (0.00001), resulting in a dollar figure (US$80/0.00001 = US$8 million) standardized to one life saved. Although the monetary value is expressed as the amount per life, it is derived by observing the actual amount of money workers sacrifice to avoid a slightly higher chance of death, and so might be better thought of as the *value of mortality risk reduction* (US Environmental Protection Agency (EPA) 2010b).[1]

After describing the theory behind VSLs, this chapter briefly summarizes various approaches used to generate VSL estimates and provides a broad overview of empirical results from the literature. VSLs can vary by income and demographic characteristics (age, gender, race), so that no single estimate is appropriate in all situations. In fact, the range of VSL estimates reported in the literature turns out to be sizeable, anywhere from US$0 to US$40 million. However, careful empirical modeling and improved risk information reduce the likely relevant range of VSLs in the United States to between US$4 million and US$10 million. For example, US Government agencies such as the EPA and US Department of Transportation (DOT) generally evaluate safety improvements using a VSL of around US$8 million.[2]

The chapter concludes with a force protection case study that examines the cost-effectiveness of two large-scale vehicle replacement programs recently implemented by the US military to increase vehicle armor protection for troops in day-to-day operations. The principal aim of the replacement programs was to reduce fatality and injury risks faced by US military personnel.

This case study illustrates a common problem when evaluating safety or force protection investments. Estimates of the benefits of risk reduction are based on engineering studies that do not consider changes in behavior that might mitigate or completely counteract the safety investment. For example, requiring drivers to wear seatbelts might reduce deaths or injuries in an accident, but could also encourage those drivers to drive faster or more recklessly, thus increasing the number of accidents. The behavioral response places drivers at greater risk, as well as increasing risks to other drivers, passengers, and pedestrians (Peltzman 1975). Simply estimating the lower probability of death or injury from using a seatbelt in a specific accident scenario will tend to overestimate the benefits of requiring seatbelt usage if behavioral responses that increase the total number of accidents are not included.

The case study presented in this chapter shows that the move from a lightly armored vehicle to a moderately armored vehicle reduced infantry fatalities at a relatively low cost of US$1 million to US$2 million per life saved for some military units. Given an estimated VSL in the range of US$4 million to US$10 million, such a force protection investment easily passes the cost-effectiveness test. Interestingly, switching to a more costly, highly armored third alternative did not appreciably reduce fatalities in any of the different military units examined, despite engineering studies that demonstrated the new vehicle was clearly safer against specific risks such as improvised explosive devices (IEDS).

An explanation for the surprising lack of life-saving benefits observed from the added armor protection in the most costly vehicle may come from offsetting behavior of our own troops or from actions by the enemy in response to the change. Both may have contributed to counteract the added force protection investment of additional armor, ultimately reflecting diminishing returns that essentially neutralized the value of the most costly safety investment. This result points to the importance of properly framing a cost–benefit study, especially when lives are at stake, and the value of VSL to help guide force protection investments.

9.2   The economic approach to valuing safety investments

The economic theory behind valuing safety is built on the assumption that people prefer not to gamble excessively with their lives or their health. Thrill seekers may seek danger for its own sake, but are in the minority. The vast majority dislike risk and are only willing to accept it if they are compensated in some way. All else being equal, a worker might choose a more hazardous workplace if he or she receives a higher wage, or a consumer might be willing to purchase a less safe product if its price is sufficiently low.[3]

On the other side of the market, it is costly for firms to improve workplace and product safety. To avoid the added costs, firms typically assess the possibility of paying higher wages (i.e. compensating wage differentials) to workers to accept slightly greater risks, or offering lower prices to customers to accept slightly more hazardous products.

Consider a labor market where there are only two types of jobs: a job with zero risk of workplace injury ($\pi = 0$) and a job with a high risk of workplace injury ($\pi = \pi_{high}$). The jobs are identical in every other respect. With the exception of thrill seekers, no worker would willingly choose the dangerous job over a safe job for the same wage. At best, the worker in the dangerous job is uninjured and earns the same as in the perfectly safe job; at worst, the worker is injured and bears the pain and cost of the injury and corresponding loss of income.[4]

For workers to accept the gamble of the dangerous job, the expected payoff if uninjured must be high enough to outweigh the expected loss if injured. This payoff might include a higher wage, better fringe benefits, or a more pleasant work environment, but for simplicity suppose the only compensation for the riskier job is a higher wage. Differences among workers in their economic circumstances, family situations, and general tastes and preferences will cause some workers to demand a very large compensating wage differential to accept extra risk, while others might be willing to accept a relatively small wage premium.

Programs that improve workplace safety have costs. Firms may need to purchase additional equipment or protective devices, install machine guards, slow down the pace of production or stop production entirely to service equipment, hire consultants to advise management or train workers in safe procedures. Those firms may also have to devote valuable management time to monitor safety.

For some employers safety-enhancing efforts may be quite expensive, but for other employers the costs may be slight. Because of inherent dangers in production, similar to the military, firms in mining, logging, fishing, and construction will need to spend relatively more than firms in manufacturing, retail trade, or financial services to achieve the same level of safety for their workers. To be willing to bear the costs of expanding safety programs firms must anticipate corresponding economic benefits such as greater worker job satisfaction (leading to lower compensation payments) or the ability to produce greater output, charge higher prices, or pay smaller insurance premiums.

If wages were the same in both safe and risky occupations, all workers (with the exception of risk seekers) would choose to work in establishments with complete safety. Workers would gain nothing from accepting any job risk, and firms would earn no economic returns from investing in safety. However, the excess supply of workers choosing safe jobs will cause their wages to fall, while excess demand by firms for workers required for risky jobs will cause wages in risky jobs to rise.

The resulting wage gap between the two types of jobs will cause some workers to improve their welfare by accepting a risky job and some firms to realize they can expand profits by investing to reduce job hazards. The decisions of workers and firms between the two types of jobs will continue until no firm can expand its profits by adjusting its expenditures on safety, and no worker can expand his or her expected utility by changing jobs.[5]

An example is provided by all-volunteer military forces. Assuming the military is the riskier occupation, all else being equal, compensating wage differentials (which might include extra job satisfaction, pride in serving the country, education and training opportunities) are required to recruit and retain individuals that have a choice of safer occupations. In turn, the military as an employer can reduce the premium (compensating wage differential) it pays soldiers through its force protection investments that reduce risk of death or injury.

Because the wage difference ($w_{high} - w_0$) seen in Figure 9.1 reflects both sides of the market, it measures both the marginal cost (the added cost of safety programs) and the marginal benefit (as measured by worker preferences) of improving safety. Notice that if job risk represents the chance of a fatal workplace injury, then the implied VSL in this market is equal to $(w_{high} - w_0)/(\pi_{high} - 0)$, which is equivalent to the earlier VSL calculation (US\$80/0.00001 = US\$8 million).

The process that sorts workers and firms among the various levels of risk is the same when there are three or more distinct levels of risk. Wages rise as risk expands, and the higher wage encourages less risk-averse workers to accept higher-risk jobs, and firms with lower costs of providing safety to eliminate hazards. In the limit, risk becomes continuous and the resulting equilibrium relationship between wages and risk is captured by a function described by a curve such as the one in Figure 9.2.[6]

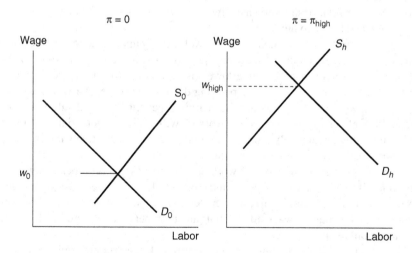

Figure 9.1 Labor market equilibrium with discrete risk.

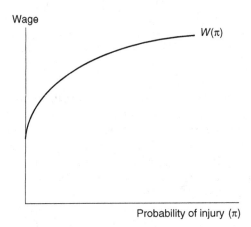

Figure 9.2 Labor market equilibrium with continuous risk.

As is well known in economics, firms maximize profits by using inputs to the point where their marginal benefits equal their marginal costs. In the case of safety inputs, marginal costs might include the expense of buying additional equipment, slowing production, or paying for safety training, while marginal benefits include the lower wages firms must pay to attract workers as risks fall.

Because the costs of providing a given level of safety vary among workplaces, the optimum level of safety in different industries (occupations) will also vary. In equilibrium, all firms tend to provide their workers a level of safety where the marginal benefits of additional safety investments match the marginal costs. Firms with lower inherent costs of reducing hazards provide a safer workplace and locate to the left along the wage relationship shown in Figure 9.2, and firms with higher costs provide less safety and locate to the right.

Similar to firms, people maximize their welfare by pursuing actions to the point where the marginal benefit of an action equals its marginal cost. In terms of safety the marginal benefit of accepting a lower-risk job is the lower chance of injury, and the marginal cost is the corresponding drop in the wage. All workers maximize their welfare by comparing the marginal benefit of added safety against the additional cost. More risk-averse workers will value the potential benefits of safety investments relatively more (or are willing to accept relatively lower wages to avoid safety risks), while the opposite is true of less risk-averse workers.

Firms tend to supply more or less workplace safety based on compensating wage differentials they must offer to recruit and retain workers, and their costs to produce a safe work environment. In turn, workers tend to sort themselves into job risk categories based on market wage differentials and their personal preferences (relative risk aversion) regarding safety.

In the end, wages must adjust along the entire risk spectrum to equilibrate supply and demand for labor. If there is a shortage of workers at any risk level, wages will rise at that risk level (in that industry), causing some firms to alter their expenditures on safety and some workers to relocate to the now better-paying jobs. The movement of firms and workers will create labor shortages elsewhere and cause wages to rise at the other levels of risk. A surplus of labor at any level of risk will cause wages to fall at that risk level, which will cascade throughout the entire risk spectrum as firms and workers adjust to the new lower wage. Equilibrium is established in the market when there is no excess demand or supply of labor at any risk level.

The slope of the wage function shown in Figure 9.2 measures the income workers must sacrifice to lower their chance of injury by a small amount (or alternatively, the amount they must be compensated to accept greater risk). Because workers maximize their well-being by equating marginal cost with marginal benefit, the slope of the wage function also equals the value workers place on small improvements in safety. Similar to the earlier case with only two levels of risk, a VSL can be calculated for a representative worker by dividing the wage premium necessary for a worker to accept a small increase in the probability of death (measured by the slope of the wage function evaluated at the mean level of risk), by the associated increase in the probability of death. An implicit value of injury can be found in a similar manner by dividing an estimated market wage increase required for a representative worker to accept a small increase in the probability of a work-related non-fatal injury or illness, by the change in that probability of injury or illness. The resulting calculation is known as the value of a statistical injury (VSI).

Market equilibrium in product markets is similar to that in labor markets, except the end result is an inverse (negative) relationship between price and risk. The added cost of producing safer products implies that the price of the product must rise as the product's risk (probability of injury from using the product) falls, compensating manufacturers for the extra costs.

Consumers value both additional safety and more goods and services, meaning that, all else being equal, they are only willing to purchase riskier products if they are sufficiently cheaper than safer products. The interaction of firms and consumers in the marketplace generates a price function where firms sort themselves based on their abilities to produce safe products, while consumers sort themselves based on their relative valuations of increased safety. In equilibrium the slope of the market price function provides an estimate of consumers' willingness to pay for added safety, which can also be used to generate a VSL or VSI (Viscusi and Aldy 2003).

9.3 Value of statistical life estimates

The majority of VSL estimates are derived from estimates of a market wage equation such as that presented in Appendix 9.1. Variation in wages is typically explained by workplace risk, controlling for other job characteristics and various demographic variables. The relationship obtained between wages and job risk, controlling for other factors, generates the data needed to estimate a VSL.

Viscusi (2004) provides a good example. For his measure of risk Viscusi relies on data drawn from the Census of Fatal Occupational Injuries (CFOI), which are discussed in more detail in Viscusi (2013). Since 1992, the Bureau of Labor Statistics (BLS) has compiled yearly data on all workplace fatalities in the United States by examining death certificates, medical examiner reports, Occupational Safety and Health Administration (OSHA) reports, and workers' compensation records. In his sample data the average fatality risk is 4/100,000, with the lowest risk level 0.6/100,000, and the highest nearly 25/100,000.[7]

Viscusi then combines the fatality risk data with individual worker demographic data from the 1997 merged outgoing rotation groups of the Current Population Survey (CPS).[8] His estimating equation assumes a linear relationship between log hourly wages and fatal injury risk (see Equation (9A.1.1) in Appendix 9.1). The VSL calculated for all workers from his baseline regression analysis is US$12.1 million.[9]

House prices provide another avenue for determining implied VSLs. All else being equal, houses located in less desirable (or riskier) areas should sell for less than houses located in more desirable areas. If desirability reflects the absence of pollution or other health hazards, then the smaller chance of premature death, injury or illness and the resulting higher price can be used to estimate a VSL.

Gayer *et al.* (2000) estimate a house market price equation to determine the implicit value of avoiding cancer. See Appendix 9.2 for the estimating equation of the relationship between house prices and environmental risks. The authors use risk information and individual housing data drawn from an area surrounding a Superfund Hazard site in the greater Grand Rapids region of Michigan to estimate the relationship between housing prices and environmental (cancer) risk.[10] They find that in the period following the EPA's release of its report, a 1.81 per 1,000,000 reduction in cancer risk (the mean level in the sample) raises the price of the average house by about US$25. The estimates imply that the household valuation of reducing one cancer is about US$13.9 million. Given an average number of household members of about 2.6, the individual value of reducing one cancer (or implicit VSL) is estimated to be about US$5.4 million.

Economists have examined a variety of products and actions to determine reasonable values for VSLs. When consumers purchase products that directly decrease risk such as bike helmets or smoke detectors, the approach is quite straightforward: simply divide the cost of the product by the lower likelihood of death. In some cases actions to expand safety may not require a monetary outlay, such as using a seat belt or driving more slowly, but even here it is often possible to generate a VSL by combining the safety effects of the action with dollar estimates of the opportunity cost of time (Viscusi and Aldy 2003).

In a particularly interesting and relevant example of the indirect approach, Rohlfs (2012) develops VSL estimates by examining two tactics used by young men during the Vietnam War to avoid the draft: enrolling in college or voluntarily enlisting. Although one might not necessarily view voluntarily enlisting in the military as a sensible strategy to avoid the draft, by volunteering men could avoid the possibility of having their careers interrupted through required military service and they could choose their branch of service, obtain specialty training, and in some cases enter as officers. Enlisting also improved one's chance of survival. From 1966 to the end of US involvement in the Vietnam War the death rates of volunteers and officers were significantly lower than the death rates for draftees.

To see how Rohlfs determines the value of avoiding the draft by voluntarily enlisting in the military consider Figure 9.3, which shows two supply curves. The first is the supply of men to the military if there were no draft. The second is the supply of men volunteering to serve in the military given a draft. At every wage, more men are willing to enlist in the military with a draft than without a draft to avoid the costs of having their careers interrupted, to be able to choose their branch of service and type of training, and to expand their odds of survival. The supply of men with the draft is everywhere to the right of the supply curve without a draft.

Given the level of pay in the military, the number of men who would enlist without a draft is E_{nd} and the number of men who would enlist with a draft is E_d. Rohlfs estimates the increase in the number of enlistees during the Vietnam War era, all else being equal, and then uses those estimates with outside estimates of the supply elasticity of men willing to enlist in the military to determine the vertical distance between the two supply curves in Figure 9.3. The vertical distance represents the increase in military pay necessary to generate the same increase in enlistments as generated from the draft. It represents the dollar value of avoiding the draft for the marginal enlistee during that period (an individual just indifferent between enlisting and taking a chance with the draft).

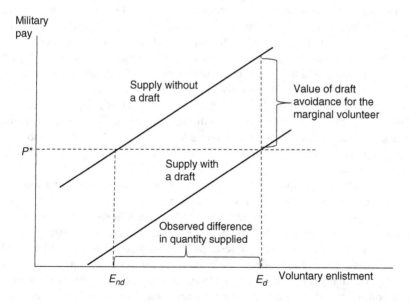

Figure 9.3 Supply of voluntary enlistments and the Vietnam draft.

Rohlfs uses a similar procedure to determine the dollar value of avoiding the draft by enrolling in college for the marginal student (an individual just indifferent between attending college and taking his chance with the draft), except that in the case of college he examines two demand curves instead of two supply curves. Based on college enrollments the cost of avoiding the draft for the marginal student was about US$30,000, and based on enlistments the cost of avoiding the draft for the marginal volunteer was about US$117,000. Rohlfs generates the implied VSLs by assuming the only cost of being drafted is the higher likelihood of death. He refers to the resulting values as upper bounds on the true VSLs. Specifically, he divides his estimates of the value of avoiding the draft by the associated differences in mortality risk and finds VSLs for young men that are in the US$1.6 million to US$5.2 million range using information from college enrollments, and VSLs that are in the US$7.4 million to US$12.1 million range using information from military enlistments. Rohlfs suggests that the higher range derived from information on voluntary enlistments may more accurately reflect the true VSL of young men at the time.[11]

9.4   Contingent valuation estimates

Besides using market data, VSLs can also be estimated using data from surveys that question individuals about their willingness to pay for small reductions in risk. Generally, the surveys used in contingent valuation (or so-called "stated preference") studies describe a base risk level that can be reduced by engaging in some activity, purchasing some product or service, or purchasing a different, safer product than the product originally described.[12]

In its simplest form, survey data provide direct values of people's willingness to pay for improvements in safety. Unlike studies using market wages or housing prices, contingent valuation studies attempt to uncover preferences directly.

Following the law of diminishing returns the marginal benefit of further gains in safety declines as safety improves. Attempting to estimate the value functions of workers or consumers that underlie market wage or housing price functions is quite difficult.[13] Because the price of safety is implicit, identifying the parameters of the structural equations underling equilibrium is more difficult than estimating a standard simultaneous equation system such as the supply and demand for a homogenous product such as milk (Brown and Rosen 1982; Epple 1987; Kahn and Lang 1988).

As with all surveys, one must ensure that respondents carefully consider the alternatives presented. Specifically, researchers should attempt to create unbiased surveys. For example, respondents tend to place a higher value on a safety device or policy when it is the only option available on a survey. Also, one must consider the order of the survey questions. Respondents often place higher values on safety devices or policies when they appear first in a set of questions. Finally, "willingness to say" does not always correspond to "willingness to pay." Such complications can undermine survey results and bias any subsequent VSL estimates.[14]

Due to inherent problems with contingent valuation surveys, many economists prefer to rely on VSLs generated from market data that reflect consumers' (or workers') actual willingness to pay (or to be compensated) for a marginal improvement (deterioration) in safety.[15]

9.5 Generating VSL estimates

The range of VSL estimates derived from the empirical literature is quite large, on the order of US$0–US$40 million (Mrozek and Taylor 2002; Viscusi and Aldy 2003; Bellavance *et al.* 2009).[16] The variation can create a dilemma for policy-makers. A proper evaluation of any program designed to improve health and safety requires accurate estimates of benefits from the program. Employing too low a VSL in workforce protection and other safety investments will underestimate the benefits of mortality risk reduction, resulting in the rejection of worthwhile programs. Setting too high a VSL will tend to overestimate the benefits of specific mortality risk reduction investments, resulting in accepting extremely costly programs and thereby diverting resources away from other more valuable uses.

One approach to solving the dilemma of the wide range of VSL estimates is to use meta-analysis to combine the various estimates into a single value that corresponds roughly to the mean of the estimates. For example, the US EPA recommends using US$8.0 million to value the lives saved from eliminating environmental hazards, based on the mean of a Weibull statistical distribution fitted to 26 separate VSL estimates (US EPA 2010a). The US DOT uses an US$8.6 million VSL to evaluate the benefits of improving transportation safety, based on the mean value of nine fairly recent labor market VSL studies (US DOT 2008).[17]

Kniesner *et al.* (2012) offer another approach and demonstrate how using the best available data and econometric tools can significantly narrow the range of VSL estimates.[18] They demonstrate how systematic econometric modeling narrows the estimated VSL from a range of US$0–US$40 million to US$4 million–US$10 million, which the authors demonstrate facilitates the choice of the proper labor market-based VSL to use for public policy (Kniesner *et al.* 2012).

Government agencies constantly make choices on how to spend scarce resources that impact public safety. Achieving complete safety, even if technologically feasible, is never possible due to resource scarcity. Economists regularly employ the monetary benefit metric of a VSL to help evaluate safety and force protection investments. As discussed earlier, the critical value of a VSL is revealed by individuals' implicit willingness to pay for reduced harm via compensating wage differentials, or lower prices paid for products that involve somewhat greater hazards.

The manner in which a death might occur and personal characteristics affecting the willingness to accept danger (for example age or education) are important in military applications, and both can play important roles in evaluating the cost-effectiveness of increased personal safety or military force protection investments. The next section offers an application of VSL in a cost–benefit study of a military force protection investment to improve the armor of TWVs. The same principles that find applications in evaluating government investments in safety improvements (EPA, DOT, DOL), and in private labor and product markets, are equally relevant and applicable to military force protection investments.

9.6   Case study: Force protection investment—armoring tactical wheeled vehicles

The following case study summarizes the methods and results presented in a recently published article by Rohlfs and Sullivan (2013a) entitled "The Cost-Effectiveness of Armored Tactical Wheeled Vehicles for Overseas US Army Operations." In their study, Rohlfs and Sullivan use a VSL cutoff of US$7.5 million to determine the cost-effectiveness of three separate armored tactical wheeled vehicles. In addition to summarizing the methods and findings, we offer a discussion of policy implications and limitations of using VSL cutoffs in evaluating tradeoffs between money spent (cost) and lives saved (benefits) for this and other military programs.

Due to the sensitive nature of the data used in Rohlfs and Sullivan (2013a), the alternative vehicles in the case study are labeled with the generic titles of Type 1, 2, or 3, the months of data are denoted 1 through 71, and the theater of operations is labeled Theater A. The US Army maintains each of the three vehicle types primarily for troop transport, and the vehicles vary in terms of maneuverability, weight, and speed. However, the primary difference among the vehicles is their armor protection.[19]

9.6.1   Background and data

As discussed in Rohlfs and Sullivan (2013a), over the course of the Global War on Terror the US Army engaged in two large-scale force protection investments that involved vehicle replacement programs to reduce fatality and injury risks for US troops. Both programs affected wheeled ground vehicles that US forces used for day-to-day operations. The first replacement program involved replacing a large number of lightly armored Type 1 TWVs, which cost roughly US$50,000 apiece, with medium armored Type 2 TWVs that cost more than three times as much, or US$170,000.[20]

The second replacement program began at the time the first program was ending, and it involved replacing about 9,000 Type 2 TWVs with heavily armored Type 3 TWVs that cost more than three times as much as the Type 2s, around US$600,000 apiece. The total investment in the Type 3 TWV force protection program was over US$50 billion, almost 10 percent of the US base defense budget at the time.[21]

To conduct an (ex-post) military CBA of alternative force protection investments requires estimates of costs (procurement, maintenance, fuel) and benefits (lives saved). The maintenance and fuel costs of Type 2 and Type 3 TWVs are typically higher than for Type 1 TWVs. Rohlfs and Sullivan estimated in-theater fuel and maintenance costs of US$5.50 per mile for Type 1 TWVs, and US$10.50 per mile for Type 2 and Type 3 TWVs.

Type 3 TWVs are also much heavier and therefore more expensive to transport overseas in comparison to the other types. Moreover, the physical depreciation (deterioration) of the vehicle types is higher in conflict conditions than in peacetime, and thus impacts expected lifetime costs, which requires further adjustments. For purposes of their study, Rohlfs and Sullivan (2013a) assume a one-way trip and three-year lifespan for all vehicle types, and that the US Army uses each vehicle in combat for all three years. The estimated costs of an average three-year vehicle deployment (including procurement and transportation) were US$143,000 for a Type 1 TWV, US$345,000 for a Type 2 TWV, and US$780,000 for a Type 3 TWV.[22]

To evaluate the force protection benefits of the three alternatives, Rohlfs and Sullivan (2013a) use casualty and unit-level characteristics in Theater A provided by the Defense Manpower Data Center (DMDC) for all Army units over a 71-month time period. They group the data at the battalion level to match up closely with how the Army assigned vehicles and tasks. They also group the data into four distinct unit types: (i) infantry, (ii) armored and cavalry, (iii) administrative and support, and (iv) other.

The Army incurred 34 deaths and 266 combat-related injuries in Theater A on average each month. The standard deviation in deaths across months is 23, while the standard deviation in combat-related injuries is 166. Total Army casualties in Theater A often changed by more than 100 from one month to the next.

Unit-level controls include detailed information on the number of troops; the fractions that are officers, Privates or Privates First Class (PFC), high school graduates, male, black, or Hispanic; average days of deployment experience; age by unit and month; and the unit's name and home state within the United States.

9.6.2 Armored vehicle case study: econometric methods and discussion of results

To evaluate the cost-effectiveness of vehicle Types 1–3, Rohlfs and Sullivan (2013a) first examine the relationship between the three vehicle types and overall unit fatalities. Specifically, they use standard econometric methods including regression analysis to estimate changes in unit-level casualty rates as a function of each unit's complement of vehicle types while controlling for other factors. Details of the modeling approach can be found in Appendix 9.3. The results are summarized below.[23]

- Preferred estimates indicate that the medium armor provided by Type 2 TWVs over the lightly protected Type 1 TWVs reduced fatalities at a cost of US$1 million to US$2 million per life saved for infantry units, well below the US$7.5 million VSL threshold set out in the study.
- For armored and cavalry units, and administrative and support units, the estimates indicate that the switch from Type 1 to Type 2 TWVs did not reduce fatalities.
- The switch from Type 2 to Type 3 TWVs did not appreciably reduce fatalities for any of the four unit types, despite the higher cost and heavier armor of Type 3 TWVs.

In terms of evaluating tradeoffs between money spent (costs) and lives saved (benefits), the policy implications are relatively straightforward. It does not appear that the extra armor protection provided by Types 2 or 3 TWVs over Type 1 TWVs provided enough benefit (in terms of lives saved) to warrant the additional costs for armored and cavalry or administration and support units. Thus, results from Rohlfs and Sullivan (2013a) suggest it would have been more cost-effective to use Type 1 TWVs in day-to-day operations for armored and cavalry, and administration and support units, and to deploy Type 2s only to infantry units. Money saved by following recommendations from the cost–benefit calculations could presumably have been better used in alternative force protection investments to save more lives, or to increase social welfare through higher compensating wage differentials.

Whereas for infantry units the results suggested Type 2 TWVs were significantly more cost-effective in comparison to Type 1 TWVs (fatalities were reduced at a relatively low cost of US$1 million to US$2 million per life saved), the additional armor protection provided by Type 3 over Type 2 TWVs did not appreciably reduce casualties. The findings suggest the preferred policy would have favored infantry units using Type 2 TWVs, rather than the less expensive Types 1s or the more expensive Type 3s.

Surprisingly, Type 3 vehicles did not appear to reduce fatalities or injuries appreciably for any of the four unit types, despite Type 3's substantially greater armor protection. The results in Rohlfs and Sullivan (2013a) therefore suggest the significantly higher investment required for Type 3s was not cost-effective in operations for any of the unit types. An important caveat is that political, psychological, operational or other benefits may exist that broaden the scope of the calculations beyond the simple evaluation of vehicle-provided force protection. Such additional considerations naturally complicate any policy recommendations that might come from a basic force protection CBA.

One key distinction between the study by Rohlfs and Sullivan (2013a) and other authors who have studied the topic (citations are withheld due to security concerns), is that the other studies tend to focus exclusively on differences in casualty rates from IEDs among the various vehicle types (with a specific focus on Type 3 TWVs). In contrast, Rohlfs and Sullivan measure the full effects of changing vehicle type, taking into account the intrinsic properties of the vehicles and any behavioral responses by the units.

For instance, other studies highlight findings that show the fraction of IED attacks resulting in death is higher for Type 1 and 2 vehicles than for Type 3 vehicles. Some authors used the IED results to suggest Type 3 TWVs saved thousands of lives in comparison to Type 1 or 2 TWVs. It should be noted, however, that several studies incorrectly assume soldiers in Type 3 TWVs are attacked by IEDs at the same rate as soldiers in other vehicle types. The other researchers also implicitly assume that the design of the extra protection provided by Type 3 TWVs does not impact the tendency for soldiers to expose themselves to attacks that do not involve IEDs or that occur outside those vehicles.

As discussed in Rohlfs and Sullivan (2013b), it appears that several implicit assumptions used in previous studies may not be appropriate. When soldiers adopted the heavily armored Type 3 vehicles, insurgents may have directed their efforts away from direct IED attacks on vehicles, and more toward indirect attacks on soldiers once they were outside their vehicles. Moreover, providing troops with safer vehicles may have increased their willingness to take certain risks, much as wearing a motorcycle helmet makes motorcycle riders somewhat more likely to take risks on the road.

In the (SDC) data, there was strong evidence of a substitution effect among armored and cavalry units. When the Army replaced their Type 1 and 2 vehicles with the heavier Type 3 vehicles, soldiers made greater use of their TWVs and less use of vehicles with more firepower, such as tanks. Anecdotal evidence also suggests that soldiers avoided certain dirt roads and bridges when driving Type 3 TWVs due to their weight. If the behavioral responses just described occurred more generally—changing the rate at which units were exposed to different types of attacks—then a more appropriate way to measure the vehicles' full benefits is to use the approach in Rohlfs and Sullivan (2013a), who examine the impact of introducing more heavily armored vehicles on a unit's overall fatalities.

A limitation of the Rohlfs and Sullivan (2013a) study is that it does not monetize all the capabilities provided by each of the three vehicles. The only benefits from the vehicles that their study monetizes are the vehicles' impacts on fatalities and injuries.

Other benefits or costs not accounted for in the study could potentially alter their estimates. For example, some vehicles may have greater maneuverability or less weight in comparison to others, which may or may not enhance operational combat capabilities. Increasing the scope of the cost–benefit calculations to capture additional capability attributes could cause the vehicles to be more or less cost-effective than indicated in Rohlfs and Sullivan.

They also acknowledge their estimates "should be interpreted with the caveat that they do not capture other potential benefits, such as increasing mission success." A more complete CBA would require monetizing any "additional benefits and costs" as outlined in US OMB (1992). For the reasons listed above, policy recommendations generated from this CBA might need to be adjusted if the scope of the research is broadened to include additional benefits and costs in evaluating the three alternative vehicles.

Capturing secondary and tertiary costs and benefits of force protection investments makes it more difficult to provide precise recommendations on optimal vehicle investments to policy-makers. A valuable extension of the original Rohlfs and Sullivan (2013a) study would be to examine other vehicle attributes that may or may not impact mission success. However, given that force protection (saving lives) was the Army's stated goal, and the principal stated aim of the vehicle procurement programs, advocating the provision of light armored Type 1 TWVs to administrative and support units, and medium armored Type 2 TWVs to infantry units, would appear to be a reasonable recommendation. The increase in armor protection provided by investments in Type 3 TWVs over Type 2 TWVs does not appear to justify their cost strictly in terms of life-saving capabilities.[24]

9.7   Concluding observations and other military applications

The VSL offers a new approach to evaluate safety and force protection investments. Applying VSL to improve force protection investments, such as the evaluation of alternative TWVs, raises an important issue. If the cost of an investment to save a life is substantially higher than the VSL threshold (US$7.5 million in the study), could the money be better used (e.g. save more lives) in alternative ways? A number of other possible military force protection investments exist and constitute important topics for future research.

Worthy topics include investments in defensive weapons systems to protect civilian populations or state-of-the-art body armor to protect soldiers. Another possible application of VSL could be more contentious. It concerns one of the costliest areas in the military—the substantial resources spent to care for wounded warriors.

Creating a list of VSL values to be applied in medical interventions based on patient characteristics (injury types, severity, ease of repair) might serve as a type of triage tool. This could potentially help evaluate tradeoffs between money spent and lives saved across numerous medical procedures to achieve the greatest possible total health benefits for the military from its limited resources.

A related opportunity to apply this cost–benefit technique is to evaluate the optimal number of medics to assign to different military units. For example, it is typical for infantry platoons (of 40 or so persons) to have only one medic with them in the field. Unfortunately, this means that some squads (usually around nine people) frequently go on patrols without medics. Would it be cost-effective to hire additional medics to help save more lives, rather than spend resources on alternative life-saving investments? This is currently an open question that could be informed using VSL.

In the current, fiscally constrained environment, the military must make difficult choices about which life-saving programs to fund. Budget constraints limit the ability to fund every safety and force protection proposal. This chapter offers a variety of techniques and examples on how VSL can be used to conduct military CBA on safety and force protection investments. Application of this powerful tool will improve the management of scarce defense resources and help determine if life-saving investments in one area might be better spent on other methods or programs to reduce overall military casualties.

Appendix 9.1: Calculating VSL through wage differentials

Estimating equation of the relationship between
wages and workplace risk

The standard estimating equation underlying most labor market VSL calculations is

$$\ln(w) = c + \sum_{i=1}^{m} \alpha_i \pi_i + \sum_{j=1}^{n} \beta_j X_j + \varepsilon, \tag{9A.1.1}$$

where $\ln(w)$ is the natural logarithm of wage; π_i are measures of workplace risk; X_i are demographic variables (such as education, race, marital status, and union membership) and job characteristics (such as wage replacement under workers' compensation insurance, and industry, occupation, or geographic location indicators); ε is an error term; and c, α_i, and β_j are parameters to be estimated. Many studies also include interaction terms between workplace risk and various X_i to determine variation in risk compensation by type of worker (union/nonunion, white/black, native/immigrant, young/old) or by level of income replacement from workers' compensation insurance (Viscusi and Aldy 2003).

Appendix 9.2: Calculating VSL through house price differentials

Estimating equation of the relationship between house prices and environmental risks

As with labor market studies, the underlying framework for generating the VSL values is a market price equation that relates house price to environmental hazards, holding other factors constant. Specifically,

$$\ln(p) = c + \sum_{i=1}^{m} \alpha_i E_i + \sum_{j=1}^{n} \beta_j C_j + \varepsilon, \tag{9A.2.1}$$

where $\ln(p)$ is the natural logarithm of price; the E_i are environmental hazards; and C_j are structure characteristics, neighborhood, and other control variables that affect price (for instance, number of rooms, number of bathrooms, lot size, neighborhood median income, and distance to central city) (Gayer *et al.* 2000).

Appendix 9.3: Calculating fatality and cost effects of armoring tactical wheeled vehicles

Estimating equations of the relationships among fatalities, expenditures, and vehicle types

For a given unit i in month t, suppose that fatalities are determined according to the following linear equation:

$$fatalities_{it} = \sum_{j=1}^{3} \alpha_{cj}^{f} \times q_{jit} + \beta_c^{f'} \mathbf{x}_{it} + \varepsilon_{it}^{f}, \tag{9A.3.1}$$

where q_{1it}, q_{2it}, and q_{3it} represent the quantities of each of three types of vehicles possessed by unit i in month t; $\mathbf{x}_{it}$ is a vector of control variables that might include other vehicle quantities, troop characteristics, or fixed effects for month, province, month by province, or unit; ε_{it}^{f} is random error; and the coefficients are allowed to vary by the unit's classification c as infantry, armored or cavalry, administrative and support, or other. Let vehicle types one, two, and three be defined as Type 1, Type 2, and Type 3 TWVs.

Because the focus of the Rohlfs and Sullivan (2013a) study is the effects of replacing one vehicle type with another, it is convenient to rearrange the terms in Equation (9A.3.1) to obtain the following specification:

$$fatalities_{it} = (\alpha_{c2}^f - \alpha_{c1}^f) \times q_{2it} + (\alpha_{c3}^f - \alpha_{c1}^f) \times q_{3it} + \alpha_{c1}^f$$

$$\times \sum_{j=1}^{3} q_{jit} + \beta_c^{f\prime} \mathbf{x}_{it} + \varepsilon_{it}^f. \tag{9A.3.2}$$

Equation (9A.3.2) serves as their main regression specification, with $\sum_{j=1}^{3} q_{jit}$, q_{2it}, q_{3it}, and varying formulations of $\mathbf{x}_{it}$ as the regressors. The differences $(\alpha_{c2}^f - \alpha_{c1}^f)$ and $(\alpha_{c3}^f - \alpha_{c1}^f)$ measure the effects of replacing Type 1 TWV with a Type 2 or Type 3 TWV.

Rohlfs and Sullivan (2013a) next focus on the costs related to the vehicles by estimating changes in expenditures by unit as a function of the different vehicle types and their usage rates. Their expenditure modeling technique follows.

To relate effects on fatalities to dollar costs, let p_{0j} denote the purchase price (including shipping cost), and let p_{1j} denote the additional cost per mile driven for a type j vehicle. Let $mileage_{jit}$ denote the miles driven of type j vehicles by unit i in month t, and define $expenditure_{it}$ as unit i's month t expense for all three vehicle types

$$expenditure_{it} = \sum_{j=1}^{3} \left(\frac{1}{36} p_{0j} \times q_{jit} + p_{1j} \times mileage_{jit} \right) \tag{9A.3.3}$$

Expenditures can be written as a linear function symmetrically to the fatalities equations:

$$expenditure_{it} = (\alpha_{c2}^e - \alpha_{c1}^e) * q_{2it} + (\alpha_{c3}^e - \alpha_{c1}^e) * q_{3it}$$

$$+ \alpha_{c1}^e * \sum_{j=1}^{3} q_{jit} + \beta_c^{e\prime} \mathbf{x}_{it} + \varepsilon_{it}^e \tag{9A.3.4}$$

where $(\alpha_{c2}^e - \alpha_{c1}^e)$ and $(\alpha_{c3}^e - \alpha_{c1}^e)$ represent the monthly costs of replacing a Type 1 TWV with a Type 2 or Type 3 TWV. Expressing the costs of changing vehicle type through Equation (9A.3.4) helps to ensure that the same factors are held constant and the same sets of observations are compared to one another for the cost as for the fatalities estimation. The mileage and expenditure data are constructed from the SDC sample and use the same sampling weights as the vehicle counts; consequently, any measurement error in vehicle quantities that affects the fatalities regressions does not affect the coefficients in Equation (9A.3.4).

The cost per life saved from replacing a Type 1 with a Type 2 TWV is $-(\alpha_{c2}^{e} - \alpha_{c1}^{e})/(\alpha_{c2}^{f} - \alpha_{c1}^{f})$, which expressed verbally is negative one times the ratio of the difference between the coefficient for Type 2 TWVs and the coefficient for Type 1 TWVs from Equation (9A.3.4), the expenditures equation, divided by the corresponding difference in coefficients from Equation (9A.3.3), the fatalities equation. The cost per life saved from replacing a Type 2 TWV with a Type 3 TWV is $-(\alpha_{c3}^{e} - \alpha_{c2}^{e})/(\alpha_{c3}^{f} - \alpha_{c2}^{f})$, which is computed as negative one times the difference between the coefficient for Type 3 TWVs and the coefficient for Type 2 TWVs from Equation (9A.3.4) divided by the corresponding difference in coefficients from Equation (9A.3.3). Other dependent variables considered in the study are combat-related injuries and miles driven by different vehicles. Rohlfs and Sullivan calculate standard errors for the ratios by estimating Equations (9A.3.3) and (9A.3.4) together using seemingly unrelated regression and applying the delta method.

Measuring effects on injuries helps to identify a benefit of changing vehicle type not included in the cost per life saved calculations. To interpret the effects on injuries better, Rohlfs and Sullivan (2013a) compute the ratios of injuries reduced per life saved as $(\alpha_{c2}^{i} - \alpha_{c1}^{i})/(\alpha_{c2}^{f} - \alpha_{c1}^{f})$ and $(\alpha_{c3}^{i} - \alpha_{c2}^{i})/(\alpha_{c3}^{f} - \alpha_{c2}^{f})$, where the i superscript denotes coefficients from the injury equation. Measuring effects on the mileage variables helps to determine the extent to which the replacement policies led units to alter their behavior.

Notes

1 Rarely do you see two jobs that are otherwise identical except for the chance of a workplace fatality. Economists derive VSL estimates econometrically using large datasets that allow them to control for other factors affecting wages or product prices to generate the *ceteris paribus* impact of risk. It is worth noting, though, that sometimes risks are explicitly priced for workers by employers—for example, with so-called hazardous duty pay in the military.

2 Implementing a safety improvement that costs more than the benefits generated can result in more lives being lost because the funding could be better spent on alternative safety improvements. Kniesner and Leeth (2004), for instance, examine safety inspections of underground coal mines by the Mine Safety and Health Administration (MSHA) and find that inspections fail the cost-benefit test. They show that eliminating one safety inspection per mine per year (MSHA inspects underground coal mines quarterly) and moving the funding to other activities such as heart disease screening or purchasing defibrillators, would save 39,700 more miners' lives. Formally, the cost-benefit test shows whether resources are allocated efficiently among competing uses, but many times a competing use can be an alternative means of improving safety and saving lives.

3 The "all else equal" requirement means that one might not always see a simple positive relationship between an occupation's pay and its level of risk. Loggers face greater risk on the job than financial analysts, but financial analysts earn more than loggers. The additional education required to become a financial analyst outweighs the added risk of logging. Economists attempt to control for other factors affecting wage rates using large datasets and multiple regression techniques. Two popular reality TV shows, The History Channel's *Ice Road Truckers* and the Discovery Channel's *Deadliest Catch*, provide nice anecdotal examples of the relationship between pay and risk holding all else equal. The two shows follow workers who face the most extreme hazards in their

professions (driving across frozen lakes and rivers in the Arctic and fishing for Alaskan king crabs in the Bering Sea) and document both the dangers they face and the very high monetary rewards they receive for facing the dangers.

4 To use an analogy, it is as if the worker is being given the choice between a dollar with certainty or a gamble where there is a $1 - \pi$ chance of a dollar payoff and a π chance of a 0 payoff. Regardless of risk preferences, rational workers would always choose the dollar payoff with certainty.

5 The wage gap sorts firms and workers into the two submarkets. The firm on the margin is indifferent between offering safe or hazardous employment. For the so-called marginal firm, the costs of the safety programs necessary to eliminate job hazards just equal the benefits of greater safety, the drop in wage. Likewise, the worker on the margin is indifferent between the two types of jobs: the utility gain from the higher wage just offsets the utility loss from the greater likelihood of a drop in income, medical expenses, and pain and suffering from an injury or illness.

6 See Kniesner and Leeth (1995, Chapter 3) for a formal derivation.

7 Viscusi uses the CFOI data to determine mortality risk by first grouping fatalities by 2-digit industry (72 industries) and then by 1-digit occupation (10 occupations) to generate a total of 720 industry-occupation cells. He then calculates the frequency of a workplace death by dividing the average number of fatalities by the average number of employees within each industry-occupation cell, using data from the period 1992 to 1997. By averaging over six years, Viscusi minimizes possible errors in characterizing risk resulting from the random fluctuation of workplace fatalities over time.

8 As is fairly typical, he excludes from his sample agricultural workers, part-time workers, workers younger than 18, and workers older than 65. Viscusi also does not include interactions between fatal injury risk and other control variables (see discussion of Equation (9A.1.1) in Appendix 9.1).

9 Although the VSL function depends on the values of the right-hand side in Equation (9A.1.1) in Appendix 9.1, most commonly considered is the mean VSL. With a fatality risk measure of deaths per 100,000 workers and a work year of 2,000 hours, the value of a statistical life is $VSL = \alpha \times \exp(\ln(w)) \times 100,000 \times 2,000$. If α is small then it is the case that $\alpha \times \exp(\ln(w)) \approx \alpha w$. (See Appendix 9.1.) All dollar figures presented have been adjusted for inflation to 2010 using the CPI-U.

10 As part of a Remedial Investigation of a Superfund site, the EPA releases an assessment of the site's risks across the various affected areas, including the elevated risk of contracting cancer (Gayer *et al.* 2000).

11 The range of values arises from differences in empirical specifications underlying the estimates of costs and risk. Rohlfs argues credit constraints prevented many young men from attending college during the period, causing the enrollment data to understate the cost of the draft and the VSL of draft-age men.

12 One example of such an approach is Vassanadumrongdee and Matsuoka (2005). They determine the VSL in Bangkok, Thailand using a survey instrument that describes the current level of air pollution in the city as resulting in annual deaths of 430 in 1,000,000. Individuals are then told that they can reduce their chance of dying from air pollution by 30 in 1,000,000 (or 60 in 1,000,000) if they take an annual health exam that detects respiratory system impairments. Each individual is randomly assigned one of four prices and asked if they would be willing to pay the amount for the annual checkup. Based on the hypothetical price that would need to be paid for the checkup and the reduction in the chance of premature death from air pollution from taking the health exam, they determine a VSL in Bangkok of about US$1 million.

13 In terms of Figure 9.2, market studies estimate the market wage equation $W(\pi)$, whereas contingent valuation studies estimate the preferences underlying the wage equation. In equilibrium, the slope of the market wage function equals the marginal benefit to the worker from a slightly safer job. The equality of the two values means it

is unnecessary to estimate underlying preferences to determine appropriate VSLs, but for more substantial improvements in safety market-determined values will overstate people's willingness to pay for greater safety.

14 Contingent valuation surveys are also more challenging to construct than other surveys because many people have difficulty properly understanding complex probability concepts and are unaccustomed to the notion of trading income for expanded safety. For example, people generally understand the simple difference in payoffs between betting on a race horse with 4:1 winning odds versus betting on a horse with 2:1 winning odds. They might have a harder time, however, understanding whether or not they would support a government policy that reduces mercury levels in the local water supply and thus decreases the risk of death for each constituent by 0.00001 at a cost of US$50 per taxpayer. If respondents do not fully understand the probability concepts in surveys then the VSL estimates from the survey may be inaccurate.

15 For further discussion see Carson *et al.* (2001) and Hausman (2012).

16 VSL estimates vary depending on both the set of control variables included in the estimating wage or price equation and the underlying population examined (Viscusi 2013). In the United States, VSL estimates are higher for union workers than for non-union workers, higher for whites than blacks, and higher for women than men (Viscusi and Aldy 2003; Viscusi 2003; Leeth and Ruser 2003). VSLs for native workers are roughly the same size as for immigrant workers, except for non-English speaking immigrants from Mexico who appear to earn little compensation for bearing very high levels of workplace risk (Hersch and Viscusi 2010). VSLs rise as people age, at least until the mid-40s, and then gradually decline (Kniesner *et al.* 2006; Aldy and Viscusi 2008). Not surprisingly given that safety is generally considered to be a normal good, VSLs are larger for higher income groups within a country at a point in time, within a country over time as the country's income increases, and within developed countries than within less developed countries (Mrozek and Taylor 2002; Viscusi and Aldy 2003; Costa and Kahn 2004; Bellavance *et al.* 2009; Kniesner *et al.* 2010). VSLs can vary across populations because of differences in risk preferences. Groups more willing to take risks will locate further to the right along the market wage function, and if the wage function is concave from below as shown in Figure 9.2, more risk-tolerant groups will have a smaller reduction in wage for a given increase in safety and a lower VSL. Alternatively, some populations may have a lower VSL because they are less careful than others and their lower safety productivity causes the wage function they face to lie below and to be flatter (resulting in a lower VSL) than the wage function faced by others. The lower ability of some workers to produce safety makes it desirable for employers to offer them smaller wage premiums for accepting risk. Discrimination may also result in two separate market wage functions, with the disadvantaged group facing not only lower wages at every level of risk but also smaller increases in wages for given changes in risk than for the advantaged group.

17 A difficulty with meta-analyses is that they include results from studies with known problems, which "imparts biases of unknown magnitude and direction" (Viscusi 2009, p. 118).

18 The authors devote particular attention to measurement errors, which have been noted in Black and Kniesner (2003), Ashenfelter and Greenstone (2004), and Ashenfelter (2006). Although they do not have information on subjective risk beliefs, they use very detailed data on objective risk measures and consider the possibility that workers are driven by risk expectations. Published industry risk beliefs are strongly correlated with subjective risk values, and they follow the standard practice of matching to workers in the sample an objective risk measure. Where Kniesner *et al.* (2012) differ from most previous studies is the pertinence of the risk data to the worker's particular job, and theirs is the first study to account for the variation of the more pertinent risk level within the context of a panel data study. Their work also distinguishes job movers from job stayers. They find

that most of the variation in risk and most of the evidence of positive VSLs stems from people changing jobs across occupations or industries rather than from variation in risk levels over time in a given job setting.

19 Rohlfs and Sullivan (2013a) used a variety of publicly available datasets from the Department of Defense (DoD) in their empirical research. They obtained vehicle data from the Theater A portion of US Army Materiel Systems Analysis Activity's Sample Data Collection (US AMSAA, SDC, 2010) and cost information from cost experts within the Army Material Command (AMC) and Cost Analysis and Program Evaluation (OSD-CAPE) departments in DoD. Some of the data used in Rohlfs and Sullivan (2013a) are considered For Official Use Only (FOUO). For another author to use the data requires that person to have an official defense-related government purpose. Rohlfs and Sullivan have made arrangements with the US Naval Postgraduate School (NPS) to sponsor potential replicators of their project, so that replicators could obtain access to the data.

20 All prices presented in the replacement vehicle case study are in 2010 dollars.

21 This is most likely an underestimate of the actual cost of the program because it does not include many costs such as maintenance and fuel. It should also be noted that the US$50 billion figure is for all Services, not just the Army, which was the focus of the study by Rohlfs and Sullivan (2013a).

22 The three cost estimates use 484 miles per month as a constant rate of usage, which is the rate observed for the average vehicle in the SDC data.

23 See Tables I–IV in Rohlfs and Sullivan (2013a) for details on their findings.

24 Exceptions, however, could be made for particularly combat-intensive units to receive heavily armored Type 3 TWVs depending on the combat environment and their specific capability requirements.

References

Aldy, J. E., and W. K. Viscusi. 2008. "Adjusting the Value of a Statistical Life for Age and Cohort Effects." *Review of Economics and Statistics* 90: 573–581.

Ashenfelter, O. 2006. "Measuring the Value of a Statistical Life: Problems and Prospects." *Economic Journal* 116: C10–C23.

Ashenfelter, O., and M. Greenstone. 2004. "Estimating the Value of a Statistical Life: The Importance of Omitted Variables and Publication Bias." *American Economic Association Papers and Proceedings* 94: 454–460.

Bellavance, Francois, Georges Dionne, and Martin Lebeau. 2009. "The Value of a Statistical Life: a Meta-Analysis with a Mixed Effects Regression Model." *Journal of Health Economics* 28.2: 444–464.

Black, D. A., and T. J. Kniesner. 2003. "On the Measurement of Job Risk in Hedonic Wage Models." *Journal of Risk and Uncertainty* 27: 205–220.

Brown, J. N., and H. S. Rosen. 1982. "On the Estimation of Structural Hedonic Price Models." *Econometrica* 50: 765–768.

Carson, R. T., N. Flores, and N. F. Meade. 2001. "Contingent Valuation: Controversies and Evidence." *Environmental and Resource Economics* 19: 173–210.

Costa, D. L., and M. E. Kahn. 2004. "Changes in the Value of Life, 1940–1980." *Journal of Risk and Uncertainty* 29: 159–180.

Epple, D. 1987. "Hedonic Prices and Implicit Markets: Estimating Supply and Demand Functions for Differentiated Products." *Journal of Political Economy* 95: 59–80.

Gayer, T., J. T. Hamilton, and W. K. Viscusi. 2000. "Private Values of Risk Tradeoffs at Superfund Sites: Housing Market Evidence on Learning about Risk." *Review of Economics and Statistics* 82: 439–451.

Hausman, J. 2012. "Contingent Valuation: From Dubious to Hopeless." *Journal of Economic Perspectives* 26: 43–56.

Hersch, J., and W. K. Viscusi. 2010. "Immigrant Status and the Value of Statistical Life." *Journal of Human Resources* 45: 749–771.

Kahn, S., and K. Lang. 1988. "Efficient Estimation of Structural Hedonic Systems." *International Economic Review* 29: 157–166.

Kniesner, T. J., and J. D. Leeth. 1995. *Simulating Workplace Safety Policy*. Boston, MA: Kluwer Academic Publishers.

——. 2004. "Data Mining Mining Data: MSHA Enforcement Efforts, Underground Coal Mine Safety, and New Health Policy Implications." *Journal of Risk and Uncertainty* 29: 83–111.

Kniesner, Thomas J., W. Kip Viscusi, and James P. Ziliak. 2006. "Life-Cycle Consumption and the Age-Adjusted Value of Life." *Contributions in Economic Analysis & Policy* 5.1.

——. 2010. "Policy Relevant Heterogeneity in the Value of Statistical Life: New Evidence from Panel Data Quantile Regressions." *Journal of Risk and Uncertainty* 40: 15–31.

Kniesner, T. J., W. K. Viscusi, C. Woock, and J. P. Ziliak. 2012. "The Value of a Statistical Life: Evidence from Panel Data." *Review of Economics and Statistics* 94: 74–87.

Leeth, J. D., and J. Ruser. 2003. "Compensating Wage Differentials for Fatal and Nonfatal Injury Risk by Gender and Race." *Journal of Risk and Uncertainty* 27: 257–277.

Mrozek, J. R., and L. O. Taylor. 2002. "What Determines the Value of Life? A Meta-Analysis." *Journal of Policy Analysis and Management* 21: 253–270.

Peltzman, S. 1975. "The Effects of Automobile Safety Regulation." *Journal of Political Economy* 83: 677–725.

Office of Management and Budget. 1992. Circular No. A-94 Revised. The White House. October 29. Available at www.whitehouse.gov/omb/circulars_a094 [last accessed November 18, 2013].

Rohlfs, C. 2012. "The Economic Cost of Conscription and an Upper Bound on the Value of a Statistical Life: Hedonic Estimates from Two Margins of Response to the Vietnam Draft." *Journal of Benefit-Cost Analysis* 3: 1–37.

Rohlfs, C., and R. Sullivan. 2013a. "The Cost-Effectiveness of Armored Tactical Wheeled Vehicles for Overseas US Army Operations." *Defence and Peace Economics* 24: 293–316.

Rohlfs, C., and R. Sullivan. 2013b. "A Comment on Evaluating the Cost-Effectiveness of Armored Tactical Wheeled Vehicles." *Defence and Peace Economics* 24: 485–494.

US Army Material Systems Analysis Activity. 2010. Theater A Sample Data Collection.

US Defense Manpower Data Center. 2008. Unit Master File. Data Request System number 23242.

US Environmental Protection Agency. 2010a. *Guidelines for Preparing Economic Analyses*. Available at http://yosemite.epa.gov/ee/epa/eerm.nsf/vwAN/EE-0568-50.pdf/ US$file/EE-0568-50.pdf [last accessed November 18, 2013].

——. 2010b. *Valuing Mortality Risk Reductions for Environmental Policy: A White Paper.* Available at http://yosemite.epa.gov/ee/epa/eerm.nsf/vwAN/EE-0563-1.pdf/US$file/EE-0563-1.pdf [last accessed November 18, 2013].

US Department of Transportation. 2008. *Revised Departmental Guidance 2013: Treatment of the Value of Preventing Fatalities and Injuries in Preparing Economic Analyses.* Available at www.dot.gov/sites/dot.dev/files/docs/VSL%20Guidance%202013.pdf [last accessed November 18, 2013].

Vassanadumrongdee, S., and S. Matsuoka. 2005. "Risk Perceptions and Value of a Statistical Life for Air Pollution and Traffic Accidents: Evidence from Bangkok, Thailand." *Journal of Risk and Uncertainty* 30: 261–287.

Viscusi, W. K. 2003. 'Racial Differences in Labor Market Values of a Statistical Life'. *Journal of Risk and Uncertainty* 27: 239–256.

——. 2004. "The Value of Life: Estimates with Risks by Occupation and Industry." *Economic Inquiry* 42: 29–48.

——. 2009. "The Devaluation of Life." *Regulation and Governance* 3: 103–127.

——. 2013. "Estimating the Value of a Statistical Life Using Census of Fatal Occupational Injuries (CFOI) Data." *Monthly Labor Review*, October. Available at http://www.bls.gov/opub/mlr/2013/article/using-data-from-the-census-of-fatal-occupational-injuries-to-estimate-the-1.htm [last accessed November 18, 2013].

Viscusi, W. K., and J. Aldy. 2003. "The Value of a Statistical Life: A Critical Review of Market Estimates throughout the World." *Journal of Risk and Uncertainty* 27: 5–76.

Part IV

New approaches to military cost–benefit analysis

10 The role of cost-effectiveness analysis in allocating defense resources

Kent D. Wall, Charles J. LaCivita, and Anke Richter

10.1 Introduction

Defense resource allocation is a multi-level resource allocation process with multiple levels within the organization making budget requests and granting approvals. Not only are there multiple levels within a defense organization, but the resource allocation process may iterate between the levels. For example, in the US PPBES system, each of the services presents its desired set of capabilities (weapons systems, personnel, new acquisitions, maintenance and readiness requirements, training, research and development, etc.) requiring a certain portion of the total Department of Defense (DoD) budget to the Office of the Secretary of Defense (OSD). OSD is then responsible for reviewing these submissions, combining the requested needs and desires into an overall proposal that will become the total requested defense budget and which will be included in the President's budget request to Congress. Given system incentives, the requests always exceed the expected available budget and OSD must decide which mix of capabilities will provide the strongest defense force for the nation within the budgetary limitations. As they decide to allocate different levels of funds to the military services, the services have the possibility to adjust their submission packages of capabilities. Each service strives for an optimal allocation among capabilities within its organization given a specific budget allocation. OSD strives for an optimal allocation of budget among the services to attain what it views as the best mix of capabilities. The process iterates among these two decision-makers (and two decision-making levels) until the services and OSD are in agreement on the capabilities that will be provided at a given allocation of the budget. (For an explanation and documentation of the PPBS process, please refer to the websites and documents provided at the end of the references.) Making the process more complex, different types and amounts of information are available to these two levels of decision-makers. Operations research, especially cost-effectiveness analysis (CEA), can provide valuable insight to this iterative programming process.

While the preceding paragraph emphasizes the interactions seen at the top level of the PPBES system, similar situations arise throughout the defense organization. At lower levels, there is competition among capability providers in a service to be included in the service's budget proposal to OSD; for example, the armored division and the infantry division in the Army; the infantry division and the field artillery in the Army; the surface navy and aircraft carriers in the Navy; or information operations and the surface navy in the Navy. At the higher level, this occurs when the DoD budget is presented to Congress as part of the overall budget for the country.

The situation is also seen outside of defense. Excellent examples are found in multi-national aid programs. For example, the majority of HIV/AIDS intervention programs implemented in Africa are funded by external sources (e.g. donor governments; UN agencies; the Global Fund to Fight AIDS, Tuberculosis, and Malaria; and the World Bank). Each of these sources chooses to allocate funding to individual countries based on their proposed interventions. The individual countries then allocate these funds to local organizations and programs to conduct these interventions. Finally, the individual organization tasked with implementing the interventions may make further allocation decisions to spend monies on prevention and treatment efforts with individual populations or geographical regions. Lasry *et al.* (2007) provides more information for these applications.

Normative or prescriptive theory tells us that decision-makers ultimately must choose among alternatives based on their benefits and their costs. For decision-makers in the public sector benefits are most often expressed in terms of effectiveness because of the difficulties in "pricing out" the "products" associated with each alternative. National defense and homeland security are prime examples. There are no markets for placing monetary value on the "products" associated with an aircraft carrier battle group, national missile defense system or counter terrorism policy. The decision-maker somehow must integrate information on cost and effectiveness and decision problems are focused on striking a balance between these two attributes. Cost-benefit analysis (CBA) is replaced by CEA and examination of tradeoffs between effectiveness and cost becomes a crucial task for the decision-maker. Unfortunately the integration of cost and effectiveness is not straightforward and there are many views on how it should be done (see Willard 1998; Fowler and Cason 1998; Thomas and Sheldon 1999; and the excellent literature review by Ruefli 1974). This issue is even further compounded and complicated in a multi-level decision process.

Mathematical programming techniques can provide vital insight into these types of optimization problems. For any optimization problem (maximize effectiveness subject to budget constraints) it is possible to develop the dual problem formulation (minimize the shadow prices—the value of each constraint—subject to desired levels of effectiveness). With basic convexity assumptions, the optimal solution of the primal problem is an optimal solution of the dual problem as well. This relationship has been extensively explored in the operations research literature (see for example Bazaraa and Shetty 1979; Hillier and Lieberman 1990; Luenberger 1973; Solow 1984) and it has been shown how the problem can be solved either by working with the primal formulation or the dual formulation. Frequently, one formulation is much easier to solve than the other. This is indeed the case when considering the multi-level resource allocation process as it can take advantage of (rather than be hindered by) the different information available at each decision-making level.

This chapter explores these two potential solution techniques in a multi-level resource allocation problem. The goal of the resource allocation is to maximize the overall effectiveness in a public sector organization through the allocation of a single limited resource (the budget). We begin with a formulation of the resource allocation decision problem in its primal form and explore practical aspects of its solution, paying special attention to information requirements. The next section presents the dual formulation of the problem and its solution. The practical implementation of the dual solution and its information requirements are compared with those of the primal solution. The third section considers the resource allocation problem from the perspective of CEA. Here we show that a decision-maker who claims to be motivated by cost-effectiveness concerns is actually implementing the dual solution. The desire to find "the best tradeoff between cost and effectiveness" is, in reality, a desire to solve the resource allocation problem via the dual formulation. Two illustrative examples are provided, one involving continuous alternatives and one involving discrete alternatives, before we end with a summary of our main points.

10.2 The primal decision problem

The public sector organization is viewed as a maximizer of overall effectiveness subject to a resource constraint. This objective is pursued by allocation of resources "downward" through its hierarchical structure. To simplify the exposition and fix ideas, we consider a single resource (money) and the simple two-level hierarchy depicted in Figure 10.1. The first level is occupied by one unit, the top-level decision-maker or manager, who decides how to allocate the resource to the units on the lower level. The second-level units are themselves decision-makers—they decide how best to use the allocated resources given to them by the upper level.

For example, in the DoD, the Secretary of Defense would be the first-level decision-maker who is responsible for allocating the defense budget to the second-level decision-makers, the military services. In this manner, in Figure 10.1 DM_0 is the Office of the Secretary of Defense, $DM_{1.1}$ is the Army, $DM_{1.2}$ is the Navy, $DM_{1.3}$ is the Air Force, etc. The military services are themselves decision-makers as they choose how best to allocate the funds within their organizations to provide the greatest amount of military capability.

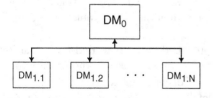

Figure 10.1 The two-level hierarchy.

A mathematical formulation of the first-level decision-maker's problem is easy. Let V denote the overall effectiveness and let x_i ($i = 1, 2, \ldots, N$) denote the funds allocated to the ith second-level unit. The decision-maker then desires to:

$$\max_{\mathbf{x}} V(\mathbf{x}) \tag{10.1}$$

subject to

$$\sum x_i = B, \tag{10.2}$$

where $\mathbf{x} = [x_1, x_2, \ldots x_n]'$ is the vector of budget of allocations and B is the available budget. The decision-maker's decision behavior is modeled as the solution to a mathematical programming problem in primal form. To solve this system optimally, the first-level decision-maker must be all-knowing, all-seeing, and in possession of prodigious computation capability. His optimal choice is determined by the first-order necessary conditions for the solution

$$\frac{\partial V(\mathbf{x}^*)}{\partial x_i} - \lambda = 0; \quad i = 1, 2, \ldots, N, \tag{10.3}$$

where $\mathbf{x}^*$ is the vector of optimal budget allocations and λ is the Lagrange multiplier associated with the budget, i.e. the marginal effectiveness of another unit of budget. The standard prescriptive result is clear. The first-level decision-maker should select an allocation such that marginal effectiveness across all second-level units is equal.

The main issue with this formulation is the amount and type of information that is available at the different levels of an organization. The "all-knowing" and "all-seeing" decision-maker necessary to formulate and solve Equation (10.3) does not exist. At the first level, the decision-maker has a strategic view (a joint view) over all of the lower levels, the capabilities they produce, and how the entire organization and portfolio of capabilities interact and contribute to the overall effectiveness of the defense force. This level of decision-maker is less knowledgeable of the operational details; exactly how this capability is best produced. That information resides with the second-level decision-makers (in our example, the military services). They have all of the operational knowledge, which is why, when given a budget allocation, they will make a further allocation that enables them to best produce the needed capabilities. The second-level decision-makers will typically have less of a strategic/joint view. These different levels of information can be captured in the mathematical formulation of the problem presented in Equations (10.1)–(10.3).

Let y_i represent the units of output produced by each second-level decision-maker if it is given an allocation x_i. This function, $y_i(x_i)$ is known only to the second-level decision-makers. The first-level decision-maker knows the x_i and can observe the y_i but does not know the details of the production function, i.e. the first-level decision-maker does not know how y_i would change with a slightly larger or slightly smaller allocation, x_i. The first-level decision-maker assesses and values the y_i and their relative strategic contribution to the overall effectiveness of the organization. Using the concepts of multi-criteria decision-making (see Belton and Stewart 2003; Kirkwood 1997), we can create an approximation for $V(\mathbf{x})$ representing the first-level decision-maker's decision process.

Let v_i express the decision-maker's valuation of the contribution y_i makes to overall effectiveness. For example, if x_i dollars are allocated to the Air Force for anti-aircraft defense then y_i interceptor squadrons can be purchased and operated over the time corresponding to the planning period. The first-level decision-maker values this contribution towards anti-aircraft defense by assigning to the y_i a number, $v_i(y_i)$. Let w_i represent the relative importance of each measure to the overall value function, $V(\mathbf{x})$, as seen through the eyes of the first-level decision-maker: in this case, the relative importance of anti-aircraft defense versus other military capabilities to overall national defense. Thus we assume the decision-maker bases allocation decisions on the maximization of $V(\mathbf{x})$ expressed as

$$V(\mathbf{x}) \simeq w_1 v_1(y_1) + w_2 v_2(y_2) + \cdots + w_N v_N(y_N).$$

Given this approximation, the first-level decision-maker is confronted with the problem of selecting $\mathbf{x}$ so as to

$$\max_{\mathbf{x}}\{w_1 v_1(y_1) + w_2 v_2(y_2) + \cdots + w_N v_N(y_N)\}, \tag{10.4}$$

subject to Equation (10.2) and $y_i = y_i(x_i)$. The theory of constrained optimization again gives the answer. The manager behaves so as to produce the maximizing budget allocation, $x_i^*(i = 1, 2, \ldots, N)$, that obeys the first-order necessary conditions:

$$w_i \frac{dv_i}{dy_i} \frac{dy_i}{dx_i}(x_i^*) - \lambda = 0; \quad i = 1, 2, \ldots, N. \tag{10.5}$$

These equations, together with the budget constraint, provide enough information to determine the best allocations and the value for the Lagrange multiplier.

While this formulation captures the information differential between the levels of decision-makers, it is not an easier problem to solve than what was presented originally. To find the optimal solution requires the calculation of the N-dimensional system defined by Equation (10.5). Second, the first-level decision-maker requires complete knowledge of the $y_i(x_i)$ and the marginal products, $dy_i(x_i^k)/dx_i$. The decision-maker must be both knowledgeable and understanding of this detailed information and be able to use it to determine individual second-level individual marginal effectiveness. This is counter to our assumption that the first-level decision-maker does not know the operational details of the second-level decision-maker's organization. Finally, if Equation (10.5) is not satisfied, the first-level decision-maker is given little direction on how to reallocate funds to satisfy the first-order necessary conditions. A sensible guide might be to allocate more funds to the sub-units that display higher marginal effectiveness and to allocate less funds to those sub-units with low marginal effectiveness. This, however, still requires the first-level decision-maker to be in possession of the detailed knowledge assumed to reside only with the second-level decision-makers.

The only way to approach this problem is through trial and error in an iterative approach. Given an initial allocation, $\mathbf{x}^0$, satisfying Equation (10.2), the top-level decision-maker then observes the resulting $\{y_i; 1 \leq i \leq N\}$ and evaluates Equation (10.4). Using the portion of Equation (10.5) which the top-level decision-maker knows, $w_i \frac{dv_i}{dy_i}$, he guesses what an improved allocation of $\mathbf{x}$ might be. The decision-maker does not know for a fact that his choice will indeed lead to a better allocation because he cannot estimate the second portion of Equation (10.5), $\frac{dy_i}{dx_i}(x_i^*)$, since only the second-level decision-maker has this information. The new allocation is implemented and the first-level decision-maker observes the new $\{y_i; 1 \leq i \leq N\}$ and evaluates Equation (10.4). This continues until an allocation is found for which Equation (10.5) is satisfied or when changes to Equation (10.4) become sufficiently small.

This entire concept can be explained graphically using a 2-dimensional example as in Figure 10.2. In the case of perfect, complete information with a single decision-maker, the iterative solution process to find the optimal allocation can be detailed on this graphic. The budget constraint, $x_1 + x_2 = B$, appears in the fourth quadrant. The first and third quadrants depict the marginal effectiveness of each x_i assuming an additive form; i.e.,

$$D_i V = \frac{\partial V}{\partial x_i} = \frac{dv_i}{dy_i} \frac{dy_i}{dx_i}(x_i). \tag{10.6}$$

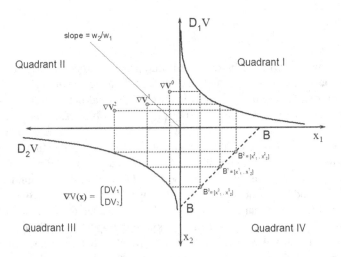

Figure 10.2 Two-dimensional example of primal solution.

The second quadrant depicts the relationship between the allocation chosen by the decision-maker and the Lagrange multiplier. The decision-maker begins by specifying $x_1^0 + x_2^0 = B$. This allocation generates $y_i^0 = y_i(x_i^0)$ and the decision-maker uses this and Equation (10.6) to compute the marginal effectiveness of each sub-unit. Since $D_1 V > D_2 V$ the first-level decision-maker decides on $x_1^1 > x_1^0$ and $x_2^1 < x_2^0$ such that $x_1^1 + x_2^1 = B$. The cycle repeats, and eventually an allocation is found for which $0 \leq V - V^k \leq \epsilon$. Now in the case of a multi-level resource allocation with differential information, the functions for the marginal effectiveness of each x_i, Equation (10.6) are not know to the first-level decision-maker. Hence quadrants I and III are blank and there is no guidance for the decision-maker's search along the budget line.

10.3 The dual decision problem

The primal formulation of the multi-level resource allocation problem is very difficult to solve directly. Another approach is to see if it is easier to solve the dual formulation of the decision problem. The dual formulation of the first-level decision-maker's problem posed by Equations (10.2) and (10.4) is (see Luenberger 1973, 318–320; or Everett 1963)

$$\min_{\lambda} \varphi(\lambda) = \min_{\lambda} \left\{ \max_{\mathbf{x}} \sum [w_i v_i(y_i(x_i)) - \lambda x_i] + \lambda B \right\}, \tag{10.7}$$

where

$$\varphi(\lambda) = \max_{\mathbf{x}} \sum \{w_i v_i(y_i(x_i)) - \lambda x_i\} + \lambda B \tag{10.8}$$

is called the dual function. The dual formulation represents the decision problem confronting the first-level decision-maker as a minimization. The decision-maker seeks that value of λ for which the dual function attains its minimum.

The dual function is composed of N separate unconstrained, one-dimensional, maximization problems that represent the decision problems faced by each of the second-level decision-makers. We find it convenient to exchange the summation and maximization so we may define this function in terms of a weighted sum of individual dual functions, $\varphi_i(\lambda)$,

$$\varphi(\lambda) = \sum \max_{x_i} \{w_i v_i(y_i(x_i)) - \lambda x_i\} + \lambda B = \sum \varphi_i(\lambda) + \lambda B. \tag{10.9}$$

While the second-level decision-makers' problem is

$$\max_{x_i} \{w_i v_i(y_i(x_i)) - \lambda x_i\}, \tag{10.10}$$

this equation is not solved in this form because its solution, x_i^*, satisfying the first-order condition

$$\frac{dv_i}{dy_i} \frac{dy_i}{dx_i}(x_i^*) = \lambda/w_i; \quad i = 1, 2, \ldots, N$$

requires knowledge of dv_i/dy_i, w_i and λ. These are known only to the first-level decision-maker.

The second-level decision-maker knows only $y_i(x_i)$ and dy_i/dx_i. However, we can define the decision problem of the second-level decision-maker as

$$\max_{x_i}\{y_i(x_i) - \lambda_i x_i\} \tag{10.11}$$

given λ_i where

$$\lambda_i = \lambda \left[w_i \frac{dv_i}{dy_i} \right]^{-1} = \lambda m_i^{-1}. \tag{10.12}$$

This λ_i is provided to the second-level decision-maker by the first-level decision-maker. In essence, λ_i is the marginal price that must be paid by the second-level decision-maker to produce more effectiveness. It is inversely proportional to the preferences of the first-level decision-maker as expressed by: (1) the marginal productivity, dv_i/dy_i; and (2) the tradeoff weight, w_i. If m_i is larger (smaller) than m_j then λ_i will be smaller (larger) than λ_j. This marginal price captures the logic that in order for one second-level decision-maker to produce more capability, he is taking budget away from something else the first-level decision-maker wants to obtain from another second-level unit. Hence λ_i is different across i, the set of second-level decision-makers. Also note that this problem is completely equivalent to that of Equation (10.10) because it has exactly the same first-order condition and, hence, solution x_i^*.

The significant difference is the information set in possession of the second-level decision-maker. This decision-maker knows only $y_i(x_i), dy_i/dx_i$. The Lagrange multiplier, λ_i, the price to be paid for additional effectiveness of the ith unit, is given to the second-level decision-makers by the first-level decision-maker. The second-level decision-maker does NOT have explicit knowledge of λ, w_i or dv_i/dy_i.

The resulting set of decisions $\{x_i^*(\lambda_i); 1 = 1, 2, \dots, N\}$ produce the set $\{\varphi_i(\lambda_i); 1 = 1, 2, \dots, N\}$ that are aggregated by the first-level decision-maker according to Equation (10.9) to define the dual function $\varphi(\lambda) = \varphi(\mathbf{x}^*(\lambda))$. Note: at the top-level $\{w_i; dv_i/dy_i; 1 = 1, 2, \dots, N\}$ are considered fixed and are left implicit for simplicity of notation.

Given the dual function, the global solution to Equation (10.7) is achieved by finding that value of λ satisfying

$$\nabla\varphi(\lambda^*) = 0, \tag{10.13}$$

where $\varphi(\lambda^*) = \varphi(\mathbf{x}^*(\lambda^*))$. The most striking aspect of the dual formulation is the fact that this gradient is the budget constraint itself (see Luenberger 1973, 313):

$$\nabla\varphi(\lambda) = \sum x_i^*(\lambda) - B. \tag{10.14}$$

In other words, when $\lambda = \lambda^*$ the resulting $\{x_i^*(\lambda^*/w_i); 1 = 1, 2, \ldots, N\}$ satisfy the budget constraint. The solution to a *1-dimensional* problem provides the answer to an *N-dimensional* allocation problem.

An iterative process involving information exchange between the first and second-level decision-makers provides a practical solution. This exchange is a price directive mechanism in which the top-level transmits downward to each sub-unit its implicit marginal cost of effectiveness, λ_i. The sub-units respond by using this parameter to solve their individual maximization problems and then transmit upward their decisions, $x_i^*()$. The top-level decision-maker then checks to see if Equation (10.13) is satisfied. This check is, however, nothing more than a check on the budget constraint, Equation (10.14). If the aggregate decision is "over" budget ("under") then the top-level decision-maker increases (decreases) λ and transmits back down "new" λ_i to each second-level decision-maker. This inter-level exchange continues until no further change in the λ_i is required; i.e., the budget constraint is met within the required precision: $|\nabla\varphi(\lambda)| \leq \delta$ for some small number δ.

The key parameter is, of course, the Lagrange multiplier, λ. It is the shadow price of the allocated asset; i.e. the value of one unit of V in terms of one unit of B. Equation (10.12) shows that the individual λ_i are a function of λ and the marginal effectiveness of the ith sub-unit in the mind of the first-level decision-maker. This means that the λ_i transmitted to the lower-level decision-makers will vary according to the preferences of the first-level decision-maker. Different Lagrange multipliers are transmitted to each second-level unit. Thus, if $m_i > m_j$ then $\lambda_i < \lambda_j$ and the ith second-level decision-maker will receive a lower "price" for effectiveness than the jth second-level decision-maker.

The search for the optimal value of λ takes the form of an iterative scheme using a simple adjustment mechanism:

$$\lambda^{k+1} = \alpha^k \lambda^k.$$

For each iteration we now replace $x_i^*(\lambda)$ with $x_i^k(\lambda^k)$ and λ_i with λ_i^k. Given $x_i^k(\lambda^k)$ we check the budget constraint. If $\sum x_i^k(\lambda^k) - B < 0$ set $\alpha^k < 1$. If $\sum x_i^k(\lambda^k) - B > 0$ set $\alpha^k > 1$ (hence $\lambda^{k+1} > \lambda^k$ when the budget is in deficit and $\lambda^{k+1} < \lambda^k$ when the budget is in surplus). Recompute the different shadow prices for each sub-unit, $\lambda_i^{k+1} = m_i^{-1}\lambda^{k+1}$. Set $k = k + 1$ and transmit the new "prices" downward to the second level and receive the "new" $x_i^k(\lambda^k)$. Go to the budget check and repeat until convergence to a satisficing solution is obtained; i.e., $|\nabla\varphi(\lambda^k)| \leq \delta$.

Figure 10.3 provides a two-dimensional illustration using the same set-up employed in illustrating the primal problem solution. The first, third and fourth quadrants of the graph are exact replicas of Figure 10.2. The second quadrant still depicts the relationship between the values of λ and the marginal effectiveness of each sub-unit. Now, however, the values of λ are those chosen by the first-level decision-maker. These, by definition, all lie on a line with slope equal to w_2/w_1. After specifying an initial value, λ^0, the first-level decision-maker gives each second-level decision-maker his Lagrange multiplier, λ_i^0. The second-level

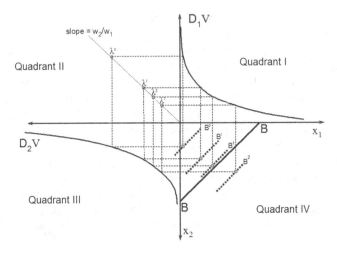

Figure 10.3 Two-dimensional example of dual solution.

decision-makers solve their maximization problems and transmit to the first-level decision-maker their proposal, y_i^0, and its cost, $(x_i^*)^0$. The corresponding budget, B^0, is observed to be far below the allowed amount so λ is reduced to λ^1. This produces new Lagrange multipliers, λ_i^1, that are used by each subunit in another round of proposals and costs. There is still a surplus so the Lagrange multiplier is lowered further to λ^2. At this value a deficit is observed so the first-level decision-maker raises the Lagrange multiplier to λ^3. Now the budget is almost completely consumed. Another adjustment of λ could be made but the first-level decision-maker may deem the current situation "good enough" and terminate adjustment of λ^k when $0 \leq |B - B^k| \leq \delta$.

A graphical comparison of Figures 10.2 and 10.3 shows that the primal approach always satisfies the budget constraint but requires iteration to seek satisfaction of Equation (10.5). The dual solution always satisfies Equation (10.5) but requires iteration to satisfy the budget constraint. Secondly, the dual problem requires a search over only one-dimension whereas the primal problem requires an N-dimensional search. Finally, the gradient of the dual solution is known and is easy to use to guide the search for λ^*. We argue that it is far easier to check for satisfaction of Equation (10.2) and iterate with the aid of Equation (10.14) than it is to attempt to satisfy the traditional first-order necessary condition.

10.4 Maximizing overall cost-effectiveness

Let us examine the problem formulation when individuals claim that decisions are made on the basis of overall cost-effectiveness. These decisions express a set of preferences that mimic those in standard microeconomic theory: allocation $\mathbf{x}^A$ is preferred to $\mathbf{x}^B$ if either $V(\mathbf{x}^A) = V(\mathbf{x}^B)$ while $\sum x_i^A < \sum x_i^B$ or $V(\mathbf{x}^A) > V(\mathbf{x}^B)$

while $\sum x_i^A = \sum x_i^B$. If two alternatives have the same overall effectiveness then the less costly alternative is said to be more cost-effective. Likewise, if two alternatives incur the same cost then the alternative with more overall effectiveness is said to be more cost-effective. If both costs and effectiveness vary, the decision-maker searches for that value of **x** that maximizes the overall cost-effectiveness measure, J:

$$J(\mathbf{x}) = \omega_E V(\mathbf{x}) - \omega_C \sum x_i. \tag{10.15}$$

Overall "cost-effectiveness," J, is a weighted difference between the effectiveness, V, and the cost. Here ω_E and ω_C are non-negative weights, summing to one, that express the decision-maker's preference for maximizing effectiveness relative to minimizing cost. A decision-maker who bases choice on maximizing overall cost-effectiveness will select that alternative representing the "best" solution to a simple two-attribute decision problem Equation (10.15) derived from the pursuit of two overriding, generally conflicting objectives: (1) the maximization of effectiveness; and (2) the minimization of cost. The solution is, of course, a function of the two key parameters, ω_E and ω_C, representing the decision-maker's preferences. The values set for these will depend on the budget constraint.

The resource allocation problem is now viewed as an unconstrained maximization problem:

$$\max_{\mathbf{x}} \left\{ \omega_E [w_1 v_1(y_1(x_1)) + w_2 v_2(y_2(x_2)) + \cdots + w_N v_N(y_N(x_N))] \right.$$
$$\left. - \omega_C \left[\sum x_i \right] \right\}$$

or

$$\max_{\mathbf{x}} \left\{ \sum [\omega_E w_i v_i(y_i(x_i)) - \omega_C x_i] \right\}.$$

The solution, as before, is determined by the first-order necessary conditions:

$$\frac{dv_i}{dy_i} \frac{dy_i(x_i^*)}{dx_i} - \frac{1}{w_i} \frac{\omega_C}{\omega_E} = 0; \quad 1 \le i \le N$$

or

$$\frac{dy_i(x_i^*)}{dx_i} - m_i^{-1} \frac{\omega_C}{\omega_E} = 0; \quad 1 \le i \le N \tag{10.16}$$

where

$$m_i = w_i \frac{dv_i}{dy_i}.$$

This solution is identical to that obtained in the dual formulation if we define $\omega_C/\omega_E = \lambda$. Thus, the maximization of overall cost-effectiveness is identical to the dual function maximization problem given by Equation (10.8): $x_i^*(m_i^{-1}\lambda^*) = x_i^*(\lambda_i^*)$. The identical solution method as presented in Section 10.2 can be used.

We find it both reasonable and natural for decision-makers to rationalize decisions by claiming to have found the "correct," "best," or "most appropriate" tradeoff between cost and effectiveness. They are stating that they have found the most effective solution given the opportunity cost of the resource (as captured by the Lagrange multipliers). The dual problem iterative solution we have presented is the basis for the communication between levels in a hierarchical organization. The first-level decision-maker transmits downward the current opportunity cost of effectiveness. In return the second-level decision-makers send the first level their solutions: $y_i(x_i^k)$ and x_i^k. The first-level decision-maker checks to see if the resource constraint is satisfied. If the constraint is satisfied (i.e., $|B - \sum x_i| \leq \delta$) then a solution has been found. If not then the first-level decision-maker sends revised opportunity cost information to the second level and the process repeats. No marginal information is exchanged. The first-level decision-maker merely checks the budget requests against the constraint and returns to the second-level decision-makers new information on the tradeoff between effectiveness and cost. All evaluations of the second-level decisions and how they integrate with the first-level decision-maker's overall tradeoff between effectiveness and cost are done implicitly.

10.5   Illustrative examples

We present two examples to demonstrate the ability of a coordinated maximization of overall cost-effectiveness in solving the multi-level resource allocation problem. The first example is the continuous case where there are an infinite number of possible alternatives for each of the second-level decision-makers. This is the situation illustrated in Figures 10.1 and 10.2. This is the world of continuous differentiability, smooth curves, very "tidy" mathematics and a closed-form solution of the second-level maximization of the cost-effectiveness function. The second example assumes each second-level decision-maker only has a finite number of possible alternatives to offer. This is the discrete case and is more representative of many real-life situations. Here we no longer have a differentiable representation for $y_i(x_i)$ and hence no closed-form solution. A solution must proceed by direct search using function values; i.e., the numerical values of $y_i(x_i)$ proposed by the second-level decision-makers. Our illustrations use a very simple adjustment procedure for the first-level decision-maker's revision of the λ, which ensures that λ increases if $\sum x_i > B$ and decreases if $\sum x_i < B$. In real-life this revision may be more involved. However, even with our very basic implementation of the solution procedure, the process finds the correct answer in very few iterations. This implies that the adjustment of λ need not be a complex procedure to be effective and makes the entire process more usable.

Both cases relate to the following scenario. Imagine the Ministry of Defense of a small country using a planning system in which its force elements, both existing and prospective, are organized into programs. The country has a coastline and land borders to it north, east and south. There are two major threat environments: (1) one originating with an aggressive regime in the country on its eastern border; and (2) one to the west originating from across the sea. Suppose there are two main programs, Program 1 for border security and Program 2 for coastal security. The director of the joint planning staff is the first-level decision-maker and the program managers of the two programs are the second-level decision-makers. The director of the joint planning staff is given a budget, B, by the Minister of Defense and must decide how to allocate these funds between the two programs. The instructions from the Minister of Defense convey to the director of joint planning a preference for addressing border security more than coastal security problems. In addition, the director of joint planning knows that both programs will provide a decreasing marginal contribution to overall national military effectiveness. The director believes, however, that Program 1 will have a higher initial marginal rate of contribution to overall national military effectiveness than does Program 2. We will assume these preferences are represented by the value function:

$$V(x_1, x_2) = 0.6[1 - e^{-2.95y_1(x_1)}] + 0.4[1 - e^{-2.10y_2(x_2)}]. \qquad (10.17)$$

Thus, the director of joint planning prefers maximization of border security effectiveness to maximization of coastal security effectiveness by a ratio of 3:2. Furthermore, the initial marginal rate of contribution to overall national military effectiveness from y_1 is 40 percent more than that from y_2.

The director of the joint planning staff requests proposals from the program managers along with instructions indicating the cost (price) of effectiveness. Each program staff then executes analyses and makes a recommendation. The recommendations become requests for funds by each program office. The information contained in $V(x_1, x_2)$ in Equation (10.17) is understood to reside completely in the mind of the first-level decision-maker and is, therefore unknown by the second-level decision-makers. The first-level decision-maker, however, provides instructions to the second-level decision-makers, using the Lagrange multiplier, as detailed in the examples that follow, that allow them to respond in a way consistent with the preferences captured in $V(x_1, x_2)$.

10.5.1 The continuous case

Let Program 1 (Border Security) be described by the effectiveness production function

$$y_1(x_1) = 1 - e^{-1.9x_1}$$

and let Program 2 (Coastal Security) be described by the effectiveness production function

$$y_2(x_2) = 1 - e^{-0.9x_2}.$$

This information resides internal to each program office and its staff. The director of the joint planning staff does not know, nor chooses to know, these details. The director possesses only the "strategic" information—that contained in $V(\mathbf{x})$. The planning process begins with the director setting a value for λ^0 based on his/her assessment of the given budget, B. If B represents a significant growth over previous budgets then λ^0 will be smaller. This will allow the program managers to propose more capabilities as the marginal cost of providing effectiveness is low. Likewise, if B represents a significant reduction from past experience then λ^0 will be larger. This will force the program managers to reduce the amount of capabilities they propose as the marginal cost of effectiveness is high. The director now uses Equation (10.16) to construct the λ_i resulting in

$$\lambda_1 = [0.6 \cdot 2.95 \cdot e^{-2.95y_1}]^{-1}\lambda^0$$

$$\lambda_2 = [0.4 \cdot 2.10 \cdot e^{-2.10y_2}]^{-1}\lambda^0,$$

where we set y_i equal to the previous proposed value given to the director by the program managers. Initially, in the beginning of the current planning period, these would be the result of the previous planning period solution.

We now illustrate the planning process derived from the overall cost-effectiveness paradigm (based on the dual formulation) by simulating the process using the following steps. Let $a_1 = 2.95, a_2 = 2.1, c_1 = 1.9, c_2 = 0.9$ and $\lambda^0 = 1/B$.

STEP 1: (Initialization) Set $k = 0, \lambda^k = \lambda^0, \Delta y_1 = \Delta y_2 = \Delta y$.
STEP 2: $\lambda_i^k = [w_i \cdot a_1 \cdot e^{-a_i \Delta y_i}]^{-1}\lambda^k = m_i^{-1}\lambda^k$.
STEP 3: $x_i^k = -c_i^{-1} \ell n \left(\frac{\lambda_i^k}{c_i}\right)$.
STEP 4: $B^k = x_1^k + x_2^k$.
STEP 5: Check for budget satisfaction. If $|B^k - B| \leq \delta$ then STOP. Otherwise
If $B^k > B + \delta$ then set $\lambda^{k+1} = \left[1 + \beta \cdot \left(\frac{B-B^k}{B}\right)\right]\lambda^k$ and $k = k+1$ and go to STEP 2.
If $B^k < B - \delta$ then set $\lambda^{k+1} = \left[1 - \beta \cdot \left(\frac{B^k-B}{B}\right)\right]\lambda^k$ and $k = k+1$ and go to STEP 2.

Step 2 represents the director's determination of each program managers's opportunity cost of effectiveness using the director's tradeoff weights for overall national military effectiveness and an estimate of the marginal contribution to $V(\mathbf{x})$ of each y_i. We assume this estimate is the result of a simple mental calculation: the evaluation of $\Delta v_i/\Delta y_i = a_i e^{-a_i \Delta y_i}$ where $\Delta y_i = \Delta y = 0.001$. Step 3 represents the individual program managers and the processes by which they determine the most cost-effective proposal given their opportunity cost of effectiveness defined by the director. In the case where $y_i(x_i) \in C^1$ we always have a closed form solution to the program manager's maximization of the cost-effectiveness function. This produces the x_i^k. Step 4 and 5 represent the director's budget check in terms of a satisficing decision rule (where η is the director's permissible percentage budget error). In the following simulation experiments we use $\delta = \eta \cdot B$ where $\eta = 0.02$ while $\beta = 1.0$.

Figures 10.4, 10.5 and 10.6 depict simulations for three budgets: $B = 2.5, 4.5$, and 6.5. Each simulation is presented in four panels: the top left shows λ^k, the top right gives the decisions x_1^k (solid line) and x_2^k (dashed line), the lower left traces $V(\mathbf{x}^k)$ and the lower right presents $B^k = x_1^k + x_2^k$. Convergence to the solution $\{\lambda^*, \mathbf{x}_1^*, \mathbf{x}_2^*\}$ is asymptotic whenever $V(\mathbf{x}^k)$ is continuous in $\mathbf{x}^k$. Convergence is always finite, however, when the decision maker employs a satisficing rule for the budget like $|B_K - B| \leq \delta$. In each case the larger is B; the smaller is λ^*. When $B = 2.5$ we obtain convergence in two iterations and when $B = 4.5$ we obtain convergence in two iterations. When $B = 6.5$ we obtain convergence in eight iterations. Rapid convergence can always be achieved by increasing β. When $\beta = 2.0$, we get convergence in three iterations, as in Figure 10.6. The convergence of λ is monotonic, either from above or below, depending upon whether $\lambda^0 = 1/B$ results in $\lambda^0 > \lambda^*$ or $\lambda^0 < \lambda^*$.

10.5.2 The discrete case

The border security program manager and staff develop an efficient set of six alternatives described in Table 10.1.

The coastal security manager and staff develop an efficient set of six alternatives given in Table 10.2.

As in the previous example, all the data in the tables are internal to each program office. The director of the joint planning staff is not in possession of these details and delegates to the program managers all responsibility for developing the data, executing the analyses and making recommendations.

The discrete case is both more representative of real-life resource allocation problems and more difficult. First, there may be no allocation (x_1^k, x_2^k) such that $B = B^k = x_1^k + x_2^k$, while $V((x_1^k, x_2^k) \geq V(x_1, x_2)$ for all other budget feasible allocations. There may be, however, several satisficing solutions; i.e., allocations for which $|B - B^k| \leq \delta$ while $V((x_1^k, x_2^k) \geq V(x_1, x_2)$. Any such alternatives are satisfactory solutions. Second, the discrete environment does not admit a closed-form solution for $x_i(\lambda_i)$. Each program manager must perform a direct search over his/her alternatives $\{y_{ij}, x_{ij}\}$ to identify that x_{ij}^* that maximizes $y_{ij} - \lambda_i x_{ij}$ for given λ_i. Here the search is over $j \in \mathcal{N}_i$, the index set for the ith program manager.

Figure 10.7 presents the complete set of alternatives in this resource allocation problem. There are 36 combinations of program proposals in cost-effectiveness space representing the set of possibilities open to choice by the director. It must be understood that this information is NOT known *a priori* by the director. The director is only presented with proposals—one from each program office so is only aware

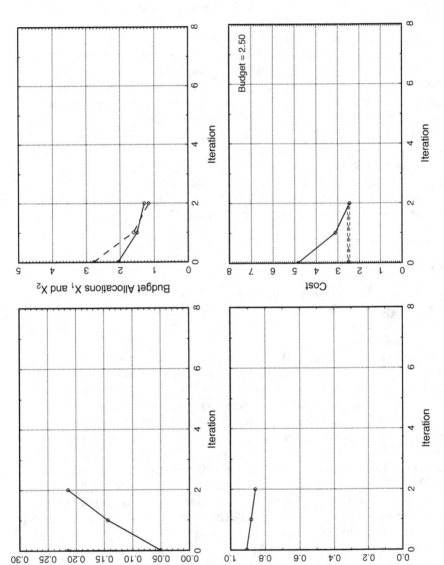

Figure 10.4 Continuous case with $B = 2.5$.

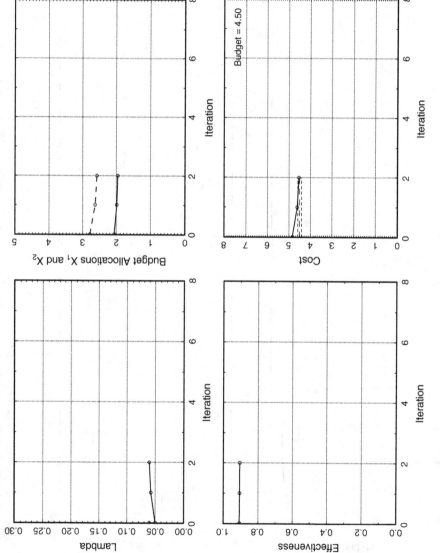

Figure 10.5 Continuous case with $B = 4.5$.

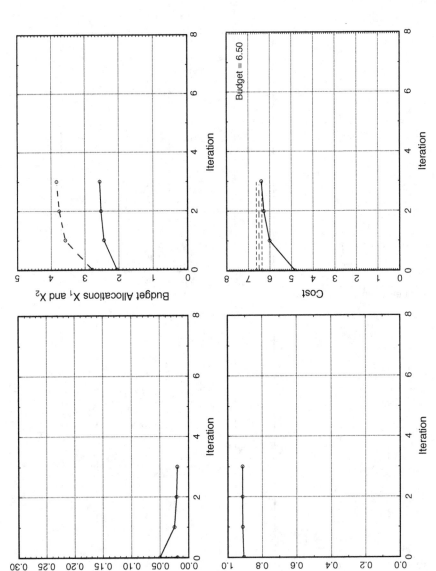

Figure 10.6 Continuous case with $B = 6.5$.

Table 10.1 Border security alternatives

Alternative	x_1	$y_1(x_1)$
1	0.50	0.15
2	0.75	0.40
3	0.81	0.49
4	1.50	0.68
5	1.79	0.75
6	3.50	0.85

Table 10.2 Coastal security alternatives

Alternative	x_2	$y_2(x_2)$
7	0.40	0.11
8	1.00	0.55
9	1.55	0.76
10	2.00	0.83
11	2.80	0.91
12	3.95	0.98

of the combinations as they are presented sequentially (by the program managers). There are 20 clearly dominated alternatives—alternatives where there exist at least one other alternative that is either less costly yet equally (or better) effective or more effective yet equally (or less) costly. We see that for small B there are clearly defined solutions but the envelop of the set of alternatives, the efficient set, becomes relatively "flat" for $B > 4.0$ making the identification of efficient solutions difficult. We present Figure 10.7 solely for the benefit of the reader to understand the challenge of each example allocation problem presented below.

As in the previous case we have $w_1 = 0.6$, $w_2 = 0.4$, $a_1 = 2.95$, and $a_2 = 2.1$. The simulation is composed of the following steps.

STEP 1: (Initialization) Set $k = 0$, $\lambda^k = \lambda^0$, $y_1^0 = y_2^0 = \delta$.

STEP 2: $\lambda_i^k = [w_i * a_1 * e^{-a_i y_i^0}]^{-1} \lambda^k = m_i^{-1} \lambda^k$.

STEP 3: $x_i^k = x_{ij}^* = $ the solution of $\max_{x_{ij}} \{y_{ij} - \lambda_i^k x_{ij}\}$

STEP 4: $B^k = x_1^k + x_2^k$.

STEP 5: If $|B^k - B| \leq \delta$ then STOP, $\{y_1(x_1^k), y_2(x_2^k)\}$ is a satisfactory solution. Otherwise

If $B^k > B + \delta$ then set $\lambda^{k+1} = \left[1 + \beta \cdot \left(\frac{B - B^k}{B}\right)\right] \lambda^k$ and $k = k + 1$ and go to STEP 2.

If $B^k < B - \delta$ then set $\lambda^{k+1} = \left[1 - \beta \cdot \left(\frac{B^k - B}{B}\right)\right] \lambda^k$ and $k = k + 1$ and go to STEP 2.

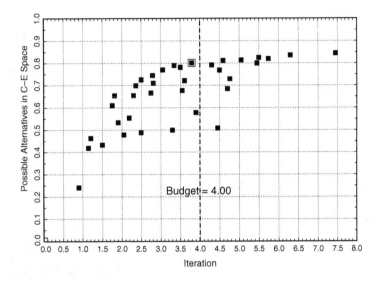

Figure 10.7 Discrete case alternatives.

Steps 1, 2, 4, and 5 again represent the director and Step 3 the program managers' maximization of cost-effectiveness, which is now a direct search over their respective finite set of solutions. Figures 10.8, 10.9, and 10.10 show the simulation results for three budgets: $B = 2.5, 4.5$, and 6.5, respectively. As in the continuous case, each simulation is presented in four panels: (1) the top left presents λ^k; (2) the top right presents the decisions x_1^k (solid line) and x_2^k (dashed line); (3) the lower left presents $V(\mathbf{x})$; and (4) $B^k = x_1^k + x_2^k$ occupies the lower right panel.

All simulations find a satisficing solution. Convergence depends on $\delta = \eta B$ and β. We use $\eta = 0.01$ and $\beta = 0.45$ for $B = 2.5$ and obtain convergence in three iterations. We use $\eta = 0.01$ and $\beta = 1.10$ for $B = 4.5$ and obtain convergence in three iterations. When $B = 6.5$ convergence is obtained in three iterations if $\eta \geq 0.02$ with $\beta = 1.0$ or $\eta = 0.01$ with $\beta = 2.0$.

The convergence indicated here compares favorably with the existing PPBES process at the DoD. Undoubtedly, convergence to a satisficing solution within a three or four level hierarchy would take longer to achieve.

10.6 Summary

The dual formulation of a multi-level public sector resource allocation problem provides a sound theoretical basis for decision-makers who rationalize their decisions with statements like "...the chosen alternative possesses the best balance between cost and effectiveness." They are expressing nothing less than the first-order necessary conditions for a solution of the dual formulation of the problem. The pivotal variable in such problems is the Lagrange multiplier, or "shadow price". This represents the marginal cost of effectiveness.

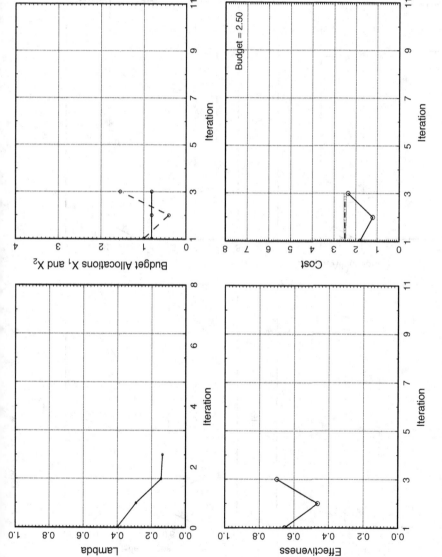

Figure 10.8 Discrete case with $B = 2.5$.

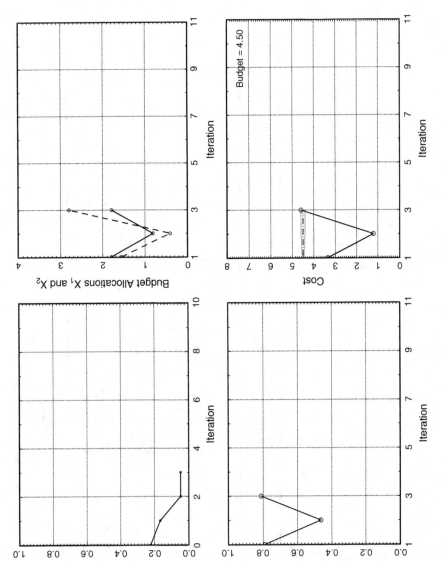

Figure 10.9 Discrete case with $B = 4.5$.

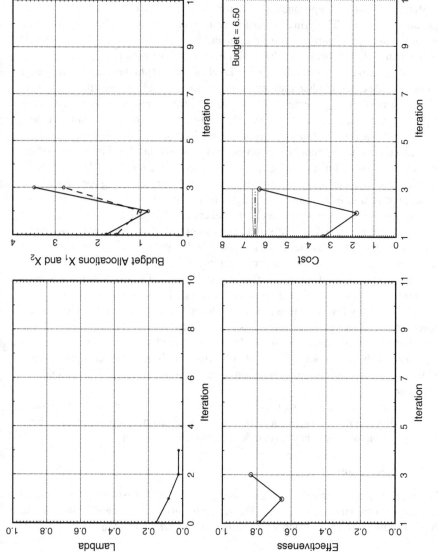

Figure 10.10 Discrete case with $B = 6.5$.

Both the traditional primal formulation and our dual formulation require an iterative procedure to obtain a solution. In the primal problem the budget constraint is always satisfied and one iterates on the budget allocation until all marginal effectiveness values are equal (to the optimum value of the Lagrange multiplier). In the dual problem the marginal effectiveness measures are always equal and one iterates on the Lagrange multiplier (the magnitude of the marginal effectiveness) until the budget constraint is met.

Mathematically the approaches are equivalent, but behaviorally there is a significant distinction. The primal solution requires the first-level decision-maker be in possession of all marginal information and be able to solve an N-dimensional search using this information. This conflicts with our assumptions on the differential information available at each level of the organization. The first-level decision-maker has neither the expertise nor the specialized and detailed operational information possessed by the second-level decision-makers. The dual approach only requires the first-level decision-maker to know the values, y_i and x_i. No marginal information is required, i.e. the first-level decision-maker does not need to know how the capabilities proposed by the second-level decision-makers will change based on a small change in the budget allocation. The first-level decision-maker solves only a one-dimensional problem, searching for the value of λ that produces satisfaction of the budget constraint, which is a much more manageable task. The second-level decision-makers are delegated complete authority to decide how to "spend" the resource, consistent with the opportunity cost transmitted to them by the first-level decision-maker. We believe this is consistent with the decentralization found in many organizations.

Of particular importance is the relative speed with which an optimal solution to the multi-level resource allocation problem can be found implementing the dual formulation. Very few iterations are needed to find acceptable results. The convergence was rapid using an extremely basic adjustment mechanism for λ. In real life, these adjustments can be made more adroitly using the first-level decision-maker's expertise and historical knowledge. This is important because in real applications, with the usual budget and time constraints, only a limited number of iterations will be possible.

We believe the dual formulation is the best way to solve a multi-level resource allocation problem and is, in fact, the way individuals naturally approach these types of problems when they wish to make cost-effective decisions.

Acknowledgement

This work benefits from the insights and interpretations of Assistant Professor David L. Rose who has since passed away. He was an inspiring teacher and brilliant mind that is fondly remembered, and sorely missed, by all who knew him.

Bibliography

Bazaraa, Mokhtar S. and C.M. Shetty. 1979. *Nonlinear Programming: Theory and Algorithms*. Toronto, Canada: John Wiley and Sons.

Belton, Valerie and T.J. Stewart. 2003. *Multiple Criteria Decision Analysis: An Integrated Approach*. Norwell, MA: Duxbury Press.

Everett III, Hugh. 1963. "Generalized Lagrange Multiplier Method for Solving Problems of Optimum Allocation of Resources." *Operations Research* 11: 399–417.

Fowler, B.W. and P.P. Cason. 1998. "The Cost Exchange Ratio: A New Aggregate Measure of Cost and Operational Effectiveness." *Journal of the Military Operations Research Society* 3: 57–64.

Hillier, Frederick S. and Gerald J. Lieberman. 1990. *Introduction to Operations Research* (5th edition). New York: McGraw-Hill Publishing Company.

Kaplan, Stanely and B. John Garrick. 1981. "On the Quantitative Definition of Risk." *Risk Analysis* 1: 11–27.

Kirkwood, Craig. W. 1997. *Strategic Decision Making: Multiobjective Decision Analysis with Spreadsheets*. Belmont, CA: Duxbury Press.

Lasry, A., G.S. Zaric, and M.W. Carter. 2007. "Multi-level Resource Allocation for HIV Prevention: A Model for Developing Countries." *European Journal of Operational Research* 180: 786–799.

Libby, R. and P.C. Fishburn. 1977. "Behavioral Models of Risk Taking in Business Decisions: A Survey and Evaluation." *Journal of Accounting Research* 15: 272–292.

Luenberger, David G. 1973. *Introduction to Linear and Nonlinear Programming*. Reading, MA: Addison-Wesley.

Payne, J.W., D.J. Laughhunn, and R. Crum. 1980. "Translation of Gambles and Aspiration Level Effects in Risky Choice Behavior." *Management Science* 10: 1039–1060.

Petty II, J.W. and D.F. Scott. 1981. "Capital Budgeting Practices in Large American Firms: A Retrospective Analysis and Update." In *Financing Issues in Corporate Project Selection*, edited by F.G.J. Derkinderen and R.L. Crum. Boston, MA: Martinus Nyhoff.

Quade, E.S. 1989. *Analysis for Public Decisions*. Englewood Cliffs, NJ: Prentice Hall.

Ruefli, T. 1971. "PPBS – An Analytical Approach." In *Studies in Budgeting*, edited by R.F. Byrne, A. Charnes, W.W. Cooper, O.A. Davis, and D. Gilford. Amsterdam: North-Holland.

Ruefli, T. 1974. "Analytic Models of Resource Allocation in Hierarchical Multi-Level Systems." *Socio-Economic Planning Sciences* 8: 353–363.

Solow, Daniel 1984. *Linear Programming: An Introduction to Finite Improvement Algorithms*. New York: Elsevier Science Publishing Company.

Thomas, C. and R.S. Sheldon. 1999. "The 'Knee of the Curve' – Useful Clue but Incomplete Support." *Journal of the Military Operations Research Society* 4: 17–29.

Willard, D. 1998. "Cost-Effectiveness, CAIV, and the Knee of the Curve." *Phalanx* 31: 24–27.

Documents and websites relating to the PPBS process

Bright, T. 2010. *PPBE at the Pentagon: Changes Coming?* Available at http://view.dau.mil/mp_pbl/dauvideo/Active_Directory-CN_Admin___MP_OU_Service_Accounts_and_Groups_OU_Ft_Belvoir_DC_DAU-ADS_DC_dau_DC_mil/MediaBin/Download/3614/PPBE_at_the_Pentagon_FEB_2010_DAU_2-16-10.pdf [last accessed November 25, 2014].

Defense Acquisition University. 2012. *Program Budget Decision (PBD) Cycle Oct.–Nov.* Available at https://dap.dau.mil/acquipedia/Pages/ArticleDetails.aspx?aid=d97f7732-4fab-414b-b49b-75caa037e304 [last accessed November 25, 2014].

Defense Acquisition University. Defense Acquisition Portal. *The Budgeting PPBE Phase.* Available at https://dap.dau.mil/aphome/ppbe/Pages/Budgeting.aspx [last accessed November 25, 2014].

DoD. Directive Number 7045.14.2013. Available at www.dtic.mil/whs/directives/corres/pdf/704514p.pdf [last accessed November 25, 2014].

Tomasini, R. *Planning, Programming, Budgeting and Execution (PPBE) Process.* Defense Acquisition University. Available at http://www.google.com/url?sa=t&rct=j&q=&esrc=s&source=web&cd=8&sqi=2&ved=0CE8QFjAH&url=http%3A%2F%2Fwww.dau.mil%2Fhomepage%2520documents%2FPPBE%2520Process%2520Brief%2C%2520with%2520Carter%2520Efficiency%2520Initiatives %2C%2520Tomasini%2C%2520Dec%252010.pptx&ei=MPI6U7bhIIKS2QWK2oHIBw&usg =AFQjCNEYOx6DNS_h9Ig1 AXVoyPJcvEwf_w&sig2=v195LBreynL0rB-O8b8gtA [last accessed November 25, 2014].

Travers, O. 2011. *Department of Defense Planning, Programming, Budgeting and Execution (PPBE) Process/Army Planning, Programming, Budgeting and Execution (PPBE) Process: An Executive Primer.* Available at https://www.documentcloud.org/documents/293931-dodarmyppbeprimernov-2011.html [last accessed November 25, 2014].

11 A risk-based approach to cost–benefit analysis

Strategic real options, Monte Carlo simulation, knowledge value added, and portfolio optimization

Johnathan C. Mun and Thomas Housel

11.1 Introduction

Games of chance have been popular throughout history. Biblical accounts even record Roman soldiers gambling for Christ's robes. In earlier times, chance was something that occurred in nature, and humans were simply subjected to it as a ship is to random waves. Until the Renaissance, the future was thought to be a chance occurrence of completely random events, beyond the control of humans.

With the advent of games of chance the study of risk and uncertainty increasingly mirrored real-life events. Although games of chance were initially played with great enthusiasm, rarely did anyone consciously determine the odds. It was not until the mid-1600s that the concept of chance was seriously studied: The first such endeavor can be credited to Blaise Pascal, a father of the study of choice, chance, and probability. Fortunately, after many centuries of mathematical and statistical innovations by visionaries such as Pascal, Bernoulli, Bayes, Gauss, Laplace, and Fermat, and with the explosion of computing technology, uncertainty can increasingly be explained with much more elegance through rigorous, methodological applications. Today, with the assistance of powerful software packages, we have the ability to apply these techniques to increase the value of cost–benefit analysis (CBA), or what might be called "risk–benefit analysis."

Humans have struggled with risk for centuries, but through trial and error and through the evolution of human knowledge, have devised ways to describe, quantify, hedge, and even take advantage of risk.[1] In the US military, risk analysis, real options analysis, and portfolio optimization techniques are enablers of a new way of approaching problems of estimating return on investment (ROI) and estimating risk-value tradeoffs of strategic real options.[2]

Several advanced quantitative risk-based concepts are introduced in this chapter, including the application of strategic real options analysis, Monte Carlo risk simulation, stochastic forecasting, portfolio optimization, and knowledge value added (KVA). These methodologies rely on standard metrics and existing techniques, such as ROI and discounted cash flow discussed in Chapter 17, and complement these techniques by pushing the envelope of analytics while not replacing them outright. These advanced techniques are used to help make the best possible decisions, to allocate budgets, forecast outcomes, and create portfolios with the highest strategic value or ROI (even when conditions surrounding these decisions are risky or uncertain). These new techniques can be used to identify, analyze, quantify, value, forecast, and manage (hedge, mitigate, optimize, allocate, and diversify) risks associated with strategically important military options (see Chapter 14 for example).

11.2   Why is risk important in making decisions?

Before we embark on a journey to review these advanced techniques, let us first consider why risk is critical when making decisions. Risk is an important part of any decision-making process. For instance, suppose projects are chosen based simply on an evaluation of returns (i.e., monetary *benefits* from the project's output) alone, or *costs* alone; clearly, the higher-return and lower-cost project will be chosen first over lower-return and higher-cost projects. Projects that produce valuable outputs that offer higher returns also often bear higher risks. Projects with significantly lower returns and higher risks will tend to be abandoned.

An exclusive focus on cost reduction can result in stifled innovation and creativity. The goal is not simply cost reduction to reduce risks. In this case, the simplest approach is to fire everyone and sell off all the assets. The real question is: how do costs compare to desired outputs/benefits—that is, "costs compared to what?"

To encourage a focus on improving processes and innovative technologies, a new way of calculating ROI that includes a unique numerator is required. ROI is a simple ratio that requires unique estimates of the numerator (i.e., monetary value such as revenues) and the denominator (i.e., monetized costs and investments). ROI estimates, however, must be placed within a larger context and a longer-term view that includes estimates of risk and the ability of management to adapt as they observe the performance of their investments over time. Therefore, instead of relying purely on immediate ROIs or costs, a project, strategy, new process innovation, or new technology should be evaluated based on its total strategic value—including updated returns, costs, and strategic options as well as its risks. Figures 11.1 and 11.2 illustrate possible errors in judgment that could occur when risks are ignored.

Figure 11.1 lists three *mutually exclusive* projects with their respective implementation costs, expected net returns (net of the costs to implement), and risk levels (all in present values).[3] Clearly, for the severely budget-constrained decision-maker, the cheaper the project the better, resulting in the selection of Project X. Assuming the budget is not a binding constraint, the returns-driven decision-maker will choose Project Y with the highest benefits. Project Z will be chosen by the risk-averse decision-maker as it provides the least amount of risk, while still providing a positive net return. The upshot is that, with three different projects and three different decision-makers, three different decisions will be made. Who is correct and why?

Figure 11.2 demonstrates when Project Z should be chosen. For purposes of illustration, suppose all three projects are independent and mutually exclusive,

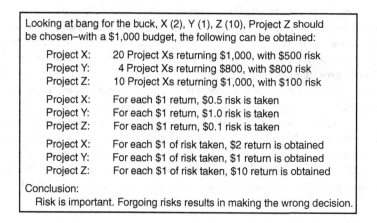

Name of Project	Cost	Returns	Risk
Project X	$50	$50	$25
Project Y	$250	$200	$200
Project Z	$100	$100	$10

Project X for the cost and budget-constrained manager
Project Y for the returns driven and nonresource-constrained manager
Project Z for the risk-averse manager
Project Z for the smart manager

Figure 11.1 Why is risk important?

Looking at bang for the buck, X (2), Y (1), Z (10), Project Z should be chosen–with a $1,000 budget, the following can be obtained:

Project X:	20 Project Xs returning $1,000, with $500 risk
Project Y:	4 Project Xs returning $800, with $800 risk
Project Z:	10 Project Xs returning $1,000, with $100 risk
Project X:	For each $1 return, $0.5 risk is taken
Project Y:	For each $1 return, $1.0 risk is taken
Project Z:	For each $1 return, $0.1 risk is taken
Project X:	For each $1 of risk taken, $2 return is obtained
Project Y:	For each $1 of risk taken, $1 return is obtained
Project Z:	For each $1 of risk taken, $10 return is obtained

Conclusion:
Risk is important. Forgoing risks results in making the wrong decision.

Figure 11.2 Adding an element of risk.

and that an unlimited number of projects from each category can be chosen (only constrained by a budget of US$1,000). With this US$1,000 budget, 20 project Xs can be chosen, yielding US$1,000 in net returns and US$500 risks, etc.

It is clear from Figure 11.2 that project Z is the best project: That is, for the same net return (US$1,000), the least amount of risk is undertaken (US$100). Another way of viewing this selection is that for each US$1 of risk, US$10 in returns are obtained on average. This example illustrates the concept of *bang for the buck* or getting the best value (net monetary benefits) with the least amount of risk.

An even more striking example is provided when there are several different projects with identical single-point average net benefit or costs of US$10 million each. Without risk analysis, a decision-maker should, in theory, be indifferent to choosing any of the projects. With risk analysis, however, a better decision can be made. For instance, suppose the first project has a 10 percent chance of exceeding US$10 million; the second, a 15 percent chance; and the third, a 55 percent chance. Then additional critical information is obtained on the riskiness and uncertainty of the project or strategy, and a better decision can be made.

11.3   From traditional risk assessment to Monte Carlo risk simulation

Military and business leaders have dealt with risk throughout the history of war and commerce. In most cases, decision-makers viewed risks of a particular project, acknowledged its existence, and moved on. Little quantification was performed. In fact, most decision-makers only focus on single-point estimates of a project's net benefit or profitability. Figure 11.3 shows an example of a single-point estimate.[4] The estimated net revenue of US$30 is simply that: a single-point estimate whose probability of occurrence is close to zero.[5]

In the simplest model shown in Figure 11.3, the effects of interdependencies are ignored, and, in modeling jargon, we have the problem of *garbage-in, garbage-out* (GIGO). As an example of interdependencies, the units sold are probably negatively correlated to the price of the product (since demand curves slope downwards), while average variable costs may be positively or negatively correlated to units sold (i.e., depending on whether there are decreasing or increasing returns to scale in production). Ignoring these effects in a single-point net revenue estimate with uncertain sales will yield grossly misleading results. There are numerous interdependencies in military options as well—for example, complex issues in logistics, beginning with the supplier all the way through to the warrior in the field.

In the commercial example illustrated in Figure 11.3, if the unit sales variable becomes 11 instead of 10, the resulting revenue may not simply be US$35. The net revenue may actually decrease if there is an increase in variable cost-per-unit, while the sale price may actually be slightly lower driving the increase in unit sales. Ignoring these interdependencies will reduce the accuracy of the model.

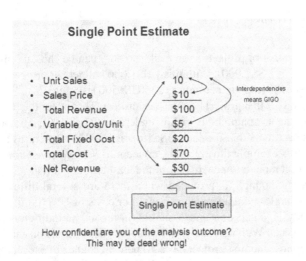

Figure 11.3 Single-point estimates.

Source: Mun (2010).

One traditional approach used to deal with risk and uncertainty is the application of *scenario* analysis. For example, scenario analysis is a central part of the capabilities-based planning approach in widespread use for developing DoD strategies (Mun 2010). In the single-point estimate example described above, suppose three scenarios were generated: the worst-case, nominal-case, and best-case scenarios. When different values are applied to the unit sales, the resulting three scenarios' net revenues are obtained. As discussed earlier, if problems of interdependencies are not addressed, then the net revenue obtained in each case is unreliable and not much confidence can be placed in the analysis.

In the military planning case, problems are exacerbated by the lack of objective ways to estimate benefits in monetary units. Without a monetary benefits analysis such as that illustrated in Chapter 8, it becomes difficult (if not impossible) to compare the net benefits of various scenarios. In addition, interdependencies must be interpreted in a largely subjective manner. This makes it impossible to apply powerful mathematical statistical tools that enable more objective portfolio analysis.[6] This is a particularly challenging problem for top leaders in the DoD required to make judgments for selection among alternatives (often referred to as "trades") about the potential benefits and risks of numerous projects and technology investments.

A related approach is to perform *sensitivity* analysis. Each variable is perturbed a pre-specified amount (e.g., unit sales is changed ±10 percent; sales price is changed ±5 percent; and so forth), and the resulting change in net benefits is captured. This approach is useful for understanding which variables drive or impact the result the most. Performing such analyses by hand or with simple Excel spreadsheets is tedious and provides incremental benefits at best. A related approach that has the same goals but uses a more powerful analytical framework is the use of computer-modeled Monte Carlo risk simulations and tornado sensitivity analysis, where all perturbations, scenarios, and sensitivities can be run hundreds of thousands of times automatically (Mun 2010).

Computer-based Monte Carlo risk simulations can be viewed as an extension of the traditional approaches of sensitivity and scenario testing. Simulations focus on critical success drivers (variables that affect bottom-line variables the most, which themselves are uncertain).

Applying simulation, interdependencies are captured using estimates of multiple regression analysis and other analytical tools. The uncertain variables are then simulated tens of thousands of times automatically to simulate all potential permutations and combinations, generating a spectrum of possible outcomes. The resulting net revenues–monetary benefits from these simulated potential outcomes are tabulated and analyzed. In its most basic form, simulation is simply an enhanced version of traditional approaches—such as sensitivity and scenario analysis—but automatically performed thousands of times while accounting for all the dynamic interactions between the simulated variables.

Based on specific assumptions, the resulting net revenue outcomes from a simulation can be displayed as in Figure 11.4. The interpretation is that there is a 90 percent probability net revenues will fall between US$19.44 and US$41.25, with

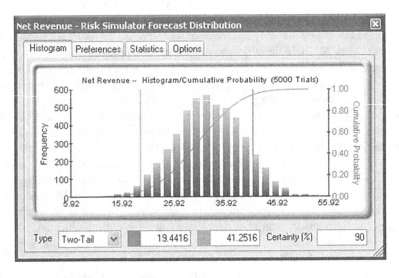

Figure 11.4 Simulation results.

Source: Mun (2010).

a 5 percent worst-case scenario of net revenues falling below US$19.44. Rather than having only three scenarios, the simulation created 5,000 scenarios, or trials, where multiple variables were changed simultaneously according to user-specified underlying functional relationships (relating unit sales, sale price, and variable cost-per-unit).

Monte Carlo risk simulation, named for the famous gambling capital of Monaco, is a very potent methodology. For the practitioner, simulation opens the door to solve difficult and complex but practical problems with relative ease.[7] In simple terms, Monte Carlo risk simulation creates virtual futures by generating thousands and even hundreds of thousands of sample paths of outcomes and analyzes their prevalent characteristics. In practice, Monte Carlo risk simulation methods are used for risk analysis, risk quantification, sensitivity analysis, and forecasting.

An alternative to simulation is the use of highly complex stochastic closed-form mathematical models (Mun 2010). A well-informed analyst would use all available statistical tools to obtain the same answer in the easiest and most practical way possible. In all cases, when modeled correctly, Monte Carlo risk simulation provides similar answers to the more mathematically elegant methods. In addition, there are many real-life applications where closed-form models do not exist and the only recourse is to apply simulation methods. So, what exactly is Monte Carlo risk simulation and how does it work?

Monte Carlo risk simulation, in its simplest form, is a random-number generator that is useful for forecasting, estimating, and analyzing risk. A simulation calculates numerous scenarios of a model by repeatedly picking values from a user-predefined *probability distribution* for the uncertain variables and it uses those values for the model. As all those scenarios produce results, the collection of results can be used to generate a forecast (based on underlying formulas, functions, and user-specified probability distributions of key variables built into the simulation).

Think of the Monte Carlo risk simulation approach as picking golf balls out of a large basket repeatedly with replacement. The size and shape of the basket depend on the distributional *input assumption* (e.g., a normal distribution with a mean of 100 and a standard deviation of 10, versus a uniform distribution or a triangular distribution) where some baskets are deeper or more symmetrical than others, allowing certain balls to be pulled out more frequently than others. The number of balls pulled repeatedly depends on the number of *trials* simulated. Each ball is indicative of an event, scenario, or condition that can occur. For a large model with multiple related assumptions, imagine the large model as a very large basket wherein many baby baskets reside. Each baby basket has its own set of colored golf balls bouncing around. Sometimes these baby baskets are linked with each other (if there is a *correlation* between the variables), forcing the golf balls to bounce in tandem—whereas in other uncorrelated cases, the balls are bouncing independently of one another. The balls that are picked each time from these interactions within the model (the large basket) are tabulated and recorded, providing a *forecast output* result of the simulation.

11.4 Knowledge value added analysis

As the US military is not in the business of making money, referring to revenues throughout this chapter may appear somewhat misleading. For non-profit organizations, especially the military, an alternative approach to those illustrated in Chapters 8 or 9 to capture benefits is to apply KVA as a proxy estimate to generate an equivalent monetary "benefit" (or "revenue") to permit ROI analysis (Cook *et al.* 2007; Housel *et al.* 2007). ROI is a basic CBA ratio with the exception that the estimated profit (revenue minus cost) is in the numerator and cost in the denominator. KVA generates ROI estimates by developing a market comparable price-per-common-unit of output, multiplied by the quantity of output, to achieve a total revenue estimate.

The primary purpose of KVA methodology is to describe all organizational outputs in common units. The use of common units provides a means to compare the outputs of all assets (human, machine, and IT). For example, the purpose of a military process may be to collect signal intelligence or to plan for a ship modification and upgrade. KVA would describe the outputs of both processes in common units; thus making their performances comparable.

KVA measures the value provided by human capital assets and IT assets by analyzing an organization, process or function at the process level. It provides insights into each dollar of IT investment by monetizing the outputs of all assets, including intangible assets (e.g., such as that produced by IT and humans). By capturing the value of knowledge embedded in an organization's core processes (i.e., employees and IT), KVA identifies the actual cost and revenue of a process, product, or service. Because it identifies every process required to produce an aggregated output in terms of historical prices and costs-per-common-unit of output of those processes, KVA allows unit costs and unit prices to be calculated. The methodology has been applied in 45 areas within the DoD: from flight scheduling, to ship maintenance and modernization (Rios *et al.* 2006; Housel *et al.* 2008; Rabelo and Housel 2008; Kendall and Housel 2004).

As a performance tool, the KVA methodology:

- compares all processes in terms of relative productivity;
- allocates revenues and costs to common units of output;
- measures value added by IT by the outputs it produces; and
- relates outputs to the cost of producing those outputs in common units.

Based on the tenets of complexity theory, KVA assumes that humans and technology in organizations add value by taking inputs and changing them (measured in units of complexity) into outputs through core processes. The amount of change an asset within a process produces can be used as a measure of its marginal value-added or benefit. The additional assumptions in KVA include the following:

- Describing all process outputs in common units (e.g., using a knowledge metaphor for descriptive language in terms of time it takes an average employee to learn how to produce the outputs) allows historical revenue and cost data to be assigned to those processes.
- All outputs can be described in terms of the time required to learn how to produce them.
- Learning time, a proxy for procedural knowledge required to produce process outputs, is measured in common units of time. Consequently, units of learning time = common units of output or "Knowledge" (K).
- A common unit of output makes it possible to compare all outputs in terms of cost-per-unit as well as price-per-unit; revenue can now be assigned at the sub-organizational level.
- Once cost and revenue streams have been assigned to sub-organizational outputs, normal accounting and financial performance and profitability metrics can be applied (Rodgers and Housel 2006; Pavlou *et al.* 2005; Housel and Kanevsky 1995).

Describing processes in common units also permits market-comparable data to be generated, a feature particularly important for non-profit organizations like the US military. Using a market-comparables approach, data from the commercial sector can be used to estimate price-per-common-unit, allowing a monetary measure of benefits or revenue estimates of process outputs for non-profit organizations. This approach also provides a common-units basis to define benefit streams regardless of the process analyzed.

KVA differs from other non-profit ROI models because it allows for revenue estimates, enabling the use of traditional accounting, financial performance, and profitability measures at the sub-organizational level. KVA can rank processes by the degree to which they add value to the organization or its outputs. This ranking assists decision-makers in identifying the value-added of various processes.

Value is quantified in two key metrics: Return-on-knowledge (ROK: revenue/cost) and ROI ((revenue-investment cost)/investment cost). The outputs from a KVA analysis become the input into the ROI models and real options analysis discussed next. By tracking the historical volatility of price- and cost-per-unit as well as ROI, it is possible to establish risk (as compared to uncertainty) distributions, which is important to accurately estimate the value of real options.

The KVA method has been applied to numerous core military processes across the services (Rios *et al.* 2006; Housel *et al.* 2008; Housel and Nelson 2005). This KVA research has provided a means for simplifying real options analysis for DoD processes discussed below. Current KVA research will provide a library of market-comparable price- and cost-per-unit of output estimates. This research will enable a more stable basis for comparisons of performance across core processes. The data also provide a means to establish risk-distribution profiles for integrated risk analysis approaches such as real options and KVA, which have been linked directly to the Real Options Super Lattice Solver and Risk Simulator software for rapid adjustments to real options valuation projections (Housel *et al.* 2010).

11.5 Strategic real options analysis

An important step in performing strategic real options analysis is the application of Monte Carlo risk simulation. By applying Monte Carlo risk simulation to simultaneously change all critical inputs in a correlated manner within a model, one can identify, quantify, and analyze risk.[8] The question then is: what next? Simply quantifying risk is useless unless you can manage it, reduce it, control it, hedge it, or mitigate it. This is where strategic real options analysis can be used. Think of real options as a strategic road map for making decisions.

Suppose you are driving from point A to point B, and you only have or know one way to get there: a straight route. Further suppose there is a lot of *uncertainty* as to what traffic conditions are like further down the road, and you *risk* being stuck in traffic (there is a 50 percent chance this will occur).

Simulation will provide you the 50 percent figure. Knowing that half the time you will get stuck in traffic is valuable information, but the question now is: so what? (especially if you must ultimately arrive at point B). Suppose you discover several alternate routes to get to point B. You could still drive the straight route; but, if you hit traffic, make a left, right, or U-turn to avoid congestion—mitigating the risk, and getting you to point B faster and more safely. There is potential value in these newly discovered real *options*.

The real options approach can help guide how much you would be willing to pay for a *strategic road map* or *global positioning satellite* investment to reveal and possibly exploit alternative routes. In military situations with high risk, real options can help identify strategies to mitigate risks. In fact, both businesses and the military have applied real option approaches for hundreds of years without fully realizing it—the military calls this approach *courses of action*. For example, do we take Hill A so that it provides us the option and ability to take Hill B and Valley C, or how should we take Valley C? Or do we avoid taking Valley C altogether? And so forth.

It is useful to discuss the formal structure (and subsequent analytics) that real options analysis provides. Using real options analysis, we can quantify and value each strategic pathway and frame strategies to hedge, mitigate, or sometimes take advantage of risk.

In the past, corporate investment decisions were relatively straightforward, applying traditional cost–benefit (NPV) analysis as in Chapter 17. Buy a new machine that is more efficient (where the discounted stream of future monetary benefits exceeds the investment cost); make more products costing a certain amount (if benefits outweigh the costs); or hire a larger pool of sales associates (if the marginal increase in forecast sales revenues exceeds the additional salary and implementation costs). Need a new manufacturing plant? Show that the construction costs can be recouped quickly and easily by the increase in revenues it will generate through new and more improved products, and the initiative is approved. Many real-life conditions, however, are more complex.

Suppose a company decides to go with an e-commerce strategy, but multiple strategic paths exist. Which path does it choose? What are the options? If the wrong path is chosen, how does it get back on the right track? How does the company value and prioritize the paths that exist? If you are a venture capitalist firm with multiple business plans to consider for possible investment, how do you value a start-up firm with no proven track record? How do you structure a mutually beneficial investment deal? What is the optimal timing to a second or third round of financing?

Real options analysis is useful not only in valuing a firm through its strategic business options: it can also be used as a strategic business tool in capital investment and acquisition decisions. For instance, should the military invest millions in a new open architecture initiative and, if so, what are the values of the various strategies for such an investment, and how do we proceed? How should the military choose among several alternative IT infrastructure projects? Should it invest billions in a risky R&D initiative? The consequences of a wrong decision can be disastrous, and lives could be at stake.

In a traditional analysis, these questions cannot be answered with any certainty. In fact, some of the answers generated through the use of traditional analysis can be misleading because most models assume a static, one-time decision-making process. The real options approach is sequential in nature, taking into consideration the strategic options certain projects create under uncertainty and a decision-maker's flexibility in exercising or abandoning these options at different points in time, as the level of uncertainty decreases or is revealed over time.

Traditional analysis assumes a static investment decision and assumes that strategic decisions are made initially with no recourse to choose other pathways or options in the future. In contrast, the real options approach incorporates a learning model such that the decision-maker makes better and more-informed strategic decisions when some levels of uncertainty are resolved through the passage of time, actions, and events (see Chapter 14 for an interesting application).

The use of the KVA methodology to monitor the performance of given options, and the adjustments to real options as leaders learn more from the execution of given options, provides an integrated methodology to help military leaders hedge their bets while taking advantage of new opportunities over time. Real options analysis can be used to frame strategies to mitigate risk, increase value, and find optimal strategic pathways to pursue. It can likewise generate options to enhance the value of a project while managing risks. Imagine real options as your guide when navigating through unfamiliar territory, providing road signs at every turn to help make the best and most informed driving decisions. This guidance is the essence of real options.

Figure 11.5 illustrates a very basic real options framing exercise—clearly more complex situations can be developed. From the options that are framed, Monte

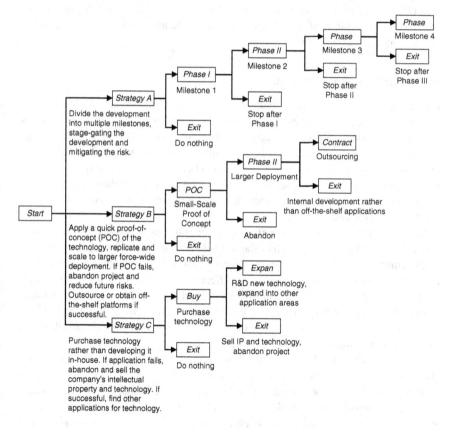

Figure 11.5 Example real options framing.

Source: Mun (2010).

Carlo risk simulation and stochastic forecasting, coupled with traditional techniques, are applied. Then, real options analytics are used to solve and value each strategic pathway allowing better-informed decisions.[9]

As mentioned previously, real options analysis can generate options to enhance the value of a project while managing risks. Sample options include the option to expand, contract, abandon, or utilize sequential compound options (phased stage-gate options, options to wait and defer investments, proof-of-concept stages, milestone development, and R&D initiatives).

Sample applications in the military include using real options for acquisitions (see Chapter 14), spiral development, and various organizational configurations, as well as the strategic importance of integrated and open architectures as real options multipliers. Under guidance of the US Office of Management and Budget (OMB) Circular A-76, comparisons using real options analysis could be applied to enhance outsourcing competitions between the Government's Most Efficient Organization (MEO) and private-sector alternatives. Real options can be used throughout strategic planning (the Joint Capabilities Integration Development System (JCIDS) requirements generation process in the United States) and in the Defense Acquisition System.[10] Many other possible applications exist in military decision-making and portfolio analysis.

11.6 Portfolio optimization

In most decisions, there are variables over which leadership has control (*control variables*), such as how to establish supply lines, modernize a ship, use network centricity to gather intelligence, and so on. Similarly, business leaders have options in what they charge for a product, how much to invest in a project, or which projects they should choose in a portfolio when they are constrained by budgets or other resources. These decisions could also include allocating financial resources, building or expanding facilities, managing inventories, and determining product-mix strategies.

Such decisions might involve thousands or millions of possible alternatives. Considering and evaluating each of them would be impractical or even impossible. These control variables are also called *decision variables*. Finding the optimal values for decision variables can make the difference between reaching an important goal and missing that goal. An optimization model can provide valuable assistance in incorporating relevant variables when analyzing decisions and finding the best solutions for making decisions. Optimization models often provide insights that intuition alone cannot.

An optimization model has three major elements: an objective, decision variables, and constraints (see Mun 2010, Chapter 4). In short, the optimization methodology finds the best combination or permutation of decision variables (e.g., best way to deploy troops, build ships, and choose which projects to execute) in every conceivable way such that the objective is maximized (e.g., strategic value, enemy assets destroyed, or ROI), or minimized (e.g., risk and costs), while still satisfying the constraints (e.g., time, budget, and other scarce resources).

Obtaining optimal values from complex models generally requires iterative or ad hoc search algorithms. This search often involves running one iteration for an initial set of values, analyzing the results, changing one or more values, rerunning the model, and repeating the process until a satisfactory solution is obtained. This process can be very tedious and time consuming even for small models and it is often not clear how to adjust values from one iteration to the next.

A more rigorous method systematically enumerates all possible alternatives (Mun 2010). This approach guarantees optimal solutions if the model is correctly specified.[11] Figures 11.6 to 11.8 illustrate a sample portfolio analysis where, in the first case, there are 20 total projects to choose from (if all projects were executed, it would cost US$10.2 billion), and where each project has its own ROI or monetary benefit measure, cost, strategic ranking, and comprehensive, tactical, and total military scores (obtained from field commanders through the Delphi Method to elicit their thoughts about the strategic value of a particular project or initiative; see Mun 2010).

The constraints are full-time equivalence resources, budget, and strategic score. In other words, to build the most strategic portfolio possible there are 20 projects or initiatives to choose from, where we want to select the top 10—subject to having enough money to pay for them, the people to do the work, etc.[12] All the while, Monte Carlo risk simulation, real options, and forecasting methodologies are applied in the optimization model (e.g., the values for each project are shown in Figure 11.6, linked from their own models with simulation and forecasting methodologies applied, and the best strategy for each project is chosen using real options analysis) (Mun 2006, 2010). Or perhaps the projects shown are nested within one another. For instance, you cannot exercise Project 2 unless you execute Project 1, but you can only exercise Project 1 without having to do Project 2, and so forth. The results are shown in Figure 11.6.

Figure 11.7 shows the optimization process done in series with some of the constraints relaxed. For instance, what would be the best portfolio and the strategic outcome if a budget of US$3.8 billion were imposed? What if it were increased to US$4.8 billion, US$5.8 billion, and so forth? The efficient frontiers depicted in Figure 11.7 illustrate the best combination and permutation of projects in the optimal portfolio. Each point on the frontier is a portfolio of various combinations of projects that provides the best allocation possible given the different budgets (requirements and constraints) (Note: This can be thought of as a stochastic analogue to the deterministic economic evaluation of alternatives (EEoA) approach to CBA introduced in Chapter 4).

Finally, Figure 11.8, another example, shows the top ten projects (based on a budget constraint) that were chosen and how the total budget is optimally allocated to provide the best and most well-balanced portfolio.

11.7 Integrated risk management

We are now able to put all the pieces together into an *Integrated Risk Management* framework to see how these different techniques are related in a risk analysis and

Project Name	ENPV	NPV	Cost	Strategy Ranking	Return to Rank Ratio	Profitability Index	Selection	Military Score	Tactical Score	FTE Resources	Comprehensive Score
Project 1	$458.00	$150.76	$1,732.44	1.20	381.67	1.09	0	8.10	2.31	1.20	1.98
Project 2	$1,954.00	$245.00	$859.00	9.80	199.39	1.29	1	1.27	4.83	2.50	1.76
Project 3	$1,599.00	$458.00	$1,845.00	9.70	164.85	1.25	0	9.88	4.75	3.60	2.77
Project 4	$2,251.00	$529.00	$1,645.00	4.50	500.22	1.32	0	8.83	1.61	4.50	2.07
Project 5	$849.00	$564.00	$458.00	10.90	77.89	2.23	0	5.02	6.25	5.50	2.94
Project 6	$758.00	$135.00	$52.00	7.40	102.43	3.60	1	3.64	5.79	9.20	3.26
Project 7	$2,845.00	$311.00	$758.00	19.80	143.69	1.41	1	5.27	6.47	12.50	4.04
Project 8	$1,235.00	$754.00	$115.00	7.50	164.67	7.56	1	9.80	7.16	5.30	3.63
Project 9	$1,945.00	$198.00	$125.00	10.80	180.09	2.58	1	5.68	2.39	6.30	2.16
Project 10	$2,250.00	$785.00	$458.00	8.50	264.71	2.71	1	8.29	4.41	4.50	2.67
Project 11	$549.00	$35.00	$45.00	4.80	114.38	1.78	0	7.52	4.65	4.90	2.75
Project 12	$525.00	$75.00	$105.00	5.90	88.98	1.71	0	5.54	5.09	5.20	2.69
Project 13	$516.00	$451.00	$48.00	2.80	184.29	10.40	0	2.51	2.17	4.60	1.66
Project 14	$499.00	$458.00	$351.00	9.40	53.09	2.30	1	9.41	9.49	9.90	4.85
Project 15	$859.00	$125.00	$421.00	6.50	132.15	1.30	1	6.91	9.62	7.20	4.25
Project 16	$884.00	$458.00	$124.00	3.90	226.67	4.69	1	7.06	9.98	7.50	4.46
Project 17	$956.00	$124.00	$521.00	15.40	62.08	1.24	1	1.25	2.50	8.60	2.07
Project 18	$854.00	$164.00	$512.00	21.00	40.67	1.32	0	3.09	2.90	4.30	1.70
Project 19	$195.00	$45.00	$5.00	1.20	162.50	10.00	0	5.25	1.22	4.10	1.86
Project 20	$210.00	$85.00	$21.00	1.00	210.00	5.05	0	2.01	4.06	5.20	2.50
Total	$14,185.00		$3,784.00	99.00			10	58.58	62.64	73.50	33.15
Profit/Rank	$143.28	Maximize	<=$3800	<=100			x <=10			<=80	
Profit*Score	$470,235.60										

Figure 11.6 Portfolio optimization and allocation.

Source: Mun (2010).

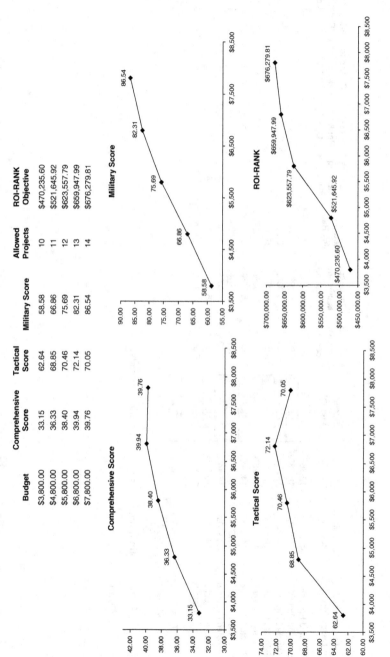

Figure 11.7 Efficient frontiers of portfolios.

Source: Mun (2010).

Asset Class Description	Annualized Returns	Volatility Risk	Allocation Weights	Required Minimum Allocation	Required Maximum Allocation	Return to Risk Ratio	Returns Ranking (Hi-Lo)	Risk Ranking (Lo-Hi)	Return to Risk Ranking (Hi-Lo)	Allocation Ranking (Hi-Lo)
Selected Project 1	10.54%	12.36%	11.09%	5.00%	35.00%	0.8524	9	2	7	4
Selected Project 2	11.25%	16.23%	6.86%	5.00%	35.00%	0.6929	7	8	10	10
Selected Project 3	11.84%	15.64%	7.78%	5.00%	35.00%	0.7570	6	7	9	9
Selected Project 4	10.64%	12.35%	11.23%	5.00%	35.00%	0.8615	8	1	5	3
Selected Project 5	13.25%	13.28%	12.09%	5.00%	35.00%	0.9977	5	4	2	2
Selected Project 6	14.21%	14.39%	11.04%	5.00%	35.00%	0.9875	3	6	3	5
Selected Project 7	15.53%	14.25%	12.30%	5.00%	35.00%	1.0898	1	5	1	1
Selected Project 8	14.95%	16.44%	8.90%	5.00%	35.00%	0.9094	2	9	4	7
Selected Project 9	14.16%	16.50%	8.37%	5.00%	35.00%	0.8584	4	10	6	8
Selected Project 10	10.06%	12.50%	10.35%	5.00%	35.00%	0.8045	10	3	8	6
Portfolio Total	**12.6919%**	**4.52%**	**100.00%**							
Return to Risk Ratio	**2.8091**									

Figure 11.8 Portfolio optimization (continuous allocation of funds).

Source: Mun (2010).

risk management context. This framework is comprised of eight distinct phases of a successful and comprehensive risk analysis implementation, going from a qualitative management-screening process, to creating clear and concise reports for management. The process was developed by the authors based on previous successful implementations of risk analysis, forecasting, real options, KVA cash-flow estimates, valuation, and optimization projects both in the consulting arena and in industry-specific problems (Mun 2010). These phases can be performed either in isolation or combined in sequence for a more robust integrated analysis.

Figure 11.9 shows the integrated risk analysis process. We can segregate the process into the following eight simple steps:

1 qualitative management screening;
2 time-series and regression forecasting;
3 base case KVA and NPV analysis;
4 Monte Carlo risk simulation;
5 real options problem framing;
6 real options modeling and analysis;
7 portfolio and resource optimization;
8 reporting and update analysis.

11.7.1   Qualitative management screening

Qualitative management screening is the first step in any integrated risk analysis process. Decision-makers have to decide which projects, assets, initiatives, or strategies are viable for further analysis in accordance with the organization's mission, vision, goal, or overall strategy. The organization's mission, vision, goal, or overall strategy may include strategies and tactics, competitive advantage, technical, acquisition, growth, or synergistic or global threat issues. That is, the initial list of projects should be qualified in terms of meeting the leadership's agenda. Often the most valuable insight is created as leaders frame the complete problem to be resolved. This is the step where risks to the organization are identified and carefully described.

11.7.2   Time-series and regression forecasting

The future is then forecasted using time-series analysis, stochastic forecasting, or multivariate regression analysis (if historical or comparable data exist). Otherwise, other qualitative forecasting methods may be used (subjective guesses, growth-rate assumptions, expert opinions, Delphi Method, and so forth).[13]

11.7.3   Base case KVA and net present value analysis

For each project that passes the initial qualitative screens, a KVA-based discounted cash-flow model is created (Rios *et al.* 2006). This model serves as the base case analysis where a NPV and ROI are calculated for each project using the forecasted

1 RISK IDENTIFICATION

List of projects and strategies to evaluate

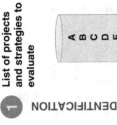

A
B
C
D
E

Start with a list of projects or strategies to be evaluated... these projects have already been through qualitative screening

2 RISK PREDICTION

Base case projections for each project

Risk Simulator

Time Series Forecasting

...with the assistance of time-series forecasting, future outcomes can be predicted...

3 RISK MODELING

Develop static financial models

Traditional analysis stops here!

...the user generates a traditional series of static base case financial (discounted cash flow) models for each project...

4 RISK ANALYSIS

Dynamic Monte Carlo simulation

Risk Simulator

Simulation

Lognormal

...Monte Carlo simulation is added to the analysis and the financial model outputs become inputs into the real options analysis...

5 RISK MITIGATION

Framing Real Options

...the relevant projects are chosen for real options analysis and the project or portfolio real options are framed...

6 RISK HEDGING

Options analytics, simulation, optimization

Simulation   Lattice

Real Options Super Lattice Solver

...real options analytics are calculated through binomial lattices and closed-form partial-differential models with simulation...

7 RISK DIVERSIFICATION

Portfolio optimization and asset allocation

Optimization   Risk Simulator

Effects of Waiting   Decision   Effects of Going

...stochastic optimization is the next optional step if multiple projects exist that require efficient asset allocation given some budgetary constraints... useful for strategic portfolio management...

8 RISK MANAGEMENT

Reports presentation and update analysis

...create reports, make decisions, and do it all again iteratively over time...

Figure 11.9 Integrated risk analysis process.

values in the previous step. This step also applies if only a single project is under consideration. This NPV is calculated using the traditional approach utilizing the forecast revenues and costs and discounting the net of these revenues and costs at an appropriate risk-adjusted rate (see Chapter 17). The ROI and other financial metrics are generated here.

11.7.4 *Monte Carlo risk simulation*[14]

Because the static discounted cash flow produces only a single-point estimate, there is often little confidence in its accuracy given that future events that affect forecasted cash flows are highly uncertain. To better estimate the actual value of a particular project, Monte Carlo risk simulation can be employed. Usually, a sensitivity analysis is first performed on the discounted cash-flow model; that is, setting the NPV or ROI as the dependent variable, we can change each significant explanatory variable and note the change in the dependent variable of interest. Explanatory variables can include revenues, costs, tax rates, discount rates, capital expenditures, depreciation, and so forth, which ultimately flow through the model to affect the NPV or ROI figure of interest. Each significant explanatory variable can be changed by a set amount to determine the effect on the resulting NPV.

A graphical representation can then be created in Risk Simulator (which is often called a tornado chart because of its shape), where the most sensitive precedent (explanatory) variables are listed first in descending order of magnitude. Armed with this information, the analyst can then decide which key variables are highly uncertain in the future and which can be assumed to be deterministic. The set of key uncertain variables that drive the NPV (and, hence, the decision) are called *critical success drivers*. These critical success drivers are prime candidates for Monte Carlo risk simulation. Because some of these critical success drivers may be correlated, a correlated and multidimensional Monte Carlo risk simulation may be required. Typically, these correlations can be obtained through historical data. Running correlated simulations provides a much closer approximation to the variables' real-life behaviors.

11.7.5 *Real options problem framing*[15]

The risk information obtained somehow needs to be converted into *actionable intelligence*. Once risk has been quantified using Monte Carlo risk simulation, what do we do about it? The answer is to use real options analysis to hedge these risks, to value these hedges, and to position the organization to take advantage of the risks.

The first step in real options analysis is to generate a strategic map through the process of framing the problem. Based on the overall problem identification occurring during the initial qualitative management-screening process, certain strategic option alternatives would have become apparent for each particular project. These so-called strategic optionalities may include (among other things) the option to expand, contract, abandon, switch, choose, and so forth. Based on the identification of strategic optionalities that exist for each project or at each stage of the project, the analyst can then choose from a list of options to analyze each in more detail. Real options can be added to the projects to hedge downside risks and to take advantage of upside swings.

11.7.6   Real options modeling and analysis

Through the use of Monte Carlo risk simulation, the resulting stochastic discounted cash-flow model will have a distribution of values. Thus, simulation models analyze and quantify the various risks and uncertainties of each project. The result is a distribution of NPVs and the project's volatility. In the real options approach, we assume that the underlying variable is the future profitability of the project, which is the future cash-flow series.

An implied volatility of the future free cash flow or underlying variable can be calculated through the results of a Monte Carlo risk simulation previously performed. Usually, the volatility is measured as the standard deviation of the logarithmic returns on the free cash-flow stream. In addition, the present value of future cash flows for the base case discounted cash-flow model is used as the initial underlying asset value in real options modeling (Mun 2006). Using these inputs, real options analysis is performed to obtain the project's strategic option values. (Note: an alternative approach is introduced in Chapter 14.)

11.7.7   Portfolio and resource optimization[16]

Portfolio optimization is an optional step in the analysis that generalizes and extends the "opportunity cost" approach in the EEoA discussed in Chapter 4. If the analysis is done on multiple projects, decision-makers should view the results as a portfolio of rolled-up projects because the projects are, in most cases, correlated with one another, and viewing them individually will not present the true picture. As most organizations do not only have single projects, portfolio optimization is crucial. Given that certain projects are related to others, there are opportunities for hedging and diversifying risks through a portfolio approach. Because firms have limited budgets and have time and other resource constraints, while at the same time they have requirements for certain overall levels of returns, risk tolerances, and so forth, portfolio optimization takes into account all these to create an optimal portfolio mix. The analysis will provide the optimal allocation of investments across multiple projects.

11.7.8   Reporting and update analysis

The analysis is not complete until reports are generated. Not only are the results presented, but the process used to obtain the results should also be described. Clear, concise, and precise explanations transform a difficult black-box set of analytics into transparent steps. Decision-makers will be reluctant to accept results coming from black boxes if they do not understand where the assumptions or data originate and what types of mathematical or analytical models have been applied. Risk analysis assumes that the future is uncertain and that decision-makers have the ability to make midcourse corrections when these uncertainties become resolved or risks become known; the analysis is usually done ahead of time and, thus, ahead of such uncertainty and risks.

Therefore, when these risks become known over the passage of time, actions, or events, the analysis should be revisited to incorporate the decisions made at each step and/or to revise any input assumptions. Sometimes, for long-horizon projects, several iterations of real options analysis should be performed, where future iterations are updated with the latest data and assumptions. Understanding the steps required to undertake an integrated risk analysis is important because it provides insight not only into the methodology itself, but also into how it evolves from traditional analyses, showing where the traditional approach ends and where the new analytics begin.

11.8 Conclusion

The leadership of ministries of defense can take advantage of more advanced analytical procedures to make strategic investment decisions and manage portfolios of projects using KVA and the real options approach. In the past, due to the lack of technological maturity, this would have been extremely difficult; hence, businesses and the government had to resort to intuition, past experience, and relatively unsophisticated models. Now, with the assistance of new technology and more mature methodologies, financial leaders have every reason to take the analysis a step further.

Corporations such as 3M, Airbus, AT&T, Boeing, BP, Chevron, Johnson & Johnson, Motorola, and many others have already successfully applied these techniques. As emphasized in this chapter (and in the real options application in Chapter 14) the military has the same opportunity. The relevant software applications, books, case studies, and public seminars have been created, including specific case studies developed exclusively for the US Navy.

The only real barrier to implementation is a lack of exposure to the potential benefits of these new methods. Hopefully, this chapter has revealed the potential benefits of these analytical techniques and tools that can complement and enhance CBA techniques currently used by leadership. In order to fully prepare for twenty-first-century challenges and create highly effective and flexible military forces, strategic real options, KVA, and risk analysis can be leveraged by leadership to improve decision making. Combining real options with KVA can help ensure maximum strategic flexibility and improve risk-based CBA.

Notes

1 To the people who lived centuries ago, risk was simply the inevitability of chance occurrence beyond the realm of human control, albeit many phony soothsayers profited from their ability to convincingly profess their clairvoyance by simply stating the obvious or reading the victims' body language and telling them what they wanted to hear. We modern-day humans—ignoring for the moment the occasional seers among us and even with our fancy technological achievements—are still susceptible to risk and uncertainty. We may be able to predict the orbital paths of planets in our solar system with astounding accuracy or the escape velocity required to shoot a man from the Earth to the Moon

or drop a smart bomb within a few feet of its target thousands of miles away, but when it comes to, say, predicting a firm's revenues the following year, we are at a loss.

2 There are many new US Department of Defense (DoD) requirements for using more advanced analytical techniques. For instance, the Clinger-Cohen Act of 1996 mandates the use of *portfolio management* for all federal agencies. The Government Accountability Office's *Assessing Risks and Returns: A Guide for Evaluating Federal Agencies' IT Investment Decision-Making* (Version 1) (February 1997) requires that IT investments apply ROI measures. DoD Directive 8115.01 issued October 2005 mandates the use of performance metrics based on outputs, with ROI analysis required for all current and planned IT investments. DoD Directive 8115.bb (2006) implements policy and assigns responsibilities for the management of DoD IT investments as portfolios within the DoD enterprise—where a portfolio is defined to include outcome performance measures and an expected ROI. The DoD *Risk Management Guidance Defense Acquisition* guidebook requires that alternatives to the traditional cost estimation need to be considered because legacy cost models tend not to adequately address costs associated with information systems or the risks associated with them.

3 Risks can be computed many ways, including volatility, standard deviation of lognormal returns, value at risk, and so forth. For more technical details, see Mun's *Modeling Risk* (2nd edition, 2010).

4 We will demonstrate how KVA combined with the traditional market comparables valuation method allows for the monetization of benefits (i.e., revenue).

5 On a continuous basis, the probability of occurrence is the area under a curve, e.g., there is a 90 percent probability revenues will be between US$10 and US$11. The area under a straight line, however, approaches zero. Therefore, the probability of hitting exactly US$10.00 is close to 0.00000001 percent.

6 See Chapter 14 for an interesting application of real options analysis in the case where benefits are not measured in monetary units.

7 Perhaps the most famous early use of Monte Carlo risk simulation was by the Nobel physicist Enrico Fermi (sometimes referred to as the father of the atomic bomb) in 1930, when he used a random method to calculate the properties of the newly discovered neutron. Monte Carlo methods were central to the simulations required for the Manhattan Project: in the 1950s Monte Carlo risk simulation was used at Los Alamos for early work relating to the development of the hydrogen bomb and became popularized in the fields of physics and operations research. The Rand Corporation and the US Air Force were two of the major organizations responsible for funding and disseminating information on Monte Carlo methods during this time, and today there is a wide application of Monte Carlo risk simulation in many different fields—including engineering, physics, research and development, business, and finance.

8 The outcomes from a Monte Carlo risk simulation include probabilities and various risk statistics that can be used to make better decisions.

9 The pathways can be valued using partial differential closed-form equations, lattices, and simulation. Various software packages are available for this task, such as the author's The Real Options SLS software by Real Options Valuation, Inc., available at www.realoptionsvaluation.com [last accessed November 21, 2014].

10 For example, in the US DOTMLPF vs New Program/Service solutions, joint integration, analysis of material alternatives (AMA), analysis of alternatives (AoA), and spiral development.

11 Suppose that an optimization model depends on only two decision variables. If each variable has 10 possible values, trying each combination requires 100 iterations (10^2 alternatives). If each iteration takes a very short amount of time (e.g., two seconds), then the entire process could take approximately three minutes of computer time. Instead of two decision variables, however, consider six; then consider that trying all combinations requires 1,000,000 iterations (10^6 alternatives). It is easily possible for complete

enumeration to take many years to carry out. Therefore, solving complex optimizations has always been a fantasy until now: With the advent of sophisticated software and computing power, coupled with smart heuristics and algorithms, such analyses can now be completed within minutes.

12 There are 2×10^{18} possible permutations for this problem and, if tested by hand, it would take years to complete. Using Risk Simulator, the problem is solved in about five seconds, or several minutes if Monte Carlo risk simulation and real options are incorporated in the analysis.

13 See Mun (2010, Chapters 8 and 9) for details on forecasting and using software to run time-series, extrapolation, stochastic process, ARIMA, and regression forecasts.

14 See Mun (2010, Chapters 4 and 5) for details on using software to run Monte Carlo simulations.

15 See Mun (2006) for more technical details on framing and solving real options problems.

16 See Mun (2010, Chapters 10 and 11) for details on using software to perform portfolio optimization.

References

Cook, G. R., T. J. Housel, J. Mun, and P. Pavlou. January 2007. "Return on Investment in Non-revenue Generating Activities: Applying KVA and Real Options to Government Operations." *Review of Business Research* 7(1): 16–19.

DoD. US Department of Defense Directive 8115. October 10, 2005. *Information Technology Portfolio Management.* NUMBER 8115.01, ASD(NII)/DoD CIO. Available at http://dtic.mil/whs/directives/corres/pdf/811501p.pdf [last accessed November 27, 2014].

DoD. US Department of Defense Directive 8115. October 30, 2006. *Information Technology Portfolio Management Implementation.* NUMBER 8115.02, ASD(NII)/DoD CIO. Available at http://www.dtic.mil/whs/directives/corres/pdf/811502p.pdf [last accessed November 27, 2014].

GAO. February 1997. *Assessing Risks and Returns: A Guide for Evaluating Federal Agencies' IT Investment Decision-Making.* Version 1. GAO/AIMD-10.1.13. Available at www.gao.gov/assets/80/76295.pdf [last accessed November 27, 2014].

Housel, T. J., and V. Kanevsky 1995. "Reengineering Business Processes: A Complexity Theory Approach to Value Added." *INFOR* 33: 248–262.

Housel, T. J., and S. K. Nelson. 2005. "Knowledge Valuation Analysis: Applications for Organizational Intellectual Capital." *Journal of Intellectual Capital* 6(4): 544–557.

Housel, T. J., W. Little, and W. Rodgers. October 29–31, 2007. "Estimating the Value of Non-Profit Organizations Using the Market Comparables Approach." In *Refereed Proceedings of the Collected Papers of the European Institute for Advanced Studies in Management (EIASM): 3RD Workshop on Visualising, Measuring and Managing Intangibles & Intellectual Capital.* Ferrara, Italy, pp. 156–162.

Housel, T. J., E. Tarantino, S. Hom, and J. Mun. 2008. "Shipyard Planning Case." In *Making Cents Out of Knowledge Management*, edited by J. Liebowitz, pp 68–90. Lanham, MD: Scarecrow Press.

Housel, T. J., V. A. Kanevsky, W. Rodgers, and W. Little. May 28, 2010. "The Use of Modern Portfolio Theory in Non-Profits and Their IT Decisions." In *Refereed Proceedings of the IC6: World Conference on Intellectual Capital for Communities in the Knowledge Economy.* Paris, France.

Kendall, T., and T. J. Housel. July 18–21, 2004. "Resolving the ROI on IT Issue (Best Session Paper)." In *Refereed Proceedings of the 8th World Multi-conference on Systemics, Cybernetics, and Informatics.* Orlando, FL.

Mun, J. 2006. *Real Options Analysis: Tools and Techniques for Valuing Strategic Investments and Decisions* (2nd edition). Hoboken, NJ: Wiley Finance.

Mun, J. 2010. *Modeling Risk: Applying Monte Carlo Risk Simulation, Strategic Real Options, Stochastic Forecasting, and Portfolio Optimization* (2nd edition). Hoboken, NJ: Wiley Finance.

OMB (Executive Office of the President; Office of Management and Budget). August 4, 1983, revised 1999. *Circular NO. A-76.* Washington DC 20503. Available at http://www.whitehouse.gov/sites/default/files/omb/assets/omb/circulars/a076.pdf   [last accessed September 30, 2014].

Pavlou, P. A., T. J. Housel, W. Rodgers, and E. Jansen. 2005. "Measuring the Return on Information Technology: A Knowledge-based Approach for Revenue Allocation at the Process and Firm Level." *Journal of the Association of Information Systems* 6: 199–226.

Rabelo, L., and T. J. Housel. May 20, 2008. "Estimating the Knowledge Value-Added of Information Technology Investments." In *Refereed Proceedings of the Institute of Industrial Engineers* (IIE) *Annual Conference.* Vancouver, British Columbia, Canada, pp. 1849–1854.

Rios, C., T. J. Housel, and J. Mun. 2006. "Real Options and KVA in Military Strategy at the United States Navy." In *Modeling Risk: Applying Monte Carlo Simulation, Real Options Analysis, Forecasting, and Optimization Techniques, Case Study*, pp. 441–452. Hoboken, NJ: Wiley Finance.

Rodgers, W., and T. J. Housel. 2006. "Improvement of Global Performance Measures Related to Intangible Assets." *Collected Papers of the 32nd European International Business Academy (EIBA) Conference (Refereed Proceedings).* December 7–9, Fribourg Switzerland.

12 Extensions of the Greenfield–Persselin optimal fleet replacement model

Application to the Canadian Forces CP-140A Arcturus Fleet

David W. Maybury

12.1 Introduction

Today's Canadian Forces operate increasingly aging military platforms, often retaining fleets for unprecedented long service lives (DND 2014). The unfamiliar territory of operating platforms well beyond expected service lifetimes presents the Canadian Department of National Defence (DND) with a central cost–benefit analysis (CBA) problem: to replace a fleet of aging vehicles or to continue an ongoing maintenance regime. As vehicles age, we expect that the overall operating and maintenance costs (O&M) will eventually reach a level prohibitive to continued operation, thereby suggesting vehicle replacement as the best alternative. Aircraft platform replacement decisions arising primarily from aging effects present a relatively new problem for global militaries. Most replacement decisions in the past have occurred largely through new capability requirements, thus limiting aging effect data. Only recently have selected platforms yielded sufficient data to allow for comprehensive studies.

The United States Air Force (USAF) faces substantial challenges in operating airframes with exceptionally long service lives and, having recognized age as a factor in O&M costs as early as the 1960s (Johnson 1962), the USAF started comprehensive fleet lifetime O&M studies in the 1990s. While limited data in early studies contributed to a confused literature in the 60s and 70s, from Johnson (1962) to Marks and Hess (1981), large datasets and the application of more sophisticated analytical methods available to the USAF in recent years has enabled investigators to draw the cautious conclusion that age effects impact O&M costs. In particular, it was demonstrated in Ramsey *et al.* (1998) that heavy-maintenance workloads have increased with the chronological age of the KC-135 tanker aircraft, and an earlier RAND study (Hildebrandt and Sze 1990) estimated that, for every year increment in the age of a USAF mission design series, O&M costs increase on average by 1.7 perent. Further studies on age effects using commercial airline data (Ramsey *et al.* 1998; Dixon 2005), data from US Navy aircraft (Johnson 1993; Jondrow *et al.* 2002; Stoll and Davis 1993; Francies and Shaw 2000) and those of the USAF (Hildebrandt and Sze 1990; Kiley 2001; Pyles 2003; Keating and Dixon 2003) in the areas of workloads, material consumption, repairs per flight hour, mean time between failures, and program depot maintenance all show positive growth with age. Investigators warn (Pyles 2003) that changing accounting practices, budget sluggishness, and relatively fixed maintenance-personnel requirements plague USAF and USN studies, creating a difficult environment in which to extract age effects from other pressures. Raymond Pyles's 2003 RAND corporation investigation for the USAF on the impact of aging airframes on maintenance represents the most comprehensive study to date (Pyles 2003). Using regression methods that address several issues simultaneously, Pyles discovered a positive relationship between maintenance requirements—in nearly all activities—with airframe age. Not only did Pyles find that different maintenance tasks realize different age effects for the same airframe, but he also found that age effects correlate with aircraft complexity and fly-a-way costs.

In light of growing evidence that suggests age impacts maintenance and hence O&M costs, DND requires a strategy to determine the optimal replacement time for a fleet of vehicles after which it becomes increasingly disadvantageous both economically and operationally to maintain the fleet. As a case study for constructing and implementing a strategy for fleet replacement, we consider the CP-140A Arcturus maritime surveillance aircraft. Acquired from the Lockheed Aircraft Corporation by DND in 1993, the CP-140A is the sister aircraft of the CP-140 Aurora, with both airframes based on the P-3 Orion. The Arcturus fleet consists of three vehicles based with 14 Wing at CFB Greenwood and, unlike the Aurora, the Arcturus does not possess anti-submarine warfare capability. Today, the Arcturus finds a primary role in pilot training, drug trafficking interdiction, search-and-rescue, and sovereignty patrols.

As part of the Canada First Defence Strategy announced in 2008, the Government of Canada has undertaken a significant renewal process for Canada's military. In late 2008, the Assistant Deputy Minister (Materiel) and the Director General Aerospace Equipment Program Management sought operations research input from the Centre for Operations Research and Analysis (CORA) on decisions surrounding the CP-140A Arcturus and the CP-140 Aurora fleets. The Government of Canada had recently altered the decade-long Aurora Incremental Modernization Program (AIMP) for CP-140 life extension to help position DND for the eventual acquisition of a new long-range maritime patrol surveillance aircraft. The Assistant Deputy Minister (Materiel) wished to better understand the expected service life of this platform.

Since acquisition, the CP-140A Arcturus fleet has seen annual O&M costs per vehicle increase dramatically since procurement. Discerning pure age effects from the upward spiralling annual O&M costs presents a highly non-trivial problem. Instead of attempting to isolate each age effect from usual inflationary pressures, operational tempo, budget processes, training programs, and random events (such as the discovery of unanticipated maintenance problems), we apply the Greenfield–Persselin model (Greenfield and Persselin 2002, 2003) by assuming that random events occur independently of airframe age, but that the aircraft's resiliency diminishes with time. Our position maintains that random events trigger O&M costs that evolve proportionally—the aircraft becomes more susceptible to damage as it ages. By focusing on economic considerations that include tradeoffs among costs, operational availability, and the effects of uncertainty, we find an optimal replacement time in a stochastic setting.

In addition to addressing fleet replacement issues, the model we apply also contains forecasting capabilities, yielding insight into future replacement decisions. Most importantly—and we cannot overstress this point—the model implicitly attaches an option value to the capacity to delay a decision. Models based solely on deterministic net present value (NPV) arguments implicitly assume that a military investment choice is either reversible, in that the military can cancel the investment if circumstances become unfavourable, or if irreversible, that the military investment choice occurs as a now or never proposition. Deterministic approaches oversimplify military fleet replacement decisions by not placing an option value on the capacity to delay.

In this paper, we model the CP-140A Arcturus O&M costs as a geometric random walk with a stochastic discount factor represented by operational availability (A_o). We apply the techniques of dynamic programming to calculate an optimal replacement time by translating the Greenfield–Persselin model into an explicit first passage time problem. The model we construct represents a prototype for a fleet replacement strategy using data from the CP-140A Arcturus as a case study. The methods we use build on the Greenfield–Persselin model and we apply the model directly to help inform Canadian military leadership on fleet-wide decisions regarding Canada's maritime surveillance capabilities.

We organize the paper in four parts. Following the introduction, we present the Greenfield–Persselin model in Section 12.2. Section 12.3 applies the model to the CP-140A Arcturus data and provides a mean first passage time approach to the replacement problem. Finally, in Section 12.4, we present a discussion concerning military impact and future research.

12.2   The Greenfield–Persselin model

Empirical evidence suggests a positive relationship between the age of military platforms and their O&M costs (Johnson 1962; Nelson 1977; Marks and Hess 1981; Ramsey *et al.* 1998; Hildebrandt and Sze 1990; Dixon 2005; Johnson 1993; Stoll and Davis 1993; Francies and Shaw 2000; Jondrow *et al.* 2002; Kiley 2001; Pyles 2003; Keating and Dixon 2003). From a modeling point of view, the most important feature emerging from RAND studies suggests that "many of the problems associated with aging material have emerged with little or no warning" (Pyles 2003). Thus, the RAND studies lead us to consider random shocks in addition to constant growth in O&M costs. Based on the ideas from the literature on forest harvesting and renewable resource management, Greenfield and Persselin suggest an infinite horizon generational replacement model in the presence of stochastic noise.

Greenfield and Persselin view the problem of fleet replacement similarly to the problem of deciding to harvest a forest for commercial purposes. As each timber stand grows, it gains in value and, at some point in the future, the forester will make the decision to harvest the stand followed by replanting. Thus, over an infinite time horizon the forester faces an infinite succession of harvest-replanting cycles. The forester must determine the holding period before harvesting. If all else remains equal over each interval, the first optimal holding period will be identical to all other periods. The military faces a similar problem in that, as a military platform ages, its O&M costs increase, eventually leading to a necessary replacement. We can imagine that the military enters a series of repair-replace cycles and, like the forester, the military must determine the optimal replacement time.

In a deterministic universe in which we exactly know the fleet O&M costs evolution function, Greenfield and Persselin construct a simple fleet replacement time model. Let us assume that a military platform has an acquisition cost, p, in an environment of a continuously compounding interest rate discount, r, with an instantaneous (known) O&M cost rate, $m(t)$. The variable t denotes the chronological age of the platform. We assume that the military looks to minimize total ownership costs, thereby determining an appropriate replacement time. The NPV life-cycle cost of a single fleet generation as a function of time reads

$$\text{NPV}(s) = p + \int_0^s dt\, m(t) \exp(-rt), \tag{12.1}$$

where s denotes the replacement time. We now imagine that the replacement process repeats *ad infinitum*. Like the simplified forester's problem, if all else remains equal, each generation faces the same O&M cost structure. Thus, we can write the total ownership cost of successively owning a series of fleets as

$$c(s) = \sum_{i=0}^{\infty} \left(p + \int_0^s dt\, m(t) \exp(-rt) \right) \exp(-rsi), \tag{12.2}$$

where s denotes the replacement time of each generation. The total ownership cost, Equation (12.2), represents a converging geometric series yielding

$$c(s) = \frac{p + \int_0^s dt\, m(t) \exp(-rt)}{1 - \exp(-rs)}. \tag{12.3}$$

Differentiating this expression with respect to the replacement time, s, we find that the military minimizes total ownership cost by applying the first order condition which yields

$$m(s^*) = rp + r \frac{\left(\int_0^{s^*} dt\, m(t) \exp(-rt) \right) + p \exp(-rs^*)}{1 - \exp(-rs^*)}. \tag{12.4}$$

As an example, if we know that the instantaneous O&M cost rate has the form $m(t) = b \exp(\alpha t)$, then we find that

$$c(s) = \frac{p + \dfrac{b(1 - \exp(-(r - \alpha)s)}{r - \alpha}}{1 - \exp(-rs)}, \qquad (12.5)$$

and

$$m(s^*) = b \exp(\alpha s^*) = rp + r \frac{\dfrac{b(1 - \exp(-(r - \alpha)s^*))}{r - \alpha} + p \exp(-rs^*)}{1 - \exp(-rs^*)}. \qquad (12.6)$$

The replacement time, s^*, can be found numerically.

While the deterministic model version of the Greenfield and Persselin model assumes that the military replaces the fleet with exactly the same vehicle at exactly the same price in constant dollars, we caution that the model does not assume this situation reflects reality. The model simply determines the total ownership cost associated with the *specific* vehicle under consideration given an infinite number of generations. The Greenfield–Persselin infinite horizon generational replacement model determines the total ownership cost curve associated with the fleet under consideration. In this regard, the model determines the length of the holding period for each generation in the infinite series.

As Greenfield and Persselin elucidate, the problem with the model outlined thus far stems not from its lack of a replacement option comparison, but from the assumption of an exactly known O&M cost evolution. While the model recognizes the irreversibility of the replacement decision, it implicitly assumes that the decision to replace occurs as a now or never proposition. According to the solution given in Equation (12.6), for every year the fleet is retained past $t = s^*$, the military incurs a known marginal cost. Thus, the model demands replacement at exactly time $t = s^*$, the now or never situation. In reality, we do not know the actual O&M cost evolution function which is further complicated by random shocks to the fleet. Since the costs evolve stochastically, there is a chance that the following year will see a *decrease* in O&M costs from random occurrences. The chance that the O&M costs can actually decrease in the following year—no matter how small that decrease might be—must factor into our decision to replace the fleet. We require a model that places an option value on the capacity to wait.

Greenfield and Persselin made three key insights into the deterministic replacement model. They noticed that Equation (12.5) contains three important factors:

- the constant p in the numerator represents the part of the total ownership cost associated with the initial procurement;
- the second term in the numerator represents a NPV contribution to the total ownership cost arising from O&M activity; and
- the denominator represents a discount factor.

Greenfield and Persselin promote the O&M cost function, the NPV, and the discount factor of Equation (12.5) to a stochastic variable and use dynamic programming to calculate the expected replacement time. By calculating the expected discount factor and the expected NPV at the expected replacement time, Greenfield and Persselin produce a boundary in the O&M costs which signals the optimal replacement point (Greenfield and Persselin 2002, 2003).

While the Greenfield–Persselin model strictly uses O&M costs as the random process that triggers replacement, we feel that the strict reliance on monetary considerations masks the military's true objective: maximize a military advantage at the best possible cost. By relying only on pure monetary issues, the Greenfield–Persselin model can call for long holding periods even in cases where the fleet fails to provide the military with operational availability. A similar problem occurs in economic modeling. Few people value money for its own sake, but rather value the consumption possibilities that wealth represents. For this reason, economic modeling usually resorts to utility functions based on consumption as opposed to wealth itself. We extend the Greenfield–Persselin model by including a stochastic discount factor with the O&M cost process. Determining an objective value function that attempts to measure degrading capability will not only prove exceedingly difficult to construct, but will also destroy the attractive feature of the Greenfield–Persselin model in that the fleet is always compared to itself. We propose using operational availability (A_o) as the stochastic discount factor. By using A_o, we penalize the fleet for failing to provide the military with a vehicle deemed necessary even if the lack of availability reduces costs.

We model the O&M costs per A_o (m_u) as a geometric random walk

$$dm_u = \alpha m_u \, dt + \sigma m_u \, dW(t), \tag{12.7}$$

where $dW(t)$ is the Weiner process, α gives the geometric growth rate, and σ sets the strength of the driving uncertainty. Following the Greenfield–Persselin model, we can calculate the expected replacement time, the expected discount factor at replacement, and the expected NPV at replacement using dynamic programming. Each part can be used to assemble an expected total ownership cost function. The expected replacement time, $a(m_u^*, m_u)$, satisfies the Bellman relation

$$da(m_u^*, m_u) = dt + a(m_u^*, m_u) + \mathbb{E}\left[da(m_u^*, m_u)\right], \tag{12.8}$$

where m_u^* is the O&M cost per A_o at replacement. (Mathematical details appear in Appendix 12.1.) Notice that the replacement time is no longer a function of time, but rather a function of O&M costs per A_o. The solution to Equation (12.8), given the boundary condition $a(m_u^*, m_u^*) = 0$, reads

$$a(m_u^*, b) = \frac{\ln\left(m_u^*/b\right)}{\alpha - (1/2)\sigma^2}, \tag{12.9}$$

where $m_u(t = 0) = b$, the initial O&M costs per A_o. We see that volatility in the O&M costs per A_o process, represented by the parameter $\sigma \geq 0$, increases the lifetime of the fleet relative to a deterministic approach. The model values the capacity to wait in an uncertain environment. We will return to this idea in the following section. Applying the Greenfield–Persselin model, the expected total cost per A_o function, $c_E(m_u)$, becomes

$$c_E(m_u) = \frac{p + \frac{b}{r-\alpha}\left(1 - \left(\frac{b}{m_u}\right)^{\beta_1 - 1}\right)}{1 - \left(\frac{b}{m_u}\right)^{\beta_1}}, \tag{12.10}$$

where

$$\beta_1 = -\left(\frac{\alpha}{\sigma^2} - \frac{1}{2}\right) + \sqrt{\left(\frac{\alpha}{\sigma^2} - \frac{1}{2}\right)^2 + \frac{2r}{\sigma^2}}, \tag{12.11}$$

and using the first order condition we find that

$$m_u^* = \frac{\beta_1}{\beta_1 - 1}(r - \alpha)p + \frac{\beta_1}{\beta_1 - 1}(r - \alpha)\frac{\frac{b}{r-\alpha}\left(1 - \left(\frac{b}{m_u^*}\right)^{\beta_1 - 1}\right) + p\left(\frac{b}{m_u^*}\right)^{\beta_1}}{1 - \left(\frac{b}{m_u^*}\right)^{\beta_1}}, \tag{12.12}$$

which determines the O&M per A_o level at replacement.

While Greenfield–Persselin focus on the expected fleet replacement time, the model can be reinterpreted entirely as a first passage time problem to the barrier m_u^*, which is set by Equation (A12.1.22). By focusing on a first passage time interpretation of the problem, along with the use of a stochastic discount factor, we find that the Greenfield–Persselin model class represents an excellent tool in assessing fleet lifetimes and in providing military leadership with a decision window for an aging fleet. We demonstrate the power of this model class with the CP-140A Arcturus fleet.

12.3 An application: the CP-140 Arcturus

Using the data obtained through the DND *Cost Factors Manual* and the Canadian Forces fleet data base PERFORMA, we analyze the CP-140A Arcturus for optimal replacement in the presence of stochastic noise. The dataset contains 13 years of data (1995–2007) on each of the three aircraft that comprise the fleet, including acquisition costs. The O&M costs include petroleum, oil, lubricants, engineering services, repairs, overhauls, and sparing costs. Since any amortization costs connected to the fleet do not involve the disbursement of funds, and since usual military activity in the form of salaries or unit support will require funding independent of vehicle age, we do not include costs associated with these effects in O&M.

Based on RAND studies, we take the position that fleet resiliency diminishes with time (e.g., metal fatigue, increased chance of corrosion discoveries), and hence problems triggered by random events—which occur independently of the CP-140A's age—compound. We apply the Greenfield–Persselin model to capture these effects with a stochastic discount factor represented by A_o. Finally, we assume a constant interest rate discount of 4.40 percent, which provides a good approximation to a risk-free interest rate in Canada over the period in consideration (see Chapter 17). We keep the discount rate fixed throughout the study.

To summarize our model input assumptions, we have:

- effects of new technology, modernization and replacement choice are not considered;
- salaries supporting DND civilian or military personnel are not included in O&M;
- direct squadron support costs are not included in O&M;
- amortization costs are not included;
- a fixed discount rate of 4.40 percent;
- the fleet becomes less resilient to random events with time;
- random events occur independently of vehicle life.

We do not include the actual dataset for the CP-140A Arcturus in this report.[1] Instead we provide a normalized dataset that sets the initial O&M per A_o at 4.4 in dimensionless units. We apply a standard likelihood analysis technique to estimate the model parameters of the geometric random walk in Equation (12.7), yielding (at two standard deviations)

$$\hat{\alpha} = 0.2 \pm 0.1 \qquad \hat{\sigma} = 0.4 \pm 0.1, \tag{12.13}$$

which generates an estimate for the O&M per A_o barrier of

$$16 < m_u^* < 39. \tag{12.14}$$

Notice that we have large uncertainty in the estimated parameters. This reflects the limited costing data we have CP-140A fleet—we have a small sample size.[2] In Figure 12.1, we see the O&M per A_o sample path (in normalized units) with the calculated barrier and its associated uncertainty represented by a hatched bar. The first passage interpretation becomes immediately clear in the presence of real data (normalized in this case). The uncertainty in the estimated barrier, m_u^*, implies uncertainty in the expected replacement time. Since the expectation is calculated conditionally on parameter estimates, the expectation itself becomes uncertain. To capture the subtleties associated with uncertainty in the parameter estimates, we treat the problem as a first passage of time to the region delineated by the upper and lower estimate bounds of m_u^*. We interpret the region between the two boundaries as a critical region for the decision-maker. Once the process enters the

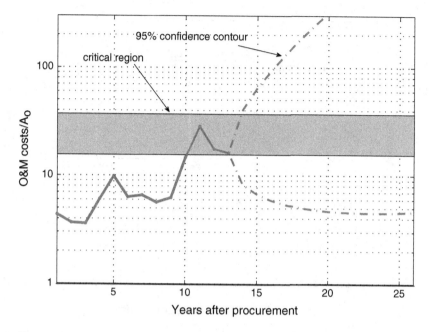

Figure 12.1 CP-140 Arcturus data with the critical region indicated.

critical region, the model calls for the decision-maker to consider a replacement or an overhaul initiative.

By interpreting entry of the critical region as a flag for initiating a decision process, we see in Figure 12.1 that the model calls for replacement consideration of the CP-140A Arcturus at year ten. Using Equation (12.8), the expected time to enter the critical region from the first year of data is at year 11. The uncertainty envelope gives the 95 percent confidence band for the future sample path.

The application of the original Greenfield–Persselin model, which does not use a utility discount, yields Figure 12.2. Without the utility discount, and again using standard likelihood techiques, we find the parameter estimates

$$\hat{\alpha} = 0.1 \pm 0.1, \qquad \hat{\sigma} = 0.2 \pm 0.1, \tag{12.15}$$

with barrier

$$9 < m_u^* < 20. \tag{12.16}$$

The expected time to the critical region jumps to 23 years, representing more than a 100 percent increase over the model without the stochastic discount factor. We see that the effect of a stochastic discount factor dramatically changes the predictions of the model. Again, we display the uncertainly envelope at the 95 percent confidence band.

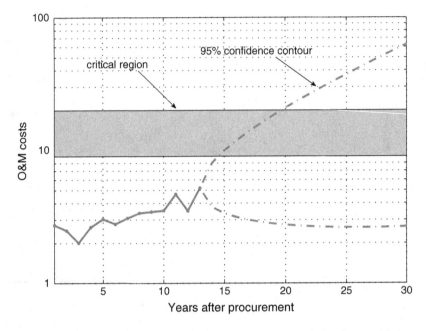

Figure 12.2 CP-140 Arcturus data with no stochastic discount factor shown with the critical region indicated.

Given the current level of the O&M per A_o process, the first passage of time interpretation allows us to calculate the expected sojourn time within the critical region, and the probability that the process will exit through the upper boundary before the lower boundary. Both pieces of information provide a clearer picture of the decision problem to military leadership. The sojourn time calculation can give decision-makers an estimate of the amount of time remaining before the model definitively calls for fleet replacement or a major overhaul.

To calculate the expected time of a drift diffusion process within a region, we can use the backward Fokker-Planck equation (see Gardiner 2003 for details), which for our model yields the differential equation for the expected time as

$$k_1 \frac{dT(\tilde{m}_u)}{d\tilde{m}_u} + \frac{1}{2}k_2 \frac{d^2T(\tilde{m}_u)}{d\tilde{m}_u^2} = -1, \tag{12.17}$$

where $\tilde{m}_u$ represents the log-transformed process, $a < \tilde{m}_u < b$, $T(a) = T(b) = 0$, and where in our model $k_1 = (1/2)\sigma^2$ and $k_2 = \alpha - (1/2)\sigma^2$. In fact, we can use Equation (12.17) to derive the Greenfield–Persselin expected replacement time result, Equation (12.8), by considering $\tilde{m}_u \in (-\infty, \tilde{m}_u^*]$, where $\tilde{m}_u^*$ represents the log-transformed boundary. Thus, the Greenfield–Persselin model is in fact a first passage time problem in the log-transformed space and it is this characterization that bears fruit in the presence of real data. Once the fleet enters the critical region, using Equation (12.17), the expected sojourn time reads

$$T(\tilde{m}_u) = \frac{1}{k_2} \left[\frac{(\tilde{U} - \tilde{L})\left(e^{\frac{-k_2}{k_1}\tilde{U}} - e^{\frac{-k_2}{k_1}\tilde{m}_u}\right)}{\left(e^{\frac{-k_2}{k_1}\tilde{L}} - e^{\frac{-k_2}{k_1}\tilde{U}}\right)} - \tilde{m}_u + \tilde{U} \right], \tag{12.18}$$

where $\tilde{L}$, and $\tilde{U}$ denote the log-transformed upper and lower boundaries of the critical region respectively. We find that the expected sojourn time within the critical region at year 11 for the CP-140A Arcturus in Figure 12.1 is 0.8 years.

As an aside, we can also calculate the probability that the O&M per A_o process will exit through the upper barrier of the critical region before the lower barrier by once again invoking the backward Fokker-Planck equation. In this case, we have

$$k_1 \frac{d^2 \pi_U(\tilde{m}_u)}{d\tilde{m}_u^2} + k_2 \frac{d\pi_U(\tilde{m}_u)}{d\tilde{m}_u} = 0, \tag{12.19}$$

where $\pi_U(\tilde{m}_u)$ represents the probability of exit through $\tilde{U}$ before $\tilde{L}$ with the condition that

$$\pi_{\tilde{U}}(\tilde{m}_u) + \pi_{\tilde{L}}(\tilde{m}_u) = 1, \tag{12.20}$$

and the condition that $\pi_{\tilde{U}}(\tilde{U}) = 1$ and $\pi_{\tilde{U}}(\tilde{L}) = 0$. The probability that the process will exit through the upper boundary $\tilde{U}$ before the lower boundary is given by the solution to Equation (12.19), namely,

$$\pi_{\tilde{U}}(\tilde{m}_u) = \frac{e^{\frac{-k_2}{k_1}\tilde{m}u} - e^{\frac{-k_2}{k_1}\tilde{L}}}{e^{\frac{-k_2}{k_1}\tilde{U}} - e^{\frac{-k_2}{k_1}\tilde{L}}}, \tag{12.21}$$

$$\pi_{\tilde{L}}(\tilde{m}_u) = 1 - \frac{e^{\frac{-k_2}{k_1}\tilde{m}u} - e^{\frac{-k_2}{k_1}\tilde{L}}}{e^{\frac{-k_2}{k_1}\tilde{U}} - e^{\frac{-k_2}{k_1}\tilde{L}}}, \tag{12.22}$$

where $\tilde{m}_u$ gives the current log-transformed value of the O&M per A_o process. The probability of exiting through the top of the critical region before the lower boundary can give the decision-maker insight into delaying the procurement initiative once the process has entered the critical region.

In addition to calculating the sojourn time and probabilities of exit, we can also calculate the distribution of the hitting time to any level. In particular, since we are working in the log-transformed space, the probability density function for the first passage time to level $\tilde{L}$ is given by

$$p(\tilde{L}, m_u; t) = \frac{(\tilde{L} - m_u)}{\sigma\sqrt{2\pi t^3}} \exp\left(-\frac{(\tilde{L} - m_u - (\alpha - 1/2\sigma^2)t)^2}{2\sigma^2 t}\right), \tag{12.23}$$

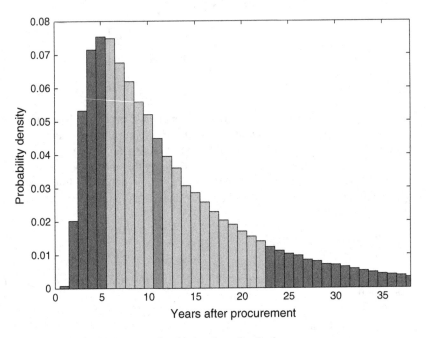

Figure 12.3 CP-140 Arcturus data hitting time distribution.

where α and σ are the growth and volatility parameters of the model. In Figure 12.3 we show the distribution of the hitting time to the lower barrier in Figure 12.1 from the first year of data. The hatched region in Figure 12.3 denotes the 60 percent confidence region around the expectation of 11 years. The hitting time calculation allows decision-makers to estimate the probability of reaching a given level which can shed light on the risks of holding the fleet longer than anticipated.

12.4 Discussion and conclusion

The stochastic discount extended Greenfield–Persselin model applied to the CP-140A Arcturus fleet replacement problem captures the random features in costs and performance that systems exhibit over long periods of time. Through dynamic programming the model extracts a critical region which delineates the optimal replacement interval. We note that replacement under uncertainty contains non-intuitive features, such as the lengthening of the expected time of replacement relative to the deterministic approach. Uncertainty plays a large role in determining the optimal replacement time.

In 2009, DND used this model as a decision input tool for restructuring the CP-140A Arcturus and CP-140 Aurora fleets until their expected replacement in the early 2020s. Our principle findings on the service life of CP-140A Arcturus fleet included the following points.

- Including the stochastic discount factor, the CP-140A entered the critical region for decision at year 11 (calendar year 2006).
- If we ignore the stochastic discount factor, the expectation time for replacement/overhaul jumps by more than 100 percent to 23 years.
- Under the assumption that the A_o represents an appropriate discount factor, the model calls for the initiation of a replacement/overhaul decision process for the CP-140A Arcturus fleet.

We should not view the critical region solely in terms of fleet replacement. The critical region simply denotes the place in O&M per A_o space where the expected total ownership costs begin to realize an expected marginal cost. We imagine that several external variables, such as queuing problems or sparing issues, can create an adverse growth environment and corrections in these areas might radically drive the sample path away from the critical region in a non-stochastic manner. Furthermore, we might find it advantageous to undertake a reset-the-clock overhaul rather than acquiring a new fleet once the sample path has drifted into the critical region. Ideally, we see the stochastic model presented in this paper used in conjunction with other decision tools.

We have treated the O&M cost per A_o as a single stochastic variable in a drift-diffusion model. The statistical tests we performed on the data gave us no compelling reason to reject this approach. In reality, the O&M costs and A_o both evolve stochastically and potentially feed back on one another. Thus, we can imagine the fleet replacement/overhaul problem as a coupled system of stochastic differential equations with O&M cost following a geometric random walk, and the A_o tracking a different process, such as a mean reverting process (e.g. an Ornstein–Uhlenbeck process with boundaries). We might also advance the model by using a stochastic interest rate with an appropriate industry specific military deflator (see Chapter 17). Finally, if military consensus is available, the stochastic discount factor could be promoted to a nonlinear function of A_o with the inclusion of potentially other relevant performance and economic measures. In particular, since the fleet will require routine maintenance work, we might imagine a stochastic discount function of A_o that turns on slowly as A_o diminishes. We view this area of research as an exciting possibility.

The application of the Greenfield–Persselin model and the model extension presented above rest on the ability to capture the statistical properties of the sample path in the data. Describing the sample path as a geometric random walk represents an approximation. If the data supports it, we can use more sophisticated models, such as jump diffusion (or more general Lévy processes). These modifications would require a new first passage time calculation along with a re-calculation of the critical region. Again, this represents exciting opportunities for further work. However, as the O&M cost per A_o is a price process that evolves over time, a geometric random walk is a good starting place. If on examination of the data, the sample path cannot be approximated by a geometric random walk, new methods will be required. Finally, as in all operational research studies, this model is an approximation of reality that endeavors to provide decision support—in this case a military cost–benefit analysis. The overall replacement/overhaul decision will require additional input, including examination of replacement alternatives, budget feasibility, and military obsolescence.

The CP-140A Arcturus fleet represents a special case in that the homogenous fleet consists of only three aircraft all delivered to the military at the same time. The application of the model to the CP-140A did not include complications from multiple aircraft variants, aircraft with different service lives, or aircraft that have seen life extension modifications. More complicated fleets will require special treatment of these circumstances to apply the Greenfield–Persselin model more generally.

Operational tempo, unforeseen engineering and maintenance problems, and budgeting processes all factor into the evolution of O&M costs of vehicle fleets. Separating specific variables that directly relate to age from other effects presents a daunting task. By treating the problem stochastically under the assumption that fleet resiliency diminishes with time, we can determine the critical time to consider fleet replacement. Most importantly, the stochastic approach implicitly attaches an option value to the capacity to delay in making the replacement decision—as more information becomes available to the decision-makers, better choices can be made. Deterministic methods that focus only on marginal costs or NPV inputs ignore this important feature. The Greenfield–Persselin model, with a stochastic discount factor, balances economic considerations, uncertainty, and fleet performance in establishing a replacement time. We feel that the Greenfield–Persselin model class represents an important step in understanding optimal fleet replacement times in military life cycle cost–benefit problems.

Appendix 12.1: The mathematical details of the Greenfield–Persselin model

The detail presented here follows Greenfield and Persselin (2002) closely. In Equation (12.5), which gives the relationship between total ownership costs and the replacement interval, we see that the numerator contains an initial procurement cost and an NPV part, and the denominator represents a discount factor. To promote the relationship to its stochastic counterpart, we need the expected age at replacement, the expected NPV at replacement, and the expected discount factor at replacement. Once we have these three expressions we can rewrite Equation (12.5) in its stochastic setting.

Expected age

First, we imagine a pre-determined cut-off cost per utility (perhaps set independently by policy) m_u^*, above which DND is not willing to pay. Once we find $m_u > m_u^*$, we consider fleet replacement or a reset-the-clock overhaul. We imagine that the process starts at initial condition b below m_u^* and, using Bellman's recursive equation from the last section, we see that the expected age, $a(m_u^*, m_u)$

evolves as

$$a(m_u^*, m_u) = dt + (a(m_u^*, m_u) + \mathbb{E}(da(m_u^*, m_u))). \tag{A12.1.1}$$

Note that Equation (A12.1.1) contains two parts: an additive time increment in the expected age from the current time increment, and a term that represents the expected age at replacement resulting from the time increment. After some manipulation, we can re-express Equation (A12.1.1) as

$$\frac{\mathbb{E}(da(m_u^*, m_u))}{dt} + 1 = 0; \tag{A12.1.2}$$

Expanding the differential using Ito's Lemma we find

$$\mathbb{E}(da(m_u^*, m_u)) = \left(\frac{1}{2}\sigma^2 m_u^2 \frac{d^2 a(m_u^*, m_u)}{dm_u^2} + \alpha m_u \frac{da(m_u^*, m_u)}{dm_u}\right), \tag{A12.1.3}$$

where we have used $\mathbb{E}(dW) = 0$. Thus, we have the differential equation for the expected age of replacement as

$$\frac{1}{2}\sigma^2 m_u^2 \frac{d^2 a(m_u^*, m_u)}{dm_u^2} + \alpha m \frac{da(m_u^*, m_u)}{dm_u} + 1 = 0. \tag{A12.1.4}$$

We should note that, while we obtained Equation (A12.1.4) through dynamic programming, we could have obtained the same result from a mean first passage time approach. If we regard the cutoff, m_u^*, as a barrier, the problem amounts to finding the expected time for m_u to diffuse from some initial starting point to the barrier. The stochastic formalism requires the backward Fokker-Planck equation (Gardiner 2003) and, in this case, results in Equation (A12.1.4). Thus, we can approach the replacement problem from either perspective, and we will use either formalism as appropriate. Since $m_u = 0$ is an absorbing point in the geometric random walk, the solution to Equation (A12.1.4) reads

$$a(m_u^*, m_u) = A + B \ln(m_u). \tag{A12.1.5}$$

If we assume the initial condition $m_u(t = 0) = b$ along with the boundary condition that the expected age at m_u^* vanishes, $a(m_u^*, m_u^*) = 0$, we find the expected time for platform replacement is

$$a(m_u^*, b) = \frac{\ln\left(m_u^*/b\right)}{\alpha - (1/2)\sigma^2}. \tag{A12.1.6}$$

Again, we can obtain the same result from calculating the mean first passage time of $a(m_u^*, m)$ from b through the barrier m_u^*.

Equation (A12.1.6) connects with the deterministic approach since setting $\sigma = 0$ recovers the deterministic result. In the deterministic case, we find the exact age at which to replace the vehicle as a function of the pre-determined boundary, m_u^*, namely

$$a(m_u^*, b) = \frac{1}{\alpha} \ln\left(m_u^*/b\right).$$ (A12.1.7)

The deterministic case determines m_u^* through the minimization of the total ownership cost function. Thus, we see that uncertainty in the system, characterized by σ, demands that we hold the platform longer than the deterministic result. We see that the stochastic approach implicitly values the capacity to wait by recognizing that there is a chance that next year's O&M cost per utility will decrease. The term, σ, reflects the size of this chance and thereby increases the waiting time. We also notice that in order for the Equation (A12.1.6) to make sense, we must have $\alpha - (1/2)\sigma^2 > 0$, otherwise the expectation time to cross the barrier m_u^* becomes infinite (implying that it will never be advantageous to replace the vehicle).

Expected discount factor

The expected discount factor at replacement calculation proceeds in a similar fashion to the expected age calculation except that we no longer have an additive increment since the discount factor appears multiplicative in the total ownership relation. Thus, we have the following Bellman equation for the expected discount factor:

$$\rho(m_u^*, m_u) = \exp(-rdt)\left[\rho(m_u^*, m_u) + \mathbb{E}(d\rho(m_u^*, m_u))\right].$$ (A12.1.8)

Rearranging, we find

$$\mathbb{E}(d\rho(m_u^*, m_u)) + (1 - \exp(rdt))\rho(m_u^*, m_u) = 0$$ (A12.1.9)

and, with the use of Ito's Lemma, we have

$$\mathbb{E}(d\rho(m_u^*, m_u)) = \left(\frac{1}{2}\sigma^2 m_u^2 \frac{d^2\rho(m_u^*, m_u)}{dm_u^2} + \alpha m_u \frac{d\rho(m_u^*, m_u)}{dm_u}\right) dt = 0.$$

(A12.1.10)

Altogether, we find that the expected discount factor obeys

$$\frac{1}{2}\sigma^2 m_u^2 \frac{d^2\rho(m_u^*, m_u)}{dm_u^2} + \alpha m_u \frac{d\rho(m_u^*, m_u)}{dm_u} - r\rho(m_u^*, m_u) = 0.$$ (A12.1.11)

Equation (A12.1.11) is a Euler-Cauchy differential equation and therefore has the solution

$$\rho(m_u^*, m_u) = Am_u^{\beta_1} + Bm_u^{\beta_2}.$$ (A12.1.12)

Substituting our solution into Equation (A12.1.11) we obtain β_1, β_2 as the roots of the quadratic equation

$$\frac{1}{2}\sigma^2(\beta-1)\beta+\alpha\beta-r=0, \tag{A12.1.13}$$

namely,

$$\beta_{1,2}=-\left(\frac{\alpha}{\sigma^2}-\frac{1}{2}\right)\pm\sqrt{\left(\frac{\alpha}{\sigma^2}-\frac{1}{2}\right)^2+\frac{2r}{\sigma^2}}. \tag{A12.1.14}$$

The boundary condition

$$\rho(m_u^*,0)=0, \tag{A12.1.15}$$

demands that the coefficient associated with negative root vanishes, and the boundary condition

$$\rho(m_u^*,m_u^*)=1 \tag{A12.1.16}$$

implies that $A=(m_u^*)^{-\beta_1}$. Thus, the full solution for the expected discount factor at replacement, in light of the boundary conditions, reads

$$\rho(m_u)=\left(\frac{m_u}{m_u^*}\right)^{\beta_1}. \tag{A12.1.17}$$

Expected net present value

We can approach the expected NPV of the life-cycle cost similarly. In this case, the recursive Bellman equation contains an additive term as the O&M cost per utility accrues over time:

$$M(m_u^*,m_u)=m_u dt+\exp(-rdt)\left(M(m_u^*,m_u)+\mathbb{E}(dM(m_u^*,m_u))\right). \tag{A12.1.18}$$

Applying Ito's Lemma once more, we find the differential equation

$$\frac{1}{2}\sigma^2 m_u^2\frac{d^2M(m_u^*,m_u)}{dm_u^2}+\alpha m_u\frac{dM(m_u^*,m_u)}{dm_u}-rM(m_u^*,m_u)+m_u=0. \tag{A12.1.19}$$

We have an inhomogeneous Euler-Cauchy differential equation, and applying the boundary conditions $M(m_u^*,m_u^*)=0$ (i.e. the life-cycle cost goes to zero as the cycle has ended) and $M(m_u^*, 0) = 0$, and including the starting value, b, at the beginning of the cycle, we find

$$M(m_u^*, b) = \frac{b}{r - \alpha}\left(1 - \left(\frac{b}{m_u^*}\right)^{\beta_1 - 1}\right). \tag{A12.1.20}$$

If we now put the expected net present life-cycle value together with the expected discount factor, we find the expected ownership cost curve as a function of the cost:

$$c(m_u) = \frac{p + \frac{b}{r - \alpha}\left(1 - \left(\frac{b}{m_u}\right)^{\beta_1 - 1}\right)}{1 - \left(\frac{b}{m_u}\right)^{\beta_1}}. \tag{A12.1.21}$$

Differentiating with respect to m_u we find the transcendental equation for m_u^*, i.e. the value of m_u that minimizes the expected total ownership cost in the presence of stochastic noise, as

$$m_u^* = \frac{\beta_1}{\beta_1 - 1}(r - \alpha)p + \frac{\beta_1}{\beta_1 - 1}(r - \alpha)\frac{\frac{b}{r - \alpha}\left(1 - \left(\frac{b}{m_u^*}\right)^{\beta_1 - 1}\right) + p\left(\frac{b}{m_u^*}\right)^{\beta_1}}{1 - \left(\frac{b}{m_u^*}\right)^{\beta_1}}. \tag{A12.1.22}$$

In the deterministic model, in which $\sigma = 0$, we find the analogous relation

$$m_u^* = rp + r\frac{\frac{b}{r - \alpha}\left(1 - \left(\frac{b}{m_u^*}\right)^{r/\alpha - 1}\right) + p\left(\frac{b}{m_u^*}\right)^{r/\alpha}}{1 - \left(\frac{b}{m_u^*}\right)^{r/\alpha}}. \tag{A12.1.23}$$

Note that Equation (A12.1.23) conveys the same information as Equation (12.6) since the deterministic case links the replacement age and the O&M cost per utility in a one-to-one manner.

Comparison of Equation (A12.1.22) and Equation (A12.1.23) reveal the essential difference concerning the value of waiting. The deterministic case balances the marginal costs and the known savings from delay through a small increment in time. On the other hand, the stochastic case balances the marginal costs and savings from delaying until the O&M costs per utility increase by a small increment. In the stochastic case, the time interval required to increment the O&M costs per utility by a given amount is random.

Notes

1 DND did not want the actual cost data included with this paper.
2 This paper elucidates an application of the Greenfield–Persselin model with extension to a Canadian Forces fleet that was already undergoing a replacement decision process by DND, and it was for this reason that we chose the CP-140A fleet.

References

Dixon, M. 2005. *The Costs of Aging Aircraft: Insights from Commercial Aviation*. RAND Dissertation, Pardee RAND Graduate School.

DND (last access July 2014). *Ch-124 Sea King: Intelligence, Surveillance and Reconnaissance Aircraft*. http://www.rcaf-arc.forces.gc.ca/en/aircraft-current/ch-124.page. Department of National Defence 2, 1.

Francies, P. and G. Shaw 2000. *Effect of Aircraft Age on Maintenance Costs*. Briefing, Center For Naval Analyses, Alexandria VA.

Gardiner, C. 2003. *Handbook Of Stochastic Methods* (3rd edition). Heidelberg: Springer.

Greenfield, V. and D.M. Persselin. 2002. *An Economic Framework For Evaluating Military Aircraft Replacement*. Santa Monica, CA: RAND MR-1489-AF.

——. 2003. "How Old Is Too Old? An Economic Approach To Replacing Military Aircraft." *Defence and Peace Economics* 14(5): 357–368.

Hildebrandt, G. and M. Sze. May 1990. *An Estimation Of USAF Aircraft Operating And Support Cost Relations*. Santa Monica, CA: RAND, N-3062-ACQ.

Johnson, J. August 1993. *Age Impacts On Operating And Support Costs: Navy Aircraft Age Analysis Methodology*. Patuxent River, MD: Naval Aviation Maintenance Office.

——. June 1962. *Forecasting The Maintenance Manpower Needs Of The Depot System*. Santa Monica, CA: RAND, RM-3163-PR.

Jondrow, J., R. Toast, M. Ye, J. Hall, P. Francis, and B. Measell. 2002. *Support Costs And Aging Aircraft: Implications For Budgeting And Procurement*. CNA Corporation.

Keating, E. and M. Dixon. 2003. *Investigating Optimal Replacement Of Aging Air Force Systems*. Santa Monica, CA: RAND MR-1763-AF.

Kiley, G. 2001. *The Effects Of Aging On The Costs Of Maintaining Military Equipment*. Washington, DC: Congressional Budget Office.

Marks, K. and R. Hess. 1981. *Estimating Aircraft Depot Maintenance Costs*. Santa Monica, CA: RAND R-2731-PA&E.

Nelson, J. 1977. *Life Cycle Analysis Of Aircraft Turbine Engines*. Santa Monica, CA: RAND, R-2103-AF.

Pyles, R. 2003. *Aging Aircraft: USAF Workload And Material Consumption Life Cycle Patterns*. Santa Monica, CA: RAND MR-1641.

Ramsey, T., C. French, and K. Sperry. 1998. *Aircraft Maintenance Trend Analysis*. Briefing, Oklahoma City Air Logistics Center, and Boeing.

Stoll, L. and S. Davis. July 1993. *Aircraft Age Impact On Individual Operating And Support Cost Elements*. Patuxent River, MD: Naval Aviation Maintenance Office.

Part V
Selected applications

13 Embedding affordability assessments in military cost–benefit analysis

Defense modernization in Bulgaria

Venelin Georgiev

13.1 Introduction

The economic reality of scarce resources combined with the human need for security requires hard choices. The challenge is to make rational, informed and effective decisions to meet existing needs with available resources[1] in a way that maximizes security. Defining, motivating, and supporting such decisions with military cost–benefit analysis (CBA) is a complex process, the implementation of which would be impossible without appropriate tools—quantitative and qualitative analytical methods and models for evaluating the effectiveness of the use of resources to meet the needs of people and society. The limited availability and competing demands for financial resources on the one hand, and the existential human need for security on the other, requires careful resource allocation decisions, and useful tools to justify and support the implementation of those decisions.

The tools to manage defense resources include various management systems (requirements generation, financial management, defense acquisition, etc.), and involves making routine and reasonable decisions. The overall effectiveness of defense spending depends on the resulting output, namely the security of society, guaranteed by the defensive capabilities obtained as a product of careful management of defense resources and innovative and technologically appropriate defense investments (see Chapter 3). The efficiency and effectiveness of management decisions depends on objective, scientifically sound and generally accepted military CBA methods and models such as those described in previous chapters, applied in practice by competent experts, managers and politicians.

Resource decisions are made within a process that in itself needs to be transparent to decision-makers, e.g., to allow the preservation of a clear audit trail from national security objectives, through defense objectives, to taxpayers' money (Tagarev 2009). Among the various questions related to resources management, the most important are:

- how to create affordable, i.e. resource constrained plans;
- how to deal with uncertainty; and

- how to support the senior civilian leadership of a defense ministry in the exercise of its authority and obligations as agents of democratic control of the armed forces.

Decisions concerning required capabilities ("defense requirements") are often resource informed (i.e. assessed as realistic), but not necessarily resource constrained (i.e. fitting within defense budget forecast—see Chapter 7). But once program decisions are made, the cost of the defense program for each future year cannot exceed the defense budget forecast for the respective year (Tagarev 2006, 2009). This chapter discusses the case of a recently inducted member of NATO, Bulgaria. An example of a military CBA is presented that involves the evaluation of a new multi-role fighter for the Bulgarian Air Force.

13.2   Description of the current situation

The coherence and integration between resources and financial management systems does not always provide for effective management. For example, the US Government Accountability Office (GAO) concludes that defense processes for determining required capabilities, in the planning, programming and budgeting system (PPBS), and for developing, manufacturing and the acquisition of defense products, are not sufficiently integrated. This leads to more defense investment programs and projects going forward than can be funded from the defense budget (GAO 2009). As a result, there are significant risks and problems in trying to achieve maximum military effectiveness with existing defense budgets.[2] Additional analytical instruments—methods, models and other decision support tools—are needed in order to overcome these deficiencies.

What are the empirical results from the implementation of expensive projects to modernize the armed forces? In many cases investment projects do not yield the intended effects in terms of defense capabilities, making it necessary to spend additional resources to extend existing or start new acquisition projects. However, unforeseen cost increases in ongoing investment projects often reduce the possibilities of funding new ones.

Another related shortcoming is the fact that delayed implementation of investment projects leads to delays in expected delivery of defense capabilities needed by the armed forces to fulfill security missions and operations. The consequences in terms of quality and effectiveness of project management outcomes, partly derived from weaknesses in the traditional application of military CBA, are illustrated in a review of the investment portfolio of the US Department of Defense (DoD) in 2007, according to which (GAO 2009):

- the total number of implemented investment programs is 95;
- the cost of research and development programs have increased unexpectedly by 40 percent;
- the total costs of investment programs has increased by 26 percent;
- the absolute value of the total contingency programs is 295 billion dollars;

- the number of programs with more than 25 percent unexpected increase in the total cost represents 44 percent of all investment programs; and
- the average delay in implementation of investment programs is 21 months.

The risk is that there exists an imbalance between the massive investment costs required to modernize armed forces, and the quality and effectiveness of current military CBA methods and models applied to the management of acquisition projects, especially relating to the evaluation and selection of projects for future funding.

Another example is provided by the recent experience of a new NATO member, Bulgaria. The country suffered a significant cut in its 2010 defense budget both in absolute terms and as a percentage of its gross domestic product (GDP). The new defense capital budget amounted to only 0.8 percent of the total defense budget in 2010, compared to an average of 20–22 percent in previous years. This sharp reduction in the amount of investment funding, among other things, increased demands on the decision-making process. It created a strong impetus to improve financial and project management, and in particular to increase the application of military CBA methods that incorporate careful economic analysis in the selection and evaluation of force modernization projects.

Bulgaria (BG) faced many of the same problems experienced by the US described above. For example, within a single planning cycle, cost estimates of the country's commitments to NATO defense and security in the form of force goals increased several times, from the time commitments were originally made to the actual assessment of costs in the programming and budgeting cycle. Adverse effects from implementing such a mechanism to plan, evaluate and implement defense programs and projects can be classified in several ways.

First, attempts to reduce investment costs can lead to the development of incomplete and therefore less effective investment projects.[3] Here it is sufficient to mention two examples of false savings. The acquisition of ships for the BG Navy was made without appropriate energy units to provide power while docked. Another example involves the purchase of training aircraft for the BG Air Force that did not include the necessary computer simulator courses required to support the initial training of pilots. The results of such oversights is that life-cycle costs of defense investments increase unexpectedly, and/or that it becomes necessary to launch new investment projects for the acquisition of additional equipment, training, services or supplies. Ultimately, this leads to lower quality investments that reduce the desired capability (effectiveness) of the program.

Second, incentives matter. There is strong motivation for program managers to complete investment projects, even if they prove costly, since cancelling them can be a career killer. This behavior can bias cost estimates. If optimistic (lower) cost estimates are systematically used in military CBAs, and future defense funding constraints are not explicitly incorporated into the analysis, then more investment projects are started than can realistically be financed by the defense budget. As a consequence, in the implementation phase financial resources have to be transferred from one investment project to another and from one major program to another, negatively impacting overall capabilities and the performance of defense forces. Ideally, such inter-program decisions should be conducted ex-ante through a properly structured CBA and not ex-post under duress.

It is often necessary to reduce the scope, or to suspend or eliminate investment projects to accommodate budget shortfalls. This was the experience of recent projects for the acquisition of transport aircraft and helicopters by the BG Air Force (BGAF), and for automotive equipment by the BG Land Forces. The ultimate result of management decisions based on biased or incomplete analysis is a delay in providing required defense capabilities, often accompanied by a reduction in the level and quality of those capabilities.

The issue of reporting the feasibility of investment projects in terms of future funding realities is becoming more urgent. The 2010 White Paper on Defense and the Armed Forces of Bulgaria declares the intention of Ministry of Defense (MoD) leadership to develop a long-term investment plan incorporating all force modernization projects aimed at building and maintaining required defense capabilities. Acknowledging future funding constraints, the plan calls for the MoD to include investment projects that are "financially feasible in the period until 2020" (MoD 2010).

Ideally, military CBAs would normally require investment plans that ensure financial feasibility of modernization projects throughout their life cycles, and thus a longer horizon of investment planning may be necessary. The designers of these plans should take account of multiple risks, including those related to future financing opportunities, the depreciation of the defense capital stock over time, economic viability, the dynamics of innovation and technology, possible changes in the security environment, and the commitments of the country to international security (see Chapter 7).

Accepting that innovation is a "new idea that works" (Tzvetkov 2004), analysts and practitioners need to look for opportunities to utilize military CBA to resolve analytically challenging tasks in defense resources management, or to approach existing analytical tasks in more effective ways. The new "real options" approach introduced in Chapters 11 and 14 in this volume offer an example.[4] No matter whether innovation is of the "push" type, implementing ideas coming from science and research, or "pulled" from needs identified in practice, the objective is to provide defense forces that maximize national (and collective) security of individuals and society.

Implementation of innovative ideas can increase the competitiveness of the defense sector in the contest for the allocation of public funds among areas such as health, education, internal order, etc. The economic evaluation of alternatives (EEoA) presented in Chapter 4 is an example of one such innovative method for performing CBA in evaluating and selecting investment projects to modernize the armed forces, under realistic budget scenarios.

One of the major differences between the traditional analysis of alternatives (AoA) and EEoA is the content of the reported input variables in the analysis (Figure 13.1). While examining operational effectiveness and the life-cycle costs of defense investments (similar to a conventional AoA), EEoA adds a new variable—the uncertainty of existing and projected future funding constraints.

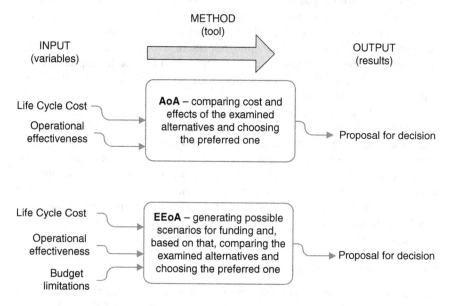

Figure 13.1 Variables used in AoA and EEoA.

Uncertainty is represented by possible budget/funding scenarios, thus explicitly incorporating the affordability of alternatives under examination. One possible strategy is to incorporate budget scenarios for 'optimistic,' 'pessimistic' and 'most likely' funding options.

13.3 Evaluation of a multi-role fighter for Bulgaria

Today, military CBAs offer a practical tool for decision support in capabilities-oriented force planning processes to determine the optimal structure of the armed forces, and for analyzing and selecting options based on defense budget realities, risk management, etc. A valuable contribution is the development of various measures of effectiveness (MoE or "effects") such as those discussed in Chapter 8 of this volume.

In response to observed capability gaps defined on the basis of scenario planning against current and future threats, planners identify weapons system requirements, (as well as doctrine, training, readiness levels, etc.). From these requirements, selected criteria are identified to help develop MoEs.

Consider the following example. The goal is to find the most suitable multi-role fighter for the BGAF. The procurement of a new multi-role fighter for the BGAF requires an evaluation of several possible alternatives using military CBA. The process consists of several phases.

The first phase of any military CBA includes the definition of goals and objectives and proper scoping of the analysis. Precise, clear and, if possible, quantitative

definitions of military goals and objectives can help to define program requirements and narrow the scope of the analysis. In this case the goal is to acquire
required operational capabilities (ROC) to perform BGAF missions and tasks
through the procurement of a new multi-role aircraft, or modernization of the current fleet. The objective is to obtain necessary capabilities for the implementation
of new missions and tasks such as air superiority, air interdiction, close air support,
kill boxing, reconnaissance, etc.

The main factors that influence the scope of the analysis are the defined needs
and requirements that have to be met, the relevant time period for the evaluation,
and the efforts and expenditures necessary to complete the military CBA. A "primary" analysis is performed when an alternative (proposal) is evaluated with the
objective of minimizing costs of satisfying existing requirements. A "secondary"
analysis involves new needs or requirements that must be met or when existing
systems can no longer satisfy current requirements. For the purpose of this military CBA, the project can be classified as a secondary analysis—required to satisfy
new needs of the BGAF.

13.3.1   *Comparing costs of competing alternatives*

Several methods exist to compare the cost of competing alternatives. Among
the more frequently applied are net present value (NPV; see Chapter 17), sav-
ings/investment ratios (SIR) and rate of return (ROR) etc. (see DOA 2001). The
main factors that determine the method to be used for the particular project and its
analysis are the amount of financial resources available, the benefit/effectiveness
measures, and the duration of the period of the analysis.

Due to the fact that the cost and the effectiveness are different for the different alternatives considered in this example, but the duration of the period for
analysis is the same for each of the alternatives, the methods recommended by
DOA (2001) for comparison of the alternatives are NPV, or annual benefit/cost
ratios (ABCR). Given the severe warnings in Chapter 4 about using benefit/cost
ratios when neither effectiveness nor costs are fixed, the EEoA offers other
approaches that will be reviewed after the discussion of MoEs and measures of
performance.

13.3.2   *Measures of effectiveness and measures of performance*

Higher level MoEs represent the customers' (or operators') perspective, usually
of a qualitative nature. They describe the customers' expectations of a product,
project or system. The MoE can be represented in the form of a hierarchical
diagram (see Figure 13.2). Weights can be attached to each component at each horizontal level in the hierarchy. Evaluation of alternate designs can be made through
the use of a method such as the weighted objective decision matrix or similar
methods (see Chapter 8). The use of MoEs enables analysts to propose the best
alternative to solve the problem under consideration.

For purposes of the military CBA for a multi-role fighter, possible measures of
effectiveness (MoEs) include survivability, vulnerability, weapon system features,

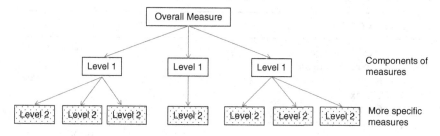

Figure 13.2 The MoE hierarchy diagram.

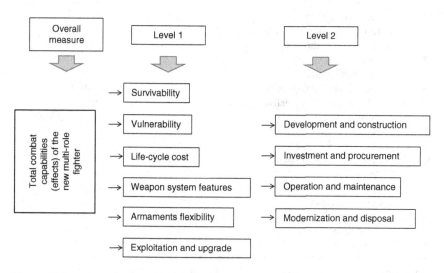

Figure 13.3 Example of an MoE hierarchy diagram.

armament flexibility, exploitation and upgrade options, shown as Level 1 in Figure 13.3. Life-cycle costs involves all the Level 2 factors.

Measures of performance (MoP) express system design specifications derived from higher level MoEs, as described in Table 13.1. MoPs are quantitative characteristics of more interest to operators and their purpose is to demonstrate what companies have done to achieve the MoE requirements (see Table 13.1).

The next phase of a military CBA includes identifying alternatives. This list of alternatives should be as comprehensive as possible, including alternatives that may not yet be available. An incomplete list of alternatives could be reason to question the validity of a military CBA. Alternatives that are not yet available should be discussed and documented, but it is not necessary to include them in subsequent work on cost and effectiveness estimation. As a general rule, alternatives can be included when they satisfy stated requirements and their realization is feasible given the period of analysis, and defense budget limitations.

Table 13.1 MoP specifications for the multi-role fighter

Specifications (MoP)		
1	Maximum speed	2,000–2,300 km/h
2	Maximum altitude	15,000–18,000 m.
3	Range	2,000–2,500 km.
4	G-max	9
5	Combat radius	500 km.
6	Combat endurance	>2 hrs.
7	Weight – empty	15–20 tons
8	Payload	3–5 tons
9	Maximum wing loading	up to 4 tons
10	Thrust–weight ratio	0.95–1.2
11	Reverse thrust of power plant	yes
12	Active power thrust vector control	yes
13	Max vertical velocity	300–350 m/s
14	Supersonic cruising speed	yes
15	Takeoff and landing distance	750–1,000 m.
16	Navigation/weapon delivery system	yes
17	Weapons loads	up to 8 pylons
18	Systems for self-defense	yes
19	Interoperability with land and air based systems	yes
20	Ability to transfer data in real time at a distance more than 150 km	yes
21	Container for air reconnaissance	yes
22	Container for electronic warfare and reconnaissance	yes
23	Aerial refueling	yes
24	Catapult system at V0 and H0	yes
25	Exploitation system	yes

Source: *Guide for Aircrafts' Tactical and Technical Characteristics*, 2000, pp. 66–82.

A set of possible alternatives to consider for military modernization could include producing systems within the MoD, purchasing or leasing new systems, purchasing or leasing used systems, or modifying/upgrading existing systems. New alternatives might also be generated from various combinations of these alternatives.

For the multi-role fighter, the list of possible alternatives includes modernization of existing fighters (MiG-21 or MiG-29), as well as purchase of new or used fighters (F-16, F-18, Gripen, etc.). The first alternatives from the list (modernization of existing fighters) are documented as part of the analysis, but were not pursued.

The next phase of military CBA requires gathering data for the cost and effectiveness of each alternative, storing them in a database and executing the necessary computations. The sources used to gather data and the results of the computations should be carefully documented as they can greatly influence the results. This phase of military CBA is one of the most critical parts of the analysis. It requires

Table 13.2 MoE/MoP for multi-role fighter alternatives

Specification	Requirements	Alt1 F-18 E/F	Alt2 F-16 C/D	Alt3 GRIPEN
1 Navigation/weapon delivery system	yes	yes	yes	yes
2 Maximum speed	2,000–2,300 km/h	1,900	2,142	2,126
3 Combat radius	500 km	722	1,252	800
4 G-max	9	9	9	9
5 Maximum wing loading	Min. 4 tons	7.7	7.2	6.5
6 Thrust–weight ratio	0.95–1.2	–	1.1	–
7 Combat endurance	>2 hrs	2.5	–	–
8 Interoperability with land and air based systems	yes	–	–	–
9 Systems for self-defense	yes	yes	yes	yes
10 Max vertical velocity	300–350 m/s	–	294	80
11 Payload	3–5 tons	–	–	–
12 Maximum altitude	15,000–18,000 m	15,200	15,300	19,000
13 Range	2,000–2,500 km	3,700	4,215	3,300
14 Ability to transfer data in real time at a distance more than 150 km	yes	–	–	–
15 Container for air reconnaissance	yes	yes	–	–
16 Weapons loads	Min. 8 pylons	9	9	8
17 Exploitation system	yes	yes	yes	yes
18 Container for electronic warfare and reconnaissance	yes	yes	–	–
19 Catapult system at V0 and H0	yes	yes	yes	yes
20 Reverse thrust of power plant	yes	yes	–	yes
21 Aerial refueling	yes	yes	yes	yes
22 Supersonic cruising speed	yes	yes	–	yes
23 Active power thrust vector control	yes	yes	–	yes
24 Takeoff and landing distance	750–1000 m	430–620	450–650	400–600
25 Weight – empty	15–20 tons	16.65	11.84	9.7

Source: *Guide for Aircrafts' Tactical and Technical Characteristics*, 2000, pp. 66–82.

sufficient time and resources since it can have a major impact on the final results (see Chapter 8). Analysts should take into account all relevant cost factors and the total expected effectiveness of each alternative. MoE/MoP results can be reported as shown in Table 13.2.

As discussed earlier in Chapter 5, analysts use a variety of methods to calculate life-cycle costs. Here, the Government Asset Management Committee (2001) recommends engineering methods when there is detailed and accurate capital and operational cost data available; direct cost estimation of particular cost elements; analogous cost methods when there exists data from similar systems of analogous size, technology, and operational characteristics; and parametric cost estimation when historical cost data is available (see Chapter 5).

13.3.3   *Approaches to compare and rank alternatives*

The next phase of the military CBA involves comparing and ranking alternatives. The literature refers to this as "the heart of the analysis." In the vocabulary of the EEoA, the multi-role fighter example is an "intra-program" analysis, and the alternatives under consideration could be constructed as competing fleets of aircraft (see Chapter 4).

One of the main challenges in defense management is to achieve a balanced portfolio of acquisition projects that, among other requirements, are feasible in terms of budgetary constraints. It is possible to address this challenge through EEoA (see Chapter 4). This method clearly distinguishes among three key variables: life cycle costs, operational effectiveness, and the budgets expected to be available to finance the program/project (funding scenarios). One of the ideas behind EEoA is to improve coordination between capabilities-based planning, programmatic defense resources management, and defense acquisition.

An innovative idea of EEoA is to use different budget scenarios to reflect forecasts for the future programming period (also see Chapter 7). EEoA prescribes an explicit optimization approach to make military investment decisions within realistic funding constraints. This parallels the optimization approach implicit in PPBS, designed to build an optimal mix of forces, equipment and supplies which maximizes national security within fiscal constraints.

In general there are six ways to structure an EEoA, as illustrated in Figure 13.4.[5]

- In the first five approaches the program or project can be analyzed independently of other programs/projects in the defense portfolio. In the sixth approach, the analysis of costs and effectiveness takes account of competing (or complementary) programs/projects included in the portfolio.
- The first three approaches assume that alternatives can be constructed by decision-makers in cooperation with analysts (endogenous alternatives); an example would be comparing alternatives fleets of multi-role fighters generated by experts and the programming team (see Chapter 15 for example).
- The last three approaches focus on evaluating previously defined alternatives (exogenous alternatives) e.g. different companies producing multi-role aircraft participating in the contest for selection of a supplier of such aircraft for the needs of the BGAF.

The next phase of a military CBA includes carefully recording assumptions and constraints. In general, a military CBA is performed in conditions of incomplete information, which requires numerous assumptions. The goal is to reduce the extent of uncertainty in the analysis. Assumptions and constraints are often defined before choosing the alternatives. Assumptions and constraints define the environment for the analysis and influence the final results of any military CBA. This is extremely important for decision-makers to recognize and for analysts to communicate.

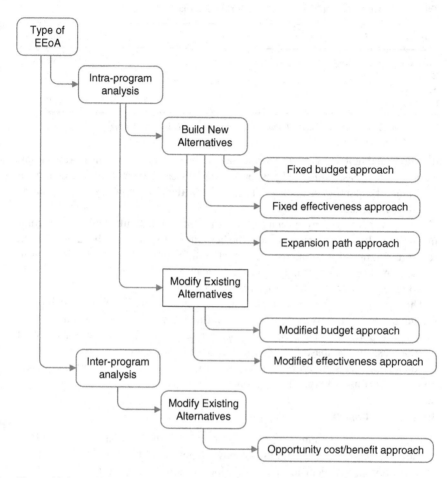

Figure 13.4 Possible approaches to structure an EEoA (see Chapter 4).

For example assumptions and constraints for the multi-role fighter could involve future budgets, the time-span of life-cycle costs and effectiveness, technical and tactical characteristics, operations and maintenance costs, etc. In discounting future costs (see Chapter 17) there are several key milestones such as a mission's life, base year, lead-time, etc. The mission's life is the period over which the system is required. The base year is the year to which costs and benefits for the alternatives will be discounted. Start year is the year in which initial investments for the considered alternatives are made. Lead-time is the time from the beginning of the start year to the beginning of the economic life of an asset for each of the alternatives. Possible values of these time characteristics for the multi-role fighter example are shown in Table 13.3.

The next to last phase of a military CBA involves exploring assumptions and constraints through sensitivity analysis. Sensitivity analysis answers "what-if"

Table 13.3 Time characteristics assumed for the alternatives

Time characteristics	Possible values
Mission's life period	15–20 years
Base year	2010
Start year	2012
Lead-time	2–3 years

Source: *Guide for Aircrafts' Tactical and Technical Characteristics*, 2000, pp. 66–82.

questions and helps to generate confidence in the results. Variations in key parameters such as costs, future budgets, or MoE/MoPs can be explored. If a change in the value of a parameter impacts the ranking of the alternatives, this needs to be carefully recorded.[6]

The *final phase* of any military CBA is to report the results and make recommendations. It is an essential phase—the best alternative needs to be identified and recommendations regarding its implementation formulated. Recommendations to decision-makers are extremely important because sometimes the rankings do not clearly demonstrate which alternatives are truly superior options.

The final results from the application of the AoA approach should be presented to decision-makers in the most attractive and intuitive manner possible. The report should include the goals, assumptions and constraints, list of alternatives, the database for life-cycle cost and effectiveness, appropriate cost-effectiveness charts, and results of the sensitivity analysis. The report should end with conclusions and recommendations.

13.4 Conclusion

In conclusion we can summarize by observing that the application of the EEoA framework offers several significant advantages in military CBA. The multi-criteria approach to decision-making, which is a basis for the traditional AoA, focuses on life-cycle costs and operational effectiveness while leaving affordability as a secondary consideration. In contrast, EEoA expands the range of variables in the analysis by explicitly including future funding constraints. In practice, this can be accomplished through the development and implementation of financial scenarios for the acquisition project. Given future funding challenges, it is imperative that all defense acquisition decisions explicitly include affordability.

Notes

1 The amount of financial resources is limited by various factors, such as the size of gross domestic product, the state of the economy as a whole, the amount of funds allocated from the state budget in the interest of building and maintaining defense capabilities, the allocation of earmarked funds for security in areas which include personnel, maintenance, training, participation in operations, investments, etc.

2 Another consequence is the adoption of investment programs and projects in defense without having sufficiently comprehensive, detailed and reliable estimates of costs and

associated resources. In a study conducted in 2009, the Business Executives for National Security (BENS) concluded that most of the requirements for defense capabilities are determined in the absence of adequate input as to the suitability of the investment programs and projects in terms of budgetary constraints.

3 In the language of project management, too often the scope of the investment project does not match the scope of the defense products, which is the subject of investment.

4 The development and implementation of improved or new methods of military CBA approaches in the evaluation and selection of investment projects to modernize the armed forces can be considered a critical part of the innovation process in defense.

5 A detailed discussion of the six approaches to structure an EEoA appears in Chapter 4. This chapter offers a decision map which significantly eases the practical work of analysts in choosing the preferred approach to structure an EEoA. Depending on specific characteristics of the particular acquisition, this decision map facilitates the analytical process and can serve as a valuable guide for analysts and decision-makers.

6 An appropriate way to find parameters that impact the results is to evaluate their influence, for example, in terms of percentages of the costs or effectiveness of the alternatives. From a practical point of view, all factors that are related to spending greater than 20 percent from the total spending for the alternative need to be considered in the sensitivity analysis.

References

DOA. 2001. *Economic Analysis Manual.* US Army Cost & Economic Analysis Center.

GAO. March 2009. Michael J. Sullivan, *Defense Acquisitions: DoD Must Prioritize its Weapon System Acquisitions and Balance Them with Available Resources,* Testimony, before the Committee on the Budget, House of Representatives, GAO-09-501T, Washington, DC.

Government Asset Management Committee. 2001. *Life Cycle Costing.* Sofia: Military Publishing House.

Guide for Aircrafts' Tactical and Technical Characteristics. 2000. Sofia: Military Publishing House.

Ministry of Defense. 2010. *White Paper on Defence and Bulgarian Armed Forces.* Sofia: Ministry of Defense.

Tagarev, Todor. Spring–Summer 2006. "Introduction to Program-based Defense Resource Management." *Connections: The Quarterly Journal* 5:1 55–69. Available at www.pfpconsortium.org/file/introduction-to-program-based-defense-resource-management-by-todor-tagarev [last accessed February 8, 2012].

Tagarev, Todor. 2009. "Introduction to Program-based Force Development." In *Defence Management: An Introduction,* edited by Hari Bucur-Marcu, Philipp Fluri, and Todor Tagarev. Geneva: DCAF, pp. 75–92.

Tzvetkov, Tzvetan. 2004. *Innovations and Investments in Defence.* Sofia: Stopanstvo.

14 Real options in military acquisition

A retrospective case study of the Javelin anti-tank missile system

Diana I. Angelis, David Ford, and John Dillard

14.1 Introduction

This chapter offers an application of the real options approach to cost–benefit analysis (CBA). The Javelin "fire-and-forget" anti-tank missile was originally designed to replace the US Army's DRAGON missile system. Introduced in the late 1970s, the DRAGON had a wired command link to guide its missile to the target that needed to be optically tracked by a gunner. Besides placing the gunner at risk, the overall effectiveness of the DRAGON was somewhat compromised due to limited range, lethality, and reliability problems. It also proved challenging for gunners to aim the missile and track the target. The goal was to replace the DRAGON with a lighter weapon with increased range, lethality, and ideally a "fire-and-forget" tracking and guidance system.

The development of the Javelin, shown in Figure 14.1, required advances in several immature technologies to achieve the desired benefits. Target locating and missile guidance subsystems represented particularly troublesome issues. Three alternative technologies were initially considered. Each of the three technologies represented realistic options that promised the desired benefits/effectiveness.

Instead of investing in a single technology, the Army decided to award three "Proof of Principle" (technology demonstration phase) contracts of US$30 million to each of three competing contractor teams to develop their technologies, followed by a "fly-off" missile competition. The Army paid US$90 million in August 1986 for these three options, each with the potential, but not a guarantee, of delivering the desired benefits. Spreading the US$90 million over three competitors, the Army in effect acquired the right, but not the obligation, to purchase the most successful technology at a later date—a textbook example of a "real option."

Section 14.2 offers a brief review of real options theory introduced in Chapter 11 of this volume. Section 14.3 follows with a more detailed description of the three Javelin guidance technology alternatives. A multi-criteria model is developed in Section 14.4 to measure the benefits or "effectiveness" of the three

Figure 14.1 The Javelin anti-tank weapon system missile and command launch unit.
Source: US Marine Corps photo 2/10/2010 by Corporal Andres Escatel.

guidance technologies. Combining cost estimates with overall measures of effectiveness (MoE) offers the ability to graph the cost-effectiveness of the three alternatives. Cost-effectiveness graphs are generated in Section 14.5 under both deterministic and probabilistic assumptions. A decision tree is used in Section 14.6 to model the value of each option, given probabilities of success and estimated costs to recover from failure. The Army's actual decision is revealed in Section 14.7, and the final section, Section 14.8, summarizes the case study.

14.2 Real options

An option offers the right, but not the obligation, to take specific future actions depending on how uncertain future conditions evolve (Brealey and Meyers 2000). The "real options" approach to CBA applies options theory to tangible assets. Real options theory offers a powerful tool in structuring and valuing flexible strategies to address uncertainty (Courtney *et al.* 1997). The central premise of real options theory is this: if future conditions are uncertain, and switching strategies at a later date would incur substantial costs, then adopting flexible strategies and delaying decisions can have significant value when compared to committing to a particular strategy early in pre-project planning (Amram and Kulatilaka 1999). Real options theory helps answer questions such as: "What are possible future actions?"; "When should we choose between these actions to maximize value based on the evolution of uncertain conditions?"; and "How much is the right to delay choosing an alternative worth at any given time?"

A real option compares one or more strategies that might be used in the future to a reference strategy that could be committed to today. Uncertain future conditions are monitored and converted into signals that can be compared to trigger conditions that exercise a decision rule to determine if the reference strategy should be abandoned and an alternative strategy adopted (i.e. to "exercise" the option). Waiting to see how uncertainty evolves (i.e. learning) in order to make better strategy choices is a key feature of the real options approach. The real options approach requires defining both the exercise signal and the exercise decision in the context of a set of observable variables.[1]

Real options can be described along several dimensions (ownership, value, complexity, availability, etc.). A common typology separates real options according to the managerial action that can be applied. This includes options to postpone a decision (hold and phasing options), change the amount of investment (growth, scaling or abandonment options), or alter the form of involvement (switching options).

The use of real options can focus on the monetary valuation of acquiring flexibility, or on the design and impacts of real options on decision-making (managerial real options). Both of these aspects of real options can improve project management and add value.

A wide variety of mathematical models have been used to estimate the monetary value of options to help select strategies (e.g. see Chapter 11, and Garvin and Cheah 2004). These models use the various benefits and costs of an option to estimate its value. Although some real options can be purchased and exercised at no cost (e.g. the option to have salaried employees work overtime), others involve significant costs to obtain, maintain or exercise flexibility that might add value.

The cost of an option is a payment for access to flexibility to change the strategy. The total costs of exercising an option must also include costs of changing the strategy if the option is exercised. Option maintenance costs include any benefits lost by delaying the decision. One simple and intuitive approach is to estimate the value of an option as the difference between the values of the project with and without the option, e.g. recognizing that uncertainty impacts future performance versus assuming a single specific and known (deterministic) future.

Managerial real options can improve decision-making. This facilitates option design and implementation by structuring risky circumstances faced by practitioners into real options. For example, Ceylan and Ford (2002) describe the use of options to manage technology development risk in the development of the National Ignition Facility by the Department of Energy. Employing managerial real options addresses many of the challenges of using real options valuation models to improve risk management (Triantis 2005; Garvin and Ford 2012).

Structuring development program risk management challenges as real options requires describing challenges with standard real options parameters and structures (Miller and Lessard 2000). This can improve management's understanding of the risks of alternative decisions, and it sets the stage for the design of risk mitigation strategies. The design of options can be improved by assessing and selecting individual and interacting sets of option parameters and their values, such as evaluating the exercise cost that would make an option very attractive or never beneficial.

Operationalizing real option components, such as the operational changes required to change strategeis and implement project monitoring signals, can enhance the implementation of real options. Real options can improve program planning and management by helping managers to recognize, design, and use flexible alternatives to manage dynamic uncertainty. A retrospective opportunity to apply the real options approach is provided by evaluating the technology development that was required for the success of the Javelin anti-tank missile system.

14.3 Javelin technology options

The Javelin is a "fire-and-forget" anti-tank missile system. This "fire-and-forget" capability came from the Joint Army/Marine Corps Source Selection Board's decision to select the development team's AAWS–M design. This design coupled a forward looking imaging infra-red (FLIR) system with a beyond state-of-the-art onboard software tracking system.[2] As mentioned earlier, the CBA involved three teams (alternatives) that were formed to develop competing guidance technologies for the Javelin. Only one team would then be chosen for follow-on advanced development and then production.

Ford Aerospace, teamed with its partner Loral Systems, offered the laser beam-riding (LBR) missile. Hughes Aircraft, teamed with Boeing, offered a fiber-optic (FO) guided missile. Texas Instruments, teamed with Martin-Marietta, offered a forward-looking infra-red (FLIR) missile system.

With the Ford/Loral LBR system, the gunner would identify the target visually and point a laser beam at the target throughout the flight. After launch, the missile continuously corrected its flight to match the line of the laser (to "ride" the laser beam) to the target.

The Hughes/Boeing FO system included a coil of very long and fine optical fiber that connected the launch unit, operated by the gunner, to a camera in the nose of the missile. The gunner would fly the missile to the target using a joystick controller device.

The TI/Martin-Marietta FLIR scanned the view in front of the gunner and generated a thermal-based image of the target area. Once observed through the Command Launch Unit, or thermal sight, the gunner switched to a starting array in the missile to acquire the target by narrowing brackets in the viewfinder around the target with a simple thumb switch. After launch, the missile would continuously correct its flight path using a tracking algorithm which employed optical correlaters oriented upon visible and distinct target features.

Once the 27-month "Proof of Principle" phase ended, each team enjoyed generally successful missile flight tests. Each flew over a dozen missiles and achieved target hit rates over 60 percent. Each candidate's system, however, offered significant advantages and disadvantages.

The Ford/Loral LBR required an exposed gunner and man-in-loop throughout its rapid flight. It was cheapest at an estimated US$90,000 "cost-per-kill," a figure comprised not only of average unit production cost estimates but also reliability and accuracy estimates. It was fairly effective in terms of potential combat utility with diminishing probability-of-hit at increasing range. "Top-attack" on armor would be dependent upon precision fusing, detonation, and accuracy of downward-firing explosively formed projectiles from shaped charges.

The Hughes/Boeing FO guide prototype enabled an unexposed gunner (once launched) and also required man-in-loop throughout its slower flight. It was judged as likely costlier, but less affected by accuracy throughout its range with an automatic lock and guidance in its terminal stage of flight—and it even offered target switching. Although requiring more intensive gunner training, it could attack targets from above at the most vulnerable part of a tank's armor.

The TI/Martin-Marietta FLIR prototype offered completely autonomous "fire-and-forget" flight to target after launch, but was perceived as both the costliest and technologically riskiest alternative. It would be easiest, however, to train and be effective at maximum ranges by means of its target acquisition sensor and guidance packages. It used "top-attack" as a more effective means of armored target defeat, but would also have a flat trajectory capability for "direct fire" against targets under cover of bridges, trees, etc.

The challenge was to evaluate the operational effectiveness and cost of each alternative, and this is explored in Section 14.4.

14.4 Effectiveness of technology options

The benefits of each alternative anti-tank missile guidance system can be measured using a simple multi-criteria effectiveness model based on acquisition objectives originally specified for the anti-tank missile: lethality, tactical advantage, gunner safety, and procurement.[3] This multi-criteria effectiveness model is based on concepts discussed earlier in the book originally developed by decision scientists (for example, see Chapter 8; Keeney 1982, 1988; Buede 1986).

The first three objectives clearly relate to the operational effectiveness of the missile. Meanwhile, the procurement objective attempts to recognize the burden of procurement and technology issues that make some alternatives more difficult to procure than others. This concern is captured as "ease of procurement."[4]

Under each objective, specific metrics are identified to measure how well the objective is achieved by a particular alternative. The objectives and their corresponding metrics (measures) appear in Table 14.1. The weights assigned to each objective, and to measures that define those objectives, reveal the relative importance of the objectives, and the relative importance of each measure with respect to an objective. In this example, it is assumed that lethality, tactical advantage, and gunner safety are equally important. Since they each receive a weight of 0.3, they are three times as important as procurement, which receives an importance weight of 0.1. All weights at each level of the hierarchy sum to one.

For lethality, the relative weight placed on the probability of a kill (i.e. the probability of a hit times the probability of a kill given a hit or $P(H) \times P(K/H)$) is 0.7. The relative weight placed on "top-attack" capability is 0.3. For tactical advantage, the most important attribute is the heaviness of the system, which receives a relative weight of 0.4. This is followed by time to engage (0.3), then time of flight

Table 14.1 Anti-tank missile guidance system effectiveness

Weight	Objective	Weight	Measure	LBR		FO		FLIR	
				Value	Score	Value	Score	Value	Score
0.3	Lethality								
		0.7	P(H) × P(K)	5	1.05	4	0.84	7	1.47
		0.3	Top attack	6	0.54	7	0.63	9	0.81
0.3	Tactical advantage								
		0.4	Weight	9	1.08	5	0.6	3	0.36
		0.3	Time to engage	8	0.72	7	0.63	5	0.45
		0.2	Time to flight	7	0.42	5	0.3	5	0.3
		0.1	Redirect capability	10	0.3	10	0.3	0	0
0.3	Gunner safety								
		0.2	Required training	5	0.3	1	0.06	10	0.6
		0.8	Exposure after launch	2	0.48	8	1.92	10	2.4
0.1	Procurement	1	Ease of procurement	8	0.8	6	0.6	4	0.4
	MoE				**5.69**		**5.88**		**6.79**

(0.2), and then redirect capability (0.1). Gunner safety is measured mostly by the gunner's exposure to enemy fire after launch (0.8) and also by the amount of training required (0.2).

In this example, actual values for each measure (computed or subjectively assigned) for each of the three competing technology alternatives (LBR; FO; FLIR) are converted (normalized) on a scale of 0 to 10. For instance, in the case of gunner safety, the objective is to minimize the amount of time the gunner is exposed to enemy fire (measured in minutes). With LBR the gunner must stay in place until the target is hit, leading to a longer exposure time, so LBR receives a low value of 2. The FO system allows the gunner to hide while guiding the missile, so he is exposed for a shorter time and, thus, FO receives a better value of 8. The FLIR system allows the gunner to conceal himself immediately after launch ("fire-and-forget") and, thus, is given the maximum value of 10. The other values shown in Table 14.1 are derived in similar fashion.

The overall MoE achieved by each of the three alternatives under the previous assumptions is shown at the bottom of Table 14.1. Individual scores shown in Table 14.1 for each measure are calculated by taking the normalized value for that measure, multiplying it by the relative weight for that measure, and multiplying again by the relative weight placed on the higher level objective.[5] The overall MoE for any given alternative is the sum of the individual metric scores.[6]

The overall MoEs reported in Table 14.1 suggest that FLIR offers the greatest benefit/effectiveness (6.79), with LBR and FO closely tied for second (offering overall MoEs of 5.69 and 5.88, respectively). This ranking turns out to be consistent with the Army's revealed preference for the three guidance technologies: They preferred FLIR over the other two guidance systems, and they perceived the FO system as being slightly better than the LBR system (J. Dillard; personal communication, November 12, 2012).

14.5   Cost-effectiveness analysis

The previous section focused on the overall operational effectiveness of the three guidance alternatives. Assuming budgets for the program are constrained, then selection of the best alternative also requires cost estimates, including technology development and manufacturing (production) costs.

The Army's estimates of the cost-per-kill for each alternative are reported in Table 14.2. This table also reveals estimates of the total program cost for each alternative assuming an Army requirement of 2,000 missiles.

A cost vs effectiveness graph, in which the MoE is plotted against total program cost for each alternative, is shown in Figure 14.2.

From Figure 14.2 we can see that no single alternative dominates another, meaning there is no alternative that is both cheaper and more effective than another. In

Table 14.2 Anti-tank missile cost

	LBR (US$m)	FO (US$m)	FLIR (US$m)
Cost/kill	0.09	0.11	0.15
Program cost	180	220	300

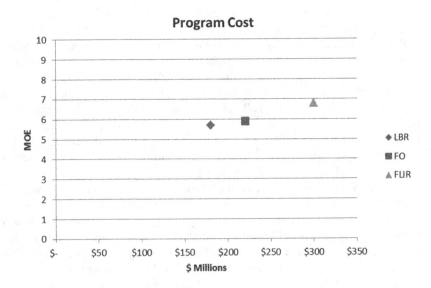

Figure 14.2 Deterministic cost-effectiveness.

this case, as discussed in Chapters 4 or 10, it is useful to examine marginal benefits and marginal costs to help evaluate alternatives.

The LBR alternative is the least costly and least effective. We compare it to the FO alternative in Table 14.3 and note that the marginal cost of choosing FO over LBR is US$40 million. Table 14.3 also shows differences in values for each of the effectiveness measures used to calculate the MoE between the two alternatives. A positive change represents an increase in effectiveness while a negative difference indicates a decrease in effectiveness. A similar analysis for FO vs FLIR is shown in Table 14.4.

While Figure 14.2 offers an overall picture of differences in cost vs effectiveness of the three alternatives, Tables 14.3 and 14.4 allow decision-makers to see specifically what they gain and lose at the margin as they go from one technology to the next. Arguably this is captured in an aggregated way in the overall MoE, but it is also important for decision-makers to understand specific benefits they receive for the money (value-for-money).[7] This marginal analysis defines the tradeoff space for decision-makers, but it is not the solution.[8]

Table 14.3 Marginal analysis of cost and effectiveness for LBR and FO

Marginal analysis	*LBR*	*FO*	*Difference*
Program cost (US$ million)	180	220	40
P(H) × P(K)	5	4	−1
Top-attack	6	7	+1
Weight	9	5	−4
Time to engage	8	7	−1
Time of flight	7	5	−2
Redirect capability	10	10	0
Required training	5	1	−4
Exposure after launch	2	8	+6
Ease of procurement	8	6	−2

Table 14.4 Marginal analysis of cost and effectiveness for FO and FLIR

Marginal analysis	*FO*	*FLIR*	*Difference*
Program cost (US$ million)	220	300	80
P(H) × P(K)	4	7	+3
Top-attack	7	9	+2
Weight	5	3	−2
Time to engage	7	5	−2
Time of flight	5	5	0
Recall capability	10	0	−10
Required training	1	10	+9
Exposure after launch	8	10	+2
Ease of procurement	6	4	−2

The previous cost vs effectiveness analysis assumed all guidance technology development efforts would be equally successful and achieve the estimated MoEs. At the start of the "Proof of Principle" effort for the project, however, there was significant uncertainty and no assurance that any of the technologies would be successfully developed.

In fact, early assessments of the probability of success differed among the three alternatives. A notional assessment of the probability of success for each option is given in Table 14.5. Table 14.5 also calculates the "expected MoE" based on the given probability of success for each option. The expected MoE is simply the overall MoE shown in Table 14.1 multiplied by the probability of success.

Given this new calculation of expected MoEs, the previous cost vs effectiveness graph can be revised as shown in Figure 14.3. Here we conclude the LBR system is superior since it is both cheaper and has a higher expected MoE than the other two (FO and FLIR), and therefore it dominates those guidance systems. Interestingly, the Army's actual cost and operational effectiveness analysis (COEA) in fact found LBR was the preferred alternative (J. Dillard; personal communication, November 12, 2012).

14.6   Value of technology real options: a retrospective assessment

The value of a real option is derived from the difference between the expected net value (i.e. expected benefits minus expected costs) of an investment and the net value of that investment given that it succeeds. The option value lies in the flexibility to terminate the project if it is not successful.

To develop a simple option valuation model for the Javelin guidance technologies, we note benefits appear as the MoEs in Table 14.1. In the absence of a real options approach, each of the alternatives has an expected cost that is simply based on the uncertainty associated with its technological development.

If the development effort fails, we assume the Army will have to pay some additional cost to complete the technology and to achieve the anticipated level of effectiveness (MoE). We refer to this additional cost as the "cost to fix" the technology.

If technology development is successful, then the cost to exercise the option will be the total program cost from Table 14.2 and, in Table 14.6, is shown as "cost to implement." If the technology development fails, the cost of the alternative will be the "cost to implement" plus the "cost to fix" the technology. The total expected cost of each alternative is given in Table 14.6.

Table 14.5 Probability of development success and expected MoE for Javelin technology options

	LBR	FO	FLIR
P (success)	0.6	0.5	0.4
Expected MoE	3.414	2.94	2.716

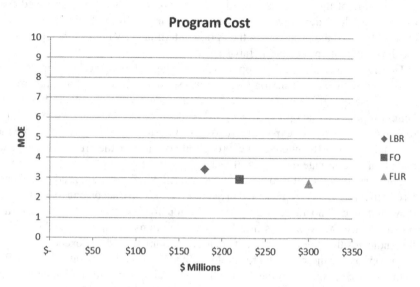

Figure 14.3 Probabilistic cost-effectiveness.

Table 14.6 Expected cost of Javelin guidance technology alternatives without option to terminate project

	LBR	FO	FLIR
Probability of success	0.6	0.5	0.4
Cost to implement (US$ million)	180	220	300
Probability of failure	0.4	0.5	0.6
Cost to fix (US$ million)	50	70	90
Total cost to implement given failure (US$ million)	230	290	390
Expected cost (US$ million)	200	255	354

The values shown in Table 14.6 assume that we do not use a real options approach. Instead, we will pick one of the technologies based on the cost vs benefit analysis presented in Section 14.5. Whichever technology we choose, we will have to pay an additional cost to achieve the anticipated effectiveness (MoE) if the development phase fails.

The real options approach allows the Army to pay for the option to find out if technology development succeeds before making its final choice. If development succeeds, the MoE shown in Table 14.1 is achieved and the Army can proceed with the project if they prefer that option based on the cost vs effectiveness analysis presented in the previous section. If development fails, the particular development project can be terminated and there is no further cost.

The value of the option is given by the difference between the expected cost of the technology development project with no option (from Table 14.6) and the expected cost of the project with the option to terminate. Values of the options for the three alternatives appear in Table 14.7.

Differences in values of the options reflect the different levels of uncertainty associated with each technology. The values shown in Table 14.7 are maximums in the sense that if we pay any more than the option value we would have been better off not using an option. If we pay less than the option value, we experience real cost savings by not expending funds on an unsuccessful technology. Note the more uncertain the technology (i.e. probability of failure), the greater the value of an option to terminate the project if technology development fails.

Let us suppose that the Army preferred the LBR technology (based on the cost vs effectiveness analysis presented in Section 14.5). Then, according to Table 14.7, they should pay no more than US$92 million for the option to terminate the project. Since the Army was in effect buying options for all three technologies, this indicates that the total amount spent on options should not exceed the value of the option for the preferred technology. Since the maximum value of the LBR option is US$92 million, if the Army allocated that option value equally across all the alternatives, they should spend no more than roughly US$30 million for each option, which is precisely what they did.

Given some technologies are more uncertain than others, a better approach is to allocate the US$92 million based on the level of uncertainty the Army is trying to resolve. Using the probability of failure data in Table 14.7 as a notional measure of risk, 27 percent of the total option value would be allocated to LBR, 33 percent to FO, and 40 percent to FLIR.

Returning to the previous example, if *ex-ante* the Army prefers the LBR technology, then the total cost of the option should not exceed US$92 million. Recognizing uncertainty (i.e. risk of failure), this means the Army should be willing to pay roughly US$25 million for the LBR option, US$30 million for the FO option, and US$37 million for the FLIR option. Doing so allocates the dollars based on risk while keeping the total cost no more than the maximum option value of the preferred alternative. Again, since US$92 million is the maximum value of the

Table 14.7 Value of Javelin guidance technology options

	LBR	FO	FLIR
Probability of success	0.6	0.5	0.4
Cost to implement (US$ million)	180	220	300
Probability of failure	0.4	0.5	0.6
Cost if project is terminated (US$ million)	0	0	0
Expected cost with option (US$ million)	108	110	120
Expected cost w/o option (US$ million)	200	255	354
Value of option (US$ million)	92	145	234

real option, to realize cost savings from this strategy, the Army would need to pay less than US$92 million for all three options.

14.7   The Army's choice revealed

The LBR candidate emerged as the winner of the original CBA based on initial assessments of relative weights on the multiple criteria. In a strange twist, the Source Selection Evaluation Board (SSEB) instead chose the FLIR candidate, partly as a result of a significant shift in the importance (relative weight) attached to gunner safety that drove a strong preference toward "fire-and-forget" in the overall MoE.[9] While time of flight and gunner survivability were not explicitly stated requirements in the original (AAWS-M) Joint Required Operational Capability document, "fire-and-forget" nevertheless translated into greatly enhanced gunner survivability, and it ultimately appealed to decision-makers (particularly to operator representatives). In June 1989, a full-scale development contract was awarded for the AAWS-M project to the FLIR team of Texas Instruments and Martin-Marietta.

The Office of the Secretary of Defense viewed the program as having an acceptable risk because of its 27-month technology development phase (which included a real options approach to develop a technical solution) and the subsequent 36-month plan for full-scale development. At the program office level, however, FLIR was known to be a high risk program in several technical areas. Focal plane array (FPA) technology was still immature, despite successful technology development phase results.[10] Since it was recognized as technologically risky, the government funded its own night-vision laboratory. In effect, it purchased an option by partially funding several companies to produce these devices. In 1991, the only five known FPA makers in the world were Rockwell International, Loral, Santa Barbara Research Corporation, Sofradir (a French firm), and Texas Instruments.[11]

As an additional gauge of technological maturity, a comparative baseline test was mandated at the second milestone upon the decision to launch the Javelin program into full-scale development. That test would pit the immature FPA technology against existing tube-launched, optically tracked, wire-guided (TOW), and DRAGON (legacy systems) night-viewing optics. Results of this test showed the Javelin's immature FPAs still outperformed the DRAGON and were almost as effective as the much larger TOW anti-tank missile system.[12]

About 18 months into the Engineering and Manufacturing Development (EMD) phase, serious technical problems doubled the expected cost of development and added about 18 more months to the originally planned 36 months to complete. This required formal re-baselining that took the better part of the next year to accomplish.[13] The program was restructured, given a new baseline, and was subsequently completed largely within the new parameters. The additional 18 months added to the original 36-month phase helped to resolve the uncertainties and complexities of system development.

Today, Javelin is viewed as a successful weapon system that delivers valuable operational effectiveness, despite its earlier developmental challenges. It is routinely used in combat operations and has enjoyed repeated full-rate production contracts.[14] In the decade from 2003 to 2013, more than 1,000 Javelin missiles were fired in Iraq and Afghanistan with close to 98 percent reliability.

14.8 Conclusions

Several observations can be drawn from the analysis of the Javelin guidance technology acquisition process. The first is that the benefit of weapon systems or, in this case, missile guidance systems, is not measured in dollars. This makes using a traditional option valuation model based on monetary benefits minus costs difficult (see Chapter 11 for example), if not impossible. Instead, a useful approach is to turn to principles of multi-criteria decision-making to develop MoEs for each alternative. The overall MoE can then be joined with cost estimates to illustrate a trade space of alternatives available to decision-makers.

Secondly, we note that the three proposed guidance systems involved different levels of risk. This information can be used to calculate an "expected MoE" for each alternative, incorporating uncertainty into the analysis. This probabilistic MoE can be combined with the alternative's expected cost to present a risk-adjusted trade space for decision-makers.

Thirdly, we show that a real options approach not only allows uncertainty to be incorporated explicitly in the analysis, but it also enables calculation of the value of real options based upon various risks. This leads to different option values for different alternatives based on technological maturity.

Using this real options approach, we conclude that the Army might have mitigated its risks by offering each development team a different amount of money to develop their proposed technology, based on probabilities of success derived from technological risk assessments. We note that the final "cost to fix" the FLIR guidance technology ultimately selected by the Army turned out to be significantly higher than the US$30 million originally paid to develop the technology. This is in line with predictions of the real options model that recognized the FLIR technology as the riskiest investment.

In conclusion, the real options approach to CBA captures the value of flexibility in acquisition decisions. Faced with significant uncertainty, implementing a real options approach can result in more efficient use of scarce resources.

Notes

1 In the classic example of stock purchase options, the exercise decision rule is to sell a stock if the price rises above a certain price, and the exercise signal is the stock price. The decision delay is incurred while the option holder waits to see if the stock price rises above the exercise price.

2 The Advanced Anti-Armor Weapon System – Medium (AAWS-M) project inspired the Javelin program. The joint Army and Marine Corps operational requirements document for the Javelin was formally approved-amended in 1986–88. The FLIR approach consisted of a laser beam-riding system, a fiber-optic guided system, and a forward-looking infra-red system.

3 The services procuring the Javelin system did not actually use this exact methodology for the selection of the Javelin guidance technology, but used something similar for a weighted decision analysis of the three alternatives.

4 This burden is sometimes termed "transaction costs" as opposed to "production costs." Note prior discussions in this volume about the interpretation of placing a weight on production costs. Ideally, the operational performance of investments should be evaluated independently of production costs in the spirit of "cost as an independent variable" (CAIV). The next section discusses a way to combine cost and effectiveness measures.

5 For example, required training has a weight of 0.2 and is a metric that supports gunner safety, which has a weight of 0.3. LBR received a value of 5 for this metric, so the score for LBR is $0.3 = (5) \times (0.2) \times (0.3)$. The score for FO is $0.060 = (1) \times (0.2) \times (0.3)$ and the score for FLIR is $0.6 = (10) \times (0.2) \times (0.3)$. All other scores in Table 14.1 are calculated in a similar manner.

6 For example, the MoE for LBR is $5.69 = 1.05 + 0.54 + 1.08 + 0.72 + 0.42 + 0.30 + 0.30 + 0.48 + 0.80$. Note that the MoE is calculated on a scale of 0 to 10 where an "ideal" alternative would receive an MoE of 10.

7 As discussed in Chapter 4, and because the MoE combines different measures that are not necessarily substitutes, it is not possible to use benefit/cost ratios (i.e. the ratio of MoE to cost) to rank alternatives.

8 Solving the cost-effectiveness problem as defined in this case could be handled by "leveling the playing field" as discussed in Chapter 4, using the fourth or fifth approaches to structuring an economic evaluation of alternatives (EEoA)—the modified budget or modified effectiveness approaches—or the sixth ("opportunity cost") approach.

9 As part of the capability formulation process, technical constraints are deliberately avoided in requirements documents to allow and encourage a maximum range of alternative solutions to a particular requirement or capability deficiency.

10 It would be gauged today at approximately Technology Readiness Level 5. DoD assesses the maturity of critical technologies on a scale from 1 (lowest) to 9 (highest) as described in the *Technology Readiness Assessment Guidance* (2011) http://www.acq. osd.mil/ddre/publications/docs/TRA2011.pdf [last accessed December 4, 2014].

11 The two-partner TI/Martin-Marietta Joint Venture in the full-scale development phase was also free to maximize competition at the subcontractor level. In their make-or-buy decision, Texas Instruments elected to make the focal plane array for both of its uses in the command launch unit and in the missile. The company had made these devices for other programs, but not in these two distinct configurations (scanning and starting arrays).

12 Around focal plane array attainment of specified sensitivity and production yield, system weight, tracker algorithm, and other areas.

13 This constituted a "Nunn-McCurdy breach" of cost and schedule thresholds, which required Congressional notifications and formal re-baselining taking the better part of the next year to accomplish. Over that next year, the program sought a new baseline with many different revised program estimates—climbing from 36 months duration and US$298 million in cost, to 48 months duration and US$372 million in cost, and finally to 54 months and US$443 million for the total cost and duration of this phase.

14 The system design has continued to be upgraded, not as blocks of capability, but with software, warhead, and producibility enhancements.

Bibliography

Amram, M. and N. Kulatilaka. 1999. *Real Options: Managing Strategic Investment in an Uncertain World*. Cambridge, MA: Harvard Business School Press.

Brealey, R. and S. Myers. 2000. *Principles of Corporate Finance* (6th edition). New York: McGraw Hill.

Buede, D. M. 1986. "Structuring Value Attributes." *Interfaces* 16(2): 52–62.

Ceylan, B. K. and D. N. Ford. 2002. "Using Options to Manage Dynamic Uncertainty in Acquisition Projects." *Acquisition Review Quarterly* 9(4): 243–58.

Courtney, H., J. Kirkland, and P. Viguerie. 1997. "Strategy under Uncertainty." *Harvard Business Review* 75(6): 67–79.

Dillard, J. and D. Ford. 2009. "From Amorphous to Defined: Balancing the Risks of Spiral Development." *Accounting Review* (52).

Ford, D. and J. Dillard. 2009. "Modeling the Integration of Open Systems and Evolutionary Acquisition in DoD Programs." *Acquisition Review Quarterly* (51).

Garvin, M. and C. Cheah. 2004. "Valuation Techniques for Infrastructure Decisions." *Construction Management & Economics* 22(5): 373–383.

Garvin, M. and D. Ford. 2012. "Real Options in Infrastructure Projects: Theory, Practice and Prospects." *Engineering Project Organization Journal* 2(1–2): 97–108.

Keeney, R. 1982. "Decision Analysis: An Overview." *Operations Research* 30(5): 803–838.

———. 1988. "Structuring Objectives for Problems of Public Interest." *Operations Research* 36(3): 396–405.

Lyons, J., D. Long, and R. Chait. 2006. *Critical Technology Events in the Development of the Stinger and Javelin Missile Systems: Project Hindsight Revisited.* Washington, DC: National Defense University Center for Technology and National Security Policy.

Miller, R. and D. Lessard. 2000. *The Strategic Management of Large Engineering Projects.* Cambridge, MA: MIT Press.

Triantis, A. 2005. "Realizing the Potential of Real Options: Does Theory Meet Practice?" *Journal of Applied Corporate Finance* 17(2): 8–16.

15 An application of military cost–benefit analysis in a major defense acquisition

The C-17 transport aircraft

William L. Greer

15.1 Introduction

This case study illustrates the traditional approach to military cost–benefit analysis (CBA) and acquisition decisions within the Department of Defense (DoD) described in Chapter 8. It specifically discusses decisions made in 1993–95 to replace C-141 transport aircraft with the C-17 strategic airlifter. It also includes a discussion of events leading up to the study, the analytical approach taken, the study participants, critical points in the analyses, decisions reached, and lessons learned.

The C-17 Globemaster II aircraft has been one of the more successful military transportation assets in history. It provides rapid delivery of cargo or passengers almost anywhere in the world. Currently it is flown by the US Air Force (USAF)'s Air Mobility Command (AMC) and by the armed forces of several other countries, including the United Kingdom's Royal Air Force, the Royal Australian Air Force, the Canadian Force's Air Command, NATO, and the Qatar Emiri Air Force. The United Arab Emirates recently ordered C-17s, and many other countries are exploring the possibility of doing so. In addition to its transoceanic strategic-lift capability, the C-17 can also perform tactical airlift, medical evacuation, and airdrop missions. It played a significant role in moving goods, vehicles, and personnel during Operation Enduring Freedom in Afghanistan and Operation Iraqi Freedom in Iraq, and it has contributed to emergency relief operations around the world. It is widely considered a success story.

That was not always the case. The program came very close to being cancelled in the early 1990s. Key decisions made around that time serve as a valuable example of the useful role of CBA in major defense investment decisions. This chapter describes cost-effectiveness analyses (CEAs) that informed the decision to retain the C-17 program, and serves as a case study in how such assessments can assist decision-makers. The focus is on the analyses but, just as important, it provides insights into how these analyses were received and used to make the decision to invest in the C-17.

The analyses depicted here are drawn from documents (Greer *et al.* 1993; Bexfield *et al.* 2001) prepared by the Institute for Defense Analyses (IDA) for the DoD. Studies such as these were referred to at that time as cost and operational effectiveness analyses (COEAs), currently called analyses of alternatives (AoAs).

These studies include many of the basic considerations of cost and effectiveness analysis discussed in this book.

15.1.1 Background

In the 1970s, the USAF launched a plan for a new cargo aircraft to carry most of the largest equipment the Army needed (e.g. tanks, large-tracked and wheeled vehicles, and Patriot batteries) into small remote airfields—many with runways shorter than 3,000 feet. Although at the time airlifters existed that could carry large equipment (the C-5) and land in small airfields (the C-130), no existing airlifters could perform both these tasks.

In December 1979, the DoD initiated the Cargo-Experimental (C-X) competition for a new strategic airlift aircraft. The C-X was to be an aircraft that could deliver a full range of combat equipment over intercontinental distances, operate from a 3,000-foot runway, possess survivability features, have excellent reliability, maintainability, and availability, and have a low life-cycle cost. Early in 1980, the DoD issued the request for proposals (RFPs) for the new C-X program. Boeing, Lockheed Martin, and McDonnell Douglas responded. After reviewing the various designs, in August 1981 the DoD selected the aircraft design proposed by McDonnell Douglas.[1] The winning design incorporated many features already demonstrated on the YC-15, a McDonnell Douglas aircraft that had been developed and flight tested in the 1970s. This chosen design was later designated the C-17. Because of the earlier testing of the YC-15, it was viewed as a program with low development and cost risk.

In addition to carrying large cargo and landing in small airfields, the C-17 was also designed to back up and turn in a small radius, thereby optimizing the use of limited ground space. It was also designed to conduct troop and cargo airdrops, replacing the aging C-141s that previously conducted those missions. It was an aircraft for all missions.

In 1982, the DoD conducted a large transportation assessment, the Mobility Study, which established the air mobility requirements at that time, based on perceived wartime needs. To meet these requirements, the USAF determined that 210 C-17s were needed. These requirements were codified in the 1983 *Air Mobility Master Plan*. Largely because of budget rather than effectiveness considerations, the number 210 was subsequently reduced by the Office of the Secretary of Defense (OSD) to 120 during the 1990 Major Airlift Review. Thus the number of C-17s under consideration in the early 1990s was 120.

Several complicating issues arose at that time. The earlier assessments of low development and cost risk proved wrong. Costs for the C-17 continued to rise, and the several aircraft delivered for testing did not demonstrate the reliability and performance expected. Static wing loading tests revealed that the wings failed at lower loads than predicted, forcing even higher costs to strengthen them.

Lockheed Martin, manufacturer of the C-5 and C-141, made an unsolicited proposal in 1991 to upgrade and extend the life of the C-141s at a cost that appeared lower than that of the troubled C-17 program. An added complication and a renewed sense of urgency was presented when it was found that C-141s had developed a large number of microscopic cracks in their wing structures—a condition that temporarily grounded the entire C-141 fleet until repairs could be made.

This raised a number of questions for DoD: Should it continue with the C-17 program despite escalating costs and lower performance than desired? Should it cancel the C-17 program and extend the life of C-141s, continuing with wing repairs until a new C-X design was chosen? Or should it investigate other alternatives? These were the issues confronting Congress and the DoD in 1993 and are the topics of this case study.

Congress mandated that the DoD conduct an independent assessment of the C-17 program and report its findings to the US Congress (Senate and House Armed Services Committees). The legislation further restricted fiscal year (FY) 1994 spending on the C-17 until such a study was completed. After reviewing the expertise and capabilities in several federally funded research and development centers (FFRDCs), the OSD selected the IDA to conduct the study. IDA completed its study in 1994. The findings were used by the DoD and duly reported to the congressional defense committees.

Table 15.1 summarizes the history of the C-17 program up to the point at which analyses were conducted to determine whether to go ahead with the program.

With the CEAs in hand, the OSD finally approved the 120-aircraft C-17 program in 1995. The road to this decision point was not an easy one. It required numerous analyses, the main one of which is the cost-effectiveness case study

Table 15.1 C-17 decision timelines

Year	Events
1970s	• USAF decided new cargo aircraft, C-X, was needed to carry heavy and large army equipment into austere airfields
1981	• McDonnell Douglas selected to build C-X, called C-17
1982	• *Mobility Study* published, calling for more airlift capability
1983	• USAF *Airlift Master Plan* estimated that 210 C-17s needed to meet needs identified in mobility study
1990	• Major Airlift Review reduced C-17 requirement from 210 to 120
1991	• Lockheed Martin proposed C-141 service life extension program (SLEP)
1992	• Joint Staff issued report, concluding that C-17 is more cost-effective than either new C-5 or C-141 SLEP
	• Joint Staff issued *Mobility Requirements Study*
1993	• Problems with aging C-141s continued
	• C-17 exhibited engineering problems and cost increases
	• Congress restricted FY94 C-17 spending pending further study
	• DoD asked IDA to conduct COEA on C-17 program
1994	• IDA completed C-17 COEA
	• COEA sent to Congress after OSD review
	• Additional DoD studies were authorized

summarized in this section. At the end of this section, we also summarize more recent decisions affecting the C-17 program.

15.1.2   Organizations involved

In 1993, strong views existed on the C-17 program. Proponents for the C-17 resided, among other places, within the Army Material Command and at McDonnell Douglas. Detractors included Lockheed Martin, manufacturer of competing aircraft like the C-5 and C-141, the Boeing Corporation, manufacturer of the commercial 747 and 767 aircraft, and other potential competitors to the C-17.

Numerous subcontractors were also interested in the outcome. Senior OSD officials were responsible for generating objective, unbiased analysis to support the Secretary of Defense on whether to continue the C-17 program. The Secretary was interested in a study that sorted through the claims and evaluated the alternatives. The report would be delivered to the Defense Acquisition Board (DAB), the OSD board that recommends acquisition actions to the Secretary of Defense, who, after review, would propose it to the House of Representatives and Senate defense committees. The CBA needed to be independent, clear, and able to withstand intense scrutiny.

The IDA study team consisted of experts in airlifter operations, computer modeling and simulation, aircraft and engine design, and cost estimating. The study team engaged in frequent interactions with aircraft and engine manufacturers, USAF operational commands, the AMC, the USAF Air Staff, the Joint Staff, and OSD.

15.1.3   Methodology

The approach taken in this study consisted of the following steps:

- identify the alternatives (fleets of aircraft to replace C-141s and upgrade strategic-lift capability);
- establish airlift requirements (criteria and attributes);
- estimate effectiveness of each alternative in the airlift mission (measures of effectiveness or MoEs);
- estimate the total ownership cost, sometimes referred to as the total system life-cycle cost, of each alternative;
- arrange the cost and effectiveness information to facilitate decision-making. Some steps (costing and determining effectiveness) were performed concurrently; and
- perform sensitivity analyses as needed.

15.1.3.1   Identify fleet alternatives

The alternatives were initially selected to have equal lift capability (equal effectiveness—see Chapter 4 in this book) as measured by one of the common capacity measures used in the airlift community: million ton-miles per day

(MTM/D) (AFPAM 10-1403 2003). When divided by the distance an airlifter must fly from the United States to the theater of interest, the MTM/D is a rough measure of the steady-state rate of delivery of cargo to the theater, provided sufficient infrastructure and parking spaces are available, including en-route and in-theater. Since the infrastructure and parking assumptions are rarely satisfied, fleet-wide MTM/D offers only a partial approach to identify comparable alternative fleets of aircraft that offer similar airlift capability. More detailed analyses further differentiate among the alternatives, identifying both higher-cost-higher-effectiveness and lower-cost-lower-effectiveness alternatives.

15.1.3.2 Establish airlift requirements

The requirements for airlift were taken from the *Mobility Requirements Study* (MRS) (Joint Staff J4 Logistics 1992). This study, completed by the Joint Staff and OSD, identified the type and tonnage of cargo and troops that were to be moved by air (as well as by land and sea) per day. Cargo was identified by a commodity code and by dimensions that allowed it to be sorted into three conventional cargo categories called outsize, oversize, and bulk.[2] The MRS established lower limits for acceptable cargo delivery rates that would meet medium-risk criteria in warfighting simulations. The final cargo delivery schedule is referred to as the Time-Phased Force Deployment Data (TPFDD).

15.1.3.3 Estimate effectiveness of each alternative

The effectiveness analysis involved estimating for each alternative fleet of airlift aircraft how much cargo and how many troops from the TPFDD were delivered to the theater within a fixed period of time. To make these estimates, the study used a detailed simulation of the aircraft loading, aircraft movement, and cargo flow. The specific models used were the Airlift Loading Model (ALM) for loading, the detailed simulation model Mobility Analysis Support System (MASS) for airlift movement and cargo flows, and the Airlift Cycle Analysis Spreadsheet (ACAS) for more aggregate but faster assessments of cargo and passenger movement.[3] The primary output of MASS and ACAS used in the report was the total cargo tonnage, separated into the three categories of bulk, oversize, and outsize cargo, delivered in 30 days by each alternative fleet.

15.1.3.4 Estimate costs

The study team also provided cost estimates including the development, procurement, and the annual operations and support (O&S) costs for each airlifter in each alternative fleet. Total life-cycle costs over a 25-year period were then estimated for each alternative. Information from the C-17 Program Office, contractors, and OSD was used to arrive at independent cost assessments, all conducted in accordance with standard costing methods.[4]

An attempt was made to make the alternatives as comparable as possible in all other measures. Specifically, all alternatives were sized to be capable of a brigade-size airdrop. All alternatives possessed comparable intra-theater tactical airlift capabilities. Since the C-17s could also substitute for C-130s in tactical airlift roles when in-theater, the study argued that mixed fleets with C-17s need not have as many C-130s for comparable overall strategic and tactical capability as those without them. Adjustments were made to the C-130 fleet size needed for each alternative with corresponding adjustments in the associated O&S costs.

*15.1.3.5   Arrange cost and effectiveness information to facilitate
        decision-making*

Finally, once cost and effectiveness measures were estimated for all alternatives, a way of displaying them simultaneously to help decision-makers quickly sort out favorable ones from less favorable ones was developed. As discussed earlier, this step is crucial in any study of this type, since it establishes the framework for the decisions that must ensue. Such a framework must be free from biases (or must clearly identify biases that would otherwise be hidden) but must emphasize the critical issues. The organization of the cost and effectiveness results is vital to the utility of the analyses. Examples will be provided later.

15.2 Alternatives

Alternatives refer to the alternative fleets, each made up of a number of different types of aircraft. This section first discusses the different types of aircraft in the alternative fleets and then describes the composition of the alternative fleets, i.e. how many of which types of aircraft are in each. Figure 15.1 provides a schematic of the aircraft under consideration to indicate the relative sizes and capacities of these airlifters. Capacity is significant for determining how much each airlifter can carry, and size proves important for airbases with restricted space or facilities.

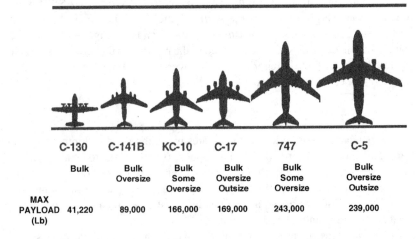

	C-130	C-141B	KC-10	C-17	747	C-5
	Bulk	Bulk Oversize	Bulk Some Oversize	Bulk Oversize Outsize	Bulk Some Oversize	Bulk Oversize Outsize
MAX PAYLOAD (Lb)	41,220	89,000	166,000	169,000	243,000	239,000

Figure 15.1 Aircraft size and capacity comparisons.

The military aircraft types considered in the study included: C-5A, C-5B, KC-10A, C-17, C-5B+, C-141, C-Y, militarized 747-400F, and militarized 767-300F. In addition, aircraft from the Civil Reserve Air Fleet (CRAF) that can be called up for duty to transport troops and bulk cargo during war conditions were also incorporated into fleet mixes. Each is discussed briefly in turn.

15.2.1 Core aircraft types

The 1993 core airlift fleet is summarized below. These aircraft would remain in the fleet no matter which new airlifter program was selected and are referred to as members of the core fleet, common to any alternatives.

15.2.1.1 C-5A/B

At the time of the study in 1993, 76 C-5As and 50 C-5Bs made up the total aircraft inventories of the active, guard, and reserve fleets.[5] Operating costs and utilization rates are slightly different for the two types, but they carry the same payloads the same distances. These are the largest airlifters of the USAF. Each C-5 can take off or land with a maximum payload of nearly 120 tons. At the time the study was conducted, the average cargo weight carried by the C-5s was 68.9 tons (these estimates are updated frequently by AMC, so more current numbers should be used in future studies), with a block speed[6] of 423 knots. C-5s can carry very heavy or very large outsize cargo, such as M-1 Abrams tanks, Patriot battery radars, or CH-47 helicopters. They can also carry smaller oversize cargo, such as wheeled vehicles (5-ton and smaller trucks, M-2 Bradley or Stryker vehicles, or high-mobility multi-purpose wheeled vehicles (HMMWVs)). Of course, the C-5 can also carry palletized bulk cargo such as ammunition, supplies and food, as well as troops.

15.2.1.2 KC-10A

The KC-10 is a dual-purpose aircraft. It serves as the largest airborne tanker in the fleet and as a cargo carrier. For purposes of this study, AMC estimated that 23 of the KC-10s would be dedicated to cargo missions. A single KC-10 can lift 83 tons of cargo, although it can carry only a fraction of oversize cargo and cannot carry any outsize cargo. The average payload assumed was 41.7 tons, and the aircraft moves with a 445-knot block speed.

15.2.1.3 Civil Reserve Air Fleet

The CRAF consists of a number of different aircraft owned and operated by various airfreight companies such as Federal Express (FedEx) and commercial passenger airlines such as United Airlines and American Airlines. The CRAF program was initiated in 1952 to provide on-call transportation assets in emergencies. These companies contract to provide aircraft and crew during specified wartime conditions in return for a guaranteed market share of DoD's peacetime airlift (US Congressional Budget Office CBO). There are three stages of wartime CRAF conditions. The Commander US Transportation Command (USTRANSCOM), with the concurrence of the Secretary of Defense, has the authority to activate each stage.

- *Stage I*: minor operations—a pre-set number of commercial aircraft on 24-hour notice. Stage I has only been used a few times, such as in 1990 to support Operation Desert Shield deployments to Southwest Asia and in 2003 to support Operation Iraqi Freedom;
- *Stage II*: theater war—additional aircraft are released for more serious emergencies. Stage II has also only been used once, for Operation Desert Storm;
- *Stage III*: national emergency or two-theater war—even more aircraft made available. This stage has never been used. Nonetheless, this is the stage assumed for this study, i.e. supporting two nearly simultaneous major wars abroad.

15.2.2   Proposed aircraft types

Proposed aircraft types represent various alternatives that compete to augment the core fleet. These alternatives include proposals to extend the life of and/or replace the C-141. This section first reviews a program to extend the life of the C-141s and then introduces a variety of new aircraft alternatives.

15.2.2.1   C-141 service life extension program

The C-141, which can carry oversize and bulk cargo, was scheduled for retirement because of its age and because outsize cargo carriers were thought to be more useful to the airlift fleet of the future. To maintain the C-141 in the fleet would have required a Service Life Extension Program (SLEP). The biggest cost items in the C-141 SLEP were to re-wing the aircraft and add a new cab top to replace serious corrosion damage. The maximum payload for the C-141 is nearly 45 tons, although the average cargo carried is 27.5 tons at a 410-knot block speed.

15.2.2.2   C-Y

The C-Y is a hypothetical new replacement airlifter for the C-141. The C-Y would have modern off-the-shelf engines and avionics, but would carry the same load as the C-141. It was used in the analyses as a potential replacement for the C-141 as each C-141 reached its terminal fuselage life span at 45,000 flying hours, a point reached before the end of the 25-year period of the analysis. Thus, two acquisition and operating costs are associated with the C-141 SLEP: the cost of SLEP itself plus the cost of the replacement airlifter when the C-141 reaches the end of its operational life.

15.2.2.3   C-17

The C-17 is smaller than the C-5, but larger than the C-141. The C-17 can carry outsize cargo, but not as much as a single C-5. The C-17 requires no more room at an airbase than the C-141 does, which is important when airbase space is limited. It can also operate from shorter runways than can the C-5, affording an opportunity to use more airfields in-theater and en-route. The C-17 can take off and land with a maximum payload of 85 tons, although the average payload assumed in the study was 48.3 tons (again, AMC sources have updated data). The C-17 block speed was estimated at 423 knots.

15.2.2.4   C-5B+

This is a new aircraft proposed as an alternative to the C-17. It is identical to the C-5B except that new GE CF6 engines would be used to reduce the high noise and pollution levels associated with the C-5 TF39 engines. The study assumed the same performance as the C-5B. Since the current C-5 line has been shut down, part of its cost involves a restart of the C-5 manufacturing line at Lockheed.

15.2.2.5   *Militarized 747 and 767*

A different approach to replacing C-141s would be to purchase commercial aircraft, such as Boeing 747-400s or 767-300s, modified (militarized) to handle some oversize as well as the traditional bulk cargo.[7] Unlike the CRAF, these aircraft would be owned and operated by the USAF. The 747s were estimated to be able to carry 73.1 tons each on average, while each 767 could carry 44.2 tons. Both aircraft types can fly at 445-knot block speeds. Two different commercial derivatives were used to explore whether large or small options might be best. As will be seen in the results, the larger 747s were significantly more cost-effective than the 767s.

When the study began, militarized commercial aircraft were not included as alternatives to the C-17. Some within the Air Force objected that these commercial (militarized) aircraft could not carry outsize cargo and only limited amounts of oversize cargo and therefore should not be considered candidates to replace the C-141. Since the C-141 SLEP was an option as a replacement for the C-17, and C-141s cannot carry outsize cargo, logic and fairness dictated that these militarized commercial derivatives be included. This inclusion turned out to play a crucial role in the ultimate decisions made, as will be demonstrated. It also underscores the importance of not prematurely eliminating alternatives, and including as broad a range as possible, since a wide set of alternatives can help highlight important variables to include in the CBA.

15.2.3   *Alternative fleets*

A total of 26 alternative fleets were considered[8] in the preliminary analysis illustrated in Table 15.2. The numbers in the table indicate how many aircraft of each type were included in each alternative. Each entry consists of two numbers, separated by a diagonal line. The larger number represents total aircraft inventory (TAI); the smaller number represents the primary aircraft authorized (PAA).[9] Each of the alternatives, identified with a numerical label ranging from 1 to 26, was designed to have the capacity to deliver 52 MTM/D.

Table 15.2 Alternatives with 52 MTM/D capacity

Categories	Alternative number	Numbers of aircraft (TAI/PAA)[a]				
		C-17	C-141 SLEP	C-5B+	747	767
One-aircraft alternatives	1	120/102	–	–	–	–
	2	–	263/225	–	–	–
	3	–	–	102/87	–	–
Two-aircraft alternatives with reduced numbers of C-17s	8	94/80	58/49	–	–	–
	9	94/80	–	21/18	–	–
	10	94/80	–	–	18/17	–
	11	94/80	–	–	–	30/28
	25	70/60	108/92	–	–	–
	26	70/60	–	42/36	–	–
	18	70/60	–	–	34/32	–
	22	70/60	–	–	–	56/53
	23	47/40	160/137	–	–	–
	24	47/40	–	62/53	–	–
	21	47/40	–	–	49/47	–
	17	47/40	–	–	–	83/78
	4	26/20	212/181	–	–	–
	5	26/20	–	82/70	–	–
	6	26/20	–	–	66/63	–
	7	26/20	–	–	–	108/103
Two-aircraft alternatives with no C-17s	12	–	136/116	49/42	–	–
	13	–	136/116	–	40/38	–
	14	–	136/116	–	–	65/62
	15	–	–	49/42	42/40	–
	16	–	–	49/42	–	69/66
	19	–	–	–	32/30	83/79
Illustrative three-aircraft alternative	20	47/40	93/79	–	21/20	–

Note
a TAI = total aircraft inventory; PAA = primary aircraft authorized.

The entries in Table 15.2 represent alternative additions to the core fleet. Each alternative also includes the then-current core fleet of C-5s, KC-10s, and Stage III CRAF forces. The alternatives are sorted into sets of categories: one-aircraft alternatives; two-aircraft alternatives with reduced numbers of C-17s; two-aircraft alternatives with no C-17s; and an illustrative three-aircraft alternative. Alternative 1 has 120 C-17s; all other alternatives have fewer, or no, C-17s.

Note that the one-aircraft alternatives involve only one new type of aircraft added to the core fleet. As already noted, Alternative 1 contains the full 120 C-17 fleet as programmed at that time by the USAF. Alternatives 2 and 3 proposed substitution of the C-17s with a SLEPed C-141 fleet or a new-start C-5 fleet, respectively.

The alternatives that included a reduced number of C-17s proposed a number of different options including some C-17s in addition to one other aircraft. For example, Alternative 8 has 94 C-17s and 58 C-141 SLEPs. The smallest number of C-17s considered in this category was 26 C-17s, the minimum number already obligated to DoD under contract without incurring termination penalties.

The two-aircraft alternatives with no C-17s include mixes of the C-141 SLEP, C-5B+, 747, and 767 aircraft, taken two at a time, that provide the same MTM/D as 120 C-17s.

The study also briefly examined a few three-aircraft alternatives, but it was felt that DoD would probably not embrace a program that called for three new airlifter types unless the benefits turned out to be dramatic for a reasonable cost. Although the results for these alternatives did not turn out to offer dramatic benefits, they served as a useful example for purposes of comparison.

15.3 Key inputs and models

This section summarizes the important data and considerations needed for the analyses. It also points to the central role played by the MASS and ACAS models to develop measures of effectiveness and the cost-oriented resource estimating (CORE) model for cost measures.

15.3.1 Scenarios and delivery requirements

The careful choice of scenarios is essential to any analysis, since this provides the context within which the system will be employed and a context for the evaluation of each alternative's effectiveness. The airlift analyses were conducted for two different types of scenarios: one massive and geographically distant, the other small, close, but intense.

The selection of scenarios offers one of many opportunities for participants to influence a military CBA. Proponents and opponents of various alternatives can attempt to manipulate the scenarios in order to focus on features that show their solution to its best advantage. It is critical to guard against this kind of bias. Scenarios must be selected to explicitly address all important features, since the purpose of the analysis is to provide objective and unbiased insights to the decision-maker on how the system is likely to perform in critical scenarios relevant to national defense.

In this case, the first scenario considered involved a concurrent, sequential deployment of forces from the United States to meet the needs first of a Major Regional Contingency (MRC)-East and subsequently of a MRC-West.[10] The designations East and West refer to the US coast from which most of the airlifters would stage for the respective MRC operations.[11] Over 550,000 tons of cargo was required within a 90-day period for both MRC scenarios.

The second scenario involved a Lesser Regional Contingency (LRC)[12] that began with a brigade-size airdrop followed by air delivery of cargo and additional

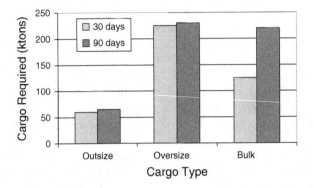

Figure 15.2 MRS airlift delivery requirements for MRC-East and MRC-West combined.

troops to the target country. In this second scenario, CRAF was not activated and the reserves were not mobilized. A total of 50,000 tons of cargo was required in four days, in addition to that delivered in the initial brigade airdrop. This case allowed the analytic team to test the robustness of the alternatives to very different requirements from those addressed by the MRCs.

The MRC scenarios dominated the analyses conducted. These scenarios required the full support of the airlifter fleet, including full augmentation by CRAF. Most of the analyses discussed in this chapter refer to the first set of scenarios. It turns out that the LRC scenario added little to the insights obtained from the two MRC scenarios.

The airlift requirements from the mobility requirements study (MRS) are summarized graphically in Figure 15.2 for two different time periods: 30 days and 90 days. Virtually all outsize and oversize cargo was required to be in-theater within the first 30 days. There are only minor differences between requirements for 30-day delivery and for 90-day delivery. To meet continuing resupply requirements, the remaining bulk cargo in each case continues to build over time. This emphasis on rapid delivery of outsize and oversize cargo will become the basis of measures of merit (or effectiveness) in the study.

15.3.2 Aircraft characteristics

Several key aircraft characteristics are essential in determining load and delivery of required cargo. These are discussed in this section.

15.3.2.1 Range-payload relationships

Figure 15.3 summarizes the range-payload curves for each of the strategic airlifter types. The payload is limited at short flying distances (ranges) by the maximum cargo weight the aircraft can lift. The maximum range is defined where an aircraft carries its maximum fuel load at takeoff and no cargo. At intermediate distances,

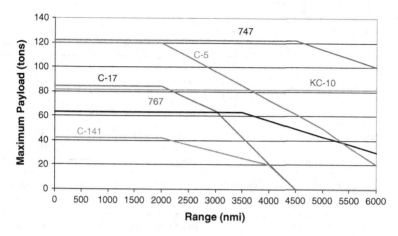

Figure 15.3 Range payload curves for airlifter types.

the range-payload relationship illustrated in Figure 15.3 depends on tradeoffs between cargo and fuel loads.

Once these relationships were established, they were used to determine the best refueling locations en route to allow an airlifter to carry as much cargo as possible. While actual operations would undoubtedly provide opportunities for in-flight refueling, payloads were assigned with the conservative assumption that the airlifter would have to use en-route bases for refueling.[13] As Figure 15.3 reveals, the 747 and KC-10 airlifters are the least constrained by the range-payload relationships.

15.3.2.2 Use rate

Surge use rates[14] are the upper limit in terms of flying hours that a fleet of aircraft can fly on any given day, applied to the first 45 days of operations. Table 15.3 reports surge use rates for each airlifter type analyzed. These numbers became major sources of disagreement as the study proceeded, resulting in sensitivity analyses using lower C-17 use rates and higher C-5B+ use rates. While each excursion requires time and resources, the use of sensitivity analysis to investigate key relationships and variables is one of the advantages of analysis. Sensitivity studies are usually conducted on a range of issues with priorities established by the key decision-makers. The need for sensitivity analyses should be anticipated and built into study timelines.

15.3.2.3 Maximum on ground and ground times

The space available at airbases is referred to as "maximum on ground" (MOG). It measures the maximum number of each specific type of airlifter that can be located at a given base to receive service at the same time.[15] The values for each airlifter type were taken from a list of worldwide MOG allotments for each airbase.

Table 15.3 Airlifter surge use rates

Airlifter category	Airlifter type	Surge use rate (hrs/day/PAA)
Military	C-5A/B	11.0 (average)
	C-141 SLEP	12.5
	C-17	15.2
	C-5B+	12.5
	KC-10	12.5
Commercial derivative	Militarized 747 or 767	12.5
CRAF	All	10.0

Table 15.4 MOG estimates maximum number of aircraft on ground simultaneously (by theater and aircraft type)

MRC theater	C-17	C-141 SLEP, 767	C-5, KC-10, 747
East	26	26	15
West	24	20	11

Table 15.4 summarizes MOG estimates for the airlifters analyzed at an aggregate theater-wide level. Note that the largest airlifters consume nearly twice the MOG space of the smaller ones. For example, a maximum of 26 C-17 aircraft can be on the ground simultaneously in the East-MRC theater of operation.[16]

Another important input is the ground time required to load and unload cargo and refuel aircraft. This reflects the amount of time each aircraft uses its allocation of MOG. Ground times vary by mission (en-route refueling, on-load, and off-load) and aircraft type. The C-5s had the longest ground times (3.75 hours on-load; 3.25 hours en route and off-load), especially when compared to 2.25 hours for en route, on-load, and off-load for the C-17 and C-141. Boeing's commercial derivatives had the longest on-load times (4–5 hours) but the shortest en route times (1.5 hours).[17]

15.3.3   *Loading and transportation effectiveness analysis*

The main models used for the estimates of how much cargo and how many passengers were delivered were ALM, MASS/AFM, and ACAS. These models are summarized briefly to give a sense of the assumptions used in the analysis.[18] Further detail on each of the models can be found in Appendix 15.1.

15.3.3.1   *Airlift loading model*

The ALM was used to determine the average cargo payload carried by each aircraft in the fleet. The MASS/Airlift Flow Model (AFM) then used this result to simulate the transport. ALM used cargo from the entire TPFDD for these estimates. The cargo was differentiated according to 26 different categories called "commodities." Each commodity could contain vehicles, pallets, and passengers

(PAX). The sequence in which the aircraft were to be loaded had to be specified as well as aircraft cargo storage dimensions, cargo door opening sizes, number of passenger seats, and maximum payload allowable by weight. Loading stopped when the weight limit was reached, or, more commonly, when cargo fully filled the cargo space in the aircraft.

15.3.3.2 MASS/AFM

The MASS/AFM was a large Monte Carlo simulation[19] that scheduled and executed each airlift mission by tail number. It incorporated a great deal of realism, such as specific routes used, airbases with MOG limitations, times for loading and off-loading, and crew duty days. It used the ALM loading results along with the nature of the TPFDD cargo and PAX at individual airbases to load the cargo. Only that part of the TPFDD available at a specific base on a specific day (plus any undelivered leftover cargo from previous days) was available for loading. The output was tons delivered per day.

15.3.3.3 Airlift cycle analysis spreadsheet

The ACAS model was a simplified approximation to the analyses produced by MASS/AFM and was used to conduct the large number of excursions needed in the study. It used aggregate data and aggregate MOG values, calibrated against MASS/AFM to provide confidence for these numerous excursions.

15.3.4 Cost analysis

The total costs for the various airlifters were estimated from numerous sources and models. The study included both the acquisition costs for new aircraft (C-17, C-5B+, C-Y, 747, or 767) and for the C-141 SLEP, as well as 25-year operating costs. All costs were expressed in constant FY 1993 dollars and were discounted to net present value (NPV) using the then-current standard discount factor of 4.5 percent per year.[20]

The study team used detailed cost information from numerous sources—the C-17 Program Office, airframe and engine contractors, and the OSD Cost Analysis Improvement Group (CAIG)—to arrive at its own independent cost estimates. When no data were available, historical data trends were used to supplement these data sources. In general, IDA cost estimates for the C-17 were somewhat higher than those of the Program Office, an issue that slowed progress during parts of the study while these differences were debated. The CAIG agreed with the IDA estimates, and these were the ones retained in the report.

15.3.4.1 General

The basic approach was first to establish acquisition schedules and C-141 retirement schedules for all alternatives and to make assumptions regarding the active/reserve aircraft mix for airlift. The study team used the C-17 schedule programmed at that time by the USAF, with C-141s retired at such a rate as to maintain a constant MTM/D capacity. Other airlift alternatives (C-5B+ and commercial derivatives) were acquired at rates consistent with their manufactures' capabilities, with the C-141s also retired at a rate to keep MTM/D constant.[21]

15.3.4.2 Acquisition

The study used the USAF C-17 acquisition schedule, with a maximum acquisition of 16 per year. Historical cost data for the C-17 were used to generate a cost-learning curve to predict future costs for C-17s. Appropriate adjustments to historical trends were added as needed, such as the cost for extra weight to strengthen the wings and higher costs associated with more realistic engine estimates for all lots after the first ones. IDA estimated the full C-17 program acquisition cost at approximately US$23 billion, about US$3 billion over the Program Office estimate. In the end, the higher-cost IDA results were used in the report, with a comparison to the Program Office estimates included as an excursion.

At the time the study was conducted, 26 C-17s were under contract with long-lead funding. The US government would have incurred a cost penalty for breach of contract if it failed to buy 26 production C-17s. Thus alternatives that included less than 26 C-17s were levied an additional termination fee associated with breaking the contract (US$1.5 billion).

Lockheed Martin Aeronautical Systems provided cost estimates for the alternative of restarting the C-5 line as well as for refurbishing the C-141s in a C-141 SLEP. IDA used these and other historical Lockheed data and made adjustments as required. Examples of adjustments include adding hush kits to dampen the sound of the engines and adding extra material to the fuselage. The cost to restart the C-5 line was estimated at US$750 million. New C-5 engines were used to reduce noise levels below those mandated by the Federal Aviation Administration (FAA).

A recently completed Scientific Advisory Board (SAB) report had recommended that the weep hole cracks in then-current C-141s could be repaired and their life extended to 45,000 flying hours. When the C-141 reached its 45,000-flying-hour life limit, the SAB determined it had to be replaced, and the cost of a new C-Y replacement was imposed to include a US$3.5 billion development cost.

Boeing supplied basic cost data for the 747 and 767 commercial derivative aircraft alternatives. Production rates from 6 to 12 per year for military acquisition were used, based on Boeing production capabilities and competing markets for new 747 or 767 aircraft. An additional 20 percent of the acquisition price was added to account for reinforced floors and rollers and widened side doors, for an estimate of US$155 million for the militarized 747 and US$88 million for the militarized 767. Since the relevant production lines were already open, no developmental costs were imposed. Over the course of the study, these same commercial derivative aircraft also became known as "non-developmental airlift aircraft."

15.3.4.3 Operating and support

The primary tool used to estimate O&S costs was the USAF CORE model. This is the standard model used for O&S cost estimates in the cost community (AFI

Table 15.5 Summary of O&S costs per PAA

Aircraft	Number of flying hours per year	CORE cost estimates ($million/year/PAA)
C-17	1,427	10.8
C-5B or B+	660	9.49
C-5A	325	6.75
C-141 SLEP	1,178	7.72
747	900	8.08
767	900	4.98
KC-10A	550	4.62
C-130E/H	637	4.01

65-503 1994). Use of the model requires aircraft to be sorted according to whether they are in the active, associate or reserve fleets. It takes into account the number of flying hours per year, the cost of the fuel burned, the cost associated with personnel needed (crew, maintenance), software costs, training costs, the cost of spares, and the cost of contractor logistics support.

O&S cost estimates from the USAF CORE model for all the aircraft types are summarized in Table 15.5. The commercial derivative aircraft were assumed to have contractor logistics support, the cost of which was included in the cost estimates for alternatives containing commercial aircraft derivatives.

15.4 Initial cost and operational effectiveness results

This section summarizes the initial results presented to the Strategic Systems Committee (SSC) and to the DAB in August 1993, along with their reaction.[22] Throughout the early stages of the analyses, key decision-makers were periodically apprised of the methodology, inputs, and results. Frequent meetings were held between the study team and working levels representing the interested DoD organizations. AMC was in continuous contact, providing all the MASS/AFM computer runs with inputs provided from IDA. This is an essential part of any analysis, which is both a process and a product. Close communication allows the analyst to understand the critical issues as viewed by the various players and decision-makers, as well as to provide the decision-makers with an opportunity to help guide the analysis.

The initial cost and operational effectiveness results are summarized in Figure 15.4. These results were developed using cargo and equipment data specified in the airlift portion of the TPFDD files from the mobility requirements study that had been completed the year before.

15.4.1 Initial results

All 26 alternative fleets of aircraft under consideration are displayed in Figure 15.4 according to their effectiveness (tons of outsize cargo[23] delivered in a 30-day period) and cost (FY 1993 25-year discounted life-cycle cost). The numbers beside

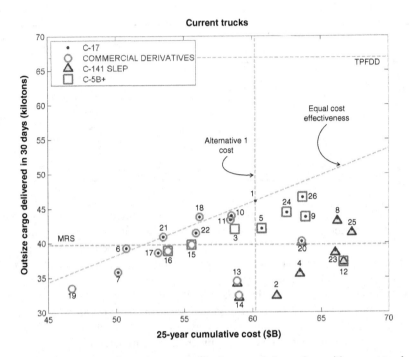

Figure 15.4 Comparison of cost and effectiveness of alternatives with current trucks.

each symbol identify the alternatives. To assist with visual interpretation, alternatives that contain any C-17s contain a small black dot; those with any C-5B+ have a square; those with any C-141 SLEP have a triangle; and those with commercial derivatives such as 747s or 767s have an open circle. For example, Alternative 1 with only a small black dot includes only C-17s (120 according to Table 15.2). In contrast, alternative 18 contains both C-17s and commercial derivatives (70 C-17s and 34 747s according to Table 15.2) as indicated by the dot inside the larger open circle.

For reference, the outsize cargo requirement of the 30-day scenario set by the MRS is shown as a horizontal dashed line. Any fleet alternatives below the line would require additional aircraft to satisfy this mission requirement. The vertical dashed line shows the cost of the 120-C-17 Alternative 1. Any fleet alternatives to the right have a higher cumulative cost than this fleet made up exclusively of C-17s. The sloping dashed line indicates a locus of alternatives that have the same cost-effectiveness as Alternative 1 (i.e. same "bang for the buck" or ratio of effectiveness to cost).[24]

This chart clarifies several things. First, the C-141 SLEP alternatives (i.e. the triangles) appear to be among the worst candidates relative to the C-17 fleet (Alternative 1), both from a cost and from an effectiveness perspective. To make them more effective by adding either C-141 aircraft or another aircraft that is part of the mix, additional costs would be incurred.[25] This seems to eliminate a whole category of alternatives immediately. Second, the fleet alternatives of C-17s combined with commercial derivatives (open circles with concentric black dots) appear to be close in cost-effectiveness. This catches our attention and elevates our consideration of militarized 747s and 767s. In particular, the 747 appears the better of the two commercial derivatives. Finally, the C-5B+ (squares) alternatives appear slightly less cost-effective in all their mixes than the C-17 mixes, but run a close second. They cannot easily be dismissed from this chart.

Based on these initial results, the DAB was impressed with the potential for using commercial derivatives such as the 747 at lower cost than the C-17 program. The study team was tasked with examining several excursions and reporting back as soon as possible. At the same time, C-17 proponents perceived the results as a threat to their program and reviewed the assumptions of the analyses in detail.

15.4.2 Changing assumptions: transportation of new army trucks

As often happens when unexpected results are presented, those most affected by the conclusion that commercial aircraft could be the most attractive alternatives began to search for flaws in the methodology and errors in the inputs. Hence they made a major discovery that seriously challenged the analysis to date. This discovery concerned the ability of commercial aircraft derivatives to transport new army trucks.

The preliminary analyses had assumed current (meaning circa 1993) army trucks (hence the subtitle in Figure 15.4 of "Current Trucks") were to be airlifted. Actually, the Army planned to replace their 2.5- and five-ton trucks with 10,843 new ones, members of the family of medium tactical vehicles (FMTV). Since trucks constituted a major component of the TPFDD, with thousands being airlifted to theater, the effect on the analyses could potentially be significant. These new trucks differed in two significant ways as far as air transportability is concerned: axel loads and truck height. Each is discussed next with its effect on transportability in the different alternatives.

The axel loads on some of the new trucks are much higher than those of the corresponding current trucks. These loads are so heavy, in fact, that a stronger reinforced floor would be needed on the militarized 747s to carry them. Thus additional costs for reinforcing commercial derivatives would be necessary if these trucks are to be carried. Since the CRAF 747s are not reinforced, they cannot carry any new trucks at all, thus reducing their utility in moving some of the oversize cargo.

Even more significant is truck height. There are two versions of the new trucks: one designed for airdrop or low-altitude extraction by parachute and the other for normal loading and unloading from a stationary airlifter. The difference is that the airdrop-capable versions have collapsible cab tops that permit them to be easily loaded through the nose of a 747; the others (the vast majority) have fixed non-removable cab tops whose heights prevent the trucks from entering through the nose door. The nose door height cannot be changed because the 747s nose space is needed for cockpit and crew and therefore limits door height. The side doors would be tall enough, but not wide enough (without alteration). The new FMTVs would, however, fit through the doors of C-17s, C-5s, C-141s, and KC-10s.

The study team investigated possible ways to address this impasse. First, the Army could spend an additional US$700 per truck to ensure that all trucks have collapsible cab tops. This would ensure that they fit on 747s. The Army objected, not just on the basis of cost, but also on operational utility. The Army deliberately chose non-collapsible cab tops for the next-generation trucks to afford greater protection in chemical environments. Thus this solution did not seem reasonable. Second, if the cab tops could not be changed, perhaps the 747 side doors could be widened. Boeing engineers estimated that the cost to widen the doors and provide additional roller reinforcements would be about US$10 million per aircraft. The materiel-handling equipment could raise the trucks to the appropriate height from the ground, and the trucks would have to maneuver with a sharp turn as they entered the fuselage. Thus, greater care in moving the trucks through the side doors would be needed, with some risk and longer loading times. This seemed technically possible, so it, along with the extra costs entailed, became the new commercial derivative design: wider side doors with additional roller and floor reinforcements.

The new trucks also affected CRAF. Civilian aircraft forced into service could not be expected to carry the new trucks because of their extra weight.

The results under the new assumptions are shown in Figure 15.5. The results assume either collapsible cab tops for the new trucks (FMTVs) or an extended side door for the Boeing 747.

Figure 15.5 is similar to Figure 15.4, except that it captures the fact that all alternatives will have lower delivery capabilities, since CRAF cannot carry the new army trucks.[26]

Figure 15.5 also contains a new alternative, Alternative 21a. This alternative was added after a second briefing to the DAB. At the DAB it was noted that, with only three additional 747s, Alternative 21 (with 47 C-17s and 49 747s) could be raised up to the MRS line and therefore meet the requirement and level the playing field.[27] With this, Alternatives 10 (with 94 C-17s), 18 (with 70 C-17s), and 21a (with 47 C-17s) could be seen as providing at least as much capability as demanded by the MRS, but at lower cost than Alternative 1 (the programmed fleet of 120 C-17s). This chart reinforces the notion that there are less costly alternatives to the C-17 program, most involving militarized commercial derivatives.

Some decision-makers wondered what the results would be if the new trucks could not be accommodated aboard militarized 747s. That was a fair question deserving an answer. Figure 15.6 summarizes results for that situation for a selected set of alternatives.

As Figure 15.6 clearly illustrates, the viability of the commercial derivatives is critically associated with the ability to load the Army's FMTV trucks onto the modified aircraft. Under these assumptions, the combined fleets of 747 and C-17 (Alternatives 10, 18, and 21) that earlier had cost-effectiveness ratios similar to Alternative 1 (made up exclusively of C-17s), no longer do so and even fall below

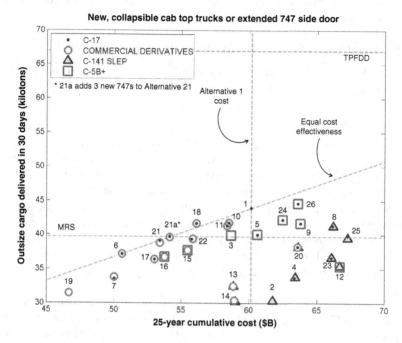

Figure 15.5 Comparison of cost and effectiveness of alternatives with new army FMTV trucks.

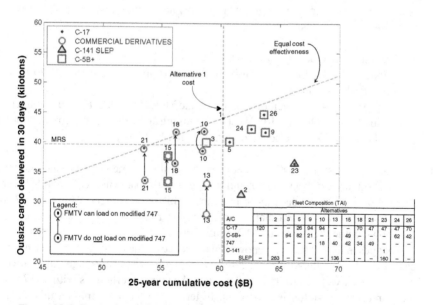

Figure 15.6 Comparison of selected alternatives with different assumptions about MTV loading on militarized 747.

the minimum effectiveness MRS scenario line. If commercial 747 derivatives cannot be loaded with new army trucks, then their effectiveness plummets.

15.5 Sensitivity analyses of other underlying assumptions

Additional analyses were conducted to gauge the sensitivity of the results to other assumptions. These are discussed here.

15.5.1 MOG and use

The analyses presented so far include specific assumptions about the space available at "en-route" and in-theater airbases and about utilization rates of aircraft. The space available for aircraft at airfields en route to a final destination is a function of the assumptions concerning other activities at those bases and in the theater and thus is subject to considerable uncertainty. The assumption regarding the utilization rates of aircraft depends on funding decisions and maintenance policies to provide specified levels of operational performance and could, in principle, be strategically altered. To gauge the sensitivity of the results to specific assumptions and data inputs, the study subjected both of these key assumptions to sensitivity analysis.

Although the values used in the study allowed for reasonably robust operating conditions, C-17 proponents cited less-than-ideal operating conditions as a key advantage of their aircraft. The C-17, with a MOG value close to that of the C-141, requires less space than the C-5 or 747. Since considerable subjectivity is inherent in the values used for any study, it seemed reasonable to explore how sensitive the results were to changes in this input. The study team thus considered the following three MOG conditions:

- robust, corresponding to the AMC values used in previous charts;
- moderate, with conditions in MRC-East that approximated the 1990 Desert Shield MOG values;
- constrained, which included the moderate MOG for MRC-East just noted and reduced the MOG in MRC-West by removing airfields near the conflict border and reducing MOG elsewhere in the theater by 50 percent.

In all cases, as the MOG was reduced, the ability of the C-17 to land and take off on short airfields, to back up, and to take up less space than C-5s and the commercial derivatives made it more favorable. This is illustrated in Figure 15.7 for five of the alternatives. For clarity, only the most robust and constrained extremes are shown while the moderate MOG case lies in between.

Changes in the MOG have a powerful influence on the results. In the constrained case, none of the alternatives meet the MRS requirements, although Alternative 1 with the most C-17s suffers less than the other fleet alternatives with C-17s and other, more space-intensive airlifters. In terms of systems thinking, this clearly points to the possibility of investing in adequate infrastructure to improve MOG as a new alternative that can be integrated with various combinations of aircraft.

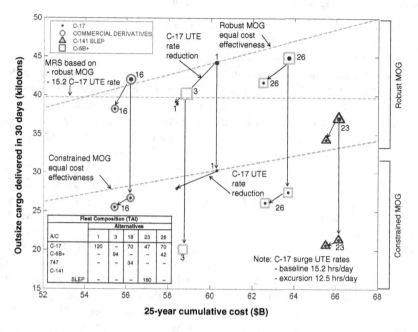

Figure 15.7 Impact of reduced MOG and reduced C-17 use rates.

It also cautions against assuming that lower cost alternatives always provide the best payoffs.

Another key assumption in the analysis was questioned by 747 proponents who objected to the assumption of higher C-17 use rates. The basic analyses assumed a 12.5-hour-per-day use rate for the 747s and a 15.2-hour-per-day rate for the C-17s under wartime surge conditions. The use rate attainable by the C-17 was still unproven when the study was conducted, so some doubted it would exceed that achievable by commercial aircraft.

Figure 15.7 also illustrates the effect of a smaller use rate for the C-17. The reduced use rate was assumed to be 12.5 hours/day—the same as the assumed use rates for the C-5B+ and the militarized commercial derivatives. The smaller use rate reduced effectiveness and also cost (because of fewer flying hours per year associated with such a lower use rate). The overall effect was noticeable but was not nearly as dramatic as that seen in the MOG assumption excursions. While it was reasonable for the study team to be skeptical about such a large projected use rate for an unfinished aircraft, deviations from that projection did not dramatically affect the cost-effectiveness measures for the C-17. Interestingly, subsequent tests two years after this original study validated the 15.2 hours/day value, rendering the arguments moot. Study teams, however, can never know these things in advance and are well served to look carefully at all key assumptions that could influence the results.

15.5.2   Assuming airlift capability other than 52 MTM/D

After the first DAB meeting in August 1993, there was a growing sense on the part of some decision-makers that commercial derivatives in conjunction with some number of C-17s might be the best solution. When the initial results were briefed to the DAB, additional airlift capability assumptions were requested. These cases were developed to determine how few C-17s might be acceptable if that program was reduced from the 120 aircraft originally assumed in Alternative 1.

IDA was asked to assess how well a number of new alternatives would fare. The result of one set of analyses is summarized in Figure 15.8. In this case, 10 new alternative fleets are introduced, with MTM/D values ranging from 46 up to 55. An attention to cost was also used to make virtually all the new alternatives no more costly than Alternative 1. Figure 15.8 illustrates cost and effectiveness measures for Alternative 1, various mixes of C-17s and commercial derivatives, and mixes of C-17s and C-5B+s. Since by the time the DAB was expected to reach its decision it was expected that 40 C-17s would already be delivered or under construction, many of the new alternatives included 40 C-17s, and none involves fewer than that number. As Figure 15.8 shows, the set of mixes of C-17s with commercial derivatives is roughly equal in cost-effectiveness to Alternative 1 with exclusively C-17s. Moreover, for roughly the same budget, the commercial and C-17 fleet mixes are well above the effectiveness of the C-17 and C-5B+ mixes.[28] This chart confirmed the sense derived from earlier charts that a mixed fleet of C-17s and commercial derivatives might have merit—provided they could carry the new army trucks.

Some decision-makers felt that a fleet size capable of generating a transportation capability of 52 MTM/D was too small. After all, the C-17 program had been born when the requirement was 66 MTM/D. As previous charts have shown, all alternatives fell significantly below the effectiveness demanded by the TPFDD line. Thus IDA was subsequently asked to examine the possibility of alternatives that generated higher MTM/D. Figure 15.9 summarizes the results of two different sets of alternatives: those with 52 MTM/D and those with 59 MTM/D, a value with historical roots when new airlift programs were initiated several years prior to this study period. The 59 MTM/D alternatives are all identified with the prefix "E" on the chart. It is interesting that the same frontier line observed earlier still carries over to these higher MTM/D cases. Namely, all alternatives fall on or below the equal cost-effectiveness ratio line that runs through Alternative 1, within statistical uncertainty.[29]

15.5.3   Another scenario: LRC-short

The foregoing analyses assumed two different MRCs. There may be a need, however, for forces to meet LRCs. The one selected for analysis was LRC-Short, involving sustained airlift to a relatively close theater (short range, hence the name Short), following an airdrop on Day 1. The baseline assumption is that all major airbases are seized by the airdropped troops and are available for operations. Since the MRC cases showed MOG to be a critical input, the study also examined an excursion in which 50 percent of these same airbases are unavailable.

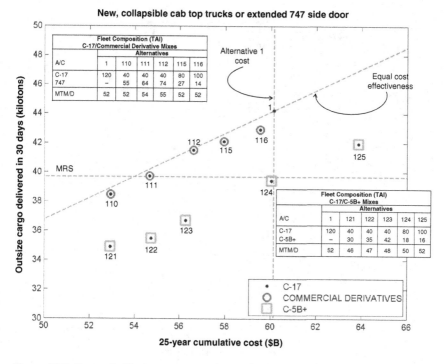

Figure 15.8 Cost and effectiveness comparisons of new alternatives.

Figure 15.10 summarizes the results for LRC-Short. In this case, the effectiveness measure is the total cargo delivered (not just outsize) in eight days after the initial first-day airdrop. The 25-year total cost is the same as before. The four-day TPFDD is used for purposes of comparison, although it has not been achieved even in eight days by any alternative.

A comparison of the amount of cargo delivered for robust (baseline) MOG conditions and for a 50 percent loss in airfields shows the same general results that appeared before in the case of the MRC scenarios: alternatives with fleets with C-5s and 747s suffering a greater reduction in capability than those with C-17s when MOG is constrained. Those with the C-5B+ seem to suffer the greatest reductions.

15.5.4 *Cost excursions*

All the sensitivity analysis excursions discussed to this point principally focused on different effectiveness assumptions including scenarios, use rates, MOG, and the composition of alternative fleets of aircraft. The cost estimates included in the study represented the best forecasts generated by the cost team. While there are many uncertainties in the cost estimates, one that became obvious to the DAB was the yearly acquisition cost assumptions for each of the alternatives.

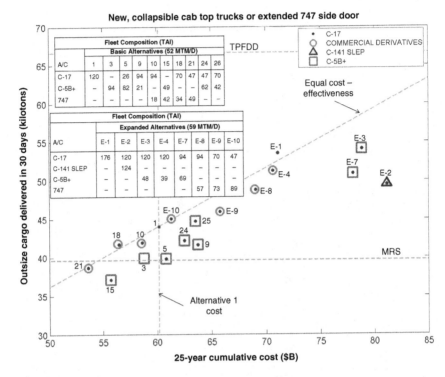

Figure 15.9 Comparison of 59 MTM/D expanded capacity alternatives with the nominal 52 MTM/D alternatives.

In the cost estimates shown earlier, each alternative was developed estimating the costs of efficient production-lines, independent of annual budgets. A more realistic approach would be to constrain all annual expenses over the six-year period of the Future Years Defense Program (FYDP) to be no greater than those associated with the C-17 program itself, as expressed in the then-current C-17 Selected Acquisition Report (SAR). This would force many of the alternatives analyzed to stretch their acquisition profiles to remain under the spending cap.[30] To test how stretching out programs and the concomitant increases in acquisition costs would influence the outcome of the analyses, a sensitivity analysis was conducted. The results for selected fleet alternatives appear in Figure 15.11.

As Figure 15.11 shows, fleet alternatives with mixes of C-17 and commercial derivatives all show increases in total cost of US$1–2 billion. The cost of Alternative 1 also increases slightly, since the cost team did not feel that the full 120 C-17 program could stay within the cost caps of the C-17 acquisition budget. The C-5B+ fleet alternatives do not increase in cost in this excursion, since the start-up time for the new C-5 line takes several years and removes it from competition with other aircraft types in those alternatives. As the figure shows, even

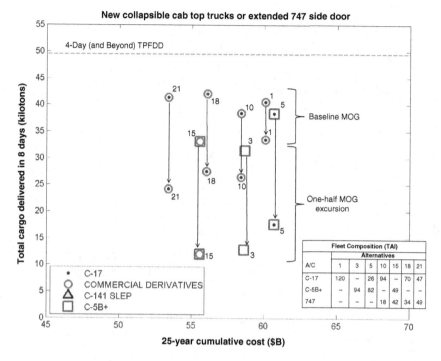

Figure 15.10 Comparisons of alternatives in LRC-Short.

though total lifetime costs do increase if the SAR serves to limit near-term funding, the C-17/commercial-derivatives fleets still dominate the cost-effectiveness comparisons.

The relative contribution from the different cost elements can be seen in Figure 15.12. Figure 15.12 also illustrates the effect of different discounting assumptions on the cost estimates. Two of the alternatives are compared in Figure 15.12: Alternative 1 with 120 C-17s, and Alternative 2 with no C-17s but with 263 C-141 SLEP/C-Ys instead. Figure 15.12 also illustrates the effect of discounting through two examples: no discounting and the baseline OMB-directed 4.5 percent discounting. Note that the large effect of O&S costs that accrue over the 25-year life-cycle cost period for all alternatives. Discounting emphasizes near-term costs, which has a bigger effect (reduction) on long-term O&S cost estimates than on near-term acquisition cost estimates.

15.6 Reported findings

The C-17 Cost–Benefit Analysis (i.e. COEA) reported the following findings, briefed to the DAB in November 1993. The findings incorporated several items reported in earlier briefings and added the sensitivity analysis excursions discussed in the previous section.

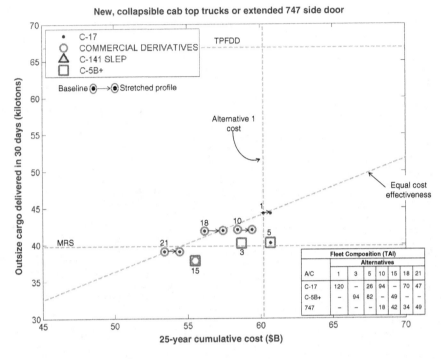

Figure 15.11 Effect of FYDP stretch-out on alternatives in MRC.

- The cost and performance of the planned C-17 fleet alternative (#1) make it the preferred military airlifter. It is more resistant to airfield constraints (i.e. MOG) than the new C-5 and possesses a higher use rate. It is far superior in both cost and effectiveness to the C-141 SLEP.
- The next most attractive alternatives after the 120 C-17s would be mixed fleets of C-17s and modified commercial aircraft with specially reinforced floors and some concession for the height of new FMTV army trucks, such as wider side doors.
- If new army trucks cannot be loaded on commercial derivatives, then the next most attractive alternatives to the 120 C-17 program would be mixes of C-17s and new C-5s.

A mixed fleet of commercial derivatives and some number of C-17s (less than 120) became a serious contender to Alternative 1, the original/baseline 120 C-17 fleet, reducing the total cost of the program. The study did caution that overall effectiveness could be compromised. The introduction of 747s would provide fewer aircraft for certain unique military operations such as airdrops, deliveries to remote and inadequate airfields, low-altitude parachute extractions, and rapid off-loading of cargo while the airlifter is still moving down the runway (combat

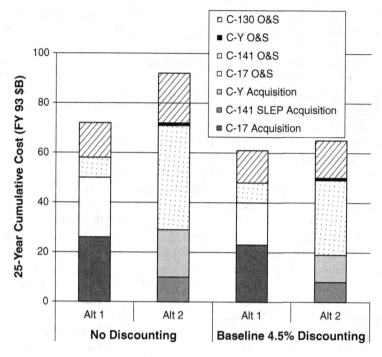

Figure 15.12 Effect of discount rates on two alternatives.

off-loading) with engines running. It also provided a fleet less well able to adapt to limited MOG conditions. Nonetheless, its lower cost recommended it for more detailed consideration.

15.7 The rest of the story: *ex-post* decisions subsequent to the analysis

15.7.1 Decisions 1994–1995

The decision ultimately reached by the DAB in January 1994 was to place a cap on C-17 production at the 40 already under development and to establish a non-developmental airlift aircraft (NDAA) program to investigate the feasibility of acquiring and operating militarized commercial derivatives in lieu of C-17s. The analyses presented in the IDA study had a major impact on this decision. After the results of the NDAA study became available, a new decision would be made. The DoD also reached a financial settlement in 1994 with the C-17 manufacturer McDonnell Douglas over past claims, setting the stage for a clean slate and new decisions.

From February through May of 1994, the IDA analysts responsible for the study briefed congressional staffers and the Government Accountability Office (GAO).

In its report that same year (US GAO 1994), the GAO favored the acquisition of 40 C-17s and 64 747s over the 120 C-17 case. In May 1994, the DoD formally released the IDA report to Congress in response to the initial congressional request for such a study.

In 1995, many events converged that influenced the ultimate decision. In January of that year, the C-17 reached its initial operational capability (IOC). It subsequently underwent formal reliability, maintainability, and availability (RM&A) testing in July, achieving the performance needed to support a 15.2 hours/year use rate. During the same year, the AMC initiated, per OSD guidance, a study of NDAA options called the Strategic Airlift Force Mix Analysis (SAFMA) USAF Air Mobility Command (1995). The aim of that study was to determine the minimum number of C-17s acceptable and to provide industry with an opportunity to make proposals for NDAA competitors to the C-17. The RFPs was released in March. Meantime, also in March, the Joint Staff and OSD released a new mobility requirements study to replace the older MRS used in the IDA C-17 Cost-Benefit Analysis (COEA) report. The new study was titled the Mobility Requirements Study Bottom Up Review Update (MRS BURU) OSD (1995) and established new cargo and troop lift requirements for the MRCs. This study provided the new delivery requirements for the SAFMA. SAFMA used essentially the same MASS model (updated) that IDA used two years earlier.

AMC conducted the SAFMA using fleet mixes of C-17s and Boeing 747s, the only contractor-proposed alternative. Data from the C-17 RM&A as well as new lower price estimates from McDonnell Douglas for the C-17 were available. IDA played an auxiliary role in this process, providing an independent validation of the models and approaches taken, although the actual analyses were conducted by AMC as part of a proprietary source selection process.

In November 1995, the results of the RM&A and the SAFMA were presented to the DAB. At this meeting, it was decided to proceed with the 120 C-17 program and not acquire any militarized 747s.

Thus, in a lengthy set of decisions, OSD arrived back at the position it started from two years before: buy 120 C-17s. Something very significant, however, had happened in the interim: the introduction of competition had compelled the C-17 manufacturer to reduce costs and improve performance in order to prevail. By revealing feasible alternatives, the IDA cost-effectiveness study contributed to the creation of what economists call a "contestable market" (Baumol *et al.* 1983, 492–496). The threat of the entry of new competitors was sufficient to reveal efficiencies that reduced aircraft costs. The new restructured C-17 program was several billion dollars lower in total cost than the older one, a significant savings for the government and its taxpayers.

15.7.2   Decisions post-1995

The C-17 program has prospered since the days of these early analyses. It has grown to nearly twice the size of the program discussed here and is now larger than the size of the original fleet envisioned in 1983 of 210 aircraft. Table 15.6

Table 15.6 Summary of C-17 acquisition decisions through FY 2010

Year	C-17 acquisition decisions	Results
2002	60 additional C-17s bought	Total 180
2005	OSD *Mobility Capabilities Study* (OSD 2005) shows no additional C-17s beyond 180 are needed.	–
2007	10 additional C-17s bought	Total 190
2008	15 additional C-17s bought	Total 205
2009	IDA study on size and mix of airlift force (Greer *et al.* 2009) shows no additional C-17s beyond 205 are needed.	–
2009	SecDef declares that no more C-17s are needed.	–
2009	8 additional C-17s bought	Total 213
2010	OSD/USTRANSCOM *Mobility Capabilities & Requirements Study* (OSD 2010) shows no additional C-17s beyond 213 are needed	–
2010	10 additional C-17s to be bought (production through 2013)	Total 223
2010	*Quadrennial Defense Review* (OSD QDR 2010) indicates that no more C-17s are needed	–
2010	Subcommittee of Senate Homeland Security & Governmental Affairs hearings (US Senate Hearing 2010) on C-17 requirements, also affirmed that no additional C-17s are needed	–
2011–14	No additional C-17s in budget	–

reports subsequent decisions made to augment the C-17 fleet from the original 120 aircraft to 223.

The impetus for adding C-17s beyond the 120 initially approved came after the attacks on September 11, 2001, and the decision to strike back at al-Qaeda and the Taliban in Afghanistan. Airfield limitations in Afghanistan and Iraq supported the case for additional C-17s that could more easily operate in austere environments.

Additional studies have continued to the present time, all addressing the issue of how many C-17s (and other airlift aircraft) are needed. Table 15.6 summarizes the conclusions reached in those studies. The programmed number in 2011 is 223 C-17s.

15.8 Lessons learned

Many lessons can be learned from this study. A selection is presented below as the conclusion of this chapter.

15.8.1 The importance of an open process to combat special interests

The results were certain to be controversial to some interested parties, so it was necessary to maintain credibility and impartiality. The C-17 COEA benefited from a continuously open process, with frequent feedback and critical commentary as the study developed. The analysts were able to maintain their independence and objectivity throughout but made their results available to others as the study evolved. In this way, all parties had an opportunity to see how the results were evolving and to recommend alternative approaches, inputs, and/or sensitivities.

15.8.2   *The value of analysis in promoting competition*

The emergence of viable competitors to the C-17 and the willingness of decision-makers to honestly consider these alternatives created positive incentives for the C-17 manufacturers to meet and exceed their cost and performance objectives. Even though in the end DoD did not select the 747, its presence, looming as an alternative on the horizon, appears to have had a salutary effect on the C-17 program and the airlift capabilities of DoD. While this cannot be proven unequiv-ocally, most observers of the decision process feel that the analysis encouraged implicit competition that may have saved the government billions of dollars.

15.8.3   *The power of sensitivity analysis and other excursions*

Every piece of data and every assumption in the analysis needs to be scrutinized to understand its effect on the conclusions. The problem must be clearly structured up front and reviewed as the analysis proceeds from an independent and broader systems perspective to avoid overlooking important factors. Future army trucks having trouble fitting in 747s is a good example. Total systems' thinking is key. It is easy for analysts to become focused on the particular program—buy C-17s—while the effect of other programs that could have a profound effect—new rigid top trucks—are overlooked.

Another example is MOG. The infrastructure investments needed to improve airfield airlift capability could overwhelm the cost of the aircraft themselves. In fact an important tradeoff exists between improving airfields and lower aircraft costs or improving aircraft so they can operate in more constrained airfields. These insights and the importance of changes in assumptions and input values can only be determined by a robust set of alternatives and sensitivity analysis excursions. Not all of these can be foreseen at the start of a study, but ensuring time and resources are included in the overall study plan to conduct sensitivity analyses can have powerful payoffs.

Appendix 15.1: Additional details on loading and transportation models and acquisition costs

The main models used for estimating how much cargo and how many passengers were delivered were ALM, MASS/AFM, and ACAS. These models are summa-rized briefly to give a sense of the assumptions used in the analysis. As noted earlier, these models have subsequently evolved to more advanced versions, but it is important to know how the transportation problem was approached in 1993.

Airlift loading model

The ALM was used to determine the average cargo payload carried by each aircraft in the fleet. The MASS/AFM then used this result to simulate the transport. ALM used cargo from the entire TPFDD for these estimates. The cargo was differentiated according to 26 different categories called "commodities." Each commodity could contain vehicles, pallets, and passengers. Examples include Air Force aircraft, Air Force support, Marine prepositioning, armored infantry, mechanized infantry, Combat Service Support (CSS), engineer, CSS medical, and ammunition. Pallets were of a common size and weight, but weight and dimensions differentiated the vehicles from one another. The sequence in which the aircraft were to be loaded had to be specified, as well as aircraft cargo storage dimensions, cargo door opening sizes, number of passenger seats, and maximum payload allowable by weight. The ALM then used user-selected rules for loading the aircraft (e.g. vehicles were sorted according to width, with the widest loaded first and pallets last for a given commodity code). Loading stopped when the weight limit was reached or, more commonly, when cargo fully filled the cargo space in the aircraft. Most airlifters reached volume constraints before they reached weight constraints, as they do in real life. From these simulations, the analysts calculated the average payload carried by each aircraft type, detailed by commodity type and by the cargo classes of out/over/bulk/PAX.

While ALM does an excellent job of estimating optimum average cargo loads, these loads are rarely achieved in actual operations. Differences in actual units—in the way cargo arrives at a port of debarkation and in the proficiency of the cargo loaders—often results in actual loads falling slightly below those predicted by the model. These inefficiencies can sometimes be noted during real exercises and operations. By establishing community agreement at the outset on the use of the same methodology for all aircraft, the study treated each alternative in a consistent manner.

MASS/AFM

The MASS/AFM was a large Monte Carlo simulation[31] that scheduled and executed each airlift mission by tail number. It incorporated a great deal of realism, such as specific routes used, airbases with MOG limitations, times for loading and off-loading, and crew duty days. It used the ALM loading results along with the nature of the TPFDD cargo and PAX at individual airbases to load the cargo. Only that part of the TPFDD available at a specific base on a specific day (plus any undelivered leftover cargo from previous days) was available for loading. User-selected priorities for loading out/over/bulk/PAX classes were considered for each airlifter. The AMC analysts ran the simulations at Scott AFB with inputs from IDA. The primary outputs for the study were tons delivered per day by commodity type and class (out/over/bulk/PAX).

As with ALM, MASS/AFM may produce results that would be viewed as optimistic in real operations. For example, the inefficiencies that often exist with high levels of congestion at en-route bases are not included (although MOG does limit the number of aircraft being serviced at the base). Again, the decision-makers and study team need to make reasonable assumptions and focus on the higher objectives of the study. If an assumption appears to have the potential for making a large impact on the results, sensitivity analysis may be required.

Airlift cycle analysis spreadsheet

The ACAS model was a simplified approximation to the analyses produced by MASS/AFM and was used to conduct the large number of excursions needed in the study. It used aggregate data and aggregate MOG values, calibrated against MASS/AFM to give confidence, for these numerous excursions.

Acquisition costs

The study used the Air Force C-17 procurement schedule, with a maximum acquisition of 16 per year. It also used multi-year procurement arrangements to reduce uncertainty and cost. From the historical cost data for the C-17, IDA derived a cost-learning curve to predict future costs for C-17s as more manufacturing experience is attained. This stage was a delicate one, requiring the cooperation of McDonnell Douglas to supply competition-sensitive information with the understanding that only aggregate levels of detail would appear in the final report. Publishing a second proprietary document for use by the government, while using the aggregate results in the COEA, attained the desired balance between a need for discussion of the methodology and a display of the aggregate results and the need to protect the legitimate interests of the source. Appropriate adjustments to historical trends were added as needed, such as the cost for extra weight to strengthen the wings and higher costs associated with more realistic engine estimates for all lots after the first ones. During the study, the C-17 Program Office disagreed strongly with the IDA estimates. The basic disagreement arose from different assumptions about the learning curves. IDA used data for the entire C-17 program, adjusting the first few low-cost lots for their later prices while the Program Office used later prices only. IDA estimated the full C-17 program acquisition cost at approximately US$23 billion, about US$3 billion over the Program Office estimate. In the end, the higher-cost IDA results were used in the report, with a comparison to the Program Office estimates included as an excursion.

At the time the study was conducted, three test C-17s (not counted as part of the 120) had been produced, an additional six production aircraft were undergoing operational test and evaluation (OT&E), and a total of 17 production aircraft had either been delivered or were in various stages of assembly at the Long Beach McDonnell Douglas facility. Moreover, aircraft through production number 26 were under contract with long-lead funding. Failing to buy 26 production C-17s would have incurred a cost penalty by the US government for a breach of contract. Thus alternatives with fewer than 26 C-17s were levied an additional cost associated with breaking the contract (US$1.5 billion).

Lockheed Martin Aeronautical Systems provided cost estimates for restarting the C-5 line as well as for refurbishing the C-141s in a C-141 SLEP. Again, only aggregate data appeared in the final report, with company-sensitive data relegated to the proprietary government-use document. IDA used these data and other historical Lockheed data and made adjustments as required. Examples of adjustments include adding hush kits to dampen the sound of the engines and extra material to the fuselage. A recently completed SAB had recommended that the weep hole cracks in then-current C-141s could be repaired and their life extended to 45,000 flying hours. When the C-141 reached its 45,000-flying-hour life limit, the SAB determined it had to be replaced, and the cost of a new C-Y replacement was imposed to include a US$3.5 billion development cost.

For the C-5 restart, a cost to restart the line was imposed on any alternatives using C-5B+ aircraft. IDA estimated that US$750 million would be needed to restart the line in Marietta, Georgia. New C-5 engines were used to reduce noise levels below those mandated by the FAA.

Boeing supplied basic cost data for the 747 and 767 commercial derivative aircraft. Production rates from six to 12 per year for military acquisition were used, based on Boeing production capabilities and competing markets for new 747 or 767 aircraft. An additional 20 percent of the acquisition price was added to account for reinforced floors and rollers and widened side doors, for an estimate of US$155 million for the militarized 747 and US$88 million for the militarized 767. Since these lines are open, no developmental costs were imposed.

Notes

1 McDonnell Douglas was subsequently merged with the Boeing Company in 1997.
2 Bulk cargo is carried on standard USAF 463L pallets and is transportable by all airlifters. A pallet holds bulk cargo measuring no more than $104'' \times 84'' \times 96''$. Oversize cargo is larger than the pallet dimensions and consists typically of wheeled vehicles. Oversize cargo is larger than a single pallet but less than $1,090'' \times 117'' \times 105''$. All oversize cargo can fit on a C-141 (or larger aircraft). Outsize cargo is the largest of these three, fitting only on C-5s and C-17s.
3 The use of a detailed model (i.e. MASS) along with a more aggregate one (i.e. ACAS) is a common approach that balances study resources and time with precision in results. Calibration of ACAS to specific MASS results allowed ACAS to be used in rapid sensitivity excursion analyses. Comparisons of ACAS runs with MASS runs for these same sensitivity excursions showed no loss in precision for using the significantly faster ACAS.
4 Costs also addressed contract claims that McDonnell Douglas had made as well as penalty charges associated with terminating the C-17 line short of then-contracted production levels.
5 In 2010, a total of 111 C-5s were in the USAF inventory. Of these, 49 were C-5Bs.
6 Block speed is the distance flown by an aircraft divided by the time spent once blocks are removed from the aircraft wheels and it taxies down the runway until it lands and comes to a complete stop with blocks again in place.
7 Bulk cargo would be no problem in the commercial non-militarized version, since that is what CRAF carries. The nature of the militarization would be to strengthen the floors to handle higher pressure points (such as under the wheels of fully loaded five-ton trucks) and possibly to modify the doors to permit wider cargo or equipment to be loaded from the side.
8 A considerable number of additional alternatives were added later in the study, not all of which had a capacity of 52 MTM/D, but these were introduced after the more powerful comparison displays (to be shown later) were developed. At that point, equal MTM/D became an interesting but marginally useful criterion. Actual performance in realistic scenarios became the more important gauge. To start the analyses, IDA first focused on these 26 equal-MTM/D alternatives.

9 The TAI entries indicate how many new aircraft are to be procured: The PAA values are the numbers available to deliver cargo and troops in the scenarios studied and the numbers used in O&S costing estimates.

10 Today the acronym MRC has been replaced by MCO (Major Combat Operation) and CC (Conventional Campaign), but the meaning is equivalent. Here, we will use the MRC notation used in the original 1993 study.

11 MRC-East refers to a theater in Southwest Asia, supported mainly by flights out of East Coast US bases. Similarly, MRC-West refers to a theater in the Western Pacific with deployments from the western US airbases. It was assumed that CRAF Stage II would be authorized at the onset of MRC-East, with Stage III activated when MRC-West deployments began.

12 Today, LRC has been replaced by IW (Irregular Warfare) or a vignette from the SSSP, the Steady State Security Posture collection of lower intensity conflicts.

13 This assumption is further supported by the heavy demand for tankers to support fighter deployments to the MRC theaters as well as the potential for supporting combat aircraft employment during and following deployment.

14 The use rate is the average number of hours per day that an aircraft flies. Its estimate depends on the amount of time it spends on the ground which, in turn, involves the mission capable rate, which is a measure of reliability. It is used in the models to place an upper limit on the amount of time an aircraft flies.

15 The MOG-value of each airbase is specified by aircraft type and is determined by the material handling equipment (MHE) available, fuel availability, and the number of service positions allotted to airlift (in-theater bases are often mostly occupied by fighter aircraft). Large aircraft may require more than one service position.

16 It suffices to show the difference in the number of spaces available for small airlifters as contrasted with larger ones. Detailed databases at the appropriate classification are maintained by AMC.

17 MOG was usually the most constraining at en-route bases. En-route MOG constraints may cause longer, less efficient routes to be used.

18 These models have subsequently evolved to more advanced versions, but it is important to know how the transportation problem was approached in 1993.

19 MASS/AFM has now been replaced at AMC by the Air Mobility Operations Model (AMOS).

20 The Office of Management and Budget (OMB) changes the discount factor every year (US OMB 1992). For cost-effectiveness analyses of Federal programs, OMB mandates the use of discounted dollars.

21 All costs prior to FY 1994 were considered "sunk" and ignored. Only future expenditures were considered.

22 The SSC provided a review of the study prior to presentation to the higher-level DAB. All offices represented in the DAB had representatives in the SSC.

23 As noted earlier in Figure 15.2, virtually all the required outsize cargo must be delivered within a 30-day time period. This category of cargo differentiates best among the alternatives because of its criticality to the early stages of battle. Excursions (not shown here) at 20 days showed no new insights, so 30-day deliveries were displayed in the study.

24 As discussed elsewhere in this book, using cost-effectiveness ratios to evaluate alternatives is generally not appropriate and can in fact be very misleading without a budget constraint or fixed level of effectiveness.

25 These are examples of the modified budget approach and the modified effectiveness approach for cost-effectiveness comparisons in which neither cost nor effectiveness are initially constrained to be equal for all alternatives. These are described by Francois Melese (Melese 2010, 40–45).

26 The reader may wonder how oversize cargo such as trucks can influence the rate of delivery of outsize cargo. The interaction is complex, involving a competition for space

aboard aircraft that does carry outsize (i.e. C-17s and C-5s) and between outsize cargo and oversize cargo. If no oversize trucks can be carried by CRAF, those same trucks begin to crowd out any outsize cargo that C-17s and C-5s would have otherwise carried, reducing their outsize delivery capability.

27 This is an example of the modified effectiveness ("level the playing field") approach described by F. Melese in Chapter 4 of this book.

28 This is an example of the fixed budget approach described by Francois Melese (2010, 33–35).

29 The use of cost-effectiveness ratios can be misleading unless the analyses are constructed under the same budget or same effectiveness frameworks (Melese 2010, 17–20). In this case, the use of a common effectiveness framework, i.e. same MTM/D confers meaning.

30 Note that the economic evaluation of alternatives (EEoA) approaches introduced in Chapter 4 of this book make a clear distinction between the "life-cycle costs" or "price" of an alternative, its operational effectiveness (schedule and performance), and the resources (funding or budget) likely to be available for the overall program.

31 MASS/AFM has now been replaced at AMC by the Air Mobility Operations Model (AMOS).

References

Baumol, W. J., J. C. Panzar, and R. D. Willig. 1983. "Contestable Markets: An Uprising in the Theory of Industry Structure: Reply." *American Economic Review* 73(3): 492–496.

Bexfield, J. M., T. A. Allen, and W. L. Greer. September 2001. *C-17 COEA Case Study* (IDA Document D-2688). Alexandria, VA: Institute for Defense Analyses.

Greer, W. L., J. N. Bexfield, J. R. Nelson, D. A. Arthur, P. B. Buck, W. C. Devers, J. L. Freeh, B. R. Harmon, D. Y. Lo, H. J. Manetti, A. Salemo, J. A. Schwartz, J. W. Stahl, V. Suchorebrow, and D. M. Utech. December 1993. *Cost and Operational Effectiveness Analysis of the C-17 Program* (IDA Report R-390). Alexandria, VA: Institute for Defense Analyses.

Greer, W. L. *et al.* February 2009. (U) *Study on Size and Mix of Airlift Force* (IDA Paper P-4425) (Classified study). Alexandria, VA: Institute for Defense Analyses. (Subject is SECET//NOFORN.)

Joint Staff J4 Logistics. 1992. *(U) Mobility Requirements Study* (Classified study). Washington, DC: Joint Staff J4.

Melese, F. January 4, 2010. *The Economic Evaluation of Alternatives (EEoA)* (NPS-GSBPP-10-002). Monterey, CA: Naval Postgraduate School.

Office of the Secretary of Defense (OSD). 1995. *(U) Mobility Requirements Study Bottom Up Review Update* (Classified study). Washington, DC: OSD.

Office of the Secretary of Defense (OSD). 2010. *Quadrennial Defense Review Report*. Washington, DC: OSD. Available at www.defense.gov/qdr/qdr%20as%20of%2029jan10%201600.pdf [last accessed July 23, 2014].

——. 2005. *(U) Mobility Capabilities Study* (Classified study). Washington, DC: OSD.

——. 2010. *(U) Mobility Capabilities and Requirements Study – 2016* (Classified study). Washington, DC: OSD.

Secretary of the Air Force. February 4, 1994. *US Air Force Cost and Planning Factors* (AF Instruction 65-503). Washington, DC: Secretary of the Air Force.

——. December 2003. *Air Mobility Planning Factors* (Air Force Pamphlet 10-1403). Scott Air Force Base, IL: USAF Air Mobility Command. (December 2003 is the most recent version of AFPAM 10-1403).

US Congressional Budget Office (CBO). October 2007. *Issues Regarding the Current and Future Use of the Civil Reserve Air Fleet*. Washington, DC: US CBO.

US Government Accountability Office (GAO). July 11, 1994. *Airlift Requirements: Commercial Freighters Can Help Meet Requirements at Greatly Reduced Costs* (GAO/NSIAD 94-209). Washington, DC: US GAO. Available at www.gpo.gov/fdsys/pkg/GAOREPORTS-NSIAD-94-209/content-detail.html [last accessed July 22, 2014].

US Office of Management and Budget (OMB). October 29, 1992. *Guidelines and Discount Rates for Benefit-Cost Analysis of Federal Programs* (OMB Circular No. A-94) (Revised annually). Washington, DC: OMB. Available at www.whitehouse.gov/omb/circulars_default [last accessed July 22, 2014].

USAF Air Mobility Command (USAF). 1995. *(U) Strategic Airlift Force Mix Analysis* (Classified study). Scott Air Force Base, IL: USAF Air Mobility Command.

US Senate Homeland Security and Governmental Affairs; Subcommittee on Federal Financial Management, Government Information, Federal Services, and International Security. July 13, 2010. *Hearing on the Cost-Effectiveness of Procuring Weapon Systems in Excess of Requirements*. Statement by Dr. William L. Greer, Assistant Director, System Evaluation Division, Institute for Defense Analyses, Alexandria, VA.

16 Cost-effectiveness analysis of autonomous aerial platforms and communication payloads

Randall E. Everly, David C. Limmer, and Cameron A. MacKenzie

16.1 Introduction

This chapter demonstrates the use of multi-criteria decision-making techniques (discussed in Chapter 8) to analyze the cost-effectiveness of autonomous aerial platforms and communication payloads for communication missions in the military. We compare the cost-effectiveness of 17 aerial platforms and 9 communication payloads across three mission scenarios.

Unmanned aerial vehicles (UAVs) can help to supply the information technology connectivity that is increasingly being demanded by technology advancements on the battlefield. Autonomous vehicles are well suited for the communication mission, which is often mundane and tedious. The advent of lightweight construction materials, high energy-density lithium battery technology, and more efficient microprocessors increase UAV capability (Department of Defense 2013). The larger payload capacities and longer endurance of modern UAVs combined with communication payloads that are more capable and efficient and weigh less make them more suitable to the communications relay role than their predecessors. UAVs are also more flexible than more permanent infrastructure such as relay and cellular towers, and they can be quickly repositioned to support warfighters on the move.

Scrutiny on discretionary spending in public budgets, including defense budgets, will continue to increase in many countries. Future acquisitions will need to be executed thoughtfully with a clear consideration of the value and cost. Although other studies (see Ferguson and Harbold 2001; Collier and Kacala 2008) have analyzed the costs and benefits of UAVs for different missions, no study has undertaken an extensive cost-effectiveness of the most modern UAVs and other aerial platforms that can support communication requirements for military operations in austere environments. This chapter seeks to remedy that deficiency by performing a cost-effectiveness analysis of aerial platforms and communication payloads for use as a communication relay in support of distributed military operations.

We conduct a multi-objective analysis of alternatives to compare the cost-effectiveness of selected aerial platforms and communication payloads across three scenarios. This chapter considers 13 different UAVs, 4 alternative aerial platforms, and 9 communication payloads suitable for the communication relay mission. UAVs range in size from the hand-launched Raven to the Triton with its 130-foot wingspan, and communication payloads vary in weight from less than a pound to over 250 pounds. We follow the approach detailed in Chapter 8 to analyze the cost-effectiveness of these alternatives. An objectives hierarchy lists the desirable attributes for aerial platforms and communication systems, and value measures and tradeoff weights lead to a numerical measure of effectiveness (MoE). The annualized life-cycle costs (LCC) are estimated for the aerial platforms, and acquisition costs are calculated for the communication payloads. Selecting the most cost-effective alternative involves consideration of the costs and MoEs. After selecting the most cost-effective aerial platforms and communication payloads for a specified scenario, we discuss whether the selected aerial platforms are compatible with the communication payloads.

Section 16.2 reviews a few applications of cost-effectiveness analysis in defense and discusses previous studies of UAV effectiveness. We briefly outline in Section 16.3 the different UAVs, alternative aerial platforms, and communication payloads. Section 16.4 discusses the cost-effectiveness model. An objectives hierarchy is presented for the aerial platform and for the communication payload in Section 16.5. After detailing the methodology for estimating costs for the aerial platforms in Section 16.6, we analyze the cost-effectiveness of all the alternatives for three different scenarios in Section 16.7, and offer concluding thoughts in Section 16.8. We rely on subject matter experts to collect and analyze data for several alternatives, and develop value measures and tradeoff weights based on our own research, expertise, and experiences. Consequently, the results should not be viewed as definitive, but the analysis does provide insights into selecting the best aerial platform for different communication relay missions. Defense decision-makers could incorporate their own preferences within this framework to determine the most cost-effective aerial platform and communication payload for a given scenario.

16.2   Literature review

Cost-effectiveness analysis seeks to evaluate costs versus the benefits of an alternative when the benefits cannot easily be measured in monetary units. The MoE can be a single numerical measure of performance if only one objective determines the effectiveness for a decision problem. Frequently, decision-makers have multiple objectives, and combining several objectives into a single MoE requires a systematic process or mathematical equation. Value-focused thinking encourages decision-makers to articulate their values and identify and structure their objectives (Keeney 1996). Multi-objective or multi-criteria decision-making provides a framework for developing value measures over those objectives and tradeoff weights among objectives in order to combine several objectives into a single MoE for a given alternative (Keeney and Raiffa 1976; Kirkwood 1997).

Some multiple objective analyses include minimizing cost as an objective and developing a multi-attribute value function over all the objectives, including cost. For example, a study to help the US Army determine which bases to close develops a value function for 40 attributes, including a few cost-related attributes (Ewing *et al.* 2006). The decision-maker selects the set of bases to remain open that maximizes the total value subject to Army capability requirements. A cost-effectiveness analysis for the Army (Buede and Bresnick 1992) constructs MoEs for several air defense alternatives and depicts the MoE and the cost of each alternative on a two-dimensional chart. Similarly, our analysis separates the cost of each alternative from its MoE and compares the cost-effectiveness of the alternatives on a two-dimensional chart.

Several studies have analyzed the use of UAVs for different military missions, but many are financial in nature. The LCC of the the Triton UAV determines the financial implications of the US Navy purchasing this system for its Broad Area Maritime Surveillance (Lawler 2010). Yilmaz (2013) compares the Reaper and the Guardian UAVs for US border security and the Israeli-manufactured Heron UAV for patrolling Turkey's border but focuses primarily on the costs of the systems as opposed to their effectiveness. Some business case analyses (Thiow Yong Dennis 2007; Fry and Tutaj 2010) determine the number of UAVs of a specified type that is necessary to achieve a mission, and the decision-maker should choose the UAV type that can accomplish the mission at the lowest total system cost. These approaches are similar to the second way to structure an economic evaluation of alternatives as described in Chapter 4.

A multiple objective analysis (Ferguson and Harbold 2001) compares the Global Hawk UAV, the manned research vehicle Proteus, and three solar powered aircraft that could be used for communications relay, intelligence, surveillance, and reconnaissance. A score is assessed for each platform based on the following objectives: instantaneous access area, endurance, survivability, feasibility, flexibility, responsiveness, and acquisition cost. A more recent analysis (Collier and Kacala 2008) measures the effectiveness of airships, UAVs, and tactical satellites based on a multi-objective framework across a range of operating environments and mission sets. The decision-maker should select a mix of different aircraft to maximize the total fleet effectiveness subject to a budget constraint (see Chapters 4 and 10).

In this chapter, we apply the principles of multi-criteria decision-making to evaluate the effectiveness of several aerial platforms, including UAVs and airships. Like Ferguson and Harbold (2001), we focus on a communication relay mission, but we use LCC for the aerial platforms as opposed to acquisition costs because LCC more accurately represents total costs (see Chapter 5). We examine more aerial platforms, which have multiplied since the Ferguson and Harbold (2001) study. A unique contribution of this chapter is the examination of the cost-effectiveness of communication payloads that can be integrated with the aerial platform. Collier and Kacala (2008) study multiple scenarios—a technique that we adopt in this chapter. Unlike Lawler (2010), Thiow Yong Dennis (2007), and Fry and Tutaj (2010), who develop models so that the benefits or effectiveness is equal across the UAV alternatives, our analysis determines unique MoEs for different aerial platforms and communication payloads and different mission scenarios.

16.3 Alternatives

Over 50 countries' militaries are developing or operating about a thousand different UAV platforms (Parsons 2013). The US Department of Defense currently has approximately 11,000 UAVs in its inventory, consisting of almost 150 different platforms (American Institute of Aeronautics and Astronautics 2013). Israel, who first deployed UAVs for military operations, manufactures approximately 45 different UAV platforms (Dobbing and Cole 2014). We focus on 13 UAVs and 4 other aerial platforms that can be used for communication missions. We separately consider several communication payloads that can be fitted to these aerial platforms. Much of the information and many of the specifications for the aerial platforms come from Nicholas and Rossi (2011).

UAVs can be divided into five categories: small, medium, large, high altitude long endurance (HALE), and vertical takeoff and landing. Small UAVs are hand-launched and include the Wasp III and RQ-11 Raven. Both UAVs are hand-launched with ranges of 3–5 miles.

We examine two medium-size UAVs, the RQ-Shadow 2000 and the RQ-21 Blackjack. The Shadow, with a wingspan of 20 ft, is launched by catapult and usually lands using a runway with a hook at the bottom of the aircraft to snag a wire across the runway. The Shadow is primarily used for reconnaissance, surveillance, target acquisition, and battle damage assessment. The RQ-21 Blackjack, with a 16 ft wingspan, is a catapult-launched, vertically arrested UAV with multimission capability and six payload bays with power and Ethernet that can be fitted with cameras, communication capabilities, or other custom payloads.

Large UAVs have wingspans exceeding 25 ft and include the MQ-1 Predator, the MQ-1C Gray Eagle, the MQ-9 Reaper, and the X-47B Unmanned Combat Air System Air Carrier Demonstration (UCAS-D). The Predator was originally designed for intelligence, surveillance, and reconnaissance (ISR) but has been enhanced to be capable of taking on many roles including targeting, forward air control, laser designation, weapons delivery, and bomb damage assessment (General Atomics Aeronautical 2013). The Gray Eagle is a larger version of the Predator used by the US Army (General Atomics Aeronautical 2012a). The Reaper, also known as Predator B, is a hunter-killer UAV designed to eliminate time-sensitive targets via onboard 500-pound bombs and Hellfire missiles (General Atomics Aeronautical 2012b). Still in the demonstration and testing phase, the UCAS-D is designed to take off and land on aircraft carriers and to perform persistent surveillance with strike capability (Naval Air Systems Command 2014).

HALE UAVs are typically large UAVs with a maximum ceiling of approximately 60,000 feet and an endurance of 24 hours or more. The RQ-4 Global Hawk is operated by the US Air Force (USAF) for long-range ISR. The MQ-4C Triton is the U.S Navy's version of the Global Hawk and has deicing capability.

Vertical takeoff and landing UAVs (which can be small, medium or large) have rotary blades. These UAVs include the MQ-8 Fire Scout, which is used on ships to provide situation awareness, targeting support, and communications relay, and the YMQ-18A Hummingbird used for ISR and carrying cargo.

Non-UAV aerial platforms considered as part of this study include rapidly erected towers and tethered balloons. Rapidly erected towers present an interesting alternative to UAVs because data link and power can be supplied via cables from the ground, which can offer near limitless endurance. Two possible towers are the Rapid Aerostat Initial Deployment (RAID) Tower System and Cerberus Tower (Army Deploys 2008). Tethered balloons, such as the TIF-25K and PTDS-74K aerostats, are capable of carrying power and data through the tether and can go significantly higher than towers (US Army Aerostat-Based PTDS 2010; Raven Aerostar 2014).

In addition to identifying the most cost-effective aerial platform, we also evaluate the cost and effectiveness of 9 communication payloads that can be used with the aerial platforms. Wave Relay is a mobile ad hoc network (MANET) solution that continuously adapts to fluctuations in terrain and the environment to maximize connectivity and communication performance (Persistent Systems 2012, 2014). We consider two Wave Relay configurations: the Wave Relay Gen4 Board and the Wave Relay Quad Radio Router. WildCat II is a tactical MANET product and can interact with two separate ground networks, bridge ground and airborne networks, or act as backhaul (TrellisWare Technologies 2014a). Ocelot is a small form module manufactured by the same company that manufactures WildCat II (TrellisWare Technologies 2014b). The Xiphos 1RU and the Xiphos 6RU radios are 4G tactical broadband solutions for mobile communication users. The radios claim a range of 5 to 7 miles on the ground and up to 62 miles via airborne deployment with clear line of sight (Oceus Networks 2014). The Falcon III RF-7800W OU440 is rated for operational uses up to 15,000 ft and includes a high level of encryption capability (Harris 2012b). The Falcon III AN/PRC-1176 is a manpack capable of UHF/VHF analog voice and digital data (Harris 2012a). Finally, the Direct Data Link is designed specifically for small UAVs and provides Internet Protocol (IP)-based communication between a ground station and the aircraft (AeroVironment 2013). The Raven UAV can come equipped with the Direct Data Link.

16.4 Cost-effectiveness model

The model for evaluating the effectiveness of the aerial platforms and communication payloads follows the approach described in Chapter 8, and interested readers are encouraged to read that chapter for more extensive details. Measuring effectiveness begins with the development of an objectives hierarchy, and the bottom level of the hierarchy consists of measurable attributes. If the attributes are mutually preferentially independent, an additive value function can be used to measure the effectiveness of an alternative (Kirkwood 1997). The MoE of the jth alternative $v(j)$ is calculated via the following equation:

$$v(j) = \sum_{i=1}^{M} w_i v_i(x_i(j)),$$

(16.1)

where w_i is the global tradeoff weight for attribute i, $v_i(\cdot)$ is a value function for attribute i, $x_i(j)$ is the level of attribute i for alternative j, and M is the total number of attributes. The range for $v_i(\cdot)$ is between 0 and 1, inclusive.

If the attribute is a numerical measure, we assess the value function using marginal analysis by asking what the incremental or marginal change in value is when the attribute is increased or decreased. We fit an exponential function to the assessed values for attribute i using a least-squares approach (see Appendix 16.1 for more details). If the attribute is composed of categorical ratings, such as "low," "medium" and "high," we directly assign values from 0 and 1 for each category.

Local tradeoff weights are weights assessed for all attributes within a single objective. We frequently use a swing weight procedure to assess local tradeoff weights among attributes within an objective (von Winterfeldt and Edwards 1986). The swing weight procedure assumes that all attributes are at the worst level, and the decision-maker is asked which attribute he or she desires to move to the best level. The selected attribute receives a score of 100 and the desirability of "swinging" the other attributes from worst to best are assessed relative to the score of 100 for the most preferred attribute and a score of 0 when all the attributes are at their worst level. Local tradeoff weights for each attribute are calculated by normalizing the scores so that these weights sum to one. Multiplying the local weights by the tradeoff weights for each objective higher up in the objectives hierarchy returns global weights w_i for $i = 1, \ldots, M$ for each attribute so that $\sum_{i=1}^{M} w_i = 1$.

After the MoE for each alternative is calculated via Equation (16.1) and Equation (A16.1.1) in the Appendix, we depict the MoE and the cost of each alternative as a point on a two-dimensional chart. We analyze the cost-effectiveness of each alternative that belongs to the efficient solution set, where the efficient set is composed of alternatives that are not dominated by another alternative. Tradeoffs between the different alternatives are discussed.[1]

16.5 Objectives hierarchy

The first step to measure the effectiveness of an alternative is to create an objectives hierarchy describing what should be done to achieve an effective solution for the aerial platform and communication payload. The aerial platform and communication payload have separate objectives hierarchies, and the bottom level for each hierarchy consists of attributes that can be measured or observed for each alternative. To keep the vocabulary simple, we call the first and second levels of the hierarchy "objectives" and the bottom or third level of the hierarchy "attributes." The hierarchies are based on our opinion after extensive research and discussions with subject matter experts.

16.5.1 Objectives hierarchy for aerial platform

Maximizing the mission effectiveness of the aerial platform is divided into four objectives: maximizing performance, flexibility, readiness, and survivability

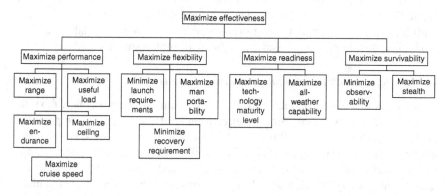

Figure 16.1 Objectives hierarchy for aerial platform.

(Figure 16.1). Performance describes the capability of an aerial platform to perform the mission and is composed of five attributes. We seek to maximize range (the distance an aerial platform can travel as stated by the manufacturer), endurance (the maximum number of hours a platform can remain aloft), ceiling (the platform's mean sea level as stated by the manufacturer), cruise speed (the highest sustained operational speed a platform can achieve), and useful load (the amount of weight a platform can carry).

Flexibility describes the ability to employ the aerial platform in different conditions. Flexibility is further divided into three attributes: launch requirement, recovery requirement, and man portability. Launch requirement describes the type of launch required by the aerial platform, and aerial platforms that need less space launching are favored over assets that require more space for launch. Recovery requirement describes the type of method utilized for recovering the aerial platform, and platforms that need less space to be recovered are favored over assets that require more space for landing. Man portability is a binary attribute, and a platform that is man portable can be transported and launched by a single operator. We seek to minimize the launch and recovery requirements and maximize man portability in order to maximize flexibility.

Readiness determines how prepared an aerial platform is to support the mission. Technology maturity level and all-weather capability are the only two attributes that define readiness. Other attributes that could also be used to measure readiness include the mishap rate and availability, but data for these attributes are generally not available for the alternatives. Technology maturity level is measured by the number of years in service for the aerial platform based on initial operating capacity, and it serves as proxy measure for the reliability of a platform. Platforms with less technology maturity lack the field testing and refinement of older and more tested designs. All-weather capability is a binary attribute, and the platform must have deicing capability to be all-weather capable.

Survivability describes the ability of an aerial platform to accomplish its mission without being harmed by the enemy. We want to minimize observability and maximize stealth in order to maximize survivability. We define observability as the ability of enemy combatants to detect the aerial platform with the naked eye. Stealth is a binary attribute. If a platform uses radar absorbent materials similar to modern stealth aircraft, we consider that the platform has stealth capability.

16.5.2   Objectives hierarchy for communication payload

As depicted in Figure 16.2, the objectives of maximizing performance, flexibility, and readiness will maximize the effectiveness of a communication payload. Performance describes the ability of the communication payload to provide a communications link during optimum conditions. We seek to maximize power output and receiver sensitivity (which measure the payload's range) and to maximize throughput. Throughput measures the connection speed between the communication payload and a single user, as reported by the vendor in raw number of bits per second. Power output is measured in watts, and receiver sensitivity is measured in decibel-milliwatts.

Flexibility describes the ability of the communication payload to operate in varying conditions and fulfill different mission requirements. Flexibility is composed of mesh capability, power consumption, weight, and traffic type. Mesh capability is a binary attribute because the radio can either execute a mesh topology—where nodes in the communication network can send and receive data and serve as a relay for other nodes—or not. We seek to minimize power consumption by the communication payload, which is measured in watts. Weight, measured in pounds, is based on the radio manufacturer's specifications. Traffic type is voice (VHF and UHF transmission), data (e.g., video, imagery), or both.

Readiness determines how prepared a communications payload is to perform the mission. As with the aerial platforms, we use technology maturity level as a proxy measure for readiness because data on the availability of the communications payloads are not available.

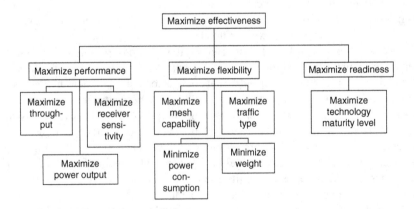

Figure 16.2 Objectives hierarchy for communication payload.

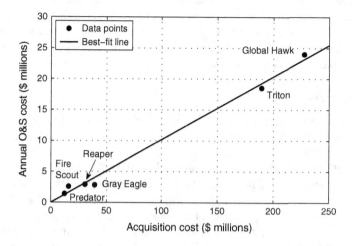

Figure 16.3 Annualized O&S cost as a function of acquisition cost.

16.6 Cost estimation

Cost-effectiveness analysis should use the LCC for each alternative, which traditionally includes research and development, acquisition, operations and sustainment (O&S), and disposal costs (see Chapter 5). The program acquisition unit cost includes research and development, procurement, and military construction costs. Disposal costs are not included in this analysis either because the aerial platforms will be used for more than 15 years or because they are assumed to be minimal.

We use the annualized LCC for each aerial platform where the LCC equals the program acquisition unit cost plus the annual O&S costs multiplied by the planned service life of each platform. The acquisition cost is based on a single UAV, tower, or aerostat. We are not able to differentiate the cost of the individual aerial platform from the launch and recovery equipment, ground control stations and other support equipment. The annual O&S cost for a platform is estimated as a linear function of the acquisition cost based on known O&S costs for six UAVs, as depicted in Figure 16.3. The annual O&S cost is 10.1 percent of the acquisition cost.

Since data on O&S costs for the communication payload alternatives are not available, we compare the costs for communication payloads only using the acquisition costs. Since O&S costs are not included for communication payloads, the costs used in this analysis underestimate the true LCCs. Even if more accurate LCCs for communication payloads were used, their costs would still be minimal compared to the costs of the aerial platforms.

16.7 Cost-effectiveness analysis

The aerial platforms and their communication payloads are evaluated under three different scenarios. The three scenarios are disaster relief, long range, and tactical user. Each scenario poses unique communication challenges, and a decision-maker's preferences differ among the scenarios. Consequently, value functions for each attribute and the tradeoff weights change under each scenario. We describe each scenario and analyze the cost-effectiveness of aerial platforms and communication payloads for each scenario.

16.7.1 Disaster relief scenario

Under the disaster relief scenario, we envision a situation similar to Hurricane Katrina or Typhoon Haiyan in which communication and cellular infrastructure has been rendered useless, and a nation's military is ordered to provide aid and coordinate relief efforts in the area. Communications links for rescue teams are needed for a fast and successful response. The disaster area is a circular area with a 100 nautical mile (NM) diameter. Task force headquarters is stationary and located at an airfield on the immediate perimeter of the disaster area. Throughput demand is expected to be more than 200 Mbps at various times and the number of concurrent users could be between 50 and 100. UHF, VHF, and data relay support is needed.

16.7.1.1 Cost-effectiveness of aerial platform

The global weights for the disaster relief scenario are presented in Table 16.1. We use the swing weight procedure to determine the tradeoff weights among the attributes that define performance. The local weights for the performance attributes are 0.28 for ceiling, 0.22 each for useful load and endurance, 0.17 for range, and 0.11 for cruise speed. Having a sufficient ceiling is necessary to ensure coverage of the entire disaster area. Endurance is important because of the long communication requirement, and useful load is important because of the large

Table 16.1 Global tradeoff weights for aerial platform for each scenario

Objective	Attribute	Tradeoff weights for each scenario		
		Disaster relief	Long range	Tactical user
Performance	Range	0.150	0.090	0.000
	Useful load	0.200	0.090	0.155
	Endurance	0.200	0.090	0.155
	Ceiling	0.250	0.113	0.000
	Cruise speed	0.100	0.113	0.000
Flexibility	Launch requirement	0.000	0.000	0.115
	Recovery requirement	0.000	0.000	0.058
	Man portability	0.000	0.000	0.173
Readiness	Technology maturity level	0.100	0.200	0.138
	All-weather capability	0.000	0.300	0.000
Survivability	Observability	0.000	0.000	0.166
	Stealth	0.000	0.000	0.041

number of first responders who need connectivity. Comparing among the objectives of performance, flexibility, readiness, and survivability, we do not assign any weight to either flexibility or survivability because the scenario assumes that headquarters is at an operational airfield and no enemy are present. We consider performance nine times more important than readiness for this scenario. Because we assume that icing is not a problem for this scenario, technology maturity level is the only attribute within flexibility to receive a non-zero weight.

Figure 16.4 depicts the cost-effectiveness of each aerial platform. Ceiling and useful load account for almost half of the MoE of the most effective solutions (the Predator, Reaper, Hummingbird, and Global Hawk). The Triton, the Navy's variant of the Global Hawk, scores equally as well as those four UAVs for ceiling and useful load but is not scheduled for its first flight until 2015. Thus, the Triton performs badly on the readiness objective. If the Triton's technology maturity level equals that of the Global Hawk, its MoE would be similar to that of Global Hawk.

As can be seen from Figure 16.4 which depicts the annualized LCC on a logarithmic scale, the efficient solution—which eliminates any alternative that is both less effective and more expensive than another alternative—includes the Raven, Cerberus Tower, TIF-25K, Predator, Hummingbird, Reaper, and Global Hawk. The Raven's endurance of only 1.5 hours and payload of 6.5 ounces make it an ineffective platform for this scenario. The Cerberus Tower's height of 30 feet allows for approximately a 7 NM radio horizon, which is inadequate coverage for this scenario.

Because the Global Hawk's effectiveness is only slightly greater than the Reaper's MoE and it costs US$30 million more per year, we prefer the Reaper to the Global Hawk. We also prefer the Predator to the Hummingbird because the Predator is only slightly less effective and costs US$64,000 less per year. The Hummingbird has a faster cruising speed but less endurance than the Predator.

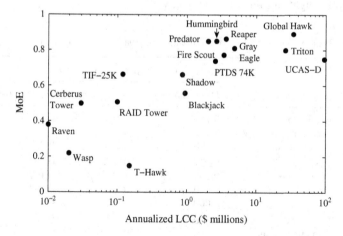

Figure 16.4 Cost-effectiveness of aerial platforms for disaster relief scenario.

Comparing the Predator and Reaper, we ask if annually spending US$1.62 million is worth the increase in effectiveness from 0.85 (Predator) to 0.86 (Reaper). The Reaper is judged more effective than Predator because the former has a higher cruising speed, but in our opinion, the higher speed is not worth the additional cost for this scenario. We examine the tradeoffs between the TIF-25K aerostat and the Predator. Although the Predator's MoE is 0.19 more than the MoE for the TIF-25K, it also costs US$1.9 million more per year. The TIF-25K's endurance of 14 days surpasses that the Predator's endurance of 40 hours. Selecting either alternative can be justified. The TIF-25K offers a low cost aerial platform with long endurance and adequate payload and ceiling, and the Predator offers more maneuverability and a larger coverage area, albeit at the expense of less endurance and a higher cost.

16.7.1.2   Cost-effectiveness of communication payload

The global tradeoff weights for the communication payload attributes for disaster relief are depicted in Table 16.2. We use a swing weight method to determine the local tradeoff weights for the three attributes (throughput, power output, and receiver sensitivity) within the performance objective. Improving power output from the worst (0 watts) to best (500 watts) level is most important and has a local tradeoff weight of 0.4. Improving throughput is almost as important, and we assign a local weight of 0.36. Finally, improving receiver sensitivity is least important, and its local weight equals 0.24. Within the flexibility objective, we assess that having mesh capable technology is most important, and we judge having mesh capable technology is twice as important as having a radio that can carry both voice and data (traffic type). The payload's weight and power consumption are not important for this scenario. Comparing the objectives of performance, flexibility, and readiness, we rank performance most important, flexibility second most important, and readiness least important. We use the rank-sum method to calculate the local tradeoff weights for these three objectives.[2]

Table 16.2 Global tradeoff weights for communication payload for each scenario

Objective	Attribute	Tradeoff weights for each scenario		
		Disaster relief	Long range	Tactical user
Performance	Throughput	0.180	0.000	0.150
	Receiver sensitivity	0.120	0.240	0.090
	Power output	0.200	0.240	0.090
Flexibility	Mesh capability	0.221	0.000	0.102
	Traffic type	0.109	0.000	0.102
	Power consumption	0.000	0.165	0.144
	Weight	0.000	0.165	0.212
Readiness	Technology maturity level	0.170	0.190	0.110

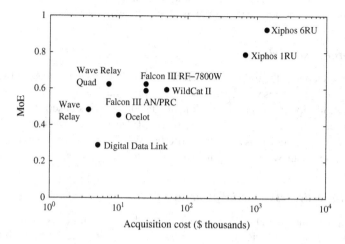

Figure 16.5 Cost-effectiveness of communication payloads for disaster relief scenario.

As can be seen from Figure 16.5, the efficient solution set comprises the Wave Relay, Wave Relay Quad, Falcon III RF-7800W, Xiphos 1RU, and Xiphos 6RU. (Figure 16.5 shows the acquisition cost for each radio on a logarithmic scale to more clearly see the differences in costs.) If the decision-maker places more importance on receiver sensitivity and traffic type relative to throughput, the Falcon III AN/PRC will replace the Falcon III RF-7800W as a member of the efficient solution set. Regardless, either of the Falcons is only slightly more effective than the Wave Relay Quad, and the Falcons cost US$18,000 more, and we prefer the Wave Relay Quad to either of the Falcons. The Xiphos 1RU and 6RU are most effective with MoEs of 0.79 and 0.93 respectively. Both radios offer high power output, high throughput, and excellent scalability for multiple users. Their superior capabilities are worth the additional cost.

16.7.1.3 Solution compatibility

Both the TIF-25K and the Predator have enough useful load to carry either of the Xiphos radio units. However, available power for the radio units is a differentiator. The Predator has 1,800 watts available for payloads. The Xiphos 6RU's power consumption is over 3,000 watts. The Predator cannot normally support the Xiphos 6RU. The TIF-25K aerostat is capable of sending power to its payload from a ground based source up the tether. The TIF-25K should be able to power the Xiphos 6RU radio unit. This may require high voltage power sent from the ground up to the aerostat to avoid high power losses over the long transmission line of the tether, but it is feasible. If a decision-maker prefers the more effective Xiphos 6RU because of its better throughput and power output, we believe the TIF-25K is the most cost-effective aerial platform. If the decision-maker prefers the less expensive Xiphos 1RU, either the Predator with its greater coverage or the TIF-25K with its long endurance can serve as an effective aerial platform.

16.7.2   Long-range scenario

In the long-range scenario, the military leadership at headquarters needs to establish UHF (voice) communications with a ship 340 NM away. The ship has lost its satellite communication capability, and we assume that headquarters is based at a large airfield near the coast. No enemy resistance is expected. The weather is cloudy with the possibility of icing conditions at higher altitudes. We assume that headquarters will need to communicate with the ship for approximately four hours.

16.7.2.1   Cost-effectiveness of aerial platform

Table 16.1 displays the global tradeoff weights for the long-range scenario. As with the disaster relief scenario, the objectives for flexibility and survivability receive zero weight because the military is operating from a large airfield and enemies are not present. Within the performance objective, we believe it is most important to improve cruising speed, and cruising speed receives a local weight equal to 0.24. Improving the ceiling is only slightly less important, and the local tradeoff weight for ceiling equals 0.23. Useful load, endurance, and range each receive local weights equal to 0.18. Within the readiness objective, the deicing capability may be crucial, and we assess local weights of 0.6 for all-weather capability and 0.4 for technology maturity level. The attributes that determine performance (useful load, ceiling, endurance, range, and cruising speed) have value functions in which the value of 0 corresponds to satisfactory requirements to complete the communication mission. Consequently, we are willing to trade off more performance in favor of readiness than we were in the disaster relief scenario. Both the performance and readiness objectives receive a tradeoff weight equal to 0.5.

The long-range scenario requires that aerial platforms satisfy a minimum ceiling of 19,102 ft. This number is calculated as a function of the 340 NM distance between the ship and military headquarters. The Shadow, Raven, Wasp, and T-Hawk UAVs, the TIF-25K aerostat, and the RAID and Cerberus Towers are excluded from this analysis because their ceilings do not meet this requirement. The Blackjack's ceiling is 19,500 ft, but its range of 55 NM is so small that it would need a much higher ceiling to be effective for this scenario. Consequently, the Blackjack is not feasible for this scenario.

The efficient solution set for the long-range scenario consists of the Predator, Reaper, and Triton (Figure 16.6). The Triton and UCAS-D are the most effective because of their deicing capability. Since the first flight for the UCAS-D is scheduled for 2019, its technology maturity level performs poorly, but even if it had the same technology maturity level as the Triton, the latter would still be more effective because the Triton has a higher ceiling than the UCAS-D. We estimate the annualized LCC of the UCAS-D at US$95 million, but its price point may come down to that of the Triton as the technology becomes more mature.

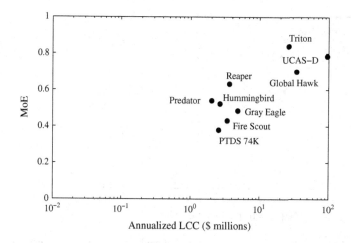

Figure 16.6 Cost-effectiveness of aerial platforms for long-range scenario.

If the UCAS-D's LCC is closer to that of the Triton, the UCAS-D could be a cost-effective alternative for the long-range scenario.

The Triton is annually US$23–25 million more expensive than the Reaper and Predator, but the Triton's MoE is 0.21 greater than that of the Reaper and 0.30 greater than that of the Predator. This gap in effectiveness is primarily due to the Triton's deicing capability. If icing conditions are not a factor, we prefer the Reaper to the Triton. The Reaper costs US$1.6 million more than the Predator, but its MoE is 0.09 greater than that of the Predator. All three UAVs will be evaluated for compatibility with the most cost-effective communication payloads.

16.7.2.2 Cost-effectiveness for communication payload

Since the headquarters needs to be able to talk with the ship, the communication payload must support voice transmission. Given this requirement, the Falcon III AN/PRC and the Wildcat II are the only feasible alternatives. Within the flexibility objective, we are indifferent between trading off between power consumption and weight, and the traffic type receives no importance because the two feasible alternatives can support both voice and data transmission (Table 16.2). We are also indifferent between trading off between power output and receiver sensitivity, and throughput is not important for this scenario. When comparing among the higher-level objectives, we prefer to increase performance, then to increase flexibility, and finally to improve readiness. We assign local weights of 0.48, 0.33, and 0.19 to those three objectives, respectively.

Figure 16.7 depicts the cost-effectiveness of the two feasible radio units. The Falcon III AN/PRC and the Wildcat II are about equally effective according to our preferences, and we prefer the less expensive Falcon III AN/PRC. If a decision-maker is unwilling to trade off as much flexibility for performance as

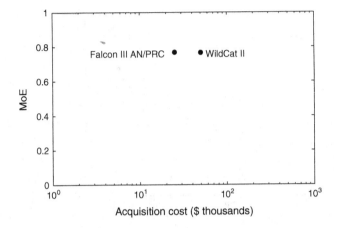

Figure 16.7 Cost-effectiveness of communication payloads for long-range scenario.

we are, the Wildcat II will be rated more effective than the Falcon III AN/PRC. A decision-maker may prefer the lighter Wildcat II that consumes less power than the Falcon III AN/PRC. The cost difference between the two communication payloads is about US$25,000, which may not be an important discriminator when the annual cost of the UAV is US$2 million or more.

16.7.2.3 Solution compatibility

The three identified cost-effective aerial platforms for the long-range scenario are the Predator, Reaper, and Triton UAVs. The Predator offers an effective low cost option. The Reaper offers twice the ceiling of the Predator and a turbine engine for a reasonable increase in cost over the Predator. The Triton offers unparalleled mission effectiveness but is also the most expensive of the three options by several orders of magnitude. Budget considerations as discussed in Chapters 4 and 7 may influence which UAV is selected. All three UAVs can easily support the Falcon III AN/PRC, which is a 12-pound, 55-watt 117G radio. Because these UAVs can easily support the Falcon III AN/PRC, a decision-maker may not want to purchase the more expensive Wildcat II for this scenario.

16.7.3 Tactical user scenario

This tactical user scenario involves a small special operations team or a single soldier trying to establish communications with higher command to coordinate extract. The tactical user, who is close to completing his mission and needs to radio back to base to arrange a helicopter extract, is about 10 NM away from the base, and a 500 ft mountain is blocking radio signals back to base. The tactical user lacks satellite communication capability. No extraction plans or time of next contact were established during the last contact between the base and the tactical user more than 24 hours ago. Only a small number of end users need to be supported. Although the primary method of communications is UHF/VHF, video may also be necessary. Additionally, the enemy is believed to be in the vicinity. The tactical user prefers to have possession and control of the aerial platform.

16.7.3.1   *Cost-effectiveness of aerial platform*

If the 500 ft mountain is located midway between the user and headquarters, the tactical user scenario requires a minimum ceiling of 1,000 ft for the aerial platform. This requirement eliminates the T-Hawk, RAID Tower, and Cerberus Tower as feasible alternatives. After meeting this requirement, an aerial platform with a higher ceiling will not necessarily perform better, and we assign a tradeoff weight equal to 0 to the ceiling attribute. The attributes range and cruising speed are not important for this scenario and also receive a weight of 0. We determine an equal preference for trading off between useful load and endurance, and each attribute receives a local weight of 0.5 within performance. Within the objective of flexibility, we use the rank-sum method to assign local weights after determining that man portability is the most important, launch method is the second most important, and recovery method is the least important. We determine that observability is much more important than stealth because the enemy is relatively low tech and decreasing observability is four times as important as moving from no stealth to stealth capability. This scenario has good weather, and deicing capability is unimportant, and technology maturity level has a local weight of 1.0.

The global weights for the attributes for the tactical user scenario are depicted in Table 16.1. We use a swing weight procedure to determine the relative importance of performance, flexibility, readiness, and survivability. Improving the flexibility of the aerial platform so that the platform can be carried and launched by a single individual is slightly more important than improving the performance (increasing the useful load and ceiling). Less important is improving the survivability (decreasing the observability), and least important is increasing the readiness (improving the technology maturity level).

The Raven is the superior solution for the tactical user scenario because it is the most effective and least expensive alternative (Figure 16.8). The Raven's small size allows it to be carried by a single individual. It can only remain in the air for 1.5 hours, but that should be enough to allow the user to communicate with higher command. If man portability is a requirement, the only other feasible platform is the Wasp. The Wasp's smaller size and lower weight may make it more portable than the Raven, but the Raven has more endurance and range.In our opinion, having more endurance is more important than the smaller size, and we select the Raven as the most cost-effective platform for this scenario.

16.7.3.2   *Cost-effectiveness of communication payload*

Because we are selecting a UAV that can be carried by a single user, we place a lot of importance on maximizing flexibility, as depicted in Table 16.2. Using a swing weight procedure, we assign tradeoff weights of 0.56 for flexibility, 0.33 for

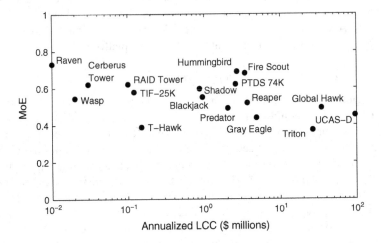

Figure 16.8 Cost-effectiveness of aerial platforms for tactical user scenario.

performance, and 0.11 for readiness. Within the flexibility objective, we believe it is important to minimize the weight of the radio, followed by minimizing power consumption. The attribute for weight has a local tradeoff weight of 0.38, and power consumption has a local weight of 0.26. Mesh capability and traffic type each have local weights of 0.18. For the performance objective, increasing throughput is the most important attribute, to allow the tactical user to transmit some video. The local weight for throughput is 0.45, and the both of the local weights for power output and receiver sensitivity are 0.27.

Figure 16.9 displays the cost-effectiveness for the communication payloads. The Wave Relay radio is the most effective and the least expensive alternative. The Wave Relay's MoE is the largest because of the radio's small weight and relatively high throughput. If a decision-maker places more importance on power consumption and receiver sensitivity relative to throughput, the Ocelot will become more effective than the Wave Relay although the former costs almost three times as much as the Wave Relay. Both communication payloads weigh less than 0.2 lbs. If a decision-maker is unwilling to trade off as much performance in favor of flexibility than in our assessment, the WildCat II may be the most effective. The WildCat II weighs 3.4 lbs, which likely makes it too heavy for the small UAVs.

16.7.3.3   Solution compatibility

The Raven and Wasp III UAVs have useful loads of 0.41 and 0.2 lbs, respectively, which excludes use of the WildCat II radio. The Wasp III would also have trouble carrying either radio. The Raven can easily accept the weight of the Ocelot and the Wave Relay card at 96 grams. However, with additional wiring, dedicated battery and antenna, either the Ocelot or Wave Relay could exceed the Raven's useful load, which could result in degraded performance of the airframe. Even

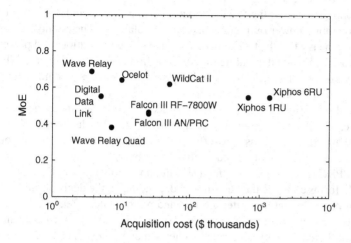

Figure 16.9 Cost-effectiveness of communication payloads for tactical user scenario.

though both communication payloads possess a small form factor, the payload compartment of the Raven may not be able to support either radio. A previous study (Menjivar 2012) tested a Raven with a Wave Relay payload. The Wave Relay radio had to be taped onto the outside of the UAV instead of being secured inside the payload compartment, which is not ideal for performance of the UAV or the communication link.

One communication payload that would work with the Raven is AeroVironment's Digital Data Link. AeroVironment offers the Digital Data Link with the Raven UAV from the factory. Digital Data Link's price is positioned between the Wave Relay and the Ocelot at US$5,000, but it has a slightly lower MoE than either one at 0.55. However, compatibility between the Digital Data Link and the Raven is assured, whereas the Ocelot and the Wave Relay units needs further testing to ensure compatibility.

16.8 Conclusions

This chapter demonstrates the use of traditional multi-criteria decision-making techniques to analyze the cost-effectiveness of aerial platforms and communication payloads for communication missions in the military. We compared the cost-effectiveness of 17 aerial platforms and 9 communication payloads across three mission scenarios.

The first scenario requires long endurance and high bandwidth capability to complete a disaster relief mission. The most cost-effective aerial platforms are the TIF-25K aerostat and the Predator UAV. The TIF-25K combines endurance measured in weeks and a high useful load with a moderate ceiling. Additionally, the TIF-25K can utilize a tether to power its payloads from the ground. The Predator is a very capable UAV platform with a relatively long endurance, long range, and reasonable cost of ownership. The most cost-effective communication payloads are the two configurations of the Oceus Networks Xiphos (1RU and 6RU) due to their high throughput, power output, and excellent scalability. The Xiphos radios can be relatively heavy (78 lbs to 276 lbs depending on configuration) and power hungry (855 to 3,275 watts depending on configuration). We select either a TIF-25K aerostat with a Xiphos 6RU connected to ground power or a Predator with a Xiphos 1RU configuration.

In the second scenario, a long-range relay is needed to connect users across a 340 NM range, which requires a minimum altitude of 19,102 ft due to radio horizon and UHF capability. The most cost-effective aerial platforms are the Predator, Reaper, and Triton. Due to its UHF capability, sensitivity, and power output, the Falcon III AN/PRC is the most cost-effective communication payload. Each of the three aerial platforms could be the best choice, depending on the decision-maker's preference for price (Predator), better altitude and performance (Reaper), or outstanding performance and deicing capability (Triton). The extra performance and capability of the Triton comes with a much higher ownership cost than the Predator or Reaper.

A covert, tactical situation where portability is preferred is the final scenario. The most cost-effective aerial platform is the Raven, which combines man portability and adequate range and endurance with the lowest cost of any aerial platform in this study. The Wave Relay is the most cost-effective communication payload for this scenario because it weighs very little and possesses a relatively high throughput for its small form factor. However, compatibility between the Raven and Wave Relay cannot be confirmed at this time. The slightly less effective and more expensive Digital Data Link is compatible with the Raven and can be an acceptable solution in the interim until more compatibility testing can be completed between the Raven and the Wave Relay communication payload.

As with any analysis, our cost-effectiveness analysis relies on a number of assumptions, which can motivate future research. We assess compatibility between the most cost-effective aerial platforms and communication payloads within each scenario based primarily on the manufacturer's provided specifications. Actual field testing would provide a proof of concept and help validate the findings of this chapter. Since complete, transparent, and reliable cost data was not always available, further research of the fully captured LCCs for UAVs, military towers, and aerostats will enable a more accurate and detailed analysis. Other missions, such as ISR, may present an interesting and useful subject for future research, and other aerial platforms currently under development could be considered. Finally, other decision-makers may have different objectives constraints, value functions, and tradeoff weights, which would change the alternatives' MoEs and the cost-effectiveness analysis.

This chapter offers a framework for comparing the cost-effectiveness of dissimilar aerial platforms and communication payloads across different mission sets. Several militaries around the world currently operate UAVs, and their use for communication will likely grow in the future. This research develops value functions and weighting parameters that change based upon mission requirements and are easily adapted to other mission sets including the traditional ISR mission. Our analysis demonstrates that the cost-effectiveness of an alternative depends on the mission requirements, and suggests the military should continue to purchase a wide array of aerial platforms and communication payloads that can be used for different missions.

Acknowledgments

We would like to thank Glen Cook and John Gibson of the Naval Postgraduate School for their advice and feedback during this research and for sharing their expertise in communication systems. Copies of the spreadsheets used to analyze the cost-effectiveness of the aerial platforms and communication payloads can be downloaded and altered to meet a decision-maker's own preferences from Cameron MacKenzie's web page at https://faculty.nps.edu/camacken/ under the tab "Thesis Supervision."

Appendix 16.1

Exponential value functions are used for the numerical attributes. The value of attribute i at a given level x_i can be calculated based on whether the decision-maker prefers "more" or "less" of an attribute:

$$v_i(x_i) = \begin{cases} \dfrac{1 - \exp(a[x_i - x_{min}]^b)}{K} & \text{if more is preferred} \\[2mm] \dfrac{1 - \exp(a[x_{max} - x_i]^b)}{K} & \text{if less is preferred,} \end{cases} \qquad \text{(A16.1.1)}$$

where $K = 1 - \exp(a[x_{max} - x_{min}]^b)$ is a normalizing constant, x_{min} is the attribute level for which $v(x_{min}) = 0$ if more is preferred and $v(x_{min}) = 1$ if less is preferred, x_{max} is the attribute level for which $v(x_{max}) = 1$ if more is preferred and $v(x_{max}) = 1$ if less is preferred, and $a \in \mathbb{R}$ and $b > 0$ are parameters selected to minimize the sum of the squared distances between $v_i(x_i)$ and the assessed values.

In order for the value function to be defined over the domain of the attribute and so that $0 \le v_i(x_i) \le 1$, we require that $v_i(x_i) = 0$ for all $x_i \le x_{min}$ and $v_i(x_i) = 1$ for all $x_i \ge x_{max}$ if more is preferred and require that $v_i(x_i) = 0$ for all $x_i \ge x_{max}$ and $v_i(x_i) = 1$ for all $x_i \le x_{min}$ if less is preferred.

Notes

1 See Chapter 4 for an alternative perspective.
2 The rank-sum only requires the decision-maker to rank the objectives rather than determining the exact tradeoff between multiple objectives. For three objectives, the most important objective receives an unnormalized weight of 3, the second most important receives a 2, and the least important receives a 1. Dividing each weight by the sum of these weights returns normalized weights of 1/2, 1/3, and 1/6 for the first, second, and third objectives, respectively.

References

AeroVironment. 2013. "Digital Data Link." Available at https://www.avinc.com/uas/small_uas/ddl/ [last accessed August 29, 2014].

American Institute of Aeronautics and Astronautics. 2013. "UAV Roundup 2013." *Aerospace America*, July/August. Available at www.aerospaceamerica.org/Documents/AerospaceAmerica-PDFs-2013/July-August-2013/UAVRoundup2013t-AA-Jul-Aug 2013.pdf [last accessed September 15, 2014].

"Army Deploys 300th RAID Tower, Supporting Forward Base Protection by Persistent Surveillance and Dissemination System PSDS2." November 23, 2008. *Defense Update*, November 23. Available at http://defense-update.com/features/2008/november/231108_psds2_raid_sensors.html [last accessed August 29, 2014].

Buede, Dennis M., and Terry A. Bresnick. 1992. "Applications of Decision Analysis to the Military Systems Acquisition Process." *Interfaces* 22: 110–125.

Collier, Corey M., and Jeffrey C. Kacala. 2008. "A Cost-Effectiveness Analysis of Tactical Satellites, High-Altitude Long-Endurance Airships, and High and Medium Altitude Unmanned Aerial Systems for ISR and Communication Missions." Master's thesis, Naval Postgraduate School.

Department of Defense. 2013. "Unmanned Systems Integrated Roadmap FY2013-2038." Reference number 14-S-0553. Available at www.defense.gov/pubs/DOD-USRM-2013.pdf [last accessed August 29, 2014].

Dobbing, Mary, and Chris Cole. 2014. *Israel and the Drone Wars: Examining Israel's Production, Use and Proliferation of UAVs*. Oxford, UK: Drone Wars UK. Available at http://dronewarsuk.files.wordpress.com/2014/01/israel-and-the-drone-wars.pdf [last accessed November 27, 2014].

Ewing Jr., Paul L., William Tarantino, and Gregory S. Parnell. 2006. "Use of Decision Analysis in the Army Base Realignment and Closure (BRAC) 2005 Military Value Analysis." *Decision Analysis* 3: 33–49.

Ferguson, Charles R., and Douglas A. Harbold. 2001. "High Altitude Long Endurance (HALE) Platforms for Tactical Wireless Communications and Sensor Use in Military Operations." Master's thesis, Naval Postgraduate School.

Fry, Jereed N., and Steven E. Tutaj. 2010. "A Business Case Analysis for the Vulture Program." MBA Professional Report, Naval Postgraduate School, Monterey, CA.

General Atomics Aeronautical. 2012a. "MQ-1C Gray Eagle." Available at www.ga-asi.com/products/aircraft/gray_eagle.php [last accessed August 29, 2014].

——. 2012b. "MQ-9 Reaper/Predator B." Available at www.ga-asi.com/products/aircraft/predator_b.php [last accessed August 29, 2014].

——. 2013. "MQ-1 Predator." Available at www.ga-asi.com/products/aircraft/predator.php [last accessed August 29, 2014].

Harris. 2012a. "AN/PRC-177G(V)1(C)." Available at http://rf.harris.com/capabilities/tactical-radios-networking/an-prc-117g/default.asp [last accessed August 29, 2014].

——. 2012b. "RF-7800W-OU440." Available at http://rf.harris.com/capabilities/tactical-radios-networking/rf-7800w.asp [last accessed August 29, 2014].

Keeney, Ralph L. 1996. *Value-Focused Thinking: A Path to Creative Decisionmaking*. Cambridge, MA: Harvard University Press.

Keeney, Ralph L., and Howard Raiffa. 1976. *Decisions with Multiple Objectives: Preferences and Value Tradeoffs*. New York: John Wiley & Sons.

Kirkwood, Craig W. 1997. *Strategic Decision Making: Multiobjective Decision Analysis with Spreadsheets*. Belmont, CA: Brooks/Cole.

Lawler, Paul P. 2010. "Cost Implications of the Broad Area Maritime Surveillance Unmanned Aircraft System for the Navy Flying Hour Program and Operation and Maintenance Budget." Master's thesis, Naval Postgraduate School.

Menjivar, Jose D. 2012. "Bridging Operational and Strategic Communication Architectures Integrating Small Unmanned Aircraft Systems as Airborne Tactical Communication Vertical Nodes." Master's thesis, Naval Postgraduate School, Monterey, CA.

Naval Air Systems Command. 2014. "Aircraft and Weapons: Unmanned Combat Air System Demonstration." Available at www.navair.navy.mil/index.cfm [last accessed May 24, 2014].

Nicholas, Ted G., and Rita Rossi. 2011. *U.S. Unmanned Aircraft Systems, 2011*. Fountain Valley, CA: Data Search Associates.

Oceus Networks. 2014. "Oceus Networks Xiphos." Available at www.oceusnetworks. com/products/xiphos [last accessed August 29, 2014].

Parsons, Dan. 2013. "Worldwide, Drones Are in High Demand." *National Defense Magazine*, May. Available at www.nationaldefensemagazine.org/archive/ 2013/May/Pages/Worldwide,DronesAreinHighDemand.aspx [last accessed September 15, 2014].

Persistent Systems. 2012. "Technology." Available at www.persistentsystems.com/ pdf/WaveRelay_ WhitePaper_Technology_01.pdf [last accessed August 29, 2014].

———. 2014. "Quad Radio Router." Available at www.persistentsystems.com/quad/ [last accessed August 29, 2014].

Raven Aerostar. 2014. "TIF-25K teathered aerostat." Available at http://raven aerostar.com/solutions/aerostats/tif-25k [last accessed August 29, 2014].

Thiow Yong Dennis, Lim. 2007. "A Methodological Approach for Conducting a Business Case Analysis (BCA) of the Global Observer Joint Capability Technology Demonstration (JCTD)." Master's thesis, Naval Postgraduate School.

TrellisWare Technologies. 2104a. "TW-130 WildCat II." Available at https://www. trellisware.com/wp-content/uploads/TW-130-WildCat-II-Product-Bulletin.pdf [last accessed March 5, 2014].

———. 2014b. "TW-600 Ocelot." Available at https://www.trellisware.com/wp-content/ uploads/TW-600_Ocelot_Product_bulletin.pdf[last accessed March 9, 2014].

"US Army Aerostat-Based PTDS Provide IED Warning." June 8, 2010. *Defense Industry Daily*. Available at www.defenseindustrydaily.com/133M-to-Lockheed-Martin-for-US-Army-Aerostat-based-Warning-System-05835/ [last accessed August 29, 2014].

von Winterfeldt, Detlof, and Ward Edwards. 1986. *Decision Analysis and Behavioral Research*. Cambridge, UK: Cambridge University Press.

Yilmaz, Bahadir. 2013. "Cost and Effectiveness Analysis on Unmanned Aerial Vehicle (UAV) Use at Border Security." In *SPIE Proceedings*, edited by Edward M. Carapezza. Paper presented at the Sensors, and Command, Control, Communications, and Intelligence (C3I) Technologies for Homeland Security and Homeland Defense XII, Baltimore, Maryland, April 29. doi:10.1117/12.2015914.

17 Time discounting in military cost–benefit analysis

Jason Hansen and Jonathan Lipow

17.1 Introduction

The proverb "a bird in the hand is worth two in the bush" can be found in John Ray's 1670 *A Handbook of Proverbs*, and remains just as valid today. People place higher value on what is certain—a bird in hand ready to eat—than they place on the uncertain—two birds in the bush that may be ready to escape. Since the past and present are by definition certain, uncertainty is really a characteristic of the future. Hence, since people value certainty over uncertainty, they also value the present over the future.

Careful accounting for the difference in value that people place on the present as opposed to the future is an important requirement of any properly conducted cost–benefit analysis (CBA). Costs incurred in the present tend to be weighted more heavily than those that can be deferred to the future. Similarly, monetary and other benefits received in the present tend to be weighted more heavily that those that will only be enjoyed at some future date.

The standard method used in military CBA to adjust costs and benefits to reflect their timing is known as "present value analysis" (PVA) or "time discounting." This chapter briefly reviews how to apply PVA to CBA, paying extra attention to the most problematic aspect—the choice of an appropriate discount rate. The next section offers a simple example of PVA applied to CBA. Section 17.3 discusses the challenge of selecting an appropriate discount rate. Risk is explicitly incorporated into the discussion in Section 17.4. Concluding comments in Section 17.5 reinforce the importance of conducting sensitivity analysis on discount rates and other key parameters in a military CBA.

17.2 Present value analysis

Suppose you have $100 in cash. You can spend that money today, or you can deposit it in a risk-free savings account offered by a local bank that offers customers 10 percent annual interest. This means you have a choice between spending $100 today, or having $110 to spend in a year's time. Of course, if you left your $110 in the account for another year, you would have even more money to spend the following year. Your $100 grows over time as described in Table 17.1.

Table 17.1 Future value of $100

Year	Growth $	Future value $
1	$100 \times (1 + 10\%) =$	110.00
2	$100 \times (1 + 10\%)(1 + 10\%) =$	121.00
3	$100 \times (1 + 10\%)(1 + 10\%)(1 + 10\%) =$	133.10

The equation that defines this growth is

$$FV = PV(1 + r)^n, \qquad (17.1)$$

where the future value (FV) is the value n years in the future of a sum of money whose present value (PV) is deposited in an account today earning interest at an annual rate of r. Solving for PV, we find that

$$PV = \frac{FV}{(1 + r)^n}. \qquad (17.2)$$

Equation (17.2) is the foundation of PVA.[1] It determines the PV of a sum (FV) that we expect to receive n years in the future. Table 17.2 calculates the PVs for $100 that we expect to receive one, two or three years in the future.

These PVA relationships can be applied to a simple CBA problem. The CBA problem here is structured as a "fixed effectiveness" approach, the second of the six economic evaluation of alternatives (EEoA) approaches described in Chapter 4. Where competing alternatives are designed to offer the same utility/benefit/effectiveness, the analysis focuses on minimizing costs. In the US Department of Defense this approach is also known as "lowest price technically acceptable" (LPTA).

Consider a CBA that involves the comparison of program costs of two equally capable helicopters—Alpha and Beta—that have a useful life of six years.[2] The procurement cost is $425 million for Alpha and only $400 million for Beta. As discussed in Chapter 5, total life-cycle costs should also include future operations and maintenance (O&M) costs.

Once acquired, operating and maintaining the Alpha will cost $50 million per year for three years, but then will increase to $100 million per year. For Beta, these

Table 17.2 Present value of $100 received in the future

Year	Conversion $	Present value $
1	$100 / (1 + 10\%)^1 =$	90.90
2	$100 / (1 + 10\%)^2 =$	82.64
3	$100 / (1 + 10\%)^3 =$	75.19

Table 17.3 Comparative life-cycle costs

| | | Alternatives | | | |
| | | Alpha | | Beta | |
	Year (1)	Cash ($m) (2)	PV ($m) (3)	Cash ($m) (4)	PV ($m) (5)
Procurement	0	425.00	425.00	400.00	400.00
Operations and	1	50.00	45.45	100.00	90.91
maintenance	2	50.00	41.32	100.00	82.64
	3	50.00	37.57	100.00	75.13
	4	100.00	68.30	50.00	34.15
	5	100.00	62.09	50.00	31.05
	6	100.00	56.45	50.00	28.22
Total		875.00	736.18	850.00	742.11
Interest rate = 10%					

operation and maintenance costs are reversed: $100 million per year for the first three years but only $50 million per year for the following three years.

Calculating the six year life-cycle costs (LCC) for each alternative, columns (2) and (4) in Table 17.3 reveals that Alpha's LCC price is $875 million, while Beta's is only $850 million. But is Beta really the "lowest price" alternative?

Comparing columns (2) and (4) in Table 17.3, we see that Beta costs less to procure but more to operate initially. Overall, however, helicopter Beta requires a lot more cash than Alpha over the first three years, and a lot less in the final three years. One possible interpretation is that if Alpha was selected, there would be excess funds freed up during those early years that could be deposited in a bank earning interest. Funds earned in that account could then be used to defray the higher costs that Alpha would incur in later years. The discounted present value calculations displayed in columns (3) and (5) of Table 17.3 take these additional funds into account. This suggests that (assuming a 10 percent interest rate) Alpha, not Beta, may be the lowest price option.

17.3 Choosing an appropriate discount rate

As we have seen, applying PVA to CBA is relatively straightforward. What is difficult is to choose an appropriate discount rate, or the value of r. For convenience, r was previously referred to as an interest rate. However, for public investment decisions, it is more accurate to characterize r as the discount rate, or even the "social rate of discount," since its value is unlikely to equal any particular interest rate observed in the capital markets or offered by banks.

What value should be used for r and how should that value be identified? A survey of over 2,000 economists did not come close to answering those questions (Weitzman 2001). While economists clearly cannot identify the correct value for r, there is a surprisingly wide consensus about what, at least in theory, the value of r ought to reflect. The foundation of this consensus is Ramsey's seminal 1928 analysis of the optimal savings rate (Ramsey 1928).

Ramsey reasoned that the optimal savings rate is the one that maximizes aggregate utility (benefits) for all present and future citizens. This can only be achieved if the marginal rate of substitution (MRS) of any two consumption goods equals the marginal rate of technical substitution (MRTS) in the production of the two goods. By choosing current aggregate consumption and future aggregate consumption as the goods in question, Ramsey then solves for the value of r that leads MRS to equal MRTS:

$$r = \alpha + \eta\lambda, \tag{17.3}$$

where α is the pure rate of time discount, λ is the rate at which per capita real consumption is expected to grow over the long term, and η is the marginal elasticity of utility with respect to real consumption. Each variable is interpreted carefully below.

We can think of α as the portion of r that discounts future utility or well-being (Heal 2007). It captures the reality that people are impatient, and "like small children... hate waiting for anything," as well as capturing the degree to which people fear unexpected death or similar, equally unforeseen as undesirable, events (Hansen and Lipow 2013). The larger α, the greater the desire to enjoy benefits earlier rather than later.

We can think of $\eta\lambda$ as the portion of r that discounts future consumption benefits (Heal 2007). The value of η captures the marginal utility of consumption, and is also a measure of risk aversion. A value of $\eta = 0$ implies that a person is risk neutral so that their marginal utility of consumption is constant over time. Hansen and Lipow (2013) point out that:

> this is the equivalent of assuming that if the prosperous Fitzwilliam Darcy (from Jane Austen's *Pride and Prejudice*) found $100 lying on the ground, it would offer him just as much utility as it would offer the impoverished Oliver Twist (from Charles Dickens' *Oliver Twist*) should he find the same sum. Clearly, this is wrong – people are risk averse and η does not equal zero.[3]

The value of λ captures the degree to which we expect consumption opportunities to be available in the future. If the value of λ is high, then future consumption is expected to be much higher than it is today. As a result, the incremental utility that this future consumption will provide will tend to be lower, and the corresponding discount rate higher (i.e. one tends to discount future consumption benefits relatively more, if it is expected there will be more available). If the value of λ is low, then future consumption is expected to be much lower. As a result, future incremental utility will be higher, and the discount rate correspondingly lower (i.e. one tends to discount future consumption benefits relatively less, if it is expected there will be less available).

If there is a widespread agreement amongst economists on the appropriate formula for the discount rate, $r = \alpha + \eta\lambda$, why can't a consensus value for the discount rate be determined? The answer is that there are bitter disagreements over the correct values for the individual variables: α, η and λ. Different assumptions and perspectives lead to parameter estimates that result in real (inflation adjusted) discount rates that range between 1 percent and 7 percent (Weitzman 2001). The contentious challenge of converging to a consensus value has led many economists to simply recommend using the government's cost of borrowing as an imperfect proxy for the discount rate (US OMB 1992).

17.4   Risk adjusted discount rates

Ramsey's analysis assumes a world of certainty, and many CBA practitioners conduct PVAs using various estimates for the value of r identified in equation (17.3). This may offer a false sense of security. To illustrate why, consider the following example described in Hansen and Lipow (2013).

Suppose a country of very like-minded people wish to maximize their collective well-being over two periods, subject to the constraint of being adequately defended by their nation's navy. To obtain an adequate defense capability, the country must add an additional submarine to the fleet in period two. In order to do so, the navy must build it during period one.

The navy can propel the submarine using one of two alternatives. One possibility is to equip the submarine with a nuclear reactor. The second is to equip it with diesel-electric propulsion. For simplicity, this CBA assumes the two alternative propulsion systems—nuclear and diesel-electric—are equally effective (i.e. the fixed effectiveness approach).

Let nuclear and diesel each have known and identical costs in the first period, where a representative agent's share (per capita) of the initial cost is g_1. Define the uncertainty in period two with two possible states of nature; war with probability π, and peace with probability $(1 - \pi)$.

During war submarines steam for many hours at high speeds, while peacetime requires little steaming.[4] Operating cost does not vary between the two states of nature for nuclear propulsion, but for diesel-electric technology more steaming means more cost. Let $\tilde{g}_2$ be the random variable describing per capita operating costs in the second period.

Consider the expected utility, or well-being, of the representative citizen. In each period the agent receives income, c, that can be consumed but not stored. Assume that the agent's benefit or "well-being" can be represented by a log-utility function. Then the expected utility of a representative agent is

$$EU = \ln(c - g_1) + \gamma E[\ln(c - g_2)], \tag{17.4}$$

where E is the expectations operator and $\gamma = 1/(\alpha + 1)$. In (17.4) the natural log operator represents a common method in economics to represent an individual's utility, or well-being. The first operator on the right hand side of the equation

Table 17.4 Parameter definitions

Symbol	Definition	Value
π	Probability of war	0.30
α	Pure rate of time discount	0.00
g_1	Agent share of initial cost	1.20
c	Citizen income	2.00

computes utility in period one based on the certain sum of money the citizen retains. The second piece of the equation does the same thing for period two, except that now the amount the citizen retains is uncertain so the expectations operator must be applied. The sum across both periods estimates the citizen's utility.

To operationalize this simple model, consider the parameters in Table 17.4.

In Table 17.5, we assume values for operating costs of both alternative propulsion systems, g_2, in both states of nature that can occur in period two (war and peace). We then plug values from Tables 17.4 and 17.5 into Equation (17.4) to obtain the expected utility of the two alternatives reported in Table 17.5.

From Table 17.5, diesel has the lowest expected cost in period two. Since cost and utility in the first period are identical for nuclear and diesel, a conventional CBA focused exclusively on minimizing expected costs of propulsion would recommend diesel-electric propulsion, regardless of the discount rate applied. However, nuclear propulsion is the choice that maximizes the expected utility, or well-being, of the representative citizen.

As the example above demonstrates, failure to take risk into account can easily lead to situations where CBA rejects the superior project or program while endorsing the inferior. The most popular methodology for correcting this problem is to modify the discount rate, r, by adding an additional "risk premium." Breeden (1979) shows the value of the risk premium (RP) that maximizes expected utility is given by

$$RP_x = - \left[\frac{1}{E(u_c)} \right] \times \text{cov}(u_c, X), \tag{17.5}$$

where X is the uncertain benefit or cost, and u_c is the marginal utility of consumption (Varian 1992, p. 379).

Table 17.5 Expected cost and utility of propulsion systems

Propulsion type	g_2 in peace	g_2 in war	Expected cost	Expected utility
Nuclear	0.3000	0.3000	0.3000	0.3075
Diesel	0.1500	0.6450	0.2985	0.2986

This approach to adjusting the discount rate is widely practiced in the private sector, and Bazelon and Smetters (1999) strongly endorse the use of similar techniques for public sector CBAs, concluding that "there is little rationale for the government to discount future costs and benefits of any particular project or program differently than the private market."

So how does the private sector estimate the RP? The standard way to estimate the RP is given by adjusting Equation (17.5) as follows:

$$RP_x = \beta_x[E(R) - r], \tag{17.6}$$

where R is a proxy for wealth or consumption (often, simply the return on a stock index such as the S&P 500), r is Ramsay's discount rate (often proxied by rates on government bonds), and β_x is the covariance of X and R.

Consistent with this approach, the US government's guidelines for CBA (US OMB 1992, 12) acknowledges that "the absolute variability of a risky outcome can be much less significant than its *correlation* with other significant determinants of social welfare, such as real national income." Surprisingly, however, Circular A-94 does not then go on to mandate use of the formula given in (17.5).

A possible explanation is that the formula works fairly well when the covariance of X and R can be estimated using historical data, but is much more difficult to apply when trying to evaluate new investments with little or no historical data. In such circumstances, a popular graduate finance textbook explains that since "you cannot hope to estimate the relative risk of assets with any precision... examine the project from a variety of angles and *look for clues* to its riskiness" (Brealey and Myers 1991, p. 200).

17.5   Conclusion

For the government analyst, "looking for clues" can be quite a challenge. For most military CBAs, "clues" may not even exist.[5] So what can be done to account for risk in a military CBA? While far from perfect—indeed far from adequate—Hansen and Lipow's (2013) proposed approach has the virtue of being relatively easy to implement in the United States. The analyst first identifies the discount rate mandated by OMB Circular A-94 (US OMB 1992). This value for r, which is based on government bond prices, is given by Appendix C of A-94 and is updated every year. The analyst then makes a *qualitative* judgment as to whether each flow of cost or benefit associated with an investment project is positively or negatively correlated with per capita consumption, and documents this judgment by writing a paragraph that explains his or her reasoning. The analyst then adds 1 percentage point to the mandated value of r used to discount benefits and costs that are positively correlated with consumption, while subtracting 1 percentage point from the value of r used to discount flows that are negatively correlated with consumption.

While such an approach is likely superior to current practice, the resultant estimates of the appropriate discount rates will still not precisely reflect the true social rate of discount. Barring a methodological breakthrough, the accounting for time and risk in discounting are likely to remain an Achilles' heel of military CBA. This reinforces the value of sensitivity analysis, including Monte Carlo simulation and other modeling efforts discussed in earlier chapters, to generate a thorough understanding of the sensitivity of military CBA to key parameters.

Notes

1 The formula to use in PVA is

$$PV = \frac{FV}{(1+r)^n}.$$

Here PV is the present value of a future value FV in n years, discounted into present terms at the rate of discount r.

2 For simplicity of exposition, assume the helicopters are fully depreciated at the end of this six year life-cycle and have no scrap value.

3 Evans (2005), for example, estimates η for 20 OECD countries and derives estimates that range from 1.08 to 1.82, with values ranging from 1.15 to 1.45 for the United States.

4 Naval pedants would be correct to point out that, formally, a diesel-electric submarine does not use steam propulsion, and hence can't "steam."

5 What exactly is the covariance of the S&P and the costs associated with building and operating an aircraft carrier? That is not an easy question. What is the covariance of the S&P and the benefits (or flows of effectiveness) that we expect to receive from that aircraft carrier? That isn't a question at all—it is a riddle worthy of the Sphinx.

References

Bazelon, C., and Smetters, K. 1999. "Discounting Inside the Washington DC Beltway." *The Journal of Economic Perspectives*, 13(4): 213–228.

Breeden, D. T. 1979. "An Intertemporal Asset Pricing Model with Stochastic Consumption and Investment Opportunities." *Journal of Financial Economics*, 7(3): 265–296.

Brealey, R. A., and Myers, S. C. 1991. *Principles of Corporate Finance* (4th edition). New York: McGraw-Hill.

Evans, D. J. 2005. "The Elasticity of Marginal Utility of Consumption: Estimates for 20 OECD Countries." *Fiscal Studies*, 26(2): 197–224.

Hansen, J., and Lipow, J. 2013. "Accounting for Systematic Risk in Benefit–Cost Analysis: A Practical Approach." *Journal of Benefit-Cost Analysis*, 4(3): 361–373.

Heal, G. 2007. "Discounting: A Review of the Basic Economics." *The University of Chicago Law Review*, 74(1): 59–77.

Ramsey, F. P. 1928. "A Mathematical Theory of Saving." *The Economic Journal*, 38(152): 543–559.

Varian, H. R. 1992. *Microeconomic Analysis* (3rd edition). New York: Norton.

US Office of Management and Budget. 1992. *Guidelines and Discount Rates for Benefit–Cost Analysis of Federal Programs*, OMB Circular No. A-94 Revised.

Weitzman, M. L. 2001. "Gamma Discounting." *American Economic Review*, 91(1): 260–271.

Index

Printed in the United States
by Baker & Taylor Publisher Services